LANGUAGE IN SOCIETY 26

African American Vernacular English

Language in Society

GENERAL EDITOR
Peter Trudgill, Chair of English Linguistics,
University of Fribourg

ADVISORY EDITORS
J.K. Chambers, Professor of Linguistics,
University of Toronto

Ralph Fasold, Professor of Linguistics,
Georgetown University

William Labov, Professor of Linguistics,
University of Pennsylvania

Lesley Milroy, Professor of Linguistics,
University of Michigan, Ann Arbor

African American Vernacular English

Features, Evolution, Educational Implications

John R. Rickford

Stanford University

First published 1999

2 4 6 8 10 9 7 5 3 1

Blackwell Publishers Inc.
350 Main Street
Malden, Massachusetts 02148
USA

Blackwell Publishers Ltd
108 Cowley Road
Oxford OX4 1JF
UK

Library of Congress Cataloging-in-Publication Data
Rickford, John R., 1949–
African American vernacular English: features, evolution,
educational implications / John R. Rickford.
p. cm. – (Language in society; 26)
Includes bibliographical references and index.
ISBN 0-631-21244-2 (alk. paper). – ISBN 0-631-21245-0 (pbk.: alk. paper)
1. Afro-Americans – Language. 2. English language – Social aspects–United States.
3. English language – Spoken English – United States. 4. Afro-Americans –
Education – Language arts. 5. Language and education – United States.
6. Afro-American students – Language. 7. Black English. I. Title. II. Series:
Language in society (Oxford, England); 26.
PE3102.N42R53 1999
427' 973'08996073 – dc21   98-47775
                                                                 CIP
British Library Cataloguing in Publication Data
A CIP catalogue record for this book is available from the British Library.

Typeset in $10^{1}/_{2}$ on 12 pt Ehrhardt
by Best-set Typesetter Ltd., Hong Kong
Printed in Great Britain by MPG Books, Victoria Square, Bodmin, Cornwall.

This book is printed on acid-free paper.

Contents

Series Editor's Preface

It is one of linguists' perennial complaints that they are not given enough recognition as experts by the rest of the world. Astronomers can pontificate about astronomy and be received respectively; physicists will be listened to attentively if they expound on the subject of physics. But if linguists talk authoritatively about language, it is very likely indeed that they will be confidently and publicly disagreed with by people who know nothing about language whatsoever except how to speak one. Indeed, there is no guarantee that linguists will even be invited to present their opinions on linguistic issues. It is just as likely that the media will call upon novelists or politicians to pronounce on matters having to do with language as it is that they will consider talking to academic linguists. Recent discussions in the United States about African American Vernacular English made this very clear. The problems caused by the mismatch between Standard English and AAVE, the ignorance of educational authorities about the true nature of AAVE, and the way in which native speakers of AAVE are and should be received by the educational system in the USA are matters of vital importance to millions of people, and yet they are as often discussed in the American media by journalists pontificating from a position of extreme ignorance as by actual experts on AAVE. One of the greatest and most highly respected authorities on AAVE is the author of this volume, John Rickford. He has over the years thought a great deal about and worked very hard in connection with the position of AAVE in the American education system. He has also been very successful at overcoming the widespread resistance in mainstream America to listening to informed views about AAVE, and has therefore been able to be very influential in leading discussions and implementing solutions to a number of associated problems. His theoretical work is also of obvious importance to all historical linguists, creolists, sociolinguists, and educational linguists. And his work on the educational implications of work on AAVE will be of interest not only in the USA but to anyone involved in issues to do with nonstandard dialects and pedagogy. As the earlier part of this book makes plain, Rickford can talk not only with passion and commitment about AAVE but also with more authority than nearly anyone on the subject. His knowledge about the structure and origins of this language variety is unparalleled, and his linguistic research has been of enormous historical linguistic, sociolinguistic, and theoretical linguistic importance. It is therefore only right that his views should be listened to and brought to the attention of an even wider audience than has already been the case. This book will hopefully help to do just that.

Peter Trudgill
University of Fribourg

Preface

The suggestion that I publish a collection of my writings on African American Vernacular English (AAVE) was first made to me about two years ago by Geneva Smitherman, who is herself a leading authority on the subject. I have been engaged in the study of AAVE for nearly 30 years, but what I've written about it is scattered in a variety of journals, conference proceedings, and edited volumes, many of them difficult to access.

The need for reliable, publicly available scientific information on AAVE was particularly evident when the Oakland Ebonics controversy broke in December 1996, and misinformation about this linguistic variety, its use, evolution, and educational significance was circulated in media reports, talk shows, private conversations and public discussions across America and around the world. For the first few days, in fact, the media consulted politicians and celebrities rather than linguists for commentary on Oakland's famous resolution of December 18, 1996. They soon learned that "linguists" might have something more authoritative to say about language, however, and began to turn to the small group of specialists on AAVE. But their reports were not always accurate (see Heilbrum's article in the January 20, 1997 issue of the *New Republic*, for example, and my letter in response in the March 3, 1997 issue), and attempts by linguists (including myself) to contribute our own Op-Eds to leading newspapers like the *New York Times* and the *Washington Post* were generally unsuccessful (see the last chapter in this volume).

In a sense, then, this book – particularly part III, which deals most directly with educational and sociopolitical issues – might be thought of as my extended opinion piece on the Ebonics controversy. But of course it is much more. As the articles in every part should demonstrate, linguists have recognized the distinctiveness and significance of AAVE for more than three decades, and during that time we have been actively researching (sometimes arguing about) its features and use, its history and ongoing development, and its educational implications. Although some people may have first heard about the African American vernacular in 1996, linguists have long known about it, and it features quite prominently in American textbooks and conferences on language variation or sociolinguistics (the study of language in society).

0.1 How I Got Involved in the Study of AAVE

My own involvement with the study of AAVE began in 1970, while I was still an undergraduate at the University of California at Santa Cruz. As a volunteer tutor of a preadolescent African American student who was not doing well in school, and as a fledgling sociolinguist, I was struck by differences between the speech and writing of my tutee and the Standard English required by schools. I also began to read the early work of Beryl Bailey, Joan Baratz, Ralph Fasold, William Labov, Roger Shuy, William Stewart, Walt Wolfram, and others on AAVE, intrigued by the connections which they were making between this linguistic variety and the difficulties which African American students were experiencing with reading and writing in Standard English (SE). The situation reminded me of the connections which Robert Le Page (1968) had made between the Creole English of students in my native Caribbean and their limited success on the English language exam which at the time was set and graded in England. That article had helped to draw me into Linguistics (from Literature), and I was further fascinated by the controversy (in its early phases then) about whether AAVE was descended from creole roots similar to those in the Caribbean.

The opportunity to spend three months teaching, doing community service, and studying the language on one of the isolated Sea Islands off the coast of South Carolina in the Spring of 1970 was the real turning point for me, as far as serious study of the vernacular of African Americans was concerned. The Gullah or Sea Island Creole spoken by island residents was similar to my native Guyanese Creole in many respects. I had no trouble understanding it, often translating and interpreting, in fact, for the Anglo-American student, Frank Smith, who accompanied me on the trip. Moreover, there were pervasive similarities between the Sea Islands and the Afro-Caribbean in terms of material and folk culture, including patterns of fishing with circular cast-nets, food preparation with the mortar and pestle, folktales featuring Brer Rabbit, legends about old higues/hags who sucked the blood of babies, and stories about slaves who flew back to Africa (see Rickford 1987c: 245–6). From my very first visit, the South Carolina Sea Islands left me with a distinct sense of returning home, and subsequent visits and research only served to deepen that sensation. At the same time, my Sea Island experience was neither idyllic nor romanticized. After working with teachers Pat Conroy and Frances Jones in the two-room schoolhouse on the island (Conroy's experiences were documented in the book, *The Water is Wide* and the film *Conrack*), I had an acute sense of how much further the bright children on the island had to go to fulfill their great potential, and wrote a senior honors thesis in 1971 entitled: " 'De train dey ridin' on is full of dead man's bones': Language, death and damnation in the two-room school-house on [D.] Island, South Carolina."

The desire to deepen my knowledge about the vernacular speech of African Americans, its history and its educational implications, led me to begin graduate study at the University of Pennsylvania in Philadelphia in 1971 with William Labov, already established as one of the leading experts in the sub-fields of sociolinguistics and AAVE. Several of my earliest publications (for instance, Rickford 1974, 1975, 1977) were written while I was a student there, drawing on data from West Philadelphia as well as the South Carolina Sea Islands.

Later on, after completing my dissertation and teaching at the University of Guyana, I moved to Stanford University, and began turning to nearby East Palo Alto and the Ravenswood School District there for research on the rela-tionship between AAVE and education, the question of whether AAVE is descended from creole roots, and the controversy about whether it is currently converging with or diverging from white and other ethnic vernaculars. Many of my publications on AAVE from 1980 to the present draw on linguistic, ethno-graphic, and classroom data from this community.

The articles which I have selected for inclusion in this volume fall into three groups: I Features and use; II Evolution; and III Educational implications. In general, I tried to choose articles which would be comprehensible to non-linguists, given the general public interest following the Ebonics controversy, and I sometimes revised them to make them more accessible. But I have also included several articles which are relatively technical because they deal in depth with issues central to the study of AAVE and need to be more readily available to linguists and other scholars interested in this subject.

0.2   Part I: Features and Use

Part I opens with a chapter providing an up-to-date list of the phonological and grammatical features of AAVE, something which was badly needed and con-stantly requested when the Ebonics controversy first broke in December 1996. Chapter 1, an extensively revised and expanded extract from a (1996) paper, will hopefully help to show why linguists continued to insist, in stiff opposition to most media commentators, that Ebonics was a systematic, regular and com-plex system, more than the slang or careless speech with which it was associated in the public's minds. The chapter also explores variability in the use of AAVE according to social class, gender, age, and style, and discusses the relationship of this variety to southern white speech and the vernaculars of other Americans.

Finally, it emphasizes that AAVE is more than a list of features, and notes the expressive use to which AAVE is put to serve a wide variety of functions by a wide cross section of people within the African American community.

Chapter 2, a reprint of a (1975) article, is the earliest publication of mine reprinted in this volume. At the time, descriptions of AAVE were equivocal at best about the importance of stress on remote time *been/bin*. Using participant observation and elicited data, I demonstrated that the remote time meaning is only associated with the stressed variant of this form (*BIN*), and clarified other aspects of the meaning and grammar of this important preverbal form, the use and understanding of which was one of the clearest dividers between Blacks and Whites. More recent work by Green (1993, 1998) and Dayton (1996) has helped to extend our understanding of the syntax, semantics, and pragmatics of stressed BIN.

Chapter 3 also deals with one of the semantically important and socio-linguistically significant preverbal tense-aspect markers of AAVE, but in this case a form which seems to have emerged or risen to prominence only more recently – the use of *had* to signal the simple past or preterit, rather than the pluperfect, as in "I was on my way to school, and I *had* slipped and fell." Attestations of this form in our East Palo Alto data come mainly from sixth-grade preadolescents, and it is through detailed quantitative and qualitative analysis of their usage that Christine Théberge Rafal and I attempt to explicate the meaning and discourse function of this form, which often marks the climactic peak of narratives, or the clauses which serve as (re)orientors or preludes to important narrative events. We also compare our data with attestations elsewhere, especially the Texas data indicating a change in progress, extensively analyzed by Cukor-Avila (1995) and Cukor-Avila and Bailey (1995).

Chapter 4 is entitled "Rappin on the Copula Coffin" for two reasons – the fact that it reopens discussion of theoretical and methodological issues in the analysis of copula contraction ("He's happy) and absence ("He Ø happy"), the most commonly examined AAVE feature, and the fact that its findings are summarized in the form of a concluding "rap." Using data from East Palo Alto, Arnetha Ball, Renée Blake, Raina Jackson, Nomi Martin and I demonstrate that the contraction and absence of *is* should be analyzed together with that of *are*, and that alternative methods of computing contraction and deletion ("Labov Deletion" versus "Straight Deletion," for instance), crucially affect the results. What is interesting about the East Palo Alto data is that it replicates almost perfectly the findings of earlier studies about the grammatical and phonological constraints on copula absence, reinforcing our sense of the robustness of this variable, and the structural similarity of AAVE from coast to coast.

Chapter 5 draws on data from the South Carolina Sea Islands to explore in theoretical terms the larger issue of the nature of ethnicity as a sociolinguistic boundary. Phonologically, the White Sea Islander (Mr King) and the Black Sea Islander (Mrs Queen) who are the focus of this chapter are very similar, but grammatically, in terms of their rules for marking plurals and passives, they are quite different. This finding contradicts the common assertion that white and black speech are identical in the South, once geography and class are controlled. After comparing my findings with the findings of black/white speech differences in other studies, I conclude that while diachronic provenience is relevant, it is the limited contact across ethnic boundaries, and the existence of different social identities and norms which accounts for the persistent linguistic (especially grammatical) differences between black and white speech.

Chapter 6, the final chapter in part I, draws on East Palo Alto data from several grammatical variables – invariant habitual *be*, copula absence, possessive *-s*, plural *-s*, and third singular present *-s* absence – to reopen the analysis of style, a neglected topic in American sociolinguistics. Using successive interviews of Foxy Boston by an African American and a European American interviewer, Faye McNair-Knox and I first examine Bell's (1984) hypothesis that speakers vary their language use primarily to suit their audience or addressee, and then his related hypothesis that the stylistic effect of topic is weaker. Although this hypothesis is basically confirmed, a number of complications arise in its investigation which indicate the need for further research on stylistic variation, especially in relation to addressee and topic shift. These and related issues are taken up by several researchers in Eckert and Rickford (forthcoming).

0.3   Part II: Evolution

Part II, which deals with the evolution of AAVE up to this point and its continuing development – one of the most contested areas in the study of AAVE – contains six papers.

Chapter 7 is an investigation of *cut-eye* and *suck-teeth*, which as words and gestures mark a major sociolinguistic boundary between American Blacks and Whites in terms of familiarity and use. Angela Rickford and I explain the gestures in detail, provide quantitative data on black/white familiarity, note Caribbean parallels, and suggest several possible sources in the languages of West (and East) Africa. Our larger point is that Africanisms in the New World are likely to reside not only in the exotic, but also – perhaps more often – in the commonplace, especially in convergences between African and English forms, and in translations into English of African forms, both of which can "pass" as English forms. "Masked Africanisms" of this type (compare Spears' 1982: 867 notion of camouflaged forms) are likely to have survived the acculturation of African peoples to European and American norms longer than direct retentions or loans, and they are worth investigating for what they can tell us about the vitality and survival of African languages and cultures in the New World, both in the present and the past.

The larger perspective of chapter 8 is the interplay of internal and external factors on linguistic diffusion and change. But this is considered through an exploration of the origins of invariant habitual *be* in AAVE – more specifically, of the common hypothesis that it represents the influence of Hiberno English *be* or *does be* through historical contact between Irish and Scotch Irish servants and African slaves and servants in the Caribbean and North America. My analysis of the historical record suggests that the contact was closer, and in ecological and emotional terms more likely to have led to Irish influence, in the seventeenth-century Caribbean, where African and Irish servants rebelled and ran away together, than in nineteenth-century America, where African American (ex-)slaves and freemen competed and fought with refugees from the Irish potato famine for limited resources. My analysis of the linguistic facts suggests that while earlier Irish and English uses of *be* and *does be* may have played some role, their influence is more likely to have been indirect, with the invariant *be* of AAVE more likely reflecting West African and creole linguistic influences. Winford (1997, 1998: 117–26), has recently concluded that although the Northern, especially the Scotch Irish or Ulster Scots presence in eighteenth-century America was more extensive than my research in this chapter had indicated, Scotch Irish was not the source of AAVE *be*; he cites forthcoming work by Montgomery and Kirk which suggests that "habitual be developed too late to have influenced American varieties of the language." (See also Montgomery and Mishoe, to appear.) Although he disagrees with some aspects of the hypothesis I support in this chapter – such as the existence of a widespread plantation creole and the traditional role of decreolization (1998: 123) – he feels that finite *be* of English settler dialects, influenced by creole *does be*, was the source of AAVE *be*.

Chapter 9 is the only paper in this volume to focus on a theme with which much of my recent work has been preoccupied – the extent to which patterns of copula absence in AAVE resemble patterns of copula absence in Caribbean Creoles and other varieties, and may therefore provide support for or against the hypothesis that AAVE has creole roots. In this case, what I provide is a reanalysis from scratch of Jamaican Creole copula data in DeCamp (1960) which had been previously analyzed by Holm (1984) in a famous paper supporting the creole hypothesis. My reanalysis of the data in two crucial categories – before _____Verb + *ing* and before _____*gonna* – shows that these categories behave much more similarly in Jamaican Creole and AAVE than had previously been supposed, increasing the likelihood that they had similar or related origins.

Chapter 10 is the last paper in this volume to deal with the creole hypothesis, this time using sociohistorical and demographic data rather than linguistic data. After listing seven types of evidence which are relevant to the creole origins issue, I explore sociohistorical data on the relative numbers of Blacks and Whites in the three primary regions of colonial America: the New England colonies, the Middle colonies (such as New York and Pennsylvania), and the South. While the possibility of pidginization and/or creolization on American soil is strongest only in the South, particularly in coastal South Carolina and Georgia, the evidence that the founder slave populations in most American colonies were brought in from the Caribbean is very strong, suggesting that the Caribbean varieties might have influenced the emerging African American vernacular in the US.

Chapters 11 and 12 both deal with the newest controversy about the development of AAVE – the question of whether it is currently diverging from white vernaculars. The divergence hypothesis was first introduced by Labov and Harris (1986), who felt that black and white vernaculars in Philadelphia had both diverged from each other because of the increased segregation which white and black middle-class suburban flight had produced in that and other cities. About the same time, Guy Bailey and Cukor-Avila began to report data from College Station and other cities in Texas which appeared to point in the same direction. At the annual NWAV (New Ways of Analyzing Variation) meeting of sociolinguists in 1986, Ralph Fasold organized a symposium on the subject, including Guy Bailey, William Labov, Arthur Spears, Fay Vaughn-Cooke, Walt Wolfram, and myself as participants.

Chapter 11 represents my contribution to that symposium, one in which I express some cautions about the hypothesis, reminding my co-participants, for instance that convergence in some features might be accompanied by divergence in others, and urging us to explore convergence/divergence in earlier centuries (for instance, with Irish/Black contact) as well as in the present. The main point of the chapter, however, was to sketch out alternative models of convergence and divergence over time so that we could have a clearer sense of their possibilities and implications. Figures 11.3 and 11.5, showing convergence followed by divergence, were important for dispelling the increasingly popular assumption that if one found evidence of late twentieth-century divergence between black and white vernaculars, this immediately undermined the creolist hypothesis that black and white vernaculars were more different in the eighteenth and nineteenth centuries, and had been gradually converging since that time.

In Chapter 12 I return to the divergence hypothesis, this time with some concrete data on language use by old, middle-aged, and young speakers in East Palo Alto's African American community with respect to six linguistic features, which allows us to assess the extent of change in "apparent time" (across age distributions). Although there are few white Americans in East Palo Alto to serve as a comparison, we do have some idea of white vernacular norms for the variables in question from studies of other communities, and with these in mind, it appears that the younger generations in East Palo Alto do "show some evidence of ongoing change away from the patterns of standard and vernacular white English." However, as I note, divergence with respect to features like invariant *be* and copula absence is matched by stability and/or convergence with respect to other features, like plural and past marking. The larger question with which I attempt to deal is *why* there should be divergence, if only in some features. Apart from residential segregation, what seems significant to me is the increased oppositional identity (Fordham and Ogbu 1986) of today's teenagers and young adults compared with older generations. Accelerated AAVE use – especially of salient features like *be* – and scathing criticism of those who "talk white" are part of a symbolic statement by today's young people of awareness of and pride in their African American identity.

0.4   Part III: Educational Implications

Part III contains only four papers, all published within the past three years (one of them may still be in press). The application of linguistic research to educational, social, and political problems is indeed the most recent but also the most deep-seated of my linguistic interests. Given that I was originally attracted to Linguistics and the study of AAVE by the promise of its potential educational applications – and this is true of most of the linguists who entered the study of AAVE in the 1960s and early 1970s – it is ironic that it has taken me so long to get around to writing about the applied side of the field. Of course my students and I have been involved in tutoring and other volunteer work over the years (see chapter 14 for further discussion), and in Rickford and Greaves (1978) I did write about the educational problems of Guyanese Creole speakers, but after writing about theoretical, descriptive and historical issues in the study of AAVE for quarter of a century, I am glad to finally be writing about its applied aspects.

Chapter 13 emphasizes how important it is for educators to be aware of attitudes towards AAVE, including their own, because of the powerful impact such attitudes often have on teacher expectations and student performance. In an attempt to go beyond the negative but superficial responses of the public which the media were fond of airing in the wake of the Oakland Ebonics resolutions, it refers to the considered opinions of African American writers as well as the several systematic studies of the attitudes of teachers, students and community members which have been conducted from the 1970s to the 1990s. Although negative attitudes still emerge in many of these studies, they are balanced by positive attitudes more often than most people might have predicted. In discussing classroom implications, I make a number of preliminary remarks about teaching reading and writing, and using contrastive analysis and dialect readers to teach Standard English, which are expanded upon in chapter 16, and I also propose some classroom exercises and strategies focusing on language diversity in literature, film, and the classroom.

Chapter 14 details what I portray as an "unequal partnership" between sociolinguistics and the African American community – how much the academic field has gained from studies of AAVE in terms of its theoretical and methodological development, but how little (in relative terms) it has given to the community in return. I indicate four areas in which I think considerably more could be done – increasing the numbers of African Americans in Linguistics, representing the African American community better in our writings, contributing to a reduction in the injustices and disparities which African Americans experience in prisons, courts, and employment, and contributing to the solution of educational problems affecting African Americans, especially in the mastery of reading, writing, and the language arts. This last area is the one I concentrate on, demonstrating the neglect of dialect readers by linguists and educators despite empirical evidence of their success in teaching reading, and urging a return to the study of this and other innovative approaches. I close with a call for increased service learning in Linguistics more generally, and for a greater commitment to ethics, advocacy, and empowerment in relations with the communities we study (cf. Cameron et al. 1992).

Chapter 15 is a popular piece, written for the educated public that reads popular science magazines like *Discover*. Following *Discover*'s rubric, the article includes no footnotes or references to earlier work in the literature, but as the other chapters in this volume indicate, the findings I present in this chapter draw on the work of many others. I basically try to show that there are more positive attitudes to AAVE or Ebonics than were reported in media coverage of the Ebonics controversy, and that AAVE is also more systematic, with a deeper history, than most commentators on the controversy assumed. Alternative Afrocentric, Eurocentric, and creolist views of the origin of AAVE are summarized, and the educational implications of the scientific study of AAVE are also noted, particularly the value of the contrastive analysis approach which Oakland was advocating.

Chapter 16 is an extensively revised version of my remarks at a conference on Ebonics held at California State University at Long Beach in 1997, one of several in which I have participated over the past two years. Long after the media stopped paying attention to Ebonics (approximately in April 1977), university faculty and students, and high school, junior high and grade school teachers have continued to grapple with the devastating rates at which schools fail African American students and the role of language therein, and conferences and symposia are a primary means of addressing these issues. In this paper, I first detail the devastating rates of African American school failure, both in California and across the nation, consider possible language and non-language factors in this failure, and go on to discuss in more detail how AAVE/Ebonics is relevant, and how it might be taken into account in teaching reading and the language arts, as Oakland originally proposed. The methods of doing this fall into three primary categories, each of which is explained and assessed in some detail: the linguistically informed approach, contrastive analysis, and introducing reading in the vernacular, then switching to the standard or mainstream variety (i.e., dialect readers). I close by citing European and Caribbean parallels to the kinds of problems which Ebonics speakers face in American schools, and the possible solutions which linguists propose for them, and suggest that allowing existing approaches which ignore Ebonics to continue, despite their abysmal record of non-success, would be a disgrace.

0.5   Terminology (AAVE, Black English (Vernacular), Ebonics)

Having covered the content of the chapters, a few remarks on terminology are in order at this point. In line with evolving trends within the larger community, linguists use "African American English" instead of "Black English" (or even older terms like "Non-Standard Negro English") for the English of African Americans, a continuum of varieties ranging from the most mainstream or standard speech (like Bryant Gumbel's, virtually indistinguishable from the formal speech of white and other Americans), to the most vernacular or non-mainstream variety. It was to focus on this latter variety – as the variety most widespread among working-class African Americans in inner-city areas, and most significant from historical and educational perspectives – and to avoid the impression that every African American would use the features associated with that variety, that Labov (1972c: xiii) first started referring to it as "black English *vernacular* [BEV]." "African American Vernacular English" is simply the most recent equivalent of that term, the one most widely used among linguists, and the older terms will be found in earlier papers reprinted in this volume.

The term "Ebonics," which was first coined in 1973 by a "group of Black scholars . . . from ebony (black) and phonics (sound, the study of sound)" (R. Williams 1975: vi), has become very popular since the Oakland controversy of December 1996. It is regarded by many if not most linguists as very similar if not identical to AAVE in terms of the features and varieties it designates. As Labov (1983: 34) noted, "The term [Ebonics] is not widely used by linguists, but discussion of Ebonics programs refer to many of the linguistic features presented at the Black English trial. There is considerable convergence between proponents of Ebonics and those who prefer the concepts Black English and Black English vernacular." This is also implicit in Ernie Smith's (1975: 77) observation that "I have spoken Ebonics, or as it has been labeled in the literature – Black English – since I was a child," and by his more recent (1997: 45) citation of structural linguistic features associated with Ebonics or

African American language which are the same as those listed as characteristic of AAVE. Smith's list includes (with the "AAVE" equivalents in chapter 1 of this volume added in square brackets):

- "the existence of heterogeneous consonant clusters (the absence of homogeneous consonant blends)"; [= #1 in table 1.1]
- "the CVCV vocalic pattern (the absence of certain consonants in coda)"; [= #2 in table 1.1]
- "the topic and comment or equative clause syntactical structure (the absence of "'copula verbals' . . .)"; [= 19a in table 1.2]
- "the existence [of] a completive aspect using the word 'done'," [= 19g in table 1.2]
- "the 'remote time construction' using the word 'been'"; [= 19f in table 1.2]
- "the existence of 'double and serial negation'"; [= 22b in table 1.2]

However, there are two respects in which the terms Ebonics and AAVE (or BEV) are different. The first is conceptual or ideological. Ebonics, like the term African American Language or African Language Systems, carries for Smith (1997: 21) and other users a strong Africanist or Afrocentrist conviction that the distinctive grammar and phonology of this variety are derived entirely from the Niger Congo African languages spoken by the ancestors of today's African Americans; and terms like "African American Vernacular English" and "Black English" are eschewed because they are thought to attribute too much genetic significance to lexical overlaps with English and to be otherwise "Eurocentric":

> The Africanists contend that, since, in its basic rules of grammar, African American speech does not in any way follow the grammar rules of English, then the term Black English is an oxymoron. That is, the grammar of African American speech is not English, yet it is called English anyhow.
>
> . . . The Africanists contend that because Ebonics is not "genetically" related to English, the term Ebonics is not a mere synonym for the more commonly used appellation "Black English." If anything, the term Ebonics is an antonym for that clearly Euro-centric appellation.

For me, "AAVE" is not Eurocentric in its orientation at all, but neutral. Certainly, many of the linguists who refer to "AAVE" or its predecessors (like "Black English (Vernacular)") have considered and endorsed African origins for specific features of this variety (see chapter 7 in this volume, and compare Alleyne 1980). But few if any of them would endorse Smith's more extreme claim that "African American speech *does not in any way* follow the grammar rules of English."

Secondly, Ebonics as originally defined (by R. Williams 1975: vi) had a broader scope than AAVE usually does, including paralinguistic features such as gesture as well as speech, and extending to Caribbean and even West African varieties:

> Ebonics may be defined as "the linguistic and paralinguistic features which on a concentric continuum represents the communicative competence of the West African, Caribbean, and United States descendant of African origin. It includes the various idioms, patois, argots, ideolects, and social dialects of black people" especially those who have been forced to adapt to colonial circumstances.

However, in practice, especially since its surge to popular usage in 1996, Ebonics is used primarily for the verbal language of African Americans in the United States, and in this sense remains pretty much the same in its reference as AAVE.

Foreword

This is a volume of sociolinguistic work that will be welcomed and absorbed by sociolinguists everywhere. To students of change and variation in the speech community, it offers a model of all the essential elements: field work based on observation and experiment, elegant quantitative analysis coupled with insightful reasoning; ethnographic insights that proceed from deep connections with the speakers of the language. For those concerned with African American English, this volume must now be considered the essential resource for any scholar who wants to do meaningful work in the field.

There is no doubt that John Rickford holds a unique position in both sociolinguistics and African American studies. He comes to the study of AAVE as an established creolist and native speaker of Guyanese Creole, who is intimately involved in the African American community of the United States. Two distinguished Caribbean scholars have followed a parallel path – Walter Edwards and Donald Winford – with important results. But as this volume shows, Rickford's contribution to our knowledge of AAVE is unequaled in scope and depth. He stands out not only for his own work, but for the contributions made by members of the research group he mobilized in East Palo Alto – particularly Faye McNair Knox, Arnetha Ball, and Renée Blake, Keith Denning, Rudolph Gaudio, Raina Jackson, Nomi Martin, Bonnie McElhinny, Faye McNair-Knox, John McWhorter, and Christine Théberge-Rafal. Most of these colleagues and former students of John's are African American, and several of them appear as co-authors in this volume. In all of his work, in Guyana and the United States, Rickford is remarkable as the linguist with an equal mastery of the techniques of variation study and ethnographic field work. Finally, Rickford stands out in his ability to carry on scholarly work in linguistic analysis without neglecting the urgent need to apply our knowledge to the serious educational problems of the United States.

It is not accidental that Rickford's first important contribution to the study of AAVE is his work on stressed *been*, which appears here as chapter 2. Though earlier studies of AAVE had noted this characteristic aspect marker, our accounts were based on occasional observations and little systematic understanding of its semantics. As a graduate student in West Philadelphia, Rickford brought hundreds of crucial observations of stressed and unstressed *been* to a class on experimental methods in the study of grammar. He then constructed the experiments that led to the remarkable results of tables 2 and 3 in chapter 2. These analyses are now the established bench mark for adequate work in the descriptive semantics of tense and aspect. The study of innovative *had*, which follows in this volume, is illuminating in another way. Linguists have come to realize that in AAVE, the *had* auxiliary often marks a simple preterit, rather than a pluperfect. Rickford approaches this problem with a sensitive analysis of observed usage, and follows with an insightful investigation of the use of *had* forms in complete narratives. He not only illuminates his own data, but is able to make sense out of the occasional remarks that we made in the early studies of 1968 in South Harlem, before we realized what was actually happening to this tense. Rickford's conclusion will certainly guide our future studies of *had*: that it is not simply a replacement of the preterit, but retains in its foreshadowing of narrative peaks something of the relational nature of its source, the English pluperfect.

Perhaps the most substantial contribution to current knowledge of the AAVE copula and auxiliary is to be found in "Rappin' on the Copula Coffin," the fourth chapter in this series of linguistic analyses. I well remember the first oral presentation of this paper at NWAVE. I was indeed carried away by the scope and power of the data provided by the four authors. When they jointly summed up their findings in a rap that was marked by precision of delivery and elegance of phrasing, I rose to my feet with others and cheered. Reassessing this chapter ten years later, I am struck by the characteristic calmness and balance of Rickford's analyses. Unlike most of us, he is never carried away. He sees that data almost always looks in two directions. Yes, the copula data is remarkably uniform across many studies throughout the United States, as table 7 shows. But no, it is not altogether uniform, and the differences among these studies are important to note. Since the various groups we studied in South Harlem did not agree in the ordering of following locatives and adjectives in their effect on copula deletion, we combined these two environments. When Holm, Baugh, and Myhill all found that a following adjective favored deletion more than locatives did, this seemed to reflect a parallel with the Caribbean syntax in which adjectives are verbs, and locatives take special, explicit copulas. But Rickford's survey showed that this hint of Caribbean/AAVE parallel did not stand up in the long run, and there are just as many studies in which the locative/adjective relationship runs the other way.

For a well-balanced view of the possible Creole origins of AAVE, we can turn to chapters 7 and 8 of this book. I am delighted to find "*Cut-Eye* and *Suck-Teeth*," co-authored by Angela Rickford. If there is anyone who does not believe that there is a strong cultural continuity between the Caribbean and the mainland Black community, this article will relieve their skepticism. It is a dramatic and fascinating account of aspects of African American culture that are not observed or noted by most Euro-Americans – but is there for them to see once their level of consciousness has been raised. The following chapter on Hiberno English and New World Black English is perhaps the most splendid example of a scholarly inquiry into a disputed question which is free from passionate or polemical thinking. Rickford begins with the need for a balanced assembly of linguistic and extra-linguistic data, and gives us a clear view of the social conditions that favor the competing influences of Hiberno English and Caribbean Creoles on the formation of AAVE. After assembling all the arguments for possible diffusion from Hiberno English, he also warns not to exaggerate what might have happened in the very small window of opportunity. He then turns to the various hypotheses about the origin of habitual *be*, weighing C.-J. Bailey's hypothesis of Irish influence against his own earlier decreolization hypothesis: that it represents the loss of *does* in earlier *does be*. Although his judicious weighing of the evidence does not find a persuasive case for Irish influence, he never eliminates this possibility, concluding that "untangling the sources of [Hiberno English/New World Black English] resemblances is a particularly challenging and rewarding enterprise. The reader is well advised to study and absorb the Rickford approach in preference to the cut-and-thrust polemics that are so common in pidgin and creole linguistics – and in the field of linguistics generally.

Rickford is objective, but that does not mean that he is an exponent of value-free science. A good portion of this volume is devoted to his efforts to apply our knowledge to the crucial educational problems of this country. Every reader should absorb the message of chapter 14: "Unequal Partnership: Sociolinguistics and the African American Speech Community." It is addressed to all of us: "we should start giving back *more*, and training our students to give back more." If Rickford ever does exhibit passion, it is in this appeal for us to justify our existence. The four final chapters are only a sampling of Rickford's efforts to put linguistics to work. When the public reaction against "Ebonics" swept upon us with all the force of madness mixed with racism, Rickford's was the clearest voice for sanity. He is the author of the resolution on Ebonics passed by the Linguistic Society of America, and his pen has rarely paused in the enterprise of restoring calmness and intelligence to the public debate.

There is no one lesson to be learned from reading this volume. It represents the varied issues put forward by a complex, penetrating and responsible scholarship. I would urge you, the reader, to pursue these matters from cover to cover. And when you are finished, I would simply urge: "Go thou, and do likewise."

William Labov, January 1999

Acknowledgments

It is a pleasure to thank the people who helped to make this book possible. The list includes Stanford students Jamillah Sabry, who worked tirelessly on the reprint requests and on the amalgamated bibliography, Naomi Levin, who helped with library runs and photocopying, and Emma Petty, who prepared the figures in the final chapter. This book was completed during a sabbatical year at the Stanford Humanities Center, and I am especially indebted to the Center's excellent facilities and their efficient, supportive staff: Keith Baker, Sue Dambrau, Susan Dunn, Gwen Lorraine, and Susan Sebbard. Gina Wein and the staff of the Stanford Linguistics Department also helped me in numerous ways over the many years that this book was written. Without the cooperation of the AAVE and creole speakers in East Palo Alto, Philadelphia, the South Carolina Sea Islands, Jamaica, Barbados, and Guyana who shared their ideas, experiences, and language with me on tape, most of the articles in this book would not have been written in the first place. I am grateful to them, and to Arnetha Ball, Renée Blake, Raina Jackson, Nomi Martin, Faye McNair-Knox, Angela Rickford, and Christine Théberge Rafal for their contributions to the jointly authored articles in this book and for permission to reprint them. I thank Geneva Smitherman (again) for suggesting this project, the anonymous reviewers for their positive feedback on the proposal, and Steve Smith and Philip Carpenter of Blackwell Publishers for saying "yes" and Helen Rappaport and other Blackwell staff for seeing this book through the various stages of production. Last but not least, I thank my loving wife Angela and my children Shiyama, Russell, Anakela, and Luke for their patience and encouragement during the preparation of this book. Angela's contributions were invaluable at every stage, from the beginning, when she helped with difficult decisions about what to include, to the end, when my brother Edward died and her emotional support helped me see the project through. I thank you all.

The author and publishers gratefully acknowledge the following for permission to reproduce copyright material:

Chapter 1: from Sandra Lee McKay and Nancy F. Hornberger (eds) *Sociolinguistics and Language Teaching*, 1998. Reprinted with the permission of Cambridge University Press. Chapter 2: from R. Fasold and R. Shuy (eds) *Analyzing Variation and Language*, 1975. Reprinted with the permission of Georgetown University Press. Chapter 3: from *American Speech* 1996 (71). Reprinted with the permission of the University of Alabama Press. Chapter 4: from *Language Variation and Change*, 1991 (3). Reprinted with the permission of Cambridge University Press. Chapter 5: from *American Speech* 1985, 60(3). Reprinted with the permission of the University of Alabama Press. Chapter 6: from *Sociolinguistic Perspectives on Register*, edited by Douglas Biber and Edward Finegan. Copyright © 1994 by Oxford University Press, Inc. Used by permission of Oxford University Press, Inc. Chapter 7: reprinted by permission of the American Anthropological Association from *Journal of American Folklore* 89: 353, July–September 1976. Not for further reproduction. Chapter 8: from *Language* 1986, 62(2). Used by permission of the Linguistic Society of America. Chapter 9: from *Towards a Social Science of Language: A Festschrift for William Labov* edited by Gregory R. Guy, John G. Baugh, Deborah Schiffrin, and Crawford Feagin, 1996. Reprinted with permission of John Benjamins B. V. Chapter 11: from *American Speech*, 1986, 62(1). Reprinted with the permission of the University of Alabama Press. Chapter 12: from *Internal and External Factors in Syntactic Change* edited by Marinel Gerritsen and Dieter Stein, 1992. Reprinted with the permission of Mouton de Gruyter. Chapter 13: from Sandra Lee McKay and Nancy F. Hornberger (eds) *Sociolinguistics and Language Teaching*, 1996. Reprinted with the permission of Cambridge University Press. Chapter 15: from *Discover* 1997, 18(12). Reprinted with the permission of *Discover* magazine. Chapter 16: from *Ebonics in the Urban Education Debate*, edited by David Ramirez, Terrence Wiley, Gerda de Klerk, and Enid Lee, forthcoming. Reprinted with the permission of the Center for Language Minority Education and Research, CSULB.

The publishers apologize for any errors or omissions in the above list and would be grateful to be notified of any corrections that should be incorporated in the next edition or reprint of this book.

Part I
Features and Use

1

Phonological and Grammatical Features of African American Vernacular English (AAVE)

1.1 Introduction

When the Ebonics controversy broke in December 1996, one of the most frequent requests from the media was for lists or descriptions of AAVE features which showed how it differed from Standard English (SE) and other American dialects, and which the general public could understand.[1] For the lexicon (vocabulary) of AAVE, this was not a problem, since in addition to the two substantive scholarly works by Major (1994) and Smitherman (1994a), there were several shorter, popular AAVE phrase books around, like Anderson (1994) and Stavsky et al. (1995).[2] For the phonology (pronunciation) and grammar of AAVE, however, the aspects which are more systematic and deepseated, less regionally variable, and more significant from a pedagogical point of view, it was much harder to recommend anything, and that remains true today.

One of the most complete and accessible (if somewhat technical) descriptions of AAVE phonology and grammar is Fasold and Wolfram's often-cited (1970) article. But besides being outdated both in terminology (it refers to AAVE as "Negro dialect") and coverage (it excludes features like *steady*, preterite *had*, and modal *come* which were not discovered or discussed until more recently), it is simply out of print. This is also true of more general introductions to AAVE like Dillard (1972), Burling (1973), and Baugh (1983), each of which includes a chapter or two on AAVE phonology and grammar. And it is true too of the classic book-length studies of Harlem, Detroit, and Washington DC conducted respectively by Labov et al. (1968), Wolfram (1969) and Fasold (1972), which report on AAVE structure as well as on variation by its users according to social class, age, gender, and style. While there are more recent works on AAVE phonology and grammar, they tend to be either less complete in their coverage (e.g. Dandy 1991), or highly specialized and technical, intended for an audience of linguists or speech pathologists (e.g. Martin 1992, Wolfram 1993, Wolfram 1994, Wolfram and Adger 1993, Dayton 1996, Bailey and Thomas 1998, Green 1993, 1998, Martin and Wolfram 1998, Mufwene 1998). One exception is the second chapter of Smitherman (1986), which covers many of the key features of AAVE in a language which most non-linguists could understand. However, Smitherman's book was originally written in 1977, and like its predecessors from the 1970s and 1980s, it doesn't cover newer features like *steady*, *come*, and *had*.

The articles, books, and monographs listed in the preceding paragraph still represent most of what we have come to know about AAVE phonology and grammar over the past three decades, and I would recommend them to readers with good library access and/or a background in linguistics. However, this article will hopefully help to fill the need for a brief, up-to-date, relatively complete and relatively non-technical description of AAVE's structural features.[3]

1.2   The Features of AAVE

Table 1.1 identifies the main distinctive phonological features of AAVE, and table 1.2 the main distinctive grammatical features of AAVE. Although it is impossible in a chapter of this length to add all the qualifying details about each

Table 1.1   Distinctive phonological (pronunciation) features of AAVE

1	Reduction of word-final consonant clusters (i.e., sequences of two or more consonants), especially those ending in *t* or *d*, as in *han'* for SE "hand," *des'* for SE "desk," *pos'* for SE "post," and *pass'* for SE "passed" (the *-ed* suffix in "passed" is pronounced as [t]).[4]
2	Deletion of word-final single consonant (especially nasals) after a vowel, as in *ma'* [mæ] for SE "man," *ca'* [kæ] for SE "cat" and ba' [bæ:] for SE "bad." Not as frequent as (1).
3	Devoicing of word-final voiced stops after a vowel, i.e., realization of [b] as [p], [d] as [t], and [g] as [k], as in [bæt] for SE "bad", and [pɪk] for SE "pig." The devoiced consonant may be followed or replaced by a glottal stop, e.g. [bætʔ] or [bæʔ]. (See Fasold and Wolfram 1970: 53–4, Wolfram et al. 1993: 10, Bailey and Thomas 1998: 89.)
4	Realization of final *ng* as *n* in gerunds, e.g. *walkin'* for SE "walking."[5]
5a	Realization of voiceless *th* [θ] as *t* or *f*, as in *tin* for SE "thin and *baf* for SE "bath."[6]
5b	Realization of voiced *th* [ð] as d or v, as in *den* for SE "then," and *bruvver* for SE "brother."
6	Realization of *thr* sequences as *th*, especially before [u] or [o], as in *thodown* [θodaun] for SE "throwdown." (See Wolfram 1993: 8).

Table 1.1   Continued

7   Deletion or vocalization (pronunciation as a weak neutral vowel) of *l* after a vowel, as in *he'p* for SE "help," and *toah* for SE "toll." May have the grammatical effect of deleting the "ll" of contracted *will*, as in "He be here tomorrow" for SE "He'll be here tomorrow," especially when the following word begins with labial *b*, *m* or *w* (Fasold and Wolfram 1970: 51–3).

8   Deletion or vocalization of *r* after a vowel, as in *sistuh* for SE "sister" or *fouh* for SE "four." This rule applies more often when the *r* comes at the end of a word and is followed by a word beginning with a consonant (*four posts*) rather than a word beginning with a vowel (*four apples*), but it can also apply when a vowel follows within the same word, as in *Ca'ol* for SE "Carol" or *sto'y* for SE "story." Grammatical effects may include the use of *they* for the SE possessive "their" (Labov et al. 1968: 99–119, Fasold and Wolfram 1970: 51–3).

9   Deletion of initial *d* and *g* in certain tense-aspect auxiliaries, as in "ah *'on* know" for SE "I *don't* know" and "ah'm *'a* do it" for SE "I'm *gonna* do it" (see Labov et al. 1968: 252); the distinctive AAVE use of *ain't* for "didn't" (ibid.: 255) probably derives historically from this rule too. Note parallels in Gullah/ Caribbean Creole English tense-aspect markers: *da* ~ *a*, *does* ~ *oes*, *ben* ~ *men* ~ *en*, *mos bii* ~ *mosii*, and *go* ~ *o* (Rickford 1974: 108).

10 Deletion of unstressed initial and medial syllables, as in *'fraid* for SE "afraid" and *sec't'ry* for SE "secretary." Strongly age-graded. According to Vaughn-Cooke (1987: 22), the unstressed syllable deletion rate for speakers over 60 years old in her Mississippi sample was 85 percent, for speakers aged 40–59 it was 70 percent, and for speakers 8–20 years old, it was 52 percent.

11 Metathesis or transposition of adjacent consonants, as in *aks* for SE "ask" (one of the biggest shibboleths of AAVE, often referred to by teachers, personnel officers, and other gatekeepers in the course of putting down the variety), and *waps* for SE "wasp."

12 Realization of SE *v* and *z* (voiced fricatives) as *d* and *z* respectively (voiced stops), especially in word-medial position before a nasal, as in *seben* for SE "seven" and *idn'* for SE "isn't" (phonetically, [ɪznt]). (See Wolfram 1993: 9, Bailey and Thomas 1998: 89).

13 Realization of syllable-initial *str* as *skr*, especially before high front vowels like "ee" [i], as in *skreet* for SE "street" and *deskroy* for "destroy" (see Dandy 1991: 44).

14 Monophthongal pronunciations of *ay* and *oy*, as in *ah* for SE "I" and *boah* for SE "boy."[7]

15 Neutralization/merger of [ɪ] and [ɛ] before nasals, as in [pɪn] for SE "pin" and "pen." (See Labov et al. 1968: 119–20.)

16 Realization of "ing" as "ang" and "ink" as "ank" in some words, as in *thang* for SE "thing," *sang* for SE "sing," and *drank* for SE "drink." (See Smitherman 1986: 18, Dandy 1991: 46).

17 Stress on first rather than second syllable, as in *pólice* instead of SE *políce*, and *hótel* instead of SE *hotél*.[8]

18 More varied intonation, with "higher pitch range and more rising and level final contours" than other American English varieties (Wolfram et al. 1993: 12; see also Rickford 1977: 205).

Table 1.2   Distinctive grammatical (morphological and syntactic) features of AAVE

19 Pre-verbal markers of tense, mood, and aspect

19a   Absence of copula/auxiliary *is* and *are* for present tense states and actions, as in
"He Ø tall" for SE "He's tall" or "They Ø running" for SE "They *are*
running."[9] (See Labov 1969 and Rickford et al. 1988, reprinted in this volume.)

19b   Use of invariant *be* (sometimes *bees*) for habitual aspect, as in "He *be* walkin"
(usually, regularly, versus "He Ø walkin" right now) for SE "He is usually
walking/usually walks." Used with auxiliary *do* in questions, negatives, and tag
questions, as in "*Do* he *be* walking every day?" or "She *don't be* sick, *do* she?"
(Fasold 1972: 150–84, Dayton 1996, Green 1998).

19c   Use of invariant *be* for future "will be," as in "He be here tomorrow." This is
essentially a result of the phonological rule deleting the contracted *'ll* of *will*
(see #7 above).

19d   Use of *steady* as an intensified continuative marker, usually after invariant
habitual *be*, but before a progressive verb, for actions that occur consistently or
persistently, as in "Ricky Bell be *steady* steppin in them number nines." (Baugh
1983: 86).

19e   Use of unstressed *been* or *bin* for SE "has/have been" (present perfects), as in
"He *been* sick" for "He has been sick." Unlike stressed BIN (see 19e),
unstressed *been* can co-occur with time adverbials (e.g. "since last week"), and
does not connote remoteness (Rickford 1975).

19f   Use of stressed *BIN* to mark remote phase (that the action happened or the
state came into being long ago) as in "She *BIN* married" for SE "She has been
married for a long time (and still is)," or "He *BIN* ate it" for SE "He ate it a
long time ago" (Rickford 1975, Baugh 1983: 80–2).

19g   Use of *done* to emphasize the completed nature of an action, as in "He *done did*
it" for SE "He's already done it." *Done* can co-occur with *been*, as in "By the
time I got there, he *been done* gone" or, in the reverse order, "They done been
sitting there an hour." (See Labov 1972c: 53–7, Baugh 1983: 74–7,
Smitherman 1986: 24, Dayton 1996, Green 1998).

19h   Use of *be done* for resultatives or the future/conditional perfect, as in "She *be
done had* her baby" for SE "She *will have had* her baby." (Baugh 1983: 77–80,
Dayton 1996, Green 1998).

19i   Use of *finna* (sometimes *fitna*, derived from "fixin' to") to mark the immediate
future, as in "He *finna* go" for SE "He's about to go."[10]

19j   Use of *come* to express the speaker's indignation about an action or event, as in
"He *come* walkin in here like he owned the damn place" (Spears 1982: 852).

19k   Use of *had* to mark the simple past (primarily among preadolescents) as in
"then we *had* went outside" for SE "then we went outside" (Rickford and
Théberge-Rafal 1989).

19l   Use of double modals,[11] as in *may can*, *might can*, and *might could* (common in
Southern White vernaculars) for SE "might be able to" or *must don't* (more
unique to AAVE) for SE "must not." (See Labov et al. 1968: 260–3, Labov
1972c: 57–9).

Table 1.2   Continued

19m Use of quasi modals *liketa* and *poseta*, as in "I *liketa* drowned" for SE "I nearly
      drowned" and "You don't *poseta* do it that way" for SE "You're not supposed
      to do it that way." (Labov 1972: 56, 59, Wolfram 1993: 13).

20 Other aspects of verbal tense marking

20a Absence of third person singular present tense *-s*, as in "He walkØ" for SE
      "He walks." The use of *don't* instead of "doesn't" as in "He *don't* sing" or *have*
      instead of "has," as in "She *have* it" is related, since "doesn't and "hasn't"
      include 3rd singular *-s* (Fasold 1972: 121–49).
20b Generalization of *is* and *was* to use with plural and second person subjects (i.e.,
      instead of *are* and *were*) as in "They *is* some crazy folk" for SE "They are crazy
      folk" or "We *was* there" for SE "We were there" (Wolfram 1993: 14).
20c Use of past tense or preterite form (V–ed) as past participle (V–en), as in "He
      had *bit*" for SE "He had bitten," or "She has *ran*" for SE "She has run." (See
      Fasold and Wolfram 1970: 62, Rickford and Théberge: 1996: 232–3, reprinted
      in this volume).
20d Use of past participle form (V–en) as past tense or preterite form (V–ed), as in
      "She *seen* him yesterday" for SE "She saw him yesterday" (Wolfram 1993: 12).
20e Use of verb stem (V) as past tense or preterite form (V–ed), as in "He *come*
      down here yesterday" for SE "He came down here yesterday."[12] (Wolfram
      1993: 12).
20f   Reduplication of a past tense or past participle suffix (also referred to
      sometimes as "double tense marking"), as in *likeded* [laɪktɪd] for SE "liked" and
      light-skinded for SE "light skinned." Only applies to a small set of verbs
      (including *liked*, *looked*, *skinned*), and more common in adolescent speech (see
      Wolfram 1993: 14).

21 Nouns and pronouns

21a Absence of possessive *-s*, as in "JohnØ house" for SE "John's house."
21b Absence of plural *-s* (much less frequent than 20a or 21a), as in "two boyØ" for
      SE "two boys."
21c Use of *and (th)em* or *nem*, usually after a proper name, to mark associative
      plurals, as in *Felicia an' (th)em* or *Felician nem* for "Felician and her friends or
      family or associates." (See Mufwene 1998: 73, who finds this more similar to
      English creoles than to other varieties of English, although southern white
      varieties use it too).
21d Appositive or pleonastic pronouns, as in "That teacher, *she* yell at the kids" for
      SE "That teacher Ø yells at the kids." (Fasold and Wolfram 1970: 81).
21e Use of *y'all* and *they* to mark second person plural and third plural possessive,
      respectively, as in "It's *y'all* ball" for SE "It's your ball" and "It's *they* house"
      for SE "It's their house" (Wolfram et al. 1993: 16).

Table 1.2   Continued

21f   Use of object pronouns (*me*, *him*, and so on) after a verb as personal datives
      (="(*for*) *myself*," "*(for*) *himself*" and so on) as in "Ahma git *me* a gig" for SE
      "I'm going to get myself some support" (Gumperz 1982b: 31, Wolfram 1993:
      16).

21g   Absence of relative pronoun (*who*, *which*, *what* or *that*) as in "That's the man Ø
      come here" for SE "That's the man who came here." Note that the omitted
      form is a subject relative pronoun (*who*). Many varieties of English allow for
      the omission of object relative pronouns, e.g. "That's the man (whom) I saw,"
      but the omission of subject relatives is rarer, and more unique to AAVE
      (Mufwene 1998: 77).

22 Negation

22a   Use of *ain'(t)* as a general preverbal negator, for SE "am not," "isn't,"
      "aren't," "hasn't," "haven't" and "didn't," as in "He *ain'* here" for SE "He
      isn't here," or "He *ain'* do it" for SE "He didn't do it."

22b   Multiple negation or negative concord (that is, negating the auxiliary verb and
      all indefinite pronouns in the sentence), as in "He *don'* do *nothin*" for SE "He
      doesn't do anything" (Labov 1972a, 1972c; 130–96).

22c   Negative inversion (inversion of the auxiliary and indefinite pronoun subject),
      as in "*Can't nobody* say nothin" (inverted from "Nobody can't say nothin") for
      SE "Nobody can say anything" or "*Ain't nobody* home" (from "Nobody ain't
      home" for SE "Nobody is home" (Sells, Rickford and Wasow 1996a, b).

22d   Use of *ain't but* and *don't but* for "only," as in "He ain't but fourteen years old"
      for SE "He's only fourteen years old" or "They didn't take but three dollars"
      for "They only took three dollars" (Wolfram et al. 1993: 14).

23 Questions

23a   Formation of direct questions without inversion of the subject and auxiliary
      verb, usually with rising intonation, as in "Why *I can't* play?" for SE "Why
      can't I play?" and "*They didn't* take it?" for SE "Didn't they take it?" (Labov et
      al. 1968: 291–6, Martin and Wolfram 1998: 29).

23b   Auxiliary verb inversion in embedded questions (without *if* or *whether*), as in "I
      asked him *could he* go with me" for SE "I asked him if he could go with me"
      (Labov et al. 1968: 296–300).

24 Existential and locative constructions

24a   Use of existential *it* (*is*, *'s*, *was*, *ain't*) instead of *there* (*is*, *'s*, *was*, *isn't*) as in "*It's*
      a school up there" for SE "There's a school up there" (Labov et al. 1968: 301–
      3).

24b   Use of existential *they got* as a plural equivalent of singular *it is*, instead of *there are*, as in "*They got* some hungry women here" (line from a Nina Simone song) for "There are some hungry women here" (Labov et al. 1968: 303).

24c   Use of *here go* as a static locative or presentational form, as in "*Here go* my own" (said by a 12-year-old girl from East Palo Alto, California as she showed me her artwork) for SE "Here is my own." (See Labov et al. 1968: 303.)

25 Complementizer/quotative *say*

25a   Use of *say* to introduce a quotation or a verb complement, as in "They told me *say* they couldn't go." Although superficially similar to the SE use of "say" to introduce quotations, note its use with verbs like *believe* and *know* (which have nothing to do with speaking) in Gullah and Caribbean creoles, and its parallels with and possible origins in the Akan complementizer *se* (Rickford 1977: 212).

feature which one would like to (but see the accompanying footnotes and references), two general comments should be made, one about the frequency with which these features occur among African American speakers, and the other about their distinctiveness vis-à-vis the colloquial or vernacular English of other Americans.

1.3   Variation in AAVE Feature Use by Social Class, Age, Gender, and Style

Not every African American speaks AAVE, and no one uses all of the features in tables 1.1 and 1.2 100 percent of the time. Although it is often said that 80 percent of African Americans speak AAVE (Dillard 1972: 229), this is a guesstimate rather than a systematic empirical finding. In general, the phonological and grammatical features depicted in tables 1.1 and 1.2 are used most often by younger lower- and working-class speakers in urban areas and in informal styles, but the extent to which this is true, and how often the features are used varies from one feature to another.

Wolfram's (1969) study of Detroit – although now 30 years old – remains one of our most comprehensive sources of information on class stratification in AAVE,[13] and table 1.3 summarizes some of the systematic class effects it revealed for several features. Note that the lower working-class (LWC) speakers' usage of these features ranged from a high of 84 percent for consonant cluster reduction to a low of 6 percent for plural -*s* absence. Note also that while

Table 1.3   Use of selected AAVE features in Detroit, by social class

FEATURE	LWC	UWC	LMC	UMC
Consonant cluster simplification NOT in past tense (60)	84%	79%	66%	51%
Voiceless th [θ] → f, t or Ø (84)	71%	59%	17%	12%
Multiple negation (156)	78%	55%	12%	8%
Absence of copula/auxiliary *is, are* (169)	57%	37%	11%	5%
Absence of third person present tense *-s* (136)	71%	57%	10%	1%
Absence of possessive *-s* (141)	27%	25%	6%	0%
Absence of plural *-s* (143)	6%	4%	1%	0%

Notes: LWC = lower working-class (e.g. laborers and other unskilled workers), UWC = upper working-class (e.g. carpenters and other skilled workers), LMC = lower middle-class (e.g. high school teachers and many white collar workers), UMC = upper middle-class (e.g. lawyers and doctors).[14] Numbers represent mean percentages of use in recordings with 12 individuals from each class.

Source: Wolfram 1969 (original page references in brackets)

the middle-class speakers used consonant cluster reduction at least half of the time, so that the distinction between them and the working-class speakers with respect to this feature was not very pronounced – Wolfram (pp. 120–1) called this "gradient stratification" – they used the other features like multiple negation and possessive *-s* absence very infrequently, so that the distinction between them and the working-class speakers with respect to these features was very pronounced – Wolfram (ibid.) called this "sharp stratification."

Investigations of AAVE also show systematic effects of style, age, gender, and linguistic environment. For instance, Foxy Boston, a teenager from East Palo Alto, deleted *is* and *are* 70 percent of the time in one interview with an African American with whom she was familiar, but only 40 percent of the time in another interview with a European American whom she had not met before (Rickford and McNair-Knox 1994: 247, reprinted in this volume). The members of the Cobras street gang in New York City, like most other AAVE speakers, deleted *is* more often when it had a pronoun subject (e.g. *He*) than when it had a noun phrase subject (e.g. *The man*), and more often when recorded with their peer group than when interviewed individually (Labov 1972c: 84). Wolfram (1969: 179) reported that the 14–17-year-old subjects in his Detroit sample deleted *is* and *are* 68 percent of the time, while the adults did so only 38 percent of the time; in my sample from East Palo Alto, California, 15-year-old Tinky Gates deleted *is* and *are* 81 percent of the time, while her 38-year-old mother, Paula Gates, did so 35 percent of the time, and 76-year-old Penelope Johnson did so only 15 percent of the time.

Finally, males are generally reported as using AAVE features more often than females, but this may be partly because the interviewers in most studies are male. For instance, Wolfram (1969: 136) reports that the lower working-class males in Detroit deleted third present -*s* 74 percent of the time compared to 69 percent for lower working-class females. But Foxy Boston and Tinky Gates, in interviews conducted in East Palo Alto by a female fieldworker (Faye McNair Knox), showed even higher rates of third present -*s* absence – 97 percent and 96 percent respectively (Rickford 1992).

1.4   The Distinctiveness of AAVE, vis-à-vis Other American Varieties

The features of AAVE that appear to be distinctive to this variety (or nearly so) are primarily grammatical. Wolfram (1991: 108) lists eight such features, and six of them (including stressed *BIN*, invariant *be*, and *is* absence) are grammatical. Many of the phonological features of AAVE (e.g. consonant cluster reduction and the deletion or vocalization of *l* and *r*), and some of its grammatical features too (e.g. multiple negation and absence of third person singular present tense -*s*) also occur in the colloquial English of Americans from other ethnic groups, especially those from the working class. Others (like the monophthongal pronunciations of *ay* and *oy*, the merger of "pin" and "pen," or the use of *done* and double modals) are characteristic of southern white vernacular speech in general (see Feagin 1979, Bailey and Thomas 1998, Wolfram and Schilling-Estes 1998.). But most of the time, the features which AAVE shares with southern and other American vernaculars occur more frequently in AAVE and/or in a wider range of linguistic environments. For instance, consonant cluster simplification appears to be more common in the AAVE of working-class African Americans than in white working-class speech, and it occurs in AAVE even when the next word begins with a vowel (e.g. *pos' office*), a position in which many other dialects retain the final consonant (Wolfram 1991: 109).[15] For some AAVE speakers, words like *des'* do not have an underlying final *k*, and the plural form is *desses* according to the same rule that applies to words ending in a final sibilant (e.g., *rose-roses*, *boss-bosses*, *church-churches*).

1.5   Concluding Remarks

While lists of vernacular, non-standard, or non-mainstream features like those in tables 1.1 and 1.2 are useful, they can also give the impression that their standard or mainstream equivalents are not characteristic of AAVE usage at all, so that if an African American speaker pronounced *past* without reducing the final *st* or used existential *there* instead of *it* ("There's a hole in the bucket") that speaker might have to be classified as speaking or switching to SE. But in practice, as Labov (1972e: 189) pointed out, a speaker might alternate between vernacular and mainstream variants many times in the course of even a brief conversation, and we have to recognize that AAVE, like most language varieties, includes a certain amount of inherent variability. That variability in turn can be adjusted in one direction or another to mark the kinds of social and stylistic distinctions discussed above, and the dynamic, shifting relationships among the interlocutors.

Finally, AAVE use, even at its most vernacular, does not consist simply of stringing together features like those in tables 1.1 and 1.2. What these lists fail to convey is the way skilled AAVE speakers use those features, together with distinctive AAVE words, prosodies and rhetorical/expressive styles, to inform, persuade, attract, praise, celebrate, chastise, entertain, educate, get over, set apart, mark identity, reflect, refute, brag, and do all the varied things for which human beings use language. It is because AAVE serves those purposes and serves them well that it continues to exist despite all the condemnations it receives from the larger society. For the preachers, novelists, storytellers, poets, playwrights, actors and actresses, street corner hustlers, church-going grandparents, working mothers and fathers and schoolyard children, rappers, singers, barber-shop and beauty-salon clients who draw on it daily, AAVE is not simply a compendium of features, but the integral whole which Claude Brown evocatively called "Spoken Soul."[16]

Notes

1   This is a considerably revised and expanded excerpt from Rickford 1996a, including a new introduction and conclusion, numerous additional references, and more than twice as many AAVE features.

2   One problem with the popular phrase books or glossaries is that they focus almost entirely on slang, the newest and most transient part of the AAVE lexicon, and the part most familiar to adolescents and teenagers. This reinforces the mistaken impression that AAVE is nothing more than slang, and that it is not known and used by adult African Americans.

3   It is difficult to provide a truly complete description in the space available, however, and difficult to avoid technical terms altogether, especially in the description of the phonology. My hope is that my description will remain relatively accessible to the educated layperson while remaining accurate and useful for the linguist or speech pathologist.

4   The systematic nature of AAVE is shown by the fact that this rule operates only when both members of the consonant cluster are either voiceless, involving no vibration of the vocal cords (as in "po*st*," "a*sk*" and "a*pt*"), or voiced, with the vocal

cords vibrating (as in "po*sed*" [*zd*], "ha*nd*" and "o*ld*"). When one member of the cluster is voiceless and the other voiced (as in "ju*mp*" or "tha*nk*") the cluster cannot be simplified, except in negative forms like *ain'* and *don'*. See Fasold and Wolfram (1970: 43–6) and Labov et al. (1968: 123–57) for further discussion.

5   This is popularly known as "dropping your g's," but it doesn't actually involve any *g*- dropping at all. What actually happens, in phonetic terms, is that one kind of nasal (an alveolar nasal – with the tongue touching the alveolar ridge right behind the top teeth) is substituted for another one (á velar nasal – with the tongue touching the velar or upper back region of the roof of the mouth). See Labov et al. (1968: 120–3).

6   As Fasold and Wolfram (1970: 49–51) point out, voiceless *th* is more often realized as *t* at the beginnings of words, and as *f* in the middle or at the ends of words. Similarly, *d* realizations of voiced *dh* are more common word-initially and *v* realizations are more common word-medially and word-finally. See also Labov et al. (1968: 92–9).

7   As Fasold and Wolfram (1970: 56) point out, this feature is common among both Blacks and Whites in the South, and occurs much more frequently before voiced sounds or pause (as in "side," "I") than before voiceless sounds (as in "site").

8   According to Fasold and Wolfram (1970: 57), this affects only a small subset of words, such as *pólice*, *hótel*, and *Júly*.

9   In the grammatical examples, Ø is used to mark the point at which a grammatical form or inflection would occur in equivalent SE examples. This is comparable to the use of an apostrophe in phonological examples (e.g. *he'p*) to mark the point at which a consonant or vowel occurs in equivalent SE forms.

10   There is no published discussion of the use of *finna* in AAVE, but see Ching (1987) for a discussion of its probable source – *fixin to* – in the South.

11   Modals are auxiliary verbs like *can*, *might*, *must* which express the speaker's mood, or attitude towards what he/she is saying, e.g. whether it is possible, likely, obligatory, and so on.

12   In general, the past tense category is well established in AAVE, as is shown by the past that most irregular or strong verbs (which undergo a stem change to mark the past) are past-marked most of the time; Fasold (1972: 39) reports that 98 percent of the 833 past tense strong verbs he examined in his Washington DC corpus were past marked. Unmarked pasts tend to come either from regular or weak verbs (like *walked*) in which the final consonant is deleted by phonological rule, or from the small set of irregular verbs (including *come, say, run, give*, and *eat*, among others) which sometimes occur without past inflection (see Wolfram et al. 1993: 12).

13   Wolfram's sample included 12 representatives of each socioeconomic class. The classes themselves were differentiated using an adapted version of Hollingshead and Redlich's (1958) scale, combining scales of education, occupation, and residency (Wolfram 1969: 32ff.). Since most African Americans in Detroit at that time were working class, Wolfram suggested (p. 36) that the speech patterns described for the LWC and UWC in his study would be characteristic of the "vast majority" of African Americans in Detroit.

14   Although illustrative occupations are given for each class to give readers a rough idea of who they designate, it should be emphasized that Wolfram's social class membership was determined in Wolfram's study (and in the parent study by Shuy,

Wolfram and Riley 1967 from which it evolved) by a combination of occupational status (weighted most heavily), education, and residency type. See Wolfram (1969: 32–41) for more details.

15 In other words, speakers of such dialects will say *pos' five letters*, deleting final t before a consonant, but *post office*, retaining the final *t* before a vowel. Similarly, some AAVE speakers delete or vocalize post-vocalic *r* before a vowel, even within the same word (so that "Carol" sounds like *Ca'ol*), but speakers of white vernaculars do not (Labov 1972c: 40).

16 In a book with this very title, Rickford and Rickford (to appear) will document the expressive use of AAVE by individuals, representing many of the categories listed in this closing sentence (writers, singers, preachers, ordinary people), in an effort to refute the widespread misimpression left by the Ebonics controversy that AAVE is not appreciated or used within the African American community.

2

Carrying the New Wave into Syntax: The Case of Black English BÍN

2.1 Introduction

Ever since the first conference on New Ways of Analyzing Variation in English was held in 1972, the abbreviated title – NWAVE – has become something of a rallying cry ("The New Wave") to those interested in the study of linguistic variation. The enthusiasm is doubtless justified. Uneasiness with categorical frameworks has been growing for some time, and the remarks made by C. -J. N. Bailey in the introduction to the papers from NWAVE I (Bailey and Shuy 1973) would probably be endorsed by a great many (though by no means all) linguists today:

> I am happy to be rid of static homogeneous models and to be rid of the fudges represented by 'my dialect', 'performance component', 'optional', and the rest. (xiv)

However, as we move beyond initial revolutionary fervour, and begin a more sober stock-taking, certain weaknesses in our line of attack become increasingly clear. One salient limitation is the extent to which we have become preoccupied with morphophonemic and phonological variation to the exclusion of everything else. Syntax and semantics, for instance, have come to represent lone islands far out at sea, increasingly untouched by any waves – old or new.

The problem is particularly acute for those "variationists" whose data consists of large samples of tape-recorded speech, covering as wide a range of stylistic contexts as possible (cf. Labov 1966, Bickerton 1973a). While the advantages of this method in terms of "accountability" etc. should be clear to most of us by now, it has a built-in limitation in providing large masses of data only on those phenomena which show up with high frequency in natural speech. In most cases, these are phonological variables; hence the disproportionate number of variation studies in phonology.

It was precisely in response to this problem that Gillian Sankoff (1973) entitled her paper presented at the first NWAVE meeting "Above and beyond phonology in variable rules." There can be little doubt about the soundness of her primary thesis – that "variability occurs, and can be dealt with, at levels of grammar above (or beyond) the phonological." However, we can hardly fail to note that the pool of data examined in some of the studies she cited (for example, *bai* in Tok Pisin) is far smaller than in the more customary studies of phonological phenomena. And that in others (Montreal *que*; cf. also the English copula as examined by Labov 1969) phonological features in the environment act as significant variable constraints. What of the other syntactic variables which show no or very little phonological conditioning? (We certainly know such cases exist.)

Finally, what of the other syntactic phenomena which tend to occur even less frequently than these – things about which not even the most basic linguistic facts are known, much less the kind of variation they display? Bickerton, in a March 1973 issue of the *Lectological Newsletter*, complained about the "reams that have been written about the different things Black speakers do with their Ds and Zs," but that "next to nothing that has been written about the different ways Black speakers organize their tense systems." But this is again because of the low frequency with which many of the most interesting Black English tense and aspect markers (e.g. Invariant *Be*, Remote *BÍN*) tend to show up in tape-recorded speech. This in turn is so not only because speakers have some awareness of the stigmatized nature of such forms, but also because the semantic conditions which they are normally introduced to express may occur rarely, if at all, in the course of a sociolinguistic interview.

Overcoming these limitations of tape-recorded data should certainly rank as one of the major challenges to riders of the "New Wave." But the problem has so far not received the attention it deserves. Innovations made in this area (cf. Labov 1973) have not sparked off a chain of repeat performances (as many of Labov's innovations in sociolinguistic interview technique did in the 1960s). And issues of validity and reliability involved in such innovations still remain to be raised.

The purpose of this paper is to draw attention to some of the innovations in methodology which have already been achieved, and to demonstrate the application of two such methods to a syntactic case about which very little has been written so far – *BÍN* in Black English. Let us first review some of the methods available for overcoming the limitations of tape-recorded data with respect to syntactic and other low-frequency phenomena.

One possibility is the method of "surreptitious" or "candid" recording. As it has been demonstrated publicly and dramatically for us most recently, this method involves tape-recording what people say without their knowledge or permission. The hope of the strongest advocates of this method is that speakers, unhampered by the constraints of the typical interview situation, will produce more of those syntactic and other variables which are normally stigmatized. While this is certainly true to the extent that other aspects of the speech-situation (for example, nature of the participants) do not have a more powerful overriding effect, it is simply the case that we cannot have our "hidden tape-recorder" with us at all times. We will always be exposed to more speech than we shall ever have the opportunity to record. The other disadvantages of this method – poor quality of recordings, discovery and its consequences, quite apart from the ethics involved, are also well known. Together, they suggest that despite its devilish appeal, this possibility will be of limited utility.

Another method involves "enriching the data of tape-recorded conversation" by including questions and topics which stimulate more frequent use of rare forms or environments than might occur naturally (Labov 1972b). The method works excellently in some cases. If you will pardon the use of a phonological example for effect, let me cite one case from recent studies at the University of Pennsylvania, of the tensing and raising of (æ). The problem was to elicit a natural production of the word "sad." One student discovered that a highly successful way of doing this was to ask interviewees if they had ever seen the movie *Love Story*. Almost inevitably the word would crop up – repeatedly – in the ensuing discussion.

The method demands careful attention to the nature of everyday conversational interaction. But it demands more. Most of the crucial syntactic/semantic variables (like BE *BÍN*) are extremely difficult to elicit, paradoxically, unless we already know a great deal about their meaning and use.

The final two methods are more immediately feasible to the researcher. Both move beyond the use of tape-recorded data, though in very different ways. The first has been used extensively by students of variation in "abstract syntax," for example, those interested in syntactic features which have no clear regional or social roots. In its more sophisticated form, this method involves eliciting the intuitions of other people and analyzing the results for patterns of variation, increasingly, with the help of implicational scales (Elliot, Legum, and Thompson 1969, C. J. Bailey 1970, Baltin 1973, Carden 1970, Sag 1973). The method has been extended, with important innovations, to the study of syntactic variation which is governed by regional and social factors (Labov 1973), and is being hailed by others (Butters 1973) as the most promising methodology for overcoming the limitations of tape-recorded data. However, as mentioned before, issues of validity and reliability are most acute with this method, and as it is usually employed, no independent check on the results is available.

The final method is one which has been used very rarely in studies to date. It involves careful and intense participant-observation. Whether our interest is in Black English, Puerto-Rican English, British English, or more abstract varieties, we exploit our contacts with native speakers to record on 3-by-5 cards every possible use of the variable in which we are interested. At the suggestion of Bill Labov, several students at the University of Pennsylvania have been using this method for some time now. We never cease to be amazed at the frequency with which even the rarest variables begin to show up once we are constantly attending to them in this way. The advances of this method over the others are also clear. Not only are we able to gather the most reliable data – from natural conversation – but we can gather it anywhere, anytime, without the need of any technical equipment. (Note too that permission to scribble away in the midst of ongoing conversations is more easily extended than permission to run a tape-recorder, partly because it is less potentially damaging to participants.)

My own studies of *BE BÍN* have depended largely on a combination of the last two methods. The "intuitive data" consists of the responses of a sample of 25 black and 25 white subjects to a questionnaire designed to explore their ability to interpret, predict, and evaluate the use of *BÍN*. This questionnaire, entitled Q-SCOM-IV, was an extension of similar ones (Q-SCOM-I to III) which had been developed and used by Bill Labov and other members of a research group in which I participated two years ago (cf. Labov 1972a). In Q-SCOM-IV, several more aspects of *BÍN* usage were attacked, and the questions about other variables served principally as "distractors." The subjects were drawn from very diverse geographical backgrounds (including Pennsylvania, New York, California, North Carolina, and Massachusetts), and were interviewed individually. (I should like to thank here Angela Rickford and Karl Reisman for their help with this time-consuming process.)

Participant-observation was carried out in two widely separate black communities – one in West Philadelphia, the other in the Sea Islands off the coast of South Carolina. Living in these communities, I was able to draw on a wide range of conversational encounters in which *BÍN*, supposedly rare, was frequently used. Although I heard many more than I was able to note down, I was able to gather about 66 sentences with stressed *BÍN*. Most of my sentences, it should be noted, come from adults over the age of 24 – providing strong contradictory evidence to the frequently voiced claim that the central syntactic structures of Black English are regularly used only by young black children or adolescents.

It is clearly impossible to present all the findings of this research in the time available to me today. I shall consider only three central aspects about *BÍN* on which there seems to be disagreement or limited information in the published literature: (a) The significance of stress (i.e. *BÍN* = bǐn?); (b) Meaning and Use; (c) Productivity–Co-occurrence Relations. I shall try to maintain a balance between substantive findings about *BÍN* itself and theoretical questions about the two methods employed. In particular I shall be interested in the internal consistency of the intuitive responses, and the extent to which they are supported by data from participant-observation.

2.2   Three Issues in the Study of Black English *BÍN*

2.2.1   *The significance of stress (i.e.* BÍN = bĭn?*)*

The *been* which we are interested in is the form which has been mentioned in the literature as signalling some "remote" past tense or perfective aspect.[1] We shall explore the precise meaning of the form in the next section. Here we simply want to know how significant stress is to the remote function with which the form has typically been associated.

Previous researchers have been quite divided on this point.[2] Stewart (1965), the first to draw attention to the form, indicated that stress was obligatory. Fasold and Wolfram (1970) feel that stress on *been* is an optional element only, its function being to "doubly emphasize the total completion of an action." Fickett (1970) shares their view on the optionality of stress, but for her its function is to distinguish *been* as a Phase Auxiliary (with remote function) from *been* as the auxiliary of a passive. The latter, in her analysis, never receives stress.

Dillard (1972) suggests that there may have existed two systems all along: one in which stressed *BÍN* is a remote, and unstressed *bĭn* a recent perfective; and another in which *been* (regardless of stress) is remote, and *done* a recent perfective. He adds that the latter system "has had most widespread influence in the U.S." but that the former "still survives in some forms of Black English."

When we turn to the intuitive responses of black subjects on this point, we find similar divisions and ambiguities. Example 1 below indicates the questions relevant to this in Q-SCOM-IV:

1   17b   Could you say 'I *bĭn* know it' (unstressed) and mean the same thing as "I *BÍN* know it' (stressed)? Yes_____ No_____
    9a   He *BÍN* had one.   9b   He *bĭn* had one. Same_____
    Different_____
    15a   He *BÍN* sick.   15b   He *bĭn* sick. Same_____
    Different_____

Question 17b for instance, was asked after subjects had responded to the meaning of stressed *BÍN*, usually with tremendous agreement on the remote function of this form. The question was whether one could say the unstressed form *bĭn* and mean the same thing. Nine said yes, ten said no. Similarly, 12 felt that 9a and 9b were the same, and ten that they were not.

As table 2.1 indicates, the number of informants who were consistent in their responses on this issue is even smaller:

Features and Use

Table 2.1 Consistency response of black subjects to 17b, 9 and 15 in Q-SCOM-IV

		Positive responses			*Negative responses*	
N	*Yes to 17b*	*Yes 17b Same 9*	*Yes 17b Same 9 Same 15*	*No to 17b*	*No 17b Diff. 9*	*No 17b Diff. 9 Diff. 15*
19	9	8	6	10	7	7

Positive responses are those which suggest that *BÍN* and *bĭn* are equivalent. Negative responses, that they are different. While there are only six informants who consistently see the two forms as equivalent, and seven who consistently see them as different, note again what an even split this is. This is the pattern that is repeated regularly, no matter how the question of *BÍN = bĭn* is put, nor how the answers are analyzed. This might be taken to suggest that Dillard (1972) is right – that there are two systems for signalling "remote" tense. In one the stress on *been* is significant, in the other it is not.

As variationists, there should be nothing uncomfortable about this conclusion. But before we accept it, let us turn to the data gathered in participant observation. From a total of 66 *BÍN* sentences, and over 200 with unstressed *bĭn*, the data is quite clear and conclusive on this point. Only stressed *BÍN* can signal remote function by itself, as is clear from the contexts in which it is used.

Unstressed *bĭn* occurs frequently with temporal adverbs or "specifiers," as in

2   I *bĭn* playing cards since I was four. (BF 38, Pa)[3]

Since this is often the case, it is possible to see how one might arrive at the mistaken impression that unstressed *bĭn* signals remote aspect. However, it is the time adverbial that signals the function in these cases, not the unstressed *bĭn* form. Not only are such time adverbials unnecessary with stressed *BÍN*, they are restricted from co-occurring with it. This syntactic consequence of the semantic difference between the two forms is illustrated most strikingly when the two follow close upon each other in the discourse:

3   I *BÍN* know you, you know. I *bĭn* knowing you *for years*. (BM 59, Pa)

The only case in which time adverbials appear to co-occur with *BÍN* is in utterances like (4):

4   He *BÍN* home – since last week. (BM 41, Pa)

However the time adverbial here does not, as in (2) or (3) occur as part of a single "sentence intonation pattern." It is separated from the main clause both by pause and by falling intonation on *home*. And in fact an analysis of (4) as derived from (4') seems quite sound:

4'   He *BÍN* home. He *bĭn* home since last week.

There is other evidence that *BÍN* and *bĭn* are different. Note the following sentence:

5   He *bĭn* doing it ever since we was teenagers, and he *still* doing it. (BM 41, Pa)

The conjoined qualification "and he *still* doing it" would be redundant if *BÍN* + V–ing were used. As we shall see in a moment, the meaning "Remote Phase Continuative" would be implicit in the form itself.

Although most of the examples with unstressed *bĭn* are not preceded by forms of *have*, there are a few which are, and seem nevertheless to carry the same semantic force. For instance:

6   Cause I've *bĭn* through it. I've *bĭn* through them changes. (BM 26, Pa)

On the basis of this, it may be possible to describe most instances of BE *bĭn* for Philadelphia, at least, as "Present Perfects." This is not the case with stressed *BÍN*.

There are also several cases of unstressed *bĭn* with *done* as first auxiliary, as in:

7   Get to work, start talking to them girls, they *done bĭn* locked up fifteen times!
    (BF 38, Pa)

There is a rare occurrence of *BÍN* + *done*, as in the Sea Island sentence:

8   Boy, if we had shrimp, we'd a *BÍN done* got us some fish! (BM 11, SI)

but none whatsoever of *done* + *BÍN*.

In the Sea Island data, stressed *BÍN* and unstressed *bĭn* must also be separated on syntactic and semantic grounds. One difference between the two forms, here as in Philadelphia, is the possibility of treating many instances of *bĭn* as "present perfects." But there are other differences here. Unstressed *bĭn* is sometimes used as a straight equivalent of *was*, indicating simple past tense. Note the close alternation between the two forms in (9):

9   I don't know if that snake *bĭn* coil, or either *was* stretch out or what. (BM 52, SI)

Used before a verb-stem, unstressed *bĭn* has the additional ambiguity of signalling either "Past" or "past before the Past":

10   But the real medicine what I *bĭn want* fuh get fuh Joo-Joo . . . (BF 78, SI)
     "But the real medicine which I *had wanted* to get for Joo-Joo . . ."

Finally, *bĭn* but not *BÍN* occurs before continuative *a*:

11   How bout that thing wuh B *bĭn a* tell you? (BM 67, SI)
     "How about that thing which B *was telling* you?"

These uses of unstressed *bĭn* are of course well known in other creole areas (cf. for Jamaican Creole, B. Bailey 1966; for Sierra Leone Krio, Jones 1968; for Guyana Creole, Bickerton 1974). The point here is not to pursue the use of *bĭn* in any detail, but simply to indicate the ways in which it differs from *BÍN* in semantic function and syntactic co-occurrence restrictions.

Enough has been said so far to demonstrate the point with which I started out, that on the basis of the participant-observation data, *BÍN* and *bĭn* must be distinguished. In the light of this, what are we to make of the intuitive judgments of black respondents, who, as indicated above, were evenly divided on this issue? It may be that those who claimed the forms were equivalent were speakers of some "other" dialect which has simply not been tapped in my own participant observation. This is possible, but I think, unlikely. First of all, the respondents were, as we shall see, in unanimous agreement on the meaning and interpretation of stressed *BÍN*. Secondly, I know that at least one of the respondents who suggested that the two forms were equivalent, consistently distinguishes them in his everyday speech. I am more inclined to think that what we are dealing with here is a weakness of the "intuitive method" itself.

Let me mention two possible sources of error which have already come to light. One is the real difficulty which some subjects had in hearing "unstressed" forms of *bĭn*. They would repeat question 9b, for instance, with lighter stress on *bin* than the stress on *BÍN* in 9a, but it would still be primary in that sentence.

This difficulty may have been the result of a second factor. For some informants, unstressed *bĭn* + *V-ed* (non-passive) is not a real possibility at all. These informants accept and say "I *BÍN* had that" but not "I *bĭn* had that." Faced with the latter, they cannot see it as contrastive, may not even hear the difference in this environment. Note that when *BÍN* and *bĭn* are contrasted in another environment in which both are possible for all informants, as in question 15: He *BÍN* sick vs. He *bĭn* sick, five of the 12 informants who had seen them as equivalent in 9 now saw them as different. It is clear that in any repeated version of this questionnaire serious attempts to overcome these difficulties will have to be made. What is demonstrated here, in this very first issue about *BÍN*, is the value of data from participant-observation in challenging and qualifying the data from intuitive responses.

2.2.2 BÍN – *meaning and use*

Previous researchers have applied a variety of labels to the Black English form *BÍN* (I ignore henceforth the issue of stress): "Completive Perfect" (Stewart op. cit.), "Remote Past" (Fasold and Wolfram 1970), "Remote Perfective" (Dillard 1972), "Perfect Phase" (Fickett 1970). What they are all trying to express via these different labels is essentially the same. That *BÍN* places the action in the distant past (relative to the present axis) and/or that it expresses "total completion of the event." One Standard English paraphrase that has been used frequently to register this fact is the time adverbial " a long time ago." This is perfectly appropriate for some of the *BÍN* sentences which I collected in Philadelphia and the Sea Islands, for instance (12):

12   She ain't tell me that today, you know. She *BÍN* tell me that. (BF 32, SI)
      "She told me that *a long time ago*"

However, this gloss, and the semantic notion of a totally completed action in the distant past, is appropriate only for a subset of the participant-observation data – those in which *BÍN* is followed by non-stative verbs. With stative verbs, or with either kind in the progressive, the function of *BÍN* is different. Instead of expressing completion of the associated process (a cover term for action or state) it asserts only that it began in the distant past and is still very much in force at the moment of speaking. In both of these cases, a better SE paraphrase would be "for a long time," e.g.:

13   I *BÍN* had this. (BM 6, Pa)
      "I've had this *for a long time*"
14   I *BÍN* treating them like that. (BF 25, Pa)
      "I've been treating them like that *for a long time*"

The similarities and differences between *BÍN* as used with non-statives on the one hand, and statives and progressives on the other, is more graphically illustrated in 15:

15

	Remote Anterior	Anterior	Point of Orientation
Statives	X_____		
Non-statives	XY		
Progressives	X_____		

In 15, X indicates the initiation of the "process" and Y the end–point.

If we wish to formulate a conjunctive definition for *BÍN* we would have to say that it places the initiation of a process at some point in the distant past. "Remote Phase" is perhaps the most appropriate label for this function.[4] It could then be extended (Remote Phase Continuative, Remote Phase Completive) to describe the particular effect of using the form with statives and progressives as against non-statives. It should be mentioned here that almost all the examples given by previous researchers involve non-stative verbs. This may be one element in their failure to perceive the more comprehensive nature of *BÍN*. This failure in turn is reflected in the labels they chose for the form – all of which suggest a Remote Phase Completive function only. Let us now turn to the intuitive responses on the meaning and use of *BÍN* to discover the extent to which they support or qualify the above analysis. In 16, the main questions in Q-SCOM-IV relevant to this issue are presented. Note that they go beyond simply asking what the form means, and try to get subjects to look through the grammar into the real world (cf. Labov 1973).

16   Q-SCOM-IV questions on the meaning of *BÍN*:
   1   Someone asked, "Is she married?" and someone else answered, "She *BÍN* married." Do you get the idea that she is married now? Yes_____ No_____
   3   Bill was about to be introduced to this guy at a party, but when he saw him, he said, "Hey, I *BÍN* know his name!" Which of these three things do you think he's most likely to say next:
      (a)   Give me a minute and I might remember it.
      (b)   He's John Jones. I saw his picture in the papers yesterday.
      (c)   He's John Jones. I've been hearing about him for years.
      So, what do you think Bill meant when he said, "I *BÍN* know his name?" Choose the one that is closest to what you think:
      (d)   Used to know.
      (e)   Already knew.
      (f)   Know, but can't quite remember.
      (g)   Know right now.
      (h)   Have known for a long time, and still do.
      (i)   Other _____.
   16   Frank asked his friend if he had paid off the bill on his new stereo, and got the answer, "I *BÍN* paid for it." Does he mean:

Table 2.2   Consistent "Remote Phase" interpretations to Qs 1, 16, 3

Group	N	Yes to 1	Yes to 1 (c) to 16	Yes to 1 (c) to 16(c) to 3	Yes to 1 (c) to 16 (c) to 3 (h) to 3
Blacks	25	23	21	19	15
Whites	25	8	4	1	1

Table 2.3   Consistent Non-"Remote Phase" interpretations to Qs 1, 16, 3

Group	N	No to 1	No to 1 ~ (c) to 16	No to 1 ~ (c) to 16 ~ (c) to 3	No to 1 ~ (c) to 16 ~ (c) to 3 ~ (h) to 3
Blacks	25	2	1	0	0
Whites	25	17	14	12	10

(a)   I've already paid for it.
(b)   I was paying for a long time, but I'm finished now.
(c)   I paid for it long ago.
(d)   I've been paying for it for a long time, and haven't finished yet.
(e)   Other _____.

The responses appropriate to a "Remote Phase" interpretation of *BÍN* were: Yes to 1, (c) and (h) to 3, (c) to 16. If we multiply the number of responses by the number of individuals in each group, we derive a total of 100 possible responses. From the start, the difference between black and white respondents on this issue is clear. For the Blacks, 87 percent of the responses were appropriate to a "Remote Phase" interpretation. Only 37 percent of the white subjects' responses were.

The overwhelming agreement among black respondents and their difference from white subjects on this issue is demonstrated even more clearly in table 2.2, which displays the number of consistent Remote Phase interpretations:

Note that while 15 of the black respondents end up giving completely consistent "Remote Phase" interpretations, only one of the white respondents manages to do so. As it turns out, he is a native of Greensboro, North Carolina, who claims to have had extensive contact with Blacks throughout his life.

The responses can be just as dramatically reviewed the other way around. In table 2.3, the consistent Non-"Remote Phase" interpretations of Blacks and Whites are tabulated:

Note that there are only two black respondents who give Non-"Remote-Phase" interpretations to 1 to begin with, and by the time non-remote interpre-

Table 2.4   Positive responses to familiarity and use questions

Group	*Have you ever heard* BÍN?	*Do you say* BÍN *yourself?*
Blacks	24/25 = 96%	17/25 = 68%
Whites	16/24 = 67%	3/22 = 13%

tations to 1, 16, and 3 are combined, none of the black respondents are involved. By contrast, 17 of the white respondents gave non-remote interpretations to 1, and ten maintained the same interpretation throughout.

Considering that a certain amount of chance error may always be present in
investigations of this type, the tremendous regularity that is revealed here is
highly significant. Both the "participant observation" and the "intuitive" data
converge strongly to endorse a "Remote Phase" interpretation for Black English *BÍN*. In addition, both data sources suggest that black and white speakers
are sharply divided in their abilities to use and interpret the form. The only
other feature which has ever been shown to differentiate the two groups so
sharply and reliably is their ability to understand the African-derived forms
"*cut-eye*" and "*suck-teeth*" and enact the non-verbal behavior to which these
refer (cf. Rickford and Rickford 1976 reprinted in this volume).

Finally, we may consider the overt responses of black and white subjects to
questions designed to explore their familiarity with and use of *BÍN*. The results
are tabulated in table 2.4.

Insofar as these results indicate what we would have suspected from
participant-observation anyway, that more Blacks have heard and use *BÍN* than
Whites, they seem generally valid. But the details are questionable. Sixteen
Whites claim to have heard *BÍN*, and three to use it themselves. But in view of
their responses on the "meaning" questions reported on above, these claims are
at least suspect. Interestingly enough, of the three Whites who claimed to "say
BÍN" themselves, two gave consistent Non-"Remote-Phase" interpretations to
all four meaning-questions, and the other one gave a similar interpretation to
two out of four. It is probable that these particular subjects were trying to claim
familiarity with what they perceived as a "black" idiom because it was in some
sense fashionable to do so.

The reverse process undoubtedly operated in the case of some black subjects. Some of those who claimed not to say the form themselves modified it in
subsequent discussion to "at least not anymore." For them, *BÍN* as a non-
standard feature had a stigma which they would just as soon avoid.[5] In any case,
the almost unanimous claim of black subjects that they had at least heard the
form is more credible, in the light of the high percentage of "Remote Phase"
interpretations on the meaning-questions.

I might only add that *BÍN* is understood by a range of black subjects considerably wider than is normally associated with the Black English vernacular. I once informally asked a few of the "meaning" questions at a dinner party. The lone black informant in this group, a Philadelphia judge, was rather surprised to discover that he was immediately distinguished from the other "subjects" by his ability to give the "correct" Remote-Phase interpretations. From his normal level of speech, one would hardly have classed him as a speaker of "Black English." But his ability to interpret *BÍN* in the same way that other BE speakers do, indicates the deep-seated sensitivity and exposure to this form that exists among black Americans, of all levels, and suggests a possible creole history. It also raises the crucial issue of whether linguistic grammars should be written on the basis of "productive" or "receptive" competence. To explore this issue at any further length is clearly beyond the scope of this paper.

2.2.3   The productivity of BÍN – co-occurrence relations

The final issue which I shall take up is the productivity of *BÍN* in the grammar of Black English. The only environment in which earlier investigators found *BÍN* to occur was before $V + ed$. Dillard (1972) also found it before $V - ing$. But the picture that emerges from the participant-observation data is that *BÍN* is far more productive in Black English than this. In addition to $V + ed$ and $V - ing$, it can be followed by:

(a) Locatives:
     17   Oh, it *BÍN* in this house. (BM 6, Pa)
(b) Adverbs:
     18   Them crab *BÍN* off. (BM 46, SI)
(c) Verb-Stem alone
     19   She *BÍN* quit school. (BM 15, SI)
(d) Passive Participles (contrary to Fickett 1970's claim), both with and without *got*:
     20   My hair *BÍN* cut. (BM 29, SI)
     21   He shoulda *BÍN* got shot. (BM 25, Pa)
(e) Modal or Done + Verb - (ed):
     22   I *BÍN* could walk on them stilts. (BF 16, SI)
     23   Boy, if we had shrimp, we'd a *BÍN* done got us some fish. (BM 11, SI)

Finally, as some of the examples here have already indicated, *BÍN* is frequently preceded by the modals *coulda*, *shoulda*, and *woulda*.
   In order to discover the reliability of co-occurrence patterns which showed up in the participant-observation data and to discover the status of patterns which had not been attested at all, we included a series of sentences (a–n) in Q-

Table 2.5   Positive acceptability ratings for sentences in Q. 18, Q-SCOM-IV

Group	N	a	b	c	d	e	f	g	h	i	j	k	l	m	n
Blacks	25	23	23	18	18	19	8	15	15	15	18	19	23	22	5
Whites	23	17	14	17	18	13	8	12	17	10	15	14	11	14	7

SCOM-IV, and asked subjects to indicate whether they found them acceptable ('Given that you could say "I *BÍN* know that," could you also say . . . ?"). The sentences themselves are reprinted in table 2.6 which displays the results in the form of an implicational array. First, however, we want to consider the extent to which black and white groups differed in their acceptability ratings in general. These data are tabulated in table 2.5.

There are one or two striking differences in the acceptability ratings given to particular sentences by members of the two groups: 23 Blacks but only 11 Whites endorsed 18 l: "They *BÍN* ended that war"; 22 Blacks but only 14 Whites endorsed 18 m: " I *BÍN* knowing that guy." But these are sentences which were already well documented from the participant observation data. On the acceptability ratings of lesser attested or unattested sentences, the difference between the two groups are virtually identical (cf. ratings for 18d and 18f). This is surprising, in view of the overwhelming difference between the two groups which was registered in their interpretations of the meaning of *BÍN*. This equivalence in the ratings of the two groups is the first piece of evidence to suggest that there is more random variation here; that somehow, in this section of the questionnaire, we have failed to elicit the richer knowledge of the syntactic relations of *BÍN* which black speakers must certainly possess in order to understand and use it as consistently as we know they do. Many different interpretations for our failure here suggest themselves. Part of the difficulty may lie in the technique of asking subjects to rate a string of sentences all at once. But Labov's (1971) remarks on idiosyncratic judgments made by informants to extremely rare alternants undoubtedly also apply here. Labov suggested that these might not be part of *langue*, but rather some kind of intuitive *parole*, and "if so, we need techniques that will enable us to stop short of (such) intuitive judgments" (1971: 447–8). Finally, it may be that both groups predict the extension of *BÍN* to other points in the grammar on the basis of their knowledge of the syntactic possibilities with Standard English un-stressed *bĕen*. If this is so, we have again failed to get at the true set of possible co-occurrence patterns with Black English *BÍN*, for as indicated in section 2.2.1 above, these can be quite different from *bĭn*.

I have not yet identified the real source of the problem here, nor have I attempted as yet any workable solutions. However, the data remain useful – if only for demonstrating the kinds of difficulties which we might encounter in asking for acceptability ratings for sentences. There are more. Disregarding the questions table 5 has already led us to raise concerning the reliability of the data we are getting here, let us go on to squeeze it, as is usually done, for all that it is worth.

Table 2.6 represents the results of the acceptability ratings of black subjects in the form of an implicational array. As usual, what this "implicational scale" implies is: (a) sentences to the left are generally more acceptable than sentences to the right; (b) if a subject finds a certain sentence acceptable, he or she will also find all sentences to the left of this (in the implicational array) acceptable.

In general, the hierarchical ranking of these sentences in terms of acceptability can be supported somewhat by the participant observation data. As already indicated, the two sentences most acceptable (furthest to the left) are well represented in the data from actual speech. And the three least acceptable (or furthest to the right): (h) He done *BÍN* locked up, (f) He *BÍN* bin gone, and (n) I have *BÍN* had that, have never been attested. The two next least acceptable sentences, including *BÍN-could* and *BÍN-done* have been attested only rarely, and only in the Sea Islands, Since none of the respondents were from this area, their low acceptability rating is understandable. However, there are a few striking surprises. For instance, "He *BÍN* got messed up," a pattern represented in the Philadelphia data, is ranked much further down the line than we would expect. And the *BÍN-NP* pattern represented in (a) He *BÍN* the leader, is ranked as third most acceptable, but has never been attested. Thus the ranking of the sentences cannot be simply taken at face value either.

To continue the discussion at this level would be to miss the whole point of the methodology of "implicational scaling" as it is usually applied to linguistic behavior or intuitions (cf. Bailey 1970, Bickerton 1973b). Implicational scales are less valuable for the ranking of particular sentences (we could achieve more or less the same results just by noting percentages of positive responses) than for isolating the "lects" (and their membership) which they may be taken to define. If we follow the solid line as it cuts upward and to the right across the table, separating mainly "positive" ratings from mainly "negative" ones, we find that no less than eleven different "lects" are found to exist among these 25 different subjects. (For instance, B15 and B5 share lect 1, the most "liberal" lect; and B1 is the only representative of lect 11, the most "conservative" one). This by itself seems highly questionable. If we could find so many "lects" among only 25 speakers, what would happen if we increased both the number of sentences, and the pool of subjects, to any significant extent? Would we truly be prepared to accept the proliferating number of "lects" as having any solid basis in reality?

Furthermore, there is absolutely no evidence in the participant-observation data for these 11 different lects. Obviously, the method here is telling us far

Table 2.6 Implicational array for black subjects' acceptability ratings to *BÍN* sentences in question 18, Q-SCOM-IV (Deviations circled, Scalability = 88.9%)

	Ved	*Ving*	*NP*	*'ve had*	*Pass.*	*knew*	*got Pass.*	*have*	*Adj.*	*Modal*	*done*	*done done*	*bin*	*have had*
	They BÍN ended that war.	I BÍN knowing him.	He BÍN the leader.	I've BÍN had that car.	The chicken BÍN ate.	I BÍN knew your name.	He BÍN got messed up.	I BÍN have that.	She BÍN nice.	I BÍN could do that.	He BÍN done gone.	He done BÍN locked up.	He BÍN bin gone.	I have BÍN had that.
Subjects	*l*	*b*	*a*	*m*	*d*	*k*	*e*	*j*	*c*	*i*	*g*	*h*	*f*	*n*
B 15	+	+	+	+	+	+	+	+	+	+	⊕	+	+	+
B 5	+	+	+	+	+	+	+	+	⊕	+	+	+	+	+
B 19	+	+	+	+	+	+	+	+	+	+	+	+	+	−
B 8	⊕	+	+	+	⊕	+	+	+	+	⊕	+	+	+	−
B 21	+	+	+	+	+	+	+	⊕	+	+	+	+	+	−
B 12	+	+	+	+	⊕	+	+	+	+	⊕	+	+	−	−
B 3	+	+	+	+	⊕	+	+	+	+	+	+	+	−	−
B 24	+	+	+	+	⊕	+	+	+	+	+	+	+	−	−
B 4	+	⊕	+	⊕	+	⊕	+	+	+	+	+	+	−	−
B 22	+	+	+	+	+	⊕	+	+	+	+	+	+	−	−
B 25	⊕	+	+	⊕	+	⊕	+	+	+	+	+	+	−	−
B 6	⊕	+	+	+	+	+	+	+	+	+	+	+	⊕	−
B 11	+	+	+	+	+	+	+	+	+	+	+	−	−	−
B 16	+	+	+	+	+	+	+	+	+	+	+	−	−	−
B 23	+	+	+	+	+	+	+	+	+	+	+	−	−	−
B 13	+	+	+	+	+	+	+	+	+	−	+	⊕	−	⊕
B 14	+	+	⊕	+	+	+	⊕	+	+	−	+	⊕	⊕	−
B 7	+	+	+	+	+	+	+	−	−	−	⊕	⊕	−	−
B 17	+	+	+	+	+	−	−	−	−	−	⊕	−	−	−
B 18	+	+	+	+	−	−	−	−	−	−	⊕	−	−	−
B 2	+	+	+	+	⊕	−	⊕	−	⊕	−	−	−	−	−
B 20	+	+	+	+	⊕	⊕	−	⊕	⊕	−	⊕	⊕	−	⊕
B 9	+	+	+	+	−	−	−	−	−	−	⊕	−	−	−
B 10	+	+	−	−	−	−	−	−	−	−	−	−	−	−
B 1	+	−	⊕	⊕	−	−	−	−	−	−	−	⊕	⊕	−

more than we can reasonably assume to be true. Its results are not supported by any of the independent evidence presently available. All this is the more striking because of the high scalability (88.9 percent) which this table manages to achieve.[6] Scalability figures like these are often included in the literature, supposedly to represent the "statistical reliability" of the implicational array. But the evidence suggests that in this case, and perhaps others, such figures may mean very little. Far more work remains to be done in developing reliable statistical and linguistic measures of the reliability and validity of implicational arrays.[7]

2.3   Conclusion

The weaknesses in the intuitive data revealed at various points in the preceding discussion of *BÍN* merit serious attention. For it is precisely the same method, eliciting judgments of the equivalence or acceptability of various sentences, and arranging the results in implicational arrays, which, as mentioned before, is most frequently used in the study of abstract syntactic "squishes," and is winning devotees among those interested in social and regional variation. The results revealed in this paper, along with other limitations previously noted (Labov 1971) should give us pause. They should also force us to consult, perhaps for the first time, a handful of research which has already explored in some detail various issues involved in the elicitation of linguistic judgments (Bolinger 1968, Gleitman 1967, Quirk and Svartvik 1966, Labov 1975, Schutze 1996). I discovered these too late to affect the course of my own elicitations. But most work involving the study of linguistic intuitions seems equally uninformed by the insights and suggestions represented in this tiny literature.

We might indicate in closing one way in which the work on *BÍN* discussed in this paper seems to relate to some of this work on "intuitive judgment methodology." Bolinger (1968: 39) had suggested:

> Perhaps we are not asking the right question when we inquire whether a given sentence or sentence-type is grammatical – we should ask instead whether it has a meaning, (and) determine what the meaning is.

The highly successful results of our "intuitive data" on the meaning of *BÍN*, contrasted with the far more ambiguous and questionable results on the acceptability of *BÍN* sentences, suggests that Bolinger may well be right on this point. (Cf. also the successful investigations of the meaning of "Cut-Eye" and "Suck-Teeth" – Rickford and Rickford 1976, reprinted in this volume). But this again is exactly the opposite of what is being done in the growing number of variation studies employing "intuitive" data.

It is clear that we shall have to be far more critical about the use of elicited intuitive data than we are presently. Intuitions can be invaluable resources. But, contrary to past and present expectations, they are not necessarily or universally so. What questions we can ask, what answers we can accept, and what we can do with such answers, are things that remain very much to be worked out, both in general, and for specific cases. There is much work to be done here, and much work to be done also in developing other methods, like participant-observation,[8] which can serve as independent "checks and balances."

The prospects for overcoming the limitations of tape-recorded data and carrying the "New Wave" into syntax, seem promising but not easy. However, there is no reason to limit our goals and methods to those that require the least effort and/or imagination. This is no way to run a revolution.

Notes

This paper is full of references to the work and influence of William Labov. It is not inordinately or accidentally so, however, for he has been in the forefront of innovations in (socio-) linguistic methodology for the past ten years. I welcome this opportunity to thank him for provoking me to a critical awareness of the importance of "methodology" and for stimulating my own work both by example and suggestion.

1   As used in this paper, *been* is an abstract form in which stress is not distinguished. It is introduced primarily to facilitate discussion of the work of previous researchers. $BÍN$ and $bĭn$ are more concrete – the former referring to the stressed form, the latter to the unstressed.

2   The work of Loflin (1970) is omitted in the body of this paper. This might be surprising to some, since Loflin does discuss $BÍN$, and his paper is often cited as a high point in the formal analysis of Black English. But we must not be "snowed" by apparent applications of the transformational-generative framework to the field of "sociolinguistic variation." Loflin "accounts" for $BÍN$ by "postulating a formative E of emphatic stress which could be given in the rule rewriting VP and which could be converted into appropriate realizations, e.g. $E + V + ed \Rightarrow BÍN + V + ed$." In recognizing the obligatory nature of stress, Loflin is justified. But his rule for generating the form is totally ad hoc and unmotivated, most seriously because the meaning of the form is not discussed at any point. Loflin's methodology, drawing on the intuitive reactions of an isolated 14-year-old informant, has also received widespread criticism.

3   The notation in parentheses following each sentence records in this order the following information: race, sex, age, and geographical community of the speaker.

4   We cannot explore here in any depth the fascinating issue of how "remote" the initiation of a process must be to justify the use of $BÍN$. One thing is certain – no absolute distance in objective time from the point of orientation can be set. What $BÍN$ expresses is the speaker's subjective feelings about the event and the "time" involved. Thus an old woman stepping out of a dentist's office she had entered only

a few minutes before said, "He finish so quick. I ask him was he finished, and he say 'I *BÍN* finished'."

There are, however, "consensus definitions" of how "remote" the initiation of a process must be, relative to certain cases. And there is a rich arena for research in the use of *BÍN* contrary to such "consensus" definitions for dramatization and self-aggrandizement, or "styling." Thus a young woman who was complimented on the fine dress she had bought only the day before replied nonchalantly, "Oh, I *BÍN* had this!" This " styling" use of *BÍN* is open to challenge, however.

These considerations are not totally irrelevant to the methodological issues with which we are concerned in this paper. For instance, Gary M. of New York hesitated before giving the "Remote Phase" interpretation to question 3 in Q-SCOM-4 (see 15 below), because, in his words "I don't know if he *BÍN* know that guy. A lot of dudes go around running off at the mouth bout how they *BÍN* know this and they *BÍN* know that. Ain't nothing but a bunch of jive!"

5   This section may be taken to illustrate the general principle that questioning people on their own use of linguistic forms or varieties which have high social effect (either positive or negative) is likely to produce unreliable results unless checked against other evidence.

6   The scalability figure is arrived at by the formula:

$$100 - \left(\frac{\text{No. of deviations}}{\text{No. of cells}} \cdot \frac{100}{1} \right)$$

In this case: $100 - (39/350 \cdot 100)$.

7   The whole question of what is to be retained, what modified in borrowing techniques like "sociometric scaling" from social-survey methodology is quite problematic. For instance, "factors" which are marked by a high number of "deviations" are often omitted in psychological and sociological work. But so far no one has suggested in linguistic circles that sentences like 18 g should be thrown out of consideration altogether. (I am thankful to Wolfgang Wölck for raising this issue.) The closest anyone has come to this is Labov (1971), see page 28 above.

8   At the risk of being accused of descending to the trivial or ephemeral, let me suggest here one or two methods for extending the method of participant-observation to include information on the frequency of pre-coded variables which occur more often than *BÍN*. The art is to develop idiosyncracies like doodling or breaking matches in half. With each occurrence of a variant (for example *que* vs. ø) one makes the appropriate "doodle" on a handy napkin or whatever, or puts the broken half of a matchstick in the appropriate pile. So long as one remembers to collect the napkins, or put the matchstick pieces into different pockets, these "extensions" can prove extremely informative and reliable. Needless to say, however, they put a tremendous strain on the "participant-observer" of natural conversation, and require some practice.

3

Preterite Had + *Verb* -ed *in the Narratives of African American Preadolescents*
(with Christine Théberge-Rafal)

In this paper, we discuss an unusual use of the pluperfect form *had* + Verb *-ed* that we first noticed in 1988 in the narratives of preadolescent African American students (primarily sixth-graders) in East Palo Alto (EPA), California. Many vernacular features, like *been*, unmarked possessives, existential *it*, and others occurred in the recorded speech and writing of the children in this urban, low-income, and predominantly African American community. However, the feature that we found most striking – because it had not previously been reported as a feature of African-American Vernacular English (AAVE) – was the use of preverbal *had* to mark the preterite rather than the pluperfect.

Our paper will proceed as follows. In section 3.1, we will explain the distinction between the preterite and the pluperfect and provide preliminary textual examples of the use of preterite *had* by the preadolescents in our EPA sample. In section 3.2 we will provide a series of quantitative and qualitative analyses of the preadolescents' usage of this form in an attempt to account for, if not predict, its occurrence. In section 3.3 we will consider the use of preterite and pluperfect *had* by other AAVE speakers, including adolescents in EPA,[1] preadolescents and adolescents from East Harlem, New York, whose usage was described by Labov et al. (1968), and adolescents and young adults from Springville, Texas, whose usage was described more recently by Cukor-Avila (1995) and by Cukor-Avila and Bailey (1995). The usage of Puerto Rican youth in New York will also be mentioned in this section. In section 3.4, we will summarize our findings on this feature, and suggest directions for further research.

3.1   The Preterite vs. the Pluperfect

It may be helpful to clarify at this point the distinction between the preterite or simple past and the pluperfect or past perfect.[2] Reichenbach (1947: 290) dia-

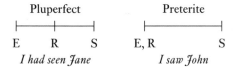

Figure 3.1 The distinction between the pluperfect and preterite tenses (after Reichenbach 1947: 290) *Note*: R = Reference Point, E = Event Point, S = Speech Point.

grams these two tenses along a left–to–right timeline (see figure 3.1), showing the Event Point (E), Reference Point (R), and Speech Point (S; or what Bybee, Perkins, and Pagliuca 1994: 55, and others refer to equivalently as the "Moment of Speech"). In both instances, the Event being described precedes the Speech Point; however, the past perfect has a Reference Point (R) between the Event and the Speech Point. That Reference Point is often defined by an adjacent clause whose verb occurs in the preterite tense, as in (1).

1   I *had seen* (E) John already by the time Mary *arrived* (R).

But the Reference Point might also be established by a time adverbial, like the phrase *by six o'clock yesterday evening* in (2) from Comrie (1985: 65).

2   John *had arrived* (E) *by six o'clock yesterday evening* (R).

Comrie's description (1985) of the difference between the preterite and pluperfect is very similar to Reichenbach's, but his conceptualization and additional detail are revealing. Comrie defines the preterite or simple past as an *absolute tense*, one which takes "the present moment as its deictic centre" (36) and simply locates a situation or event "prior to the present moment" (41). The pluperfect, by contrast, is an *absolute-relative tense*, insofar as it situates a reference point in the past (the *absolute* component) and locates an event "prior to that reference point" or "past in the past" (the *relative* component, 65). Comrie makes the point that since the event "referred to by the pluperfect is itself located in the past" (see figure 3.1) and since "the time points that can be referred to by the pluperfect can in principle be referred to by the past," it might at first seem puzzling why the relatively complex pluperfect should exist at all. He explains:

> in locating situations in time, it is necessary not only to relate situations relative to the present moment, but also to relate them chronologically to one another. A simple sequence of past tense fails to do this, e.g. "John arrived; Mary left," which leaves open whether John's arrival preceded or followed Mary's departure. Given the tendency for linear order of clauses to follow chronological order of events, the example just given is most likely to be interpreted as meaning that

John's arrival took place first, then Mary's departure. If for some reason it is desired to represent events in other than chronological order, the pluperfect is an ideal mechanism for indicating this, as when the previous example is changed to "John arrived; Mary had left." (Comrie 1985: 67)

What is interesting about the EPA children's use of *had* is that it is *not* used in the pluperfect-favoring situation which Comrie describes – for indicating an event which is later in narrative time than another one but earlier in real time.[3] On the contrary, *had* + V -*ed* is used as an absolute tense and in situations where a preterite or simple past form occurs regularly in English narratives. In describing this usage as "preterite *had*," we are trying to convey the point that it has the *form* of the standard English (SE) pluperfect but the *function* of the SE preterite.

One common context for preterite *had* in our data, for instance, is to mark the *first* complicating action in a narrative, ruling out the possibility that it could be serving the "flashback" function referred to above. For our definition of narratives we draw on the following cogent characterization by Schiffrin (1981), which draws on earlier work by Labov (1972c) and Labov and Waletzky (1967):

> Narratives are oral versions of experience in which events are relayed in the order in which they presumably occurred. Their defining characteristic is a relationship of *temporal juncture* between at least two clauses: if a change in the order of the two clauses results in a change in the interpretation of what actually happened, then those two clauses are *narrative clauses*, and the events reported are *narrative events*. (Schiffrin 1981: 47)

In the following narratives from 12-year-old Dafina and 12-year-old Nathan, preterite *had* occurs in the first narrative or complicating action clause, marked as "a." In presenting these and subsequent texts, we adhere to the conventions of Schiffrin (1981: 45n1), according to which narrative or complicating action clauses are lettered,[4] while non-narrative clauses are unlettered, but labeled as abstract, orientation, evaluation, embedded evaluation, or coda clauses:[5]

3   This is a story that happened to me Monday, not too long ago [*Abstract*]
    I was on my way to school [*Orientation*]
    (a)   and I *had* slipped [cf. "and I *slipped*"]
    (b)   and fell[6]
    (c)   and I ran back in the house to change my clothes and I almos' – [laughs]
    (d)   And, and my mother told me to be more careful around myself because
           I always slip and fall
           And that's all my story. [*Coda*] (Dafina, 12, EPA)

4   I was riding home from school, and on my way home I was, when I was up in
    the driveway [*Orientation*],

(a)   a car *had* backed up [cf. "a car *backed* up"]
(b)   and it ran over my bike
(c)   and I tried to run.
(d)   Then, it just ran over me.
(e)   I tried to, I tried to get up from under,
(f)   but it kept on going forwards and backwards, riding all over me.
(g)   Yeah, that's when I woke up. [*Coda*] (Nathan, 12, EPA)

Of course, as Comrie (1986: 18–19) has noted, the English pluperfect is not *restricted* to "flashback" situations in which narrative order diverges from chronological or event order. With respect to the following example:

5   Old Sam's boat approached the other side of the pier. He *had* docked before I began fishing.

Comrie (1986: 18) observes that

> the three relevant events are actually narrated in their chronological order, but nonetheless the pluperfect is (correctly) used for the second of the three events.
>   There is a single, simple characterization of the meaning of the pluperfect that captures the full range of its uses. . . . *The pluperfect locates a situation prior to a contextually given reference point, this reference point itself being located in the past.* . . . With respect to the reference point, apart from locating it chronologically relative to the situation in question and relative to the present moment, all that the pluperfect tells us is that such a reference point exists in the context. It does not in itself give us any indication as to how we should find that reference point – this is part of the interpretation of the pluperfect in a particular context, not part of its meaning. [emphasis added]

Bearing this in mind, one might argue that the *had* predicates in 3a and 4a are functioning as regular pluperfects since their reference is to a point chronologically prior to the reference of the verbs (*fell, ran over,* and so on) in the immediately following and subsequent clauses. Although we consider it important to note that these and other instances of preterite *had* in our data *are* prior to subsequent reference points, since this helps to explain their grammaticalization from and connection with English pluperfects,[7] the East Palo Alto tokens differ from conventional English usage in several ways. For one thing, unlike the example in 5, the *had* clauses in our EPA data are *not* linked to the reference points of subsequent clauses by anterior-marking conjunctions like *before*. Second, the EPA tokens of preterite *had* are *not* used in the out-of-sequence or look-back function in which the pluperfect is favored in English. Third, in conventional American English narratives, comparable sequences of actions are sufficiently and most commonly expressed by sequences of preterite forms (sometimes also by "historical presents"; see Wolfson 1979 and Schiffrin 1981) rather than by pluperfect forms.

To understand the functions of the preterite *had* tokens in our EPA corpus, we will, in the next section, analyze them both quantitatively and qualitatively.

3.2   Quantitative and Qualitative Analysis of the EPA Examples

In the Appendix, we list all of the preterite *had* examples (52 in all) which we recorded in narratives from African American school children (nine in all) in East Palo Alto in 1988. On the basis of these examples and on the evidence of all the past-reference verbs that occur in these narratives (281 cases in all[8]), it is possible to make some quantitative generalizations which extend our understanding of preterite *had* and its role in the tense-aspect system and narrative structure of its users. We will also consider some individual texts in detail to understand the qualitative functions of preterite *had* therein.

3.2.1   Relative frequency of past reference forms

Table 3.1 shows the frequencies of all past-reference verb forms in those EPA narratives which included at least one occurrence of preterite *had*. Note, first of all, that most of the past-reference verbs in these narratives – two-thirds – are standard, morphologically marked preterites (e.g., *walked*) and that unmarked forms (e.g., *walk*) occur only 5 percent of the time. One of our initial hypoth-

Table 3.1   Frequency of past markers* in narratives with preterite *had* + V *-ed*

	Total		With *then*
Had + V *-ed* (*had walked*) as preterite[†]	52	(19%)	27 (52%)
V-*ed* (*walked, fell, started*) as preterite[‡]	185	(66%)	53 (29%)
V-Ø (*walk, fall, start*) as preterite§	13	(5%)	7 (54%)
Had + V *-ed* (*had walked*) as pluperfect	2	(1%)	0 (0%)
Had as main verb preterite (*had a cat*)	16	(5%)	2 (13%)
No change (*hit*) as preterite	13	(4%)	6 (46%)
TOTAL	281	(100%)	95 (N/A)

* Excludes past tense copulas (151), modals (6), and *didn't* (5), which do not vary with preterite *had* + V *-ed* in our corpus (i.e., *had been sick "was sick").
[†] Includes one token of *had* + V *-Ø* (*had push*).
[‡] V-*ed* verbs: regular (*walked*) = 31 (17%); irregular (*fell*) = 145 (78%); syllabic (*started*) = 9 (5%).
§ V-Ø verbs: regular (*walk*) = 4 (31%); irregular (*fall*) = 6 (46%); syllabic (*start*) = 3 (23%).

eses was that the standard marking of the preterite (V -*ed*) might have been weakening in this variety and that preterite *had* + V -*ed* might have entered the dialect as a compensatory process. However, the low frequency of unmarked preterites in these narratives casts some doubt on this hypothesis, as does the fact that zero past marking is relatively infrequent in AAVE in general, particularly so with strong or irregular verbs (e.g., *came*). Labov et al. (1968: 138), describing their Harlem, New York City data, noted, "The great majority of verbs in text occurrence are irregular, and these show the past tense forms." In a similar vein, Fasold (1972: 38–9) reported that only 1.6 percent of the strong or irregular past reference verbs examined in his AAVE corpus from Washington, DC, were unmarked, and Rickford (1992: 189) found that only 6 percent of irregular past forms were unmarked in samples recorded from AAVE speakers in EPA ranging in age from 13 to 88.

The possibility that preterite *had* might have emerged in this variety to compensate for the weakening of V -*ed* is further minimized by the data in table 3.2, which show both the relative frequency of unmarked preterites in the narratives by verb type and the distribution of *had* + V -*ed* tokens by verb type. If the preterite weakening hypothesis were correct, we might have expected the verb type with the highest frequency of zero marking to be most commonly represented among the *had* + V -*ed* tokens, but in fact the opposite is true. Irregular verbs, which are *least* frequently unmarked (4 percent), are *most* commonly represented among the *had* + V -*ed* tokens (56 percent), and syllabic verbs, which are *most* frequently unmarked (25 percent), are *least* commonly represented among the *had* + V -*ed* tokens (2 percent).

3.2.2   *Verbs marked with* had *and their form*

Table 3.3 shows the specific verbs which co-occur with preterite *had* in our corpus, in the forms in which they occur and with their respective frequencies. One noteworthy point is that all but one of these predicates (*had a fight*) are nonstative or action verbs, the kind that are conventionally found in complicating action rather than orientation clauses in narrative. Another point worth noting is that the form of the main verb is always V-*ed* (*had came, had went, had threw, had bit*) rather than V-*en* (*had come, had gone, had thrown, had bitten*). The morphological distinction which SE draws between preterite or past tense (V -*ed*) and past participle (V -*en*) forms is weak in many English vernaculars,[9] but it is particularly unmarked in AAVE, as noted by Fasold and Wolfram (1970: 62):

> In standard English, most past participles are formed with the -*ed* suffix and so are identical with the past tense form. But there are a number of semi-regular and irregular verbs for which the past participle and past tense are formally distin-

Table 3.2 Relative frequency of unmarked preterite verbs (V-Ø/[V-Ø + V -ed]) by verb type and distribution of preterite *had* + V -ed tokens by verb type

Verb Type	Unmarked (V-Ø)	*had* + V -ed
Regular (*walk*)	4/35 (11%)	13/52 (25%)
Irregular (*tell*)	6/151 (4%)	29/52 (56%)
Syllabic (*start*)	3/12 (25%)	1/52 (2%)
No change/ambiguous (*hit*)	13 (N/A)	9/52 (17%)

Table 3.3 Verbs occurring with preterite *had* in EPA corpus

asked	1	kicked	1
backed (up)	1	left	3
bit	1	messed	1
broke (up)	1	missed	1
came (around/in)	3	pushed/push	4
crashed	1	put	1
drove	1	said	1
gave (up)	2	slipped	1
got (Ø/wet/out/mad/		took	2
up/him)	6	threw	1
grabbed	1	uppercut	1
had (a fight)	1	walked (off)	1
hit	6	went (home/outside/	
hurt	1	inside/somewhere)	6
kept	1	won	1

guished (e.g., *came* versus *has come*, *ate* versus *has eaten*, etc.) In [AAVE], however, it seems that there may not be any irregular verbs for which the past tense and past participle are distinct. Sometimes the standard English past participle form is generalized to serve both functions (*He taken it*; *He have taken it*), but *more commonly the simple past form is used in both kinds of constructions* (e.g., *He came*; *He have came*). [emphasis added]

3.2.3   *Occurrence in* then *clauses*

Table 3.1 shows the relatively high frequency (52 percent) with which preterite *had* occurs in clauses which begin with *then*, marking the action as chronologically subsequent to the previously related event or events (cf. Schiffrin 1990: 254).[10] It is significant that these occurrences of *then* are all clause-initial, since, as Schiffrin (1990: 255; 1992: 756) has shown, initial *then* marks successive shifts in reference time from one clause to another while clause-final *then* marks overlapping occurrences. Comparably high frequencies of co-occurrence with *then* are found for virtually all the other preterite tokens in these narratives,[11] and the frequencies are especially similar in the case of the unmarked (V + Ø) and no-change preterites – 54 percent and 46 percent respectively – where there might similarly be some question about their preterite reference. By contrast, neither of the two pluperfect tokens in our corpus co-occurs with *then*.[12]

In this connection, it is interesting to note the following observation by Fleischman (1990: 157), which establishes the semantic relationship between the temporal conjunction *then* and the use of the preterite tense in narrative and which supports our classification of the *had* tokens in our corpus as preterites rather than pluperfects:

> Narrative events are separated from each other by *temporal juncture*, which is semantically equivalent to the temporal conjunction "then": *a* happened, then *b*, then *c*, and so forth. . . . It will be observed that the events reported in the lettered narrative clauses are all punctual and completed; their time reference is conventionally assumed to be that of the "current narrative plane" of the story (i.e., past). The expected tense–aspect category is therefore the [Preterite].

3.2.4 Narrative function of preterite had forms

Another pattern of the use of preterite *had*, which is apparent from the narratives in (3) and (4) above and which receives confirmation from quantitative analysis of the entire data set (see table 3.4), is the high frequency (94 percent, 49 of 52 tokens) with which it occurs in narrative or complicating action clauses, where the preterite, as noted above, is the expected tense. In many languages, the pluperfect is more common in orientation and other backgrounding clauses, as Fleischman (1990: 140) observes:

> Also common in Orientation are before-pasts (PLP [Pluperfect] or PA [Past anterior]) for explanatory circumstantial material – what had already happened to produce the situation in which the events of the story will take place, . . .

Cukor-Avila and Bailey (1995) have argued that what we call here preterite *had* + V -ed and what they call "innovative *had* + past" represents a re-analysis of the conventional English pluperfect by AAVE speakers and its grammaticalization as a simple past or preterite. We agree with them on this but feel that the occurrences of this innovative preterite *had* need closer analysis to understand why and how the grammaticalization occurs – that is, what connection there is between conventional (pluperfect) and innovative (preterite)

Table 3.4   Preterite *had* + V *-ed* tokens by discourse function in narratives

Orientation	1 (2%)
Embedded Orientation	1 (2%)
Complicating Action	49 (94%)
Incomplete/Unclear	1 (2%)

had usage, and why SOME preterites are more likely to be marked with *had* than others.

Cukor-Avila and Bailey (1995) hypothesize that the reanalysis/grammaticalization process which produced preterite *had* began in orientation and similar backgrounding clauses and subsequently spread to complicating action or narrative clauses. Forty percent (40/99) of their preterite *had* tokens from Springville, Texas, occur in orientation clauses. By contrast, only 4 percent (2/52) of the tokens in our EPA corpus occur in orientation clauses. However, the Springville corpus includes older speakers like Vanessa,[13] who was between 27 and 30 years old when her examples, including the following one, were recorded:[14]

6   (a)   When I was working at Billups
     (b)   me an' the manager we *had became* real good friends
     (c)   and so she *had started* callin' me her sister.
     (d)   So I liked workin' there
     (e)   because uh, we did the work together.
     (f)   We made it easy for each other. (Vanessa, about 27, Springville, Texas, from Cukor-Avila and Bailey, 1995: 407, example 22)

Discussing this example, Cukor-Avila and Bailey (1995: 407) observe that

> Vanessa's use of *had* + past suggests that she views the events of "becoming friends" and the manager "calling her her sister" not as sequenced events, but as a result of some other action, perhaps the fact that they worked together a lot and got along so well. In this brief orientation section to a much longer narrative, Vanessa is offering background information, in essence "setting the scene" for the rest of the narrative. Additionally, there is no explicit reference point stated in conjunction with the use of these forms. Instead there is an implied reference time which is the beginning of the actions that comprise the narrative. . . . In both examples (22) and (23), then, innovative *had* + past functions as a type of remote past signaling that the events described occurred prior to the telling of the narrative.

We agree (with the authors here, and with the extended discussion of this example which Cukor-Avila has kindly provided us via electronic mail) that the explicit reference point which would favor the use of a conventional "pluper-fect" in this narrative is not obvious. The real-time reference of the *had* predicates in lines (b) and (c) could not have preceded the reference of *working* in line (a), and Standard-English speakers would probably encode them both as simple preterites (*we* BECAME *good friends; she* STARTED *calling me her sister*). However, the preterite *had*s in this intriguing example are not only prior to the start of the complicating action of the narrative; they are also prior (at least in part) to the stative (and evaluative) predicate *liked working there* in line (d), with the conjunctive *so* helping to reinforce this earlier/later, cause/effect relation-ship. To the extent that this is in fact the case, we can see something of the pluperfect's "relativeness" in the grammaticalization of *had* as a preterite.

The following narrative from the EPA corpus similarly reveals how the relativity of the English pluperfect carries over into the preterite *had* usage of AAVE:

7   One time my mom and my dad HAD went somewhere [*Orientation*]
    And she left me and my brother and my little sister at home.
(a)   And my brother he HAD got mad at me
      'cause I was on the phone.
(b)   And so he threw a pillow
(c)   and I ducked
(d)   and he hit the table
      and my mom's crystal was on it
(e)   and he broke it.
      And I got in trouble for it [*Evaluation*]
      and he didn't.
      I couldn't get back on the phone for like about three weeks.
      I was so mad.
      Then when he HAD broke it,
      I was trying to clean it up, and, you know, stick it back together.
      But some of it was just broken [into] too many pieces.
      I couldn't put it back together.
(f)   Then she came home.
(g)   It [She] was like, "Uh, uh, who broke this?"
(h)   I'm like, "I don't know." (Laughs.)
(i)   Then so my brother, he said, "She was on the phone and then she came
      in here and hit me and then I threw the pillow."
(j)   And so she said, "Well, it's really your fault because you ain't supposed
      to be on the phone." (Cathy, 12, EPA)

The *had broke* preterite in the evaluation section (see Labov 1972: 370–5) of the narrative – where the action is suspended while the narrator reveals her frustra-tion at the injustice of the situation – was classified by us as a conventional pluperfect, fulfilling the classic flashback function of marking a time prior to the reference point of the immediately preceding clauses (GOT *in trouble*;

COULDN'T GET back; WAS so mad). The other *had* predicates in the opening lines of this story – *had went; had got mad* – were classified by us and by others whom we polled on this issue as preterites rather than pluperfects, since the reference points to which they might establish anterior reference do not precede them textually and they could just as well be encoded as conventional preterites (*WENT somewhere; GOT MAD at me*). Note, however, that the parents' going out marks a crucial part of the orientation phase of this narrative (this is the single orientation clause tabulated in table 3.4), providing an essential backdrop for the brother's getting mad and throwing a pillow at the narrator. Although the brother's getting mad may be legitimately interpreted as the first complicating action in the narrative (this is how we have interpreted and coded it), it could also be seen as another part of the orientation section, the final precursor to his throwing the pillow and breaking the vase. These initial *had* predicates, then, provide good examples of the use of preterite *had* to mark events prior to the first complicating action in a narrative (cf. Cukor-Avila and Bailey 1995 on this point above), and while they might most naturally be encoded in standard English as conventional preterites, at least some of the linguists whom we asked felt that they could also be encoded as conventional pluperfects in standard English (*had gone; had gotten mad*).

Relatedly, it is interesting to note that several of the preterite *had*s in our data, although they are part of the complicating action of the narrative, also mark temporary (re)orientation points or what Schiffrin (1992: 763), following Psathas (1979), calls "landmarks": "locations that the speaker uses as a base from which to orient the next action." Examples include the sentences 1–6 in the Appendix, from a relatively long narrative by Tabitha. Like other (re)orienting markers, these predicates include motion verbs (*had walked off; had came; had went; had left*) which describe the location of the protagonists as one episode ends and another begins, with a new set of complicating actions:

8 (n)   And then she hit kinda hard in his face, but not that hard . . .
   (p)   And then so they *had walked* off.
   (q)   And Gerald started walking off, said, "I'ma bring my peoples!"
   (r)   Then Corey walked up to him,
   (s)   Corey Corey walked up to him and decked him in the eye, I mean in the jaw.
   (t)   And then he said, "I'ma bring my people."
   (u)   And then and um, we *had came* around a corner,
         And then we *had came* around a corner,
   (v)   We *had went* home,
   (w)   And then Gerald mother and him come up, and Gerald was crying.
         (Tabitha, 12, EPA)

Sometimes, the reorientation does not involve movement to a new location but the temporary cessation or resolution of a conflict (e.g., *had broke up* in the following example), which re-erupts with greater intensity in successive clauses:

9 (j)   And then she take him off the pole
   (k)   And then she was jus' beating him up.
   (l)   And then they *had broke up*.
   (m)   And then she walked back over to him
   (n)   And then she slapped him in the face
   (o)   And she had him on the fence, just punchin him and stuff. (Clinton, 12, EPA)

The following example is particularly interesting because while the first *had* precedes the climactic *peak* of the narrative (the protagonist/narrator being "whupped" by her aunt for having gone to the bathroom in a bumper car at Disneyland), the subsequent *had*s precede and reinforce the sad *point* of the narrative – that everyone remained mad at the narrator for this accidental by-product of her excitement while on the bumper cars, and that in the middle of all the activities that Disneyland had to offer, the physically and emotionally exhausted family members went to their motel room and slept:

10 (b)   And then, and then (I was around eight), I used the bathroom.
    (c)   And then I got off the bumper cars.
    (d)   And that man he have to wipe it off and everything.
    (e)   And so, um, my auntie, she *had took* me to the bathroom,
    (f)   And she whupped me and everything.
          I was crying. [*Evaluation*]
          I was crying.
          We was staying at Disneyland for around for around three days.
          I was crying and everything.
    (g)   And then, so, and then, so she *had just took* me up to the car,
    (h)   And we *had just left*, 'cause they was mad at me and everything.
    (i)   And we just went to our motel room
    (j)   and slept. (Angie, 12, EPA)

Cases like these, where the *had* precedes the descriptive peak or the emotional/moral point of the narrative, represent yet another instance of the "subjectification" which commonly occurs in grammaticalization, the pragmatic-semantic process whereby "meanings become increasingly based in the speaker's subjective belief state/attitude toward the proposition" (Traugott 1989: 35; 1994: 4). Although they do not exactly resemble English pluperfects, they exploit the pluperfect's characteristic of "locating a situation prior to a contextually given reference point" (Comrie 1986: 16) to direct our attention to key complicating actions and evaluative points in a narrative. Strategically, the *had* predicates function as foreshadowers of key actions and points in the narrative, directing us to seek in adjacent clauses the reference points which occurrences of *had* would normally require.

Another way of understanding 9 and 10, and several other texts in our corpus, is to recognize that the *had* predicates presage the evaluative component of the narrative, what Labov (1972c, 366) describes as "the means used by the narrator to indicate the point of the narrative, its raison d'être: Why it was told, and what the narrator was getting at." Sometimes, the evaluation is external, by explicit statement ("I was crying," "they was mad at me and everything"), and, sometimes, the evaluation is embedded in the actions described ("we just went to our motel room and slept"). In 10, the external evaluation is provided at a point at which the action is suspended (Labov 1972c: 374), and the following example is also of this type:

11 (l)   And then he *had messed* –
    (m)   And then he *had pushed* the referee,
    (n)   so I uh, let Anthony win.
           Because I'm the referee and I make the decidings. [*Evaluation*]
           Because whoever mess with the referee, he can make the decide . . .
           (David, 10, EPA)

Altogether, 42 percent of our *had* marked predicates (22/52) are of this (re)orienting or point-preceding type. It is perhaps just a short step from using *had* to mark the *prelude* to a particularly intense complicating action to using it for the *first* such complicating action itself (as in examples 3 and 4 above), or to mark the particularly dramatic or emotionally intense developments themselves, as in the following two narratives.[15]

12   One day, I was, I was jus' sleepin' [*Orientation*]
            and then I, I had, I was sleep,
            and my mother, my mother, she was whuppin me.
            She was whuppin me.
            She was whuppin me
            and I was hollerin an everything.
    (a)   And then all of a sudden this, this man was, this man come in my
            room,
            he had blood over his face and everything.
    (b)   And he *had* grabbed my mother [cf. "he *grabbed* my mother"]
    (c)   and slammed her down to the ground
            and I was hollerin an everything [*Evaluation*]
            And then all of a sudden –
            and that was the end of my dream.
    (d)   I woke up
            I was goin, "Ma! Ma!"
    (e)   And then she *had* just came, came in there [cf. "she just *came*"]
    (f)   and then she *had* threw water on me and stuff [cf. "she *threw* water"]
    (g)   and told me to wake up, right?

(h)   She just went, "Angie, wake up! Wake up! Wake up! It was just a
      dream! It was just a dream! Wake up!"
(i)   And then I, I just woke up
      And I was crying. [*Evaluation*] (Angie, 12, EPA)

13   Well, one day I was like, I was riding my [bike] over . . . Dumbarton
      [bridge]. [*Orientation*]
      This was a scary dream. [*Evaluation*]
(a)   And then I fell.
      And I was, I was like,
      the water had like,
      it was sort of hard a little bit [*Re-orientation*]
      and I was riding my bike
(b)   and then it [the bridge] broke.
      And then this big old shark was chasing me.
      And I was trying to ride on my bike under water,
      But I wasn't going nowhere [*Embedded evaluation*]
(c)   so I tried to start swimming.
(d)   And then the shark *had* bit, *had* got my leg [cf. "*bit*," "*got*"],
      and it was biting me.
(e)   And then it, another shark came
(f)   And grabbed my other leg,
      And they was just chewing off my legs,
(g)   And um they chewed my legs off . . . (Clinton, 12, EPA; narrative
      continues)

Following Fleischman (1990) we may describe these dramatic high-points of
the narrative as constituting a Peak, "a point in the Complicating Action in
which discourse tension reaches a climax" (141). The significance of this is that
Peaks "are frequently marked in surface syntax by various devices" including
tense shifting:

> Observing that Peaks are typically zones of linguistic turbulence (marked dis-
> course micro-contexts) where predictable correlations between grammatical fea-
> tures and levels of information relevance operative elsewhere in the text are often
> cancelled or even reversed, Longacre (1976: 219ff) notes that a frequent strategy
> for achieving the highlighted vividness of narrative Peaks is through tense switch-
> ing, in particular through a shift into the PR [Present]. (Fleischman 1990: 142)

In the case of the EPA texts, the tense shift is marked with preterite *had*
rather than the present tense. The usage is not entirely unprecedented, however, since, according to Fleischman (1989), Paceño Spanish (the Spanish of La
Paz, Bolivia) "uses the *pluperfect* as a non-relative tense . . . to express 'surprise
and nonpersonal knowledge upon encountering an unknown or something seen
for the first time that occurred without one realizing it' (Laprade 1981: 223)"
(29). Examples from Fleischman (1989: 30, drawing on Laprade 1981) are
provided in 14 and 15:

14   Te habías casado [*Plup.*]
     "You got married! (and I hadn't heard)"
15   Había sabido [*Plup.*] hablar Aymara muy bien
     "It turned out he *did* know how to speak Aymara very well"

The parallels are not exact – for one thing this unusual Spanish use of the pluperfect for the preterite can occur in a single sentence without its being in a sequence, and for another, its nonpersonal function is not shared with the EPA usage. But in both cases it can be said that the use of a pluperfect form marks a surprising or unexpected development, and one which, in at least the immediately preceding EPA texts, corresponds to a narrative Peak.

Having described preterite *had* as sometimes marking the landmarks to actions in new episodes of narratives, sometimes marking the preludes to dramatic peaks or moral/emotional *points*, and sometimes marking those dramatic peaks themselves, it must be admitted that in a number of examples – about 38 percent or 20 of our 52 tokens – preterite *had* appears to be simply used as a variant of V-*ed*, with absolute time reference and none of the relative time reference which would link it, however tenuously, to its pluperfect source. This is particularly true of the usage of David, a prolific *had* user whose single extended narrative accounts for just over a third of our preterite *had* examples (34–52, Appendix), many of them alternating in preceding or successive lines with simple preterites (e.g., *hit . . . had hit*; *push . . . had push*).

16   (x)   Cause when he *hit* me like this. . . .
     (y)   he *had uppercut* me like that,
     (z)   and then he *had hit* me like that
     (aa)   He had kicked me,
     (ab)   It was half-wrestling
     (ac)   And then one I was tired
     (ad)   then he just beat me,
     (ae)   And *push* me down.
     (af)   That's when he *had push* me down. [David, 10, EPA]

These examples resemble the use of *had* for unsequenced listings and single events which Cukor-Avila and Bailey (1995) describe as later stages of the grammaticalization process.

3.3   Use of Preterite and Pluperfect *had* by Other Speakers

Our analysis of the narratives of the nine preadolescents from East Palo Alto who provided the data for this paper – all but two of them 12 years old[16] – has so far established that they use preterite *had* quite commonly and pluperfect *had* quite rarely. How does this compare with the usage of other groups of speakers? We have four primary groups for comparison: 1 African American adolescents and adults in East Palo Alto; 2 African American preadolescents and adolescents in Harlem whose usage a quarter century ago was reported by Labov et al. (1968); 3 African American adolescents and young adults whose usage is discussed in Cukor-Avila (1995) and Cukor-Avila and Bailey (1995; 1996); 4 Puerto Rican teenagers and young adults in New York City, as reported to us by Ana Celia Zentella (1989).

3.3.1   Contemporary Usage among African American Adolescents and Adults in East Palo Alto

A computer search of the transcripts of recordings made separately in 1986–7 with two East Palo Alto adolescents, Foxy Boston, 13, and Tinky Gates, 15,[17] turned up *no* instances of preterite *had*, but several instances of pluperfect *had*. One of Foxy Boston's pluperfect *had* tokens occurred in a narrative about the shooting of Greg, a friend of hers:

17 . . . they was playin cards, right, an' Greg paid all his money but 'cept a quarter, cause he didn't have change, and he *tol' him* [R] that he had – he *had give it back* [E] to him, but – an Alabama wuh – Alabama, he didn' mean to shoot him . . . (Foxy Boston, 13, EPA 7: 9)

Note that the event (E) referred to in *had give it back* in (17) is chronologically earlier than the reference point (R) established by *tol' him* but that E occurs later than R in narrative time – precisely the pluperfect favoring situation described by Comrie (1985: 65).[18]

Tinky has ten tokens of pluperfect *had*, and they are all similar to Foxy's, insofar as they describe events (E) which are chronologically earlier, but later in narrative time, than another event which serves as the reference point (R). We will give three examples:

18 Then the Black girl came back, an they was tearin her up. So then tha' thing got turned out, an' I *was tryin' to fin'* [R] my cousin Ruth. Ruth *had already left* [E]. [Tinky Gates, 15, EPA 12: 26.]

19 But you know what, mama? Tell her 'bout that time yo' mama left you there to cook them beans an [laughter] – you ran off an the beans was burnt. An y'all had to go get some new beans and *tell her* [R] that them was the ol' beans that y'all *had cook* [E] . . . [Tinky Gates, 15, EPA 12: 77.]

20 Steven's fifteen. An we all *got sent home* [R]. Okay, this wha' happen. Okay, all day, he – we *had been* [E] with each other all day long. (Tinky Gates, 15, EPA 12: 80.)

Finally, a search of the transcript of a contemporaneously recorded interview with Penelope Johnson, a 76-year-old woman from EPA, turned up nine
instances of *had*, all of them used as regular English pluperfects, for instance:

21 You know, he finally decided [E], he – because he *had* retired [R], you know,
    from work. (Penelope Johnson, 76, EPA 5: 9)

Tentatively, in the light of this evidence from Foxy, Tinky, and Penelope
Johnson, we conclude that the use of preterite *had* in EPA is restricted to
preadolescents. A related respect in which the preadolescents differ from the
adolescents and adults in this area is that the preadolescents do not use present
perfect *have*, while the older speakers use it at least some of the time (two
tokens from Foxy, one from Tinky, and four from Penelope Johnson), as in
these examples:[19]

22 I don't know how long I've been staying here. (Foxy Boston, 13, EPA 7: 2)
23 An today – today I *haven't* seen – (Tinky Gates, 15, EPA 12: 79)[20]
24 I *have* seen the next house . . . change owners or whatever a lot. (Penelope
    Johnson, 76, EPA 5: 22)

One must be careful about the negative evidence from the preadolescents
because their recordings are generally shorter and restricted to narrative, which
is not an ideal site for the present perfect. But it is possible that the adolescents
and adults have acquired both pluperfect *had* and present perfect *have* as part
of a system of oppositions which the younger AAVE-speaking children do not
yet control. This possibility is reinforced by the fact that the two African-
American adults whose voices are heard on the Foxy/Tinky recordings – Faye
McNair-Knox, the interviewer, and Paula Gates, Tinky's mom – use the
present perfect forms even more often than the adolescents do, suggesting that
we may indeed be dealing with a developmental or age-graded phenomenon.

3.3.2 Usage 25 years ago among African American preadolescents and adolescents in East Harlem

Although Labov et al. (1968) do not discuss preterite *had* directly, we can glean
from their study several interesting facts about the use of auxiliary *have* and *had*
among African American preadolescents and adolescents in East Harlem, New
York City, just over a quarter of a century ago.

For one thing, they note (224–5) that, as a verbal auxiliary, *had* was
more common than *have*, *had* occurring 150 times in recordings with the
Thunderbirds (8–13 yrs old), Cobras (11–17 yrs old), Jets (12–19 yrs old), Oscar

Brothers (16–18 yrs old) and Lames (9–13 yrs old), while *have* occurred only 66 times. In this respect, Labov et al.'s data agree with our East Palo Alto data.[21] Although their data are not presented in a way that would allow us to see whether it was also true at that time that use of the present perfect increased with age, there are several hints that this may have been the case, as it is in our data. The authors note, for instance that "adults use more *have* than adolescents" (226). And the three examples of present perfect *have* which they present from Harlem peer-group members are from adolescents aged 13 and 15,[22] while the one example they present to show that some native speakers may not have ready access to the present perfect is from a younger, ten-year-old peer-group member:[23]

25   I was *been* in Detroit. [10, T-Birds, #498, Labov et al. 1968: 254]

With respect to the semantic function of auxiliary *had*, Labov et al. identify it as the "past perfect" and suggest that both "preadolescent and pre-pre-adolescent speakers" use it "with appropriate semantic force" (254). They provide the following example from an eight-year-old Thunderbird member to support this point:

26   [How did the fight start?]
     I *had came* over . . . (8, Thunderbirds, #933, Labov et al. 1968: 254)

But note that as the initial predicate in a narrative, this would represent an unusual use of the English pluperfect. However, the fact that it occurs with a motion verb, the fact that it's the first complicating action in the narrative, and the fact that it appears to serve as a foreshadower of some other action are all characteristic of EPA preterite *had*. The authors provide only two other full examples of *had* + V -ed, and of these the first (27 below) seems to us to be an example of preterite *had*, while the second, in context, might well be a pluperfect.

27   When I went down there – they almost *had took* me away. (13, Jets, #606, Labov et al. 1968: 225)
28   I never *had got* tol' on. [14, Jets, #527, Labov et al. 1968: 254]

If examples 26 and 27 really are tokens of preterite *had* – and we would need the entire narrative context to be certain – this usage may have been in existence for a quarter of a century or more.
     One final feature of Labov et al.'s discussion of the use of *had* and *have* that is worth noting is their observation, "the perfect forms do not seem to be clearly

distinct . . . from the preterit forms" (258). They cite in support of this, ex-amples like *Have you ever SAW; He hadn't SEED; she had SWAM out; we had RAN down; she had CAME over; I had THREW UP.* As noted above, this is also the case in our recent East Palo Alto data, where the canonical form is *had* + V *-ed* rather than *had* + V *-en.*

3.3.3 Usage among African American Adolescents and Adults in Springville, Texas

We have already noted (in section 3.2.4) the claim of Cukor-Avila (1995), and Cukor-Avila and Bailey (1995) that "innovative" *had* + PAST (= preterite *had*) in Springville, Texas, represents a re-analysis of the conventional English pluperfect by AAVE speakers and its grammaticalization as a simple past or preterite. What remains to be added in this section, and related to the EPA data, is their specific claim that this grammaticalization represents an ongoing change which began about half a century ago. Figure 3.2 (= figure 3 in Cukor-Avila and Bailey 1995), showing the percentage of innovative or preterite *had* + PAST as a proportion of all *had* + PASTs (traditional pluperfects and innova-tive preterites), provides the crucial data for this claim. Note that the first evidence of innovative *had* + PAST (20 percent) is found among speakers born pre-WWII (between 1918 and 1945) and that its percentage use increases (to about 40 percent) among speakers born post-WWII (1945–69) and increases yet again (to about 70 percent) among speakers born in 1970 or later.

Given the fact that the comparable percentage of preterite *had* for our EPA preadolescents is 96 percent (52/54 tokens, see table 3.1), one might hypoth-esize that they represent an even more advanced stage of the change depicted in figure 3.1. However, apart from the fact that the proportion of preterite *had*s in the EPA data would drop somewhat if computed against the total of all narra-tives or all recorded speech from these speakers,[24] there is the problem that our two adolescent speakers (Foxy and Tinky) show no traces of this innovative usage.[25] Since they were also born in the post-1970 period, we might have expected them to show some evidence of preterite *had*, the more so because we have longer recordings with them than we have with the preadolescents, and because the adolescent recordings include many narratives, the context which favors preterite *had*. On the basis of the EPA data alone, we would be hard-pressed to distinguish between preterite *had* as an age-graded feature (dimin-ishing or dropping out of use as the speakers got older, and perhaps gained firmer control of the opposition between present and pluperfect) or as change in progress (remaining in the speech of these preadolescents as they grew older, and increasing in frequency in the speech of successive preadolescent cohorts). Given the ancillary evidence of Labov et al. (1968) that innovations resembling preterite *had* were attested in New York over 25 years ago, we are tempted to

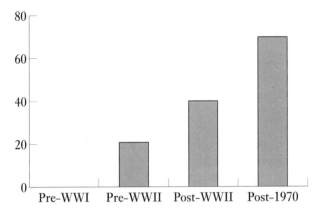

Figure 3.2 Preterite *had* as a percentage of all *had* + V -ed forms (After Cukor-Avila and Bailey 1995, fig. 3)

conclude that preterite *had* represents change in progress in AAVE more generally, but we would need additional data both from the EPA and New York communities to confirm this.

3.3.4 *Usage among Puerto Ricans in New York City*

Since 1989, when we first presented this paper, we have received reports of preterite *had* being used elsewhere in the United States by African American youth or Puerto Rican youth in contact with African Americans. Some of the reports, like those of Cukor-Avila (1995) and Cukor-Avila and Bailey (1995; 1996) are formal, with attestations and analysis. Most are informal, without accompanying attestations. However, one scholar who has given us actual attestations is Ana Celia Zentella (of the City University of New York, Graduate Center) who reported similar usage among young Puerto Ricans in New York City (1989). To illustrate the similarity, Zentella shared with us a book report written by a 19-year-old Puerto Rican woman, born and raised in New York City, which was replete with *had* + V -ed constructions. Some of these were pluperfects, as in 29, where reading and reflecting on *A Time with a Future* establish a reference point between the earlier events involving the student's grandparents and the moment of writing.

29   Reading *A Time with a Future*, I began to think of how my grandmother *had planned* my grandmother's life after my grandfather died. Like Carmela, my grandmother *had been married* to my grandfather for over 45 years. They *had lived* a happy and fantastic life most of the time. (19-year-old NYC Puerto Rican, in writing; from Zentella 1989)

But many others were preterites or simple pasts, without clear intervening reference points, as in examples 30 and 31. And in her comments on the paper Zentella suggested that the student contact a writing instructor "to go over the differences in meaning between 'had + _____ed' and the regular past tense."

30 *Happy Birthday Lucia had brought* tears to my eyes. . . . What *had troubled* me was when Virginia *had simply up and left* Mateo and the kids.
31 Aunt Rosanna's Rocker was a story which I *hadn't necessarily liked* or understood. The story *had appeared* to be a good one, up until the point when Zoraida's rocking chair *had been taken* away.

From this limited evidence, it appears that preterite *had* usage has a wider social distribution, in terms of geography and age-range, than our East Palo Alto data indicate, that it might indeed have increased in frequency since Labov et al. (1968) made their recordings with African American youth in New York in the mid-1960s, and that it might have spread to other ethnic groups in contact with African American youth.

3.4   Conclusions and Directions for Future Research

In this paper, we have drawn attention to the innovative use of *had* + V *-ed* in the narratives of African American preadolescents from East Palo Alto as a preterite rather than a pluperfect tense, that is, without the relational reference point (usually earlier in narrative time) which the standard English pluperfect requires. However, close analysis of the preterite *had* tokens reveals that more than half of them serve the function of marking a narrative reorientation or peak, or of foreshadowing a narrative peak or evaluative point. In these respects, the grammaticalization of *had* as a preterite retains something of the relational nature of its source, the English pluperfect.

Comparisons with the usage of other speakers are quite revealing. On the evidence of Labov et al. (1968), preterite *had* appears to have been attested in New York City over a quarter century ago, and to the extent that more recent usage among Puerto Rican students in New York is any indication, the innovation may have increased in frequency and spread to other ethnic groups in the interim. Data from Springville, Texas (as reported in Cukor-Avila and Bailey 1995), suggest that the grammaticalization of *had* as a preterite may have begun in the orientation clauses of narratives and spread from there to complicating action clauses and even to single events and unsequenced listings outside of narratives. Moreover, the Springville data suggest that the innovation began with speakers born before World War II and that it has increased steadily in its frequency with successive generations. It is tempting to see in the Springville and New York City data a more general pattern of change in progress and to assume that the EPA preadolescents represent the vanguard of such a process. However, the fact that EPA adolescents do not (yet) show any evidence of this innovation gives us pause, since age-grading is also a possibility.

Some of the directions for future research on this feature – which constitutes yet another exciting development in the study of AAVE's tense-aspect markers (compare how much we have learned about *done, be done*, stressed *BIN*, invariant *be, steady*, and *come* in the past quarter century) – are already implicit if not explicit in what we have written above. We need larger corpora of preterite *had* tokens, from EPA, Springville, Texas, New York City, and other American cities, and we need qualitative exegesis of their functions both within narratives and without, combined with quantitative tabulations of their use in relation to other past-reference predicates. We also need more substantive data on preterite and pluperfect *had* usage among older speakers (adolescents, young, middle-aged, and old adults), combined with data on present-perfect and completive usage, to distinguish between age-grading and change in progress. Finally, we need better data and analysis of the English pluperfect, as used in spontaneous and informal speech, for the innovation represented by preadolescent AAVE usage might reflect or might have helped to initiate a more general change in American English usage which is not (yet) documented in grammatical handbooks and formal studies in linguistics.

Appendix
Sentences with Preterite *had* + Verb *-ed* in
East Palo Alto Corpus

Parenthetical information includes name, age, and example number in our list of narrative predicates. An asterisk indicates a written narrative.

1   . . . And then so they *had* walked off and Gerald started walking off. . . . (Tabitha, 12, #65)
2   . . . and um we *had* came around a corner. . . . (Tabitha, 12, #70)
3   . . . and then um we *had* came around a corner. . . . (Tabitha, 12, #71)
4   . . . we *had* went home. . . . (Tabitha, 12, #72)
5   . . . and then um we *had* went outside. . . . (Tabitha, 12, #84)
6   . . . and then we *had* left. . . . (Tabitha, 12, #87)
7   . . . and um um after that we *had* missed the bus. . . . (Tabitha, 12, #93)
8   . . . and then me and Roné came and we *had* got wet too. . . . (Tabitha, 12, #105)
9   . . . I was on my way to school and I *had* slipped and fell. . . . (Dafina, 12, #3)
10   . . . Adie said . . . and then um I *had* went home. . . . (Anita, 12, #29)
11   . . . and then my cousin *had* asked me. . . . (Anita, 12, #30)

12   . . . and then um Jeanine *had* said . . . (Anita, 12, #34)

13   . . . she drove cars, then she *had* drove some that looked like bubber cars. . . . (Jane*, 13, #299)

14   . . . and then they *had* broke up. . . . (Clinton, 12, #124)

15   . . . and then all of a sudden this man come into my room, he had blood over his face and everything and he *had* grabbed my mother. . . . (Angie, 12, #137)

16   . . . I was goin' "Ma! Ma!", and then she *had* just came, came in there. . . . (Angie, 12, #143)

17   . . . and then she *had* threw water on me and stuff. . . . (Angie, 12, #144)

18   . . . And then the shark *had* bit, . . . (Clinton, 12, #175)

19   . . . *had* got my leg . . . (Clinton, 12, #176)

20   . . . when I was up in the driveway, a car *had* backed up and it ran over my bike. . . . (Nathan, 12, #219)

21   . . . I was drivin' and then when we *had* got . . . (Angie, 12, #230)

22   . . . my auntie, she *had* took me to the bathroom. . . . (Angie, 12, #238)

23   . . . she *had* just took me up to the car. . . . (Angie, 12, #244)

24   . . . and we *had* just left. . . . (Angie, 12, #245)

25   . . . and they blew this thing up and it *had* crashed. . . . (Clinton, 12, #255)

26   . . . and it *had* went inside this place and this lady had him captured. . . . (Clinton, 12, #256)

27   . . . and then he *had* put the organ together and he start playing. . . . (Clinton, 12, #261)

28   . . . One time my mom and my dad *had* went somewhere and she left me. . . . (Cathy, 12, #277)

29   . . . and my brother he *had* got mad at me 'cause I was on the phone. . . . (Cathy, 12, #277)

30   I said "No," and then so she *had* left me alone. . . . (Cathy, 12, #317)

31   . . . and then (she) *had* went home on our way. (Cathy, 12, #318)

32   . . . she pushed me and I fell and I *had* hurt my leg. . . . (Cathy, 12, #332)

33   . . . and then so I *had* got up so we started fighting. . . . (Cathy, 12, #334)

34   . . . I *had* got him on the ground and I had him like this. . . . (David, 10, #351)

35   We was playing yesterday and then after that him and his brother *had* had a fight. . . . (David, 10, #363)

36   . . . and he *had* gave up. (David, 10, #364)

37   . . . I said, "Man he messed you up, . . . and then he *had* messed . . ." (David, 10, #374)

38   . . . then he *had* pushed the referee so I uh let Anthony win. (David, 10, #375)

39   . . . and then uh Anthony *had* won. . . . (David, 10, #379)

40   . . . he made him uh give up cause he *had* hit him. . . . (David, 10, #382)

41   . . . he *had* hit him in his nose. . . . (David, 10, #383)

42   . . . and Jojo *had* gave up. (David, 10, #384)

43   . . . and then when it was my turn to fight him I *had* kept on hitting him. . . . (David, 10, #387)

44   . . . cause we was half wrestling, half boxing and he *had* pushed me down. . . . (David, 10, #411)

45   . . . after he *had* hit me in my jaw then I hit him back. . . . (David, 10, #412)

46   . . . and then he *had* just pushed me down. . . . (David, 10, #415)

47   . . . and I run go backwards and once he *had* uppercut me like that. . . . (David, 10, #419)
48   . . . and then he *had* hit me like that. . . . (David, 10, #420)
49   . . . and he *had* kicked me. (David, 10, #421)
50   . . . that's when he *had* push me down. (David, 10, #426)
51   And I *had* hit him in his nose. (David, 10, #458)
52   I *had* hit him in his nose, though. (David, 10, #460)

Notes

This paper represents an extensive revision of a paper, "Preterite *had* in the BEV of Elementary School Children," which we presented at the eighteenth annual Conference on New Ways of Analyzing Variation in English (NWAVE 18), held at Duke University in October 1989. That paper in turn drew on data originally included in Théberge (1988), a senior honors essay. We are grateful to Raina Jackson, Arnetha Ball, and Bonnie McElhinny for allowing us to use narratives they recorded in East Palo Alto; these provided a substantial number of the preterite *had* tokens in our data set. We are also grateful to Renée Blake for transcription and to Jabrina Walker for helping us to analyze the usage of older EPA speakers. We are also grateful to Educational Testing Service for supporting Christine's later work on this paper through a postdoctoral fellowship. Finally, we are indebted to Elizabeth Closs Traugott for helpful discussion of several critical points in the analysis and to Angela Rickford and Howard Rafal for their encouragement and support.

1   We follow Labov (1972c: 393) in classifying speakers 10 to 12 years old as preadolescents and speakers 13 to 16 years old as adolescents. By this criterion, Jane, one of the "preadolescents" in our sample, is technically an adolescent, but her lone token of preterite *had* is included with those of the 12-year-olds because she was a member of their peer group and in the same elementary school grade (sixth) as them.

2   According to Binnick (1991: 6, 11), the term *preterite* comes from Latin *praeteritum* "gone by," while the term *pluperfect* comes from the Latin *plusquam-perfectus* "more than perfect (i.e., completely done)."

3   Fleischman (1990: 132) describes this pluperfect-favoring situation in terms similar to those of Comrie. Of the sequence *I finished writing my paper, I went to bed*, she notes that "a minimal narrative is produced by simply juxtaposing two clauses whose order is iconic to the assumed real-world chronology of the events they report." By contrast, the sentence *I went to bed after I had finished writing my paper* is described as configuring "the same scenario in terms of a foregrounded action in the main clause ('going to bed') to which the action of 'finishing the paper' is backgrounded by means of a subordinating conjunction ('after') and a tense of anteriority – the [pluperfect]."

4   Additionally, following the conventions of Labov (1972c: 362) and Schiffrin (1981: 46), subordinate clauses and quotations are not considered narrative clauses and are therefore unlettered.

5   Labov (1972c: 370) provides the following convenient characterizations of each of
     the major components of a narrative as answers to different underlying questions:
     Abstract: What was this about? *Orientation:* Who, what, when, where? *Complicat-
     ing action:* Then what happened? *Evaluation:* So what? *Result* (= *Resolution*): What
     finally happened? To this we may add, from Fleischman (1990: 135), *Peak:* What
     was the highpoint? *Coda:* What is the relation to the present context?

6   In conjoined verb phrases, as in 3a and 3b, *had* occurs with the first verb only, and
     not the second (**I HAD SLIPPED and HAD FELL*). This is true even when the conjuncts
     are clausal and the second verb has an overt subject, as in 4a and 4b (*a car HAD
     BACKED up and it RAN over*).

7   On grammaticalization in general, see Traugott and Heine (1991) and Hopper and
     Traugott (1993).

8   Not included in the count of past reference verbs, because they show no variation
     with preterite *had* + V *-ed*, are past tense copulas (151 tokens), modals (six tokens),
     and instances of *didn't* (five tokens). Past reference verbs within the dialogue
     rather than the narrative clauses of the story (e.g., "Mom, Andrew cracked his
     head open") were also excluded because they showed no variation with preterite
     had + V *-ed*.

9   We have recorded a number of present and past perfect examples from white
     Americans recently which include V *-ed* rather than V *-en*.

10   In one additional case (number 7 in the Appendix), preterite *had* + V *-ed* occurs in
     a clause beginning with *after that* instead of *then*. In another case (number 15 in the
     Appendix), the preterite *had* + V *-ed* clause is separated from *then* by two interven-
     ing clauses but still appears to be governed by it. Neither of these tokens was
     included in the *then* clause count for table 3.1, which includes only clear and
     unambiguous cases.

11   The one exception is main verb *had* as a preterite, which co-occurs with *then* only
     13 percent of the time. This may be due to the fact that this is a stative predicate,
     since virtually all of the *had* + V *-ed* preterites are nonstative verbs, referring to
     actions which are more likely to be described as subsequent to other actions.

12   One of the two pluperfect tokens appears to occur in a *then when* time clause (e.g.,
     Then when he HAD BROKE it, I was trying to clean it up), but as we can see from the
     larger context of the narrative (example 7 on page 43) in which this clause occurs,
     this *then* is equivalent to *moreover* and serves the function of discourse-marking
     rather than that of an anaphoric reference-point shifter. Note that the time frame
     of this *then* clause is not subsequent to the time frame of the immediately preced-
     ing clause or clauses (as it is in the case of the 25 tokens of *then*-clauses with
     preterite *had*), but that it takes us back to a point somewhere in the middle of the
     preceding sequence (see example 7 on page 43).

13   The data in Cukor-Avila and Bailey (1995) were collected in a rural east-central
     community of Texas (Springville) in the late 1980s and early 1990s. Although
     Vanessa is older (born in 1961) and her relatively high percentage of preterite *had*
     use in orientation clauses (48 percent, 13/27) accords with the hypothesis, the
     correlation between age and use of preterite *had* in orientation clauses is relatively
     weak in the Springville corpus, at least to the extent that we were able to compute
     it from the data in Cukor-Avila and Bailey (1995, table 1). Brandy, born in 1982,
     shows an equally high percentage of *had* use in orientation clauses (46 percent,

6/13), and Lamar, born in 1976, shows categorical use (100 percent, 4/4) in orientation clauses. Sheila, born in 1979, uses preterite *had* in orientation clauses less often (29 percent, 11/38) than Vanessa does, as the hypothesis would lead us to expect, but the older speaker Travis, born in 1965, showed categorical *non*-use (0 percent, 0/7) in orientation clauses, contrary to the hypothesis. These fluctuations, of course, may be due to the relatively small number of tokens and speakers. If we restrict ourselves only to speakers with 25 tokens or more, we get a relatively clear contrast between Vanessa (born in 1961), with 48 percent *had* use in orientation clauses, and Sheila (born in 1979), with only 29 percent. It will be interesting to see if this correlation holds up with additional data.

14 For convenience, we retain the line lettering of Cukor-Avila and Bailey (1995) in this and other examples, which follows the conventions of Labov (1972) insofar as both narrative and non-narrative clauses are lettered as long as they are independent clauses. Our own practice, as noted above, is to follow the convention of Schiffrin (1981) and letter only the narrative or complicating action clauses.

15 Dream narratives, such as those in 12 and 13, can be temporally complex. Whether the reference point is related to tense in the dream itself or in the consciousness of the dreamer after waking is not always clear. Note, however, particularly in 12, that the analysis of the use of *had* + V *-ed* to mark a particularly intense complicating action holds for both the narration of the dream and for the narration of an event that took place after waking.

16 The exceptions were David, a fourth-grader who was about ten when he was recorded, and Jane, a sixth-grader who, at 13, was just one year older than most of her classmates.

17 In Foxy's case, only the transcript of the first reel-to-reel tape resulting from her first interview (EPA 7) was searched; in Tinky's case, the transcripts of both reel-to-reel tapes from her first interview (EPA 12 and 13) were searched. Searches were done for these strings: *had, hadn', 'd, have, haven', 've, done,* and *been.*

18 In this respect, the *had give it back* clause would also be anterior in Caribbean English creoles, eligible for marking with *bin* (in the basilect) or with *did* or *had* (in the mesolect). On this point, compare Givón (1982): "It [*bin*] marks out of sequence clauses in the narrative, specifically those which 'look back' and relate events that occurred earlier than the preceding clause in the narrative" (121). See also Bickerton (1975: 109) and Rickford (1987c: 141–3).

19 Other present perfect forms used by Foxy and Tinky include Ø *been, done,* and *ain'*. See Winford (1993) for a related analysis of these and other present perfect variants in Trinidadian English Creole (TEC).

20 Tinky's other three tokens all involved modals (e.g., *shoulda been* and *would have changed*), suggesting that Winford's suggestion (1993) that these forms serve as entry points for the acquisition of the present perfect in TEC might also be applicable to AAVE.

21 This does not mean that we agree with their primary explanation for this fact – that the lone *d* remaining from the contraction of *had* is less subject to deletion than the lone *v* or *z* remaining from the contraction of *have* or *has* (225). Whether or not this phonetic explanation turns out to be valid, we suspect that auxiliary *had* as a category is acquired before auxiliary *have*, so that the grammar provides more *had* forms than *have* forms as input to the phonetic reduction rules.

22 A fourth example is from an 11-year-old New Yorker who is not a peer-group member.

23 Of course, Loflin (1967) had earlier asserted that AAVE had no underlying *have* at all. Labov et al. (1968) argue persuasively against this sweeping generalization, although they themselves conclude that "one cannot say that the position of *have* in [AAVE] is entirely secure" (223).

24 Recall that table 3.1 shows frequencies only in narratives containing at least one occurrence of preterite *had.*

25 Penelope Johnson's non-use of preterite *had* is, of course, precisely what we would expect if Cukor-Avila and Bailey's hypothesis about the time course of this change applied more generally, since she was born before World War I.

4

Rappin on the Copula Coffin: Theoretical and Methodological Issues in the Analysis of Copula Variation in African American Vernacular English
(with Arnetha Ball, Renée Blake, Raina Jackson, and Nomi Martin)

In this article, we reopen the analysis of one of the oldest and most frequently examined variables in the paradigm of quantitative sociolinguistics: variation between full, contracted, and zero forms of inflected copula and auxiliary *be* (henceforth "the copula") in African American Vernacular English (AAVE), as in "Sue *is* the leader," "She's happy," "He Ø talkin." For convenience, we use the term *copula* from this point on in its broad sense, to include what we would have to distinguish in a narrow sense as copula *be* (before a noun phrase, adjective, or locative) and auxiliary *be* (before Verb + *ing* or *gon(na)* Verb).

The copula is an important feature for sociolinguistics and American dialectology for several reasons. First, copula absence sets AAVE apart from all other American dialects, especially with respect to *is* absence. European American vernacular varieties as far apart as Mississippi, New York, and Palo Alto, California, show some *are* absence, but little or no *is* absence (see Labov 1969; McElhinny 1993; Wolfram, 1974); by contrast, *is* absence for African American vernacular speakers in the same areas runs to 80 percent or more. Second, the copula has played a crucial role in determining whether AAVE derives from an earlier plantation creole, as AAVE resembles some Caribbean creoles in its patterns of copula absence, especially as affected by following grammatical categories (see Alleyne 1980; Bailey 1965; Baugh 1979, 1980; Bickerton 1973; Holm 1976, 1984; Poplack and Sankoff 1987; Rickford and Blake, 1990; Stewart 1970b; Winford 1988). Third, the copula has figured significantly in other controversies – the Ann Arbor court case, for instance (Labov, 1982; Smitherman, 1981b), and the issue of whether AAVE is currently diverging

from European American Vernacular English (Bailey and Maynor 1989; Butters 1989; Fasold et al. 1987; Rickford, 1992. Fourth, Labov's (1969) classic
study of the AAVE copula constituted one of the earliest and richest demon-
strations of the need for and the nature of the quantitative sociolinguistics
paradigm. For these reasons, the AAVE copula is a showcase variable in American dialectology and quantitative sociolinguistics. It is one of the most studied
variables in the quantitative paradigm and one of the best-known to linguists in
other subfields (see Akmajian, Demers, and Harnish 1984: 295ff).

But if the AAVE copula has been this well studied, why return to it now?
Initially, the copula was only one of several variables we were investigating in
East Palo Alto, for the light they might shed on the currently controversial
divergence issue. However, as we began to comb through the literature in
preparation for analyzing our own data, we discovered that there was considerable variation among previous copula researchers on matters as basic as what
forms to count and how they should be counted. Moreover, although Labov
(1969) had explicitly considered some of the theoretical and methodological
alternatives, most subsequent copula analysts had not, choosing one approach
or another without explicit discussion or justification. As the effects of the
different alternatives were potentially significant, we decided that we could not
adequately investigate the "live" issues of substance without simultaneously
returning to the neglected or "dead" issues of methodology. Hence, the title of
this article: "Rappin on the Copula Coffin."

Of the many theoretical and methodological issues on which copula researchers have differed, two are particularly significant, and they are the ones
we focus on in this article.

4.1   Which Forms Constitute the Variable?

Virtually all AAVE copula researchers agree that non-finite and past tense
forms of the copula are almost invariably present in full form ("She will *be* here
tomorrow"; "She *was* here yesterday"); that *am* is almost categorically present
in contracted form ("I'*m* here"); and that the only forms that regularly allow
full, contracted, and zero options are the remaining present tense forms, *is*
and *are*. However, as table 4.1 shows, researchers have differed according to
whether their copula tabulations included *is* only, *is* and *are* separately (treating
them as two variables), or *is* and *are* together (treating them as one variable).

The earliest position, represented by Labov, Cohen, Robbins, and Lewis
(1968), was that the deletion of second person and plural *are* could be handled
by a general *r*- vocalization or desulcalization rule, the kind that produces *po'*
and *they* from *poor* and *their*; this left only *is* as a target for the copula deletion
rule. All statistics on the copula in Labov's work, and in the work of other early

Table 4.1 Previous contraction/deletion tabulations of *is* and *are*

	is	*are*	*is + are*
Labov et al. (1968); Labov (1969)[a]; Pfaff (1971)	+		
Wolfram (1974); Baugh (1979)	+	+	
Wolfram (1969); Poplack & Sankoff (1987)[b]			+

[a] *Are-* deletion handled by *r-* vocalization/desulcalization rule.
[b] However, subject factor group permits some separation of *is* and *are*.

copula researchers like Pfaff (1971), were therefore based entirely on *is* and its variants. However, Wolfram (1974) argued persuasively that the deletion of second person and plural *are* should *not* be handled by a general desulcalization rule; part of his evidence was that desulcalization in *po'* and similar forms was strongly favored by a following consonant, whereas the deletion of copulative *are* was not. The tendency thereafter, as shown in table 4.1, was either to tabulate statistics on *are* deletion and *is* deletion separately, as if they were two variables (Baugh 1974, Wolfram 1974), or to pool them, as if they were one (Poplack and Sankoff, 1987). But the theoretical rationale for either choice, and its statistical effects, were never systematically discussed.

4.2 How Should Frequencies of "Contraction" and "Deletion" be Computed?

Assuming that the AAVE copula is underlying (this has been challenged by creolists, but we accept it initially) and that an accountable analysis requires us to count full, contracted, and deleted forms, how should we do this? At first, this seems straightforward. For contraction, report the number of contracted tokens as a proportion of *all* the tokens in which contraction could have occurred (we refer to this as "Straight Contraction"); for deletion, do likewise (we refer to this as "Straight Deletion"). So that if, as shown in table 4.2, we had 10 Full Forms (F), 10 Contractions (C), and 10 Deletions (D), the formula for computing the relative frequency of Straight Contraction would be

$$\frac{C}{F+C+D} = \frac{10}{30} = 33\%$$

and the formula for Straight Deletion would be

$$\frac{D}{F+C+D} = \frac{10}{30} = 33\%$$

Table 4.2   Alternative formulae for computing the percentages of contraction and deletion

---

Straight Contraction:
$$\frac{C}{F+C+D} = \frac{10}{30} = 33\%$$

Straight Deletion:
$$\frac{D}{F+C+D} = \frac{10}{30} = 33\%$$

Labov Contraction:
$$\frac{C+D}{F+C+D} = \frac{20}{30} = 67\%$$

Labov Deletion:
$$\frac{D}{C+D} = \frac{10}{20} = 50\%$$

Romaine Contraction:
$$\frac{C}{F+C} = \frac{10}{20} = 50\%$$

Note: Hypothetical data set: 10 tokens of *is* or *are* (Full Forms, F), 10 tokens of *'s* or *'re* (Contractions, C), 10 tokens of Ø (Deletions, D).

However, these straightforward formulae were *not* the ones used by Labov (1969). Arguing that AAVE could only delete where contraction was possible and that every deleted copula had prior contraction in its history, Labov proposed that "deletions" should be included in the contraction count, yielding the computational formula shown in table 4.2:

$$\frac{C+D}{F+C+D}$$

which we refer to as "Labov Contraction." And as the only candidates for deletion were previously contracted forms, he proposed that full forms be excluded from the denominator to yield the computational formula:

$$\frac{D}{C+D}$$

which we refer to as "Labov Deletion."

Labov Contraction and Labov Deletion are the formulae most often used in the study of the AAVE copula, although they are referred to simply as contraction and deletion, as though there were no other formulae and no controversy about choice of formulae. However, Romaine (1982), arguing for a rule schema in which deletions took place first and were then removed from the pool of copula forms eligible for contraction, proposed another formula for contraction:

$$\frac{C}{F+C}$$

which we refer to as "Romaine Contraction." As even the small example in table 4.2 indicates, the formula one adopts can significantly affect the results, with contraction rates ranging from 33 percent to 50 percent to 67 percent *for the same data*. If different researchers use different formulae (as they *do*), comparisons across studies might be difficult if not impossible to interpret (as they sometimes *are*).

We consider both of these issues in more detail, drawing for our discussion on nine different variable rule analyses of 1,424 tokens of the copula.[1] These copula tokens were extracted from recorded spontaneous interviews and peer group sessions with approximately 30 AAVE speakers from East Palo Alto (EPA), California. EPA is a low-income, predominantly (62 percent) African American community of approximately 18,000 people, located a few miles east of Stanford.

As we present our quantitative results, we comment on some of the substantive findings about copula variation in this community as well as the methodological issues sketched earlier. But before introducing our results, we note that, like previous researchers, our quantitative analysis excluded nonfinite and past tense forms of *be* and approximately 2,000 "Don't Count" present tense copula tokens. Although such tokens are important for arguments that AAVE has an underlying copula, they were excluded from the variable analysis either because they were indeterminate (e.g., tokens of contracted *is* followed by a sibilant, as in "He's sick," which, in rapid speech, are phonetically difficult to distinguish from deletions, as in "He Ø sick") or because they showed invariant copula presence (e.g., *am*, which occurs in contracted form almost 100 percent of the time).[2] As Wolfram (1969: 166) noted (see also Labov et al. 1968: 184): "In the quantitative measurement of copula absence, it is essential to separate environments where there is no variability from those where there is legitimate variation between the presence and absence of the copula. Failure to distinguish these environments would skew the figures of systematic variation."

The following extract (1) from one of our EPA recordings shows the kinds of present tense tokens of the copula that were included in (Counts) and excluded from (Don't Counts) our quantitative analysis. It also exemplifies the vernacular ambience of our data. The extract is from a recording with 14-year-old Tinky and her friends.[3] Faye McNair-Knox, the interviewer, has lived in EPA since grade school and is excellent at eliciting the vernacular.

1   From an interview with Tinky Gates, 14, East Palo Alto, CA
(T = *Tinky*; I = *Interviewer, Faye McNair-Knox*; R = *Roberta, a friend*; Ø = *zero copula*; C = *Count token of the copula, present tense*; DC = *Don't Count present tense copula token*)
My buddy Gina came down here from Stockton. We was all cool, right? An' I tol' – An' they was wantin' to fight her. They wanted to fight her cause she was bran' new, over some Michael Washington they don' even know nutten

about. (R: Nahhhh! Not Michael!) An' they – they was all wantin' to fight her over some Michael Washington. I said, "Lemme tell you somep'n." I said, "Michael *ain't* [DC, neg] gettin' yo' education." Everybody was crackin' up! I was – I was – I wa' – they said, "Tanya – duh – Tanya – y'all all – y'all – y'all got her started now, she Ø [C] finna [<fixing to] give y'all a lecture!" (Laughter.) An' everybody – I said, "For real, now, look on the realistic side." I said, "We got four more months o' school – actually, three more months o' school." I said, "We Ø [C] trippin' aroun wi' somep'n' bout – while Michael Washington Ø [C] out here sellin' his rocks, an' he Ø [C] doin' his little stuff!" I said, "What we – we each – we Ø [C] still at the middle school. We ain' [DC, neg] even got over the hill yet." I said, "We Ø [C] waitin' for the fourteenth to get graduation time, see who Ø [C] (g)on be ridin' the boat, an' we Ø [C] sittin here actin' crazy." I said, "Nuh-uh," I said, "I don' know 'bout y'all, but I'm [DC, *am*] (g)on be ridin the boat." I said, "Cause, uh, like – like them – like that man say, 'Let freedom ring'?" I say, "Nuh-uh, naw, I'ma [DC, *am*] be lettin freedom ring wi' my – (laughter) – wi' my vote!" Everybody was crackin' up. They said, "Tanya Ø [DC, following sibilant] stupid." I said, "Nuh uh, I – I – I am [DC, *am*] serious, y'all."

4.3   *Is* and *Are*

As Wolfram's (1974) arguments for disassociating *are* deletion from *r*-desulcalization have been generally accepted, the issue of what forms should constitute the variable boils down to the issue of whether the contraction and deletion of *is* should be considered separately from the contraction and deletion of *are*, that is, as two variables, separately tabulated; or with their tabulations combined, as one variable. No one has considered this issue in any detail to date. One theoretical justification for a two-variable analysis is that this could account for the tendency of some speakers to delete *are* but not *is* (see Labov, 1969: 754, fn. 38) or to delete *are* more frequently than *is* (Wolfram, 1974: 512). That is, we could say that such speakers have the *are* deletion but not the *is* deletion rule or that the overall application or input probability of the former is higher than that of the latter.

However, if copula form were itself treated as a constraint on copula variation by creating a subject or person–number factor group distinguishing plural and second person subjects (yielding *are*) from third singular ones (yielding *is*), the difference in application possibilities and factor weights for *is* and *are* could still be represented in a one-variable framework (Poplack and Sankoff 1987). The advantage of a one-variable framework is that – to the extent that the constraints on the contraction and deletion of these two forms are similar – these constraints would have to be stated only once. The pool of copula tokens would also be increased, permitting more robust statistical manipulation.

The issue then is whether the *constraints* on these two forms are similar enough to allow us to consider them together. Poplack and Sankoff (1987) did not provide separate data on each form, so we cannot tell whether their pooled analysis is fully justified. However, Wolfram (1974) did provide separate straight deletion frequencies for *is* and *are* according to preceding and following grammatical environment, and he found them similar enough to propose a single copula deletion rule. Baugh (1979) did not explicitly consider the issue of one rule or two, but he did provide separate Labov Contraction and Labov Deletion data on the two forms, considering a broader set of constraints than Wolfram did, and using the variable computer program to estimate constraint effects. His results for contraction (1979: 177, 187) reveal similar effects for the two forms. In the subject factor group, for instance, a personal pronoun favors copula contraction more than a noun phrase for both *is* and *are*. However, his results for deletion are mixed: parallel for *is* and *are* insofar as the hierarchy of constraints in the following phonological factor group is concerned, but divergent insofar as the constraints in the following grammatical and subject factor groups are ordered differently for *is* than they are for *are*.

In order to assess this issue adequately, we decided to do our own separate tabulations of *is* and *are*, using the four internal factor groups considered by Baugh, plus a fifth, external one for age group. Because we are not interested at this point in the difference between Straight Contraction, Labov Contraction, and the like, we use as a basis for comparison the most commonly followed computation formulae in the literature to date – Labov Contraction and Deletion. Table 4.3 shows separate Labov Contraction data for *is* and *are*, and table 4.4 shows comparable Labov Deletion data for the same two forms. Before we discuss the data in these two tables, however, we need to explain briefly what they represent and how they were computed.

The statistics in tables 4.3 and 4.4 (actually, in tables 4.3–8) are not simply the observed frequencies of Labov Contraction and Deletion in the data but probability coefficients or factor weights calculated by the variable rule computer program (Cedergren and Sankoff 1974; Sankoff 1988).[4] The particular variable rule model we used is the logistic model, represented by 1 (from Rousseau and Sankoff 1978: 62). Here, p_0 represents the input probability (the overall likelihood of rule application) and p_i, p_j, p_k, and so on represent the effect of factors i, j, and k present in the environment.

(1) $$\left(\frac{p}{1-p}\right) = \left(\frac{p_0}{1-p_0}\right) \times \left(\frac{p_i}{1-p_i}\right) \times \left(\frac{p_j}{1-p_j}\right) \times \cdots \times \left(\frac{p_k}{1-p_k}\right)$$

Higher factor weights favor rule application, and lower ones disfavor it. Factor weights enclosed in parentheses correspond to factors that were "not selected" by the stepwise regression routine within the variable rule program, because they did not significantly affect the observed variation.[5] Although nonsignifi-

Table 4.3 Labov Contraction of *is* and Labov Contraction of *are* in East Palo Alto (variable rule factor weights)

Factor group	Constraints	Run 1: Labov Contraction of *is*	Run 2: Labov Contraction of *are*
Following Grammatical	*gonna*	.84	.93
environment	Verb + -*ing*	.64	.54
	Locative	.50	.55
	Adjective	.44	.38
	Noun phrase	.31	.23
	Miscellaneous	.23	.24
Subject	Personal pronoun[a]	.78	.82
	Other pronoun	.39	.44
	Noun phrase	.31	.22
Following Phonological	___Consonant	(.48)[b]	(.52)
environment	___Vowel	(.52)	(.48)
Preceding Phonological	Consonant___	.36	(.41)
environment	Vowel___	.64	(.59)
Age group	Old	.41	.41
	Middle	.41	.33
	Young	.67	.74
Data on each run:			
Computation formulae		$\dfrac{C+D}{F+C+D}$	$\dfrac{C+D}{F+C+D}$
Overall frequency (*ns* in parentheses)		68% (715)	90% (709)
Input probability		.60	.75

[a] Personal pronoun: *you, he, she, we, they*. Other pronoun: *these, somebody*, etc.
[b] Parentheses indicate values for factors "not selected" as significant during variable rule regression (step down) analysis.

cant for the current analysis, nonselected factor groups may reveal weak linguistic effects and including them facilitates comparison with other studies.

With these preliminaries aside, we can turn now to table 4.3, which shows factor weights for Labov Contraction of *is* and *are*.[6]

The general picture that emerges from table 4.3 is that although *are* contraction is more likely than *is* contraction, the constraints on the contraction of these forms are virtually identical. In the Following Grammatical factor group, contraction is strongly favored by *gonna* and strongly disfavored by a noun phrase, both in run 1 (*is*) and run 2 (*are*), with locative and adjective showing

Table 4.4 Labov Deletion of *is* and Labov Deletion of *are* in East Palo Alto (variable rule factor weights)

Factor group	Constraints	Run 3: Labov Deletion of *is*	Run 4: Labov Deletion of *are*
Following Grammatical environment	*gonna*	.81	.76
	Verb + -*ing*	.72	.60
	Locative	.42	.41
	Adjective	.43	.47
	Noun phrase	.30	.30
	Miscellaneous	.27	.45
Subject	Personal pronoun[a]	.61	.23
	Other pronoun	.27	.76
	Noun phrase	.63	.53
Following Phonological environment	___Consonant	(.50)[b]	(.47)
	___Vowel	(.50)	(.53)
Preceding Phonological environment	Consonant___	(.57)	.66
	Vowel___	(.43)	.34
Age group	Old	.25	.21
	Middle	.32	.51
	Young	.87	.79
Data on each run:			
Computation formulae		$\dfrac{D}{C+D}$	$\dfrac{D}{C+D}$
Overall frequency (*ns* in parentheses)		53% (483)	78% (636)
Input probability		.32	.94

[a] Personal pronoun: *you, he, she, we, they*. Other pronoun: *these, somebody*, etc.
[b] Parentheses indicate values for factors "not selected" as significant during variable rule regression (step down) analysis.

comparable intermediate effects. Similarly, in the Subject factor group, contraction is favored by a personal pronoun (e.g., *he, we, you*) and disfavored by a noun phrase (e.g., *the man*). Other pronouns (e.g., *these* and *somebody*) are somewhat less disfavorable to contraction than the personal pronouns.[7] The Following Phonological environment is nonsignificant for both forms, the factor group as a whole not being selected in the regression analysis. And although Preceding Phonological environment is significant for the contraction of *is* and nonsignificant for *are*, the results for the latter point in the right direction: preceding vowel more favorable than consonant, as we would expect with contraction, which involves the removal of the copula *vowel*.

Ignoring the Age Group factor group for the moment, note that the internal constraints on the contraction of these two forms pattern precisely as they did in Labov's *is-* contraction data from the New York City Jets 20 years ago. Labov (1969: 731–2, 746) found that contraction was most favored by a preceding vowel, by a pronoun subject, and by a following *gonna*. Furthermore, Labov, like us, did not find following phonological environment a significant constraint on contraction. Our *is/are* contraction data also agree substantially with Baugh's (1979) contraction results for Los Angeles speakers. In short, the data in table 4.3 not only establish that *is-* contraction and *are-* contraction are similarly constrained; their similarity to the results of other independent studies also reinforces our confidence in the nonrandomness and significance of the quantitative patterns we found, and in the basic uniformity of AAVE nationwide.

Table 4.4 shows the Labov Deletion statistics for *is* and *are* in EPA. The similarities between the two columns are not as striking as they were in the case of contraction, but the variable rule results for the two forms are still comparable, particularly with respect to Following Grammatical environment, Following Phonological environment, and age. Preceding Phonological environment is significant for *are* instead of *is*, but the factor weights for *is* again point in the right direction: preceding consonant more favorable than preceding vowel, because deletion in Labov's framework involves removal of the sibilant consonant.[8] The biggest point of difference between the runs for Labov Deletion of *is* and Labov Deletion of *are* occurs in the Subject factor group, and it may be a function of the skewed distribution of tokens in the *are* data – the fact that pronouns account for 573 of the 634 tokens (90 percent) in this factor group – close to the 95 percent danger point at which it becomes difficult to separate the effect of a particular factor from the overall application rate or input probability (Guy, 1988: 131). This anomaly deserves further consideration, but we may conclude tentatively that *is* and *are* behave similarly enough to be treated together, as they were in Poplack and Sankoff (1987), making the data pool larger and more robust and ensuring that their similarities in constraint effects need be stated only once. In subsequent tables, *is* and *are* tabulations are pooled, but a person–number factor group allows us to show the differential effect of *is* versus *are*, capturing both the similarities and the differences between these forms.

4.4   Labov, Straight, and Romaine Contraction, *Is* + *Are* Combined

We turn now to the second major methodological issue of this article, the differences between computing contraction and deletion by means of Labov

Contraction, Straight Contraction, and the other formulae illustrated in table 4.2. Theoretical assumptions govern the choice of one formula or another too, but we postpone critical discussion of their theoretical rationales for the moment and simply inquire in this section about their quantitative effects. Again, this issue has not been adequately considered in the literature, and because researchers usually present their data already computed by one method or the other, and in a way that permits little recalculation by alternative methods, it is difficult to estimate the methodological effect of alternative computations from previous studies. Starting afresh with a new data set, however, and using the variable rule program, it is relatively easy to redefine contraction or deletion in different ways and have the program work out the different effects of alternative computations or rule orderings (see Sankoff and Rousseau 1989).

Table 4.5 shows variable rule results for the different methods of computing contraction of *is* and *are*, combined. The different contraction formulae are reprinted under each column as a reminder of what each method involves. For three factor groups, there is little difference among these alternative methods of computing contraction. Following Phonological environment plays a nonsignificant role in all three cases, as it did in our separate Labov Contraction analyses of *is* and *are* (runs 1 and 2, table 4.3) and as it did, too, in earlier Labov Contraction analyses of copula contraction in Los Angeles (Baugh 1979: 177, 187) and Samaná (Poplack and Sankoff 1987: 306). The results for the Subject and Preceding Phonological factor groups are also very similar across runs 5, 6, and 7, as graphically illustrated in figures 4.1 and 4.2. As figure 4.1 shows, personal pronoun subjects are most favorable to contraction and noun phrase subjects least favorable, regardless of which contraction formulae you use. Similarly, in figure 4.2, a preceding vowel favors contraction over a preceding consonant across the board.

However, beyond these two factor groups, big differences emerge. For the Person factor group, Romaine and Straight Contraction methods both show significant effects (third singular *is* favoring contraction over plural and second person *are*), whereas Labov Contraction does not. For the Age factor group (see figure 4.3), we get different results from virtually every run. Labov Contraction shows the young age group strongly favoring contraction, whereas the other groups disfavor it; Romaine Contraction shows no significant effects; and Straight Contraction is the mirror image of Labov Contraction, with the oldest group in the lead and the youngest far behind.

Results for the important Following Grammatical factor group are shown in figure 4.4.[9] Here, it is Labov Contraction and Romaine Contraction that are now parallel, both showing *gonna* as the most favorable constraint and adjective and noun phrase as the least. In the case of Straight Contraction, however, we get an ordering that is diametrically opposed to the others, showing noun phrase as the most favorable environment and *gonna* the least. This reversal of the ordering for Following Grammatical environments depending on whether

Table 4.5 Labov, Romaine, and Straight Contraction runs, *is* and *are* combined, East Palo Alto (variable rule factor weights)

Factor group	Constraints	Run 5: Labov Contraction	Run 6: Romaine Contraction	Run7: Straight Contraction
Following	*gonna*	.87	.72	.33
Grammatical	Verb + -*ing*	.60	.50	.41
environment	Locative	.51	.57	.58
	Adjective	.43	.46	.52
	Noun phrase	.28	.39	.61
	Miscellaneous	.24	.35	.55
Subject	Personal pronoun[a]	.79	.79	.62
	Other pronoun	.41	.43	.51
	Noun phrase	.28	.26	.37
Person-Number	2nd person and Plural	(.53)[b]	.43	.36
	3rd person singular	(.47)	.57	.64
Following	___Consonant	(.49)	(.49)	(.52)
Phonological environment	___Vowel	(.51)	(.51)	(.48)
Preceding	Consonant___	.36	.32	.36
Phonological environment	Vowel___	.64	.68	.64
Age group	Old	.41	(.50)	.72
	Middle	.39	(.45)	.54
	Young	.70	(.55)	.25
Data on each run:				
Computation formulae		$\dfrac{C+D}{F+C+D}$	$\dfrac{C}{F+C}$	$\dfrac{C}{F+C+D}$
Overall frequency (*ns* in parentheses)		79% (1,424)	55% (675)	26% (1,424)
Input probability		.74	.46	.19

[a] Personal pronoun: *you, he, she, we, they*. Other pronoun: *these, somebody*, etc.
[b] Parentheses indicate values for factors "not selected" as significant during variable rule regression (step down) analysis.

one uses Labov Contraction or Straight Contraction is a phenomenon that Labov himself commented on explicitly two decades ago (1969: 732–3). We discuss it further in section 4.6.

One other point worth making is that the input probabilities – the overall measures of the likelihood of rule application – vary quite dramatically (from

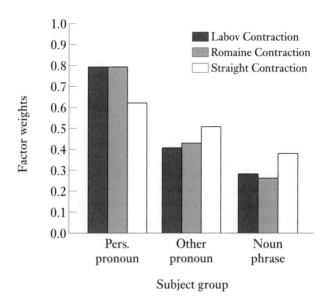

Figure 4.1   Contraction – Subject factor group, EPA.

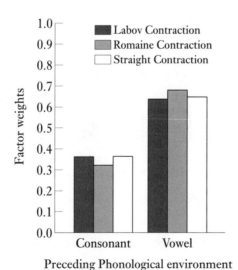

Figure 4.2   Contraction – Preceding Phonological environment, EPA.

Features and Use

Figure 4.3   Contraction – Age factor group, EPA.

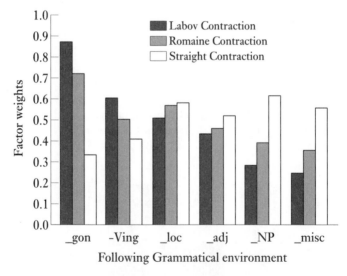

Figure 4.4   Contraction – Following Grammatical environment, EPA.

.74 to .46 to .19) across the three runs in table 4.5. Although we are dealing with the same forms (*is* and *are* as a joint variable), the different computational methods make quite different predictions about the tendency for contraction to apply in this sample.[10]

Table 4.6 Labov Deletion and Straight Deletion, *is* and *are* combined, East Palo Alto (variable rule factor weights)

Factor group	Constraints	Run 8: Labov Deletion	Run 9: Straight Deletion
Following Grammatical	*gonna*	.77	.83
environment	Verb + *-ing*	.66	.67
	Locative	.42	.47
	Adjective	.47	.45
	Noun phrase	.29	.27
	Miscellaneous	.37	.29
Subject	Personal pronoun[a]	(.51)[b]	.62
	Other pronoun	(.44)	.46
	Noun phrase	(.54)	.42
Person–Number	2nd person and Plural	.67	.64
	3rd person singular	.33	.36
Following Phonological	___Consonant	(.48)	(.48)
environment	___Vowel	(.52)	(.52)
Preceding Phonological	Consonant___	.59	(.47)
environment	Vowel___	.41	(.53)
Age group	Old	.22	.23
	Middle	.42	.42
	Young	.83	.82
Data on each run:			
Computation formulae		$\dfrac{D}{C+D}$	$\dfrac{D}{F+C+D}$
Overall frequency (*ns* in parentheses)		67% (1,119)	53% (1,424)
Input probability		.62	.35

[a] Personal pronoun: *you, he, she, we, they.* Other pronoun: *these, somebody,* etc.
[b] Parentheses indicate values for factors "not selected" as significant during variable rule regression (step down) analysis.

4.5 Labov Deletion and Straight Deletion of *Is* + *Are*

With respect to the deletion of *is* and *are*, we only have two runs, one for Labov Deletion and one for Straight Deletion. Romaine's proposal that deletion apply before contraction to the total pool of copula tokens is equivalent to Straight Deletion, so there is no separate Romaine Deletion formula for us to consider.

Table 4.6 shows the *is* + *are* results for Labov Deletion and Straight Deletion (runs 8 and 9). In general, the runs are highly convergent, more so than the

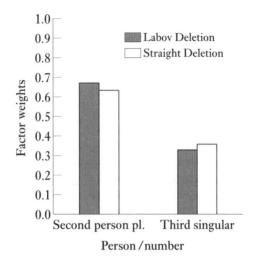

Figure 4.5   Deletion – Person-Number factor group, EPA.

contraction runs in table 4.5. On reflection, however, this is not so surprising, as the only difference between Labov Deletion and Straight Deletion is the absence or presence of full forms in the denominator, and full forms constitute only 205 or 14 percent of the tokens in our sample. In data sets with more full forms, the difference between a Labov Deletion and a Straight Deletion analysis would be more substantial.

The differences that *do* emerge in our sample are in the Preceding Phonological and Subject factor groups. Preceding Phonological environment is significant for Labov Deletion, as we would expect in Labov's formulation, where deletion involves the removal of the lone consonant remaining after contraction, a process favored by a preceding consonant. Straight Deletion – which involves the removal of the copula vowel and consonant simultaneously, as a *grammatical* rather than *phonological* variable – shows no significant phonological conditioning, so each method's theoretical assumptions are supported by *its* respective quantitative results. In the case of Subject, Labov Deletion shows no significant effect, whereas Straight Deletion shows the favoring effect of a personal pronoun that Labov (1969: 730) originally found. But the deletion results for this factor group may be confounded by the distributional problem to which we alluded when discussing table 4.4 – the fact that personal pronouns constitute the overwhelming majority of subject tokens in this factor group.

Overall, as noted, the *similarities* between runs 8 and 9 are more striking than their differences. As shown in figure 4.5 for the person–number factor group, second person and plural *are* is more favorable to deletion than third person *is*, for Labov Deletion as well as Straight Deletion (the factor weights are almost

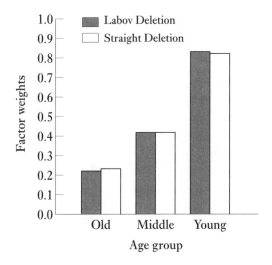

Figure 4.6 Deletion – Age factor group, EPA.

identical!) and as Wolfram (1974: 512) also found to be true in his Straight
Deletion copula data from Mississippi. With respect to Age, depicted in figure
4.6, both runs show a linear correlation, the youngest speakers strongly favoring deletion, whereas the oldest age group disfavors deletion strongly and the
middle group is intermediate. This is directly in line with other evidence we
have (see the section on age-grading, to follow, and Rickford, 1992) that teenage AAVE speakers tend to use vernacular variants more frequently than their
parents and grandparents, partly as assertions of their ethnicity and youthful-
ness and in response to the more significant pressure they experience from their
peers to avoid "acting white" (see Fordham and Ogbu, 1986). Finally, the
Following Grammatical hierarchy, shown in figure 4.7, agrees in both cases,
except in the relative positions of locative and adjectives. However, the weights
for these two factors are close together in both runs anyway, and as table 4.7
indicates, the relative ordering of these two constraints is subject to more
fluctuation than that of any other two constraints in earlier studies of copula
deletion in AAVE. Our two deletion runs also follow most previous studies of
AAVE in finding that *gonna* is the most favorable following grammatical constraint and noun phrase the least.

4.6 Implications

In this section, we consider the implications of the preceding discussion for two
larger issues: 4.6.1 the theoretical issue of the relation between the contraction

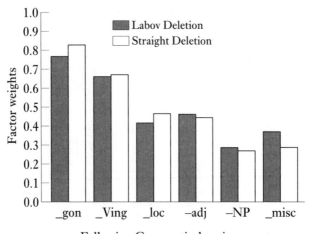

Figure 4.7   Deletion – Following Grammatical environment, EPA.

and deletion rules in the grammar, and 4.6.2 the substantive issue of whether the age differences we have observed symbolize change in progress.

4.6.1   The relation between the contraction and deletion rules

With respect to the rule–ordering issue, Labov (1969: 728) suggested that there were several possible ordering relations for the optional or variable contraction and deletion rules in AAVE, the primary ones being those shown in 2.

2   Possible orderings for contraction and deletion (Labov 1969: 728)

	Case 1	*Case 2*
	1 Contraction	1 Deletion
	2 Deletion	2 Contraction
	əz → z/ . . .	əz → Ø/ . . .
	z → Ø . . .	əz → z/ . . .

In case 1, contraction and deletion are both phonological rules, affecting only one segment at a time; contraction applies first to the full form əz (itself weakened from ɪz), yielding z ("He əz here" becomes "He'z here"), and deletion, fed by the contraction rule, applies to the remaining z, yielding zero ("He'z here" becomes "He Ø here"). Of course, these formulations would have to be revised to include *are*, but this does not affect the point. In case 2, deletion applies first, and contraction applies second to any remaining full forms that have not been bled away by the deletion rule. Deletion in the case 2 formulation

Table 4.7 Copula absence by Following Grammatical category in various AAVE studies, showing variability in Loc./Adj. orderings

Variable and study	NP	Loc.	Adj.	V ing	Gonna
is, NYC T'Birds (Labov 1969: 732)	.23	.36	.48	.66	.88
is, NYC Jets (Labov 1969: 732)	.32	.52	>[a].36	.74	.93
is, NYC Cobras (Baugh 1979: 180	.14	.31	.72	>.59	.78
is + are, Detroit working class (Wolfram 1969: 172)[b]	.37	.44	.47	.50	.79
is + are, Detroit middle class (Wolfram 1969: 172)[b]	.02	.13	>.04	.11	.33
is, Rita, Berkeley (Mitchell-Kernan 1971: 117–18)[c]	.09	.14	.20	.71	.75
is, Los Angeles (Baugh 1979: 181)[d]	.32	≥.29	.56	.66	.69
are, Los Angeles (Baugh 1979: 189)[d]	.25	.69	>.35	.62	.64
is + are, Texas kids (Bailey and Maynor, 1987: 457)[e]	.12	.19	.25	.41	.89
is + are, Texas adults (Bailey and Maynor 1987: 457)[e]	.09	.15	≥.14	.73	>.68

[a] The greater than sign (>) has been placed between any adjacent constraint columns that deviate from the majority pattern in showing the relative frequency or probability of copula absence decreasing rather than increasing from left to right. The locative/adjective orderings show four such deviations in the ten sets of studies surveyed, compared with one each for other adjacent environments. Note that whereas two of these deviations are relatively small (.01 and .03 apart, indicated by ≥), the others are more substantial, especially those involving locative and adjective (differences of .34, .09, and .16).
[b] The zero realization columns for the Adj. and Loc. statistics in Wolfram's (1969: 172) figure 49 need reversing, as the accompanying graphs make clear. Statistics are rounded to two decimal points.
[c] Labov (1982: 182, table 2) reported the *is*- deletion percentage for adjective in Mitchell-Kernan's study as .03, but it should be .09 (4 out of 46, Mitchell-Kernan 1971: 117–18).
[d] Variable rule factor weights. Frequency data not available.
[e] Bailey and Maynor are unique in including invariant *be* in their count (in the total out of which the percentage of zero forms is calculated).

is a grammatical rule, affecting the entire copula formative, but contraction is a phonological rule, removing only the vocalic segment of the copula.

One of Labov's major arguments for case 1 and against case 2 was the nature of the associated quantitative results. Case 1 required computation by Labov Contraction and Labov Deletion methods, and the resultant statistical patterns

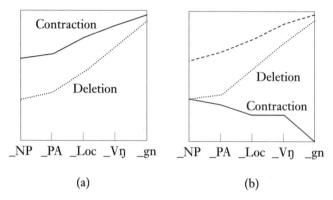

_NP _PA _Loc _Vŋ _gn   _NP _PA _Loc _Vŋ _gn

(a)   (b)

Figure 4.8   (a) Case 1 (Jets, Labov 1969: 732). (b) Case 2 (Jets, Labov 1969: 733).

showed contraction and deletion responding in *parallel* ways to following grammatical environments, as in figure 4.8a. Case 2, however, seemed to require
Straight Contraction and Straight Deletion methods, and the resultant statistical patterns showed contraction and deletion responding in diametrically
opposed ways to following grammatical constraints, as in figure 4.8b. Labov
regarded this latter result as "very implausible," presumably because the *qualitative* parallels between contraction and deletion that he had insightfully noted
– the fact that neither rule applied in exposed or stressed positions, for instance
(1969: 722) – argued for making them *quantitatively* parallel too.

    However, Wolfram (1975: 84) suggested that "the motivation for this order
(case 1 rather than case 2) cannot be justified from the quantitative dimensions
of the rules, since either order can be accommodated by them." We tend to
agree with this assessment. Note, for instance, that the *only* reason the contraction percentages in figure 4.8a rise in tandem with the deletion percentages
as one goes from noun phrase to *gonna* is because they are boosted by the
deletion percentages at every point; there is no theory-independent or method-
independent parallel between the contraction and deletion percentages "out
there in the real world."

    Romaine (1982: 218–21) argued that the quantitative results were neutral in
a different way – by showing that if the second rule in case 2 operated only on
the pool of *un*deleted forms (in our terms, if you used Romaine Contraction
instead of Straight Contraction to tabulate the corresponding frequencies), the
orderings for contraction and deletion would remain parallel, as in figure 4.9.
Figure 4.9 does not quite show this, because the black contraction bar for *gon*
drops to .50 instead of rising above the .71 for −Ving.[11] But we have already
seen from our data that Romaine Contraction and Labov Contraction yield
relatively similar results, so her basic argument still holds.

    Furthermore, suppose we assumed the legitimacy of the creolist hypothesis

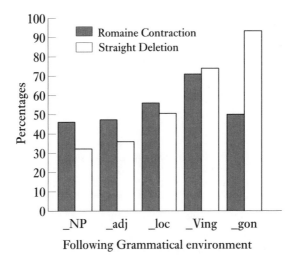

Figure 4.9 Romaine Contraction and Straight Deletion of *is*, NYC Jets.
(*Source*: Romaine 1982: 219, table 8.1, case 2, corrected.)

and assumed that AAVE, in common with other decreolizing varieties, has been changing to include a grammatical *insertion* rule for *is* and *are*, followed by phonological contraction (both optional/variable in application), as depicted in case 3:

3　Case 3
　　1　Insertion
　　2　Contraction
　　Ø → əz/ . . .
　　əz → z/ . . .

The computation formula for the insertion rule would be identical to Labov Contraction

$$\left(\frac{C+D}{F+C+D} \right)$$

and the subsequent contraction rule would clearly have to be computed by the equivalent of Romaine Contraction

$$\left(\frac{C}{C+F} \right)$$

as we already do for speakers whose copula outputs include no deletions, for instance, most speakers of European American Vernacular English in the United States. The point is that there is valid reason to use a formula like Romaine Contraction even if we do not accept Romaine's specific arguments

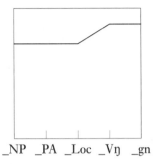

_NP _PA _Loc _Vŋ _gn

Figure 4.10 Labov Contraction of *is*, European Americans, Inwood, NY.
(*Source*: Labov, 1969: 733.)

for doing so. Moreover, if we return to table 4.6 and compute the reciprocals of the figures for run 9 (.17 for *gonna*, .33 for verb + *ing*, and so on), which is what a copula *insertion* rule (as in case 3) would produce, they turn out to be quite plausible. The absence of phonological constraints would be in line with the grammatical status of the insertion rule; insertion would be favored most by a following noun phrase and least by *gonna*, and so on.

A second reason for preferring the case 1/figure 4.8a formulation proposed by Labov was the resultant similarity between the AAVE *is-* contraction pattern and the comparable pattern for European American Inwood speakers in New York, shown in figure 4.10.[12] The case 2/figure 4.8b formulation would make the African American and European American copula contraction patterns seem dissimilar, and Labov regarded this as implausible.

But there are several rebuttals to this line of argument. First, the European American pattern of figure 4.10 shows only a copula/auxiliary disjunction (verb + *ing* and *gonna* separated from noun phrase, adjective, and locative), whereas the AAVE pattern shows a finer separation of all five following environments, probably due to qualitative differences in the kind of copula each environment took (including zero) in the West African and Creole languages from which AAVE derives (Alleyne, 1980; Baugh, 1979; Holm, 1976; Dennis and Scott, 1975).

Second, the putative European American pattern was based on *is-* contraction data from only eight Inwood, New York, speakers. When Stanford University student Bonnie McElhinny (1993) attempted to replicate Labov's results with *is-* contraction data from nine European American Vernacular English (EAVE) speakers from California, Pennsylvania, New York, and Indiana, she found that individuals varied widely in terms of the relative effects of the following grammatical categories, unlike the case in AAVE. And although their pooled *is-* contraction data, shown in table 4.8, is somewhat parallel to figure 4.10 in showing noun phrase less favorable to contraction than verb +

Table 4.8 Straight Contraction of *is* by Following Grammatical environment for nine European American speakers (%s and variable rule probabilities)

Environment	Probability	Percentage
gonna (*n* = 19)	.34	58
Verb + *ing* (*n* = 84)	.73	76
Locative (*n* = 66)	.66	65
Adjective (*n* = 194)	.60	69
Noun (*n* = 211)	.39	36
Miscellaneous (*n* = 38)	.28	21

Source: McElhinny 1993: table 4, p. 26

Table 4.9 Variable rule weightings assuming a contraction rule by Following Grammatical environment

Following environment	Variable rule weighting
gonna	.73
Verb + *ing*	.30
Locative	.74
Predicate adjective	.40
Noun phrase	.32

Source: Fasold 1990: table 3, p. 12

-ing, it diverges from it quite dramatically in showing *gonna* as the most disfavoring environment rather than the most favorable one.[13] Fasold's (1990) Varbrul results for contraction of *is + are* among 14 European American speakers from the Washington, DC, area, shown in table 4.9, reveal some expected orderings, too (noun phrase less favorable than adjective, for instance), but also several surprises (verb + *-ing* as the least favorable environment, locative as the most), so much so that, "It was a relief that the regression component of VARBRUL 2S discarded the entire following environment factor group, as failing to contribute significantly to the predictive power of the analysis. The significance level did not approach the required .05" (Fasold 1990: 12).

All in all, what these replication studies suggest is that there really *is* no stable, significant, and well-established following grammatical contraction hierarchy for EAVE speakers with which AAVE contraction and deletion patterns should agree, even if we considered such agreement a theoretically desirable end (see figure 4.11).[14] Furthermore, although there is valid explanation for at least part of the deletion/insertion hierarchy if a prior creole ancestry for AAVE is assumed (Creole *go/gon* is a future marker that *never* takes a preceding copula, Creole noun phrases always require an *a* or *da* copula, and so

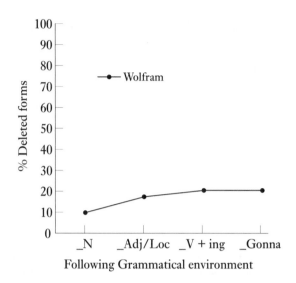

Figure 4.11 Straight Deletion of *is*, European American Mississippi speakers. (*Source*: Wolfram 1974: 514.)

on; see Holm, 1984: 298), there is no persuasive reason to expect AAVE or EAVE *contraction* to follow a similar pattern.

The other reason to expect African American deletion and European American contraction patterns to match is, of course, Labov's (1982: 180) qualitative observation that, "Where other dialects of English can contract, BEV can delete or contract the copula; but where other dialects cannot contract, BEV cannot delete or contract." But Ferguson (1971) showed that Russian, Arabic, Haitian Creole, and other "Type B" languages that usually do not have an overt copula in present tense contexts nevertheless require one in some of the same places that AAVE and other English dialects do: exposed or clause-final position, past tense, stressed position, and so on. To the extent that such similarities turn out to be universal, they undermine the argument for manipulating the quantitative contraction/deletion frequencies of AAVE to match those of EAVE. At present, we are following up on Ferguson (1971) by looking more intensively at constraints on copula contraction and absence in languages around the world, exploring the possibility that the AAVE patterns might reflect universal grammatical constraints.

4.6.2   Change in progress or age-grading?

Let us turn briefly now to the second issue, of whether the significant age effect for deletion shown in table 4.6 and figure 4.6 signifies change in progress, perhaps increasing divergence from Standard English of the type Labov,

Bailey, and their colleagues reported for other areas (see Fasold et al. 1987). As table 4.10 (from Rickford, 1992) shows, the copula is only one of several variables that show strong age correlations in EPA. Invariant *be* and zero possessive *-s* also show the adolescents clearly ahead in terms of vernacular or nonstandard values. But in the case of plural *-s*, there is no difference among the age groups, and in the case of past marking the old people are actually *more* nonstandard than the young ones. So, evidence of divergence needs to be balanced against evidence for convergence, as Denning (1989) and others have noted.

Furthermore, with no reference point in real time, it is difficult to tell whether the copula patterns represent change in progress or stable age-grading. Our openness to the latter possibility has been increased by the discovery of a new AAVE variable, the use of *had* to mark simple past instead of pluperfect, as in 4.

4   I was goin, "Ma! Ma!" And then she *had* just came, came in there, and then she *had* threw water on me and stuff. (Sixth-grader, East Palo Alto)

Here, *had* simply marks successive narrative events rather than an earlier but out-of-sequence one as it does in Standard English ("Before we came around a corner, we *had* gone home"). This "simple past" *had* is common among fifth- and sixth-graders but seems to disappear by the end of the first year in middle school (Rickford and Théberge-Rafal 1996; Théberge 1988).[15] Recent reinterview data on Foxy Boston, the most vernacular speaker in our East Palo Alto sample, also seems to suggest that age-grading might be at work, at least where copula absence is concerned. When she was first interviewed in 1987, just having turned 14, Foxy omitted the copula 90 percent of the time, but when reinterviewed in 1990, under similar circumstances and with the same interviewers (Faye McNair-Knox and her teenage daughter), Foxy's overall copula absence had dropped to 70 percent. Interestingly enough, her *are*-absence frequency had remained high (99 percent in 1987, 86 percent in 1990); what had changed in the interim is that her *is*- absence frequency had dropped dramatically (79 percent to 44 percent), making her more similar to her mother (Dotsy Boston) and other adults, who favor *are*- deletion significantly more than *is*- deletion.[16]

We plan to continue considering the issue of whether high copula absence rates in EPA represent stable age-grading or an ongoing change in progress that will eventually alter the community norm for all age groups (see Rickford, 1992, for further discussion). But note that in either case, a copula *insertion* (rather than deletion) rule seems the most reasonable way of accounting for the limited *is/are* use of the youngest speakers in our sample, like Tinky. For older speakers, who use overt forms of the copula more often, the assumption that it is underlying, but sometimes deleted, is more plausible. If we took frequency of usage considerations into account in this way, we might well have to represent

Table 4.10 Six Vernacular Black English variables as used by six African American East Palo Altans, grouped by age

Speaker, age, tape no.	Invariant be	is, are absence	Possessive –s absence	3rd sg. –s absence	Plural –s absence	Unmarked past tense
Old Folk						
John Carbon, 88 EPA 1, 2	1	19% (123)	0% (5)	63% (117)	12% (112)	20% (245)
Penelope Johnson, 76 EPA 5, 6	0	15% (55)	13% (23)	57% (75)	10% (242)	14% (372)
Mid Age						
Dotsy Boston, 42 EPA 24–26	1	18% (77)	0% (2)	54% (65)	3% (124)	10% (69)
Paula Gates, 38 EPA 14	0[a]	35% (115)	36% (11)	44% (34)	1% (145)	12% (135)
Teenagers						
Tinky Gates, 15 EPA 12, 13	50	81% (256)	53% (15)	96% (56)	11% (167)	11% (132)
Foxy Boston, 14 EPA 7, 8	146	90% (154)	86% (22)	97% (69)	13% (107)	9% (147)

[a] In a subsequent interview, Paula Gates did use a few tokens of invariant *be*, however.
Source: Rickford 1992: table 1, p. 37

different age groups in this small intercommunicating speech community by means of widely different rule schema, as is necessary in some creole continua. This poses a number of theoretical and methodological challenges that we hope to explore in future work.

4.7 Summary

In the spirit of the title of this article, and in tribute to one of the most distinctive art forms to have emerged in America in recent years, we present our summary in the form of the rhymed rap that we "performed" at the end of our presentation at NWAVE-XVII in Montreal:

> Folks who study the copula tend to forget
> That the method you use, 'fects the results that you get.
> In the case of *is* and *are*, it doesn't seem to matter,
> Whether you study 'em apart, or study 'em together.

> Labov Contraction versus Straight is the biggest gap we found;
> In following grammatical, the differences abound.
> Labov Deletion versus Straight is really no big deal,
> But if we had more full forms, the differences might be real.

> The larger question raised by these quantitative tools,
> Is the relation of the contraction and deletion rules.
> The pioneer of the copula, his name's Labov, you know,
> Said contraction 'fore deletion, the figures seemed to show.

> But the order of the rules really don't affect the game.
> If you use Romaine's methods, results come out the same.
> In short, the AAVE rules, and their relation to SE,
> Are still open to discussion, as far as we can see.

> One effect we found is due to differences in age.
> Young groups delete the most, and this may represent a stage.
> To know if age-grading is a factor here,
> We need to study these kids as they advance in years.

> THE COPULA AIN'T DEAD, AS WE HAVE TRIED TO SHOW –
> THERE'S A LOT TO BE LEARNED 'BOUT THIS VARIABLE, YOU
> KNOW!

Notes

This article is a revised version of a paper originally presented at the Seventeenth Annual Conference on New Ways of Analyzing Variation in Language (NWAVE-

XVII), held at the University of Montreal, Quebec, October 27–9, 1988, and presented subsequently at linguistics colloquia at Stanford University and the University of California, Santa Cruz. The final version was completed while the senior author was a Fellow at the Center for Advanced Study in the Behavioral Sciences, at Stanford University, and the financial support provided by NSF grants BNS-8700864 and BNS-8913104 is gratefully acknowledged. We are grateful to the Irvine Foundation for supporting the research done by the student co-authors (two graduate students and two undergraduates) and for funding their travel to Montreal. Finally, we wish to thank the following for their assistance and/or comments: Keith Denning, Ralph Fasold, Gregory Guy, Faye McNair-Knox, K. P. Mohanan, Angela Rickford, Don Winford, the editors of *Language Variation and Change*, and the anonymous referees.

1 Our sample is comparable in token size to Labov's (1969) sample from four adolescent groups in New York City in the 1960s, which included 1,455 copula tokens.

2 The list of Don't Count (DC) present tense cases excluded from our quantitative analysis is very similar to the DC lists of Wolfram (1969) and Labov et al. (1968). They include: clause finals; tokens of *is* followed by *s*; tokens of *are* followed by *r*; tokens of *am*; tokens of *what's*, *it's*, and *that's*; tokens under primary stress; and *ain't* and other negatives. Blake (1992) provided a separate analysis of these DC forms in a sample of our data.

3 Tinky's high copula absence rate (100 percent in this extract, 80 percent to 90 percent more generally) erodes the stereotype that AAVE is restricted to inner-city males. It is typical of EPA *youth*, both male and female.

4 The variable rule computer program we used is a Macintosh version (MACVARB) developed by Gregory Guy and Bill Lipa at Stanford University. It is a pleasure to acknowledge their assistance.

5 In general, these are factors whose probabilities are close to each other and close to the .5 level; excluding them does not make a statistically significant difference to the analysis.

6 The factor weights or values in tables 4.3–8 are taken from the run in which all the factor groups are included to provide data on the nonselected factor groups. Corresponding values for the runs that include only the significant/selected factor groups are either identical or very similar (usually differing by only a decimal point or two). The only difference worth noting is that the input probabilities for runs 1 and 2 are .67 and .80 (instead of .60 and .75, respectively) when only the significant factor groups are retained.

7 Incidentally, we separated other pronouns from the personal pronouns because we wanted to see whether the strong favoring effect on contraction reported for subject pronouns in earlier work was due entirely to the fact that most of them end in a vowel – which also favors contraction; all of our personal pronouns end in a vowel, and their high probabilities (.78, .82) suggest that their strong favoring effect is due to more than the fact that they end in vowels, because the probabilities for the latter are lower (compare .64, .59 for preceding vowels in table 4.4).

8 Recall that contraction removes the copula vowel (iz → z); deletion removes the remaining sibilant (z → Ø).

9 This factor group is important because of the crucial role it has played in the creole origins and divergence issues.

10 This is also true of the Labov Deletion and Straight Deletion runs in table 4.6, although the variation in the input probability there is somewhat smaller (.62 vs. .35).

11 Romaine's (1982: 219) table 8.1 shows *gonna* rising to .76, but this is a mistake, because the fraction of contracted over contracted plus full forms in this environment for the Jets is $\frac{2}{4}$ (Labov, 1969: 732) rather than $\frac{3}{4}$ (the fraction in Romaine's table 8.1).

12 Because the white speakers in Labov's and McElhinny's studies never deleted the copula, contraction results in either case would be the same whether computed by Straight Contraction or Labov Contraction (see table 4.1). To allow for the possibility of deletions among some white speakers (see Wolfram 1974), it might be best to think of these studies as depicting Straight Contraction.

13 Table 4.8 depicts both relative frequencies and variable rule probabilities or factor weights. In general we refer to the probabilities because they take into account the simultaneous effect of other constraints (such as subject), whereas the frequencies do not.

14 Note that Wolfram's (1974: 524) Straight *is-* deletion statistics for white Mississippi speakers (he gives no contraction data) essentially only discriminate between noun phrase and other following environments, again raising doubts about the robustness of the white patterns.

15 The use of simple past *had*, similarly age-graded, has also been reported for African American speakers in Houston, Texas (Karin Cordell, personal communication).

16 With respect to the use of invariant habitual *be*, however, Foxy had become no less vernacular, and indeed more, using over 385 tokens in 1990 compared with 146 in 1987 (see Rickford and McNair-Knox 1994, for discussion).

5

Ethnicity as a Sociolinguistic Boundary

Despite the flood of research on Vernacular Black English (VBE) beginning in the 1960s, it is fair to say that American sociolinguistics has made less progress in understanding the role of ethnicity as a sociolinguistic boundary than it has in understanding other social variables like socioeconomic status and sex or gender. In part this is because more work on VBE has been devoted to fine-tuning the description of its phonological and grammatical features than to exploring the social and linguistic relations between neighboring black and white speakers.

One result of this limited progress is that positions on the issue of black–white speech relationships in the United States remained stalemated for a long time, one group of linguists insisting that the ethnic differences are merely regional patterns which disappear when geography and social class are held constant, and the other group asserting that the ethnic differences are more intractable. (See Davis 1983, Dillard 1972, Fasold 1981, Wolfram 1974, and Wolfram and Clarke 1971 for statements and summaries of these positions.) Another is that the investigation of this issue has neither benefitted sufficiently from, nor contributed sufficiently to, more general discussions of the relationship between language and ethnic identity (Fishman 1977, Giles 1979), or the role of social contact in linguistic convergence (Weinreich 1953).

More recently, however, there have been encouraging signs of change. Quantitative studies of Southern white speech communities have begun to appear (Wolfram 1974, Feagin 1979), as have comparisons of contiguous black and white communities in the rural South (Nichols 1983, and several papers in Montgomery and Bailey 1985, including those by Bailey and Bassett, Butters and Nix, Dorrill, and Nichols). At the same time, detailed investigations of black–white contact and linguistic diffusion in urban Northern neighborhoods have been undertaken (Ash and Myhill 1983, Hatala 1976, Labov 1984b), these studies, like the preceding ones, involving quantitative analysis of specific phonological and grammatical features based on data recorded within the speech community. The work of Gumperz (1982a), Heath (1983), and Michaels (1981) has also made novel contributions to our understanding of black–white speech relationships, but at the level of discourse patterns and ways of speaking rather than individual grammatical features.

This paper has been written in the spirit of this emerging tradition. It deals with the language of one black and one white speaker of comparable social status who, at the time they were recorded, had spent virtually all their lives in the same isolated South Carolina community. As it turns out, these speakers differ in some fundamental grammatical respects, and before examining possible explanations, we will consider other evidence of contact and diffusion between American Blacks and Whites and between other ethnic groups elsewhere.

5.1   A Sea Island Example: Mrs Queen and Mr King

The individuals whose speech we will compare in this section are both from one of the Sea Islands off the coast of South Carolina and Georgia. As a group, these islands are famous as the home of Gullah or Sea Island Creole (Gonzales 1922, Turner 1949, Cunningham 1970, Nichols 1976, Jones-Jackson 1978), and for other distinctive features of Afro-American history and culture (Jackson et al. 1974). The island on which Mrs Queen and Mr King lived (the names are pseudonyms) is off the coast of South Carolina. No bridge connects it to the mainland. The approximately 100 people who live there travel by boat to Bluffton, South Carolina or Savannah, Georgia, for grocery shopping, medical attention, and so on.

At 84, Mrs Queen was the oldest resident of the island when I tape-recorded her at her home in 1970, in a sociolinguistic interview lasting over an hour and eliciting considerable casual or spontaneous speech. As I have noted in Rickford (1986d), it would be inappropriate to apply multi-index scales of social stratification designed for urban communities to this isolated island community, but on scales of this type, Mrs Queen would probably rank fairly low. Like many of the residents on the island, she shucked oysters in the local oyster factory until it was closed down by pollution of the coastal waters from industries in Savannah, and, like others, she depended for subsistence on the fish she caught, the poultry and cattle she raised, and the vegetables she grew. Growing up at a time when every hand in the family was needed at harvest time, she was not given the opportunity to go beyond third grade in elementary school:

> Da's it. I stop right dey. . . . I had to go on de fa'm, go to wo'k an' he'p to make a livin.

However, her training and long years of service as a midwife, her active participation in the island's church and burial society, and her popularity with local and visiting Whites gave her a higher-than-average social status compared with other Blacks on the island.

Mr King was 81 years old when I interviewed him at his home in 1981. A white man born in Bluffton, South Carolina, he was brought over to the island at the age of two. He couldn't remember for sure how far he'd managed to go in school, but since his account of his school days matches Mrs Queen's own so closely, it is doubtful whether he got any further than she did:

> I don'know what grade I did finish complete. Because, dem days, de olda chi'ren had to he'p raise de younga ones. . . . I'd go to school maybe a week an den have to be put in de fiel'to wo'k bout two weeks an – time you got back to school an got interested in it an caught up wid de odda chi'ren . . . you was outa school again to go back in de fiel'. Da's de way I wen'to school. I come up ha'd, son.

Like some of the men on the island (Blacks and Whites included), he was fortunate to get a job on the dredges which used to ply the coastal waterways to keep the channels open. The work was hard ("Sometimes you stay out in de ma'sh like a pig in de pen. It was a terrible life, I tell you") but Mr King, with more doors open to him than the average black Sea Islander, gradually worked his way up the ladder:

> Sta'ted at de bottom. I was just a extra man aroun de engine room. Den I got to be an oila, an I was an oila fuh – fuh yea's. An den I got to be a head oila. . . . But I finally got promoted to third assistant engineer. An dat – da's de bigges' money I ever made. Dat was one hundred an twenty dolla's a mont an board. Dat was big money den.

Despite the fact that he held this relatively good job for a while, Mr King, the son of a farmer who raised cows for sale, supplemented his income with subsistence farming and fishing. His reference (above) to having to catch up with "de odda chi'ren" suggests that he was less privileged than other white children (no Blacks were in the class) on the island. His more privileged classmates went to school all year and undoubtedly went further than he did, finding more lucrative occupations in Southern cities on the mainland. Even today, when there are only a handful of Whites on the island, Mr King does not live close to the other Whites, and his is the only home surrounded by black families.

In all the preceding respects, Mr King and Mrs Queen's socioeconomic backgrounds are more nearly comparable than those of almost any black/white pair of individuals on the island.[1] They are also generally respected on account of their age and well liked on account of their geniality. And since they both seem to have had above-average frequency of contact with members of the other race, one would expect that – other things being equal – their speech would show the effects of mutual linguistic influence and diffusion across ethnic lines. Mr King's speech, in particular, had always struck me, impressionistically, as more nonstandard and Gullah-like than that of other local Whites. And I was delighted at the opportunity to record him in 1981, believing that careful analysis would confirm my prior subjective impression.

5.1.1   Phonology

With respect to phonological features this impression was largely confirmed. As the orthography of the preceding quotation suggests, both speakers have voiced dental stops rather than interdental fricatives in word-initial position (/dɪs/ "this"), the vocalization or deletion of postvocalic /r/ and /l/ (/we/"where", /ɔraɪt/"allright"), and the simplification of word-final consonant clusters (/faɪn/"find", /kɛp/"kept"). In both speakers these nonstandard features – which Fasold (1981, 167) regards as common in both black and white speech, particularly in the South – were categorical or nearly so, occurring 80 percent of the time or more.

Mr King and Mrs Queen also shared the variable realization of other phonological features which are perhaps more unique to the Sea Island or coastal Carolina area, and which have striking parallels in the Caribbean English creoles. These include the realization of *can't* as /kjaːn/ – with palatalization of the velar consonant before /a/ and the negation signalled by a combination of vowel length and pitch (see Allsopp 1972, Carter 1983); the occasional affrication of /tr/ sequences (/tʃrut/ "[in] truth"); the variable laxing of open-syllable vowels in the personal pronouns and other high-frequency function words (/dɪ/ "they", /tʊ/ "to, on, at" – see Rickford 1979); the production of *here* as /je/, /jɛ/, and /jə/; and the occasional deletion of the initial dental in *dem, dat* and a few other function words. A major element in the Gullah quality of Mr King's speech is undoubtedly the distinctive intonation and other prosodic features which he appears to share with black Sea Islanders. (See Turner 1949: 249–53.) One of the few respects in which Mr King seems phonologically different from Mrs Queen is in his use of a more rounded vowel in the realization of words with *ar* sequences in Standard English, so that he pronounces *parking* as [pɔːkɪn] or [pɒːkɪn] where she would more typically say [paːkɪn]. In many other respects, however, he sounds like a black Sea Islander; one West Indian overhearing his recording even wondered whether he was a fellow West Indian.

5.1.2   Morphosyntax

When we turn from phonology to morphosyntax, the similarities between Mr King and Mrs Queen evaporate. This can be seen clearly by comparing their patterns with respect to plural formation and the marking of the passive.

Table 5.1 Plural formation in the speech of two Sea Islanders

Speaker	Noun ## dem	Noun # Ø	Noun # s
Mrs Queen (n = 128)	.01	.76	.23
Mr King (n = 114)	.00	.06	.94

The three primary realizations of semantically plural nouns which we have to consider are the following:

5.1.2.1 Noun##dem, as in *de masa dem*[2]   This is the system found in many creoles when no plural numeral or quantifier accompanies the noun (Alleyne 1980, Dijkhoff 1982) and a definite article or possessive precedes (Mufwene 1984), although it should be noted that these syntactic restrictions keep the relative frequency of this type low – less than 20 percent – even among the most basilectal creole speakers (Rickford 1986d).

5.1.2.2 Noun# Ø as in *dey raise hog* or *sixty cent*   This is the basic creole system when the noun is nonspecific, indefinite, or generic in reference, or where it is specific in reference but preceded by a plural numeral, plural quantifier, or plural deictic/demonstrative modifier (Alleyne 1980: 100–1; Bickerton 1981, Dijkhoff 1982, Mufwene 1986). As noted in Rickford (1986d), morphologically unmarked plurals have also been reported for non-creole English dialects, especially where nouns of measure are concerned, and when preceded by a plural cardinal number (McDavid 1972: 268; Wright 1905: 263).

5.1.2.3 Noun#s as in *the oysters*[3]   This is, of course, the Standard English system for plural individuated or count nouns (Mufwene 1981), approximated if not exactly followed by many English dialects. Note that the instances of *s* tabulated above include only the regular or weak nouns (*cats*, *dogs*, *roses*), but data on plural marking in the irregular or strong nouns (*mice*, *feet*, and so on) will also be considered.

The relative frequency of these types in the recorded speech of Mrs Queen and Mr King is indicated in table 5.1. Clearly, Mrs Queen and Mr King are quite different where plural formation is concerned. The vast majority of her semantically plural nouns are morphologically unmarked and in this respect creole-like, while virtually all of his are marked with -*s*, approximating the Standard English ideal. I had hypothesized at first that Mrs Queen's variation between Ø and -*s* might be subject to the same constraints that govern the choice between Ø and postnominal *dem* in the ideal creole system outlined above. On the basis of individual examples like the following, this would certainly seem to be the case:

I got two bruddaØ. [Ø after plural numeral]

TingØ change. [Ø where nonspecific; here equivalent to "Things have changed"]

We had jus' finish buyin' de tings fuh de weddin. [-*s* where creole postnominal *dem* is possible]

But one can also locate individual counterexamples:

My mudda had . . . five girl*s* and three boy*s*. [-*s* with a preceding plural numeral, where Ø would be expected]

The only way to determine what is really going on is to code every realization of plural -*s* or Ø according to the hypothesized constraints and do a quantitative, multivariate analysis. I did this for Mrs Queen's data, using a recent logistic version of the variable rule computer program designed by David Sankoff, and the results indicated that the primary constraints were not semantic or syntactic, but phonological.[4] The single most powerful constraint was whether the immediately following segment was a vowel (favoring -*s*) or a consonant or pause (disfavoring -*s*).[5]

Mrs Queen's variation between -*s* and Ø may not be governed by the subtle creole semantic/syntactic factors which one might have expected or hoped to find, but it still differs from Mr King's variation between these alternatives, which is not subject to the same phonological conditioning. For Mr King, -*s* absence is nonexistent (that is, the suffix was present in all 45 instances) in his sample before a consonant – precisely where we would expect it to be highest (i.e., where we would expect the least -*s*).[6] Before a vowel or pause, Mr King deleted -*s* 10 percent of the time (seven of 69 instances).

The difference between the grammars of Mrs Queen and Mr King looms even larger when we consider their means of passive formation. We will restrict our attention here to sentences which meet the commonly accepted definition of the passive as a construction in which "the grammatical subject is typically the recipient or "goal" of the action denoted by the verb" (Crystal 1980: 259).[7] The three primary types which we have to consider here are these:

1   Unmarked Passives. This is the classic creole type. The passive relation between the surface subject and a transitive verb is not overtly signalled (by the presence of *be* V + *en* and/or an agent phrase), but must be semantically inferred from the fact that the grammatical or surface subject is not a possible agent or feasible subject of the action denoted by the verb and must therefore be the deep structure object or theme (Allsopp 1983: 153). The clearest and most common examples involve inanimate surface subjects with transitive verbs which subcategorize for animate or human agents, as in Mrs Queen's: *Dis house Ø build since I married.* The agent is rarely if ever expressed in passives of this type, and in this respect they are like truncated *be* or *get* passives.[8]

Table 5.2   Passives in the speech of two Sea Islanders

Speaker	Unmarked Passives	*Get* Passives	*Be* Passives
Mrs Queen (n = 17)	.71	.23	.06
Mr King (n = 11)	.00	.36	.64

2   *Get* Passives. This type, involving inflected forms of *get* V + *en*, is common in colloquial English (see Feagin 1979), especially where the active involvement of the surface subject in the event referred to by the verb is implied (Lakoff 1971): *He got arrested to test the law.* In Guyanese and other English creoles, it is commonest with human subjects, with both *get* and the main verb uninflected: *i get lik dong* "He was knocked down" (Bickerton 1971: 479).

3   *Be* Passives. This is, of course, the basic modern English type, involving inflected forms of *be* V + *en*, as in Mr King's example: *A lot o' dis lan' on dis islan' is bein' sold fuh taxes.* Mrs Queen's single example of this type occurs in the following dialogue:

JRR:	Who leave . . . de lan dat dey use fuh de cemetery . . . ? Who lan dat was?
MRS QUEEN:	Dat was bought.
JRR:	By de – ?
MRS QUEEN:	By de people o' de islan.

In five subsequent references to this same event within the next minute, she uses corresponding active forms instead ("de people bought dat"). The relative frequency of these various kinds of passive in the recorded speech of Mrs Queen and Mr King is shown in table 5.2. Although both speakers use the *get* passive to a limited extent, they differ sharply in their usage of the other subcategories. The unmarked creole passives are Mrs Queen's primary type, but they are completely absent from the speech of Mr King. The standard English *be* passives are Mr King's primary type, but Mrs Queen uses only one such example.

5.2   Black–White Speech Differences in Other Studies

We have seen that Mrs Queen and Mr King are similar with respect to phonological features, but different with respect to morphosyntactic ones. In this section we will review the findings of other studies of the English of Blacks and Whites in the USA, beginning with those which focus, like ours, on coastal South Carolina.

Stewart's (1974) black–white comparisons are based on textual evidence from earlier periods rather than tape recordings of present-day speech, but they are valuable nonetheless. One of his key points was that "in those areas in which the Whites were greatly outnumbered by the Negroes, there is ample evidence that they acquired Creole English (usually in childhood) and used it habitually with their slaves. In fact, there is anecdotal evidence that Whites in some places actually used Creole English with each other as well" (16). He gives two examples from coastal South Carolinian (Gullah) territory in support of this claim, one of them including this piece of dialogue between two Whites (Heyward 1937: 162–3; Stewart's translations appear in square brackets):

> "My Lawd, Boss," she exclaimed, "how oonuh know dat? Pa dead too long!"
> [How do you know that? Father has been dead for a very long time.]
>   Replying in her own Gullah dialect, I said, "Gal, enty you fabor yo' pa? Enty you en him all-two stan' same fashi'n?" [Girl, don't you resemble your father? Don't you and he both have the same looks?]

This is a striking indication of the extent to which some whites acquired some of the features of the Gullah speech native to black Carolinians on the coast. But the acquisition was most marked with respect to lexical and phonological features. Stewart notes subsequently (25) that while "whites were implicated along with Negroes in the establishment and maintenance of pidgin and creole forms of English, both in Africa and the New World," their varieties were generally not *structurally* identical. For instance, where West Africans would distinguish between *I get book* (with nonspecific reference, and therefore zero article) and *I get one book* (with indefinite but specific reference, therefore accompanied by the article *one*), Whites might merge these into *I get one book*, equating *one* semantically with the English indefinite article.[9] Stewart argued that "there must always have been 'racial' dialects" like these, "the product of the fact that virtually all the whites were also fluent speakers of European English, while some of the Negroes were native speakers of African languages."

Nichols (1983), in a study of neighboring black and white communities with comparable socioeconomic characteristics in coastal South Carolina, found that there was a major difference between them with respect to pronominal usage. While both groups used *it* as neuter subject and object at least some of the time, "The nonstandard pronoun forms used by the black community are *ee* in subject position, for most black speakers, and *um* in object position. The nonstandard forms for the white community are *hit* in subject position and sometimes in object position" (206). The only area of convergence between the two communities was represented by a subgroup of younger persons who used the standard variant *it* categorically both as subject and object. To the extent that speakers retained vernacular, non-standard forms, black–white differences persisted.

In earlier studies, Nichols found other morpho-lexical and morpho-syntactic differences between these two communities: in tense-marking of strong verbs, in their use of expletive *there*, and in their use of the locative prepositions *at* and *to*. (See Nichols 1983: 213, for references.) On the whole, she attributes the synchronic differences to the retention of features of an older northern British dialect within the white community. Although both groups appear to be increasing their use of Standard English forms in response to a number of external forces (decreased isolation, increased education, tourism, and so on), she finds little diffusion of vernacular features across ethnic lines.

Wolfram (1974) compared the tape-recorded speech of Whites in rural Franklin county, Mississippi with conventional descriptions of northern Vernacular Black English, and found both similarities and differences. The Whites didn't use the distinctive distributive or habitual *be* of VBE at all, although they did have some instances of *be* which seemed to be derivable from the deletion of an underlying *will* or *would*. The Whites showed a high frequency of *are*-deletion, comparable to that reported for VBE: 64.2 percent overall in a sample of 33 speakers (but varying according to socioeconomic status and linguistic environment). With respect to *is*-deletion, however, the Whites were further from VBE norms. Most speakers (30 out of 45) had no *is*-deletion at all; the others did show some *is*-deletion, but at a somewhat lower frequency than normally reported for northern VBE: 14.6 percent among the 15 white deleters, compared with 17 percent and 37 percent respectively for upper and lower working-class black speakers in Detroit (Wolfram 1969: 174).[10]

Wolfram concludes that VBE is a decreolized variety, with copula deletion and the use of distributive *be* among Blacks reflecting the influence of an earlier creole. He suggests that the Whites of Franklin county show selective rather than full assimilation of black features because of structural factors. Assimilation of copula deletion at an earlier stage in which syntactic rather than phonological constraints were dominant would have involved "rather serious *syntactical* modifications of the grammar," and the integration of distributive *be* with the rest of the VBE tense-aspect system "may have made the price tag of assimilation too costly."[11]

Fasold (1981) is an invaluable survey of earlier studies of black–white differences, some of which, in consequence, need not be resummarized here. It also includes some experimental data from Fasold's work in Washington, DC, which indicate that black adolescents and children there often do not use possessive *-s*. In response to test items requiring the use of possessive forms, many of them produce unmarked possessives like *Jack Johnson car* and *mouse cheese*. These data agree with earlier tape-recorded data from Labov et al. (1968:

169) indicating that black peer-group members in New York City omitted possessive -*s* 62.3 percent of the time in attributive position, as in *people houses* (from a 14-year-old member of the Jets). Fasold has no comparable experimental data for northern white speakers, but cites Southern (Augusta and Atlanta, Georgia) data from Miller (1977) and Sommer and Trammell (1980) indicating a sharp disjunction between the Blacks and Whites studied, with the Blacks using zero possessives commonly (52.2 percent in the lower-class Blacks studied by Sommer and Trammell), and the Whites always having the possessive -*s* intact.

A similar disjunction shows up – even more dramatically – in comparisons of our Sea Island pair on this feature. It is questionable whether Mrs Queen's grammar includes possessive -*s* as an underlying category at all. Out of 25 possible nominal possessives in her recorded speech, 22, or 88 percent, were unmarked, and the three cases with possessive -*s* could all be regarded as formulaic, including two instances of the place-name *Benjie's Point* and one of *Oyster's Union Society*.[12] By contrast, only one of Mr King's seven nominal possessives, or 14.2 percent, is unmarked; the others all have -*s*.

The most detailed comparative work on the speech of Blacks and Whites in the North is that being done by Labov and his associates in Philadelphia, Pennsylvania and Camden, New Jersey. Labov reports that "In general, the black community of Philadelphia does not participate in any of the phonological or grammatical processes that define the white vernacular, nor share the norms of interpretation" (1980: 373–4). The features in question – shared by virtually all Whites who were born and grew up in Philadelphia or moved there before the age of eight – include: the use and interpretation of positive *anymore* to mean "nowadays," the use of *be* as a present perfect auxiliary with *done* and *finished* (*When can you* be done *five shirts?*), and the fronting of /uw/ and /ow/. At the same time, the black vernacular of Philadelphia includes forms like stressed *been*, *steady* and *be done V-ed* which are found across the nation, but are either not used by Whites, or interpreted differently (Rickford 1975, Baugh 1984). Labov refers to this linguistic divergence between Blacks and Whites as a "cleavage" (374), one which is bridged only when the members of each group shift towards the national network standard rather than the local vernacular. This latter finding agrees precisely with that of Nichols' study (1983) of South Carolina, summarized above.

In the same paper, Labov reports on the intriguing case of a 13-year-old white girl, Carla, in a black neighborhood of Camden, New Jersey. Carla, originally described in Hatala (1976), had assimilated much of the surrounding black culture (dancing, verbal skills, and so on), was apparently accepted and liked by black youth, and sounded black to both white and black listeners. However, when her recorded speech was examined in detail, according to Labov, it was found to contain only a "selected subset of syntactic, lexical and prosodic features" of the black vernacular, and to include features which are

generally absent from the VBE tense-aspect system, such as the copula/
auxiliary *be* and third singular present tense -*s*. As Labov (379) notes, this case
highlights the difference between the social or symbolic definition of the notion
speaks Black English and the linguistic definition. From the viewpoint of the
social/symbolic definition (still poorly understood), Carla appears to share the
norms of the black speech community, but from the viewpoint of Labov's
linguistic definition – in which priority is given to "central" grammatical
features – it appears she does not.

Ash and Myhill (1983) have further increased our understanding of the
relation between black–white speech differences and contact by studying the
relative values of several linguistic variables in the speech of four groups of
Philadelphians. The variables included (but were not limited to) the following
features commonly associated with VBE: the monophthongization of /ay/, the
nasalization of preceding vowel and loss of final /n/, absence of the copula, and
absence of third singular and possessive -*s*. The groups studied were: Blacks
with little contact with Whites, Blacks with considerable contact with Whites,
Whites with considerable contact with Blacks, and Whites with little contact
with Blacks.[13] Their results, summarized in Labov (1984), indicate that Whites
generally show less effect of interracial contact than Blacks; Whites with considerable black contact are differentiated from the sole White with little black
contact only with regard to knowledge of 24 lexical items and use of some of the
phonological variables (such as /ay/). With respect to the grammatical
variables, the Whites are undifferentiated, bunched up against the white vernacular and Standard English norm (the two are identical on these variables).
On the other hand, not only do the Blacks with considerable white contact show
a greater general effect of interracial contact, but the effect is most dramatic for
the grammatical variables, with respect to which "the Blacks with little contact
are at the extreme end of the scale, and all others are closest to white dialect
position, with minimal use of the BEV features." Labov suggests both internal
and external reasons for the increased approximation of white speech which
Blacks show on the grammatical variables. We will refer to them in the next
section, when we survey the possible explanations for black–white speech
differences more critically, and attempt to reach a more general understanding
of the nature of ethnicity as a sociolinguistic boundary.

5.3   In Search of Explanations

In an attempt to understand the divergence between the grammars of Mrs
Queen and Mr King and the patterns of black–white speech differences revealed in the studies summarized above, we will explore a number of potential
explanations in this section.

5.3.1   *Anatomy, geography, socioeconomic status*

These are all non-starters. Claims about the linguistic effect of anatomical or genetic differences – Gonzales' (1922) references to the "clumsy tongues," "flat noses and thick lips" of "Gullahs" learning English provide the stock example – have long been regarded as racist and/or uninformed. The family background experiments conducted by Labov and his colleagues in New York City (Labov et al. 1968, 2: 266–85, summarized in Trudgill 1983b: 51–2) have further discredited them.

It has also been suggested, more rationally, that black–white differences might reflect urban–rural or regional differences, or differences in socioeconomic status or education rather than ethnicity (Kurath 1949, McDavid and McDavid 1951, David 1969). It is easy to imagine cases in which this might be true, and some of the ethnic differences reported in the literature may well mask possible effects from these variables.[14] But the data from Mr King and Mrs Queen, the data from Nichols' studies in coastal South Carolina, and the Philadelphia data from Labov and his colleagues all indicate that major black–white differences persist even when socioeconomic status, education, and geography are relatively well-controlled.

5.3.2   *Diachronic provenience*

The most common explanation for black–white speech differences – at least among those who recognize such differences – is that the linguistic systems used by each group have different diachronic origins: a creole, perhaps influenced by West African linguistic patterns in the case of Blacks, and British or colonial white American dialects in the case of Whites. This is one of the primary explanations advanced by Stewart (1974), Wolfram (1974), Fasold (1981), and Nichols (1983) for the black–white speech differences identified in their studies, and the grammatical comparison of Mrs Queen and Mr King leads us naturally to similar considerations. The respects in which these two speakers differ are respects in which creoles and their lexically related standards differ in many parts of the world. Mrs Queen shows some degree of decreolization or movement away from basilectal Gullah norms, notably in her use of phonologically conditioned plural -*s* (albeit at a relatively low frequency level), and in her use of a single *be* passive. But her *Noun # dem* plural and her unmarked passives and possessives are clear Gullah features, and in an area long associated with Gullah speech, it would be foolhardy not to regard them as such. On the other hand, Mr King's plurals, passives, and possessives are clearly in accord with the system of Standard English, with occasional exceptions of a sort commonly encountered in white dialects of English both in Britain and the United States.

But if we think about it carefully, this appeal to diachronic provenience refines our understanding of the *nature* of the black–white speech differences (the dependent variable) without *explaining* why or how they persist (the independent variable). There is no inherent reason why an individual from a creole-speaking tradition must acquire that creole or be restricted to it, and dozens of counterexamples militate against any assumption of this kind.

For instance, Giles (1979: 261), drawing on earlier research by Giles and Bourhis (1976) and Bourhis and Giles (1977), found that many second- and third-generation West Indians in Cardiff, Wales, "had assimilated to such an extent that tape recordings of their speech were labelled as 'White.'" Giles contrasts this explicitly with the United States, where Blacks have resided for many more generations but can still be ethnically identified from speech 80 percent of the time. Another example is provided by Katherine, a 14-year-old Indo-Guyanese girl from a rural village whose case I described in Rickford (1983a: 306–7). Her mother and father are both strong creole speakers, but on the basis of repeated tape recordings, participant observation, and overt elicitation, I concluded, "Katherine, who goes to school at one of the country's best secondary schools in the capital city of Georgetown, speaks an almost (grammatically) flawless acrolect, and . . . seems *incapable* of using the basilectal and lower mesolectal varieties of creole that her parents can use."

There is also no inherent reason why virtually flawless acquisition of creole speech should be restricted to Blacks, even if it is true, along the Atlantic seaboard, that creoles developed earliest and were spoken most extensively by black populations. Katherine's parents and other creole-speaking East Indians in Guyana furnish a case in point. Their grandparents and great-grandparents came to Guyana as indentured servants in successive waves beginning in the 1830s, after the emancipation of African slaves deprived sugar plantations of their captive labor force. By 1917, when the indenture system itself came to an end, thousands and thousands of East Indians resident in the (then) colony had essentially acquired the creole speech of Afro-Guyanese. Today, the basilectal English creole of rural Indo-Guyanese shows little if any influence from Bhojpuri or the languages native to the early indentured immigrants (Gambhir 1981) and provides an excellent index to nineteenth-century Afro-Guyanese usage.[15] Similarly, Holm (1980: 59–63) found that whites in the Bahamas had acquired some of the tense-aspect features of black speech, including durative *be*, and Warantz (1983: 74) reported that, on the Bay Islands off the coast of Honduras, in the southwestern Caribbean "Bay Islanders do not attribute differences in BIE [Bay Island English] speech styles to membership in different racial groups. In the words of one islander, 'Black and white, we all speaks the same.'"[16]

In order to demonstrate that substratal influence or inherited linguistic tradition is not sufficient to explain the persistence of inter-ethnic differences, we could also refer to the acquisition of English by Norwegian and other immigrants (Haugen 1956) or other instances of second-language acquisition worldwide. But the creole-based examples furnished above serve to illustrate particularly well that other factors must be taken into account. The examples themselves suggest that these other factors should include opportunity (contact) and motivation for language learning or linguistic diffusion across ethnic lines. We will get to these, but in the tradition of Weinreich (1953), let us first consider potential internal or structural constraints.

5.3.3   Structural constraints

Although he considered their judgments premature, Weinreich (1953: 67) noted that many writers before him had expressed opinions on the susceptibility of the different domains of language to borrowing. The writers he cites – Whitney (1881), Dauzat (1927), Pritzwald (1938) – all list vocabulary as the first and most easily diffused domain. This accords with our data on diffusion across ethnic lines (Stewart 1974, Labov 1980a, Ash and Myhill 1983), and might be attributed in part to the relative independence of lexical elements, especially open-class items which are not intimately involved in the grammatical subsystems of the language. However, there is internal disagreement among the writers cited by Weinreich with respect to the likelihood of diffusion or mixture in the other domains, with Dauzat and Pritzwald opposed to Whitney in ranking phonology before morphosyntax, but disagreeing among themselves on the relative ordering of morphology and syntax.

In any case, the data on Mr King and Mrs Queen, together with some of the data from the other studies summarized above, suggest that nonstandard phonological features diffuse more readily across ethnic lines than nonstandard grammatical features do.[17] We will return to this point below, but one initial explanation for the more limited diffusion of grammatical elements might be that they are more tightly imbricated in semantic oppositions and morphosyntactic relationships in each language. As noted above, Wolfram (1974) has suggested that "the syntactical nature of copula absence at earlier stages in the decreolization of Vernacular Black English may have made wholesale assimilation [by Whites] very difficult at that point." We could make a similar argument with regard to the assimilation of *be*-passives by Mrs Queen, suggesting that these would not become more productive until the English copula had rooted more firmly in her grammar.

Important though internal considerations like these might be, it is clear that they do not always work as predicted and cannot by themselves tell the whole story. Again, Wolfram's argument (1974) that the assimilation of distributive *be* might have been structurally difficult for Whites in the South is less persuasive in the light of Bailey and Bassett's evidence (1985) that some southern Whites do use distributive *be*. Labov (1984b: 20–1) has noted that Blacks with considerable contact with Whites show mastery of third singular -*s* although "the structural apparatus needed to acquire it – the existence of subject-verb agreement – is almost missing from the [VBE] grammar." Gumperz and Wilson's study (1971) of language mixing in Kupwar is even more revealing, for the local varieties of Urdu, Marathi, Kannada and Telugu – their speakers in contact, code-switching, and borrowing among themselves in this village over 400 years – have actually diverged from their respective standards and converged to each other in semantic distinctions and morphosyntax. Bynon (1977: 253–6), noting that the non-Bantu Mbugu language in Tanzania "has acquired the complex nominal and verbal morphology of the surrounding Bantu languages," has concluded that "given a certain intensity and duration of language contact, there is nothing that may not be diffused across language boundaries." Thomason (1981) reaches exactly this conclusion on the evidence of several other language-contact situations. And so we turn, quite naturally, to contact – to opportunities for the acquisition or diffusion of linguistic features across ethnic boundaries.

5.3.4   Contact: opportunity for linguistic diffusion

Of all the factors we have considered so far, contact is clearly the most important one for explaining inter-ethnic differences. The most common explanation for *regional* differences in language is that physical or geographical barriers (distance, mountains, rivers) keep regional populations separate, and "it is axiomatic in dialectology that the isolation of peoples breeds linguistic development along different lines" (Davis 1983: 4). Trudgill has suggested (1983b: 35, 54) that social class and ethnic differentiation in language might be partly like regional differentiation, maintained by social distance and barriers to interaction almost as palpable in effect as geographical ones. That this might indeed be the case is shown by Ash and Myhill's finding (1983) that the Blacks who had little contact with Whites were the best exemplars of VBE and showed little acquisition of white vernacular or SE norms.

Contrariwise, when conventional barriers to inter-ethnic interaction are eroded, the linguistic differences between ethnic groups are often minimized. Ash and Myhill also found that Blacks with considerable white contact had converged towards white linguistic norms, particularly in grammar. Wolfram (1974) reported, "For Puerto Ricans with extensive black peer contact, we found that virtually all the features of Vernacular Black English were adopted, but for those with restricted black contacts, we found that only certain ones were assimilated." And Frederick Douglass' autobiography (1881) – cited in Stewart (1974: 5) – revealed that close association between Douglass and Daniel Lloyd, the son of his white master, was responsible for his control of white dialect: "I have often been asked during the earlier part of my life in the North how I happened to have so little of the slave accent in my speech. The mystery is in some measure explained by my association with Daniel Lloyd, the youngest son of Col. Edward Lloyd" (33). In an earlier version of his autobiography, as Stewart pointed out, Douglass also asserted that the convergent effects of Daniel's contact with the slaves worked the other way too: "Even 'Mas' Daniel, by his association with his father's slaves, had measurably adopted their dialect" (1855: 77).

Further evidence of the significance of contact for inter-ethnic convergence is provided by the situations noted above: the linguistically convergent ethnic groups in Kupwar have been in close contact for several hundred years; the East Indians who came to Guyana essentially learned their Creole English from the Blacks among whom they worked daily in the fields (but see Rickford 1987c for relevant questions about this contact); Katherine's mastery of the Guyanese English acrolect is to be attributed in part to extensive contact with acrolect-speaking friends and teachers in school; the second- and third-generation West Indians in Cardiff are in Cardiff, not the West Indies, and have been thoroughly exposed to Cardiff dialect patterns from birth.

In the context of these examples, the persistent grammatical differences between Mr King and Mrs Queen at first seem paradoxical. At the time they were recorded, they had both been in continuous residence on this isolated island for more than 80 years. In the first two decades of this century, when they were acquiring their respective vernaculars, the island "was lousy wid people," in the words of Mr King, with more than 50 people on an island about nine miles long and five miles wide. There was the same disproportionate number of Blacks to Whites as there is now, but the fact that the raw numbers were considerably greater means that Mr King might have had even more opportunity to be exposed to the speech of Blacks, and Mrs Queen to the speech of Whites, than they do now.

However, strict racial segregation – recall that they went to separate schools – would have seriously limited their exposure to and acquisition of each other's speech patterns, particularly where subtle grammatical conditioning or semantic distinctions were concerned. The intimate association of Blacks and Whites as playmates which Douglass experienced, and which led white children to "imbibe" the "manners and broken speech" of the blacks (in the words of an eighteenth-century observer cited in Read 1933: 329 and Stewart 1974: 17), did not seem to have been the norm when Mr King and Mrs Queen were growing up, and they are still not the norm today. The handful of white children now resident on the island do go to school with black children, but they don't hang out with them after school or join them for deer-hunting expeditions at night.

Adults of both races exchange greetings and small talk when they pass on the road or meet at the dock, but rarely if ever do they meet for religious worship, socializing at home, or drinking and relaxation at the local clubhouse. As a result, while there is ample opportunity for hearing each others' speech, there is little for intimate interaction of the kind which encourages dialect diffusion.[18]

But it is not clear that increased interaction would necessarily have led to greater convergence. What close contact and interaction provide is good input – models – for language learning. Whether *input* will become *intake*, or be reflected in *output*, depends in part on the attitudes of the groups in contact, as Schumann (1978b: 372) has noted: "Even when there is sufficient social contact for second language acquisition to take place, for attitudinal and affective reasons there may be such psychological distance that 'input' generated in the contact situation never becomes 'intake' for the learner." Whinnom (1971: 92–3), recognizing the import of attitude, described it as the "ethological or emotional" barrier to linguistic convergence, distinguishing it from the "ecological" barrier of contact. It is the role of this ethological barrier to inter-ethnic convergence on the Sea Islands and elsewhere that we will finally consider.

5.3.5   *Motivation, identity*

The nonlinguistic boundary between Blacks and Whites is relatively hard, in the sense of being "so overt and consensually distinctive of the social category that interethnic mobility is physically impossible" (Giles 1979: 275, drawing on Banton 1978). Given the salience of this particular ethnic boundary in the United States in general and along the South Carolina seaboard in particular, it is only natural that diachronically inherited differences of language should have come to serve as part of the identifying or identity-reinforcing characteristics of ethnic difference (Trudgill 1983b: 54–5). As Fishman (1977: 21) has noted, "Language is commonly among the conscious 'do' and 'don'ts' as well as among the unconscious ones: that is , it is among the evaluated dimensions of ethnicity membership (whether consciously or not)." More specifically, Stewart (1974: 19), arguing against the common assumption that "greater opportunities for acculturation to European norms offered by the presence of greater numbers of whites would naturally be taken advantage of to the maximum possible degree by New World Negroes," points out that "other acculturative mechanisms might have operated to modify this outcome. . . . One would be the organization of whites and Negroes into separate classes or castes, with the possible retention of European and African cultural differences (together with later innovations within either group) consequently acquiring the status of 'appropriate' behaviors for members of each group." The claim that differences originally derived from divergent substrata or diachronic provenience might be perpetuated not only by lack of contact but also by socially generated expectations that this is how

Blacks *should* talk, and this is how Whites *should* talk, is quite compelling. On the Sea Islands, Blacks and Whites, for all their lack of intimate interaction, are aware that each group follows different norms, and *should*. Talking Gullah is part of black identity, not white, as is *rapping* or *telling lies* on Saturday night (Rickford 1986e) and *folk-praying* on Sunday morning (Jones-Jackson 1983, Rickford 1972). Approximation to or adoption of the other group's linguistic norms may be negatively viewed as *crossing-over*; frequent inter-ethnic rather than intra-ethnic communication may itself be viewed as *crossing-over* and regarded with suspicion or hostility (Fishman 1977: 21). The linguistic acts of identity (Le Page and Tabouret-Keller 1985) which black and white Sea Islanders make are usually with respect to members of their own ethnic group; there is little motivation for either to adopt the vernacular norms of the other. The strong desire of West Indians in Cardiff for cultural assimilation, which is reflected in the attenuation of their ethnic speech markers (Giles and Bourhis 1976), is not present on either side of the ethnic divide on the Sea Islands.

These considerations, taken together with relative absence of interaction and inherited/diachronic differences, would explain why black and white speech on the Sea Islands is different, but not why these differences are more marked at the level of morphosyntax than at the level of phonology. However, there is considerable precedent from other Caribbean communities for sharp social differentiation with respect to morphosyntax but gradual or very little social differentiation with respect to phonology. Both in Guyana (Rickford 1987c) and Belize (Escure 1981), decreolization is primarily reflected in morpho-syntax, with socially prominent individuals who consider themselves to be speakers of acrolectal or so-called good English evincing non-standard creole phonological features – like consonant cluster simplification and the pronuncia-tion of *town* as /tʌŋ/ – in their speech. A similar situation exists in Surinam, where the prestige local norm involves Dutch syntax but Sranan phonology (Eersel 1971). In all of these cases the non-standard phonological norms are either unconsciously accepted or taken as representative of regional or national norms, and the notion of speaking creole, with its attendant social connotations, is reflected primarily in morphosyntax. The South Carolina Sea Islands appear to be similar in this respect. Non-standard phonological features are part of a regional Sea Island identity in which both Blacks and Whites participate, but non-standard morphosyntactic features are more heavily marked as creole and serve as ethnic markers.

At the same time, standard morphosyntactic features are also prestigious, and while there is little evidence of white speakers increasingly moving in the direction of creole grammar, there is evidence of both Blacks and Whites moving in the direction of Standard English with increasing education and exposure. Nichols' study (1983) of two South Carolina speech communities shows this most clearly, with black/white pronominal differences disappearing as young educated Blacks and Whites adopt standard forms. Mr King and Mrs

Queen, both older, more isolated, less educated and less upwardly mobile than Nichols' young subjects, are different, but one can note in Mrs Queen's phonologically conditioned use of plural -*s* and in other respects (see n. 12) some degree of decreolization – movement away from creole norms and towards Standard English.[19] From this point of view I would not agree with Labov's (1984b) rejection of differential prestige as an explanation for grammatical convergence between blacks and whites on standard norms, although his interpretation of standard grammatical variables as "claims to generalized rights and privileges" could probably be equated with differential prestige in the context of the Sea Islands, if not in Philadelphia.[20]

5.4   Summary

In line with a relatively new tradition, we have compared the speech of one black and one white speaker on an isolated South Carolina Sea Island and found that they are similar phonologically, but different with respect to three grammatical variables: plural formation, passivization, and the marking of nominal possessives. After a survey of earlier data-based studies of black–white speech differences in the United States, we have considered individually a number of possible explanations for their persistence. Anatomy, geography, and socio-economic status are less significant than they often have been alleged to be. Diachronic provenience and structural considerations are relevant, but not in themselves explanatory. Contact and social identity – or the limited availability of opportunity and motivation for adopting the patterns of other ethnic groups besides one's own – loom largest in the maintenance of inter-ethnic linguistic differences, but, in accord with a pattern which shows up in other creole communities, the social differentiation is marked primarily at the morpho-syntactic level.

It would be useful to refine our understanding of ethnicity as a sociolinguistic boundary by comparing variation in intra-ethnic communication contexts with variation in inter-ethnic ones (see Escure 1982).[21] But on the basis of available evidence from the Sea Islands and elsewhere, ethnicity appears to be like regional or social class boundaries insofar as it involves social *distance*, and like the boundary of sex or gender (Trudgill 1983b: 88) insofar as it reflects *difference* in socially expected norms.

Notes

1   Although Mrs Queen is now deceased, I will use the present tense for convenience.
    I am grateful to Michael Montgomery and the funding agencies of the 1981 University of South Carolina conference on language variety in the South for the

grant which facilitated my attendance at that conference and my return visit to the Sea Islands. (See Montgomery and Bailey 1986 for a number of the conference papers.) It is also a pleasure to acknowledge the helpful comments on an earlier draft of this paper which I received from Ron Butters, Salikoko Mufwene, and Angela Rickford.

2   ## = word boundary, # = morpheme boundary.

3   I have chosen to use -*s* to indicate the plural morpheme in this paper although I used -*z* in Rickford 1986d. In both cases, the symbol includes morphophonemic variation between /z/, /s/ and /əz/.

4   The program uses maximum likelihood methods to assign a probability coefficient to each factor representing its INDEPENDENT contribution to the overall probability of rule application. It is important to have some means of measuring the independent effects of each factor, for the apparent regularity of one factor – for instance, preceding quantifiers – might mask or be masked by the effect of another – for instance, the following phonological environment. In my earlier and more detailed study of Mrs Queen's plural marking (Rickford 1986d, n. 19), I provided the probability coefficients for all of the four factor groups investigated, even though the program indicated that the phonological factor groups accounted adequately for the variance in the data and that the inclusion of the syntactic factor groups did not significantly enhance our ability to predict or regenerate the data. Not only were the syntactic factor groups less significant, overall, than the phonological ones, but the ordering of individual factors within the syntactic factor groups was not what I had predicted. For instance, a preceding plural quantifier favored the omission of plural -*s* very slightly, but a preceding *dem* – also inherently plural – had the opposite effect, contrary to expectation. Readers who wish to review the detailed coefficients in the earlier paper should be reminded that probabilities above .5 favor -*s* absence, and those below .5 disfavor -*s* absence.

5   In Rickford (1986d), I opted for assuming an underlying plural -*s* for Mrs Queen, removed by a phonological deletion rule. But this was only after considerable discussion, taking into account the limited evidence of her strong plurals and the difficulty of incorporating a phonologically constrained grammatical insertion rule in currently available grammatical models, almost all of which treat phonology as interpretive and post-syntactic. Nevertheless, I expressed even then reservations about the fact that Mrs Queen had three times more cases of -*s* presence, and although Mufwene (1986) does not do justice to the quantitative evidence and theoretical argument which had led me to posit a phonologically constrained deletion rule, and I still differ from him on certain points, I am persuaded enough by his discussion of the often-singular reference of *children* and similar cases to discount the evidence of the strong plurals. Once we can adopt a model in which grammatical insertion can be phonologically conditioned (Kiparsky's lexical phonology is a possible candidate), I would be happy to accept a plural -*s* insertion rule for Mrs Queen. This would have the additional advantage of matching the diachronic development of Mrs Queen's grammar (and that of Gullah as a whole) more accurately.

6   In view of the fact that Mr King had so few unmarked plurals, it was neither possible nor necessary to replicate the four-factor multivariate analysis which we did on Mrs Queen's data; the data represent simple relative frequencies. It is

difficult to locate any persuasive constraint on Mr King's use of plural Ø. The only constraint which seems to have a (weak) systematic effect is occurrence in a partitive construction, as in *all kindØ o' stuff* and *all sortØ o' stuff*. The absence of plural marking on the head noun of the following idiomatic expression may be related: *dem sonØ of a guns*.

7 This excludes active sentences with generalized indefinite subjects like *Dey used to call de big oystas de selec's* (Mr King) and *You could catch dem anytime den* (Mrs Queen), which are treated as variants of the agentless passive by Weiner and Labov (1982). Compare the possible but nonoccurrent *De big oystas used to be called de selec's* and *Dey could be caught anytime den*.

8 See Alleyne (1980: 97–100), Allsopp (1983), and Markey and Fodale (1983) for further discussion of the creole passive, and Traugott (1972: 14) for discussion of similar examples involving the present participle in Early Modern English.

9 Stewart's (1974) formulation of this distinction is the earliest I know of in the literature, even though the subsequent discussions of Bickerton (1981) and Dijkhoff (1982) are more detailed. In this, as in many other respects, Stewart's paper has received less citation and commendation in the literature than it deserves.

10 As Fasold (1981) has noted, Feagin's study (1979) of Whites in Anniston, Alabama agrees substantially with Wolfram's findings. Her rural working-class subjects have 56.3 percent *are*-deletion and 6.8 percent *is*-deletion.

11 The structural explanation is less persuasive in the face of Bailey and Bassett's evidence (1986) of white distributive *be* use.

12 She does mark suppletive pronominal possessives, however: *my* instead of *me* (17 out of 17 cases), *our* instead of *we* (one case out of two), *his* instead of *he* (four times out of seven). Labov et al. (1968: 170) report similar data for black peer group members in New York City, who use *my*, *her*, and *our* categorically in possessive position.

13 In the Ash and Myhill study, degree of contact was determined according to four variables: "the racial composition of the speaker's present neighborhoods, the racial composition of the speaker's high school, the number of friends the speaker has from the opposite group, and the number of spouses and/or lovers of the other ethnic group that the speaker had had" (Labov 1984: 16). For some reservations about Labov's conclusions about Carla, see Butters (1984).

14 Devonish (1978) has argued, quite persuasively, that the differences which Bickerton (1973) claimed were ethnic (Indo-Guyanese vs. Afro-Guyanese) were really primarily urban/rural differences.

15 Cruickshank (1905) includes several turn-of-the-century texts of Indo-Guyanese usage which illustrate this point, but they also include one or two features (like a transitivizing or object agreement marker *am/um*) which were not present in Afro-Guyanese speech and may reflect Indic influence. See Devonish (1978), Gambhir (1981), and Rickford (1987c) for further discussion.

16 Warantz also mentions that they don't consider their language a creole, reserving that term for the "unintelligible" speech of Jamaicans and Belizeans. Her texts reveal a mesolectal variety, close to Standard English in some ways, but also containing distinctive creole features.

17 Of course, some phonetic features do not diffuse, as evidenced by the findings of

Dorrill (1982) and Labov (1984b); the latter suggests that there may be structural reasons why the fronting of /aw/ has not spread to Philadelphia VBE.

18 Labov (1984b: 14) notes that exposure to television, even four to eight hours a day, does not appear to have any effect on the VBE of isolated black speakers in Philadelphia. The kind of contact which he considers relevant includes: "face-to-face interactions of speakers who know each other; who have something to gain or lose from the contact; and are not so different in power that the symmetrical use of language is impeded."

19 The situation is complex, both on the Sea Islands and in the Caribbean, for creole speech does have solidarity-reaffirming values of its own, and synchronically there are forces which impel speakers in different situations both forwards to the acrolect and backwards to the basilect. In overall diachronic terms, however, the gradual tendency is a decreolizing one, not that the basilectal variants have disappeared, but that the relative numbers who use it are diminishing, and the numbers using mesolectal or acrolectal features are increasing. See Rickford (1983a, 1983b).

20 Labov's reason for rejecting a general appeal to "differential prestige" is that while Blacks with extensive white contacts adoped standard grammatical variables used by Whites, they didn't adopt sound changes characteristic of Philadelphia white speech which might also be considered prestigious insofar as they were used by the local upper middle-class. In place of a general appeal to prestige, Labov proposes instead that sound changes are associated with local identity and serve as symbolic claims to "local rights and privileges," including "access to local jobs, to renting or buying houses in closely held areas, obtaining variances from local political bodies, obtaining the use of public space for play, streets, parades, markets and ceremonies," etc. Grammatical variables, by contrast, serve as claims to "generalized rights and privileges," including "those goods that are available by social convention to any individual who can satisfy general regulations for access to them set by social convention, irrespective of membership in particular sub-groups. Such generalized resources include money, ownership of goods sold on the open market, education, and legal, financial and technical knowledge." The distinction may be useful but can be handled equally well by distinguishing between *local* and *generalized prestige*, given the common definition of *prestige* as "standing or estimation in the eyes of people" (*Webster's Third International Dictionary*) and Weinreich's more particular definition of it with respect to language as "value in social advance" (1953: 79). We also have to be cautious about automatically equating *local* with *phonological* and *generalized* with *grammatical*, since some phonological variables like /ð/ > [d], /θ/ > [t], -*ing* > *in'* (perhaps precisely because of their relative stability) do have generalized prestige, while, on Labov's own showing (1980), grammatical features like positive *anymore* or perfect *be* have local (Philadelphian) but not generalized prestige, and do not diffuse to the black community.

21 Giles (1979: 278) has predicted that the combination of a hard nonlinguistic and a relatively soft linguistic boundary will lead to the accentuated use of ethnic speech markers by subordinate ethnic groups in inter-ethnic communication. This is obviously relevant to us and worth investigation.

6

Addressee- and Topic-Influenced Style Shift: A Quantitative Sociolinguistic Study
(with Faye McNair-Knox)

6.1 Introduction

This chapter is a study of addressee- and topic-influenced style shift in language, within the framework of quantitative or "variationist" sociolinguistics.

The first section is written from a theoretical, history-of-science perspective; we begin by contrasting the taxonomic, polydimensional approach of sociolinguists such as Hymes (1972) and Halliday (1978) with the empirical, unidimensional approach of Labov (1966: 90–135, 1972a: 70–109), for whom styles were ordered on a single dimension, involving *attention* paid to speech. We suggest that the neglect of style within the American variationist school from the 1970s onward was due in part to methodological and theoretical difficulties with this approach. As we note, an alternative unidimensional approach, considering style as *audience* accommodation (Giles and Powesland 1975, Bell 1984), is more promising, but although several quantitative studies within this framework have been made over the past decade and a half, most of them were done outside the United States, primarily in Britain.

In the second section, we introduce some new data on addressee and topic style shift in language, drawn from our ongoing study of sociolinguistic variation in East Palo Alto (EPA), California, a multiethnic, low-income community of over 18,000 people, located just east of Stanford University. The data are from our two most recent interviews with Foxy Boston, an 18-year-old African American teenager whose vernacular language use we have been chronicling, through successive recordings, since she was 13.[1] The two interviews which form the empirical focus of this paper were recorded about eight months apart in 1990 and 1991 within the same setting (Foxy's home), but with different interviewers. The 1990 interview was done by Faye (coauthor of this paper), a

41-year-old African American lecturer at Stanford, who was familiar to Foxy as a community resident and from earlier interviews. Faye was accompanied by her 16-year-old daughter, Roberta (a pseudonym), a native of East Palo Alto, who served primarily as cointerviewee and peer for Foxy (see section 6.2.1). Since this was the third interview with Foxy, we'll refer to it as interview III. The 1991 interview (referred to as IV) was conducted by Beth (a pseudonym), a 25-year-old European American who was a graduate student at Stanford and a stranger to Foxy. Although the latter interview was ostensibly being done for Faye, and Beth was able to trade on "inside knowledge" from Faye's earlier interviews, Foxy's language in the second interview was less vernacular and more standard than it was in the former.

We investigate Foxy's style shift across the two interview contexts by means of quantitative analyses of her usage of several variables, including zero copula, invariant *be*, plural *-s*, third singular present *-s*, and possessive *-s*. The fact that (most of) these variables *are* sensitive to style-shifting is itself of interest, since the earlier literature on African American Vernacular English (AAVE) is either ambiguous or negative on this point. The fact that the style-shifting is primarily a function of the race of the interviewer(s) is also of methodological interest, for, with only a few exceptions (Anshen 1969, Fasold 1972, Terrell et al. 1977, Edwards 1986), race-of-interviewer or -addressee effects have been neglected within sociolinguistics,[2] although they have been the focus of lively discussion in other social sciences, where the focus is on the content of interviewees' responses rather than their language (see, for instance, Schumann and Kalton 1985, Anderson et al. 1988). In fact, the effect of interviewer attributes on interviewee speech – although privately recognized as important by everyone – has received little systematic discussion in the sociolinguistics literature. The primary exceptions have been studies of the effects of addressee status or solidarity (Brown and Gilman 1960, Payne 1976, Baugh 1979, Hindle 1979, Coupland 1984), gender (Walters 1989a and b), and insider versus outsider status (Van den Broeck 1977, Bickerton 1980b, Russell 1982, Rickford 1983a).

We also argue that the variable rule computer program, which we use for the analysis of zero copula, allows us to disentangle the effect of audience-design from the effect of internal grammatical constraints with a precision that other approaches do not, and we recommend it as a general means of studying stylistic variation. Finally, we consider variation by topic within each interview, attempting to assess whether this can be related to audience-design, as Bell (1984: 178–82) suggests, and its relative importance vis-à-vis addressee-influenced style shift.

In our conclusion, we summarize our main findings and stress the importance of encouraging quantitative sociolinguists to return to the study of stylistic variation and of encouraging students of style in spoken language to exploit the assets of the quantitative approach (see Eckert and Rickford, in press).

6.2   The Study of Style in Quantitative Sociolinguistics

Stylistic or intraspeaker variation has certainly received less attention within American sociolinguistics than has social or interspeaker variation.[3] This is less true of British sociolinguistics, where the concept of *register* (variety "according to *use*") has been as firmly established as the concept of *dialect* (variety "according to the *user*"), and where the concepts of *field* (subject-matter), *tenor* (addressee and other participant relations), and *mode* (communication channel) have encouraged attention to the subdimensions of register (Gregory and Carroll 1978: 7–11, Halliday 1978: 33).

Within American sociolinguistics, heuristic sociolinguistic taxonomies (for instance, Ervin-Tripp 1964, Hymes 1972, Preston 1986) have also provided for the analysis of stylistic or intraspeaker variation, via their inclusion of categories such as message content, setting, purposes, and key, alongside interspeaker categories such as speaker's age, sex, ethnicity, and region. Such taxonomies are typically wide-ranging; for instance, Hymes (1972) includes 16 components, while Preston (1986) expands the number of potentially relevant categories to 50.

By contrast, empirical studies within the framework of quantitative sociolinguistics, whether in Britain or the United States, have usually taken a more parsimonious approach, attempting to relate stylistic variation to one primary underlying dimension.[4] In the 1960s and early 1970s, *attention paid to speech* (Labov 1966) reflected in varying degrees of formality, was the underlying dimension on which styles ranging from casual to careful to reading and wordlists were delimited. In the late 1970s and 1980s, to the extent that stylistic variation in speech has figured in quantitative sociolinguistics, it has primarily involved the study of the effects of the *addressee*. However, as noted, most of this work was done outside the United States.

6.2.1   Attention paid to speech

It is instructive to trace the rise and fall of style as a central area of interest in American quantitative sociolinguistics, and of attention paid to speech as its principal theoretical conceptualization. Labov is clearly the major pioneer in this framework, but in his earliest (1963) study, of Martha's Vineyard, style-shifting was basically ignored, because the majority of his subjects did not show stylistic variation for the variables under investigation: "Sometimes the conversation will take a livelier tone, or a more formal aspect, but the percentage of centralized forms is not significantly affected" (Labov 1972e: 21).

In his 1966 study of the pronunciation of (*r*) and other variables in New York City, however, Labov found that it was critical to attend to stylistic variation, and particularly to net *casual speech*, "the everyday speech used in informal situations, where no attention is directed to language" (100), for only casual speech adequately revealed the regularity of everyday synchronic and diachronic processes – the nature of social stratification, for instance, or the direction and status of ongoing linguistic change. Although casual speech (appropriately called style A) could be easily separated from *reading* style (style C), *word lists* (style D), and *minimal pairs* (style D), the task of distinguishing it from *careful speech* (style B), "the type of speech which normally occurs when the subject is answering questions which are formally recognized as 'part of the interview'" (92), was more difficult, and it was to this problem that Labov devoted most of his attention.

Labov's solution, well known by now, was to define certain contexts – for instance, speech with a third person (A2), speech on the topic of childhood rhymes and customs (A4), and speech on the topic of the danger of death (A5) – as *potential* casual speech contexts, and to classify speech in these contexts as *actual* examples of style A when it was accompanied by "channel cues" such as a change in tempo, pitch, volume, breathing, or laughter.

One problem, however, was that researchers usually found this method of distinguishing casual speech difficult to apply in an objective and reliable way. As Wolfram (1969: 58–9) noted in discussing the Detroit dialect survey:

> An exploratory attempt to distinguish careful from casual speech based on Labov's criteria was *rejected* for several reasons. [i] In the first place, any of the paralinguistic channel cues cited as indications of casual speech can also be indications that the informant feels an increased awareness of the artificiality or formality of the interview situation. Can nervous laughter reliably be distinguished from relaxed or casual laughter? [ii] Also, the subjective interpretation of the paralinguistic cues tends to bias the interpretation of casual speech even though the channel cues are theoretically supposed to be independent of the measurement of linguistic variables. To what extent must there be a change of pitch or rhythm and how close to the actual feature being tabulated must it occur? [iii] Further, for some informants, the incidence of casual speech, based on Labov's cues, is so infrequent that it is difficult to base statistics on so few examples. (emphasis and numbering added)

Other researchers, like Trudgill (1974), avoided the indeterminacy of channel cues altogether, depending instead on earlier versus later sections of interviews or topical contexts alone to separate careful and casual speech. But most overcame the methodological problem by ignoring the distinction between these styles altogether. This was true even in the Philadelphia neighborhood studies of the Linguistic Change and Variation (LCV) project – the principal research focus of Labov and his associates from 1980 onward. As Labov (1989:

11) notes, in a paper originally presented in 1982, "The main data base is the set of tense/lax ratings of all short *a* words in the *spontaneous speech* recorded from the 100 subjects. *This includes both 'casual' and 'careful' speech as defined in Labov 1966*" (emphasis added). What came to define the sociolinguistic/variationist approach to language was its use of recorded corpora of *spontaneous* (real, natural, conversational) speech in the new (Labov 1989) sense. There was an unspoken consensus that while it was valuable to try to get as much *casual* speech (in the old sense) as possible, the operational difficulties of separating casual from *careful* speech made further attachment to the theoretical distinction unrealistic. In any case, even where the recordings of quantitative sociolinguists were primarily careful speech, in the old sense (Labov 1989: 50), they were still able to identify regular internal and external constraints on linguistic variation and change, and to distinguish themselves theoretically from those who depended instead on "introspection – and the elicitation of others' introspections" (Labov 1989: 51).

   Although most quantitative sociolinguists came to ignore the casual/careful distinction – and to attend less and less to stylistic variation in general – for practical, operational reasons like these,[5] there were also empirical and theoretical arguments against studying stylistic variation principally or only in terms of attention paid to speech.[6] Many of these arguments have been summarized by Milroy (1987: 172–83), but the primary ones are worth repeating. Wolfson (1976) expressed the view that the "spontaneous" speech produced in response to requests for danger of death narratives often had a "performed" quality and challenged the assumption that natural/absolute speech existed as an absolute entity. Macaulay (1977), Romaine (1978, 1980), and Milroy (1980) presented evidence which suggested that reading did not lie on the same continuum as speech, at least not in the British varieties they investigated.[7] Baugh (1979: 25) noted that styles delimited according to attention paid to speech were the products of linguistic inquiry rather than social circumstance and chose to study situational style-shifting because it was likely to be closer to realistic stylistic variation in everyday conversation. Cheshire (1982), Dressler and Wodak (1982), and Finegan and Biber (1994) questioned whether "attention paid to speech" really underlay the kinds of formality Labov distinguished. In a related vein, Traugott and Romaine (1985) criticized the attention-paid-to-speech approach for its unidimensionality (see also Irvine 1979, 1985: 560) and for its implicit view of the speaker as passive respondent rather than active strategist. And Bell (1984), critiquing the experimental work on monitoring by George Mahl which Labov (1966: 134, 1972: 97–9) had cited, and summarizing empirical evidence from other researchers, concluded that "empirical foundation for the attention variable is notably lacking" and that "attention is at most a mechanism of response intervening between a situation and a style. This explains both why it seemed a plausible correlative of style shift, and why it could never be a satisfactory explanation of style" (1984: 148). By and large these critiques came from outside the main tradition of American quantitative sociolinguistics, and they came *after* most quantitativists had already begun to shy away from distinguishing styles in terms of interview contexts and channel cues, but they perhaps contributed to the decline in the study of style in terms of attention paid to speech.

6.2.2 Addressee and other audience design effects

When Labov et al. (1968) turned to the study of AAVE in Harlem, they were still interested in eliciting casual or vernacular speech, for "the most systematic and regular form of language is that of basic vernacular" (167). But as their primary means of achieving this goal, they adopted a new approach – recording group-sessions, in which adolescent and preadolescent AAVE speakers were "in spontaneous interaction with each other" (57).[8] To the extent that Labov et al. discuss stylistic variation in this study, it is by comparing speakers' outputs in the individual interviews with their outputs in the group sessions ("single style" vs "group style"). Theirs is actually one of the earliest empirical sociolinguistic studies of stylistic variation to use addressee rather than topic or attention as the primary variable. Anshen (1969) and Fasold (1972) also reported quantitative variation in the output of AAVE speakers according to (race of) addressee, although it was not a major theme of their work. However, for Blom and Gumperz (1972), stylistic variation among Norwegian speakers in Hemnesberget according to whether they were speaking to locals or outsiders was of central significance, leading them to introduce (424–5) the theoretical distinction between *situational* switching, primarily influenced by addressee, and *metaphorical* switching, primarily influenced by shifts in topic and role relationship while addressee and other situational features remain constant.[9]

From the late 1970s on, there have been several quantitative studies of stylistic variation in the recorded speech of individuals according to addressee. The list includes, in chronological order, Bell (1977, 1982, 1991), Van den Broeck (1977), Douglas-Cowie (1978), Baugh (1979, 1983), Payne (1976), Hindle (1979), Rickford (1979, 1987b), Bickerton (1980b), Coupland (1980, 1981, 1984), Trudgill (1981), Russell (1982), Thelander (1982), Purcell (1984), Lucas and Borders (1987), Walters (1989a, b), and Youssef (1991). The typical approach was to record one or more individuals speaking to someone who was a local insider or someone relatively familiar and compare this with their recorded outputs when speaking to an outsider or a stranger. The parallels with the work of Labov et al. (1968) and Blom and Gumperz (1972) are striking, but while some of the new studies (for instance, those by Baugh and Rickford) acknowledged an intellectual link with these earlier works, others (for instance, Douglas-Cowie and Bickerton) did not, almost as if their authors had independently hit upon an operationally clear-cut way of distinguishing styles which they knew from informal observation and experience to exist. Moreover, with only a few exceptions, the new studies drew on data from Great Britain and other communities outside the continental United States, and some were also outside the American variationist/Labovian tradition.[10]

One theoretical source of this approach to stylistic variation which *was* acknowledged by some of the researchers (Coupland, Russell, and Trudgill, for instance) was the speech accommodation model of British social psychologist Howard Giles and his associates (Giles and Powesland 1975, Giles and Smith 1979, Thakerar et al. 1982, Giles 1984). In this model, the theoretical significance of the addressee is paramount, since speakers are seen either as converging with or diverging from their addressees depending on their relationship to them and their desire to gain social approval or achieve "communication efficiency." The speech accommodation model, recently reconceptualized in broader terms as "communication accommodation theory" (Coupland and Giles 1988: 176), makes explicit links with theoretical frameworks in psychology and other behavioral sciences and has undergone several revisions and refinements over the years. It has inspired many empirical studies – see Giles, Coupland and Coupland (1991) for some of the most recent – although critiques have been made of the limited linguistic analysis in some studies and of the tendency to refer to accommodation theory post hoc.

Bell's extended (1984) discussion of style as audience design, which provided an integrative review of many of the addressee-based studies mentioned above, and has undergone some refinements of its own (see Bell 1991), has received relatively little attention at variationist conferences (like NWAVE) or in the quantitative sociolinguistics literature.[11] This neglect is unfortunate, however, for in its integration and explication of diverse strands of earlier sociolinguistic work, and in its bold hypotheses and predictions, Bell (1984) strikes us as one of the most theoretically interesting works to emerge in the study of style-shifting – and in sociolinguistics more generally – since the work of Labov in the early 1960s.

Space will not permit us to recapitulate all the ideas and data that Bell (1984) presented – and we would, in any case, encourage readers unfamiliar with the paper to read it themselves – but we summarize some of its key elements and explain how it relates to the empirical study to be presented in this paper.

A central feature of Bell's paper is its attempt to relate interspeaker (social) and intraspeaker (stylistic) variation by means of the *style axiom*: "Variation on the style dimension within the speech of a single speaker derives from and echoes the variation which exists between speakers on the 'social' dimension" (151). As Bell notes, this axiom explains a number of previously unexplained facts about sociolinguistic structure, including the fact that "some linguistic variables will have both social and style variation, some only social variation, but none style variation only" (151); the fact that the degree of style variation never exceeds the degree of social variation (152ff.); the fact that audience effects are most strongly marked for addressees and are progressively weaker for auditors, overhearers, and eavesdroppers (162ff.); and the fact that stylistic variation by topic and other nonaudience factors presupposes and is weaker than variation according to addressee (178ff.). While these generalizations are shown to be tenable as "facts," on the basis of earlier studies, they also constitute working hypotheses against which all current and future work can be judged. They are therefore empirical and falsifiable claims, with theoretical import. Although it is easy to criticize an essentially monodimensional approach to style such as this one for neglecting potentially relevant factors, we believe that sociolinguistics needs the integrative and predictive approach to theory testing and development which Bell's paper represents.

Before turning to the empirical East Palo Alto study which will occupy us for the rest of this paper, we should note some of the questions which Bell's paper specifically led us to pursue. Why do some variables show significant addressee-based shift between the two interviews while others do not? Can we account for this differential accommodation by appealing to the variables' role in social or *interspeaker* variation, as Bell (166–7) suggests? What is Foxy reacting to as she style shifts between one interview and the other – her interlocutors' personal characteristics (race and familiarity, for instance) or their specific linguistic usage (Bell, 167–9)?[12] What of the role of *topic shifts* within each interview? Can these be viewed as proxies for audience-design, as Bell (178–82) asserts? And does Foxy's vernacular use in our very earliest interviews (1986, 1988) square with the evidence and analyses we present from interviews III and IV? These are some of the questions we attempt to answer in the next section of this chapter.

6.3   Empirical Study of Style Shift in Foxy's Interviews

Following Bell (1984: 146–8), we treat linguistic differences in the speech of a single speaker (*intraspeaker* variation) as stylistic, in contrast with differences between the speech of two or more speakers, which is *interspeaker* or social variation (as, for instance, in social class or ethnic dialects). Stylistic differences between Foxy Boston's speech in interviews III (EPA 55–6) and IV (EPA 114B), taken as wholes, will be regarded as instances of addressee-influenced style shift, since the primary situational differences between the interviews are the race and familiarity of the interviewers.

Section 6.3.1 gives further information about the two interviews which provide the new data for this paper. Section 6.3.2 discusses *addressee*-influenced differences in Foxy's quantitative usage of five vernacular variables, comparing them with earlier studies of these variables in relation to race and

style. Section 6.3.3 considers the interviewers' usage of the same variables to
see whether Foxy is accommodating to the linguistic usage of her addressees, or
their personal/social characteristics (Bell 1984: 167). Section 6.3.4 explores
topic-controlled variation in vernacular usage within Foxy's two interviews,
assessing whether such nonpersonal style design can be related to and derived
from interpersonal addressee design (Bell 1984: 178–82). Finally, section 6.3.5
briefly discusses Foxy's usage in two earlier interviews with Faye and Roberta,
one of which suggests that the setting, scene, and key (Hymes 1972), as well as
the strategic use of style, have to be given more prominence than Bell's approach perhaps allows them.

6.3.1   Further information about the two interviews

The two interviews described in general terms in the introduction were comparable insofar as both were conducted in Foxy's home and focused on conversing
with Foxy as the primary interviewee. However, they differed with respect to
logistics, tempo and key, participants, and topics. Interview III was recorded in
June 1990 on a UHER 2600 stereo reel-to-reel tape-recorder; it lasted about 96
minutes and produced a one-and-a-half spaced transcript of 88 pages. Interview IV was recorded in February 1991 on a Sony TCD-5M stereo cassette
recorder; it lasted 75 minutes and produced a one-and-a-half spaced transcript
of 42 pages. The fact that the transcript of interview III is twice as long as that
of interview IV while the recording itself was only slightly longer indicates that
III was a livelier and more informal interaction, with a faster tempo and more
give-and-take among the participants. This was in turn related to differences in
who the participants were, their relation to Foxy, and the distribution of topics
in each interview, which the next two subsections discuss.

6.3.1.1   Interview III   Besides Foxy (F), the primary participants in interview III were two African American females who were familiar to Foxy from
the community and from previous interviews. Faye, the adult, served as the
interviewer (I), introducing most of the initial topics, but she employed a
bantering approach which encouraged informality and often led to laughter, for
instance, from an early section of the interview (2, transcript), dealing with
college plans:

1 I: What kinds of plans you have for college? Where – Where have you been
       thinking about going?
   F: Prob – . . . I don' wanna go far away.
   I: Really? You wanna hang around with mom?
   F: Mm-hmm[=yes][laughter]
   I: Are you scared to get out there on your own?
   F: No! [laughter] I's jus' that . . . we just too close, I guess.

Faye's intimate knowledge of places, people, and events in the community also stimulated Foxy to talk excitedly about events and individuals which she might not have mentioned to a stranger.[13] For instance, Faye's reference to a recent gang-related killing on Xavier Street led Foxy to note (15, transcript) that three of her friends had been killed similarly, including, most recently, Jimmy (name changed):

2 F: Oh, and then Jimmy. . . . Jimmy got killed at Shakedown's.
    I: Is that that shooting they had over there? [high-pitched]
    I: Yeah, that – that was my good – good friend. I was like, "WAIT A MINUTE!" . . . I was like, "Y'all lying! No! I just talked to Jimmy, the other night."

Another factor which contributed to the animated conversational quality of interview III was the presence of Roberta (R), Faye's daughter. Roberta was primarily a cointerviewee, talking about her own teenage experiences in Oakland (where she had attended high school) and often stimulating Foxy to use teenage slang spontaneously and to share aspects of their peer-group knowledge about boys and other topics, as in this extract (23, transcript):

3 F: This one [Black Student Union (BSU) convention] was in Bakersfield. And we met so many GUYYYS, from uh – ooh, now lemme tell you what high school got – got it going on.
    R: Saint Mary's! Saint Joe's!
    F: YES, YES! St. Mary's! [laughter]
    I: Oh yeah!
    F: St. Mary's is HITTIN! IT'S HITTIN!
    R: [To I] St. Mary's is an all boy's school in Oakland –
    F: [Overlapping with R] St. Mary's is HITTIN! They be like, "Ooh, yes. Wha's your name?" Ooh! Blah, blah, blah, this. [laughter] I be like, "Ooh, yeah – you – you come here?" I be like – Tanya was like "Wha – wha's your name? Uh, WHERE YOU GOING TO SCHOOL AT NEXT YEAR?!" [laughter] . . . I'm like, "Y'all is a fool."

In this informal atmosphere, Foxy produced long stretches of excited speech, often overlapping with or interrupting other participants' turns, and bringing narrated events to life through extensive use of direct quotations and sound effects, as in the preceding quotation and in this account of repeated phone calls from an admirer (49–50, transcript):

4 F: an' she – ma – I be on the telephone and he be going, [breathlessly and fast] "Where you went today? I – I know you wasn't at home! I called you. You wasn't at home! I left a message! You wasn't at home. Where you was at today? Uhn-uhn, Uhn-uhn, you got to get a beeper or something so I can

page you. You have to call me back. Where was you?!" [laughter] And everyday – everyday, "Did you go shopping today? What you go buy? You bought this? You bought that? You like it?" And I be going, "Yep, yep, yep."

I: Mm-mm-mm-mm.

F: "Okay." Then he hang up.

I: Mm-mm-mm-mm.

F: Then [pause] – THIRTY minutes later –, BRRINNNG [telephone]! "Hello." "Oh, I'm just calling to see if you in the house." My ma be like, "DANG! That boy on your TIP!"

Most of interview III was occupied by personal and/or controversial topics (see section 6.3.4 for further details), such as male–female relationships and drug-dealing and related violence in the community, and these succeeded in engaging the interviewee's enthusiastic participation.

6.3.1.2   Interview IV   Beth's interview IV was actually modeled quite closely on interview III (to which Beth had listened beforehand), so that many of the topics and subtopics overlapped, including high school life, college and career plans, boyfriends, girlfriends, teenage pregnancies, recreation activities, race relations, boy–girl relationships, and slang terms. Both interviews naturally included distinctive topics of their own (community homicides in III, the Gulf War in IV), but this was less significant than the relative time spent on related topics, Foxy's personal and emotive involvement in each, and her relation to her interlocutor as she talked. For instance, both interviews began with school life and college plans, a relatively formal and nonpersonal topic, exemplified by the following extract (p. 7, transcript interview IV):

5   F: . . . my teacher, his name is Mr Segal and he's like – really hard. And he's like, "You guys[??]" he teaches you – he teaches us like we're in college, and my um Biology – when I had Biology? This guy named Mr Cross – I mean he teaches you like you're in college. He gives you – he gives you all your book and he assigns you ALL this work. It's like sooo much work . . . and it's – it's done in a week and you're like, "OH MY GOSH!"

However, this topic constituted only 7 percent of interview III but 19 percent of interview IV (see section 6.3.4). The next topic in IV, the Gulf War and related events at school, produces the same information-giving register from Foxy and goes on for another 13 percent of the transcript, whereas the next topics in III are drugs, murders, and thefts in the community, producing much more excitement and involvement on Foxy's part. As we'll see in a moment and explore further in section 6.3.4, the topic of boy–girl relationships ("wives and slamming partners") produces equally involved dialogue and vernacular usage in both interviews, but Foxy simply gives more topics this personalized, animated treatment in interview III than she does in interview IV.

This is in turn related to the fact that Foxy's interlocutor in interview IV is European American and a stranger, and the fact that she is unaccompanied by a teenager like Roberta to whom Foxy can relate as a peer-group insider. Although Beth opens the interview by saying that Faye "asked me to talk to you" and draws artfully on terms and events which Foxy had mentioned in her previous interview, her status as an outsider is clear from the fact that she doesn't know specific individuals and institutions that Foxy mentions, as in this excerpt (3, transcript):

6   F: You might know Alice [name changed]. She used to work at Stanford with Faye?

     B: I haven't met her.

     F: Oh. Well, she goes to Howard.

Moreover, while she is skillful at keeping up her end of the conversation and usually reacts fluidly to what Foxy says in any one segment of the interview, Beth's transitions between topics are sometimes awkward, marked by long pauses and hesitation fillers as she tries to decide what to turn to next. And sometimes, perhaps because of dialect differences, Beth's questions are misunderstood, as in this excerpt (16, transcript):

7   B: I mean, do you think they maybe talk more to girls than they –

     F: Talk to girls?

     B: Do you think they're like, yeah, like more open with other – with girls than they are with other guys? You see what I'm saying? Like do you think they, um –

     F: Do I think, um, guys are open with – girls than guys?

     B: Yeah.

These misfirings in interlocutor communications, added to their ethnic distance, help to hold interviewer and interviewee at arm's length, so to speak, for at least the first third of interview IV. Even where Foxy goes *on* about something at some length, as in her account of acquaintances who are in the Gulf or scheduled to go there, she doesn't get *into* it as fully as she might, as she often does in interview III. And she sometimes deals with topics sparingly in interview IV, as in this discussion of teen pregnancies, which occupies only a few lines (15, transcript):

8   B: Do you have many friends who are pregnant?

     F: Yeah, a lot of my friends do have kids – [pause] or are pregnant, yeah.

     B: How do you feel about that?

F: I don't know. I was like, "They're CUTE," but then, I was like, "I'm not ready to have kids, oh my gosh."

B: Do you think they're ready – do you feel like they're ready to have kids?

F: No, but [laughter] – I 'on know. [laughter]

In interview III, by contrast, the same topic goes on for one and a half pages; Foxy's contributions to this topic are not only longer, but more personal (note her references to specific individuals), and animated with more dialogue and sound effects (6, transcript):

9 F: . . . when I be driving, it seem like every corner I drive around – there go somebody you know pushing a baby.

   I: Mm. Mm. Mm.

   F: [Quoting] "Hi, F.! Beep-beep!" [Car horn; laughter]

   I: Mm. Mm. Mm. Mm-hmm.

   F: Me and T. and them be like, "Tha's a SHAME, huh?!" . . . Cause like, you know Elizabeth? [Name changed] I be like, "Dang, T., she in the same grade with me and SHE HAVE 3 KIDS!"

   I: Oh my GOD!

   R: She got three kids?!

   F: She got three kids!!

Interview IV does have its animated highlights, however. The most notable one is Foxy's discussion of "wives and slamming partners," which, interestingly enough, occurs in response to Beth's question about whether these terms, which she said Faye had told her about, were still in use. Foxy's response to this display of insider knowledge is not only long (going on for five full pages) but also lively, packed with as much dialogue as in interview III, with as much copula absence, and with even more risqué lexicon (a point we return to in section 6.3.4), as this segment (from pp. 21–2, transcript B) illustrates:

10 F: Well, all guys have a main girl that they really like – that they really, you know, spend time with ['n] stuff, and that's the one they call – their *wife*. And it's like, the other girls, they just . . . It's just like – you know, it's just that, they don't really care about 'em, they just – they just *slam* – that's just they work. [Background laughter] *Work* just means "sex" too. That's just they work and stuff like that. But, like – if you talking to a guy on a phone and all his friends come in, "Hey blood, blood! Who you talking to? Who's that on the phone? Who's that on the phone?" They be like, " . . .Maybe I can get my hit in." [Background laughter] *Hit* means "slam." And then the boy be saying, "Blood, you better go on. This the wife. This the wife. I'm talking to my wife on the phone." Then they be like, "Oh for real? I'm sorry, I'm sorry, I'm sorry, blood, I'm sorry. I didn't know it was the wife."

Table 6.1   Foxy's vernacular usage interviews III and IV

Variable	Foxy: Interview III (1990, African/ American Interviewer)	Foxy: Interview IV 1991, European/ American Interviewer)
Possessive -*s* absence	67% (6/9)	50% (5/10) N.S.
Plural -*s* absence	1% (4/282)	0% (0/230) N.S.
Third singular present -*s* absence	73% (83/114)	36% (45/124)*
Copula *is/are* absence	70% (197/283)	40% (70/176)*
Invariant habitual *be*	385 (= 241 per hr)	97 (= 78 per hr)*

Note: Number of tokens in parentheses; *significant by chi-square test, <.001; N.S. = Not Significant.

6.3.2   Addressee-*influenced style shift: differences between Foxy's vernacular usage in interviews III and IV*

In this section we'll consider Foxy's addressee-influenced style shift between interviews III and IV, as reflected in quantitative differences in her use of the following variables.[14]

(a)   Possessive -*s* absence, as in: "the teacher'∅ clerk" [Int. IV];[15]
(b)   Plural -*s* absence, as in: "They just our friend∅" [Int. III];
(c)   Absence of third person singular present tense -*s*, as in: "At first it seem∅ like it wasn't no drugs" [Int. IV];
(d)   Absence of copula/auxiliary *is* and *are*, as in: "He ∅ on the phone" [Int. III]; "You go there when you ∅ pregnant" [Int. IV];[16]
(e)   Use of invariant habitual *be*, as in: "He always *be* coming down here" [Int. III] and "I *be* tripping off of boys" [Int. IV].

Table 6.1 shows the relative frequency with which Foxy used the vernacular variants of these variables in each of the two interviews, without regard to internal constraints.[17] We discuss each of the variables in turn, relating our findings concerning style-shifting to the findings of earlier researchers (including Bell 1984) and discussing the effects of internal constraints where known.

6.3.2.1   Possessive -s *absence*   Although Foxy's possessive -*s* absence is 17 percent higher in interview III than in interview IV, indicating a style shift in the hypothesized direction, the difference is not statistically significant, because of the small number of tokens on which the percentages are based.[18] This case illustrates the need to provide both the number of tokens on which relative

frequencies are based and chi-square or other measures of statistical significance, information which is not always provided in variationist studies of
AAVE and other dialects.

Labov et al. (1968: 169–70) was the first study of AAVE to provide information about possessive -*s* absence in relation to style. Combining data from all
their African American New York City peer groups (44 youths, excluding
the "Lames"), the authors reported 72 percent (23/32) possessive -*s* absence
for single style, and 57 percent (32/56) for group style. Again, the percentage
gap seems relatively large, but it is statistically insignificant (chi-square = 1.89,
$p > .05$).

How can we explain the absence of statistically significant style-shifting for
this variable?[19] Bell (1984: 167) has advanced the following strong hypothesis:

11   A sociolinguistic variable which is differentiated by certain speaker charac-
     teristics (e.g. by class or gender or age) tends to be differentiated in speech
     to addressees with those same characteristics. That is, if an old person uses
     a given linguistic variable differently than a young person, then individuals
     will use that variable differently when speaking to an old person than to a
     young person . . . and mutatis mutandis, for gender, race and so on.

Since urban European American vernaculars typically show little or no absence
of possessive -*s*, in contrast with urban AAVE (Ash and Myhill 1986: 38–9,
Labov and Harris 1986: 11–12), one might expect from Bell's hypothesis that
AAVE speakers would show significantly lower rates of -*s* absence when speaking to European Americans than to African Americans. The fact that Foxy does
not do so, at least not to a statistically significant degree, suggests the need for
a rider to Bell's hypothesis: If the variable is relatively rare in speech, its value
and exploitation as a symbolic counter in style-shifting may be reduced.[20]

Another tack we might take on this problem is to interpret the evidence of
Labov et al. (1968) as suggesting that possessive -*s* absence in AAVE is an
indicator, showing social but not stylistic differentiation, instead of a *marker*,
showing differentiation by social class *and* style (Labov 1972e: 179). As Bell
notes (1984: 166), features established as indicators on the basis of limited style
shifting among speech, reading, and word lists will tend to show little or no
addressee style shift. This argument is somewhat tautologous, however, and it
also potentially contradicts the hypothesis in 11, since features that are indicators insofar as they show little differentiation in terms of more monitored or less
monitored speech might still show addressee style shift if they are differentially
used by a speaker's interlocutors or the ethnic/class/gender groups to which
the interlocutors belong. A final reason for not allowing the evidence of earlier
data sets to *define* the status of variables in new data sets (as indicators or
markers) is that the evidence of previous studies might be limited or mixed, and
there is always the possibility that the older and newer data sets might differ

regionally, or in terms of social class and recording situation, or insofar as they represent change in the intervening time period.

Baugh (1979: 215–17) in fact provides quite a different kind of evidence from Labov et al. (1968), because possessive *-s* absence among his Pacoima (Los Angeles) AAVE speakers is influenced most strongly by a situational/stylistic factor – whether the addressee is familiar to the interviewer (favoring *s*-absence) or not (disfavoring *-s* absence). We don't have the Ns on which Baugh's probability coefficients are based, but he does note that "possessive *-s* occurs less frequently than plural *-s* or third person singular *-s*" (215). Whether tokens of this variable occurred *more* frequently in Baugh's study than in our study or Labov's, allowing us to attribute its stylistic significance to this, is unclear.

6.3.2.2 Plural -s *absence* In the case of plural *-s* absence, sample size is not a problem, but the one percentage point (1 percent) difference between Foxy's usage in interviews III and IV is too slight to achieve statistical significance.[21] Here we can argue, however, that we would *not* expect significant addressee shift on the basis of Bell's hypothesis (11), since AAVE usage rates on this variable tend to be low. Labov and associates' (1968: 161) New York City peer-group members displayed 7 percent (75/1059) plural *-s* absence overall in single style and 9 percent (57/648) for the same members in group style; Wolfram's (1968: 150) upper- and lower-working-class Detroit teenagers had 3 percent and 7 percent plural absence, respectively; and, more germanely, AAVE speakers recorded in East Palo Alto in 1986–7 (Rickford 1992) showed frequencies of plural *-s* absence ranging from 1 percent to 13 percent.[22] This is not a major vernacular variable for AAVE speakers, and as such its insignificant role in style-shifting between European American and African American addressees in interviews III and IV is not surprising. Bell (1984: 166) cites a similar case from the work of Douglas-Cowie (1978: 41–2); five of her speakers rarely used the local variant of two variables, (ɔ:) and (aye), so, as Bell notes, "had little distance to shift when addressing the English outsider." However, Baugh (1979) points in a different direction; although he notes (223) that "the plural marker, as has been observed in many BEV communities, is very rarely deleted," he nevertheless finds style-shifting significant for plural *-s* absence in the speech of his Pacoima (Los Angeles) AAVE speakers (219).

6.3.2.3 Third singular -s *absence* Unlike the preceding two variants, this variable and its vernacular variant occur frequently enough to allow us to consider its internal conditioning, a potentially significant factor which many quantitative studies of style (for instance, those by Douglas-Cowie, Bickerton, Coupland, Russell, and Thelander referred to earlier) unfortunately do not take into account. The omission is unfortunate because a shift in a speaker's usage from one situation to the next might have little relation to addressee or other differences, and more to the effect of internal constraints, differentially distrib-

Table 6.2   Foxy's third person singular present -*s* absence by verb type

Verb Type	Interview III	Interview IV
Regular verbs (*walk*)	67% (57/85)	31% (27/87)
Have	75% (3/4)	11% (1/9)
Do	60% (3/5)	40% (2/5)
Don't	100% (15/15)	50% (8/16)
Say	100% (5/5)	100% (7/7)
TOTAL, all verbs	73% (83/114)	36% (46/124)

uted in the two situations. Without systematic data on internal constraints, it is difficult to know for sure.[23] Without such data, it is also impossible to test the "status" extension of Bell's "style" hypothesis, in which Preston (1991: 36) proposes, "Variation on the 'status' dimension derives from and echoes [and will be less than/contained within] the variation which exists within the 'linguistic' dimension."

Table 6.2 shows the percentage of third singular -*s* absence in Foxy's two interviews in relation to the primary internal factor which seems to affect this variable locally (cf. Rickford 1992): verb type. The percentage of -*s* absence is higher in interview III than interview IV in every case except *say*, and the relative effect of verb type is similar in both interviews, with *don't* (versus *doesn't*) and *say* favoring -*s* absence more than regular verbs and *have* (versus *has*) do. Furthermore, the distributions of verb types within each interview are comparable – the verbs less favorable to -*s* absence (regular verbs and *have*) constitute 78 percent (89/114) and 77 percent (96/124) of the total set of third singular present stems in interviews III and IV, respectively, and the stems more favorable to -*s* absence (*don't* and *say*) account for 18 percent of the total in interview III (20/114) and 19 percent in interview IV (23/124). Clearly, the tendency for Foxy to omit third singular -*s* more often in interview III than interview IV remains true when the effect of verb type is taken into account; we can conclude that the overall percentages of -*s* absence in interviews III and IV are robust indicators of a fundamental style shift between the interviews.

Given what we know about the very limited third singular -*s* absence in European American Vernacular English (Ash and Myhill 1986: 38–9), a marked style shift of this type is again consistent with Bell's "differential accommodation" hypothesis (see 11 above). But what do earlier studies indicate about AAVE style-shifting in relation to this variable?

The most directly comparable study is Fasold (1978: 214), which reports race-of-interviewer effects on the speech of 47 working-class AAVE interviewees from Washington, DC. Those who were interviewed by African

Americans exhibited higher rates of third singular -*s* absence (68 percent) than those who were interviewed by European Americans (63.8 percent), but the difference was not statistically significant.[24] The fact that Fasold's African American interviewers were mostly "middle-class, standard English speaking young women (a few were conducted by a working class black man)" may have had something to do with this unexpected result, especially if they failed to establish the kind of insider's rapport which Faye and Roberta had with Foxy Boston.

Although Baugh (1979) does not provide data on the effects of African American versus European interviewers – an African American, he interviewed all his Pacoima speakers himself – his important study of style-shifting in AAVE also includes data on third person -*s*. Styles in Baugh's study were delimited along the intersections of two dimensions. The first was the relative *familiarity* (or solidarity) of interviewer and interviewee, ranging from his outsider status during the first year of his fieldwork to his insider status in the third or fourth year, when he was living in the community itself, had "gained access to a number of social domains," and had become "active in the day to day lives" (30) of community members.[25] The second, related to the first, was whether the speech events that were being manifested in the presence of the interviewer were primarily *vernacular* or nonvernacular. Baugh found significant stylistic variation for suffix -*s*, especially third singular present -*s* (212–15). Baugh's variable rule probability coefficients for stylistic factors for third person -*s* absence (see table 6.3) in fact outweigh and contain those for internal linguistic factors (the variation space or range for style is .184, compared with .092 for following phonological environment and .158 for preceding phonological environment), contrary to Preston's (1991: 36–7) predictions that the scope of the latter would outstrip that of the former. After noting that stylistic factors are also significant for postvocalic *r*-deletion, but not for copula absence or *t, d* deletion, Baugh suggests (225) that *r*'s "lack of grammatical function" allows it to be used as a stylistic device, since "little if any confusion results from post vocalic /r/loss." The argument with respect to suffix -*s* is similar, though not made as directly (225–7): Discourse context can usually provide the grammatical information provided by suffix -*s*, so it is free to be variably absent in accord with situational or stylistic factors. This is reminiscent of Hymes' (1974: 160) observation that strong versus weak aspiration of an initial stop in English has stylistic but not referential meaning – in fact, it is free to have the former because it lacks the latter. However, nothing in Bell's theory would predict the general argument, and since it isn't confirmed by our results (third singular -*s* absence, copula absence, and invariant *be* all show significant style-shifting although they are bearers of potentially significant grammatical information), we do not pursue this interesting hypothesis any further.

However, it is worth noting that, contrary to his expectations, Baugh found more significant style-shifting for -*s* absence according to whether he was

Table 6.3 Constraints on third singular *s*-absence, Pacoima

Situation/Style	Foll. Phon. Env.	Prec. Phon. Env.
Familiar Vernacular: .601	—Consonant: .546	Nasal—: .490
Unfamiliar Vernacular: .443	—Vowel: .454	Voiced Consonant—: .567
Familiar Non-Vernacular: .538		Voiceless Consonant—: .427
Unfamiliar Non-Vernacular: .417		ts-cluster—: .430
		Vowel—: .585

Source: Baugh 1979: 215

familiar or nonfamiliar to his interlocutors than whether he used AAVE or not (235).[26] As we will see later, Faye used some of the AAVE variants, but nowhere near as often as Foxy did, and Foxy's differential vernacular usage in interviews III and IV must be taken as a combined accommodation to the race and familiarity of her interviewers. Since Beth is both non-African American and a stranger, it's difficult to say which feature Foxy is primarily responding to, but Baugh's study reminds us that familiarity can be a significant addressee variable in and of itself.

Another study which reports style-shifting data for third singular -*s* absence in AAVE is Wolfram (1969), which reported (147) a significant style shift effect among his working-class Detroit speakers, who had much higher third person -*s* absence rates in spoken interview style (61.3 percent) than in reading style (15.6 percent). Of course, since the text of his reading passage was fixed and did not deliberately exclude instances of third person -*s*, the scope for stylistic variability was limited, and this method does not in any case provide direct information on style as *audience design*. However, Wolfram's results are of interest because they led him to exactly the opposite conclusion from Baugh (1979). After noting (177) that zero copula also shows significant style-shifting among his working-class speakers, Wolfram comments, "For other grammatical features, the working class showed significant stylistic shift between the interview and reading styles but in the phonological variables there is generally slight variation between interview and reading style." Since our study did not look at phonological variables, we're in no position to arbitrate on this issue, but it's an interesting one which deserves further research. As Wolfram (1969: 204) notes, grammatical variables generally show sharp stratification while phonological variables show gradient stratification. If Bell's hypothesis (see extract 11) is right, the former would therefore be more likely to show marked style shift.

The final study of relevance is Labov et al. (1968), who, discussing third person present -*s* absence in the speech of their New York City adolescent peer groups, observe (164), "There is no stylistic shift observable in moving from group style to single sessions." This statement is corroborated by combined data from the T-Birds, Aces, Cobras, Jets, and Oscar Bros, across both preconsonantal and prevocalic environments, which show a third singular -*s* absence rate of 66 percent (208/316) in group style, compared with 69 (384/560) in single interview style (161). The absence of style-shifting for this variable runs counter to the findings of the present study as well as to the results of Baugh and Wolfram reported earlier, but it may be related to Labov et al.'s claim, based on a high overall percentage of third singular present -*s* absence and the irregular effects of following phonological segments, that "there is no underlying third singular -*s* in AAVE" (164).

6.3.2.4 Absence of copula/auxiliary is and are   In the case of copula absence, the set of internal factors which could affect the distribution of the variable is too large to keep track of with percentages and one-dimensional tables.[27] So we turned instead to the variable rule program (Gregory Guy's MACVARB, based on David Sankoff's VARBRUL 2S), which, on the basis of inputted information about observed frequencies of copula absence in different environments, estimates the independent contribution of each factor to rule application, expressed as a probability coefficient (see Sankoff 1988).[28]

Table 6.4 shows the outputs of three analyses of Foxy's copula absence data using the variable rule program.[29] The first two runs are for interviews III and IV considered separately; they show us first of all that Foxy's copula absence is similarly affected by internal constraints in both interviews; the same factor groups are selected as significant by the regression routine of the program, and the ordering of factors within each group is comparable, with second person and plural *are*, for instance, much more likely to be absent (.74, .67) than third singular *is* (.26, .33).[30] But what is even more significant are the input probabilities (corrected means), shown in the first row of this table: .49 for interview III and .20 for interview IV.[31] These represent "the probability that the rule will apply regardless of environment" (Guy 1975: 60) and indicate that there remain big differences between interviews III and IV even when the cross-cutting effect of internal factors is taken into account. The final column of table 6.4 provides a similar indication, in a different way – by pooling the data from both interviews and contrasting interviews III and IV as factors in a new INTERVIEW factor group. The effect of this external constraint is shown to be as pronounced as the effect of the PERSON/NUMBER factor group, with interview III much more favorable to copula absence (.72) than interview IV (.28).[32]

Given the much higher frequencies of copula absence in AAVE than in European American Vernacular English (Wolfram 1974, Ash and Myhill 1986: 38–9, McElhinny 1993), we would of course expect higher rates in speech to African Americans than European Americans, given Bell's hypothesis (see 11), and Foxy's behavior in interviews III and IV conforms perfectly to this prediction. However, earlier studies are quite mixed with regard to the significance of style-shifting for copula absence in AAVE more generally. As noted, Baugh (1979: 183–91) found that situational factors were of minimal importance for

Table 6.4 Probability coefficients for Foxy's copula absence, interviews III and IV separately and combined

Factor Group Constraints		Interview III	Interview IV	Interview III + IV
Input probability		.49	.20	.33
Following Grammatical	Gonna	[100%]	.79	.90
	Verb-*ing*	.59	.66	.59
	Locative	.87	.52	.61
	Adjective	.39	.29	.29
	Noun phrase	.24	.32	.21
	Miscellaneous	.34	.40	.31
Subject	Personal pronoun	.81	.81	.83
	Other pronouns	.27		.26
	Noun phrase	.39	.19	.37
Person/number	Second person plural	.74	.67	.71
	Third person singular	.26	.33	.29
Interview	III (African American interviewer)			.72
	IV (European American interviewer)			.28
Overall %'s (Ns)		70% (283)	40% (176)	58% (459)

this variable as used by his Pacoima interviewees, less influential than the internal linguistic constraints, and less influential than in the case of suffix -*s* absence. By contrast, Wolfram (1969: 177) found a sharp decline in copula absence among his working-class Detroit interviewees between their spoken interview style (41.8 percent) and reading style (7.9 percent).

Labov et al. (1968: 191), who considered only absence of *is*, not *are*, suggested that "stylistic shifts are minor effects among the [NYC] pre-adolescent and adolescent peer-groups, and only begin to assume importance with the older adolescents and adults." This appears to be generally true of their data in table 6.5, although the adults show less style-shifting than they'd lead us to expect,[33] and it is certainly true from other evidence in their study that internal linguistic constraints have a greater effect on variability in copula absence than external factors do (as in Baugh's study).

Note, however, that when the effect of a noun phrase versus pronoun subject is controlled for, as in table 6.6, the style effects generally *increase*.[34]

This supports our general point that it is critical to control for the effects of internal constraints when considering style-shifting. Since we don't have a

Table 6.5   % *Is* absence, by style, Central Harlem, New York

Peer group	T-Birds (9–13 yrs)	Cobras (11–17 yrs)	Jets (12–16 yrs)	Oscar Bros (15–19 yrs)	Adults (20+ yrs)
Single style	36%	44%	27%	31%	11%
Group style	41%	42%	45%	44%	17%
Style effect	5%	2%*	18%	13%	6%

* Instance in which group style shows less copula absence than single style, rather than more.
Source: Adapted from table 3.12, Labov et al. 1968: 192

Table 6.6   % *Is* absence, by subject and style, Central Harlem, New York

Peer group	T-Birds		Cobras		Jets		Oscar Bros		Adults	
	NP	Pro	NP	Pro	NP	Pro	NP	Pro	NP	Pro
Single style	12%	51	18	67	18	61	04	15	08	16
Group style	42%	60	36	77	27	58	26	64	14	27
Style effect	30%	09	18	10	09	03*	22	49	06	11

* Instance in which group style shows less copula absence than single style, rather than more.
Source: Adapted from table 3.12a, Labov et al. 1968: 194

variable rule analysis of the New York City data which includes style as a constraint (Labov 1972 and Cedergren and Sankoff 1974 consider internal factors only), we can't tell for sure whether it would remain significant when all the cross-cutting internal constraints are controlled for, but table 6.6 at least suggests that it might have been more important than Labov et al. (1968) originally suggested, and more in line with what Bell's differential accommodation hypothesis would lead us to expect.

6.3.2.5   Invariant habitual be   The first thing that must be said about Foxy's use of invariant habitual *be* in these interviews is that it exceeds anything reported in the literature to date. For instance, Labov et al. (1968: 236) recorded a total of 95 *be* tokens from 18 members of the Thunderbirds gang in New York City; Wolfram (1969: 198) recorded 94 from his sample of 48 speakers in Detroit (most were from younger, working-class speakers); and, more recently, Bailey and Maynor (1987: 457) reported a total of 119 from their sample of 20 12- and 13-year-old children in the Brazos Valley, Texas. Foxy had singlehandedly surpassed these group totals since Faye's first interview with her in 1986, producing 146 tokens of invariant habitual *be* on that occasion. Her *be* frequency of 385 in her most recent reinterview with Faye (interview III) surpasses even this earlier high-water mark, and her 97 tokens with Beth (in interview IV), although representative of a style shift away from AAVE, is still higher than reported for African American individuals in other studies.

As first noted by Wolfram (1969: 196), invariant *be* "presents special problems" if one attempts to quantify its occurrences in relative terms, that is, "on the basis of actual and potential realizations of particular variants of a variable." Bailey and Maynor (1987) quantify it as a percentage of all present tense forms of *be*, including *is*, *are*, and zero copula, but this ignores the fact that *be* is a variant of noncopula forms as well, in particular, the English present tense (Richardson 1988, Rickford 1989). Until the relationship of *be* to the full set of its potential alternants is better understood, it is best to report its occurrence in absolute terms.

Because we have absolute rather than relative data on this variable, we cannot analyze the effect of internal constraints on its occurrence as we did for third singular present *-s* of copula absence. But the statistical significance of Foxy's per hour rate of invariant *be* usage (230 in interview III versus 78 in interview IV) is, in any case, so massive as to make it unlikely that it would be due entirely to any internal factors.

Although they shed no light on style-shifting per se, two correlates of Foxy's *be* usage in these interviews are worth noting briefly for their potential interest to other researchers. One is that, as in earlier studies by Labov et al. (1968: 234) and Bailey and Maynor (1987: 453–4), Foxy's *be* in both interviews is most frequent with second person and plural subjects, next with first person singular subjects, and least with third person singular subjects. Second, in terms of Following Grammatical environments, Foxy uses *be* in both interviews much more often with a following verb + *ing* than with a following noun phrase, locative, or adjective. This much is consistent with earlier findings (see Bailey and Maynor 1987: 457–9). However, what is new is that many of those verb + *ing* forms are *going* and *saying*, used as quotative introducers, as in

12   My mother jus *be* going, "You – tha's a shame." (III, line 56-481.5b)
13   They *be* saying, "If I can't be with you . . ." (IV, line 876)

And there is a huge set of invariant *be* tokens before *like* (44 percent interview III, 54 percent interview IV), used as a quotative introducer, as in[35]

14   He be like, "What you talking bout?" (III, line 56-028d)
15   I be like, "FOR REAL?!" (IV, line 852)

This latter feature was not characteristic of Foxy's *be* use when she was first interviewed.

Table 6.7   Invariant habitual *be*, Central Harlem, New York

Peer group	T-Birds (9–13 yrs)	Cobras (11–17 yrs)	Jets (12–16 yrs)	Oscar Bros (15–19 yrs)	Adults (Over 20 yrs)
Single style	83	95	100	18	00
Group style	12	6	29	09	00

Source: Labov et al. 1968: 236

With the exception of speakers over 75 years old from east Louisiana and Mississippi whose dialect atlas data are discussed in Bailey and Bassett (1986), European Americans generally do *not* use invariant habitual *be* (Labov et al. 1968: 235, Wolfram 1974, Sommer 1986, Nichols 1991). On the basis of this fact, together with Bell's (1984) differential accommodation hypothesis (11), we would expect the decreased use of the form between interview III and IV which Foxy displays. But do earlier studies similarly indicate that this feature is sensitive to style shift?

Labov et al. (1968: 235) report some style shift for invariant habitual *be* (called be_2) use in New York City, but it is the opposite of what we'd expect from a vernacular feature, with "very little use of be_2 in the group sessions" and more in single style, as table 6.7 shows. The authors conclude that, for the peer group members, "be_2 is an emphatic form used in deliberate speech." Whether or not this analysis was valid for New York City peer groups at the time (it is certainly not valid for Foxy and her peers today), one possible explanation for the unexpected result may simply have been the fact that Labov and his colleagues may have had more data from individual interviews than group sessions, producing more opportunities for tokens of *be* to occur. With an absolute rather than relative frequency count, the relative length of the interviews can make a critical difference. Given the magnitude of the single versus group style distributions in table 6.7, this clearly cannot be the only explanation, but it is worth considering.

A more significant factor is that invariant *be* use has simply increased by leaps and bounds since the 1960s (either that, or we have better data), and its increased frequency and salience (Butters 1989: 15, Bailey and Maynor 1987) may make it available as a counter in strategic style-shifting to an extent that was simply not possible in the 1960s. This hypothesis receives some support from the studies by Fasold (1972) and Baugh (1979) reported on below, which show increased use of *be* with African American and familiar addressees, although the extent of the style shift is less dramatic than in the case of Foxy Boston. To the extent that this hypothesis receives further support, it would of course complement and strengthen the related hypothesis which we suggested in relation to possessive *-s* – that a variable which is relatively rare in speech will tend to be exploited less frequently and regularly in strategic style-shifting.

Wolfram (1969), who depended on spoken versus reading contexts for his analysis of style, had nothing to report about invariant *be* in relation to style, because "no instances of invariant *be* occur in the reading passages" (199–200). Fasold (1972: 214), whose Washington, DC, data were most similar to ours insofar as they used both African American and European American interviewers, noted that

> a higher percentage of speakers who were interviewed by white interviewers used *be* than those who were interviewed by black interviewers – 67.7 percent, as against 62.5 percent. However, *the speakers who used* be *at least once were somewhat freer in their use of the form when talking to a black interviewer. Those interviewed by black interviewers averaged 4.7 instances per speaker; those who talked with a white interviewer had an average of 3.4* (emphasis added)

The italicized portion of this quotation certainly agrees with our data on Foxy Boston, although the extent of the difference in *be* use was much weaker in Fasold's data than in ours. Baugh's (1979: 144) comment that invariant *be* "occurs with much greater frequency in colloquial contexts where all interactants are aware of the non-standard form" also matches Foxy's behavior in interviews III and IV. Overall, we can take Fasold's and Baugh's studies as evidence of a trend which reaches its high point in Foxy's 1990s data – for *be* to function more systematically as a vernacular style marker as its frequency of use increases.

6.3.3   *Interviewers' usage: what is Foxy accommodating to?*

We have seen from section 6.3.2 that Foxy's vernacular usage is significantly lower in interview IV than it is in interview III, for three of the variables we considered: third person present *-s*, *is/are* (copula) absence, and invariant habitual *be*. We attribute this intraspeaker or stylistic variation, plausibly enough, to Foxy's accommodation to the different addressees whom she faces in each interview. But Bell's (1984: 167) question then arises: "What is it in the addressee (or other audience members) that the speaker is responding to?" Bell (1984: 167) suggests three "increasingly specific" possibilities:

16 1   Speakers assess the personal characteristics of their addressees and design their style to suit.

2   Speakers assess the general level of their addressees' speech and shift relative to it.

3   Speakers assess their addressees' levels for specific linguistic variables and shift relative to these levels.

Table 6.8   Interviewers' vernacular usage, interviews III and IV

	Third Person Present -s	is + are *Absence*	*Invariant* be
Foxy: Interview III	73% (83/114)	70% (197/283)	385
Faye: Interview III	30% (13/43)	22% (29/130)	5
Roberta: Interview III	12% (2/17)	30% (14/46)	12
Foxy: Interview IV	36% (45/124)	40% (70/176)	97
Beth: Interview IV	0% (0/17)	1% (1/81)	0

As Bell notes (168), it is difficult to distinguish between possibilities 2 and 3, "since the general speech impression of level (2) largely derives from the combined assessment of many individual variables." Operationally, we will consider level 3 to be satisfied to the extent that we can show that there is specific matching between interviewer and interviewee speech with respect to the variables under investigation, even while admitting that the influence could have been, in theory and to some extent, bidirectional.

Table 6.8, showing the vernacular usage of Foxy's addressees in interviews III and IV,[36] suggests that the third possibility is not tenable in our case. Although Beth essentially follows Standard English grammar for the variables in question, while Faye and Roberta use the AAVE variants to some extent, their levels are considerably lower than those of Foxy in the same interview. One might still maintain that Foxy was shifting *relative* to her addressees' levels (about 30 percent to 40 percent higher, for third person -*s* and copula absence, in each case), but the absolute differences are so great, especially for invariant *be*, that possibility 2 is more likely.[37]

Possibility 2 and possibility 1 seem to represent the more valid general statement in the light of Fasold's (1972: 214) finding that African American interviewees from Washington, DC, used vernacular variants more frequently with African American interviewers than with European American interviewers (significantly so in the case of past tense [*d*]-deletion). This was so, Fasold noted, "despite the fact that most of the black interviewers were middle-class, standard English speaking young men (a few were conducted by a working-class black man)."

But although it may be the personal characteristics of her addressees that Foxy is responding to, it is impossible to say without further interviews and experiments how much of Foxy's vernacular use should be attributed to the various distinctive aspects of her addressees. Their race and relative familiarity seem significant enough, from this study and from the earlier work of Anshen (1969), Fasold (1972), and Baugh (1979), but how *much* to attribute to race and how much to familiarity is difficult to say, and the contributory effects of residential community membership, personality, and age are even harder to assess (see Bell 1984: 168–9 on this point).

6.3.4   *Topic-influenced style shift in Foxy's vernacular usage,*
interviews III and IV

Although Bell (1984) suggests that the nature of the addressee and other audience members is the primary factor in a speaker's style shift, he does acknowledge that "nonpersonal" factors such as topic and setting also have some influence. However, he argues that "the direction and strength of style shift caused by these factors originate in their derivation from audience-designed shift" (178). This general argument leads him to these three specific hypotheses which can be tested against Foxy's data:

17   1   Variation according to topic . . . presupposes variation according to
         addressee. (179)
     2   The degree of topic-designed shift will not exceed that of audience-
         designed shift. (180)
     3   Speakers associate classes of topics or settings with classes of persons.
         They therefore shift style when talking on those topics or in those
         settings as if they were talking to addressees whom they associate with
         the topic or setting.

Hypothesis 17.1 is trivially correct. Since we know from section 6.3.2 that Foxy does show addressee style shift, the presupposition which the hypothesis embodies is satisfied, and any variation by topic which we find in her data would be consistent with it.

As tables 6.9 and 6.10 show, Foxy does display variation by topic in both interviews III and IV, and the data they contain allow us to address hypothesis 17.2. This hypothesis does not fare as well as the first, however, since the amounts of zero copula shift caused by addressee differences (calculated by subtracting the percentages in the Total row of table 6.10 from their counterparts in table 6.9) range from 22 percent (zero *is*) to 30 percent (zero *is* + *are*), while the amounts caused by topic changes within each interview are much higher: for instance, 75 percent for zero *is* in table 6.9 (from 0 percent for topic I to 75 percent for topic G) and 73 percent for zero *is* + *are* in table 6.10 (from 9 percent for topic G to 82 percent, topic F).[38]

One of the speakers in Douglas-Cowie's (1978: 41, 42, 45) study similarly showed more topic shift than addressee shift, and Bell (1984: 180), commenting on this exception, suggested that the expected ratios were more likely to hold for grouped data, as in Coupland (1981). To the extent that this means that cells with low token counts can be expected to show random variability, Bell is right,

Table 6.9 Foxy's zero copula and invariant *be* use by topic, interview III, with Faye and Roberta

Topic		*Zero* is		*Zero* are		*Zero* is + are		be$_2$
A:	School, including teen pregnancies (6½ pages, 7% transcript)	60%	(5)	50%	(4)	56%	(9)	7
B:	Drugs, thefts, murders, EPA (11 pages, 12% transcript)	10%	(10)	96%	(26)	72%	(36)	12
C:	Skating, meeting boys, slang (7½ pages, 9% transcript)	25%	(4)	100%	(4)	63%	(8)	19
D:	School, including teachers and drugs (3½ pages, 4% transcript)	40%	(10)	100%	(5)	60%	(15)	1
E:	Graduation, college/career (5 pages, 6% transcript)	33%	(6)	100%	(1)	43%	(7)	0
F:	Wives, slamming partners (10½ pages, 12% transcript)	54%	(13)	90%	(20)	76%	(33)	53
G:	Boy–girl conflicts and relations (7½ pages, 9% transcript)	75%	(16)	95%	(21)	86%	(37)	78
H:	Foxy's friends: girls, guys (9 pages, 10% transcript)	31%	(26)	96%	(28)	65%	(54)	61
I:	Vietnamese/foreign friends (4 pages, 5% transcript)	0%	(3)	100%	(7)	70%	(10)	10
J:	Boys, and how to treat them (9 pages, 10% transcript)	30%	(10)	69%	(16)	54%	(26)	61
K:	Race relations at school (9 pages, 10% transcript)	44%	(9)	88%	(24)	76%	(33)	48
L:	Fun at school (5 pages, 6% transcript)	3%	(6)	100%	(9)	73%	(15)	37
Total, all topics (87½ pages, 100% transcript)		39%	(118)	91%	(165)	70%	(283)	387

and we might note that the categorical cells in tables 6.9 and 6.10 – the ones with values of 0 percent and 100 percent which could be interpreted as indicators of extreme topic shift – all contain ten or fewer tokens (one cell has 12). But individuals with sufficient data should be expected to exemplify the expected ratios as well as groups. If we followed Guy (1980: 26) and accepted 30 tokens per factor as the cut-off point for reliability, hypothesis 17.2 would be sustained; table 6.10 has only one such cell for zero *is/are* (topic F), and the five qualifying *is/are* cells in table 6.9 (topics B, F, G, H, K) between them show a maximum topic-influenced shift of only 21 percent (from 65 percent for topic

Table 6.10   Foxy's zero copula and invariant *be* use by topic, interview IV, with Beth

Topic	Zero *is*	Zero *are*	Zero *is* + *are*	*be₂*
A: School, college/career plans (8 pages, 19% transcript)	9% (11)	23% (13)	17% (24)	0
B: The Persian Gulf War ($5\frac{1}{2}$ pages, 13% transcript)	11% (9)	10% (10)	11% (19)	0
C: Foxy's boyfriend, girlfriends (2 pages, 5% transcript)	0% (3)	33% (6)	22% (9)	1
D: Boy–girl differences (3 pages, 7% transcript)	0% (0)	14% (7)	14% (7)	2
E: Slang terms ($2\frac{1}{2}$ pages, 6% transcript)	0% (3)	100% (12)	80% (15)	13
F: Wives, slamming partners (5 pages, 12% transcript)	60% (15)	96% (24)	82% (39)	46
G: Recreation, F as role model (2 pages, 5% transcript)	10% (8)	33% (3)	9% (11)	16
H: AIDS, other teen problems ($3\frac{1}{2}$ pages, 8% transcript)	17% (12)	29% (7)	21% (19)	0
I: Races, other groups at school (7 pages, 17% transcript)	10% (6)	58% (12)	39% (18)	16
J: Popular music and dances ($3\frac{1}{2}$ pages, 8% transcript)	0% (8)	71% (7)	31% (15)	3
Total, all topics (42 pages, 100% transcript)	17% (75)	56% (101)	40% (176)	97

H to 86 percent for topic G) – less than the 30 percent addressee-influenced shift in *is/are* absence which separates interviews III and IV. However, if we also accepted the evidence of cells just slightly below Guy's cut-off point – specifically, the cells with 26 and 24 tokens in the zero *is/are* columns of tables 6.9 and 6.10 – hypothesis 17.2 would *not* be sustained, since the maximum topic shift in table 6.9 would be 32 percent (from 54 percent for topic J to 86 percent for topic G), and the maximum topic shift in table 6.10 would be 65 percent (from 17 percent for topic A to 82 percent for topic F), both higher (the former admittedly just slightly higher) than the addressee shift of 30 percent between interviews III and IV. We feel that the evidence of such cells should be accepted. In the case of the 24-token cell in table 6.10 (interview IV) at least, an additional six tokens would not alter the picture, whatever their realization, and zero copula fluctuations in this table accord with the very strong impression we get from listening to the tape (and attending to other variables) that Foxy makes some remarkable topic shifts within interview IV.

In the rest of this section, we concentrate on Foxy's shift between topics A and F in interview IV, using it to consider hypothesis 17.3, and comparing it with a smaller but related shift in interview III.

Elaborating on 17.3, which he offers as an *explanation* for the direction of topic style shifts rather than as a *hypothesis*, Bell (1984: 181) suggests, "Topics such as occupation or education . . . cause shifts to a style suitable to address an employer or teacher. Similarly, intimate topics . . . elicit speech appropriate for intimate addressees – family or friends." Foxy's shift between topics A and F in interview IV corresponds perfectly to Bell's hypothetical example, since A deals with school, college, and career plans and is predictably more standard, while F deals with "wives and slamming partners" (see quotation 10), the kind of topic one is most likely to discuss with friends, and one which predictably elicits the most vernacular speech. Foxy's shift in interview III between topics A and E, which deal with her academic progress and plans, and topic F, which deals with "wives and slamming partners," is comparable, although the shift is quantitatively smaller, since Foxy's baseline vernacular use with Faye and Roberta in this interview is higher.

But while the direction of shift which Foxy displays in both interviews fits Bell's predictions, it doesn't really show that Foxy style shifts when talking on various topics *as if talking to addressees associated with the topic*. If we had data on Foxy's actually talking to her teachers and closest friends, and those data matched her language use on academic versus "slamming partners" topics in our two interviews, that would provide some support for hypothesis 17.3, although Bell is careful to note (182) that the association between addressee and topic shift is relatively abstract; speakers need not be "conscious of an associated addressee when style shifting for a particular topic."

One relevant difference between Foxy's language in the college/career and "wives/slamming partner" sections of both interviews is the absence of direct quotes in the former and their prevalence in the latter. The absence of quotes, the absence of invariant habitual *be*, and the low zero copula rates in the college and career sections are all manifestations of a relatively detached information-presenting style, the kind that one might use when talking to a teacher or a stranger:

18 F: Miss R. *is* the one that – [laughter] Miss R Ø the one help me get into this program, and my – and this guy name Mr O at our school, he'*s* Chinese. [interview III, with Faye and Roberta]

19 F: M., she goes to DeAnza's nursing school. And R. and T., they'*re* going to, um, CSM, and my friend A, she's going to be going with me when I go. . . . (interview IV, with Beth)

By contrast, in the "wives and slamming partner" sections (F) of both interviews, Foxy is extremely animated and involved, frequently quoting the remarks of real and hypothetical teenagers, as in extracts 4 and 10 above. Significantly enough, both sections contain high frequencies of invariant habitual *be* (53 in interview III, 46 in interview IV), and most of these (60 percent in interview III, 72 percent in interview IV) precede quotative introducers, as in

> 20   F: I *be* like, "for real?" I *be* going, "Tramp, you're stuuupid. You Ø just DUMB! Uhhh! Get away from me! You Ø stupid!" [Interview III]
> 21   F: You be in your car with your friends and they *be* like, "Hey, F, ain't that that girl they – um – B slammed the other night?" You *be* like, "Yeah, that IS her." [Interview IV]

In the sections in which Foxy's vernacular language use reaches its peak, therefore, Foxy is not just behaving *as if* speaking to teenagers; she is, through extensive quotations, dramatically reenacting the speaking *of* teenagers.[39]

Many of the copula tokens in the "slamming partners" (topic F) sections of both interviews in fact occur within quotations. And, in interview III, copula tokens within quotations show a higher *is/are* absence rate (13/15 = 87 percent) than those not in quotations (12/18 = 67 percent), although this is not true for interview IV: 7/9 (78 percent) zero *is/are* within quotations, versus 25/30 (83 percent) zero *is/are* outside quotations. In any event, it seems reasonable to interpret the heavy use of quotations in these sections of the interviews as providing some support for Bell's hypothesis 17.3; to attribute Foxy's high zero copula and *be* use frequencies in these sections to her speaking as if speaking to (and on behalf of) her teenage friends and peers.

Whether it is theoretically *necessary* to do so is another matter. One could alternatively appeal to differences in one or more of Finegan and Biber's (1989) situational parameters (for instance, an informational communication purpose for the academic topic versus an interpersonal, affective purpose for the slamming partner topic) to characterize the topic-influenced variation which Foxy displays in these interviews. But it must be admitted that there are theoretical benefits to Bell's approach (the linking of previously unconnected social and stylistic variation), and that it squares with the empirical evidence.

One point which remains to be made before we leave this issue is that whatever vicarious identification with typical but absent addressees various topics might involve, the effect of the actual and present addressees remains stronger. (What we're doing here is essentially returning to 17.2 from a different perspective.) This is evident in the fact that although the race and familiarity of Faye and Roberta elicit more vernacular grammar, Faye's role as an adult and mother appears to lead Foxy to refer to sex allusively and indirectly in interview III (you just *do everything with 'em except that*), while using four-letter words (in quotation) with the younger Beth in interview IV:[40] Note that topic does not override addressee. For all that Foxy talks animatedly about sex and boy–girl relations in interview III, she never uses obscenities with Faye. Contrariwise, even when playing a profane rap song and discussing music and dances with Beth at the end of interview IV, Foxy's zero *is/are* and *be* rates remain low.[41]

6.3.5 Foxy's earlier interviews (1986, 1988)

We have now explored the salient aspects of Foxy's stylistic variation, as influenced by addressee and topic, in interviews III and IV. One could obviously attempt to squeeze other insights from these interviews – by considering phonological variables, for instance, or alternative influences on style shift – but it's more theoretically fruitful to look briefly at Foxy's style levels in her two earlier interviews with Faye and Roberta, as reflected in copula absence and invariant *be* use, the main variables explored in this paper.

The very first interview, which we'll refer to as interview I (= EPA 7, 8), was recorded in 1986, when Foxy was 13. Up to this point, she had been schooled entirely in East Palo Alto, in schools with exclusively or primarily African American populations, and her vernacular usage was at a peak. Interview I lasted about an hour and a half, and in it Foxy used 146 tokens of invariant *be* and exhibited whopping copula absence rates: 79 percent (N = 72) for zero *is*, 99 percent (N = 82) for zero *are*, and 90 percent for zero *is* and *are* combined (N = 154). Although these rates differ somewhat from those in interview III, it is possible to attribute the latter to change over time, especially since the intervening four years represent the teenage years – a period in which, as Eckert (1988) shows, major readjustments in an individual's social identity and linguistic usage can take place. Moreover, interview I, when contrasted with interview IV, still shows significantly higher rates of vernacular usage, and we could attribute the stylistic contrast between them to differences in the race and familiarity of the addressees, as we did in contrasting interviews III and IV above.

However, the second interview, which we'll refer to as interview II (= EPA 42, 43), is another story. This interview, recorded in 1988, when Foxy was 15, was shorter than the other interviews (55 minutes), and in it Foxy used 81 tokens of invariant *be* (= 88 per hour) and exhibited relatively low copula absence rates: 18 percent (N = 48) for zero *is*, 48 percent (N = 46) for zero *are*, and 34 percent (N = 94) for zero *is* and *are* combined. These rates are not significantly different from those in interview IV, when Foxy was addressing Beth, a European American stranger, and they therefore require some explanation.

There are several potential explanations for Foxy's reduced AAVE use in interview II. At this point she had completed her first year at a predominantly European American high school outside the EPA community. She had also taken part in a live-in summer Upward Bound program at Stanford and had been involved in several tutorial, college motivational, and preprofessional programs (Higher Horizons, MESA, TOPS, SASI) which exposed her to consistent Standard English models. We wouldn't want to overestimate the influence of these factors on her language development, but Foxy mentions in interview II that African American students at school are beginning to say that she sounds "like a white person." She does not believe that she does, but she concedes that the extensive contact she's been having with European Americans outside EPA may have had some effect.[42] For all her attempts to rebuff it, Foxy may also have been affected by the apparent prejudice she encountered at her school against her race and community; she talks of schoolmates who say they are forbidden to go to East Palo Alto because "the black people's gonna get us!" and of the school's spirit squad rejecting *all* the African American girls who try out for it. One response to such prejudice might have been a temporary diminution in her distinctively African American language and behavior.[43] By the time Foxy is interviewed again, in 1990, she seems much more secure about her background and identity; she is president of the BSU, has won respect from teachers and students on her own terms, and has seen her African American friend T. crowned as homecoming queen ("We was all happy. . . . All of us was cryin" – interview III). And her language has returned close to the vernacular levels of her early adolescent years.

There are also a number of factors within the interview situation which may have produced the reduced vernacular usage which Foxy exhibits in interview II. For one thing the setting was different. This was the only interview conducted in Faye's home, and neither Faye nor Foxy appears to relax as much as in the interviews conducted at Foxy's. Faye's status as mother and authority figure comes across much more clearly as she attends to household matters, and her role as interview director is much more sharply delineated, as she deploys more prefabricated questions than usual ("If you could pass a message on to a 15-year-old in Nigeria about life in America, what would you tell her to look out for?") and switches abruptly from one topic to another when they fail to elicit much interest ("I see I ain't gettin no information outta y'all 'bout the boys, so I'ma drop that subject"). Foxy does get more excited about some topics – sexuality, teen pregnancies, and teen slang predictably lead to elevated copula absence and invariant *be* rates – but in general she is more subdued and detached than she is in her other interviews with Faye and Roberta, and her reduced AAVE use is very much in keeping with that.

One way of accounting for Foxy's reduced vernacular usage within interview II is to consider it *initiative* style design, which, instead of occurring "in response to a change in the extralinguistic situation . . . itself initiates a change in the situation" (Bell 1984: 182). As in the cases of metaphorical switching discussed by Blom and Gumperz (1972), Foxy's more standard usage might be seen "as a claim to intellectual authority" (Bell 1984) or as a reflection of the fact that, because of her exposure to Stanford and the motivational programs referred to previously, she is now responding to Faye more in terms of her association with this institution than in terms of her race or community membership. It might even be argued that her initiative style shift in this case is partly an instance of "outgroup referee design" (Bell 1984: 188–9) – that she is now more conscious of absent Stanford people who might listen to the interview than she was in interviews I and III. To the extent that Foxy's stylistic level in interview II represents initiative style shift, the most we can do is attempt to interpret it after the fact (cf. Bell 1984: 185).

Despite our extensive discussion of this issue, our purpose is *not* to explain away the unusualness of interview II nor to view it as aberrant. Whatever the stage-of-life, intra-interview, or other factors which made it happen in interview II, Foxy has as much "right" to shift away from the vernacular with familiar African Americans such as Faye and Roberta as she does with unfamiliar European Americans such as Beth. We can't say that Foxy has one fixed register for African Americans and another for European Americans, or that she has one register for familiars and another for nonfamiliars, any more than we might expect anyone *always* to talk to a spouse or workmate in the same way. While these addressee variables do set up some valid expectations about the kind of language that Foxy (or anyone else) might use, we have to allow for the use of style as a resource and strategy, as an interactive and dynamic process (Coupland 1984, Traugott and Romaine 1985) which can vary between different situations, and for the intersecting effects of setting, scene, key, and the other multidimensional factors that Hymes (1972) and others have identified. This recognition may help us account for the fluctuating views of their intersection with style which earlier studies of AAVE variables have yielded (see sec. 6.3.2). It's not enough to say that groups A and B differ significantly with respect to a specific feature and *therefore* we should always expect the feature to display significant style-shifting when addressees from groups A versus B are involved. The features of a dialect are a resource which individuals and groups have some freedom to use as their mood and inclination dictate, although Bell's addressee-based principles do help us to predict in general ways what they are likely to do.

6.4   Summary and Conclusion

We have documented and attempted to explain the decline of intraspeaker or stylistic variation as a focus of research in quantitative sociolinguistics. We suggested that a primary reason for this decline was the fact that investigators found it difficult to separate "careful" from "casual" speech in reliable and objective ways, and that they also found it possible to continue doing quantitative "sociolinguistics" (identifying internal and external constraints on linguistic variation, for instance, or studying ongoing linguistic change) *without* attending to this operationally difficult distinction.

Whether other quantitative sociolinguists will agree with the explanation or not, it is clear that style is too central to the methodological and theoretical concerns of our sub-field for us to neglect it any longer. For one thing, Labov's original assertions that the most informal or peer group-influenced speech offers the clearest view of social differentiation and linguistic change have never been refuted, and in a sub-field where recorded corpora are the primary means of studying such phenomena, the styles represented in such corpora can hardly be ignored. If, for instance, we had used Foxy's copula and third singular -*s* absence rates in interview IV (40 percent and 36 percent, respectively) to assess the nature of current adolescent usage of African American Vernacular English in East Palo Alto, we would have had a very different picture than if we had used her corresponding rates in interview II (70 percent and 73 percent, respectively), leading us to radically different inferences about the nature of regional and gender differences in the dialect and its convergence with or divergence from other ethnic vernaculars.[44] Douglas-Cowie's (1978: 39) motivation for studying addressee-influenced style shifts among villagers in the Northern Irish village of Articlave was also rooted in a methodological concern – "to reveal the possible linguistic limitations of being a well-educated English investigator in a Northern Ireland rural community." Quantitative sociolinguists simply do not discuss these issues these days. We have become almost as bad as generative syntacticians in avoiding critical discussions about our data, making us perhaps as vulnerable to the charge of developing strong theories with weak foundations (cf. Labov 1975).

With respect to theory development, stylistic variation seems to offer more potential for the integration of past findings and the establishment of productive research agendas than virtually any other area in sociolinguistics.[45] This is because of its ubiquity (maybe even universality) and its relation to other central topics within our field, including social or status variation and internal linguistic conditioning, as explored in recent articles by Bell (1984), Finegan and Biber (1994), and Preston (1991). By the same token, quantitative sociolinguistics offers a precision to the study of style shift and accommodation that is unmatched by other approaches (cf. Coupland 1984: 53), and a means of disentangling the effects of internal and external constraints, via the variable rule program, that other approaches could fruitfully adopt. We hope that these benefits have been exemplified in our discussion of Foxy's style-shifting, particularly with respect to copula and third singular -*s* absence.

If quantitative sociolinguistics is to return to the study of style, as we urge, an approach based on the re-recording of speakers with different addressees

(Rickford 1987b) seems most promising, especially if coupled with the theoretical conceptualization of style as audience design which Bell (1984) offers. Several of Bell's hypotheses and predictions about addressee design were confirmed by the data on Foxy's style-shifting examined in this chapter. His predictions about differential accommodation (which variables might be expected to show significant style shift with different classes of addressees and which might not) were generally confirmed, once riders about absolute and relative frequencies of occurrence were added: that low rates (as with possessive and plural *-s* absence) reduce the probability that a variable will figure significantly in style shift, and high rates (as with *be* use in the 1990s) increase that probability. Preston's "status" axiom was also confirmed, along with Bell's "style" axiom.

Bell's hypotheses about the primacy of addressee over topic shift were also confirmed, more or less; more if 30 tokens per cell (Guy 1980) was accepted as a minimum cut-off point, less if cells with slightly fewer tokens were also considered. We were impressed by the dramatic topic shift (17 percent to 72 percent copula absence) which Foxy displayed when talking about "school and career" versus "wives and slamming partners" with Beth in interview IV (recorded in 1991), but we were convinced about the primacy of addressee by the fact that she generally used higher frequencies on each topic when talking to Faye and Roberta in interview III (recorded in 1990).

Bell's hypothesis that speakers shift style when talking on particular topics *as if* talking to addressees whom they associate with that topic was more difficult to investigate empirically, but it seemed to receive some support from the fact that Foxy's most vigorous vernacular usage in both interviews occurred where she was quoting extensively from teenage friends and peer group members, dramatically reenacting their actual and hypothetical conversations. Whether it was theoretically necessary to appeal to Bell's hypothesis to explain the increased vernacular usage in such sections was, however, less clear.

The single greatest challenge to Bell's audience design approach came from consideration of interviews I and II, which Faye and Roberta recorded with Foxy in 1986 and 1988. The former was no problem, since Foxy's style remained closer to the AAVE vernacular than it did in interview IV, as Bell's hypotheses would predict for an African American versus European American addressee. However, Foxy's stylistic level in interview II was *not* significantly closer to the vernacular than in interview IV, and this ran counter to Bell's predictions about responsive addressee style shift. We proposed several possible explanations for this unexpected result, including appeals to Bell's notion of "initiative" style shift (cf. Blom and Gumperz's "metaphorical switching") and consideration of components such as setting, scene, and key (Hymes 1972), which we had previously ignored. However persuasive our arguments, we were clearly engaging in post hoc interpretation by this stage and moving away from the powerful predictions which lie at the heart of Bell's (1984) approach. This may be acceptable, even necessary, for some kinds of stylistic variation, as Bell himself (1984: 185) suggests. But we would urge in closing that sociolinguists who return to or enter into the study of style attempt to push the predictive parts of Bell's model as far as possible, testing them against other data sets, and revising and refining them where necessary. Sociolinguistics needs fewer laissez-faire generalizations and more falsifiable predictions if it is to answer to recent calls for more explicit theory building (Cheshire 1987: 257, Finegan and Biber 1989: 3), and style is one area in which we have already begun to make good progress toward this goal.

Notes

This paper was prepared while the senior author was a Fellow at the Center for Advanced Study in the Behavioral Sciences, at Stanford. The financial support provided by NSF grants BNS-8700864 and BNS-8913104 is gratefully acknowledged. It is a pleasure to acknowledge, too, the assistance and encouragement which we have received from Renée Blake, Daria Ilunga, Rashida Knox, Anakela Rickford and Angela Rickford, and our forbearing families. We would like to thank those who provided feedback on the first draft of this paper, regretting only that we were not always able to incorporate their suggestions or follow their advice: John Baugh, Allan Bell, Doug Biber, Ed Finegan, Nik Coupland, Greg Guy, Dennis Preston, Suzanne Romaine, Elizabeth Closs Traugott, and Malcah Yaeger-Dror. We would also like to thank others who sent relevant papers: Marianna Di Paolo, Barbara Horvath, and Keith Walters.

1 Foxy's father, who does not live with the family, is a construction worker. Her mother, a single parent household head, is a construction planner at a Bay Area aeronautical corporation. "Foxy Boston" is a pseudonym.
2 Dubois and Horvath (1991) approach the issue from another direction, varying not the race of the interviewer, but the race of the interviewee. The questioning strategies of their Anglo interviewers in Sydney, Australia, turned out to be significantly different with Greek, Italian, and Anglo/Celtic interviewees. Their conclusion that "the negotiation of tension is most easily achieved when both members of the interview come from the same culture" (MS., 11) parallels the finding of Terrell et al. (1977: 381) that "speaking to one's own ethnic group has a facilitating effect on both the total number of words used and the complexity of the sentences used." These experimental results do not of course imply that same-race interviewers will always have a facilitating effect nor that different-race interviewers will never have a facilitating effect.
3 Of course several individual sociolinguists – Labov (1972e), Baugh (1979), Irvine . (1979, 1985), Biber (1988), to name only a few – have provided important theoretical or empirical studies of stylistic or intraspeaker variation, but the major focus of attention in the United States has been on intergroup variation – by socioeconomic class, ethnicity, sex/gender, and age. In this respect, one might say that the (partial) roots of American sociolinguistics in dialect geography have remained

evident, with social groups replacing geographical regions as the primary external variable.

4   See, however, Biber (1988), who emphasizes that a multidimensional perspective is essential to adequate analyses of register (or style) variation.

5   The diminution in American quantitativist studies of stylistic variation had started since the mid-1970s, but as shown by the published proceedings of recent NWAVE conferences (for instance, Denning et al. 1987, Ferrare et al. 1988), or the new variationist journal, *Language Variation and Change*, it is really marked from the mid-1980s on, since variationist papers in these and subsequent publications contain little or no reference to style.

6   However, some researchers – for instance, Tarone (1985), Di Paolo (1992), and Yaeger-Dror (1991) – have continued to make productive use of a Labovian-like distinction between relatively monitored and unmonitored or prescriptive and vernacular styles, involving attention paid to speech. Yaeger-Dror (1991) distinguishes terminologically between "attention-related 'style' and target-related 'register'."

7   Nikolas Coupland (personal communication) notes additional evidence in this regard, from recent research in Wales conducted by one of his students, Penny Rowlands, on stylistic variation in young children's speech, especially in relation to addressee effects over different ages: "One point to emerge very clearly in her work is that 'reading aloud' does have truly generic characteristics in that kids quickly learn prosodic and, it seems, segmental phonological conventions for doing it."

8   Labov has noted (personal communication) that his decision to use group recordings in Harlem was directly influenced by the successful use which Gumperz had made of this technique in Hemnesberget, Norway, as reported in Gumperz (1964) and elsewhere.

9   The distinction between situational and metaphorical switching – although in practice often involving change of addressee and topic, respectively – is theoretically more complex. The former "involves clear changes in the participants' definition of each other's rights and obligation," while the latter does not involve "any significant change in definition of participants' mutual rights and obligations," but usually occurs in situations which "allow for the enactment of two or more different relationships among the same set of individuals" (Blom and Gumperz 1972: 424–5). Dennis Preston (personal communication) restates it as follows: "Situational shifting occurs when a change exploits the range of options predicted by the linguistic, status, and style boundaries of an interaction. Metaphoric shift occurs when such shift occurs outside this predictability . . . it is an exploitation of the unexpected."

10 This was not true of the studies by Baugh, Hindle, Payne, and Rickford, whose dissertations were supervised by Labov.

11 Exceptions include Milroy (1987), Wilson (1987), Finegan and Biber (1994), and Preston (1991). Bell himself (personal communication) offers the following comment: "I guess if I am disappointed in anything about the lack of follow-up on audience design it is the lack of theoretical building on or critique of it rather than of empirical studies within the framework (although the two are probably linked)."

12 Bell notes (personal communication) that the question of whether speakers style shift in reaction to the general persona of their interlocutors or in relation to their

specific linguistic performance was first raised by Coupland (1981, 1984) before he picked it up. For a subsequent and more detailed analysis of the motivations for code-switching, see Coupland (1985).

13 As Labov (1972d: 52) notes, in discussing the importance of the feedback principle, the more an interviewer knows when talking about a topic, the more interviewees are likely to tell you: "Once he [the investigator] has entered far enough into the subject to ask an 'insider's question,' he will obtain richer results." Gossip, of course, exemplifies the principle perfectly.

14 All variables were tabulated in accordance with Labov's (1969: 738, 1972e: 72) accountability principle, which requires the observer to report the actual occurrences of a variant against the total of all the possible cases in which it might have occurred, excluding categorical or indeterminate contexts (see notes 15 and 16).

15 In the case of possessive, plural, and third person singular -*s* absence, tokens followed by a word beginning with *s* (as in "John's son") were not counted, since these make it difficult to tell whether the inflectional -*s* is present or not.

16 The list of "don't count" cases excluded from consideration in the analysis of copula absence is quite large (see Labov et al. 1968, Wolfram 1969, Rickford et al. 1991, Blake 1997), but they include the following cases in which the variable is either categorical or indeterminate: clause-finals; tokens under primary stress; instances of "what's," "that's," or "it's"; negatives; tokens of *is* preceded or followed by *s*; tokens of *are* followed by *r*.

17 In the case of invariant *be*, for which we have absolute rather than relative frequency data (see section 6.3.2.3), significance was calculated on the per hour rate of *be* use.

18 As noted by Rickford (1992), the relative rarity of nominal possessives in speech has been a problem for most studies of AAVE.

19 In response to this point, Suzanne Romaine (personal communication) has raised some interesting questions about the differences between production and perception and between statistical and other kinds of significance. We do not as yet have definitive answers but think her remarks on this issue are worth quoting in full: "This point raises a question that hasn't been addressed in the literature on style shifting: How much of a difference is significant in terms of *perception* by the listener? One needs to know this to determine if the variable is being used symbolically in a successful way. Tests of statistical significance only indicate *production*-related differences."

20 Of course, we also know that even a single occurrence of a stereotyped, salient (Trudgill 1986), or strongly marked feature can be enough to register a style shift, or to mark its user as speaking in a special (preferred or dispreferred) style. See Gumperz's (1983) discussion of the student who said "Ahma git me a gig," and note the following quote from Reggie, an African American teenager (cited in Rickford 1992): "Over at my school, if they – first time they catch you talkin' white, they'll never let it go. Even if you just quit talking like that, they'll never let it go!" (EPA50: A530–2). Finally, Allan Bell (personal communication) notes that in his analyses of initiative style shift in media language, "rare variants are all the more valuable just because of their rarity. Just one token can act as a marker of identity." Together these "counterexamples" to the proposed frequency rider indicate that one task for a theory of style is to determine in a principled and

predictable way the difference between rare but stylistically salient variables and rare and nonsalient ones.

21 However, it could be argued that the difference is, in this case, *qualitatively* interesting, insofar as Foxy *never* omits plural *-s* in interview IV.

22 Foxy's plural absence rate, when she was first interviewed in 1986, was 13 percent (14/107), so she has become more standard in the interim. This is also true of her copula absence rate; see section 6.3.5.

23 Le Page and Tabouret-Keller's (1985) "Acts of Identity" model, which treats linguistic behavior "as a series of acts of identity in which people reveal both their personal identity and their search for social roles" (14), is admirable in several respects, but it tends to slight or ignore internal constraints in favor of external or sociopsychological ones.

24 The difference *was* significant for percentage of [*d*]-deletion but not for cluster simplification, the other variables discussed with respect to race-of-interviewer effects (ibid.).

25 As Baugh notes (1979: 106–8), the familiarization process does not proceed uniformly for all individuals; some, like David W., became familiar with the interviewer and used vernacular styles relatively rapidly; others, like James D., remained suspicious for a longer period and took correspondingly longer to begin using his vernacular.

26 Baugh (1979) states it more generally: "The adults under analysis therefore consistently altered their speech toward SE in the presence of people with whom they were newly acquainted, regardless of their race." But since Baugh was the principal interviewer in each case, and non-African Americans were only present in peripheral roles in some of his interviews, the statement should not be taken to imply that variation by race of *addressee* is unimportant.

27 In addition to the factor groups in table 6.4, we also considered the effect of the preceding and following phonological environment, but these turned out to be nonsignificant.

28 The particular model we used is the logistic model (ibid.), in which "values above .500 favor the rule, values of less than .500 disfavor the rule and a value of .500 means a constraint has no effect" (Fasold 1978: 93).

29 In table 6.4, as in table 6.1, copula absence is calculated as "straight deletion" – the proportion of zero copulas against the total of all zero, contracted, and full forms, excluding "don't count" cases (see note 16). See Rickford et al. (1991) for further discussion of "straight deletion" and for comparison with "Labov deletion," which calculates the proportion of zero copulas against the total of zero and contracted forms only, for reasons outlined in Labov (1969). Although space prevents us from presenting all the results, we have in fact made "Labov deletion" runs for interviews III and IV; these modify the significance and ordering of some of the internal factors but do not affect the external factor (addressee-based style shift) under consideration. Interviews III and IV have input probabilities of .73 and .44 in separate "Labov deletion" runs; in the pooled (III + IV) interview run, they remain sharply differentiated as factors within a factor group, with associated factor weights of .74 and .26, respectively.

30 The only differences are in the following grammatical factor group, where minor differences from the usual ordering and from each other are shown.

31   The percentage and raw frequency data at the bottom of table 6.4 are based on the
      copula absence data prior to the removal of knockout (categorical) factors. The
      coefficients are taken from the variable rule runs containing only the significant
      factor groups.

32   Note that the data in the "Interview III + IV" column of table 6.4 confirm
      Preston's (1991: 36) prediction, since the range and limits of two of the three
      internal factors (FOLLOWING GRAMMATICAL = .21–.90, SUBJECT = .26–
      .83) exceed the range and limits of the single external variable (INTERVIEW =
      .28–.72). Dennis Preston (personal communication) has made the following addi-
      tional observation about these data: "Foxy's data here show that her stylistic
      performance (.28–.72) . . . is contained within the variation space for age within
      her speech community (.22–.83, as presented in Rickford et al. 1991: 117, table 6;
      and cited in Preston 1991: 40, table 5). This suggests that Foxy's 'models' for
      speech behavior, although perhaps triggered by audience factors, need not have
      been derived from the audience of interview IV since her own speech community
      (namely older speakers) provide a score (.22) which could predict her performance
      in setting IV (.28)."

33   To make it consistent with the data of table 6.4, tables 6.5 and 6.6 consider the ratio
      of deleted forms to full, contracted, and deleted forms (=Rickford et al.'s 1992
      "straight deletion"). Although Labov et al. claim (191) that "the feature which is
      correlated with style shift from single to group sessions is the ratio of deleted to
      originally contracted forms – that is, $D/D + C$" ("Labov deletion" in our terms),
      these alternative computations do not significantly affect their argument. The
      "straight deletion" data in fact support their claims about older/younger style-
      shifting differences better than the "Labov deletion" data do.

34   It should be noted that the data in tables 6.5 and 6.6 are not completely comparable
      because the number of forms and subjects represented in each group sometimes
      changes from one table to the other. For instance, the single style figure for the
      Cobras in table 6.5 is based on 230 tokens from eleven subjects, while the single
      style figure for the Cobras in table 6.6 is based on 141 tokens from nine subjects.

35   For analysis of constraints on variation between *say*, *go*, and *be like* as quotative
      introducers in American English, see Blyth et al. 1990.

36   For shorthand we say "interviewers' usage" in the table 6.8 title but Roberta was
      of course a cointerviewee rather than an interviewer in interviews I, II, and III.

37   Of course, there's a certain amount of mutual accommodation – Roberta and
      Faye's accommodating to Foxy, and vice versa (cf. Coupland 1984: 54) – but in the
      absence of independent data on Roberta and Faye's (or Beth's) speech in other
      contexts, we can't measure the extent of *their* accommodation, and our focus is, in
      any case, on *Foxy's* style shifts.

38   Since the invariant habitual *be* data are absolute rather than relative, they have
      no bearing on this issue; the overall "addressee" difference between interviews III
      and IV (290 tokens) will always exceed the maximum topic shift within either
      interview.

39   As Bell (personal communication) notes: "This is very much what I would regard
      as an initiative use of language: Deliberate declaring of an ingroup identity."

40   At the end of interview IV, Foxy also plays a rap song called "Bitches" for Beth,
      which, by Foxy's own admission, is extremely "profane."

41 One could also point to the fact that when Foxy's copula absence for equivalent topics in interviews III and IV is compared, it is higher in interview III than in interview IV (e.g., 76 percent versus 39 percent for race relations), but the status of these comparisons is questionable insofar as none of them passes the minimum 30-token requirement in both interviews.

42 Foxy returns to this theme in 1991 in interview IV, observing that "When I get home, I use slang and everything; when I'm at school, I talk different," and that friends still accuse her of "talking like a white girl." It appears that the latter impression might derive primarily from her phonology, from her adoption of some of the distinctive characteristics of European American pronunciation in the area.

43 And an interview with Beth or any other European American, at the time, might have shown even lower rates of vernacular usage than Faye and Roberta elicited, posing no problem for Bell's hypothesis (11).

44 There is every reason to believe that the problem would remain whether we used individual or group data, as long as we did not measure and take into account the addressee/interviewer effect.

45 See Eckert and Rickford (in press) for an updated theoretical and empirical discussion of style in sociolinguistic variation, including papers by several of the key figures cited in this article: Allan Bell, Nik Coupland, Ed Finegan and Doug Biber, Judith Irvine, and William Labov.

Part II
Evolution

7

Cut-Eye *and* Suck-Teeth*: African Words and Gestures in New World Guise*

(with Angela E. Rickford)

In the New World, things African are usually associated with the unusual and the exotic. Thus *cumfa*, with its frenzied drumming, would seem a natural candidate for inclusion in any list of African "survivals." So also would a folktale or folksong which included several lines of obscure incantation. Or a word which made use of very un-English phonotactics, like *kpoli*, or was matched against a more standard equivalent (*nyam* versus *eat*).

Our suspicions would be particularly aroused if the cultural or linguistic item were rarely used, if, for instance, we "got" it for the first and only time from the aging grandchild of some erstwhile slave, now living an isolated life far from the masses of the people. For academics and laymen alike, it is of such stuff that true New World Africanisms are made.

In keeping with this pattern of intuition and reasoning, we never attached any historical significance to *cut-eye* and *suck-teeth*. The gestures to which these refer are performed daily in our native Guyana by all kinds of people, in urban center and rural area alike. And the compounds we use to describe them could hardly be more ordinary, composed as they are of simple English words – *cut*, *eye*, *suck*, and *teeth*. With such unpromising clues to go by, it is hardly surprising that we used them everyday without giving any thought to their source.

However, while doing graduate work in Philadelphia in 1971, we happened to notice a curious division between American Whites and Blacks with respect to these very gestures. While the Blacks would "cut their eyes" and "suck their teeth" in much the same way that people did in our native community, Whites apparently never did, and were often ignorant of the meanings of these gestures when they were directed at them.

On the basis of this chance observation, we began to consider the possibility that both the gestures and the words we used to describe them might represent African "survivals," and we began to study more systematically the extent to which they were used and recognized across three broad areas: the Caribbean, the United States, and Africa. This paper reports on the results of this investigation.

We shall first briefly describe the methods we used to obtain data on these areas and then summarize the findings for *cut-eye* and *suck-teeth* under separate headings. In the conclusion, we discuss some of the larger implications and research directions which grew out of our research.

7.1   Method

Data on the use of *cut-eye* and *suck-teeth* in the Caribbean area were obtained from several sources. For the detailed physical and ethnographic descriptions of the gestures in Guyana we drew mainly on our own observations and experience, supported by comments and criticisms from fellow Guyanese. For other areas in the West Indies, we first consulted available dictionaries and glossaries,[1] then carried out our own interviews with several West Indians, representing Antigua, Barbados, Haiti, Jamaica, Trinidad, and St Kitts.

Data from the United States are based on original fieldwork conducted by the authors. Within the framework of a questionnaire designed to explore linguistic and cultural differences between black and white Americans, we asked the following question:[2]

> Now we want to consider some things that people say and use a lot. Do you know
> what the following things mean (in terms of the actions and "social significance"):
> (1)   To "cut your eyes" on someone _____
> (2)   To "suck your teeth" _____

In each case, the informant was asked to give a physical demonstration and to discuss the meaning freely. A corpus of 70 American informants was interviewed, in Philadelphia, Boston, and New York. Thirty-five of these were Black, and 35 were White. Within each group, there were 18 males and 17 females. Informants represented a diverse range of native geographical backgrounds, including Pennsylvania, New York, California, Alabama, Georgia, Illinois, and Massachusetts.

Our African data were limited by the small number of accessible informants, and by the fact that so few dictionaries of African languages had entries classified in terms of English. Nevertheless, among students at the University of Pennsylvania and in Guyana, we managed to locate speakers of the following languages: Twi, Temne, Mende, Igbo, Yoruba, Swahili, Luo, Banyang, Krio, and Cameroon Pidgin. They were first asked if they were familiar with the gestures, and then asked to provide data on their use and equivalent terms from their native languages if any existed.

7.2 *Cut-Eye*

In Guyana, *cut-eye* is a visual gesture which communicates hostility, displeasure, disapproval, or a general rejection of the person at whom it is directed. The very existence of a well-known term for this particular gesture indicates its centrality in the wide range of gestures in the culture, not all of which have comparable verbal labels.

The basic *cut-eye* gesture is initiated by directing a hostile look or glare in the other person's direction. This may be delivered with the person directly facing, or slightly to one side. In the latter position, the person is seen out of the corners of the eyes, and some people deliberately turn their bodies sideways to achieve this effect. After the initial glare, the eyeballs are moved in a highly coordinated and controlled movement down or diagonally across the line of the person's body. This "cut" with the eyes is the heart of the gesture, and may involve the single downward movement described above, or several sharp up-and-down movements. Both are generally completed by a final glare, and then the entire head may be turned away contemptuously from the person, to the accompaniment of a loud *suck-teeth*. See figure 7.1 for the main stages of this sequence.

Part of the effectiveness of a *cut-eye* as a visual "put-down" lies in its violation of what Goffman (1972) has called the "information preserve" of the individual, one of his important "territories of the self." The information preserve is "the set of facts about himself to which an individual expects to control access while in the presence of others" (39), including "what can be directly perceived about an individual, his body's sheath and his current behaviour, the issue here being his right *not to be stared at or examined* (our emphasis)." As Goffman goes on to point out, since staring constitutes an invasion of informational preserve, it can then be used as "a warranted negative sanction against somebody who has misbehaved" (61).

A *cut-eye* provides even more of a "negative sanction," since one not only invades, but with the eyes, rummages up, down, and about in another's preserve. It is as if the recipient has no power to prevent this visual assault, the very fact that someone else's eyes can run right over him like this proclaiming his worthlessness. The "cut" is made even deeper when the eyes are finally turned away – the implication here being that the victim is not even worth further attention.

This kind of visual "put-down" or "cut-down" comes to the fore in "buseings" or fierce arguments between two or more protagonists, especially between women. The argument is waged as much with words as with eyes, each protagonist "cutting up the eyes" on the other in a threatening and belligerent fashion. But there may not be any verbal argument at all. In any situation where one wishes to censure, or challenge someone else, or convey

Figure 7.1   Sequence of movements in a *cut-eye*. Note accompanying *suck-teeth* (in this case, closure is made with the tongue against the alveolar ridge).

to him that he is not admired or respected, a *cut-eye* may be conveniently employed.

Thus an old woman rebuking an eight-year-old for hitting her younger brother on the street might receive a *cut-eye* from the child (challenging her authority to intervene) in response. Similarly, a male who whistles at a female may be met with a cold *cut-eye* suggesting that she does not appreciate this form of greeting, and that he fails to win her interest or favor. In both these cases, the recipient is guilty of some infringement of what the sender considers his "rights," and the provocation for the *cut-eye* is clear (whether others consider it justified or appropriate is another matter).

Sometimes however, the "misbehavior" which earns someone a *cut-eye* is not as obvious on the surface. The recipient need not have said or done anything to the person who directs the gesture to him. But there is something in the way he dresses, looks, or behaves, which, while not necessarily intended, rubs someone else the "wrong way." This is particularly true if others around interpret the situation as one in which the recipient is trying to "show off." If, for instance, someone drives up in a big new car or arrives at a party in expensive clothes on the arm of a well-known figure, others around might cut their eyes on that person as a way of suggesting that they are not really impressed. The *cut-eye* is a way of saying "you're no big thing at all, not to my mind at least."

In fact, however, it frequently is the case that the recipient *is* someone in a situation which many people, including the sender, respect and envy. Thus, while the gesture might express genuine resentment and dislike, it is some-times an attempt to nullify the appeal of another's attributes or circumstances when these are precisely what the sender would like to have. This is clearer when the sense in which people also talk of cutting their eyes on *something* is considered. A woman who sees a prohibitively expensive dress in a store window might report to her friends that she had to "cut her eyes" on it and walk away. The phrase is used here to symbolize a rejection of something one would really like to have, but cannot or should not, because of personal circumstance.

The gesture of *cut-eye* is performed most frequently (and most skillfully!) by women. Men do not use this gesture as often and may experience real difficulty in trying to imitate the darting, highly coordinated movement which women can control. The gesture is often used when the other party in an encounter, conversation, or dispute, is enjoying his "turn" to talk, and may prompt the latter to interrupt his turn to give a more powerful *cut-eye* or some form of verbal retort in return. One common verbal retort is "Look, *cut-eye* na a kill daag" ("*Cut-eye* doesn't kill dogs"). This acknowledges that an invasion or affront has been made but attempts to vindicate the recipient by claiming that it can do him or her no bodily harm.[3]

Another pattern can be seen in a turn-of-the-century description (McTurk 1881) of a classic type of court dispute. In the course of giving his testimony, the complainant notices that the defendant has "cut his eye" on him. He interrupts his testimony to ask, "A who you a cut you yiye pon?" ("Who are you cutting your eyes on?"), to which the defendant simply replies, "you see um" (which is roughly equivalent to "If the shoe fits, wear it!"). In this particular incident, the exchange was followed by further verbal provocation and retort which is often called "shotting" or "rhyming" in Guyana, "talking broad" or "rhyming" (Abrahams 1972) in other Caribbean territories.

The physical and ethnographic account of *cut-eye* given above still does not tell the whole story, but we have attempted to make it reasonably detailed, partly because of the limited data available on patterns of nonverbal communication generally, and also because we hope it might be more easily recognizable elsewhere by other researchers. As we ourselves discovered since beginning this study, it is certainly known and used in other parts of the Caribbean. The term is listed in the *Dictionary of Jamaican English* (Cassidy and Le Page 1967: 13) for what is clearly the same gesture with the same meaning:[4]

> *Cut-Eye*: to catch (someone or something) with the eyes, then quickly close them and turn or toss the eyes aside. The purpose of the action may be to avoid temptation . . . but it is usually directed against another person . . . and is usually insulting.

The editors also add that the action may combine insult and temptation into provocation, and they cite (ibid.) the following definition from Miss Joyce Nation:

> To cut one's eyes is to toss one's head away from a man's glance in a contemptuous but sexually provoking fashion: Little girl to a little boy, "You come a me yard" (cutting her eyes) "come if you name man."[5]

While this "provocative" use of *cut-eye* is also found in Guyana, it is usually distinguished from the more hostile use of the gesture in very subtle ways, involving different privileges of co-occurrence with other paralinguistic features or "kinesic markers" (cf. Birdwhistell 1970). The difference may reside in nothing more than whether the *cut-eye* is accompanied by a slight smile, or by a *suck-teeth*, and sometimes males misread the meaning of a female's *cut-eye*, to their own embarrassment.

The term, the gesture, and its meaning, as discussed above were all instantly recognized by the various West Indians whom we interviewed. From Karl Reisman (personal communication), we also learned that it can be frequently observed in Antigua. A Haitian informant provided a dramatic demonstration of the gesture as soon as it was mentioned and explained that it was known in Haiti as *couper yeux* – literally "to cut (or cutting) the eyes." We find it very striking that the Haitian expression for this gesture should consist of morphemes which literally refer to *cut* and *eye*. The same phenomenon may be observed in Saramaccan (example provided by Ian Hancock): *a ta koti woyo* – "she's cutting eye." These examples seem to suggest different New World relexifications of an expression which existed either in one or more African languages or in a Proto-Pidgin, and which included morphemes for *cut* and *eye*. We will return to this point briefly when considering the data from African languages.

The results of our questionnaire investigation of familiarity with *cut-eye* in the United States were more dramatic than we expected. As table 7.1 indicates, almost all the black informants were familiar with the term. Among the "meanings" volunteered were "a look of disgust"; "expression of hostility"; "to threaten"; "act of defiance or disapproval"; "bad feelings"; "when you're mad at someone"; "to show you don't like somebody." All the black women understood the term and were able to perform the gesture easily and expertly.

Two of the black men were not familiar with the term. The other sixteen, although clearly aware of the meaning of the gesture, could not execute it as skillfully as their female counterparts, and they kept excusing themselves by saying, "Mostly women do that." As we have noted above, this situation is paralleled in the Caribbean. Some of the men felt it would be a "cop-out" for a man to keep using this gesture to express his feelings – physical or verbal expression ("sounding") would be the more masculine thing to do. Barring this, one should simply "keep one's cool" – remain silent, apparently unperturbed.

As table 7.1 also indicates, *cut-eye* as a lexical item and as a cultural form of behavior is almost totally unknown to white Americans. Only four of the 35 white informants displayed familiarity with the term. Of these, three said "to stare at someone," and one suggested "to look at someone out of the corner of the eye." These are good descriptions of the initial stage of the gesture, but not

Table 7.1   Number of American informants familiar with *cut-eye* according to race and sex

Sex		Blacks		Whites
Males	(n = 18)	16	(n = 18)	2
Females	(n = 17)	17	(n = 17)	2
Total	(n = 35)	33	(n = 35)	4

of the complete sequence. And in none of the cases could a white informant execute the full gesture.

Sixteen Whites plainly admitted that they had never heard the term before and had no idea of its meaning. The other 15 in the sample provided idiosyncratic and highly varied responses: "expression of religious ecstasy"; "to go to sleep on someone"; "to stop looking at someone"; "expression of horror"; "to look at someone attractively for a long time." This sharp divergence between the responses of Blacks and Whites is all the more revealing because many of the black informants were middle-class individuals completing their college education and might otherwise be considered highly acculturated to the mainstream American culture.

Some of the black informants mentioned that "rolling the eyes" is sometimes used instead of "cutting the eyes" in black American communities to refer to the very same gesture. This is confirmed in Kenneth Johnson's (1971: 17–20) description of "rolling the eyes" among American Blacks, which accords with our own description of *cut-eye* in Guyana on several points. Unless it omits certain details, however, the following description from another researcher (Cooke 1972) would suggest that the physical movements involved in "rolling the eyes" might be slightly different:

> If a girl in a lounge does not want to be bothered when a cat comes up to rap, she might lift up one shoulder slightly, rolling her eyes upward in her head as though saying, "what a drag!"

Whether or not this is the case, note that the meaning and usage of the gesture still register dislike, disapproval, or hostility. The fact that the general public usually associates "rolling the eyes" with ingratiation and "Uncle Tom" behavior (an image partly propagated by television and the cinema) suggests that Blacks might have endowed the gesture with a systematic ambiguity which they exploited to permit safe and subtle expression of their more genuine feelings. As we shall see later, *suck-teeth* can be similarly used with a strategic ambiguity.

Before presenting the results of our research on *cut-eye* with African informants, we feel a few remarks are in order. Several scholars have attempted to pinpoint the African languages which, for various historical reasons, may be assumed to have had the greatest influence on the New World pidgins and creoles. The lists are somewhat different from one scholar to another, and the relative importance of particular languages (like Wolof) is a matter of some dispute.[6]

The absence of universal agreement in this area is sometimes problematic. When considering possible etymologies for New World forms, it can be difficult to determine which languages must be examined and what weight must be assigned to the evidence of one language as against another. However, this problem is not always as critical as it might seem, because as many observers have noted (Alleyne 1971: 175; Hancock 1971: 652), many New World Africanisms go back to generalized features of West Africa, even of sub-saharan Africa as a whole. Given the multiplicity of areas from which slaves were taken, it is easy to see why this might have been so. "Survivals" were more likely to occur if they were supported by the common experience of Africans from several areas and tribal affiliations, rather than restricted to a single group.

We cannot claim to have exhausted all the "key" languages in the lists referred to above. However, the picture which emerges from the languages for which we do have data is that the concept of a *cut-eye* or *suck-teeth* gesture is familiar in several areas of both West and East Africa, and it is described by a verbal label in many of the languages spoken there.

The Mende, Banyang, and Luo examples make use of morphemes with the literal meaning of "cutting the eyes" or "sucking the teeth," and thus provide the kind of models we would need to classify our New World compounds as straight cases of loan-translation. However, we are in no position to claim that any one of these provided a particular immediate source. Neither Banyang (a "minor" language spoken in Cameroon) nor Luo (an East Coast language) are normally rated as "key" languages where the business of seeking etymologies for New World forms is concerned. Mende certainly is a "key" language in this sense, but several others for which we do not have data may provide equally plausible prototypes for loan-translation. The whole point of our discussion is that all this is not crucial. We shall probably never know which language or languages provided the immediate source; wherever the particular description of "cutting the eyes" may have come from, it received support from the fact that what it referred to was familiar everywhere.

All of the African informants with whom we talked, for instance, recognized the *cut-eye* gesture immediately. They provided the following equivalent expressions:

TWI:	*obu ma ni kyi* – "He breaks the backs of the eye on me."[7]
YORUBA:	*mólójú* – "making expressions with your eyes to show disapproval."[8] R. Abraham (1958: 423–42) also lists *mǫ́nlójú* cross-referenced to *mǫn* (D. 2) under which the following items are listed: (I) *ó mǫ́njú* – "he looked away contemptuously." (II) *ó mǫ́n mi lójú* – "he looked at me in scorn." (III) *àwòmǫn ' jú* – "a scornful look."
CAMEROON PIDGIN:	*no kɔt yɔ ai fɔ mi* – "Don't cut your eye on me."
BANYANG:	*a kpot a mek ne me* – "She cut her eyes on me."
LUO:	*kik ilokna wangi* – "he is cutting his eyes."
SWAHILI:	*usinioloka macho* – "to roll one's eyes."

The last two languages provide an interesting comparison. They are both spoken in Kenya, Swahili as the more widespread and better known East African lingua franca. The terms in Luo and Swahili correspond to the two American variants: to "cut" and to "roll" the eyes respectively. Data from other languages may provide other possible sources for the alternation between these terms.

7.3 Suck-Teeth

Suck-teeth refers to the gesture of drawing air through the teeth and into the mouth to produce a loud sucking sound. In the basic *suck-teeth* gesture, the back of the tongue is raised toward the soft palate and a vacuum created behind a closure formed in the front part of the mouth. This closure may be made with the lower lip against the upper teeth (as in figure 7.2), or with the tip or blade of the tongue just behind the upper teeth, on the alveolar ridge (as in figure 7.1, although not clearly seen). When the closure is suddenly relaxed, air outside the mouth rushes in audibly.

The gesture is accomplished by the same velaric ingressive mechanism used to produce the "clicks" of Khoisan and Southern Bantu languages (Ladefoged 1967; Westerman and Ward 1957). The differences lie mainly in the fact that the closure for "clicks" may be formed at several other points in the mouth, and that while "clicks" are stops – produced by one sharp release of the closure, a *suck-teeth* is more like a prolonged fricative – after the closure is relaxed, air continues to rush in turbulently through the narrow opening.

There are all kinds of minor variations in the way the gesture is produced. It can be made with the lips tensely pouted, or with them spread out, or pulled to one side. There are variations in the duration and intensity of the sound produced depending on the tightness of the closure and the pressure of the

Figure 7.2   A *suck-teeth* made with the inner surface of the lower lip pressed against the upper teeth.

inrushing air. These variations depend to some extent on personal habit, but are governed also by the situation – how angry one is, whether one is in a place (like a church) or in company (a circle of parents' friends) in which a loud *suck-teeth* might be frowned on. In general however, the longer and louder the *suck-teeth*, the more forceful and expressive its "meaning."

Suck-teeth, also known in Guyana and the Caribbean as *stchoops* (*-teeth*) or *chups* (*-teeth*), is an expression of anger, impatience, exasperation or annoyance. It shares some of the semantics of *cut-eye* and, as mentioned before, is often used in combination with the latter. It can be more open and powerful however, and it is considered ill-mannered in certain situations. For instance, while people of all ages do it when something annoys them or someone makes them angry, its use by children in the presence of their parents or other adults is considered rude and insubordinate. As Cruickshank (1916: 50) noted: "A sulking child is told sharply, 'Wha you suck you teeth fo?' . . . With eyes lowered and lips pouting, it pictures disgust, discontent – rebellion with the lid on."

The prohibitions against the use of this gesture are sometimes justified by the claim that it means "kiss my ass" or "kiss my private parts." This meaning may have become attached to it because of the close resemblance between the sound made in producing a *suck-teeth* and the sound sometimes made for "calling off" a girl on the street. This latter sound is made with pouted lips (the teeth not involved as articulators), and is supposed to represent a forceful kiss (among other things). It has much cruder sexual connotations than other ways of attracting a girl's attention (like whistling, or saying *pssssss*), and these seem to be attached also to the *suck-teeth* sound.

To avoid actually sucking the teeth in situations where it might be considered vulgar or ill-mannered, people sometimes say the words *stchoops* or *chups* without making the sound itself. Other interjections like *cha*, *cho*, or *shoots* may also be used, and children in particular will purse or pout their lips as if preparing to make a *suck-teeth*, but again, without making any audible sound. The advantage of this latter strategy is that it can be carried out behind the back of a reproachful adult without fear of discovery or reprimand.

Interviews with informants from Jamaica, Trinidad, Barbados, Antigua, and even Haiti (where, we understand, it is sometimes referred to as *tuiper* or *cuiper*) confirmed familiarity with this oral gesture, its meaning, and the social prohibitions against its use as outlined above. In Antigua, according to Karl Reisman (personal communication), *stchoops* to describe the action of sucking one's teeth is convergent with the word for "stupid," and the ambiguity is well exploited ("Wuh yuh *stchoopsin* yuh teeth fuh? Yuh *stchoops* or wuh?"). This reinforces the negative social connotations of the gesture.

The West Indian dictionaries and glossaries all contain some reference to *suck-teeth* or the alternate terms *stchoops* and *chups*. The *Dictionary of Jamaican English* defines *suck-teeth* as "a sound of annoyance, displeasure, ill nature or disrespect (made) by sucking air audibly through the teeth and over the tongue." (Cassidy and Le Page 1967: 428) Rodman (1971: 235) refers to it as an "expression of disdain or mild disgust," and gives as an example of its usage: "When I suggested that she visit them, she said *stchoops*."

Collymore (1970: 30–1) writing on Barbados, describes it as indicative of distrust or sulking, but attempts also a more detailed classification of the different kinds of *chupses* or *suck-teeth* which is worth reprinting:

> (i) the *chupse* of "amused tolerance," used in retort to some absurd remark or statement, a sort of oral shrugging of the shoulders; (ii) the *chupse* "self-admonitory" when the chupser has done something of which he has no occasion to be proud; (iii) the *chupse* "disdainful," accompanied by a raising of the eyebrow; (iv) the *chupse* "disgusted," in the performance of which the eyebrows are almost closed; (v) the *chupse* "sorrowful," in reality a series of quickly emitted chupses, the head being shaken slowly from side to side; (vi) the *chupse* "offensive and abusive"; (vii) the *chupse* "provocative," a combination of (iii), (iv) and (vi) which often leads to blows.

This description certainly seems to justify the statement, attributed by Collymore (ibid.) to the lead-writer of the *Barbados Advocate*, that "the *chupse* is not a word, it is a whole language . . . the passport to confidence from Jamaica to British South America."

The immediately preceding statement appears, however, to have set too closely the northern limits of the area in which *chupse* or *suck-teeth* is known. This is clear from table 7.2, which reveals that many black Americans are also familiar with it.

If we compare table 7.2 with table 7.1, it is clear that black Americans are slightly less familiar with *suck-teeth* than with *cut-eye* (nine persons who recog-

Table 7.2   Number of American informants familiar with *suck-teeth* according to race
and sex

Sex		Blacks		Whites
Males	(n = 18)	10	(n = 18)	0
Females	(n = 17)	14	(n = 17)	1
Total	(n = 35)	24	(n = 35)	1

nized the latter failed to recognize the former). But the recognition rate is still
quite high (68.5 percent), with the black females again slightly in the lead.[9]
Among the "meanings" given by black informants were: "when disgusted";
"act of defiance, disapproval"; "sign of frustration"; "impatience"; "to show
disappointment."

What is particularly striking about table 7.2, however, is that only *one* white
American, a woman, was familiar with *suck-teeth*. Twenty-six of the white
informants did not even attempt to suggest possible meanings, and the eight
who did were far off the intended track: "to shut up"; "to stammer"; "to
express that you like food"; "after eating to clean teeth." This last "meaning"
was suggested by four informants, and in fact is the only one given for "sucking
the teeth" in the *Oxford English Dictionary*. Under entry 10b for the verb *suck*
is listed: "to apply one's tongue and inner sides of the lips to (one's teeth) so as
to extract particles of food."

Now while West Indians rarely speak of "sucking the teeth" in this
"Standard English" sense, they sometimes use it as a cover or excuse for the
everyday *suck-teeth* of annoyance or insubordination. For example, a student
who responds to the teacher's instructions to write an essay in class with
an inadvertent *suck-teeth*, might claim as she approaches him with an icy
stare, that he was just "trying to clear out his teeth." Given the demonstrated
divergences between what black and white Americans most commonly understand by this gesture, it is not at all difficult to imagine that many a slave might
have been able to use it on his masters with equally feigned innocence,
to express feelings of exasperation and rage for which there was no other
outlet.

As early as 1951, Richard Allsopp (25) had observed that "words exist in
West and East African languages which contain a sound produced by sucking air between the teeth. What connection this may have with sulking or
defiance, however, as it does in our (Guyana) dialect, I do not know." It is not
clear whether Allsopp is referring here to the "clicks" of certain African languages, which so far as we know have no connection with rudeness or defiance
(see now Allsopp 1996: 538). However our interviews with African informants

some two decades later confirmed that they were in fact familiar with the gesture, and that many of their languages had verbal labels referring to it. Some of the African informants pointed out spontaneously that "sucking your teeth" in front of your parents was very rude, likely to earn you a slap or a whipping. This is, as we pointed out before, also true of Guyana and the rest of the Caribbean.

The African equivalents for *suck-teeth* which we collected were the following:

MENDE:	*i ngi yongoi ɣofoin lɔ nya ma* – "He sucked his teeth on me" (literally, "He his teeth sucked me on").[10]
TEMNE:	*tós nɛ̀* – "to suck to self"
IGBO:	*íma osò* – "to make a sucking noise with the mouth"
YORUBA:	*kp̀oše ʹ* – (vb.) "to make a sucking noise with the mouth" *òše ʹ* – (n.) "sucking noise made with the mouth"[11]
LUO:	*ichiya* – (vb.) "to make suck-teeth noise" *chiyo* – (n.) "suck-teeth noise"
KRIO:	*no sɔk yu tit pan mi* – "Don't suck your teeth on me" *no sɔk tit mi* – "Don't suck-teeth me"
CAMEROON PIDGIN:	*no sɔk yɔ tif fɔ mi* – "Don't suck your teeth on me."

There is the possibility too that *chups* and *stchoops* also have their roots in an African expression for the gesture involving the word "suck." We had always assumed that these were merely onomatopoeic creations for the sound made in sucking one's teeth. But as Hancock points out (personal communication), the Papiamentu and Sranan expressions for the gesture include a morpheme *tšupa*, which is very similar, of course, to *chups* or *stchoops*. It may derive from the Portuguese *chupar*, which, not surprisingly, means "to suck." But it is also significant that in Gambian Krio ("Aku"), the term for *suck-teeth* is *tšipú*, adopted from Wolof. As Hancock himself was the first to suggest, the Caribbean forms *chups* and *stchoops* may possibly represent a convergence of the Portuguese and Wolof forms.

If *chups* and *stchoops* turn out to be more than mere onomatopoeic New World creations, so also do the other equivalents or substitutes mentioned above: *cho*, *chu*, and *tcha*. There is first the possibility that these are merely abbreviated forms of *chups*. But there are other possibilities. The *Dictionary of Jamaican English* (Cassidy and Le Page 1967: 441) describes *cho* (with variants /cho, cha, chut, chu/) as "an exclamation expressing scorn, disagreement, expostulation, etc.," and provides two possible West African sources: "Ewe *tsóò* – interjection of astonishment, anger, impatience, disappointment," and "Twi *twéaa* – interjection of uttermost contempt." The editors (ibid.) add that "English *tcha* can hardly be the source," because the earliest citations for *tcha* in the *Oxford English Dictionary* are later (1844, 1887) than the Jamaican attestations (1827, 1835). In fact, far from being the source, English *tcha* may well be a later reflex of the Ewe or Twi interjections, perhaps via the Caribbean forms *cho* and *cha*.

This expanding network of possible African derivations which grew out of our original research into *suck-teeth* does not end here. After reading an earlier version of this paper, Ian Hancock mentioned that the Yoruba have a term (*šumú, šùtì*) for the gesture we discussed above of pursing the lips for a *suck-teeth* without actually making the sound. We wrote back, without taking it too seriously, that people sometimes refer to this in Guyana as *faul biti maut* ("mouth shaped like a fowl's behind"). When Hancock replied excitedly that speakers of Krio in Sierra Leone also use this very metaphor – *luk we yu de mek yu mɔt lɛkɛ fol yon* ("look how you make your mouth like a fowl's behind"), we felt the similarity could hardly be due to coincidence. Once again we were struck by the pervasiveness of the African influence which lurks behind so many of the symbols, patterns, and institutions we manipulate in the New World from day to day.

7.4   Conclusion

Cut-eye and *suck-teeth* provide clear evidence that "Africanisms" in the New World may reside not only in the exotic, but also (and perhaps more frequently) in the commonplace. (See Holloway 1990, Holloway and Vass 1993.) In general, the identity of such items will not be obvious, either to "natives" or "outsiders." However, it may be revealed by careful attention to disparities in usage between Whites and Blacks, and to the recurrence of the same patterns in different communities which have sizable African-derived populations.

To discover other nonverbal patterns, we need to be interested not just in rare and elaborate rites, but also in the more "ordinary" rituals involved in everyday behavior: how people walk and stand; how they greet and take their leave of each other; what they do with their faces and hands when conversing, narrating, or arguing, and so on. Reisman (1970: 132–3) discusses some examples of just this type in Antigua, and of course Herskovits (1941) had suggested several others which still warrant further investigation.

In terms of linguistic survivals, we can translate the need to look for the commonplace into an increased alertness for loan-translations and cases of convergence between English (or other European) and African forms. Like *cut-eye* and *suck-teeth*, these will look like ordinary English words; sometimes it is only the subtlest "non-English" shades of meaning and usage which will help to give them away.[12] In fact, where a particular form and meaning have become generalized to almost every part of the English-speaking world, such as "OK," the informal signal of assent or agreement, discussed in Dalby (1972), we will not have even this clue. Difficulties of this sort (and others) can make the search for loan-translations and convergences more harrowing than the search for direct loans of the *nyam* and *goober* type.

On the other hand, the very English facade which makes them difficult to recognize today has undoubtedly helped them to survive in larger numbers. Like *cut-eye* and *suck-teeth* they may be actively used even among those people who are striving most consciously toward the prestigious "standard" language and culture, and in whose speech direct African loans like *nyam* are unlikely to be found.

There is an additional significance to the study of loan-translations and convergences. As Dalby (1972: 174) has suggested, they must have been invaluable in the creation and maintenance of a subtle code by means of which slaves could communicate with each other without fear of detection or punishment by Whites. From our suggestions above, too, of the ways in which the gestures discussed in this paper might have been passed off with more acceptable "meanings" (*cut-eye* as ingratiation, *suck-teeth* as the effort to remove food from the teeth), it is clear that the code was not restricted to linguistic material. Both verbal and nonverbal resources were utilized for its creation. *Cut-eye* and *suck-teeth*, Africanisms both as words and as gestures, are themselves evidence of this.

Other examples abound. Reisman (1970: 132–3) notes the existence of a side-up turn of the head in Antigua which seems to be of African origin; it is used today as a greeting, but it also resembles a Euro-American head-gesture which might have been used as a command ("Come over here!") in the plantation environment. Investing the latter gesture with the "African" interpretation of a salutation would have provided a measure of personal satisfaction, "a way to redress the harshness of the slavery situation" (Reisman 1970: 133). Similar to this is the story told to us by Richmond Wiley, a native of the South Carolina Sea Islands, of a slave who used to answer his master's queries and commands with the words "You-ass, sir!" The insult, so obvious to his fellow slaves, was passed off on the master as the slave's slurred pronunciation of "Yes, sir."

More urgently and directly communicative was the way slaves would raise the spiritual refrain "Wait in the water" from one plantation to the next to warn a runaway that bloodhounds were on his trail – a signal interpreted by the masters as their expression of religious zeal. In all these cases, the existence of public and more "acceptable" interpretations is exploited by Blacks for the communication of more private or "unacceptable" meanings.[13] The value of Africanisms in this more general strategy is that they provided one of the sources (though not the only one) of its fuel.

As we hope this paper has itself been able to demonstrate, there is more to be done with "Africanisms" than presenting them in a list with possible sources. Viewed from the standpoint of different cultures and social groupings in both the present and the past, they have much to tell us about how peoples of African descent adapted to the experience of the New World, and how much they were understood by their social and political superiors. Finally, as we should like to stress again, the most telling Africanisms from this point of view might involve the most ordinary items of everyday behavior – how that person is looking at you across a room, or what that woman is yelling down the street.[14]

Notes

1 These include *Dictionary of Jamaican English*, ed. Frederic G. Cassidy and Robert B. Le Page (London: Cambridge University Press, 1967); Frank Collymore, *Notes for a Glossary of Words and Phrases of Barbadian Dialect* (Bridgetown: Advocate, 1970); J. Graham Cruickshank, *Black Talk, being Notes on Negro Dialect in British Guiana* (Georgetown, Demerara: Argosy, 1916); Carlton R. Ottley, *Creole Talk of Trinidad and Tobago* (Port of Spain: Ottley, 1971); and the glossary in Hyman Rodman, *Lower-Class Families in the Culture of Poverty in Negro Trinidad* (New York: Oxford University Press, 1971).

2 Discussion of some of the other items which appeared in this questionnaire and provided evidence of sharp discontinuities in the linguistic competence of Blacks and Whites is contained in Rickford (1975, reprinted in this volume).

3 Compare one of the standard rejoinders to *verbal* insult or mockery:

> "Sticks and stones can break my bones,
> But words can never hurt me."

4 Compare also the brief descriptions in Collymore (1970: 38), and Cruickshank (1916: 31).

5 Miss Nation's contributions to the *Dictionary* were made on the basis of her analysis of the spontaneous conversation of Jamaican children.

6 Compare the list of "key" languages in Turner (1949) with the list in Dalby (1972).

7 This metaphorical reference to "breaking the back of the eye" is evocative of the straining of the eye muscles which one actually feels when delivering a good *cut-eye*.

8 For all Yoruba examples cited in this paper, $\acute{v}$ = high tone, v = mid tone, $\grave{v}$ = low tone, and v' = mid-high rising tone.

9 Some of the black females pointed out that "titting your teeth" is sometimes used instead of "sucking your teeth" for the same gesture.

10 We wish to thank Richard Allsopp for contributing this example. See now his (1996: 184) entry on *cut-eye*: "A woman's gesture of contempt for sb[somebody], shown by looking at the person and closing her eyes while turning her face sharply away."

11 Abraham (1958: 490) describes *òṣe'* (1a) as "a sign denoting unhappiness." Delano (1969: 91) glosses *pòṣé* thus: "to express impatience or dissatisfaction by saying 'pshaw.'"

12 On this point, see Cassidy (1966) and Edwards (1974).

13 Reisman (1970) provides the most detailed discussion of the different ways in

which all kinds of linguistic and cultural symbols in Antigua have been subject to a process of remodelling and reinterpretation which allows them to "mediate at least two sets of cultural identities and meanings."

14 This paper represents a revised version of a paper entitled "Cut-Eye and Suck-Teeth" originally prepared in June 1973, and circulated in mimeo. We wish to thank Karl Reisman and Ian Hancock, who helped with data collection and provided both encouragement and criticism. We should also like to thank the many Americans who participated in our questionnaire, and the various West Indian and African informants, too numerous to mention by name.

8

Social Contact and Linguistic Diffusion: Hiberno English and New World Black English

8.1 Introduction

The view of language as an autonomous system is a persistent one in linguistics – see Newmeyer 1983 for synchronically based arguments in its favor – but an adequate theoretical understanding of linguistic variation and change must clearly attend both to internal factors (e.g. analogy and phonological environment) and to external ones (e.g. geography and social context). This recognition was implicit in the work of the nineteenth-century historical linguists and dialectologists, and it has been reinforced by the studies of change in progress carried out by Labov and other sociolinguists since the 1960s (cf. Gumperz 1982b: 23–4).

Labov's teacher, Weinreich, had been convinced even earlier (1953) of the need to consider both structural and "extralinguistic" factors in the study of language diffusion and shift. Others studying similar language contact phenomena have consistently reached the same conclusion (cf. Haugen 1953, Ferguson and Gumperz 1960, Fishman et al. 1968, Dorian 1981, Gal 1979). Some, indeed, have been led by the force of the empirical evidence to turn the autonomous view of language on its head, concluding that 'linguistic interference is conditioned in the first instance by social factors, not linguistic ones' (Thomason 1981 and Thomason).

Although the general importance of social context in linguistic diffusion is well-recognized, many details about the relationship between them still require clarification, and the subject is currently attracting considerable research. This research has two main strands. On the one hand, studies are being made of linguistic diffusion (or its absence) across different urban centers, social classes, sexes, and ethnic or age groups, usually on the basis of quantitative analyses of tape-recorded speech (Labov 1984a, b; Nichols 1983; Rickford 1985; Trudgill 1983a, 1984b). On the other hand, studies are attempting to account for current areal or social distributions of linguistic features in terms of settlement and contact patterns in preceding centuries, usually by attending to the geography and social history of the region and/or by detailed comparison of linguistic features in the languages concerned (Baker 1982a, Bickerton 1984b, Greenberg 1984, Hancock 1987, Holm 1984).

This paper is intended as a contribution to the second strand of research. Its focus is the possible diffusion of (*does*) *be*, as a marker of habitual or iterative aspect, from Hiberno or Irish English to New World Black English (including the West Atlantic English-based creoles and American Vernacular Black English).[1] This possibility is repeatedly raised in the literature (cf. Stewart 1970a: 246, Davis 1971: 93, Wolfram 1971: 60, Traugott 1972: 191, Sledd 1973, Rickford 1974: 106–9, Hill 1975, C.-J. N. Bailey 1982). Linguistic comparisons of this and other features in Hiberno-English (HE) and New World Black English (NWBE) are usually cursory, however; and details about the sociohistorical context in which such diffusion is presumed to have occurred are almost non-existent. In the light of the literature on linguistic change and diffusion, these are serious limitations, and ones which this paper will attempt to redress.

I will proceed as follows. In the rest of this introduction, I will briefly distinguish some of the sources which NWBE features might have, then summarize the most recent proposal that NWBE *be* might represent diffusion from HE – that of C.-J. N. Bailey. Successive sections represent evaluations of his proposal. In section 8.2, I will consider the conditions under which Irish and African populations might have come into contact in the New World, and the possibilities of diffusion between them. Available evidence suggests that HE influence on NWBE was most likely both in the Caribbean and North America in the seventeenth century, when Catholic bond servants from the southern provinces of Ireland worked alongside African servants and slaves on colonial plantations. But we must also take into account the fact that Irish immigration into eighteenth-century North America was primarily from Ulster, rather than the southern provinces of Ireland, and that NWBE was subject to other influences. In section 8.3, I will examine the merits of Bailey's diffusion proposal in terms of its internal linguistic assumptions, and will review other possible explanations for the origin of NWBE *be*. The hypothesis that this form represents decreolization from creole *does be* will turn out to be the single most persuasive one; however, this hypothesis incorporates the insights of revised diffusion hypotheses which distinguish between northern and southern HE, and include possible influence from British dialects. In section 8.4, I suggest directions for further research.

Both HE and NWBE are continua rather than single discrete varieties, originating in the acquisition of English by native speakers of Gaelic (Todd 1974: 9) and of West African languages (Alleyne 1980), respectively. To say that a feature of NWBE represents diffusion from HE is to suggest that, at some point, speakers of varieties of HE and NWBE were in contact – and that black speakers borrowed the feature from Irish speakers in its original form, meaning, or both. (The diffusion could also have been indirect, via some third population; but since this possibility is not in question, I will not consider it.) Alternatively, the feature might represent the influence of other British dialects present in the contact situation, or transfer/continuity from the native languages of the West Africans who came to the New World (substrate influence). Finally, the feature might be the result of creolization or decreolization processes which took place in the course of the acquisition of English by these West Africans, or it might represent more general universals of language acquisition. (See Alleyne 1980 for the acquisition of English by West Africans in the New World; and cf. Hymes 1971: 84; Bickerton 1975, 1981; Mühlhäusler 1980; Andersen 1983; Rickford 1983a; Schumann and Stauble 1983 for models of pidginization, creolization, and decreolization in relation to language acquisition.)

As some linguists have noted (Traugott 1972: 189–90, Bailey 1982), hypotheses that features of NWBE represent diffusion from earlier Irish English or British dialects are not automatically incompatible with hypotheses of decreolization or substratal influence, since the British dialects may have served as source or reinforcement for the creole feature. Bailey makes just this point about NWBE habitual *be*;[2] and since this form and his hypothesis about its origin are pivotal elements in this paper, I will summarize his arguments.

Bailey refers, on the one hand (238), to "the large numbers of Irishmen that Cromwell shipped to Jamaica in the 1650s, before the heyday of the African slave trade," and, on the other, to "the astonishing similarities in every detail . . . between Irish *be* and Vernacular Black English *be*." Putting the historical and linguistic information together, he suggests that Irish English might have been the source of these and other features of NWBE, and he goes on to castigate "opponents of the Irish source" for failures of "logical argumentation":

> Not everyone seems to realize that there is no logical connection between accepting an Irish source for consuetudinary *be* in vernacular black English and rejecting the Afro-Creole hypothesis about the origin of the dialect . . . *Be* could have come into Caribbean Creole from Irish English BEFORE the slaves were brought to the States. Thus vernacular black English could have derived *be* from Irish English and still have a creole source.

To evaluate this claim about the origin of VBE *be* – frequently cited as the most distinctive feature of this variety of NWBE – it will be necessary to provide more detail about Irish/African contact in the New World than Bailey does, and to explore alternative hypotheses which he does not consider.[3] It is to these tasks that I will now turn.

8.2   Contact between Irish and African Populations in the New World

Ideally, the examination of sociohistorical data on the issue of HE/NWBE diffusion should be guided by a well-developed theory of constraints on linguistic diffusion. Despite recent progress in this direction, such a theory does not yet exist, particularly with respect to external factors.[4] However, Whinnom's discussion of barriers to hybridization (1971: 92–7) provides a useful framework for determining what might be relevant, particularly if supplemented by the evidence of case studies.

Whinnom's first barrier is "ecological," dealing with the nature of the contact between linguistic groups. One factor in this category is population size: the fewer the speakers of language A, relative to B, the less likely and the slower will be diffusions from A to B (Bloomfield 1933: 462). Another relevant factor is the length and intimacy of contact. Gumperz and Wilson 1971 show that local varieties of Urdu, Marathi, Kannada, and Telugu in the South Indian village of Kupwar have converged dramatically as a result of close contact and code-switching between their speakers for over 400 years. The acquisition of neighboring Bantu features by non-Bantu Mbugu in Tanzania is another case in point – leading Bynon (1977: 255–6) to conclude that, "given a certain intensity and duration of language contact, there is nothing that may not be diffused across language boundaries." Other relevant factors in this category are physical, demographic, geographic, and political constraints on the diffusion of features (see Bloomfield 1933: 321–45; Trudgill 1983a: 31–87). Less commonly mentioned, but particularly relevant here, is the relative order in which immigrant populations settle in a new area. Thus Le Page (1960: 65–6) argues that Twi-speaking slaves significantly influenced the lexicon of Jamaican Creole – not because they were in the majority (they were not), but because they established their leadership earliest, "and by the time the slave trade expanded in the eighteenth century there had been several generations of their creole descendants whose linguistic habits were already formed to cope with life in the plantations." Other examples are provided by Bickerton (1975: 8) and by Mintz and Price (1976: 25).

Whinnom's second barrier is "ethological," or emotional, involving the attitudes of populations in contact toward each other, and toward each other's languages. Schumann 1978a considers factors of this type under the heading of "social and psychological distance" between second language learners and target language speakers, while Niles (1980: 71–2) refers to them as "psycho-linguistic/psycho-cultural" factors. More specifically, Weinreich (1953: 84–5) noted that, because of the higher prestige of German in Switzerland, "While German elements in Romansh speech are tolerated practically without any limit, the reverse trend – Romansh influence in German speech – is kept within bounds." In general, we would expect positive attitudes toward a group to favor adoption of its norms, and negative attitudes to disfavor it (Rickford 1985, Le Pate and Tabouret-Keller 1985); however, the linguistic effects of these attitudinal factors may be relatively weak (Labov 1980a: 379), and sometimes imperceptible (Labov 1972e: 318, Blom and Gumperz 1972, Cooper 1982: 11). Social prohibitions against the imitation of features across groups, despite frequent interaction (Stewart 1974: 19; Gumperz 1982d: 39), are also a subtype of ethological barrier.

Whinnom's third and fourth barriers are "mechanical" (factors of outer or phonological form) and "conceptual" (inner form – perception as shaped by syntactic and semantic structure). They can be grouped together as internal constraints on diffusion. Although still not perfectly understood (Weinreich 1953: 103–4), internal factors of this type have been more thoroughly explored than external constraints. On internal grounds, invariant *be* and similar habitual markers have an intermediate likelihood of diffusion across language boundaries: less than if they had purely lexical and no grammatical meaning, but more than if they were bound morphemes (Haugen 1956: 66–7).

The preceding factors do not exhaust the set of possible influences on interlingual diffusion (cf. Weinreich 1953: 83–110); but they allow us to hypothesize the kinds of Irish/African contact which would have favored HE/NWBE diffusion. For example, the presence of large numbers of Irish in the English colonies before Africans started to arrive – followed by relatively close, sustained, and harmonious contact between the groups – would have favored the diffusion of *be* and other features. We will attend to factors like these as we go through the relevant histories of the Caribbean and American colonies.

8.2.1   The Caribbean

I will concentrate in this section on the early settlement history of Barbados – generally regarded as a very favorable English colonial setting for the acquisition of white dialect features by Blacks, because of the high proportion of Whites there from early on (Hancock 1980: 22, Niles 1980). For comparison, I will also provide briefer sketches of the situation in two other colonial settings: Jamaica and the Leeward Islands.

In the first quarter century of Barbados's colonization by the English (1627–52), tobacco and cotton were the main crops; farms were small and numerous; and Blacks were outnumbered by Whites, many of whom were servants serving indentures of four or five years. As the island shifted to sugar cultivation, however, the importation of African slaves stepped up considerably; at the same time, white immigration decreased and white emigration increased (Sheppard 1977: 27–39). By the 1670s, Blacks outnumbered Whites by two to

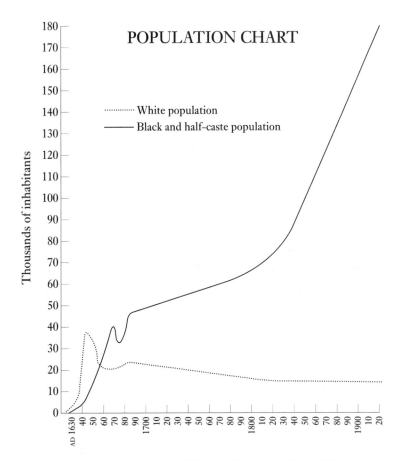

Figure 8.1   Population of Blacks and Whites in Barbados, 1630–1920.
Source: Harlow 1926: 339

one, as shown in figure 8.1; and the margin kept increasing (Handler and Lange 1978: 28).

Niles (58–60) suggests that black/white contact continued on the plantations into the second half of the eighteenth century, but the demographic conditions for direct white influence on black speech were clearly most favorable in the first quarter century of Barbados's settlement by the English, becoming steadily less so thereafter. This is also evident from the data on an even more pertinent ecological unit, namely the individual plantation. In 1646, Sir Anthony Ashley Cooper's 205-acre plantation included 21 white servants and nine black slaves; but in 1654, Robert Hooper's 200-acre plantation included 35 servants and 66 slaves; and in 1667, the 350-acre plantation of an unidentified planter included five servants and 125 slaves (Dunn 1972: 68). As Dunn notes, the statistics for these plantations may not be entirely representative, but they convey the general population trends over time. It is possible, of course, that Blacks who acquired white linguistic features in the earliest and most favorable contact period could have continued to diffuse them among later black populations (compare the case of Twi speakers in Jamaica, cited above); but direct linguistic diffusion from Whites to Blacks after the mid-seventeenth century is less likely than before – and after the mid-eighteenth century, even less so. There are no exact statistics on how many white servants in the first quarter century were Irish, but they were apparently numerous. By the 1630s, "Ireland was already a prime source of supply for servants" (Dunn 1972: 56–7). In 1652, there were 8,000 white indentured servants in Barbados, said to be "mainly Scots and Irish" (Smith 1947: 332–3). Although emphasizing the meagerness of the evidence, Bridenbaugh and Bridenbaugh (1972: 17) conclude that, "in the English West Indies in 1650, the Irish settlers constituted more than half of the entire population and outnumbered even the English."

Furthermore, Irish servants worked alongside African slaves, as other white servants did on Barbadian plantations (Dunn 1972: 69; Smith 1947: 256; Wood 1975: 54). They were also more similar to them than any other white group in terms of social standing and political rebelliousness. Of all white servants, the Catholic Irish were the least favored, and the most restricted and reviled by their Protestant English masters (Bridenbaugh and Bridenbaugh 1972: 364; Smith 1947: 289). There are reports, from the mid-1650s on, that they joined black slaves in running away, rebelling, and conspiring against the English planters (Sheppard 1977: 23; Cruickshank 1916: 65; Burns 1954: 396).

Under these relatively favorable ecological and ethological contact conditions, we might imagine that the acquisition of white dialectal varieties of English by Blacks (if not the reverse) might have proceeded quite expeditiously, and early reports appear to confirm this:

> As early as 1667 a writer from Barbados claimed that, there being so many white servants in the island and poor whites who worked in the fields, and so many Negroes having become tradesmen, "now there are many thousands of slaves that speak English." (Le Page 1960: 18)

Some scholars suggest more specifically that the *Irish* influence was particularly strong and lasting:

> The "Salt-Water" Negro picked up what he could of his master's English, but learned most of his speech from white bond servants – the first field hands – hence the Irish brogue so prevalent in the West Indies today. (Bridenbaugh and Bridenbaugh 1972: 352)

Table 8.1   Estimated distribution of major language groups in Barbados about 1675

	White Population 22,000		Black Population 33,000	
Native region:	Southwest England	Other Great Britain	Africa born: Gold Coast Senegal, Gambia, Sierra Leone Windward Coast Whydaw Other Africa	Barbados born
Languages:	Southwest English dialects	Other English dialects, Irish, Scots	(1) African languages and dialects (2) Some English	(1) English (2) Some African

Source: Niles 1980: 77

Sanguine though all this sounds for the proposal that HE might have influenced NWBE in the seventeenth century, two major considerations reduce this possibility. One is that, even if the ecological and ethological conditions of black/white contact were as favorable as some scholars have suggested (and there are reasons to be skeptical about this),[5] Africans were more likely to have been exposed to native English dialects than to HE. Drawing on the historical evidence of white indentured servants shipped out of London and Bristol from the 1640s onward, Niles (1980: 22–54) concludes that most Whites in seventeenth-century Barbados were from the southwest of England. Table 8.1 graphically displays her conclusion that Somerset and other southwestern English dialects were the main varieties spoken among the white population – outnumbering other English, Irish, and Scots dialects. This is an important point, to which we will return below.

The second key consideration is that most Irish indentured servants arriving in Barbados during this period probably spoke varieties of Irish or Gaelic, rather than English. Bliss 1977 reminds us that, although English was first introduced to Ireland during the Norman invasion in the twelfth century, it did not become widespread; modern HE developed in Ireland only after the Cromwellian settlement of the 1650s. He concludes (16) that "the general acquisition of the English language by the people of Ireland hardly began until after 1800." De Fréine (1977: 75) reaches the same conclusion, indicating that, in 1800, three-quarters of the Irish coastline – including ports such as Limerick and Kinsale, from which many indentured servants had been shipped to

Barbados – "was practically all Irish speaking." Lockhart (1976: 128) has suggested that one of the reasons for the relatively slow absorption of Irish servants in colonial America (compared with other immigrants from the British Isles) was their "use of the Irish language," which helped to make them "as distinctive among the colonial population as the negro." By the mid-eighteenth century, there is documentary evidence, at least for the American mainland, that Irish bond servants were speaking varieties of English, from the "very broken and backward" speech of one Mr M'Innis (Smith 1947: 290) to the "good English" of one James Mackelliek, who could also "talk Irish" (Read 1937: 97). But in British colonies of the seventeenth century, it was probably true for Irish servants, as for African slaves, that most knew little or no English when they came.[6] Since Irish servants were present in Barbados before African slaves began to arrive, they would have had a head start in learning English; and distinctive features of their English – perhaps influenced by their native Irish, in ways similar to the HE which was to become established in Ireland later – could have been diffused to the new arrivals. However, contrary to widespread opinion, no cohesive, well-established model of HE existed for Irish bond servants to bring with them from Ireland to the seventeenth-century Caribbean or America. Major influences on the English acquired by both the Irish and the Africans would have been the dialects of British speakers in the colonies, and the grammars of their own native languages.

Since we have explored the ramifications of the situation in Barbados in such detail, I will say less about the Leeward Islands and Jamaica, merely highlighting some pertinent historical and linguistic aspects of the Irish presence in both regions.

The Irish presence in the Leewards – particularly in Montserrat – was proportionately greater than in other British colonies in the late seventeenth century, and also more dramatic. The French invasion in 1689 of St Christopher (later renamed St Kitts) was facilitated by an armed uprising in which "130 armed Irish servants rose up in the name of King James and sacked the English plantations on the windward side" (Dunn 1972: 134). Table 8.2 (overleaf) shows the exceptional preponderance of the Irish in Montserrat. But apropos of the point made in the discussion of Barbados, and contrary to the claim of Bridenbaugh and Bridenbaugh cited above, note that the English outnumbered the Irish significantly in each of the other Leeward Islands, and that Blacks were the single biggest sector of the population in every territory except Montserrat.

From the demographic evidence, Montserrat would seem to have been an ideal setting for the acquisition of HE features by the local African population. But after comparing features of present-day Montserrat Creole English with those of southern HE, Wells (1983: 129) reached the following negative conclusion:

Table 8.2   Population of the Leeward Islands, 1678

	Nevis		Antigua		St Christopher		Montserrat		Total	
English	2,670	(36%)	1,600	(36%)	1,322	(40%)	761	(21%)	6,353	(34%)
Irish	800	(11%)	610	(14%)	187	(5%)	1,869	(51%)	3,466	(18%)
Other Whites	51	(1%)	98	(2%)	388	(12%)	52	(1%)	589	(3%)
Blacks	3,849	(52%)	2,172	(48%)	1,436	(43%)	992	(27%)	8,449	(45%)
TOTALS	7,370		4,480		3,333		3,674		18,857	

Source: Adapted from table 12 in Dunn 1972: 134

In terms of linguistic influence, then, the Irish contribution to Montserrat has been vanishingly small. Of the vaunted "soft Irish brogue", the Emerald Isle of the Caribbean retains barely the tiniest trace.

Jamaica was not colonized by the British until 1654, when an expedition sent by Cromwell to attack Hispaniola (unsuccessfully, retreating after a loss of 1,000 men) turned instead to the more poorly defended island of Jamaica. It is not clear how many of the 8,200 men in the Cromwellian force were Irish; since 3,500 of them were recruited in Barbados, and 1,200 in the Leeward Islands – both with large Irish servant populations at the time – we may assume that a considerable number were Irish. But through starvation, disease, and other factors, only 2,200 men remained by 1660 (Dunn 1972: 152–3). Smith also mentions (1947: 169) a notorious Cromwellian proposal in 1655 to transport 2,000 boys and 1,000 girls to Jamaica "to breed up a population for that newly acquired possession"; but as he notes, there is no evidence that this scheme ever materialized.

Although Jamaica attracted white servants from other parts of the Caribbean and the British Isles in the last 30 years of the seventeenth century (Dunn 1972: 157), and received more well into the eighteenth century (Smith 1947: 310), the striking feature of seventeenth- to eighteenth-century Jamaica is not how *many* white servants it had, but how *few*. Smith's statistics (1947: 335) support Dunn's observation (1972: 157):

> By 1713 Jamaica had a larger slave population than Barbados and a far higher ratio of blacks to whites . . . The large block of poor whites to be found in all of the eastern Caribbean was missing.

Similarly, Le Page (1960: 18) has noted:

> In this slow growth of the English-speaking community in Jamaica, compared with the rapid growth of the slave population, is to be found one of the major

factors which has differentiated the Creole dialect of this island from that of Barbados.

In the circumstances, there was probably less influence from HE or other white dialects on the speech of the African population in Jamaica.[7]

8.2.2   The North American Colonies

Some Irish English might have come to North America during the colonial period by way of the West Indies – through Irish servants who migrated to the North American colonies after completing their indentures in the Caribbean, or through slaves who were imported from the Caribbean after being "seasoned" and perhaps influenced by Irish English there (C.-J. N. Bailey, 238). But by the eighteenth century, North American colonies were generally getting most of their slaves from Africa rather than the West Indies (Turner 1949: 24; Wood 1975: 340–1). Since so many Irish immigrants came directly to North America between the seventeenth and nineteenth centuries, the possibility of Irish English influence on Black English there can be considered quite independently.

The flow of emigrants between Ireland and the North American colonies lasted so much longer than it did in the Caribbean, was so much more voluminous, and displayed such differences from one colony or state to the other, that there is virtually no end to the details which one could include in its description. I will depict only the most general trends, and urge interested readers to consult the cited references (and now Winford 1997) for more information.

In the seventeenth century, most Irish emigrants to North America, like those who went to the Caribbean, were "native Irish" from the southern and overwhelmingly Catholic provinces of Connacht, Munster, and Leinster (see map 8.1). In both areas, white servants at first constituted the bulk of the plantation labor force (Lockhart 1976: 10). They were soon joined, however, by increasing numbers of Africans, who came first as servants with fixed terms, later as slaves for life (Foner 1975: 190).

Similarities with the Caribbean were most marked in the southern colonies: both in Barbados and South Carolina, Blacks constituted over 60 percent of the total population within 50 years of initial settlement by the British. In New York, they were only 16 percent of the population as late as the 1750s, 100 years after British settlement; and in Boston the comparable figure was only 8 percent (Foner 1975: 256). Virginia, a tobacco-growing Chesapeake colony, had intermediate statistics: the black population was 2 percent in 1625 (Smith 1947: 328), but 25 percent by 1730, and 47 percent by 1776 (Foner 1975: 189) – making it comparable to the Leewards in 1678 (table 8.2). From these figures, we may assume that linguistic diffusion from white to black was most likely in

Map 8.1   Ireland, showing historical provinces.

the North, and least likely in the deep South; most likely in the first years of settlement, and least likely thereafter.

Many of the Whites in the northern and Chesapeake colonies, where diffusion was most likely, may have been Irish; but this impression is derived from qualitative assessments rather than precise figures. Smith (1947: 324) cites a contemporary estimate that 600 or 700 servants, "chiefly Irish," were imported to Maryland in 1698. Lockhart (1976: 4) notes that the trade in Irish servants to Virginia was established on a regular basis earlier (1619–20) than in any other British colony, and that "By 1700 the Irish were common in every colony from Newfoundland southwards to the Carolinas" (10). But even if the white servants included many Irish, who had reasonably good contact with Africans, we should remember once again that adoption of HE features by Africans would have been limited by sociopsychological factors (Herskovits 1941: 115, Stewart 1974: 17–20), and by the fact that both groups would have been learning English from British speakers in the colonies.

Irish immigration to the Caribbean had declined considerably by the dawn of the eighteenth century; but in North America, it actually increased. Some of the Irish who came in during this period were "native Irish" from the southern provinces (Lockhart 1976: 50); but the vast majority of them were Presbyterian "Ulster Scots" or "Scotch Irish" from the northern province of Ulster (Dickson 1966). The estimates of Scotch Irish immigration during this period are huge: 250,000 to 300,000 between 1717 and 1766 (Nichols 1985, Doyle 1981: 59), and 385,000 to 400,000 for the entire eighteenth century (estimates cited by Lockhart 1976: 60).[8]

These immigrants were frequently referred to simply as 'Irish' in America, and modern scholars sometimes fail to distinguish the "Scotch Irish" from the "native Irish"; but it is important to observe the distinction. The roots of the Scotch Irish go back to the "plantation of Ulster" in the early 1600s, after an Irish/Catholic revolt was crushed by the English, and Ulster land was distributed to Scottish and English settlers as a means of ensuring security (Fallows 1979: 13). By 1640, some 100,000 Scottish and 20,000 English settlers had been established in Ulster (Dickson 1966: 3), and 50,000 more Scottish families settled there between 1689 and 1715 (Lockhart 1976: 19). The Scottish settlers, who came primarily from southwestern counties of Scotland, outnumbered the English settlers by almost six to one; and the Ulster Scots dialect consequently shows considerable influence from Lowland Scots (Aitken 1984: 518–19, Harris 1984).

This is important from our perspective: when the Scotch Irish emigrated from Ireland to America in huge numbers between 1718 to 1775 – settling primarily in Pennsylvania, South Carolina, and Georgia (Crozier 1984: 313–16) – it was this Ulster Scots variety of HE which the majority must have brought with them, rather than the southern HE characteristic of earlier Irish emigrants to the Caribbean and North America. Descriptions of HE dialects are available in Braidwood 1964, Gregg 1964, Adams 1977, Bliss 1984, and Harris 1984; and one of the most important differences among them is that habitual *be* is characteristically northern, while *do be* is characteristically southern (Bliss 1972, Guilfoyle 1983). In 8.3.2, we will consider a revised version of the HE diffusion hypothesis which takes this northern/southern difference into account, but for now we can simply note its existence.

Having emphasized that most eighteenth-century Irish immigrants to America were Scotch Irish, and that they must have spoken a northern (Ulster Scots) variety of HE, we must still ask what kinds of opportunities they had for social contact with Blacks – and linguistic diffusion to them – during this period. Scotch Irish immigrants were better-off as a group than native Irish. More of them emigrated as families rather than individuals; and more traveled as redemptioners or fee-paying passengers, rather than bond servants, particularly in the 1770s (Dickson 1966: 97). More of them worked in skilled occupations, becoming backwoods frontiersmen or successful landowners. Thus, they are likely to have had less contact with and linguistic influence on American Blacks than the native Irish servants who had preceded them. However, the sheer volume of Scotch Irish immigration is significant (Winford 1997: 335).

Moreover the Scotch Irish would generally have been fluent speakers of English, unlike seventeenth-century native Irish immigrants; and eighteenth-century reports do show Irish and African populations cooperating and working together in a number of ways. For instance, the group that attacked the British soldiers in the Boston Massacre of 1770 was, in the words of John Adams (quoted in Franklin 1974: 86), "a motley rabble of saucy boys, Negroes and mulattoes, Irish Teagues and outlandish Jack Tars." Foner reports (1975: 277) that black slaves "worked side by side with white indentured servants" in Pennsylvania; and that fugitive slaves of the 1790s obtained forged passes from some Whites, "among whom the Irish were most often mentioned" (503). We do not know how many of these "Irish" were Scotch Irish (Doyle 1981: 73, suggests that two-thirds of the Irish population in America in 1790 were Scotch Irish), or how much social contact they had with Blacks in everyday life; but cooperative relations of the type referred to in this paragraph would have favored linguistic diffusion.

In the nineteenth century, the flow of Irish immigrants to America increased astronomically, largely as a result of crop failures in Ireland from the 1830s onward. Over 200,000 Irish are estimated to have arrived in America in the 1830s; between 1847 and 1855, 892,000 Irish immigrants arrived in New York alone (Coleman 1972: 325; Fallows 1979: 23). Wakin (1976: 8) estimates that 4,500,000 people emigrated from Ireland in the nineteenth century, and that most went to America. Unlike their eighteenth-century counterparts, these immigrants were predominantly Catholic, almost half of them coming from six counties in Munster and Connacht: Cork, Kerry, Tipperary, Limerick, Galway, and Mayo (Wakin 1976: 20). As a result, most of them would have spoken southern HE.

Despite the huge volume of nineteenth-century Irish immigrants, their English is less likely to have diffused among black Americans (and vice versa) than might have been the case in preceding centuries. In the first place, nineteenth-century Irish immigrants settled primarily in northern cities at a time when many Blacks were still rural and southern. According to the 1880 US census, 46 percent of all foreign born Irish were concentrated in only four northern cities: Boston, Brooklyn, New York, and Philadelphia (Wakin 1976: 65). To the extent that free Blacks lived in these cities, both they and the Catholic Irish were commonly reviled; thus an advertisement in the 1830 New York *Courier and Enquirer* included the notorious words "No Blacks or Irish Need Apply" (ibid., 52). But whereas common oppression in the "closed" plantation environment of the seventeenth-century colonies had led to common identification, joint conspiracy, and rebellion, the Blacks and Irish scrambling for employment in the "open market" of nineteenth-century America viewed each other as competitors and enemies, kept to themselves, and expressed open hostility toward each other across the ethnic divide. In the 1850s, Frederick Douglass lamented the fact that Blacks were being "elbowed out of employment" by immigrants "whose hunger and color" favored them (Foner 1983a: 214–15). As early as 1834, Irish shipwrights "hostile to the Negroes as job competitors" formed part of the mob which set fire to the Shelter for Colored Orphans and attacked the black Bethel Church in Philadelphia (Foner 1983a: 432). By the 1860s, black/Irish riots over limited jobs were raging in many of the major cities, including Toledo, Cincinnati, and Brooklyn (Foner 1983b: 392–5).[9]

In the years to follow, as Blacks in the post-emancipation period migrated to northern and western cities, they joined ethnic enclaves with others of their own kind, just as the waves of Irish immigrants who continued to pour in found their way to Five Points, New York, and other Irish neighborhoods (Fallows 1979: 33). Labov 1984a, b and Labov and Harris 1986 report that the speech patterns of working-class Blacks and Whites in Philadelphia still remain separate – and in fact become increasingly so, as each group identifies more narrowly with neighborhood values in the face of increasing economic recession and unemployment.[10] From the sociohistorical evidence, a similar situation obtained in nineteenth-century cities. We can reasonably conclude that if HE had a significant impact on VBE, it was *before* the nineteenth century.

8.2.3   Summary

Irish populations were more numerous in colonial America and the Caribbean than their present-day representation in both places might lead us to expect. Opportunities for social contact and linguistic diffusion between Irish and African populations in British colonies were most favorable in the seventeenth century, when African slaves and native Irish servants – who would have been speakers of southern HE – worked side by side on Caribbean and American plantations. Beyond the seventeenth century, the Irish presence was insignificant in the Caribbean, but the next two centuries brought increasing floods of Irish settlers to America. The eighteenth-century group came primarily from Ulster (the Scotch Irish), bringing with them northern varieties of HE. The nineteenth-century Irish immigrants to America were mainly from the southern provinces of Ireland. They were more numerous than in any previous century, but their speech is likely to have had less influence on the speech of Afro-Americans because the two groups were separated by geographical area, ethnic neighborhood, and hostile relations.

Although the preceding facts support the possibility that diffusion from HE to NWBE might have taken place, particularly in the seventeenth century, other considerations caution us against exaggerating it. One is the very short time period – one to two decades, in the initial settlement periods of each colony – in which white servants would have outnumbered black slaves, particularly in the Caribbean and the American South. An even more important one is that British servants and settlers were present in the colonies in numbers equal to or larger than their Irish counterparts; thus their English dialects might have had an even greater influence on the English of Africans and Afro-Americans in the New World. This is particularly so since many native Irish immigrants in the seventeenth century would themselves have been learning English as a second language from the English settlers in the colonies. The major linguistic implication of these facts is that, while we certainly need to consider HE (northern and southern varieties) in seeking the source of features of NWBE, other influences – English dialects, and West African or creole substrata – are likely to have been as important, if not more so. This will become even clearer as we assess proposals regarding the origins of VBE *be* and other NWBE habitual markers in section 8.3.

8.3 Hypotheses about the Origin of VBE Habitual *Be*

We will here explore alternative hypotheses about the origin of the habitual markers in NWBE, particularly VBE *be*. Their respective strengths and weaknesses will be evaluated with regard to internal as well as external considerations.

The first three hypotheses to be considered all involve diffusion. Beginning with C.-J. N. Bailey's hypothesis that *be* was diffused from HE to NWBE, I will show that it suffers from two major weaknesses, which force us to reject it as it stands. A second diffusion hypothesis differentiates between northern and southern HE, suggesting that the prevalence of habitual *be* in VBE may represent the influence of the numerous Scotch Irish northern-HE speakers who emigrated to North America, while the instantiation of the habitual category by *da* and *does* (*be*) instead of *be* in the Caribbean may represent the influence of the numerous native Irish southern-HE speakers who worked and settled there. A third diffusion hypothesis adds, to the influence of the above varieties, the models of non-standard British English – in particular southern and southwestern English varieties – to which Africans and Afro-Americans may have been exposed in colonial times. Although both these expanded diffusion hypotheses overcome the weaknesses of Bailey's proposal, they have weaknesses of their own which force us to seek other alternatives.

The alternative which provides the single best hypothesis about the emergence of VBE *be* is one which considers the development of habitual markers in NWBE in the light of processes of pidginization, creolization, and decreolization accompanying the acquisition of English by African and Afro-American populations in the New World. According to this hypothesis, VBE *be* may result, by decreolization, from creole habitual markers like *does be* and (*d*)*a* which are still in active use in the Sea Islands of South Carolina and Georgia, and in the Caribbean. Potential demerits of this proposal are outnumbered by merits – including the fact that it is capable of incorporating the strengths of both expanded diffusion hypotheses, while overcoming their weaknesses.

Finally, we will briefly consider three hypotheses about the emergence of VBE *be* which are worth mentioning, but are not viable on their own terms: decreolization from *am*, the influence of creole universals, and independent innovation.

8.3.1   Bailey's diffusion proposal

Bailey proposes that VBE habitual *be* represents diffusion from HE. One attraction of this proposal is the obvious similarity of VBE and some varieties of HE with respect to habitual *be*, reflected in sentences such as the following:

1   *Even when I be round there with friends, I be scared.*
2   *Christmas Day, well, everybody be so choked up over gifts and everything, they don't be too hungry anyway.*

The first example is from northern HE (Harris 1982: 9), and the second from a VBE speaker in Washington, DC (Fasold 1972: 171); but without this information, it would be difficult to distinguish them. If we assumed that northern HE *be* diffused to New World Blacks through contact on colonial plantations, this similarity between HE and VBE would be neatly explained.

Against this plus for Bailey's proposal, there are two major minuses.[11] One is the fact that *be* (by itself) is not used as a habitual marker in any of the Caribbean varieties of NWBE. The second is the fact that the proposal does not consider the role of habitual *do* in HE.

The first difficulty represents a real stumbling block to Bailey's suggestion that habitual *be* could have come into the Caribbean creoles from HE and thence into VBE – since *be* is not used as a habitual marker in the Caribbean English creoles today, and does not appear to have been so used in the past. The most basilectal or non-standard Caribbean Creole varieties typically mark both habitual and continuative aspect with preverbal (*d*)*e* or (*d*)*a* (Alleyne 1980: 80–3, 192–4; Bickerton 1975: 60–9, 116–20; Hancock 1984; Holm 1983: 16–18):

3   *He (d)a sing* "He usually sings; He is singing."

Mesolectal varieties closer to standard English typically employ preverbal *does* for the non-continuative habitual, and suffixed *-ing* without *does* for the non-habitual continuative:

4   *He does sing* "He usually sings."
5   *He Ø singing* "He is singing."

The closest similarity which mesolectal Caribbean varieties bear to VBE and northern HE with respect to habitual *be* is the fact that – when a predicate is an adjective, a locative/prepositional phrase, or a continuative verb (VERB + *ing*) – they sometimes employ *be* as a grammatical filler between habitual *does* and the predicate:

6   *He does be sick* "He is usually sick."
7   *He does be in the house* "He is usually in the house."
8   *He does be singing* "He is usually singing."

The synchronic differences between northern HE, VBE, and the Caribbean creoles do not mean that it is impossible to relate them diachronically (we will consider alternative means below); but they imperil Bailey's specific proposal for doing so.

The second major difficulty with Bailey's proposal is that it does not consider the role of habitual *do* in HE. From grammatical descriptions of HE like O'Donovan 1845 and Taniguchi 1956 – and from the works of Irish writers such as Joyce, Synge, and Yeats (all from the Dublin area, and thus speakers of southern HE) – *do* appears to be the primary HE habitual marker, co-occurring with *be* before Verb + *ing* and in other environments, much as reported above for Caribbean *does be*:

9   *For it's a raw beastly day we do have each day.* (Synge, *The Well of the Saints*)
10 *They do be cheering when the horses take the water well.* (Yeats, *Cathleen ni Houlihan*)

The synchronic distribution of *do* and *be* in HE still requires further empirical investigation;[12] but recent works (Guilfoyle 1983: 24; Harris 1985) have helped to clarify the situation. Both indicate that habitual *be* is characteristic of HE as spoken in northern parts of Ulster, while *do be* is characteristic of HE as spoken in the geographically more extensive southern provinces (compare Bliss 1972: 80). However, Guilfoyle's additional claim that northern HE lacks habitual *do* has been challenged. Harris (1982: 9) indicates that *do* occurs with verbs other than *be* both in the north and the south, and examples like these bear him out:

11   *When you put the turf pieces on to the barrow, you do have them in heaps and then you do spread them.* (northern HE speaker quoted by Harris)
12   *He does come when he hears the noise.* (southern HE speaker quoted by Henry 1957: 171)

Any hypothesis that seeks to relate HE and NWBE through their habitual markers must therefore take *do (be)* into account. The fact that Bailey's hypothesis fails to do this is especially problematic because the seventeenth-century Irish servants whom he sees as a key link in the diffusion process would have been southern HE speakers, undoubtedly favoring *do (be)* over *be*. These two weaknesses of Bailey's diffusion hypothesis force us to reject it as it stands.

8.3.2   A revised diffusion hypothesis

This hypothesis, which differentiates northern and southern HE, can be used to develop a more sophisticated version. Its starting point is the geographical distribution of the habitual markers in HE as reported above.

As noted in section 8.2, Ulster had a high proportion of Scottish settlers; and the prevalence of habitual *be* there, instead of *do be*, probably represents the influence of Scottish English dialects in the seventeenth century. On the one hand, these dialects "were extremely resistant to periphrasitic *do*" (Guilfoyle 1983: 28, citing Ellegård 1953: 164) – in sharp contrast to the southwestern English dialects which were more prevalent in the southern provinces of Ireland. On the other hand, the Scots dialects also retained, later than other English dialects, a distinction between *I be* (predictive, habitual) and *I am* (immediate present, eternal truths); this goes back to the Old English distinction between *beo-* and *wes-*. Traugott (1972: 116), who discusses the issue in more detail, cites the following example from a sixteenth-century Scottish English text:

13   *Traist weill . . . the feild this da beis ouris* "Trust well . . . the field this day will-be ours."

Northern HE *be(es)* may have come directly from Scots derivatives of *beo-*, or may represent the convergent influence of these Scots derivatives and the Irish habitual *bí(dh)* (see Bliss 1972: 75, fn. 75; Guilfoyle 1983: 29).

By contrast, the southern provinces of Ireland did not have so high a proportion of Scottish settlers; the prevalence there of habitual *do* (*be*) is usually attributed to transfer from native Irish and the influence of southwestern English dialects, in which periphrastic *do* was common. Bliss 1972 and Guilfoyle disagree on the role played by morphological changes in seventeenth-century Irish in this transfer (see Harris 1985 for a convenient summary of the issues); but the geographical distribution of *be* and *do* (*be*) in HE offers a neat explanation for the geographical distribution of *be* and *does* (*be*) in NWBE.

We concluded from our survey of Irish/African contact that the seventeenth and eighteenth centuries were most propitious for linguistic diffusion in the New World. During this period, the primary difference between Irish emigration to North America and the Caribbean was that northern HE (Scotch Irish) speakers went in large numbers to the former region, but not to the latter. Given these considerations, it is possible to frame the following hypothesis: VBE *be* might represent diffusion from the large body of northern HE speakers who emigrated to North America in the colonial period (as Traugott 1972: 190–1 first suggested); and the *does* (*be*) of Caribbean English Creoles might represent diffusion from the southern HE (native Irish) speakers who constituted the overwhelming majority of "Irish" immigrants to this region. To put it another way: the current distribution of habitual markers in VBE and the Caribbean English Creoles might reflect the relative distribution of northern and southern HE speakers in the colonial New World.

This hypothesis – an extension of Traugott's Scotch Irish diffusion proposal – at once eliminates the major weaknesses of Bailey's proposal, and accords with the social history summarized above. In these respects, it is an attractive hypothesis; but it does have its demerits.

One is that *do* is apparently more common with *be* than with other verbs in southern HE (Bliss 1972: 77; Guilfoyle 1983: 24); but in Gullah and the Caribbean Creoles, where we would expect heavy southern HE influence, *does* is more common with other verbs than with *be*. The difference may result in part from the fact that Irish marks the habitual/non-habitual distinction only on *be* (the "substantive" verb), and in part from the fact that creole predicates either do not require *be* at all, or do so in fewer contexts than Hibernian or British varieties of English (see section 8.3.4 below). In either case, we are reminded to beware of assuming outright diffusion between HE and NWBE. Aspectual markers of the former must have been filtered through African and creole semantic and syntactic categories, when borrowed by NWBE speakers; and unless we consider this, we will find mismatches between HE and NWBE usage which are otherwise inexplicable.

A second demerit is that, while we can be fairly certain that northern HE *be* was not diffused to the Caribbean (since few Scotch Irish went there), we cannot be sure that southern HE *do* (*be*) was not introduced to the North American colonies. As noted above, native Irish servants were present in colonial North America in significant numbers, and we would expect them to have left a *do*(*es*) *be* legacy in VBE as well as in the Caribbean Creoles. This is especially true since the native Irish were present in North America earlier than the Scotch Irish, and had closer social contact with African and Afro-American slaves.

Not only must we allow for the introduction of habitual *do* (*be*) to America, but we also need to account for its subsequent disappearance – since habitual-marking reflexes of *do* survive in the USA today only in the Sea Islands. The decreolization hypothesis to be presented in section 8.3.4 offers a convincing means of overcoming this difficulty; but first we need to consider a further expansion.

8.3.3   A further expansion of the diffusion hypothesis

It has been known for some time that periphrastic *do* was common in British English between 1500 and 1700 (OED s.v. *do*, 25a), and that it continued long afterward in southwestern English dialects (Engblom 1938; Ellegård 1953). Given the strong representation of southwestern dialects among the white colonial population of the Caribbean (see table 8.1 above), it is plausible to suggest that these may have played some role in the development of habitual *does* and *does be* in the Caribbean English Creoles – perhaps reinforcing the model of southern HE *do* (*be*) habituals used by native Irish servants. Niles (1980: 125–6) makes precisely this point, citing the following examples among others (from Elworthy 1886: xx, xlvi) to show that "uninflected *do* marked the present habitual" in non-standard southwestern English:

14   *I du zay zom prayers now and again.* (Devon)
15   *He do markety* "He usually attends market." (Dorset)

Harris 1985 independently advances a similar thesis. Drawing on Elworthy 1879, Ihalainen 1976, and other sources, he argues that there were non-standard British dialects, particularly in the south and southwest, which probably served as a model for habitual *do* (*be*) both in southern HE and Caribbean mesolectal creoles. In addition to southwestern English examples like those given by Niles, Harris cites habitual *do be* examples like these from Wright (1898: 99):[13]

16   *She do be strict with us gals.* (Oxfordshire)
17   *The childer do be laffen at me.* (Cornwall)

Harris 1985 expresses the view that the revised diffusion hypothesis of section 8.3.2, above, is strengthened by the British dialect evidence, since the existence of *do* (*be*) habituals in the Caribbean could be jointly attributed to the influence of southern HE and southwestern English dialects. However, my feeling is that, while the British dialect evidence is important for our efforts to unravel the origin of NWBE habituals,[14] it increases the difficulty noted at the end of section 8.3.2 – since southern and southwestern English speakers were plentiful in America as well as the Caribbean, and would probably have carried habitual *do* (*be*) to both regions. Thus statistics in Smith (1947: 309) indicate that, between 1654 and 1686, more white servants emigrated from Bristol to Virginia (4,874) than to Barbados (2,678). In eighteenth-century America, British immigrants were almost as numerous as the Irish, and sometimes even more so. Between 1745 and 1775, 4,116 servants entered Annapolis from London and Bristol, compared with 5,835 from Ireland (Smith 1947: 325); between 1746 and 1778, 8,707 convicts were transported to Maryland from London and Bristol, compared with only 83 from Ireland (ibid., 329).

In short, whether we consider possible influence from native Irish or southwestern British immigrants, we must allow for the introduction of habitual *do* (*be*) to America – and for the subsequent loss of reflexes of *do*, except in *do* support contexts. As suggested above, the decreolization hypothesis to be considered next overcomes this difficulty of both expanded diffusion hypotheses, but is compatible with their insights and evidence.

8.3.4   A decreolization hypothesis

The hypothesis with creole *does* (*be*) as source (first formulated in Rickford 1974), is that *be* emerged as a VBE habitual marker as part of a decreolization process involving the loss of *does* – a habitual marker with which *be* co-occurred in some environments in an earlier American plantation creole. The emergence of *be* as a replacement for *does* should, according to this theory, be seen as only one of a series of English-approximating shifts in the language of Africans in the New World: *does* itself replaces a basilectal creole habitual marker (*d*)*a*, (*d*)*e*, (*t*)*e*, or *blan*(*g*), and the existence of the habitual category in the basilect perhaps represents substratal influence from the native languages of the earliest West African slaves, several of which have an explicitly marked category of habitual aspect (Stewart 1970a: 247, Dalby 1972, Welmers 1973: 393, Alleyne 1980: 163–4). The marking of habituality in the basilect may also be a creole universal (see section 8.3.6, below).[15]

Taking (*d*)*a* as a basilectal starting point, and allowing for minor differences according to the kind of predicate it precedes, we might represent the major decreolizing stages as follows.

18   Habitual aspect with a prepositional phrase or locative:
     Stage 1: *He (d)a de [dɛ] in the bed.* (basilect)[16]
     Stage 2: *He does de in the bed.* (hab. *(d)a → does*)
     Stage 3: *He does be in the bed.* (loc. cop. *de → be*)
     Stage 4: *He Ø be in the bed.* (*does → Ø; be* "habitual")
19   Habitual aspect with a continuative or progressive verb:
     Stage 1: *He (d)a de {(d)a/pon} work.* (basilect)[17]
     Stage 2: *He does de {(d)a/pon} work.* (hab. *(d)a → does*)
     Stage 3: *He does be working.* (*de → be*; also, progressive *(d)a* V or *pon* V →
          V + *ing*)
     Stage 4: *He Ø be working.* (*does → Ø; be* "habitual")
20   Habitual aspect with an adjective:
     Stage 1: *He (d)a quiet.* (basilect)[18]
     Stage 2: *He does quiet.* (*(d)a → does*)
     Stage 3: *He does be quiet.* (with *quiet* re-analysed as adj., not verb, necessitat-
          ing introduction of cop. *be*)
     Stage 4: *He Ø be quiet.* (*does → Ø; be* "habitual")

Even though the successive lines of these derivations are described as different "stages," two or more stages could have coexisted simultaneously, as they do in some parts of the Caribbean. Given that some slaves had more exposure to English than others from the very start of black/white contact in the New World (e.g. house slaves, or those on plantations with a high proportion of Whites; Stewart 1967, Alleyne 1971), it is possible that stages 1–3 (and perhaps pidgin stages as well) might have existed on American plantations from the seventeenth century. What undoubtedly would have changed over time, however, is the relative proportion of speakers controlling each level or stage; those controlling the levels closer to English would have increased, as opportunity and motivation for approximating English increased, while the basilect and lower mesolectal stages would have fallen away, as the number of people who spoke them dwindled (Alleyne 1980: 192, Rickford 1983a).[19] In most Afro-American speech communities today, all but stage 4 have been lost. On the Sea Islands, however, earlier stages survive, allowing us to reconstruct the general process.

   One merit of this hypothesis, compared with the preceding diffusion hypotheses, is that it does not require the incredible assumption that Blacks in America were empty slates on which the dialect features of Whites were faithfully and flawlessly transcribed. On the contrary, it recognizes (a) that white varieties of English, as acquired by generations of West African slaves who arrived on American plantations speaking no English (Read 1939: 250), would often have been influenced by the structures and categories of their native languages (Alleyne 1980); (b) that they did not always have good access to or interaction with native speakers of English in this new environment, and (c) that they were a displaced multilingual population, needing to communicate with each other via this alien tongue before they had developed extensive competence in it. These are the kinds of conditions for second language acquisition in which pidgin and creole varieties develop (Andersen 1983: 3); and if the earliest Africans learned their English from Irish servants who were themselves learning English, pidginization in the form of "tertiary hybridization" (Whinnom 1971: 105) would have been even more likely. Furthermore, some Africans must have arrived from the Caribbean or the Guinea Coast already speaking an English pidgin or creole (Stewart 1967, Hancock 1986, Rickford 1997a). In either case, there is independent documentary and other evidence that pidgin and creole varieties were among the forerunners of modern VBE (Walser 1955, Stewart 1967, 1974, Dillard 1972, Traugott 1976, Rickford 1977, Fasold 1981, Baugh 1983, Holm 1984, Rickford 1998, Winford 1997, 1998).

A second merit of this hypothesis is that its decreolizing route – involving increasing formal approximations to English, while creole semantic/syntactic categories are essentially retained – fits in with theoretical formulations of decreolization in linguistics (Stewart 1962, Bickerton 1980: 113) and of cultural assimilation in anthropology.[20] It is in accord with Herskovits's concept of cultural reinterpretation, for instance, summarized by Stewart (1974: 36, fn. 2) as follows:

> In the Herskovitsian sense, "reinterpretation" is an acculturative mechanism involving the association of newly borrowed forms with older functions and meanings. In this way, non-prestigious Old World cultural traits can be retained under disguise as prestigious New World ones.

A third merit of this hypothesis is that it can account not only for the development of invariant *be Verb + ing* as the VBE habitual marker for verbal continuatives (as in 19 above), but also for the emergence of the *verb* as a habitual marker for verbal non-continuatives (see Bickerton 1975: 117 for GC parallels). The derivation is as follows.[21]

21 Habitual aspect with a verbal non-continuative predicate:
   Stage 1: *He (d)a work.* (basilect)
   Stage 2: *He does work.* ((d)a → does)
   Stage 3: *He does work.* (nothing new; no need to introduce *be* as main verb, since S already has one)
   Stage 4a: *He Ø work.* (does → Ø)

Note that the habitual marker at stage 1, as well as the transitions between stages 1–2 and stages 3–4, are exactly the same as in 18–20; what leads to a different result in 21 is the fact that the predicate here is a non-continuative main verb, and continues to be analyzed as such throughout the derivation; this obviates the need for the introduction of *be* at stage 3.[22]

A fourth merit of this hypothesis is that the decreolizing stages or levels set out in 18–20 (and the processes which link them) are attested in creoles which are regional neighbors if not relatives of VBE, enhancing the plausibility of the diachronic derivation proposed for VBE *be*. Since these stages are so central to this proposal, we will examine the evidence in some detail.

The basilectal or stage 1 form (*d*)*a* (and related variants, like *ta* in Saramaccan, *de* in Sierra Leone, *di* in Cameroon Pidgin, *e* in Sranan and Djuka), is attested in pidgins and creoles on both sides of the Atlantic: from Suriname, Guyana, Barbados, and South Carolina to Liberia, Nigeria, Cameroon, and Sierra Leone Creole (Alleyne 1980: 80–5; Hancock 1987). Gullah or Sea Island Creole, as spoken in South Carolina and Georgia, is sometimes reported as lacking *da* in habitual function (Alleyne, ibid.); but Brasch (1981: 62) cites a nineteenth-century discussion of its use on St Helena Island, and Turner (1949: 264) includes a text from Diana Brown of Edisto Island in which several examples occur, including this one:

22   [an dɛm ca əm ɟi dɪ ɲɒŋ pipl wɒt d̲ə̲ wʌk dɛ ɒn dɛm ples] "and them carry
      it give the young people what work there on them place."

The (*d*)*a* of stage 1 probably represents convergence between Eng. habitual *do* and similar West African forms: Yoruba (*a*)*máá*, Ewe *-na*, Twi *re*, *da*, Ibo *de*, Wolof *di* (see Alleyne 1980: 90, 163–4; Turner 1949: 214; Stewart 1970: 247; Cassidy and Le Page 1980: 141). Such convergence is frequent with pidgin/creole forms (Cassidy 1966, Hall 1966: 61, Rickford 1974, Mühlhäusler 1982).[23]

The stage 2 form – unstressed habitual *does* – is modeled on Eng. *does* rather than *do*, but is morphologically invariant.[24] It is not found in the Suriname creoles, or in other areas where decreolization has been minimal; but it occurs as a mesolectal variant of basilectal (*d*)*a* in communities like Guyana and in the Sea Islands. It also occurs instead of (*d*)*a* in places like the Bahamas and St Kitts, where decreolization is more advanced. A Sea Islands example in a non-continuative verbal environment is:

23   *But I does go to see people when they sick.*

(This and other Sea Islands examples below, not otherwise referenced, were recorded by me in 1970, from elderly speakers who are now deceased.) Like (*d*)*a*, *does* is neutral at first between past and non-past; but as decreolization proceeds, it becomes increasingly restricted to non-past (Rickford 1974: 99, Bickerton 1975: 116).

Stage 3, involving the introduction of non-finite *be* after *does* – either as a replacement for the creole copula *de*, or as a replacement for Ø (in the case of the re-analyzed adjectives) – is crucial in this proposal. It is attested in the Caribbean mesolects (Alleyne 1980: 213) and in the Sea Islands:

24 *I'll miss C, cause she does be here and write letter for me sometimes.*
25 *He does be up and cut wood sometimes.*

While inflected forms of the copula like *is* and *were* carry person/number and tense information, the invariant *be* which is introduced at this stage is semantically "empty," required merely as a syntactic link between *does* (or a modal auxiliary) and an adjective or similar predicate – a past participle, prepositional phrase, VERB + *ing*, or NP.[25]

The stage 4 demise of *does* in the creole predecessors of VBE may have resulted from realization of its non-standard character; but it was undoubtedly facilitated by phonological reduction processes, as synchronic style shifts and decreolization changes often are in creole continua (Rickford 1980; Singler 1984). The central rule in this process is the one providing for the loss of the initial voiced stop in a tense/aspect auxiliary – a rule which is relatively rare in white colloquial varieties of English,[26] but common enough in VBE and the West Atlantic creoles. As evidence for it, note VBE [õ no] for "don't know," [ãmə] for "I'm gonna" and *ain't* for "didn't." Compare variation in the Sea Islands and in many Caribbean creoles between progressive/habitual *da* and *a*, *de*, *te* and *e*; habitual *does* and *oes*; anterior *bin* and *in*; irrealis *go* and *o*, etc. Once the initial stop of *does* is assimilated by this rule, the remaining [əz] is subject to further contraction and deletion, as in the following Sea Island sentence – which I had filed as an example of habitual *be*, before I listened to the recording again and detected the lone sibilant which was the remnant of *does*:

26 *Sometimes you* [z] *be in the bed . . .*

The plausibility of the central claim in this proposal – that VBE habitual *be* emerged through the loss of *does* at stage 4 – is substantially enhanced by the fact that the process can still be observed. On the Sea Islands, *does* (*be*) is used as a marker of habitual aspect (as in 24–6) among adults over 60; but zero (before non-continuative verbs) and *be* (before nominals, locatives, adjectives and VERB + *ing*) are used instead by the youngest generation:

27 *But I Ø go to see people when they sick.*
28 *He Ø be up and cut wood sometimes.*

What seems clearly to have happened – the stages are set out in detail in Rickford 1980 – is that, partly because of the constant morphophonemic condensation and deletion of *does* by the older speakers, as in 26 – the form has not been transmitted to younger Sea Islanders. In the absence of *does*, they have reinterpreted zero as the habitual marker in the case of verb-stem environments like 27, and *be* as the habitual marker in other environments like 28.[27]

The fifth merit of this hypothesis is that it can incorporate the strengths of the revised diffusion hypotheses presented in sections 8.3.2–3.3 above, while overcoming their weaknesses. Since the lexicon of pidgins and creoles usually derives primarily from the superstrate, the possibility that available HE or British dialects might have served as models for the lexical instantiation of the habitual in earlier pidgin or creole varieties of NWBE is no problem for this hypothesis. At the same time, the fact that the habitual category was incorporated into the Atlantic creoles, while other semantic/syntactic features of the English models were not (see section 8.4 below and Harris 1985), can be explained by reference to substratal influence – several West African languages have a habitual, continuative, or non-punctual category – and creole universals: creoles frequently have a non-punctual aspectual category which simultaneously mediates between habituals and continuatives. These factors also help to explain why the basilectal $(d)a$ of Atlantic creoles is used for both continuative and habitual functions (i.e. is a true non-punctual), while the *do* of HE and British dialects marks habitual alone; why $(d)a$ does not retain the inflectional morphology of HE and British *do* (creoles typically have no inflectional morphology); and why it assumes phonological shapes which the English equivalent does not (forms like *de* and *di* represent convergence between English and West African inputs, while *a* and *e* result from applications of the pan-creole rule which deletes initial voiced stops in tense/aspect auxiliaries).

At the mesolectal level, either Hibernian or British varieties of English must have served as models for the choice of *does* as replacement for $(d)a$ in decreolizing varieties of NWBE. But the fact that the mesolectal creole form shows no person/number inflection can be attributed to the general invariance of creole verb stems.[28] The fact that it is realized in phonologically reduced forms ([əz, z]) and eventually disappears can be accounted for by reference to decreolization and the creole phonological reduction rules which this process exploits.

But what of cases in which the superstrate input to NWBE varieties was not habitual *do*, but *be*? Recall from sections 8.3.2–3.3 that this is most likely to have come from northern HE (southern HE and British varieties use *do be* in equivalent environments); it would have affected only locative/prepositional, adjectival, and continuative predicates (British and Hibernian varieties of English all use habitual *do* with non-continuative main verbs). Since northern HE speakers went in significant numbers to North America but not to the Caribbean, their influence might be partly responsible for the fact that decreolization has resulted in the emergence of invariant *be* as the habitual marker in VBE, but not in the Caribbean creoles.

Though it is valuable to bear this possible HE influence in mind, there are at least two other independent explanations. The first – which helps to account for one weakness of the revised diffusion hypothesis discussed in section 8.3.2

above – is that the Caribbean mesolects often do NOT employ *be* after tense/ aspect and modal auxiliaries where British and Hibernian varieties require it. Note the following recorded examples:

29 *Well Sunday you say you does Ø busy.* (Guyana)
30 *Holiday gon Ø too far from now.* (Guyana)
31 *ai waan Ø nors* "I want to be a nurse." (Jamaica, reported in Craig 1980: 113)

Clearly, if no *be* is present in pre-adjectival and other environments, it cannot emerge as the habitual marker if and when the habitual *does* disappears. Note too that the tenacity of the creole locative verb *de* in the Caribbean, as in *She does de in the room* instead of *She does be in the room* (see Bickerton 1973: 651–2), also militates against the emergence of *be* as habitual. The second explanation is that, in the Caribbean, creole speakers represent a vast majority of the local population;[29] full forms of *does* are heard too often for it to lose its foothold as the regular habitual marker. Occasional instances of *does*-deletion leaving an invariant *be* do occur:

32 *These days the sun be down fast.* (overheard in a hire-car, just outside Georgetown, Guyana, 1974)

But such instances are immediately relatable to stable synchronic variation involving *does*, and the possibility of reinterpreting *be* as the real habitual marker is slight.[30] By contrast, even in the early 1970s, the proportion of regular *does* users in the Sea Island community where I worked was small; the reduction and deletion rules affecting it frequently applied; and the conditions for the diachronic loss of *does* and reinterpretation of *be* were ideal. At present, virtually all the *does* users whom I recorded in the 1970s have died, and *be* has emerged as the primary habitual marker. If the intermediate developments, involving the reduction and deletion of *does*, had not been recorded in the 1970s, the emergence of *be* as a habitual marker on the Sea Islands might have been as much of a mystery as its emergence in VBE is usually assumed to be, and the former development would not have been able to shed any light on the latter.

One possible demerit of this hypothesis is that it will not work (unless we assume diffusion among Afro-Americans) for areas in which pidgin and creole varieties did not develop. This is most likely to have happened in the American north. In places like Pennsylvania, where a low ratio of Blacks to Whites and other conditions favored relatively successful and rapid acculturation,[31] it is possible that markedly pidginized and creolized varieties of English might not have developed among Africans and Afro-Americans. Their acquisition of white varieties of English, including those spoken by the Scotch Irish (who were the dominant white immigrants and indentured servants in the eighteenth century) might have been more like "ordinary" second language acquisition (Andersen 1983: 1–56), with some substratal transfer and a series of interlingual stages, but less opportunity for tertiary hybridization and creolization. The emergence of habitual *be* in the speech of Blacks from this region could be attributed in a rather straightforward fashion to the influence of northern HE models. However, even if we concede the possibility that pidginization and creolization might not have occurred in the American north – and there are theoretical and empirical reasons for not doing so too readily (see Stewart 1974: 19ff.) – we cannot claim that northern VBE has no creole roots, for "black speech in the north is a consequence of migration from the South" (Bailey and Naylor 1983). The possibility that pidgin or creole speech was widespread among Blacks in the south is very strong, given black/white ratios comparable to those of the Caribbean;[32] and as late as 1880, more than 75 percent of the American black population was in the south (Franklin 1974: 290).

A second possible demerit is that the English-speaking Caribbean, the Sea Islands, and the mainland USA may differ sufficiently in the sources of their African populations to make us hesitant about assuming the similar creole starting points which this proposal requires. Hancock 1980 and Nichols (1983: 209) have pointed out that the Sea Islands imported more slaves from Senegambia and Angola than did the American mainland and/or the Caribbean; and statistics in Curtin 1969 and Le Page 1960 reveal other demographic differences in the sources of Africans sent to different parts of the New World. Jamaica and Virginia imported higher proportions of slaves from the Bight of Biafra and the Niger Delta than either South Carolina or Guyana, while Guyana and Jamaica imported higher proportions from the Gold Coast and the Bight of Benin than either Virginia or South Carolina.

Although there *are* linguistic differences between the North American mainland, the Sea Islands, and individual territories within the Caribbean (Hancock 1980: 28), and some of these *may* go back to differences in the sources of their African populations,[33] the similarities between the most archaic varieties of NWBE attested for these areas are striking enough to suggest that they derive ultimately from similar, if not identical, pidgin/creole roots.[34] This point has recently been made for the lexicon by Cassidy 1980, comparing Sranan, Jamaican, and Gullah; and for phonology and morphosyntax by Alleyne 1980 and by Brasch – the former concentrating on evidence from the Caribbean Creoles, the latter on documentary evidence from the USA. Of particular relevance to our present concerns is the fact that the NWBE varieties of these areas share a rule for the deletion of initial voiced stops in tense/aspect auxiliaries (Rickford 1980), facilitating the reduction and loss of habitual (*d*)*a* and *does*.

Furthermore, since this hypothesis assumes that the choice of *does* (*be*) as the mesolectal *form* of the habitual derives, at least in part, from British or Hibernian varieties of English, inter-territorial differences in the African origins of

New World black populations are less significant than they might otherwise be (if we were looking at straight "Africanisms," for instance). The fact that Jamaican lacks habitual *does* may, as suggested in note 7, have more to do with the relative size and origins of its *white* population in the formative period.

A third potential demerit of this hypothesis is that, while good synchronic evidence exists for its derivational stages from the Atlantic Creoles, we do not have quite as much diachronic evidence for them from the North American mainland. Brasch (1981: 36, 62) provides several nineteenth-century attestations of habitual *da, do,* or *does* (reduced to *'s*) from the Sea Island area, but only one example (120) from "southern plantation speech" more generally. Oomen 1985 has found examples of iterative *does* in the narratives of 17 ex-slaves from South Carolina, but its occurrence there is reported to be "generally infrequent." One example of *does be* in these narratives (56) is:

33 *You know some people does be right fast in catchin chillun* (i.e. getting pregnant).

In considering this limited documentary evidence, however, we should bear in mind several mitigating considerations. First, documentation on the language and culture of New World slave populations, particularly from the seventeenth century,[35] is extremely limited. As Ascher (1974: 11) has noted, there is less direct documentation on American slaves than on any other American group. Second, such documentation as exists has not yet been carefully and systematically examined for the existence of *da* and *does* (*be*) in VBE.[36] Third, existing grammatical descriptions and texts from Caribbean and Sea Island communities typically show *da* and *does* as occurring less often than they do in casual everyday speech. This may reflect upward code-switching by the creole speakers on whose usage the texts and descriptions are based (Turner 1949: 12; Bickerton 1981: 305); or mishearings by field workers unfamiliar with the usage (Turner 1949: 14); or failure to notice the forms because their nonstandardness is masked or camouflaged (Rickford and Rickford 1976, Spears 1982); or the fact that the semantic conditions which occasion the use of these forms are rare in recorded texts. Sentences in which habitual or generic conditions are expressed occur very infrequently in the texts cited by Brasch, and even habitual *be* is attested only a few times (27).[37] These mitigating considerations should not discourage us from searching for documentary evidence, but they make the immediate absence of such evidence less damaging than might otherwise be the case.

The strength of the merits associated with this decreolization hypothesis, and the weakness of its potential demerits, establish it as the single best explanation for the origin of VBE *be.* Before summarizing the discussion in this section and going on to my conclusion, however, we must briefly consider three minor alternative hypotheses.

Table 8.3

Time 1		*am*	Plantation Creole
Time 2		*am/be*	early BE
Time 3		*be*	early BE
Time 4	*I*	*am/be*	present-day BE

8.3.5   *Decreolization from creole* am

The only other alternative advanced in the literature to date is Brewer's suggestion (1974) that *be* was a replacement for durative (continuative/iterative) *am*
in early VBE. Drawing on WPA slave narratives recorded in the 1930s (see
Yetman 1967), she concludes that *am* was used in early VBE very much like
invariant *be*, and suggests (80) the process of change shown in table 8.3.

Am is introduced at time 1, according to this proposal, as an invariant "first-
replacement form for an earlier base creole form such as *de* or *da*." After varying
with *be*, and then being replaced by *be* (times 2 and 3), it is reintroduced at time
4 as a "form marked to occur with *I*."

This proposal shares with the preceding decreolization proposal the merit of
providing for the dynamic evolution of VBE over time, via a process (constant
meaning, changing form) in harmony with existing theories of cultural reinterpretation and decreolization. It also has the merit of being built on accessible
documentary evidence. However, its plausibility rests to a considerable extent
on the similarity between *am* and *be* in early VBE. Brewer shows that the forms
were similar in that they were used with a variety of person/number subjects,[38]
and with a variety of predicates. She also argues that *am* shared with *be* the
function of indicating habitual, iterative, or extended states of affairs; but the
evidence for this central claim is less convincing. Some of the *am* sentences
which she cites do have clear habitual or iterative meanings of the type usually
associated with *be*:

34   *But lots of times when us sposed to mind de calves, us am out eating watermillions*
     in de bresh. (Texas; Brewer 1974: ex. 34)
35   *De women am off Friday afternoon to wash clothes.* (Texas: ibid. ex. 36)

But many others do not, including examples like the following – which are
regarded by Brewer herself (78) as counter-examples, because they refer to
single occurrences at one point in time:[39]

36   *I's 21 year old den, but it am de first time I's gone any place, 'cept to de neighbors.*
     (Texas; ex. 71)

37   . . . *de next morning dat Delbridge am shunt off de place, cause Massa Haley seed*
       he niggers was all gaunt. (Texas; ex. 70)

Another demerit of this proposal, when compared with the preceding decreolization proposal, is that the transition from *da* to *be* via *am* is not attested in other creole communities; it does not build on existing phonological similarities and processes within the continuum, as decreolization typically does. Finally, although this decreolization hypothesis might account for VBE habitual *be*, it does not account for the emergence and persistence of habitual *does* in the Sea Islands and the Caribbean.

In sum, while Brewer has drawn attention to a potential habitual marker (*am*) which was more frequent and significant in the grammar of early VBE than previously recognized, her hypothesis about the origin of VBE *be* is not as attractive as the decreolization and revised diffusion proposals considered above.

8.3.6   Universals of creolization

A plausible argument for influence from creole universals can be made with respect to the semantics of *be*. As noted above, a non-punctual category, covering both habitual and continuative aspect, is a universal feature of creole tense/ aspect systems – perhaps a part of an innate linguistic bio-program (Bickerton 1981: 27–30). But it is clear that the nature of the superstrate targets shapes the selection of intermediate forms; and such targets are the result of historical accidents rather than universal principles. The presence of Scots English speakers in Ulster apparently influenced the emergence of invariant *be* as habitual in northern HE, and the presence of northern HE speakers in America might have helped to ensure a similar development in VBE. Arguments from universals, then, take us only part of the way in accounting for the emergence of VBE habitual *be*; they help to explain its semantics, but not its form. Moreover, the positive features of a universals hypothesis have already been incorporated in the decreolization hypothesis explored in section 8.3.4 above.

8.3.7   Independent development

A final alternative is to consider *be* as an independent development of VBE, virtually unrelated to features of HE or British English or the Caribbean Creoles. Spears (1982: 867) has raised this possibility with respect to semi-auxiliary *come*;[40] and the development of stressed *bin* as a remote-phase marker also represents a VBE innovation (Rickford 1977: 207), even though its interaction with the stative/non-stative distinction and its parallels to *done* and *bin* in the Caribbean reveal creole connections.

But it is difficult to see why habitual *be* should have emerged in VBE, or where it might have come from, *without* reference to any of the central elements in the competing hypotheses: substratal transfer, superstratal influence, diffusion or decreolization. The evidence and arguments in favor of decreolization from *does* (*be*) clearly make it a superior hypothesis.

8.3.8   Summary

C.-J. N. Bailey's proposal that (undifferentiated) HE might have been the source of NWBE habitual *be* founders on the facts that *does* (*be*), rather than *be*, is the primary habitual marker in mesolectal Caribbean Creoles – and that *do* (*be*), rather than *be*, is the primary habitual marker in southern HE. Six alternatives have been discussed in turn; but only three are sufficiently congruent with relevant internal (formal, semantic) and external (geographical, historical) considerations to be entertained seriously.

One is a revised diffusion proposal, according to which northern HE is seen as a source of VBE *be* and southern HE as a source of Caribbean *does* (*be*). This accounts neatly for the absence of habitual *be* in the Caribbean, since few northern HE speakers went there. However, since many southern HE speakers emigrated to North America, and may have had close contact with Africans and Afro-Americans in the seventeenth to eighteenth centuries, it does not account for the absence of habitual *do* or *does* in VBE.

This problem also plagues the expanded diffusion hypothesis, according to which southern and southwestern British dialects are seen as other possible sources for habitual *does* (and (*d*)*a*) in the Caribbean. These dialects were also well represented in the USA, and might be expected to have left habitual *does* in VBE as well.

A decreolization proposal which relates VBE *be* to an earlier creole *does be* emerges as the strongest single hypothesis. Its assumption that the acquisition of English by Africans in the New World was often accompanied by substratal transfer, pidginization, creolization, and decreolization is more credible than the opposing assumption that it was not. Its decreolizing stages accord with independently formulated theories of cultural assimilation and contact-induced linguistic change, and are attested in Atlantic creoles which are neighbors if not relatives of VBE. Like the diffusion proposals, it assumes that HE and British dialects served as models for mesolectal creole *does* (*be*) both in the Caribbean and North America. But unlike these proposals, it has no difficulty in accounting for the loss of *does* and the emergence of habitual *be* in VBE. This is attributed to decreolization and associated phonological processes which are well-attested from the Sea Islands. Potential demerits of this hypothesis – e.g.

the fact that prior creolization is less likely to have occurred in the American north than the south – are relatively few; they are attenuated by mitigating factors (in this case the fact that the Afro-American roots of modern VBE are primarily southern), and are offset by the hypothesis's several strengths.

8.4   Conclusion

The diffusion of linguistic features between HE and NWBE was identified at the beginning of this paper as a potentially fruitful site for research on social contact and linguistic diffusion – a topic of considerable current interest within linguistics. We may now ask (a) whether further exploration of this issue seems profitable, and (b) what directions it might take.

The answer to (a) is a clear yes, because of the specific issues which remain to be settled about HE/NWBE diffusion, as well as their relevance to larger theoretical concerns. HE and NWBE both represent instances of convergence or admixture (Hymes 1971a 74ff.) between superstratal varieties of English, on the one hand, and one or more substratal languages, on the other (Irish and Scottish Gaelic in the former case; Twi, Yoruba, and other West African languages in the latter). Both HE and NWBE were in active formation and flux when contact between their respective speakers was most intense; here we can raise the general question of whether languages are especially subject to external influences at times like these (birth, death, rapid social/political change). Untangling the sources of HE/NWBE resemblances is a particularly challenging and rewarding enterprise for the historical linguist or sociolinguist, as this detailed survey of habitual *does* (*be*) and *be* has shown. Do such resemblances reflect the influence of a common superstrate? This conclusion has been favored recently by researchers working on distinctive features of HE (Guilfoyle 1983; Harris 1982) and NWBE (Bailey and Maynor 1987; Mufwene 1996); and it is supported, in the case of the habitual markers, by the possibility that southern British dialects might have provided a common model for southern HE and Caribbean *do(es) be*, while northern British dialects (especially Scots) were the model for northern HE and VBE *be*. At the same time, the contributions of the substrate languages are inescapable, especially insofar as the retention of a habitual or non-punctual category in the new hybrid languages is concerned. Creolization and decreolization were very likely in many varieties of NWBE; and since these processes could have independently produced some of the resemblances between HE and NWBE, these must be actively considered, and reconciled with alternative explanations.

The way in which preverbal markers like *do(es)* and *be* meet their demise in New World English-speaking communities may be as fruitful to study as the way they arise. For the Old World, we have research by Ihalainen and by

Weltens 1983 (summarized in Trudgill 1984b, Harris 1985), indicating that the habitual/punctual distinction in southwestern English – traditionally signalled by *do* = V vs. V (*do go* vs. *go*) and *did* + V vs. V-*ed* (*did go* vs. *went*) – is being weakened and lost among middle-aged and younger speakers. For the Sea Islands, there is the evidence on the erosion and loss of *does* reported above. But for other parts of the New World, we need to know when and how similar habitual forms – as used by southwestern British, Irish, and African speakers – ceased to be adopted by their younger generations, and what motivations and linguistic mechanisms facilitated this development. Are the forms themselves replaced or eroded, as in decreolization? Or do they remain, but undergo semantic shift, as appears to be the result of dialect contact in southwest England? Understanding the process of individual feature loss may contribute to an understanding of the larger and more complex process of language death (cf. Dorian), and both will contribute to the understanding of language change in general.

Apart from linguistic details about habitual markers, questions remain about the sociolinguistic characteristics of Irish/African relations in the New World. Were features like *do(es)* and *be* merely the linguistic correlates of sparks of discontent and rebellion which crossed between colonial slaves and bond servants as they worked together in the fields? In the terminology of Le Page's social-psychological model (1978), did a relatively "focused" Irish/African speech community emerge in British colonies in the seventeenth to eighteenth centuries, with class solidarity overriding ethnic distinctiveness? Was it accompanied by linguistic convergence from both sides? When and how did the social concord give way to conflict or disinterest? If linguistic divergence followed, was this an undoing of earlier convergence, or simply a failure to share innovations? These are fascinating questions, with potential theoretical insights for sociolinguistics and historical linguistics. And since we have by no means exhausted the relevant data or theory, the promise that insightful answers can be reached is strong.

Insofar as further research is concerned, one major need is for historical work which utilizes primary rather than secondary sources. The latter are invaluable for indicating that Irish and African populations were in the same place at the same time, with more or less the same status; but to go beyond general inferences from these facts, we need more specifics about the origins of the Irish and Africans who settled there, and what their working arrangements and inter-ethnic relations were like. We also need more contemporary references to and samples of their speech. Newspaper advertisements (Read 1937), the records of shipping companies and plantations, the letters and commentaries of contemporary observers and participants, the literary works of earlier periods, and the oral histories of aged survivors will yield more information along these lines (cf. Brasch); but locating and sifting through them will require the historian's methods, patience, and dedication – a rarity among linguists (Le

Page 1960 and Baker 1982 (a and b) are exceptions). For maximum depth, this documentary research should be limited to one colony or city at a time. In the course of this paper, Barbados, Jamaica, Virginia, the Sea Islands, and Philadelphia have each emerged as significant in some way; linguistically oriented documentary research on any one of them would be valuable.

Unknown to many scholars, and an obvious locus for further research, are other synchronic resemblances between HE and NWBE. With respect to phonology, some HE and Caribbean English dialects are similar in their pronunciations of standard /ʌ/ as [ɔ] or something similar (C.-J. Bailey 1982: 237–8; Cassidy and Le Page 1968: lii; Hancock 1969: 36ff.; Le Page 1972: 103, 111, 167, 185; Wells 1982a: 422, 1982b: 576; Winford 1979: 5–28) and in their palatalization of velar consonants before *a* (C.-J. Bailey 1982: 238–9; Cassidy and Le Page 1980: lvii; Edwards 1976; Wells 1982b: 569). VBE resembles English as spoken in some parts of western Ireland in the neutralization of /ɪ/ and /ɛ/ before nasals (Fasold and Wolfram 1970, Wells 1982a: 423). In syntax, southern HE and Caribbean BE both have a focusing rule involving clefting and the use of the copula, instead of (or in addition to) constituent fronting. Compare the HE ex. 38 (from Henry, cited by Sullivan 1973) with its basilectal GC equivalent (ex. 39):

38   'Twas a bullock we had.
39   a wan bul kau awi bin gat.

In terms of the ethnography of speaking, the description of Irish *blarney* as the use of verbal eloquence to outsmart a more powerful opponent (cf. Wakin 1976) recalls NWBE parallels in Caribbean folktales about Brer Rabbit and Anansi, and in the VBE speech event known as *coppin a plea* (Kochman 1970, Abrahams 1978).

These and other similarities will not be worth pursuing, however, if we forget to balance them against differences in other areas of phonology or syntax,[41] to question the closeness of the similarities, and to consider sources of resemblance other than diffusion. For instance, on the evidence of Cassidy and Le Page (1980: lviii), the HE and Caribbean English resemblances with respect to palatalization of velars appear to derive from the common superstratal influence of seventeenth- to eighteenth-century native English dialects, with possible West African substrate reinforcement in the Caribbean varieties. Similarly, focusing in HE turns out to differ from its Caribbean counterpart under closer inspection: the latter requires, in focused verbs and adjectives, that the focused constituent be *copied*, not simply moved, from the extraction site. Contrast the GC ex. 40 with its southern HE equivalent (ex. 41):

40   iz vizit yu kom fu vizit?
41   Is it visiting you came Ø? (Molloy 1946: 35, cited by Sullivan 1973)

Compare also Kwa languages like Twi which front *with* copying, reminding us of the possible effects of substratal influence:[42]

42   *hwe na Kwasi hwe ase* "Kwasi actually fell," lit. "Fall is Kwasi fell down."
     (Alleyne 1980: 172)

Finally, it is unlikely that resemblances between Irish *blarney* and Afro-American *coppin a plea* (whether in Caribbean folktales or the streets of New York) result from diffusion. The Anansi stories have West African roots (Tanna 1984: 77); but verbal beguilement is probably a universal which surfaces more frequently and artfully among the powerless than the powerful. (Children, for instance, are typically better at it than adults.) Wakin (1976: 9) suggests that *blarney* and double-talk may represent strategies which the Irish used to compensate for weakness via-à-vis the English: "On one side, the powerful invader; on the other, the witty evader." And given that *coppin a plea* was often an Afro-American strategy for *puttin on ole massa* (Osofsky 1969), we may be dealing here with independent but parallel linguistic developments, resulting from parallel sociopolitical conditions.[43]

The ultimate goal of the research exemplified and advocated in this paper is not simply to solve historical riddles about the relation between HE and NWBE, but to enrich our understanding of how linguistic diffusion and change proceed – bearing in mind Weinreich's still relevant dictum (1953: 3) that this requires attention to both linguistic and "extralinguistic" factors.

Notes

John Harris and I exchanged versions of this paper and his 1985 one, and were delighted to find that we had independently arrived at conclusions which were either convergent or complementary (see text for specific references to his work). It is a pleasure to acknowledge his correspondence and assistance, and to thank the following scholars for their suggestions and inputs as well: Roger Andersen, Frederic G. Cassidy, Ian F. Hancock, Nannette Morgan, Pat Nichols, Angela E. Rickford, Suzanne Romaine, John V. Singler, William A. Stewart, Sarah G. Thomason, and Elizabeth Closs Traugott. As usual, they should not be held responsible for any shortcomings of this paper. I am also grateful to Melissa Moyer and John Rawlings for bibliographic assistance, and to the Center for Research on International Studies, Stanford, for a grant which aided completion of this paper.

1   "Hiberno English" (HE) refers collectively to distinctive varieties of English spoken in "Ireland" (if one adopts the holistic Irish republican view) or the "Republic of Ireland" and "Northern Ireland" (according to the British partition). "Irish English" is sometimes used with roughly the same meaning, but is sometimes restricted to the English of people who speak Irish Gaelic as a first language.

"Northern HE" refers to varieties spoken in the historical province of Ulster. "Southern HE" refers to varieties spoken in the historical provinces of Connacht, Leinster, and Munster (see map 8.1).

2 I shall use "habitual" rather than "consuetudinary" (Bailey's term) for events which happen repeatedly, regularly, or habitually. VBE *be* and creole *does* are sometimes referred to by other labels, including "iterative" and "distributive" – as defined and used in relation to these forms, mean essentially the same thing. Thus Bickerton (1975: 63) describes *does* as "clearly limited to iterative ('habitual') expressions." Similarly, Fasold's observation (1972: 151) that "distributive *be*" is only used in iterative contexts to refer to states or events "which are periodically discontinued and again resumed" accords with my characterization of "habitual" above. However, the extent to which *does* and *be* are used for single events which are prolonged in time, but not habitual in the preceding sense, still requires further research. Baugh (1983: 71–2) cites some VBE *be* examples of this type, and it might be possible to include them under Comrie's broad definition of habituals (1976: 27) as "characteristic of an extended period of time."

3 These remarks are not meant to belittle Bailey's contribution, which was intended as a suggestive note rather than a definitive statement. The point remains, however, that his hypotheses can be assessed only in the light of more extensive sociohistorical and linguistic evidence.

4 As Heath (1984: 382) has noted, research on language-mixing tends to involve particularistic case studies rather than the synthesizing of general principles. Heath's paper itself shows that synthesizing, when it does occur, deals with linguistic patterns of diffusion rather than social constraints.

5 Although the Irish servants were sometimes referred to as "white slaves" (Lockhart 1976: 63), the two groups apparently did not live together (Smith 1947: 256); this lends support to Stewart's contention (1974: 23) that, "in terms of total time speaking, the amount of verbal interaction with whites must have been minimal for most plantation Negroes." Furthermore, there were important legal, socioeconomic, and political differences between white servants and black slaves (Galenson 1981: 172). The white servants' freedom was virtually guaranteed after their indenture terms were over; they were entitled to take their masters to court and serve in the militia; and so on. Smith (1947: 264) observes that the indentured servants were "practically never 'class-conscious' to the point of seriously threatening the order of society" – and that, despite a vague fear of slave/servant uprisings, planters "soon became convinced that white men would stick together, and looked upon the importation of more servants as adding to the security of the islands rather than imperiling it." Finally, the picture of black/white relations in Barbados which one gets from Handler and Lange (1978: 41) and from Sheppard (1977: 119) is less rosy than the one painted by Niles (1980: 10ff.) and by Williams (1985: 37); this suggests that class solidarity did not always outweigh ethnic distinctiveness.

6 Contemporary reports cited in Bridenbaugh and Bridenbaugh (1972: 352), Littlefield (1981: 117), and Rickford 1985b indicate that many Africans arriving in the Caribbean in the seventeenth to nineteenth centuries knew no English. Some slaves probably arrived knowing Guinea Coast Creole English or something similar, but as Hancock himself suggests (1980: 32, fn. 15), "only a tiny minority

of slaves would have come into prolonged contact with GCCE in Africa." See Hancock 1986 for further discussion.

7 One salient grammatical difference between Jamaican and most of the other Caribbean English creoles is that, while it does have preverbal durative or continuative *de*, it does not appear to use this morpheme as a habitual – or to have habitual *does*. Jamaica does not differ significantly from other Caribbean territories with English creoles in terms of the sources of its African slave population, and its lack of this feature may relate instead to its historically low white servant population. This is a tantalizing possibility, which would have to be assessed in the light of documentary evidence (examples in Cassidy and Le Page 1980 suggest that preverbal *da* is sometimes habitual, and we are not sure that habitual *does* was *never* used there), and with a view to other possible explanations (see Bickerton 1981: 255–6). But if it turns out to be valid, it would suggest that diffusion from pre-existing or co-existing white groups might have been an important influence on the *forms* in which the habitual was realized in NWBE (compare the hypothesis in 8.3.2).

8 Motivations for this emigration included economic suffering and religious persecution in Ireland, and hope of religious freedom and economic improvement in America (Dickson 1966: 80–1).

9 Although Foner (1975: 219) reports that eighteenth-century white craftsmen in Charleston protested against competition from skilled black mechanics and ship-wrights, their contention seems to have been primarily with the white masters who hired out their skilled slaves.

10 This conclusion is supported by evidence of sound shifts and other ongoing changes, within each ethnic group, which are not being diffused to the other; however, the notion of increasing divergence seems to be partly metaphorical, since it does not involve comparison of present-day data with equivalent data from an earlier reference point in real time.

11 Another possible objection to Bailey's proposal is this: If HE habitual markers were sufficiently prevalent in the New World to be diffused to and retained among black speakers, why aren't they also retained among present-day descendants of the original HE speakers? (Cf. Stewart 1970a: 246, fn. 6.) Although it would still be good to get corroborative evidence from other North American communities, this objection is partly offset by the finding of Dillon (1972: 131), reported by Harris 1985, that HE habitual markers survive in a white community on the southern shore of Newfoundland in which Irish immigration was concentrated. VBE *be* could also be a case of secondary acculturation (Alleyne 1980: 199–200; Bickerton 1971: 464, fn. 7) – in which group B, for ecological and other reasons, retains linguistic or cultural features originally borrowed from group A after many members of group A have "lost" it.

12 In addition to the issue of their geographical distribution, there is a question about their semantic relationship. Henry 1957 claims there are fine semantic differences between *I do go* (iterative), *I be going* (iterative durative), and *I do be going* (frequentative durative) in the HE of County Roscommon (Connacht); but Harris (1982: 9) feels that, while these fine distinctions between *do* and *do (be)* may be maintained in the Roscommon dialect, "in many other parts of Ireland, they are not."

13 As Harris 1985 notes, these are particularly striking because Bliss (1972: 77) used the putative non-existence of *do be* forms to argue that earlier British English could not have provided the stimulus for the development of comparable HE forms.

14 Niles (1980: 121) notes: "The seventeenth and eighteenth century dialects of southwestern England commonly used the uninflected 'be' conjugation in the present tense." Harris 1985 also points out that *be* occurs as *be* and *bis(t)* in a number of southwestern English dialects, and appears to have been more widespread in earlier times. However, although examples of British English *be* occur in both the *English Dialect Dictionary* (Wright, 1898: 197–201) and the *Dictionary of American Regional English* (Cassidy 1985: 175–80), they are rarely used with habitual meaning, and are poor candidates as sources for VBE *be*.

15 The focus in this paper is on habitual marking by means of *be* and *does be*; but NWBE varieties sometimes encode habitual aspect by other means. There is room for an accountable, quantitative investigation of the subject which starts from semantics, and charts the relationships among all potential forms. Alternants not discussed in this paper, or discussed only briefly, are:

Zero, as in G[uyanese] C[reole]: *rait hee a di maarkit wii Ø de* "We're usually right here at the market." Since *de* is stative, the absence of *a* or *does* here might be treated as an instance of the rule deleting continuative and iterative markers in temporal and conditional clauses, and before statives and modals (Bickerton 1975: 33). But this "rule" has frequent exceptions (see fn. 16, below), and zero is used for the habitual throughout the Atlantic creoles in other environments (Devonish 1978: 245ff.).

Will (be) and *would* (*be*). The tendency in the literature on VBE is to set aside instances of habitual *be* which result from deleted *will* or *would*, but everyone acknowledges that there is semantic overlap and considerable ambiguity (Fasold 1972: 153–9, G. Bailey and Naylor 1983, Dayton 1996: 216). In mesolectal varieties of creole on the Sea Islands and in the Caribbean, *would* often alternates with *useta* for past habituals; e.g., "We use tuh dance all the time tuh duh drums, . . . We would dance roun and roun" (Georgia 1940: 118).

Kin (*<can*). Well-known for its use as a habitual in Liberian English and Sierra Leone (Singler 1984); but instances of *kin* on the Sea Islands are ambiguous between habituality and modality, and the semantic domains overlap anyway: "I kin speak tuh dead folk in song and dey kin unduhstan me" (Georgia, 7).

Verb + ing. Devonish (1978: 230–1) points out that mesolectal and acrolectal *Verb + ing* in GC, like basilectal *a*, sometimes "straddles a semantic area covering both the continuative and the habitual/iterative." Indications that the situation is similar in VBE come from W. Stewart (personal communication), from John Myhill (personal communication), and from examples in Hancock 1984; the issue is worth careful investigation.

16 The co-occurrence of habitual *a* with the basilectal copula *de* here violates Bickerton's Main Stative Rule (1975), which prevents the co-occurrence of non-punctual aspect markers with stative predicates. However, violations of this type are attested in virtually every body of GC data, including Bickerton's; note his *evribadi a de aal abaut a rood* (Bickerton 1975: 34; cf. Gibson 1982, Rickford 1985b).

17 Attestations in GC of the durative part of the basilectal structure proposed for this stage (*de + a* or *de + pon*) are plentiful: *mi DE A luk mi kau* "I was (there) looking for my cow" (Bickerton 1973: 650), *Jan DE A riid im lesn* "John is busy reading his lesson" (Devonish, cited in Mufwene 1982), *mi DE PON wash mi mout* "I was in the process of washing my mouth" (Rickford 1985b). However, attestations of this durative preceded by habitual (*d*)*a* are rare. An example from Saramaccan with habitual *ta* occurs in Alleyne (1980: 87): *ini wan te mi ta si en, a TA DE TA hondi fisi* "Anytime I see him, he is fishing."

18 Although examples of both are given by Bickerton (1975: 28, 118) and by Gibson (1982: 131–2), the occurrence of *a* with "adjectives" is rarer and more awkward in GC than that of *does*, and is subject to more internal constraints. Both authors suggest, for instance, that the adjective should be "dynamic" (e.g. *jealous*) rather than "stative" (e.g. *tall*), used in reference to qualities which are relatively open to change rather than permanent. Gibson also notes, however, that *a* can occur with stative adjectives if the subject NP refers to a class of people, as in: *bos-draiva dem a taal* "Not all bus drivers are tall, but some of them are usually tall." The issue requires further research, both in GC and other creoles.

19 Bickerton 1984b has suggested that, because of their relatively small numbers, the very first Africans arriving in New World colonies may have had a better chance of approximating the English of whites in the colonies than the large numbers who came later, who learned their English from the Africans before them. But instead of replacing an across-the-board "basilect to acrolect" chronology with an across-the-board "acrolect to basilect" chronology, we need to remember Alleyne's point that varying degrees of English language acquisition would have been exemplified among the Africans at every chronological stage; his conclusion that quantitative movement away from the basilect would have increased over time still appears valid. For a more fundamental critique of decreolization, however, see Mufwene 1992.

20 Note that, since basilectal creole (*d*)*a* in 18–21 covers both progressive and habitual aspect, while mesolectal *does* is restricted to habitual, the mesolectal replacement retains only part of the meaning of the basilectal form. Incidentally, the combined durative and habitual functions of basilectal creole *a* would help to explain the occasionally durative uses of VBE *be* referred to in fn. 3 – at least if the former is seen as the ancestral relation of the latter, as proposed here.

21 In the final line of derivation 21, *does* is deleted completely, and the verb stem (*work*) is left to signal habituality by itself. However, VBE often uses *verb + s* for the habitual instead of *verb* alone; and Scott 1973 has proposed that the VBE *-s* suffix might represent systematic expression of the habitual, rather than irregular realization of the English present. It is possible to capture this intuition by deriving *verb + s* from *does verb*, via affix hopping and cliticization of the final sibilant; but, as noted by Rickford 1980, it is virtually impossible to distinguish between an *-s* suffix which is habitual and one which marks the English present, since the latter signals generic or habitual aspect most of the time.

22 The distinction of basilectal (*d*)*a work* vs. (*d*)*a de* (*d*)*a work* and of mesolectal (*does*) *work* vs. (*does*) *be working* recalls Henry's distinction between the iterative *do go* and frequentative durative *do be going* in the HE of County Roscommon (see n. 12, above). However, this distinction is probably not consistently made in everyday

creole and VBE usage, just as it apparently is not in most varieties of HE (Harris 1982: 9). Stewart (personal communication) has suggested that the motivation for the development of this distinction in the history of VBE is elusive, "since the proto-system seems at some point to have done quite well with the simpler Habituative/Progressive differentiation (and perhaps even with a single Habituative/Progressive category, e.g. as in Sranan)."

23 Mufwene has suggested English etyma for creole continuative *a* (<*at*) and locative/durative *de* (<*there*); and he supports Cassidy and Le Page's suggestion that Jamaican durative/continuative *da* may represent coalescence of *de* + *a* (see note 17 above.)

24 The adoption of *both* forms would be ruled out by the categorical invariance rule for creole verb stems – which applies even when marked past forms serve as the model, as in GC *lef* "leave" or *brok* "break." The non-adoption of periphrastic *did* as a past habitual in VBE can be accounted for by reference to GC synchronic evidence – in which *does* is used among lower mesolectal speakers just as (*d*)*a* is, for both present and past; *yuuzta* "used to" serves as the explicit past habitual at all levels of the continuum; and *did* serves as a first replacement form for anterior *bin* (Bickerton 1975: 70). The prior existence of *used to* in HE is also adopted by Guilfoyle as an explanation for the fact that English periphrastic *did* was not adopted as a past habitual in HE.

25 Gibson (1982: 62) suggests that I have treated *does be* as a "syntactic unit"; but my discussion here and elsewhere should indicate that I regard them as separate items which happen to co-occur in some environments because of syntactic requirements. It is precisely because they are separable that *be* can remain to assume the habitual function of *does*, once the latter is lost.

26 J. Sledd (personal communication) reports that, in his native southern white colloquial speech, "a long nasalized [õ:] can represent either *don't* or *going to*." This is contrary to the claim of Labov et al. (1968: 251ff.) that the assimilation of the stop of *going* to the nasal of *I'm* is unusual, and restricted within America to VBE. We clearly need field records and additional evidence on this point; but as both Stewart and Dillard have often emphasized, the occurrence of VBE features in southern white English does not preclude the possibility that the direction of influence may have been from the former to the latter. A reader has also pointed out that English support *do* is occasionally reduced: *What's your father do for a living?*

27 In view of the fact that some of these younger Sea Islanders do have contact with mainland VBE speakers, for whom *be* is the normal habitual, direct diffusion cannot be ruled out. But since they encounter instances of habitual *be* resulting from the erosion of *does* in their own communities (i.e. in their grandparents' usage), the effects of decreolization cannot be ruled out either; and it can be argued that mainland VBE *be* could not root well in Sea Island grammars unless the latter already had an inherited semantic/syntactic space available for it.

28 Tables 2–3 in Bickerton (1973: 651–2) indicate that locative/existential *de* is the very last basilectal copula or quasi-copula to be replaced by Ø or *be* in decreolization.

29 By contrast, the speakers of mainland VBE varieties constitute a minority surrounded by, and subject to acculturating pressures from, a white majority among

whom more standard varieties of English are spoken. This is not true in the Caribbean (interestingly enough, the cases that come closest – e.g. Barbados and the Bahamas – also appear to have decreolized the most). We would therefore expect decreolization to have gone further, and even to have produced different results, in America.

30   Bickerton (1975: 119–20), expanding on my original hypothesis about the relation of *does be* and *be*, discusses the reasons for the non-emergence of *be* in GC in related but somewhat different terms.

31   Data in Foner (1975: 226–32) on the proportions and relations of Blacks and Whites in Pennsylvania support the kind of linguistic acculturation proposed here. Pennsylvania as a whole had only 400–500 slaves in 1700; and the number of slaves in Philadelphia in 1767 was only 1400, or 9 percent of the city's population. Slaveholders in Pennsylvania typically had only had one or two slaves each; the largest slaveholder in Philadelphia in the 1750s had only 13 slaves. Most of these slaves were household servants, with young ones preferred "so that they could be trained at an early age and devote the largest portions of their lives to serving the master and his family." Many of those who were not household servants were skilled artisans, working alongside white indentured servants in the iron industry:

> In a report on Pennsylvania's iron manufactories in 1750, Pastor Israel Acrelius of Sweden observed that the "laborers are generally composed partly of Negroes [slaves], partly of servants from Germany or Ireland brought for a term of years."

Other slaves enjoyed contact with the larger society in their roles as bakers, masons, carpenters, butchers, painters, sailmakers, and sailors. When we consider these facts in the light of complementary evidence that Scotch Irish immigrants constituted a significant proportion of the white population in eighteenth-century Pennsylvania (Smith 1947: 314, 318; Leyburn 1962: 170–1), it is easy to see why northern HE *be* and other white features might have been directly acquired by Afro-Americans. The data summarized here might also help to explain why the black Philadelphia dialect of the 1820s which was exported to Samaná in the Dominican Republic shows so few surviving creole forms (Poplack and Sankoff 1983). At the time the Samaná emigration took place, Philadelphia had not yet been affected by the flood of Afro-American migrants who were to come up from the south in the 1880s and 1940s (Franklin 1974: 291–2, 350–1).

32   According to Foner (1975: 203), there were 10,500 Blacks in South Carolina in 1715 (compared with 6,250 Whites) – more than 60 percent of the colony's total population. By 1776, there were 90,000 Blacks and 40,000 Whites; Blacks then constituted nearly 70 percent of the total population.

33   Some result from the period in which slaves from one region or another arrived, rather than from their relative numbers. Some result from other factors, including differences in the relative proportions of black and white speakers, the contributions made by other ethnic groups, and the degree of urbanization and socio-economic mobility.

34   Features claimed in recent conference papers to demonstrate *differences* between Atlantic creoles – and so probably relatable to the sources of their African popula-

tions – turn out to be shared by the creoles in question and thus to serve as demonstration of their basic *similarity*. One such feature is counterfactual conditional markers, said to be absent from all anglophone creoles except modern Krio and Sranan. But such counterfactuals do occur in GC, marked by *bin* in combination with either *sa* or *go* at the basilectal level (Bickerton 1981: 83). It has also been suggested that GC differs from Gullah in not having a [fa] pronunciation for its infinitival complementizer, and that the Sea Island folklore motif about a hag who sheds her skin to do mischief is not found in Guyana. But this is again contrary to fact. Not only does Guyanese folklore share the old hag (*ool haig*) myth found in the Sea Islands and the Bahamas, but the hag utters virtually the same refrain when she discovers that people have sprinkled salt and pepper on her skin:

> *skin, da mii!! yu no noo mii?* "Skin, it's me!! Don't you know me?" ("Mother," 80-year-old Guyanese; see Rickford 1987c: 255 for complete text.)

35   The only contemporary records for this period cited in Brasch (1981: 3) are the court transcripts of the Salem witch trials of 1692, recorded by Magistrate John Hawthorne, and not published until 1866. Stewart (1974: 35) suggests that the use of markedly creole linguistic structures would have diminished considerably outside of the Deep South by 1776, because of decreolization; and he has pointed out (personal communication) that the lateness of the WPA narratives used as data by Schneider 1983 weakens his arguments against a creole ancestry for VBE.

36   Several sources – e.g. the nineteenth-century slave correspondence and recordings under investigation by Joseph F. Towns, III, of Cambridge University (see *The Carrier Pidgin* newsletter, September 1983: 6) – are not easily accessible.

37   Even for GC, the texts of Rickford 1987c give no attestations for *does* from earlier centuries; the earliest occurrence is in McTurk 1881, but it undoubtedly existed prior to this.

38   The forms were used with 1st, 2nd, and 3rd person subjects, both singular and plural – although this was truer of the narrators from Texas than of those from Tennessee, Mississippi, or South Carolina.

39   In addition to these examples, others are given to show that *am* expresses an "extended period or state," but they strike me as possible counter-examples with [+ punctual] reference:

> (a)   *Massa Haley seed he niggers was all gaunt and lots am run off and de fields am not plowed right.* (Texas; Brewer 1974: ex. 65)
>
> (b)   *De New Orleans folks say it am de accidentment, but de rest say de rope am cut.* (Texas; ibid. ex. 67)

40   Spears (1982: 867) cites me as saying that I had not noticed the *come* of indignation in Guyanese speech. I did, however, say that it seemed intuitively familiar; subsequently I located several examples in my GC corpus, and passed them on to him. Such examples of course challenge the status of *come* as an independent American innovation.

41 For instance, the immediate perfect construction involving *after* in conjunction
    with a progressive verb (Harris 1982) appears to be restricted to HE; and the rule
    for deleting initial voiced obstruents in tense/aspect markers (Rickford 1980)
    appears to be restricted to NWBE.

42 As Alleyne (1980: 171–2) notes, however, one difference between Twi (and more
    generally Akan) topicalization and that of creole is that the copula *follows* the
    topicalized constituent instead of *preceding* it. Alleyne attributes the creole order to
    the influence of English.

43 In reading Fallows, I came across the following characterization of Irish Catholics:

> well-versed in the survival techniques of the oppressed. They were able to
> maintain a sense of dignity only by perfecting their skills as masters of
> deception and dodgers of the law whose verbal skills confused and exasper-
> ated their overlords while amusing the knowing Irish. (1979: 13–14)

I immediately recalled stories which Richmond Wiley of the Sea Islands had told
me about slaves who deceived their masters, and delighted their fellow slaves, with
verbal trickery of various kinds. For examples, see Rickford and Rickford (1976,
reprinted in this volume).

9

Copula Variability in Jamaican Creole and African American Vernacular English: A Reanalysis of DeCamp's Texts

9.1 Introduction

The purpose of this paper is to reanalyze copula variability in the four Anansi story texts in DeCamp (1960), the classic Jamaican Creole (JC) data-set which Holm (1976, 1984) first used to show synchronic parallelisms, and therefore potential diachronic links, between creoles and African American Vernacular English (AAVE). To anticipate my major finding: after reanalysis, the quantitative patterns of copula absence by following syntactic environment in JC turn out to be much more similar to those in AAVE, lending even further weight to the hypothesis that AAVE is a decreolized form of an earlier plantation creole that was typologically similar to JC.

Before turning to the substantive issues, I wish to make a few remarks about why I chose to submit this particular paper for a volume honoring William Labov. There is, first of all, the fact that Labov's (1969) analysis of the AAVE copula remains a high point of his career; key elements of that analysis (for instance, the regular relation between contraction and deletion) are familiar to very many linguists, within sociolinguistics as well as other sub-fields, and the analysis itself introduced the variable rule framework, which remains quite central within variation theory. Secondly, the creole origins hypothesis – particularly as affected by the similarity between copula absence in AAVE and various Caribbean Creoles – is one Labov addresses in several major publications, including Labov (1972c: 36–64) and Labov (1982). Thirdly, this paper involves quantitative analysis of data drawn from recorded samples of natural speech, adhering scrupulously to Labov's important (1969: 737, fn. 20) principle of accountability. Finally, while focussing on specific analytical problems, it illustrates Labov's general point (1969: 728) that decisions about what to count and how to define the envelope of variation for a linguistic variable pose

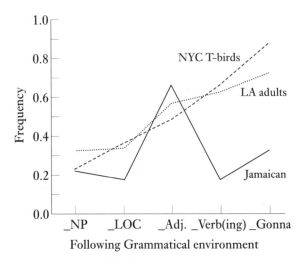

Figure 9.1   Copula absence in three African American dialects.

"subtle and difficult problems" for the variationist, but also crucial and substantive ones.

Copula variability in Jamaican Creole (JC) has played a major role in debates about the history of African American Vernacular English (AAVE). In particular, the fact that JC (and Gullah) displayed a pattern familiar from studies of AAVE – more copula absence before adjectives than before locatives and noun phrases – was taken as strong evidence for the creole ancestry of the latter by Holm (1976, 1984), Baugh (1979, 1980) and Labov (1982). Figure 9.1, drawing on data from Jamaica, NYC and LA, shows the high adj./low NP and locative pattern which John Sledd regarded as "the first serious evidence for the creole hypothesis" (Labov 1982: 198, fn. 26).

However, as further study of figure 1 will confirm, the Jamaican data were also an embarrassment for the creole hypothesis in showing relatively *low* rates of zero copula before ____Verb (+ *ing*) and ____*gonna*, where AAVE typically showed its *highest* rates of *is/are* absence. Except for Holm (1984: 293–4), no one really drew attention to this disparity, but it bothered me for years, since low zero copula rates before ____Verb + *ing* and ____*gonna* did not accord with my intuitions as a native speaker of Guyanese Creole (GC), nor with my research experience with Gullah, spoken on the South Carolina Sea Islands.

In a 1990 paper on Barbadian (first presented at the 1988 NWAV meeting in Montreal), Renée Blake and I suggested that the low zero figures for JC ____ Verb (+ *ing*) and ____*gonna* might have resulted from the way in which the envelope of variants was drawn in Holm's original (1976, 1984) analysis of JC.[1] As we noted:

In the _____Verb + *ing* case, for instance, only Ø and inflected *is* or *are* can occur in equivalent syntactic slots; basilectal *de* and *a* cannot co-occur with Verb + *ing* (*"dem *de* waakin") but only with Verb ("dem *de* go") and therefore tokens with these variants should not be considered along with the others. However, 82% of the variants in Holm's preverbal subcategory for Jamaican come from *de* and *a*; if these are removed, leaving only tokens of inflected *be* and Ø, the proportion of zero for Verb + *ing* climbs to 89% . . . A similar categorization or computation error probably accounts for the low _____*gonna* figure which Holm reports for Jamaica. (Rickford and Blake 1990: 261)

This paper is essentially an amplification of this suggestion, but one in which I have recoded and tabulated *every* copula variant in the DeCamp (1960) data-set that Holm (1976) first analyzed. One reason for doing this is to recover the full information on sample sizes and "don't count" tokens per subcategory which Holm's analysis of relative frequencies – though valuable – did not provide. Another reason is to see whether other factors besides Following Grammatical environment might be involved. I will present VARBRUL analyses of these towards the end of my paper. A final reason is to have this reanalysis of DeCamp's texts serve as a pilot for the analysis of new data which I recorded in March 1991 in Jamaica and Barbados, as part of a larger study of copula variability in AAVE, the creoles, and other languages.

Before presenting any new analysis, however, I wish to say some more about the JC data-set being used in this paper. In 1960 David DeCamp published phonetic transcripts and translations of four stories which he had recorded in Accompong village, a former Maroon stronghold, in Jamaica. The stories, ranging in length from about a quarter of an hour to half an hour each, were told by Mr Emanuel "Baba" Rowe, who was nearly 80 years old at the time. Although the stories contain some elevated, Standard English (SE) elements which probably represent Mr Rowe's adjustments to his high-status American interlocutor, they are dramatically delivered, and replete with basilectal or "deep creole" elements (See B. Bailey 1971, Holm 1984). The following brief extract from one of his stories – entitled "Andrew and the Old Witch" – will give an idea of what DeCamp's stories, transcripts and glosses are like:

1   From Emanuel Rowe's JC story "Andrew and the Old Witch" (DeCamp 1960: 159): (Text, accents and gloss as in original; but copula tokens which were counted in my analysis are indicated in boldface.)
    di uol 'liedi 'tiek op in 'rieza. him 'waip di 'rieza, 'wen in '**de** go 'shaapin di 'rieza. a 'so in 'shaapin. in 'waip di 'rieza. hin sie, 'shaapin mi 'rieza! 'shaapin mi 'rieza! 'shakam! 'shii! 'shakam! di 'rieza Ø 'shaap 'tel if a 'flai 'pich 'pan i, i 'kot im. so wen in 'draa 'op 'tuu di 'bed fi go 'kot di 'gyal 'truot, 'andro 'nuo 'wa 'hin **de** go. 'andro 'sing 'out. 'andro 'tan de, 'luk 'pan im, an 'sii wa **de** 'don. 'andro sie,

      'oo! mi 'madam 'kwii'nan 'oo!
      'wie! 'sali'oo! mi 'jienan 'ei!
      'wai yo! 'an mi 'niem Ø 'andro!

Gloss: "The old lady take up her razor. She wipe the razor, when she is going to sharpen the razor. It is so that she sharpens. She wipe the razor. She say, 'Sharpen, my razor! Sharpen, my razor! Shakam! Shee! Shakam!' [merely imitative syllables . . . DDeC.] The razor sharp until if a fly pitch upon it, it cut him. So when she draw up to the bed, to go cut the girls' throats, Andrew know what she is going to do. Andrew sing out. Andrew stand there, look upon her and see what is being done. Andrew say,

> 'Oh, my Madame Queen Anne, oh!
> Wake, Sally, oh! My dear Jane Anne, hey!
> And my name Andrew.'"

9.2   Holm's (1976, 1984) Analysis

The beauty of DeCamp's (1960) data set is that his transcripts are publicly available for inspection and reanalysis, and that copies of his original recording are also available – a rarity in our field. The first person to code and analyze copula tokens from this data-set in terms of Following Grammatical environment was John Holm, who published a preliminary analysis in 1976 and a more detailed discussion in 1984. Holm's later paper does not say anything about copula tokens which he had to exclude from consideration, but since his analysis is based on only 343 copula tokens whereas nearly 500 copula slots occur in the transcripts, he clearly did exclude some "don't count" cases, as everyone does when doing a variation analysis. Holm (1976) gives some indication of what those exclusions were: passives, cases with expletive *there*, and modals ("They are to arrive").

Table 9.1 shows the relative frequency of copula variants by following environment which Holm (1984) found among the tokens he considered. The percentages in the "zero" row are of course the data points for the Jamaican line in figure 9.1, but the other variants are also critical, and we will see how their percentages match up with our reanalysis below. Holm's analysis of DeCamp's data was extremely valuable in its own right, and insofar as it provided a basis for comparison in Baugh's significant (1979, 1980) reanalysis of Labov et al.'s NYC data and his own LA data, which further strengthened the argument for a creole origin for AAVE.

9.3   My Reanalysis

Following on some preliminary work on DeCamp's texts by my students,[2] I undertook to reexamine every potential copula token in the transcripts myself

Table 9.1   Copula variants by Following Grammatical environment in DeCamp's JC
texts (Holm's analysis)

Variant	___Noun Phr	___Locative	___Adjective	___Verb	___Gonna
Ø	22%	17%	66%	17%	32%
a	31%	–	9%	6%	–
de	0%	45%	2%	76%	– (68%?)
be	47%	17%	23%	2%	–
ben	–	17%	–	–	–

Notes: N = 323; adapted from Holm 1984: 292 (table 1) and 293 (table 2); *be* here and in
subsequent tables includes conjugated forms (*iz, ar, waz, wor*).

– coding each token in terms of Following Grammatical environment, person
and subject type, tense, and other factors. In each case, however, my codings
were based on the recording rather than the transcript, which, although generally accurate, does contain occasional errors. I should add that I also numbered
every line of the phonetic transcript sequentially from 1 to 842, and that these
are the numbers I will use to identify examples employed in this paper, should
anyone wish to return to the transcripts to study them in context.

One of the first analytical issues I had to deal with is deciding which copula
tokens to set aside as "don't count" (DC) cases, either because they were
difficult to classify reliably (indeterminate) or because they behaved more
categorically and less variably than the tokens I was going to count and analyze
in detail.[3] Unlike Holm, I did not exclude the eight existentials in the text,
which occur with both full and contracted tokens of conjugated *be*, as in "der iz
a drai goli" (36) and "das a neks stuori" (284). Nor did I exclude passives, which
occur with full, contracted and zero realizations of English *be*. Nor did I find
copulas preceding modals, unless we count as modal the *fi*-phrase in "wa Ø fi
don tide" (687), which I counted as a DC-Miscellaneous case. In general my
DC tokens were ones in which one or more variants did not or could not occur.
Table 9.2a shows the various DC types, and their frequency in my data,
beginning with the most frequent category of exclusions – tokens of highlighter
or focussing *a* (in one case *iz*), as in "*a* de di haks-dem wok" (Line 266).[4] Table
9.2b shows the frequency of copula variants among the DC tokens by Following Grammatical environment. In all, there were 127 DC cases in the texts,
leaving a total of 368 "count" cases, just 25 more than Holm found. In the rest
of the paper, I will concentrate on these 368 "count" tokens.

Table 9.3 shows the relative frequency of copula variants in the eight
subcategories I think it is necessary to recognize, and table 9.4 provides examples of each subcategory. As table 9.2b indicates, there is also a small ninth

Table 9.2a Frequency of "don't count" types (my reanalysis)

DC type	Example	Freq.
Highlighter/cleft (HI)	a de di haks-dem wok ("It was there . . ." L266)	54
No overt subject (NS)	wen Ø going doun tuu di goli, in go up (L43–4)	31
Anterior *ben* (ben)	di uol liedi no ben hie se . . . (L198)	17
Clause final (CF)	wat di ting iz, (L151)	9
Unclear (UN)	wen mi du huom (=de? L477–8)	7
Future w/o *go*, *gwain* (FU)	a Ø kil yu tidie (L225)	3
Miscell. foll. envir. (MISC)	dem a fi-hyar fiidn (L423)	4
Incomplete (IN)	yu naa iibm de . . . (L676)	2

Table 9.2b Copula variant realizations of "don't count" tokens by Following Grammatical environment (my reanalysis)

Variant	___NP	___Loc	___Adj	___V (+ ed)	___V + ing	___V + con	___goV	___Other	Total
Ø	0	0	5	11	1	0	0	1	18
a	34	5	1	0	0	1	0	16	57
de	0	4	0	0	0	13	2	9	28
be (= iz)	3	0	1	0	0	0	0	3	7
ben	0	8	0	7	0	0	0	2	17
TOTAL	37	17	7	18	1	14	2	31	127

miscellaneous subcategory, for adverbs and so on, but we can safely ignore it from this point on. Beginning with NP, I will now go on to comment on the results in each subcategory and how they compare with Holm's.

9.3.1   ___Noun phrase

The results in the ___NP column are not too suprising, and not very different from Holm's results (28 percent zero versus 22 percent, see table 9.1), although it is impossible to do a chi-square comparison to confirm this because we don't have the column Ns for Holm's data. The biggest difference is the higher percentage he reports for the creole nominal copula *a* (31 percent vs my 18 percent). However, the ___NP column in my table 9.2b suggests where the difference may lie: in his recognition of at least some of the 34 tokens of highlighter *a* before NP which I set aside because they have a different semantic function (topicalizing, equivalent to "It is" rather than "is") and are not usually replaceable by Ø.

Table 9.3   Copula variants by Following Grammatical environment in DeCamp's texts (my first reanalysis)

Variant	__NP n = 68	__Loc n = 40	__Adj n = 48	__V (+ed) n = 34	__V + ing n = 21	__V + con n = 85	__gwain V n = 25	__go V n = 47
Ø	28%	18%	81%	76%	86%	0%	100%	0%
a	18%	0%	0%	3%	0%	12%	0%	2%
de	0%	65%	0%	0%	5%	88%	0%	98%
be	54%	18%	18%	21%	9%	0%	0%	0%

N = 368, excluding 127 "Don't Count" cases.

Table 9.4   Examples of copula variants in each environment

__NP	shii <u>iz</u> a uol wich (132); mii Ø kwaku (712); mi <u>a</u> kwaku (749)
__Loc	dem <u>waz</u> der (353); hin <u>de</u> pan di trii (194); mi Ø doun a katn trii (638)
__Adj	shii <u>iz</u> def (147); him Ø def (202); di trii gyol <u>wor</u> jobial (9); in Ø so big (808)
__V(+ ed)	di trii Ø kot (221); babiabuo <u>a</u> ded (839); kwaku <u>waz</u> haili rekomendid (839a)
__V + ing	we Ø gwaing at nou (1); him <u>de</u> digin a di kantri (666); dem <u>wo</u> taaking (173)
__V [+ contin]	dat tida gyal <u>de</u> kom ya (16); it <u>a</u> bwail (24); andro <u>de</u> sliip (459)
__gwain (tu) V	yu Ø gwain fain out (12); a Ø gwain tu get (438); hin Ø gwaing kil dem (326a)
__go V	mi <u>de</u> go tel yu nou (49); a de im <u>a</u> go tan (643a); hin <u>de</u> go signal kwaku (768)

It should also be noted that eight of the 19 NP tokens which make up the 28 percent figure for zero in table 9.3 involve *niem*, as in the last line of the JC text above: "an mi *niem* Ø andro." The justification for analyzing these as Ø followed by NP is a single variant with *a* before NP: "mi niem <u>a</u> andro" (line 1896 – on tape but not in the transcript). But these cases could also be analyzed as Ø followed by verbal *niem* (which Bailey 1966 treated as a special "naming" verb, in contrast with the equating verb *a* and the locative verb *de*), or as "Don't Count" (unclear analysis) cases. If, on either count, they were removed from the NP pool (as I now think they should be), the relative frequency of zero copula before ____NP would drop from 28 percent (19/68) to 18 percent (11/60), a figure even lower than Holm's.

The larger point – of a piece with the distinctions between "Labov Deletion," "Straight Deletion" and so on which were introduced in Rickford et al.

(1991) – is that the classification and counting decisions which lie behind the statistics that variationists present and publish are sometimes problematic, and that how we solve the problems posed by our data crucially affects what we find.

9.3.2 ＿＿＿Locative

In the case of the locative column in table 9.3, my 18 percent figure for copula absence (Ø) is virtually identical to Holm's corresponding figure of 17 percent. The major difference between our analyses of the distribution of variants in this subcategory is that he includes *ben*, while I do not. From table 9.2b, we see that there are eight "DC" tokens of *ben* with locatives; if we added these to the sample of 40 "count" tokens in the locative subcategory (table 9.3) and recalculated the relative frequencies of the prelocative variants accordingly, the relative frequency of *de* would drop to 54 percent (closer to his 45 percent in table 9.1), and *ben* would account for 17 percent of the tokens in this subcategory (identical to his 17 percent in table 9.1).

However, one sound reason for excluding *ben* tokens was given by Holm himself (1984: 303, fn. 3): that it marks anterior tense and has little to do with the copula beyond its etymology.[5] This is clearest in the case of the seven verb stems which *ben* precedes in these texts, which translate into Standard English equivalents with *did V, had V* or *V + ed* rather than (copulative) *was V + ed*, and have the textual anterior or past-before-the-past semantics (especially with non-statives) associated with creole *bin* (Bickerton 1975: 28–9, 46–7; Rickford 1987c: 137–43) as in this example from DeCamp's fourth text, the story of "Babiabou":

2   mi no <u>ben</u> tel yu sie yu mos tan todi an wach wa de go hapm? (line 837)
     "<u>Didn't</u> I tell you that you must stand steady and watch what was going to happen?"

For the seven locatives preceded by *ben*, the case is somewhat less clear-cut, since these sometimes do vary with and translate into copulative and simple past *waz*, as in:

3   we unu <u>ben</u> de? (line 277) "Where <u>were</u> you guys?" (Compare 'dem <u>waz</u> der,' L 353)

But in other cases, *ben* clearly does not vary with copulative *waz*, carrying instead an anterior preverbal sense similar to that in (2):

4   an di wata mount di gyal siem plies we im <u>ben</u> de, . . . (lines 118–19) "And the water mounted the girl to the same place where it had been (previously)"

Six of the seven prelocatives with *ben* in these texts in fact precede a form *de* which seems to function unambiguously as a locative verb (locative copula) rather than adverb (i.e. in example 3 the tensed locative copula is *ben de* and the locative adverb is *we*), making them simply the past tense equivalent of the primary copula variant in this subcategory, non-tensed *de*, as in:

5   wen mi <u>de</u> a huom . . . (line 371) "When I <u>am</u> at home . . ."

If they were to be counted as copula tokens (which is not the analysis I favor at present), they might be better considered as tokens of *de* or at least *bin de* rather than *bin*.

One very important point to note about the distribution of the copula variants in the Jamaican data is that although the percent of zero copula for locatives is lower than that for _____ NP – something virtually unparalleled in studies of African American Vernacular English – it is the persistence of the creole copula *de* (65 percent in table 9.3) rather than *be* that is responsible for the low rate of copula absence before locative in the Jamaican data. A comparison of the *be* percentages for NP and Loc in the Jamaican data (54 percent *be* for NP, 18 percent *be* for Loc, table 9.3) replicates the relationship between the two environments that is generally found in AAVE (more *be* with noun phrases than with locatives), where the *be* percentage is simply the reciprocal (all full and contracted forms) of the percentage of copula absence. Compare, for instance, these relative frequencies which Labov (1969: 732, table 2) reported for the NYC Jets: 68 percent *be* with NP; 48 percent *be* with Loc. As Bickerton (1973b: 651–2) showed in his study of Guyanese Creole, *de* is the most persistent of the creole copulas. It must be the variable redistribution of this persistent, high frequency form to Ø and *be* later in the decreolization process which produces the fluctuations in the locative/adjective ordering that many studies of New World African English report (see Rickford et al. 1991: 121) and which Singler (1991) also reports from Liberia.

9.3.3   _____ *Adjective*

The high frequency of copula absence for adjectives that Holm first found in the Jamaican data emerges even more dramatically in my reanalysis, as zero climbs from 66 percent (in his study) to 81 percent (in mine). The difference seems to lie in his inclusion of several tokens of *a* which I discounted – cases before *so* and *how*, perhaps, which I classed as adverbs and put in the "Other" category of table 9.2b.

The classical creole analysis of adjectives (Bickerton 1972: 648, Holm 1984: 295–6) is of course as a sub-type of stative verb, which from this point of view would no more require a copula than a stative verb (e.g., *know*) would. The

Table 9.5a	V(+ *ing*) comparison		
	Holm ___*Verb*	*Rickford* ___*V + ing &* ___*V + contin.*	
Ø	17%	17%	
a	6%	9%	
de	76%	72%	
be	2%	2%	

Table 9.5b	___*gonna* comparison		
	Holm ___*Gonna*	*Rickford* ___*Gwain V* & ___*Go V*	
Ø	32%	35%	
a	–	1%	
de	(68%?)	64%	
be	–	0%	

justification for treating the Adjective as a special category, however, is that it does occur with overt *be* copulas some of the time (18 percent, representing reanalysis), and that, as Bailey (1966: 42) pointed out, adjectives differ from true verbs in several syntactic respects, including their co-occurrence with intensifiers (*so, thus*).

9.3.4   ____*Verb* (+ ed)

Column 4 in table 9.3 shows a separate analysis of stative Verb (+ *ed*) predicates – forms like *engage* and *recommended* which many linguists classify with adjectives in their copula analyses as a matter of course. (I'm not sure what Holm did with them; since most of these are passives, they might have been excluded.) Note that the statistics in the ____Adj. and ____V (+ *ed*) columns match very closely. If combined, the percentage of zeros for 'Adj./V + ed' would be 79 percent.[6]

9.3.5   ____*Verb* + *ing* and ____*Verb* (+ continuative)

We come now to the heart of the differences between Holm's analysis and mine – the ____V + *ing* and continuative verb predicates that occur next in table 9.3. As suggested earlier, I have long suspected that the "Verb" statistics that Holm compared with the "Verb + ing" of African American Vernacular English were an improper mixture of ____Verb and ____Verb + *ing*. That this is so is clear from table 9.5a, where I collapse these two categories in my data and reproduce his figures almost exactly. Collapsing the categories is improper, however, not only because they are syntactically incommensurate, but because their copula patterns are as different as chalk and cheese, as table 9.3 makes clear. V + *ing* occurs with Ø 86 percent of the time, while continuative verbs without an -*ing* suffix NEVER do so, taking instead the creole continuative markers *a* and *de* 86 percent of the time. Except for one case of *de* V + ing ("him *de digin* a di katn

Table 9.6 Copula variants by following grammatical environment in DeCamp's texts (my reanalysis, eliminating ___V + *con* and ___*go V*, and collapsing ___Adj. and ___V(+ *ed*))

Variant	___Noun Phr. n = 68	___Locative n = 40	___Adj. and ___V(ed) n = 82	___V + ing n = 21	___Gwain V n = 25
Ø	28%	18%	79%	86%	100%
a	18%	0%	1%	0%	0%
de	0%	65%	0%	5%	0%
be	54%	18%	18%	2%	0%

N = 236

tri" (666)) the two predicate types are almost in complementary distribution. The emergence of Ø V + *ing* represents a reanalysis of creole *de V*. The two predicates should be separated in a variation analysis, and only the ____V + *ing* statistics are properly comparable with ____V + *ing* in AAVE.

9.3.6   ____gwain V *and* ____go V

A similar argument applies to the future marker. Table 9.5b shows that Holm's low Ø figure for ____*gonna* – which has puzzled me for years – represents a conflation of tokens of *gwain V* (which occur categorically with Ø) and *go V* (which occurs almost as categorically, with *de*). The 35 percent Ø which we get for this conflation in table 9.5b comes entirely – as table 9.3 shows – from tokens of *gwain*, the form equivalent to ____*gonna* and ____*gon* in representing a frozen reduction of ____*go* + *ing*. Interestingly enough, the *go V* cases behave almost exactly like the continuative verb cases insofar as they occur exclusively with *de* and *a*; they are of course just a special case of continuatives like *im de go waak*, corresponding to "He is going to walk" in Standard English.

9.3.7   *Copula absence by following syntactic environment reconsidered*

If we now consider only the equivalent syntactic categories in AAVE and JC, their zero copula figures match even more closely, as shown in figure 9.2 (JC percentages there based on table 9.6). Furthermore, even the minor ____NP/ ____Loc disparity in the comparison would be ironed out if, as suggested earlier, we compared their relative frequencies of *be*, rather than Ø, treating copula variation as an insertion rather than deletion process.

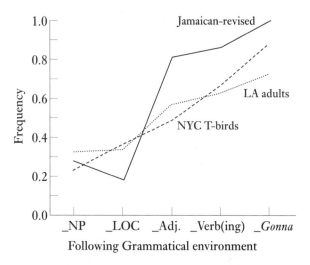

Figure 9.2 Copula absence in three African American dialects (Jamaican revised)

Table 9.7 Varbrul run for JC copula absence, sharing significant factor groups

Input: 0.52	
SUBJECT:	Personal Pro.____: .60 Other Pro.____: .23 NP____ .70
FOLL. GR. ENV.:	____NP: .23 ____Loc.: .12 ____Adj.: .75 ____V(+ed): .69
	____V + *ing*: .79
TENSE:	Present tense: .61 Past tense: .39

9.3.8   *Variable rule analysis of the grammatical constraints on copula absence*

I wish to turn briefly now to the results of a variable rule analysis of Ø in the first five subcategories of table 9.3.[7] Table 9.7 shows the results. The most significant factor group was *Following Grammatical environment*, with the factors following the order ____V + *ing* (most favorable to copula absence), ____ _V (+ *ed*), ____Adj., ____Loc., and ____NP (least favorable to copula absence). This at least establishes that the following grammatical hierarchy that emerged from the percentage figures in table 9.3 is robust, and not the effect of other intersecting factors. The second selected factor is *subject*, with 'other pronouns' (forms like *dat*, *der*, *wat*, *wich* and *hu*) strongly disfavoring zero copula; one reason for this may be that *is* often occurs in contracted forms like *das*, although *dat iz* and *wat iz* do occur). For some reason a preceding NP is the most favorable environment for zero copula, unlike AAVE studies in which a personal pronoun is the most favorable.[8] Note, however, that, in contrast with AAVE studies, "personal pronouns" do not all end in a vowel, since *him, which,* and *it* occur also as subject pronouns in JC. The third selected factor is *tense,* with present tense favoring Ø over past, as we'd expect, but note past tense still allows a healthy amount of Ø (unlike AAVE).

Not selected by the regression analysis were person (whether the subject was first, second/plural, or third; AM never occurred in the data), and text (1–4). Coded, but not included in the variable run, were the effects of preceding and following phonological environment.

9.4 Summary and Conclusion

In a complete recoding and reanalysis of copula absence in DeCamp's 1960 texts, I essentially replicate Holm's (1984) low zero copula percentages for a following Noun Phrase and Locative and his high zero copula percentages for a following adjective. In the ____Verb + *ing* and ____*gwain/gon(na)* V category, however, I find dramatically high zero copula percentages once syntactically non-equivalent forms are peeled off, and the resulting copula deletion hierarchy for Jamaican becomes dramatically more similar to that of AAVE, reinforcing arguments for the creole origins hypothesis.[9] On the other hand, there is a reanalysis process that takes place for locatives and other forms, and the effects of Subject and Tense do *not* operate in JC in quite the same way they do in AAVE. Person is also irrelevant to copula absence in JC, but is of crucial importance for the corresponding variable in AAVE. We will clearly need to examine other data sets from Jamaica (see Rickford 1998 and Rickford, to appear, for a start), and we will need to follow the evolution from basilectal to upper mesolect in Jamaica in more detail than DeCamp's texts permit us to. But in the process of providing the crucial quantitative evidence that we need to understand variability in the JC and AAVE copula for its synchronic and diachronic significance, we cannot afford to neglect fundamental issues about how to define and count tokens of our variables, or we may see oases which turn out to be mirages, and we may miss mountains that are literally staring us in the face.

Notes

This paper is a revised version of one originally presented at NWAVE-19 in October 1990 at the University of Pennsylvania. It is a pleasure to acknowledge the assistance of Renée Blake and Angela E. Rickford. The paper was prepared while the author was a Fellow at the Center for Advanced Study in the Behavioral Sciences, at Stanford, and the financial support provided by NSF Grants BNS-8700864 and BNS8913104 is gratefully acknowledged.

1   For the benefit of those who consult the published version of Rickford and Blake (1991), it should be noted that the order of pages 261 and 262 should be reversed.

2   In 1988, three undergraduate students of mine at Stanford – Jennifer Knobel, Diana Loo, and Michelle Robinson – attempted, at my suggestion, a recoding and analysis of copula variability in DeCamp's data, but their useful preliminary work could not be incorporated in this paper for several reasons. One of the most important was that JC past tense and other tokens of the copula which were excluded in line with earlier analyses of AAVE should not have been, since they were almost as susceptible to zero and other copula variants as present tense tokens were. The students' unfamiliarity with creole speech also led to a number of missed tokens and coding errors.

3   See Blake (1997) for a comprehensive review of the issue of "don't count" cases in the analysis of copula absence in AAVE.

4   There were also seven cases of actual or potential non-finite *be*, as in "yu wuda Ø supraiz," line 347, which I've excluded from the DC count because non-finites are not usually included in discussions of the copula anyway.

5   Holm makes this claim too in relation to *was*, but I don't think it applies to this form, which never, for instance, precedes (non-passive) verb stems. That is, one finds "im *bin* waan di tri gyal" (527), but not *"im *waz* waan di tri gyal," equivalent to "He (had) wanted the three girls."

6   Note incidentally that overt *-ed* tokens occur in only two cases, *contented, recommended*, both following dentals and therefore syllabic, and that there's one token of *duon('t)* for *wasn('t)* in the data.

7   The last three subcategories all show categorical copula absence or non-absence (that is, Ø = 100 percent or 0 percent) and would serve as knockout factors in the variable rule analysis, needing to be removed from the data pool before further analysis could continue.

8   This point is discussed in more detail in Rickford (1998).

9   In a new data set examined in Rickford (1991) – drawing on the speech of Jack and Gertrude Harris (pseudonyms) of St Mary, Jamaica, recorded in 1991 – these results are essentially replicated, except that _____V + *ing* shows about the same frequency of copula absence as _____Adj. See Rickford (1998: 190 and Rickford (to appear)) for these results. Quantitative analyses of copula absence in *other* Caribbean Anglophone creoles have appeared recently, e.g Rickford (1992) on Barbadian and Winford (1992a) on Trinidadian Creole, and these also show closer similarities with AAVE and boost the case for the creole hypothesis.

10

Prior Creolization of African American Vernacular English? Sociohistorical and Textual Evidence from the Seventeenth and Eighteenth Centuries

10.1 Introduction

This paper is intended as a contribution to the ongoing debate about the question of prior creolization in African American Vernacular English (AAVE), which has become more heated in recent years. In an earlier paper (Rickford 1995), I identified the kinds of evidence that bear on the possible creole origins of AAVE – see table 10.1 – and provided quantitative evidence from copula usage in creoles, diaspora recordings, and English dialects. As I noted in that paper (see also Rickford 1998), if you look at the time line for the development of AAVE (table 10.2), most of the evidence, at least as used in variationist discussions of the creole origins issue, comes from the last two centuries, especially the twentieth century. This is true of the ex-slave narratives and diaspora recordings (Samaná, Liberia, Nova Scotia), and it is true too of the twentieth-century Hoodoo (voodoo) texts analyzed in Ewers (1996).

However, in order to consider the formative period of AAVE, we need to go further back in time, to the seventeenth and eighteenth centuries, utilizing sociohistorical and textual evidence to assess the likelihood of prior creolization. Yet, surprisingly, this is where variationists have looked the least, concentrating instead on the lengthy texts and recordings which twentieth-century materials provide. The situation is reminiscent of the drunk who lost his wallet in a dark field, but was looking for it under a street light two blocks away because the light there was better.

In this paper I attempt to fill this void in the research literature by returning to the dim and distant seventeenth and eighteenth centuries to determine the likelihood that early AAVE included creole speech. With respect to literary texts and traveler's commentaries from these periods, considered by Brasch

Table 10.1   Types of evidence bearing on issue of creole origins of AAVE

1 Sociohistorical conditions (suitable for pidginization and/or creolization)
2 Historical attestations (literary texts; ex-slave narratives and recordings)
3 Diaspora recordings (Samaná, Liberian Settler, African Nova Scotian English)
4 Creole similarities (between AAVE and Caribbean creoles, Gullah, Hawaiian, etc.)
5 African language similarities (between AAVE and West African varieties)
6 English dialect differences (between AAVE and British/white American dialects)
7 Age group comparisons (across different generations of AAVE speakers)

(1981), Dillard (1972) and Stewart (1967, 1968), among others, there are certainly difficulties in determining their authenticity. But we cannot dismiss them out of hand, and there are means of assessing their relative value (cf. Rickford 1986b). With respect to sociohistorical conditions for pidgin/creole formation or transmission, considered by Schneider (1989), Mufwene (1996) and Winford (1997), among others, the light is brighter than we may have thought. I have spent the past year burrowing through historical texts like Kulikoff (1986) and Kay and Cary (1995), and as I hope to show in this paper, I believe that they can illuminate the issues of prior creolization with which we have been wrestling for so long.

10.2   Sociohistorical Conditions

One aspect of sociohistorical conditions which is relevant is the *relative numbers* of Blacks and Whites during the colonial period. In general, high numbers of African substrate speakers and low numbers of English-speaking superstrate or target language speakers would have favored pidginization and creolization of English (cf. Ferguson and DeBose 1997: 18; Schneider 1989: 33), since the Africans would not have had good access to native speaker norms of English. In the terms of Hymes (1971: 66), the pidginization-favoring element of "distance from the norm(s) of the language(s)" being learned or adapted would have been present. Bearing demographic considerations like these in mind, Bickerton (1981: 4) restricts the term "creole" to languages which arose in situations where substrate speakers constituted at least 80 percent of the population. This minimum has certainly been met in the case of some of the best-known creoles – Africans constituted 93 percent of the population in Suriname in 1700 (Migge 1993: 28) and 92 percent of the population in Jamaica in 1746 (Le Page and Tabouret Keller 1985: 47) – and it constitutes a good baseline from which to consider American demographics.

Table 10.2 Historical periods and linguistic evidence regarding the development of AAVE (literary texts shown for seventeenth–eighteenth century only)

Period	Dates	Linguistic evidence
17th C.	1610–29	(20 Africans arrive in Virginia in 1619)
	1630–49	
	1650–69	
	1670–89	
	1690–99	Literary text: Tituba's 1692 Salem Witch Trial testimony (Breslaw 1996)
18th C.	1700–19	Literary texts, e.g. Knight 1704 (1865)
	1720–39	Literary texts, e.g. Mather 1721
	1740–59	Literary texts, e.g. Horsmanden 1741 (1810)
	1760–79	Literary texts, e.g. Leacock 1776
		End of Dillard's (1972) 1st period, the Early Period (1620–1770)
	1780–99	Literary texts, e.g. Smyth 1784
		End of Dillard's 2nd period, the Late Eighteenth Century (1771–99)
19th C.	1800–19	
	1820–39	Period represented by Samaná and Liberian evidence (assumes little change since)
		End of Dillard's 3rd period, the Early Nineteenth Century (1800–1830s)
	1840–59	Period represented by ex-slave recordings (assuming little change over lifetime)
	1860–79	
		End of Dillard's 4th period, the Civil War Period (1830s–1860s)
	1880–99	
20th C.	1900–19	
	1920–39	Most ex-slave recordings and Hoodoo interviews
	1940–59	Most ex-slave recordings and Hoodoo interviews
	1960–79	New ex-slave recordings (2) and Hoodoo interviews (14)
		End of Dillard's 5th period, the Post-emancipation Period (1860s–1960s)
		Start of Dillard's 6th period, the Future (= the Present)
	1980–99	Samaná, Liberian and Nova Scotian English recordings

Hoodoo interviews = interviews conducted by H. M. Hyatt between 1936 and 1942 with Blacks concerning voodoo and witchcraft, see Ewers 1996

However, the 80 percent figure should not be considered an absolute minimum for pidgin/creole genesis, and I will not consider it so in this paper. In the first place, in Jamaica, Haiti, and Martinique, where the existence of creoles has never been in doubt, Africans constituted less than 80 percent of the population more than 35 years, 50 years, and 80 years respectively after the founding of these colonies (Williams 1985: 31; Singler 1995: 210–11). By 1690, 35 years after the settlement of Jamaica, Blacks constituted 75 percent of the population (Williams 1985: 31) – that is, they had not yet satisfied Bickerton's 80 percent criterion, although they were clearly close to doing so. In Haiti, the black population was only 34.8 percent 25 years after the colony's founding, and in Martinique, only 51.5 percent (Singler 1995), dispelling the assumption that if substrate speakers do not constitute 80 percent of the population in the first quarter century, the possibility of creole formation is doomed.

Moreover, as Dillard (1992: 64–5, 71) and McWhorter (1997: 11) have noted, the nature of the social context is as important as demographic disproportion in favoring pidgin-creole genesis. Recent studies of black/white contact on isolated islands off the coast of South Carolina (Rickford 1985) and North Carolina (Wolfram, Hazen, and Tamburro 1997) have shown that individuals from different ethnic groups can remain linguistically isolated and distinct from a surrounding majority even over long periods of time, and working-class African Americans continue to speak differently from Whites virtually everywhere in the United States although they constitute no more than 12 percent of the general population. These considerations, which remind us of the importance of "ethological/emotional" barriers to transmission and/or hybridization (Whinnom 1971: 93) should be borne in mind as we turn to demographic data from earlier periods.

The proportions of black/white contact in colonial America were radically different between its three main regions, shown in map 10.1 and table 10.3, and they varied to some extent over time. In the New England colonies, Blacks in 1750 constituted only 3 percent of the population; in the Middle colonies, they constituted twice as much (7 percent); and in the Southern colonies, they constituted *13* times as much (39.8 percent).

10.2.1   *The New England colonies*

In New England, given the low proportions of Blacks to Whites, it is unlikely that either a pidgin or creole *developed* there on a widespread scale, even though the overall proportion of 3 percent was surpassed in some places (e.g. Blacks constituted 20 percent of the population in Newport, Rhode Island), and even though segregation laws kept Blacks separate from Whites in schools, churches, and everyday life (Foner 1975: 246, 252–3). The low proportion of Blacks to Whites was particularly marked in New England's founding years (approximately the first half century), which if Hancock (1986) and Mufwene (1996) are right, are crucial for creole genesis. According to Greene (1971: 73): "Taking the section as a whole, the Negro population was comparatively small, particularly in the seventeenth century. . . in 1700, when the total inhabitants of New England were estimated at 90,000, the Negro population was probably not more than a thousand [1.1%]. The first general census of New England's

Map 10.1　Colonial America in the mid-eighteenth century (source: Foner 1975: 278, adapted)

population by race was made in 1715. At that time there were approximately 158,000 Whites and 4,150 Blacks [=2.6% of total population of 162,150].

In the light of these demographics, what are we to make of the following attestations of pidgin/creole-like speech from Massachusetts which are cited by Brasch (1981: 3) and Dillard (1972: 79–80, 1992: 67)?

1　He tell me he Ø God. (1692 Testimony of Tituba, see Breslaw 1996: 195)
2　By and by you Ø die. (1732–1783 speech of Cuff, quoted in Hobart 1866)
3　And we nevver see our mudders any more. (Jin, native of Guinea, recorded in Sheldon 1895–6)

Examples 1 and 3 contain *unmarked non-stative verbs, tell* and *see* respectively (= anterior or past in the classic creole system described by Bickerton 1975) and example 1 also contains an instance of *zero copula.* In Rickford (1998: 187) I

Table 10.3   White and Black population in the colonies, 1750 (estimated)

Colony	White	Black	Total	% Black in colony or region	% Black of all Blacks in 13 colonies
New Hampshire	26,955	550	27,505	2.0%	0.2%
Massachusetts	183,925	4,075	188,000	2.2%	1.7%
Rhode Island	29,879	3,347	33,226	10.1%	1.4%
Connecticut	108,270	3,010	111,280	2.7%	1.3%
New England	349,029	10,982	360,011	3.1%	4.6%
New York	65,682	11,014	76,696	14.4%	4.7%
New Jersey	66,039	5,354	71,393	7.5%	2.3%
Pennsylvania	116,794	2,872	119,666	2.4%	1.2%
Delaware	27,208	1,496	28,704	5.2%	0.6%
Middle colonies	275,723	20,736	296,459	7.0%	8.8%
Maryland	97,623	43,450	141,073	30.8%	18.4%
Virginia	129,581	101,452	231,033	43.9%	42.9%
N. Carolina	53,184	19,800	72,984	27.1%	8.4%
S. Carolina	25,000	39,000	64,000	60.9%	16.5%
Georgia	4,200	1,000	5,200	19.2%	0.4%
Southern colonies	309,588	204,702	514,290	39.8%	86.6%
ALL COLONIES	934,340	236,420	1,170,760	20.2%	100%

Source: Adapted from *From Slavery to Freedom* by John Hope Franklin and Alfred A. Moss, 1988: 61, drawn from Bureau of the Census: 1975. Copyright (c) 1980 by Alfred A. Knopf Inc. Reprinted by permission of the publisher

noted that zero copula is pretty much unattested in English dialects except where creole speakers have left their mark. Example 2 contains the prototypical pidgin *future adverbial "By and by"* and (on one analysis), the *absence of a future auxiliary* (zero *will*) which we see also in early Guyanese (Rickford 1987a: 86) and New Guinea Pidgin (Sankoff and Laberge 1974).

To the extent that these samples accurately attest to the presence of early pidgin/creole varieties in New England, *they were more likely to have been imported than home-grown*. Tituba, the speaker in 1, a key figure in the Salem witch trial, was an Amerindian slave from Barbados who "would have lived with and been nurtured by an African family" (Breslaw 1996: 43) before being transported to Massachusetts in 1680, in her teenage years. As Rickford and Handler (1994: 228–9) suggest, it is likely that mesolectal creole speech was present in Barbados even from the seventeenth century; it is certainly well evidenced there in the eighteenth century. Jin, the speaker in 3, was a native of

Guinea who may have arrived in America speaking a variety of Guinea Coast Creole English – the scenario favored by Hancock (1986), McWhorter (1995) and others. And Cuff, the speaker in 2, may also have been from West Africa; his name, as Dillard (1992: 62) notes, was "probably based on Cuffee, the day name for Friday among the Ashanti, with other meanings in other West African languages." As we will see, in the founding periods of most of the American colonies, slaves from the Caribbean colonies were very frequent – recall that New York and the Carolinas were British colonies on a par with Jamaica and Barbados, and that the British often drew on the Caribbean colonies to stock the labor supply of the American colonies. The Caribbean slaves unquestionably brought in varieties of pidgin and creole, and could have had a significant impact on the English acquired and used by newly arrived Africans in America.

10.2.2   The Middle colonies

In the Middle colonies of New York, New Jersey, Pennsylvania and Delaware, it is also possible that black slaves and servants who arrived knowing little or no English might have acquired the English dialects of the Whites among whom they lived without any significant pidginization or creolization. The proportions of Blacks in the population of the Middle colonies, while bigger than those in New England, were still quite limited (from 2.4 percent in Pennsylvania to 14.4 percent in New York, in 1750) and there were other factors which might have increased their exposure and possible acculturation to white norms. One was the fact that the typical slave-owner in this region was a small farmer or householder with only one or two slaves. As McManus (1966: 45) notes:

> A census taken in 1755 [in New York], about one third complete, reveals the interesting fact that the 2,456 adult slaves belonged to 1,137 owners. . . . The average owner in Rye held only two slaves, and in New Paltz, no one owned more than seven.

Moreover, the large number of white indentured servants in the Middle colonies, and the fact that many of the Blacks were skilled laborers with considerable freedom of movement, would have increased the amount of daily interaction between Blacks and Whites.

But, as in New England, while the likelihood that pidginization and creolization took place *in* the Middle colonies is very low, the likelihood that pidgin or creole speech entered these colonies from *the Caribbean* is very high, particularly in New York. McManus (1966: 24) indicates that between 1701 and 1726, twice as many slaves were imported from the West Indies (1570) as from Africa (802). As he observes (28):

Because of their emphasis on skilled labor, the English traders, like the Dutch, concentrated on West Indian imports. During the first half of the eighteenth century, thousands of slaves were transported to New York from Barbados and Jamaica. Relatively few were imported directly from Africa prior to 1750, except for occasional shipments of African children under the age of thirteen.

These statistics run contra to the claim of Schneider (1989: 32) that, although "No exact figures are available, yet the accessible information indicates that this proportion [of 'slaves coming from the West Indies, as compared to those brought directly from West Africa'] was apparently rather low."

The following creole-like examples and references to distinctive black New York speech in the 1740s which Dillard (1992: 63–4) cites from Horsmanden (1810) may well represent Caribbean creole influence:

4   "and then they would be rich like the *backarara*" [Horsmanden's note: "Negro language, signifies white people."][1]
5   "His master live in tall house Broadway. Ben ride the fat horse." [Spoken by Jack, a suspected ring-leader in the "Negro Plot," who is described by Horsmanden as speaking "a dialect so perfectly negro and unintelligible, it was thought that it would be impossible to make anything of him without an interpreter." Dillard 1992: 63, 65]

Moreover, the relative cultural and social autonomy of eighteenth-century New York Blacks, noted by Dillard (1992: 64), might also have helped to spread and preserve creole speech. In some Long Island townships, Blacks constituted 21 percent of the population by 1738, and as McManus (1966: 85–6) has noted, "The concentration of population afforded the slaves numerous opportunities to meet together in violation of the law. Most New York City slaves were artisans who were relatively free of supervision during their leisure time."

10.2.3   The Southern colonies

So far we have concluded that while pidgin or creole speech might have been imported into New England and the Middle colonies from West Africa or the Caribbean, the likelihood of indigenous pidginization and creolization in either area was small. It is important to remember, however, as shown by the rightmost column in table 10.3, that Blacks in these northern areas constituted just 13.4 percent of all Blacks in the North American colonies in the mid-eighteenth century. By contrast, Blacks in the Southern colonies constituted 86.6 percent of all North American Blacks in the mid-eighteenth century, a proportion which had grown to 89 percent by 1790 (Franklin and Moss 1988: 79). It is in the South that we should look most closely for the possibility that pidginization and creolization took place in the US, although we also have to take variation by state and county into account.

10.2.3.1 South Carolina Within the South, South Carolina stood out in colonial times as the North American colony with the largest proportion of Blacks, leading one observer to remark in 1737 that it "looks more like a negro country than like a country settled by white people" (Samuel Dyssli, quoted in Wood 1975: 132). Blacks constituted 65 percent of the colony's population in 1720 (11,828/18,393: see table II in Wood 1975: 146–7); and 69 percent in 1730 (21,600/33,400: see table 1, Wood 1989: 38). Were these proportions high enough for pidginization or creolization to have taken place? The answer is clearly yes in the case of the Sea Islands and the coast, where black proportions were as high as 79 percent in some parishes and even higher (93 percent) on individual islands and plantations.[2] The creole status of "Gullah," which was spoken and continues to be spoken on these islands (see Turner 1949, Jones-Jackson 1987) is not in doubt.

Since Blacks outnumbered Whites in South Carolina for most of the eighteenth century, it is likely that a creole was either developed or maintained in this colony more generally, and not just on the coast. But we also have to take into account the fact that Blacks did not become a majority in the colony as a whole until about 1708, 45 years after the colony's founding, when the shift to plantation-based rice-cultivation was well under way. The proportion of Blacks in the population of South Carolina in its first 25 years has been estimated at between 27 and 30 percent (Wood 1975: 25).

Historian Peter Wood suggested in 1974 that because of these early demographics, and the fact that slaves in this early period "lived and worked on intimate terms with their English-speaking masters" in the early period, "Ironically, *the first generation of slaves in South Carolina may have spoken a more standard English than those who followed them*" (Wood 1975: 175). Mufwene (1996), in formulating the general "founder principle" shown below, agrees:[3]

> *The Founder principle:* "structural features of creoles have been predetermined to a large extent (but not exclusively!) by characteristics of the vernaculars spoken by the populations that founded the colonies in which they developed." (Mufwene 1996: 84)

Mufwene argues (98–9) that the length of the homestead phase in South Carolina, as in Virginia and Reunion, would have prevented the development of basilectal creole vernaculars among black South Carolinians until the early eighteenth century, when Blacks became the colonial majority and race segregation kept them further separated from Whites.

Two caveats should be added to this argument, however. The first is that the early black population in South Carolina, as in New York, came almost entirely from the West Indies, especially from Barbados, and they might have arrived already speaking a pidgin or mesolectal creole (Rickford and Handler 1994), particularly if they had been in Barbados for some time and were not merely trans-shipments from West Africa. As Wood (1975) notes:

> During the first twenty-five years after the founding of South Carolina [1670–95], roughly one out of every four settlers was a Negro. These first Black Carolinians, scarcely more than a thousand in number, came from the West Indies, and most were retained as slaves by a small number of aspiring white immigrants from Barbados. (130)
>
> Because of the direction of Carolina's mercantile ties and the broader patterns of the English slave trade, Barbados served as the main source for this small scale commerce in Negro labor. (45)

Although Turner (1949: 2–4) and Schneider (1989: 32) emphasize eighteenth- and nineteenth-century legislative enactments in South Carolina which made it more expensive to import West Indian than African slaves (West Indian imports were actually prohibited after 1803), these developments came rather late in the history of the colony, and do not detract from the fact that the founding black population in South Carolina came from the West Indies. For instance, although some Africans were brought in illegally after 1808 (Turner 1949: 1), the slave trade was officially abolished in that year, five years after the importation of West Indians was prohibited.

The second caveat is that even if Wood and Mufwene are right about their claims that the black vernacular of early South Carolina colony may have been closer to the English of white settlers, it clearly did not remain so throughout the subsequent history of the colony. Wood himself (1975: 187) suggested, in an assessment that predates the similar conclusion of Bickerton (1984a) by nearly a decade, that:

> after the first generation, contrary to accepted dogma, most new Negroes learned the local language not from English-men but from other slaves, a fact which reinforced the distinctiveness of the dialect.

And Mufwene (1996: 101) refers to the "basilectalization" of the colony's vernacular which occurred in the eighteenth century, as "newly arrived Africans learned the colonial vernacular mostly from the creole and 'seasoned' slaves." Others have suggested that a similar linguistic shift took place in other creole communities.[4]

Moreover, note that in 1685, when the black proportion of the population was low (26 percent), the overall population of South Carolina was only 1,900; but that by 1740, when the black proportion had risen to 66 percent (Wood 1989: 38), the colony's population had risen to 59,155. It is unlikely that this 30-fold population increase simply preserved the linguistic status quo which existed 55 years earlier. One challenge for the founder hypothesis, in fact, is to distinguish between places like New England in which low initial black proportions remained low in subsequent decades, and places like South Carolina and Haiti (Singler 1995: 210) in which the proportions increased dramatically over time.

10.2.3.2 North Carolina In North Carolina, Blacks constituted between 22 percent and 27 percent of the population by the middle of the eighteenth century, and close to 30 percent by 1775 (Kay and Cary 1995: 22). In the coastal Lower Cape Fear region, which accounted for about 14 percent of the colony's Blacks at the time, that proportion was even higher – 62 percent in 1755. Except perhaps in the Cape Fear region, these black proportions, while considerably higher than in the North, do not reach the 80 percent level associated with creolization in situ. And yet there are reasons not to rule out the possibility of some creolization in this colony. For one thing, unlike the situation in New York, North Carolina slaves were quite densely concentrated:

> the concentration of slaves [in NC] who lived on units with ten or more rose from 51 percent in 1748–1755 to 62% in 1763, and those on plantations of twenty or more climbed from 19 to 29 percent. In . . . three coastal regions – the Albemarle Sound, Neuse-Pamlico, and Lower Cape Fear – an average of 63% of the slaves lived on plantations with ten or more slaves during the years 1748–55, and 32% resided on plantations with twenty or more slaves. (Kay and Cary 1995: 23–4)

In addition, black proportions relative to white servants, the segment of the white population with which they might be expected to have had the most contact, were even higher. Black slaves outnumbered white servants in North Carolina by 3.5 to 1 from 1755 to 1769, constituting about 76 percent of the unfree population (Kay and Cary 1995: 238).

Kay and Cary (1995: 148) believe that it is very likely that pidgin or Creole English developed, not only in North Carolina, "but also for the other southern colonies from Delaware to Virginia."[5] One reason is that there appears to have been "a great need among the colony's slaves for a lingua franca even as late as 1748–75" since 46.5 percent of North Carolina slave runaways spoke either no English (13.9 percent) or only "some" (32.7 percent). Moreover, they cite (149–50) the following references to distinctive black speech from contemporary travelers (quotations in double quote marks are from the authorities cited):

6a Philip Reading, Anglican minister in Delaware [actually a Middle colony rather than a Southern colony], wrote in 1748 of the difficulty of converting the slaves because of the "difficulty of conversing with the majority of the Negroes" for "they have a language peculiar to themselves, a wild confused medley of Negro and corrupt English which makes them unintelligible except to those who conversed with them for many years."

6b   J. F. D. Smyth, "an English visitor to the colonies at the beginning of the American revolution," described the language used by Virginia and North Carolina slaves in the 1770s as "a mixed dialect between the Guinea and the English."

6c   As late as the nineteenth century, Dr Edward Warren observed that slaves in the North Carolina region of Albemarle Sound included "many old 'Guinea Negroes'" who spoke what he called an unintelligible "gibberish which was a medley of their original dialect and the English language."

6d   Joseph Ottolenghe wrote from Savannah, Georgia in 1754 that it was difficult to convert slaves to Christianity because "our Negroes are so ignorant of the English language, and none can be found to talk in their own, that it is a great while before you can get them to understand what the Meaning of Words is."[6]

6e   The Reverend James Marye, Jr., wrote from Orange County, Virginia in 1754 that "there are great Quantities of those Negroes imported here yearly from Africa, who have languages peculiar to themselves, who are here many years before they understand English; & great Numbers there are that never do understand it, well enough to reap any Benefit from what is said in Church . . ."

These contemporary observations clearly indicate that the acculturation of Africans to English norms was neither as swift nor as complete as one might expect from the fact that they remained a minority of the population in North Carolina and in every other Southern colony except South Carolina. Contrary to the suggestions of Winford (1997: 322) for North Carolina, the slaves referred to in these quotations were not speaking "close approximations to the dialects of the whites with whom they were in contact."[7] They were evidently at early, in some cases fossilized, stages of English language acquisition, and the references to their speech as mixed and unintelligible suggests that it may well have been creolized. Kay and Cary themselves conclude (1995: 150–1) that:

> These observations of contemporaries plus the statistics cited earlier concerning the linguistic characteristics of slave runaways in North Carolina demonstrate that substantial numbers of slaves throughout the southern colonies spoke little or no English up to the Revolution. Moreover, Smyth's, Reading's and Warren's comments, taken together, describe widely spoken pidgin-creole languages in Delaware, Virginia and North Carolina that were derived substantially from African languages and were comprised of words taken from both English and a variety of African tongues.

10.2.3.3 Georgia   The statistics on Georgia in table 10.3 are misleading in suggesting that this colony had a low absolute and relative number of Blacks in the seventeenth century. It is certainly true that Blacks numbered only 1,000 and constituted only 19.2 percent of Georgia's population in 1750. But Georgia, founded in 1733, was settled at least 70 years later than any of the 13 British

North American colonies, and a 1735 act had prohibited the legal importation of "Black slaves or Negroes." Once this act was repealed in 1750, and Georgia became a royal province in 1752, the situation changed dramatically (Smith 1985: 22):

> The era of the royal governors (1752–1776) witnessed a spectacular growth in population and economic prosperity. In 1750, 4,200 whites and 1,000 Negro slaves [19.2% of the population] were in Georgia; in 1760, 6,000 whites and 3,578 Negro slaves [37%]; in 1770, 12,750 whites and 10,625 Negro slaves [45%]; by 1776, 17,000 whites and 16,000 Negro slaves [48%]. . . . The black population was concentrated along the coast, where the creation of rice plantations had transformed the area into a tidewater society inhabited by a preponderance of Negro slaves and a small elite planter class composed of crown officials, their associates, and migrants from South Carolina and abroad.

The Sea Islands and coastal rice-growing regions of Georgia rapidly became similar to those of South Carolina in many respects, including their high proportions of Blacks. By 1790, Blacks constituted 76 percent and 77 percent of the population in coastal Liberty and Chatham counties, respectively. These of course, are the kinds of demographic proportions associated with creolization elsewhere, and it is therefore no surprise that Gullah or Sea Island Creole is attested both on the coast of South Carolina *and* Georgia (Turner 1949: 1). As Smith (1985: 172) notes, referring specifically to the situation in tidewater Georgia:

> When Africans arrived in America, they were not taught English; they had to acquire a sufficient grasp of the language to understand others, but then were left to themselves to communicate with one another in their vernacular tongue. The syntax or word construction of their African language was unlike that of the English. They retained this structure and blended with it English words to communicate in English. The result of the adaptation [was] . . . the Gullah dialect.

What is more striking than the Sea Island situation is the fact that the combined total of 12,226 Blacks in coastal Liberty and Chatham counties in 1790 represented 42 percent of the colony's Black population of 29,264 (Smith 1985: 216, table A-4),[8] suggesting that nearly half of the colony's Blacks in this critical founding period may have been creole speakers. Moreover, since some of the slaves imported to Georgia in the early period were from the West Indies – from Antigua, Barbados, Guadeloupe, Jamaica, Saint Croix, Saint Kitts, and Saint Martin – they may have brought with them already developed creole varieties from those colonies. Table 1 in Smith (1985: 94) shows that from 1755 to 1765, 790 of 1,020 slaves imported into Georgia (77.5 percent) were from the West Indies, and the other 230 from America.[9]

Thus, far from what table 10.3 might suggest – that Georgia was the Southern colony in which eighteenth-century Blacks were numerically the least well-represented, and *least* likely to have been speaking Creole English – they were, by the 1790s, among the *most* likely to have been speaking a creole. Seventy years later, in 1860, there were 465,736 Blacks (3,500 of them free) in Georgia, representing 46.1 percent of the total population of 1,057,286 (Smith 1985: 218, table A-6). In the coastal rice belt counties of Chatham, Bryan, Liberty, McIntosh, Glynn and Camden, slaves constituted 70 percent of the combined population of 58,250 in 1860 (Smith, 1985: 32–4). By this time, new slave imports were coming from the Carolinas, Maryland, and Virginia, while Georgia slaves, in turn, were being exported "to markets in Memphis, Natchez, and New Orleans to supply planters in the newer plantation belts of Alabama, Arkansas, Florida, Louisiana, Mississippi, and Texas, where opportunities to use slaves profitably on cheaper fertile land were greater than in Georgia" (Smith 1985: 104). In short, by the ante-bellum period, Georgia itself may have been a factor in the wider dissemination of creole-like varieties.

10.2.3.4 Virginia and Maryland (the Chesapeake)   The situation in Virginia and Maryland, which are often treated together in historical accounts as "Chesapeake" colonies, is of considerable interest because slaves from these colonies together comprised a major proportion (61 percent) of all Blacks in the 13 colonies in 1750 – an effect, in turn, of the high total population of these colonies (table 10.3). Although that proportion declined as the century wore on and the slave population of other Southern colonies expanded, it is still fair to say that Chesapeake slaves represented the bulk of both Southern and American slaves in the eighteenth century.

One of the striking characteristics of the Chesapeake area, compared with other Southern colonies, is how long it took for Blacks to become a sizable part of the population. From their respective foundings in 1607 and 1634 up until about 1690, Virginia and Maryland consisted largely of small tobacco farmers, a relatively large number of English indentured servants, and a relatively small number of African slaves. According to Kulikoff (1986: 319), "blacks constituted a small part of the Chesapeake population, only about 3 percent of the people in 1650 and 15 percent in 1690. Most lived on plantations of fewer than eleven blacks." Kulikoff concludes that under these conditions "Blacks assimilated the norms of white society," particularly before 1660. Mufwene (1996) refers to this initial period in which white planters and indentured servants predominate on small farms as the "homestead phase." Building on earlier work by Baker (1991) and Chaudenson (1979), he argues that in this initial phase, "it is very unlikely that anything close to today's creoles was then developing on a large scale" (Mufwene 1996: 100).[10] He also argues (109) that the length of the European-dominated homestead phase in Virginia and Barbados and its relative shortness in Jamaica, Guyana, and coastal South Carolina, helps to explain the attestations of creole speech in the latter regions but not the former.

But if varieties of pidgin or Creole English were unlikely to have developed locally in the Chesapeake prior to 1690, they may certainly have been imported by slaves coming from the Caribbean in this early period, since, as Davis (1986: 8) has noted:

> Until the mid-1670s, when slaves were first shipped directly from Africa, most of the Chesapeake's blacks came from Barbados and other Caribbean colonies or from the Dutch colony of New Netherland (which the English conquered in 1664 and renamed New York).

The next major period of early Chesapeake history, from 1690 to 1740, "was an era of heavy slave imports, small plantation sizes, and social conflicts among blacks" (Kulikoff 1986: 319). In areas of Maryland where white servants had "outnumbered Black slaves nearly four to one" in 1670, black slaves "out-numbered servants nearly four to one" by the late 1690s (Davis 1986: 8). Not only did the black population increase dramatically during this period, but most of the new slaves came directly from Africa: "Africans continued to pour into the Chesapeake: from 1700 to 1740, slavers brought fifty-four thousand blacks into Virginia and Maryland, about forty-nine thousand of whom [= 90.7 percent] were Africans" (Kulikoff 1986: 320).

It was this flood of African imports that raised the black proportions of the population in Maryland and Virginia to nearly 31 percent and 44 percent respectively by 1750 (table 10.3). These figures do not approximate the 80 percent level associated with local creolization as well as contemporary coastal South Carolina did, but it is likely that some creole restructuring or "basilectalization" (Mufwene 1996: 101) did take place in the two to three years (Mullin 1972: 46) that it took African arrivals to acquire the English of their new locale. The historian Allan Kulikoff (1986: 327–8) speculates that not only may some of these African arrivals have come speaking a West African pidgin, but also that:[11]

> A new creole language may have emerged in the Chesapeake region combining the vocabulary of several African languages common among the immigrants, African linguistic structures, and the few English words needed for communication with the master.

One of the contemporary references to Virginia does suggest that:[12]

7   slaves "that are born there [in the colonies] talk good English and reflect our Language, Habits, and Cussoms." (Rev. Hugh Jones, *The Present State of Virginia*, 1724: 75, cited in Brasch 1981: 5)

However, support for Kulikoff's claim comes from the contrary evidence of the Virginia slave represented in Daniel Defoe's novel, *Colonel Jacque*, 1722 cited in Dillard (1972: 78):

> 8 "Yes, yes . . . me know, but me want speak, me tell something. O! me no let him makee de great master angry." (Defoe 1722, *Colonel Jacque*: 152)

Referring to this sample, Dillard (1972: 78) makes the telling observation that:

> The Virginia and Maryland Negroes in *The Life of Colonel Jacque* speak the same Pidgin English which Defoe attributes to his other Africans. *The white indentured servants who work beside them speak an entirely different variety of English.* (emphasis added)

Defoe's differentiation of black and white speech is likely to have been an accurate representation of the eighteenth-century situation in Virginia, since it is paralleled by contemporary observations on other aspects of black culture by the end of the eighteenth century:

> White observers agreed that the music, dance, and religiosity of black slaves [in the Chesapeake] differed remarkably from those of whites. . . . The practice of a distinctive culture within their own quarters gave them some small power over their own lives and destinies . . .' (Kulikoff 1986: 351)

Kulikoff (1986: 219) is referring here to the third and final phase in the development of early Chesapeake black society, one lasting from 1740 to 1790, a period in which "[slave] imports declined and then stopped, plantation sizes increased, the proportion of blacks in the population grew, and divisions among slaves disappeared." By the 1780s, "one-third to two-thirds of the slaves in eleven tidewater counties lived on farms of more than twenty slaves, and only a sixth to a tenth lived on units of fewer than six" (Kulikoff 1986: 337). This increase in plantation size and the relative autonomy of slave life may have helped to increase the linguistic differences between Blacks and Whites.

That the English of Chesapeake slaves at the end of the eighteenth century might have included more pidgin or creole-like elements than that of Whites did, despite the long acculturation which the demographics of the seventeenth century might have facilitated, is suggested by the speech of the Maryland slave, Cuff, represented in Brackenridge's 1792 novel, *Modern Chivalry*:

> 9 Massa shentiman; I be cash crab in de Wye river; find ting in de mud; tone big a man's foot: holes like to he; fetch massa; massa saym it be de Indian moccasin . . . (H. H. Brackenridge, *Modern Chivalry*, 1792: 291; cited in Brasch 1981: 18)

10.3   Summary and Conclusion

Considering sociohistorical demographics alone, the possibility of indigenous pidginization and/or creolization of English among Blacks arriving in the North American colonies in the seventeenth and eighteenth centuries is strongest in the South, particularly in coastal South Carolina and Georgia, where black proportions reached above the 70 percent mark, and weakest in the New England and Middle colonies, where the low black proportions and the opportunities for black/white contact would have been more favorable to the conventional acquisition of English as a second language. Within the Southern colonies, Virginia and Maryland occupy an intermediate status. Although their black proportions in the mid-eighteenth century were two or three times higher than those of New York, they were still only a half to two-thirds those of South Carolina, and their long initial "homestead" phase may have reduced the possibility of pidginization and creolization in the founding period. However, the increase in their African populations later on may have increased the possibility of creole development, and plantation density, cultural autonomy and separation may account for the distinctiveness of black/white language and culture which contemporary observers have repeatedly noted.

Most striking in the historical record is the evidence that *slaves brought in from Caribbean colonies where Creole English is spoken were the predominant segments of the early black population in so many American colonies*, including Massachusetts, New York, South Carolina, Georgia, Virginia, and Maryland in particular. These may be the sources of the scattered pidgin/creole attestations of black speech which Stewart (1967, 1968), Dillard (1972, 1992) and Brasch (1981) report from American colonies as distant as Massachusetts and Georgia. Moreover, if Mufwene (1996), Chaudenson (1992) and others are right about the importance of the early, founding populations, these Caribbean imports may have had an important creolizing influence on the colonies to which they came.

Can we assume that *every* African and African American in the seventeenth- and eighteenth-century American colonies spoke a basilectal or primordial creole, as is sometimes assumed to be the creolist position? From the sociohistorical and textual evidence, clearly no, and it should be noted that even prototypical creolists like Dillard (1972: 85) suggest that Blacks varied at least between pidgin, creole and standard speech in this early period. But there can be absolutely no doubt that *some* pidgin/creole speech – whether home-grown or imported – was an element in the formative stage of African American Vernacular English. In some colonies, it was clearly a very influential element, and it may be the source of the haunting similarities with Caribbean Creole English which we find in AAVE even today.

Notes

This paper is a revised version of a paper originally presented at the twenty-fifth annual conference on New Ways of Analyzing Variation in language (NWAV-25) held in Las Vegas October 17–20, 1996, and draws on ongoing research for the historical chapter in Green and Rickford (forthcoming). It is a pleasure to thank Angela Rickford for her encouragement and support. I also wish to acknowledge valuable feedback from Ira Berlin, Katarina Brett, Andrew Brown, Lorin Lee Cary, George Frederickson, Jerry Handler, John McWhorter, Pat Nichols, and Peter Wood, while absolving them of any responsibility for the ideas or claims in this paper, since I did not always heed their counsel. Although Edgar Schneider did not see the manuscript in its preparation stages, his related work on the earlier history of Black English (Schneider 1989) is noteworthy; I cite it in several places in this paper. I am indebted too to all of those who made useful comments and suggestions after my NWAV presentation, including Gregory Guy, Michael Montgomery, Salikoko Mufwene, Peter Patrick, and the referees for this journal.

1   Compare West Indian and Gullah attestations of *buckra* or *backra*, and possible sources in Ibo and Efik $m_1ba_1ká_2ra_2$ "he who surrounds or governs" (Turner 1949: 191; Cassidy and Le Page 1980: 18; Allsopp 1996: 61). Note that 1 and 2 refer to low level tone and mid level tone respectively.

2   Cf. Wood 1974: 159, describing St George's Parish in 1726, where slaves consti-tuted by then more than 70 percent of the population: "Two thirds of the slaves resided on only 18 plantations in groups ranging in size from 25 to 94, and more than 20 percent were located on the largest three of these. [In] five sixths of the total population, slaves outnumbered whites by nearly four to one . . . On the seven plantations . . . having over 50 residents, . . . there were more than 13 slaves for every white person [=92.9 percent of the population on those plantations]."

3   Although Mufwene (1996) formulates this principle more explicitly than his predecessors, provides more supporting sociohistorical evidence, and draws out its linguistic implications more fully, the essence of the principle was formulated earlier by other linguists, including Le Page (1960), Cassidy (1961), Hancock (1986) and Chaudenson (1992).

4   Wood credits Cassidy (1961: 19) and Dillard (1972: 97) for even earlier formula-tions of the idea that eighteenth- and nineteenth-century Africans arriving in the New World must have learned their English from other Africans rather than Whites. For more general discussion of the notion that English, French, and other plantation creole continua may have formed "backwards," with the first non-Europeans acquiring varieties closer to those spoken by the Europeans, and marked creolization occurring later as slaves and workers learned primarily from each other, see Baker (1982b, 1991), Bickerton (1983, 1986) and Chaudenson (1979).

5   With respect to this issue, they are critical (Kay and Cary 1995: 148) of scholars like Menard (1975) and Berlin (1980) who have "rejected, played down, or ignored the evolution of pidgin-creole languages in these colonies." By contrast, in fn. 23, p. 354, they commend Dillard (1972) for his emphasis on "the widespread devel-

opment of pidgin-creole languages among colonial blacks," although they note that "Dillard does not adequately document where and when pidgin-creole languages developed in particular colonies or regions and probably stresses too much the carryover of West African pidgin English to the colonies."

6   Kay and Cary (1995: 151) suggest that, given Ottolenghe's failure to mention Gullah, which appears to have developed in Georgia as well as South Carolina, his "dwelling on the continued impact of African languages" suggests "the distinct possibility that Ottolenghe often failed to understand that what he heard was slaves speaking creole rather than African languages."

7   Winford (1997: 321–7) rightfully observes that in North Carolina as in South Carolina and Georgia, Africans were more likely to have been significantly outnumbered by Whites and to have acquired white varieties of English in upcountry, inland areas than along the coast. However, because upcountry Blacks were in each case only a minority of the total population of Blacks in each colony (most were concentrated along the coast), we should be careful about regarding their sociolinguistic situation as prototypical.

8   The combined total for Liberty and Chatham counties includes 139 "Free Negroes" and the black population for Georgia as a whole includes 398 "Free Negroes." Smith's book is relatively unique in providing a statistical accounting of the Free Negro population. Most of the other sources I have consulted mention them without indicating their numbers, or oscillate between references to "slaves" and "Blacks" without indicating what proportion of the latter were free.

9   However, as Smith notes (1985: 94) "the figures in the table do not represent the total influx of slaves into Georgia during these years. Georgians purchased slaves in Charleston . . . and Carolinians migrated with their slaves to Georgia to develop new lands." Table 2, p. 95, shows that between 1766 and 1771, the picture changed dramatically, with 75 percent of the slave imports (2,487) coming from Africa, 21 percent (693) from the West Indies, and only 4 percent (136) from America.

10 Mufwene seems to draw quite heavily on the Chesapeake model for his more general description of the "homestead" phase of colonial development, and one should be wary of over-generalizing its applicability.

11 Note also the view of Menard (1975: 30) that a creole language was unlikely to have developed in the Chesapeake, and the views of Kay and Cary (1995: 147–52) – summarized above in the section on North Carolina – that Menard is wrong on this score, and that pidgin-creole speech is likely to have developed in all Southern colonies from Delaware to Virginia.

12 As Michael Montgomery (personal communication) has noted, Jones's statement should be treated with caution because his book was a piece of "colonial propaganda," intended "to entice more immigrants to come from England to Virginia." Assuming that Jones overstated the prevalence of "good English" among the slaves would make the situation closer to what Kulikoff (1986) suggests – that forms of pidgin/creole English were used to some extent among the slave population.

11

Are Black and White Vernaculars Diverging?

11.1 Introduction

Important considerations about the divergence of black and white vernaculars are raised by the work of Bill Labov and his associates, and by the work of Guy Bailey and his associates, with many implications. Obviously, there are purely linguistic issues that have to do with the description of black and white dialects; these give rise in turn to much larger, particularly intriguing, theoretical and methodological issues about how we analyze linguistic variation and how we study sociolinguistics. There are also, of course, a great many applied sociolinguistics issues. Professors Spears and Vaughn-Cooke have both spoken eloquently about the educational and political issues that are involved, and I want to talk instead about some of the theoretical and methodological issues that are raised, and maybe introduce a little additional data at the end.

The points that arise from studies of this nature fall into two groups, the linguistic and the social, even though (as always) it's very hard to keep the two apart.

11.2 Linguistic Issues

Within the linguistic group, the first point is the importance of a distinction between real time and apparent time. Other speakers have said so much about this issue that I hardly need to say anything about it, except to stress, as Vaughn-Cooke has already done, that it was Labov himself who pointed out the critical importance of having comparison points in real time.

Data in apparent time can be misleading, particularly with some of these variables, because of a second point which sociolinguists in general fail to take into account: the old competence vs. performance distinction (see Rickford 1987b for more discussion). For years we've been running around feeling that because we use elaborate techniques for getting at the vernacular, the evidence that we have of what speakers *do* do is perfect evidence of what speakers *can* do; even when we make qualifications to the contrary, deep down in our hearts we believe that we have come close to their real systems. But these matters are usually more complicated. Take the matter of age-grading. When I first entered the field of linguistics and read the early work, I was led to believe that age-grading was a reality, that Black English was spoken mainly if not exclusively by black children and adolescents. But after moving to Philadelphia, and living right in the middle of the black community, I heard all these people – 20, 30, 40, 50, 60 years old – who were using all the forms that they were supposed to have been age-graded out of many years before. One has to ask: what comes with increasing age? Is it a loss of forms that one knew before, or is it an extension of repertoire that allows you then to do different things with the way you present yourself in public life, a development of sociolinguistic competence that allows you greater freedom to represent what you can and cannot do? It's very clear that adults in the black community have a wider range of styles in which they can present themselves to the outside world than do children aged six, seven, eight, nine, or ten. Now we *know* these things, and yet we tend to *forget* them. There are parallel examples in macrosociolinguistics; Fishman et al. reported recently (1985: 107–94, 508–13) that a 1970 census shows a much higher proportion of mother-tongue speakers, people who claimed competence in a non-English mother tongue, than he found to be the case in 1960. Well, is it true that in ten years there was a massive rise in the number of people who in fact had a non-English mother tongue? If anything, our experience with language would lead us to expect the opposite. I think what was happening in that case is that we were witnessing the tail end of a whole series of political movements in the 1960s which made ethnicity something that it was much more acceptable to claim and to display and to talk about. And Fishman's own work has explored some of the ways in which factors of this type operate.

Another important linguistic point is the question of the differences between lexicon, phonology, and grammar which has arisen, I think in some very revealing ways, in the work of Labov and his associates. Given the differences that we find in the degree to which lexical, phonological, and syntactic features are diffused, it really becomes difficult to sum these all together and talk about Variety A and Variety B becoming on the whole more different or more similar. As some people have noted, you may have convergence at one level and divergence at another. So in the end we really have to restrict our research and our conclusions to one feature at a time.

Now the fourth point I want to talk about is the possible types of relationships between black speech and white speech which we might expect to find over time. This is an important matter, since it is easy to jump to larger (or smaller) inferences than the data warrant. I should say at the outset that I came

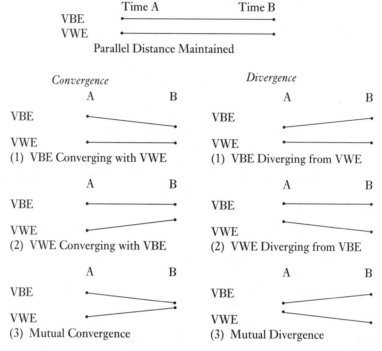

Figure 11.1 Positions on the developing relationship of Vernacular Black English and White English (Source Wolfram 1987: 41)

up quite independently with diagrams which are very similar to the ones which Wolfram (1987) has just presented (see figure 11.1), so I'll make reference to his where possible and introduce new diagrams of my own only where they differ from his in one or more respects.

Between any two points in time (A and B in Wolfram's diagrams, v, w, x, y, and z in mine) there are basically only three possible relationships which VBE and VWE (or any other pair of varieties) might exhibit with respect to a particular feature: equidistance (Walt's "parallel distance"), convergence, and divergence. Walt's first diagram is a good characterization of equidistance over time without change in either variety. To this I would add only that equidistance could equally well be maintained through parallel change in both varieties, as depicted in figure 11.2. That is, we have to be careful not to equate equidistance over time with absence of change over time. Equidistance with parallel change would suggest a closer relationship between VBE and VWE than equidistance without change, since (barring coincidence) members of each community would have to know about and follow developments in each other's

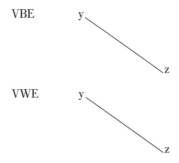

Figure 11.2   Equidistance over time with parallel change in VBE and VWE

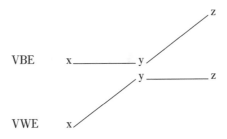

Figure 11.3   Initial convergence over brief time period through approximating change in VWE, subsequent divergence over brief time period through distancing change in VBE

communities throughout the time period to retain the same degree of similarity or difference as change occurred, whereas equidistance could be maintained without further contact if no change occurred in either community over time.

Wolfram's diagrams provide an excellent characterization of the different types of convergence and divergence which are possible. There is an additional wrinkle to these relationships which we tend to forget, however, which is that convergence between varieties over one time period might be followed in the next time period by divergence. Figure 11.3 is one possible model of this relationship, and it is not entirely hypothetical. The adoption by Whites of erstwhile black slang terms like *hip* during the late 1960s was a common talking point among Blacks, and may have been in part responsible for the subsequent replacement of *hip* by *live*/layv/and *fresh* among some black adolescents and young adults. Whether or not this was actually the case, figure 11.3 models a fully plausible possibility, parallel to the pursuit-followed-by-flight metaphor which Joos (1952) introduced, but without the references to elites and masses present in his discussion. Figure 11.4 (from Labov 1987) is another means of depicting convergence followed by divergence, with the additional assumption

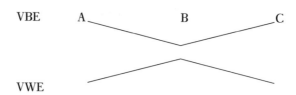

Figure 11.4   Convergence/Divergence (Source Labov 1987: 76)

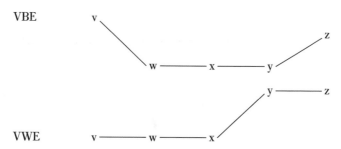

Figure 11.5   Convergence, equidistance, convergence and divergence over brief time periods (e.g., 30 years each)

that *both* varieties have undergone movement towards or away from each other at each stage.

Figure 11.5 demonstrates that if the time period is long enough, and we have evidence about the shorter time periods which comprise it, we might find that the two varieties have gone through virtually all the different possible relationships (equidistance, convergence, and divergence). The reason it is important to keep figure 11.5 in mind is that if it is in fact true that VBE and VWE are currently diverging in a number of respects – and I have still not seen the real-time evidence to clinch the case – some researchers will leap to the larger, unjustifiable conclusion that it is evidence of a long-term trend, supporting the anticreolist position that black-white speech was more similar in slavery days but has become more different because of increased segregation since then (the third theoretical combination of positions on the extent-of-differences and creole-origin position presented by Wolfram 1971, as well as by Fasold 1981: 163–4). In figure 11.1, Wolfram represents this trend as "Mutual Divergence," and his "Mutual Convergence" illustrates the opposing decreolization hypothesis – that black and white varieties were more different during the days of slavery but have been becoming more similar since then because of increased social mobility and acculturating pressures from the white majority. Proponents of either position (and the other theoretical possibilities outlined by Wolfram 1971) will undoubtedly continue to argue the merits of their respective views, but figure 11.5 should remind us all that it is treacherous to base arguments for long-term hypotheses on current developments or short-term trends.

11.3   Social Issues

I've talked a bit about the linguistic factors. I just want to say something briefly now about the social factors, and I think these fall under two main categories. First, there are the *ecological* factors (Whinnom 1971: 92), the factors having to do with the nature of the contact: how many Blacks, how many Whites, where are the neighborhoods located, what is the nature of their interrelations? It is not a priori clear to me (and I would certainly like to see more data on this) that the contact situation that exists, in the different places that have been talked about, is in fact representative of an *increase* in segregation. The second factor that's relevant here is what Whinnom (1971: 93) calls *ethological* factors, including emotional and attitudinal factors. There's a general assumption (which, of course, deep in our hearts we don't believe) that contact alone will lead to input, so that – if you get enough exposure – input from the outside will become intake, which in turn will become output. However, this is not always the case. Labov (1984b: 14–15) and his colleagues have shown very clearly that this isn't the case with data from TV or the mass media. But it isn't necessarily the case with interactional data either. The recent study I've done (Rickford 1985) of one black and one white speaker in the South who've lived together on an island nine miles by five miles, an area of maybe 45 miles in all, for 70 years, who showed very strong convergence and similarity in phonology, with marked divergence in grammar, led me to question the normal assumptions about the effects of contact. If you live on that island, you see that there are very strong social notions of the way Whites should speak and the way Blacks should speak. And this is reflected both in the forms that each group uses and the kinds of speech events in which they participate (see also Wolfram et al. 1997).

Now, the other thing is that, although we have very nice work going on in modern-day speech communities, we have a real challenge to go back in time, both to the historical records and as far as possible to all of the other available evidence to see what was going on. In this respect I particularly like Guy Bailey's attempt to get at those early periods. Recently, I've been looking in detail (Rickford 1986c) at the relations of the Blacks and the Irish, northern Scotch Irish vs. southern Catholic Irish, in the Caribbean and in the United States. The findings are extremely interesting. One can ask, even without looking at the linguistic data, what kinds of diffusion one might have expected from the sociohistorical record of Irish/African contact.

It turns out that in the seventeenth century, throughout the Caribbean and in different parts of the United States, Blacks and southern Catholic Irish worked together and were commonly reviled. Initially, both were servant groups; the Africans weren't brought in initially as slaves. There's a lot of evidence that these two groups rebelled together; in some cases they conspired together; they were hanged together as public examples. And while there are limitations from one place to another that require caution about saying they were identical kinds of populations, there's considerable evidence that there was a good deal of cohesion. And I think one would expect, although there have been disclaimers to the contrary as a general principle, that the high level of sociopolitical solidarity would have led to greater linguistic diffusion between Blacks and Whites.

In the eighteenth century America started to get the northern Scotch Irish group, which differs from the southern group in a number of ways. Their relations with local black populations in some places are very interesting. For instance, early eighteenth-century Pennsylvania, in particular Philadelphia, shows situations and conditions which were more favorable to convergence in social terms, between Blacks and Whites, than those in other parts of the country at the same time, or in the same place at later periods. For instance, Pennsylvania as a whole in 1700 had only 400 to 500 slaves. The number of slaves in Philadelphia in 1767 was only 1400, or 9 percent of the city's population. Slave-holders in Pennsylvania typically had only one or two slaves each. Furthermore, most of these slaves were household servants, with young ones explicitly preferred "so they could be trained at an early age and devote the largest portion of their lives to serving their master and his family" (Foner 1975: 227). Those who were not household servants were skilled artisans. And one visitor commented on the fact that, in Pennsylvania's iron factories in the 1750s, there were a great many Blacks and Whites (servants from Ireland and Germany) working together. Now whether they communicated also outside of the work environment is another matter. But there is evidence that there were fairly close relations in that century.

The nineteenth century presents an interesting schism between the contact or ecological factors and the ethological factors. On the one hand, there are the huge numbers of nineteenth-century Irish immigrants, mainly southern and Catholic, coming to America in the wake of the various Irish potato famines and failures. There were hundreds of thousands of them, mainly concentrated in northern cities. By the middle of the nineteenth century, 46 percent of all foreign-born Irish were in four northern cities: Boston, Brooklyn, New York, and Philadelphia. Now, to the extent that there were Blacks in those cities, both they and the Irish were commonly reviled, as in the seventeenth century. One finds ads in the *New York Courier and Enquirer* which said, "No Blacks or Irish need apply." But whereas common oppression in the closed plantation environment of the seventeenth century had led to Black/Irish solidarity and joint rebellion, the Blacks and the Irish in the nineteenth century were scrambling for open employment opportunities – it was a very different sociocultural climate – and in fact what the record reveals is tremendous hostility between the two groups. In 1834, Irish shipwrights set fire to the Shelter for Colored Orphans and attacked the black Bethel Church in Philadelphia (Foner 1983a: 432). In the 1850s, the luminary Frederick Douglass lamented the fact that every day brought hundreds of new immigrants "whose hunger and color" seemed to favor them most (Foner 1983a: 214–15). By the 1860s, black/Irish job riots were commonplace in northern cities (Foner 1983b: 392–5). Because of the hostile climate in which Blacks and Irish were interacting during this period, it's very unlikely that there existed the intimate contact that would have provided opportunities for linguistic diffusion between the two groups. Even if there were opportunities for linguistic input, putting it out as output and talking like an Irish White if you were black or like a Black if you were Irish White would have been highly unlikely.

Now the ideal thing would be to find linguistic features which allow us to test these hypotheses about the effects of social relations on linguistic diffusion, and in fact there are some. One of them involves variation between *be* and *do(es) be* as habitual aspect markers. The eighteenth-century Irish immigrants who came in smaller numbers than their nineteenth-century counterparts but had closer relations with Blacks were largely from northern Ireland, probably using a form of Irish English in which habituality was expressed by *be* without a preceding *do* as in *He be happy* (Harris 1985: 77). The nineteenth-century Irish immigrants were primarily southern Irish, probably using an Irish English variety in which habituality was expressed by *do(es) be*, as in *He does be happy*. Now there were far more nineteenth-century Irish immigrants than eighteenth-century ones, and if numbers were more important than solidarity, we would expect *do be* to have been fairly strong in nineteenth-century northern cities and to have diffused quite readily to northern Blacks. But in fact the evidence for *be*, both now and in the past, is much stronger, suggesting that the nineteenth-century southern Irish users of *(do)es be* had little linguistic influence on the black community in northern cities of the United States.

The issue is actually more complicated than I've been able to suggest here, because we have to take into account the effect of massive black migration from the South and remember that the evidence for creole-based *does be* habituals and decreolizing *'s be* and *be* forms is much stronger in parts of the South (see Rickford 1986c reprinted in this volume, for more details). My overall point, however, is that the kinds of questions raised by the work of Labov, Bailey, and their colleagues should force us not only to re-examine synchronically and in real time what is happening in communities today but also to attempt to reconstruct the social relations and linguistic processes of earlier times – to make specific hypotheses and then try as hard as possible to test them with the data that's available. I think if we take both approaches and bear in mind all the points that have been raised in this panel discussion, the result will not only be to shed light on the sociolinguistic relations of Blacks and Whites in Philadelphia, but also to increase the scope of sociolinguistic analysis as a whole.

12

Grammatical Variation and Divergence in Vernacular Black English

12.1 Introduction

The study of linguistic change as it is taking place – particularly if based on natural speech data – provides one of the best opportunities we have for understanding its internal and external constraints. In contrast with the study of changes that have long since been completed, we do not have to depend on written texts, with all their limitations. And we can, with more hope of success, keep collecting data until we have the critical linguistic environments, sociological categories, and subjective attitudes we need to solve the transition, embedding, evaluation, and actuation problems of linguistic change (see Weinreich, Labov, and Herzog 1968).

The one disadvantage which the study of change in progress has over the study of completed changes is that synchronic variability might offer misleading evidence on change in the linguistic system or community norm. Apparent-time data (distributions across different age-groups) which suggest that the system is changing might actually reflect stable age-grading, in which "differences between older and younger speakers . . . are repeated in each generation" (Labov 1966: 320). Contrariwise, if older speakers can change their speech in line with innovations introduced by younger ones – which seems to happen more often with syntactic variables – apparent-time data might suggest stability while changes in community norms are actually taking place. These and other problems of interpreting synchronic evidence of change are discussed at length by Labov (1981: 103), who proposed that the best solution is to combine apparent-time data with evidence of change in real time derived from a trend study, involving random samples of the community at intervals of about ten to 40 years.[1]

With this in mind, let us turn now to an issue about diachronic interpretations which is generating considerable controversy in American sociolinguistics and is particularly relevant to this workshop since its primary focus is grammatical variability. The issue is whether US Vernacular Black English is currently diverging from Standard English and local white vernaculars,[2] as Labov and Harris first claimed to be true in a 1983 conference paper (1986: 2): "The English spoken by Black Philadelphians is quite distinct from that of Whites, and the differences appear to us to be increasing." Citing data on the absence of third singular /s/, possessive /s/, and the copula, among other variables, Labov and his colleagues (Ash and Myhill 1986, Myhill and Harris 1986, Graff, Labov, and Harris 1986) argued that increasing racial segregation in Philadelphia had produced "a BEV [Black English Vernacular] that is more remote from other dialects than . . . reported before" (Labov and Harris 1986: 4). The work of Bailey and Maynor (1987, 1989) in the Brazos Valley, Texas, which concentrated on conjugated and invariant *be*, appeared to provide independent support for Labov's divergence hypothesis, and suggested that it might be a general urban pattern.

The divergence hypothesis was discussed in some detail at a symposium in 1985, the proceedings of which were published as Fasold et al. (1987). The primary critique of the hypothesis which was raised there – in Vaughn-Cooke's contribution in particular (Fasold et al. 1987: 12–32) – is that Labov and his colleagues had failed to provide comparison points in either real or apparent time, and that Bailey and Maynor needed an intermediate age group to minimize the possibility of age-grading.[3]

In this paper I will report preliminary results from ongoing research in East Palo Alto, California, which attempts to overcome the limitations of earlier divergence studies by providing comparisons across three age groups (evidence of change in apparent time) as well as comparisons with earlier studies in other cities (approximate evidence of change in real time). Ideally, we should have real-time evidence from East Palo itself, but, like Labov and his colleagues in Philadelphia, we have not (yet) been able to locate or draw on data about local usage from earlier periods. Implicit in Labov and Harris's original claims about divergence, however, was the assumption that urban Vernacular Black English was pretty similar from one city to the next, so that comparisons with earlier studies in other cities could serve as evidence of change in real time.[4] This is by no means an ideal strategy, since the assumption of uniformity might be invalid for specific variables, and the social dynamics of change might be quite different from one city to the next.[5] However, since no major grammatical differences have emerged from the study of Vernacular Black English in Detroit. New York City, Philadelphia, Washington DC, Atlanta, Wilmington, Berkeley, and Los Angeles, it seems reasonable to accept comparisons with earlier studies in other cities as preliminary real-time evidence, and I will accordingly compare synchronic East Palo Alto data with data from New York City and Detroit gathered 20 years ago (Labov et al. 1968; Wolfram 1969).

East Palo Alto is a low-income, newly incorporated city just east of Stanford University and Palo Alto, with a population of 18,000, over 60 percent of whom are black. Our data on vernacular-language use there come primarily from highly naturalistic spontaneous interviews and interactions recorded by insiders to the community, principally Faye McNair-Knox, a research associate on the project who is herself black and who grew up in East Palo Alto from the age of 12.[6]

The primary data I shall discuss – shown in table 12.1 – are from six black East Palo Altans from working-class backgrounds, although I shall also draw on a larger sample of 33 black speakers when discussing the copula. The six core speakers are evenly divided into old (76 years and over), middle-aged (38–42 years), and young/teenager (14–15 years) age-groups, permitting intergenerational comparisons and inferences about change in apparent time.[7] The features considered are classic ones in the study of Vernacular Black English. They include:[8]

(a)   The use of invariant *be* to mark habitual or durative aspect, as in *He be studyin all the time* "He studies/is studying all the time."

(b)   Absence of inflected *is* and *are* in copulative and auxiliary constructions, as in: *You Ø sick* and *She Ø workin right now.*[9]

(c)   Absence of possessive *-s* in Noun–Noun possessive constructions, as in: *JohnØ hat, the ladyØ house.*

(d)   Absence of third-person *-s* on present-tense singular verb forms, as in *The man walkØ there every morning.*

(e)   Absence of the regular plural *-s* suffix on semantically plural nouns, as in: *four dogØ, many houseØ.*

(f)   Absence of past-tense marking (by suffixation of *ed*, stem change, and other inflections) on semantically past verbs, as in: *he walkØ there yesterday, he tellØ me so before.*

The first four variables are ones examined in articles on the divergence hypothesis by Labov, Bailey, and their colleagues, and as it turns out, two of these provide support for the hypothesis. The other two variables have not been considered in discussions of the divergence hypothesis, and do not appear to support it. I will now discuss each feature in turn.

12.2   Invariant Habitual *be*

The data on invariant habitual *be* – probably the best-known feature of Vernacular Black English – provide the strongest local support for the divergence hypothesis, because the difference between the teenagers and the older

Table 12.1 Six Vernacular Black English variables as used by six Black East Palo Altans, grouped by age

Speaker, age, tape #	Invar. be	is, are absence	poss. -s absence	3rd sg. -s absence	plur. -s absence	unmarked past tense
John Carbon, 88 EPA 1, 2	1	19% (123)	0% (5)	63% (117)	12% (112)	20% (245)
Penelope Johnson, 76 EPA 5, 6	0	15% (55)	13% (23)	57% (75)	10% (242)	14% (372)
Dotsy Boston, 42 EPA 24–26	1	18% (77)	0% (2)	54% (65)	3% (124)	10% (69)
Paula Gates, 38 EPA 14	0*	35% (115)	36% (11)	44% (34)	1% (145)	12% (135)
Tinky Gates, 15 EPA 12, 13	50	81% (256)	53% (15)	96% (56)	11% (167)	11% (132)
Foxy Boston, 14 EPA 7, 8	146	90% (154)	86% (22)	97% (69)	13% (107)	9% (147)

(Row group labels in left margin: O L D; F O L K; M I D; A G E; T E E N; A G E R)

generations is qualitative (the adults virtually never use the form), and because the frequency with which the teenagers use *be* outstrips anything reported in the literature to date.[10] In some parts of her interview, for instance, Foxy uses *be* in almost every sentence:

1   "Shoot, I know I do, cause I *be* wakin' up and I *be* slurpin' an' I *be* goin', 'DANG, THA'S SERIOUS!' " (Foxy B., East Palo Alto 7: 686ff.)

The 146 tokens which she produced in an interview lasting less than two hours exceed the total of 98 which Labov et al. (1968: 236) recorded from the 18 members of the New York City Thunderbirds street gang in all individual and group sessions, and the total of 94 which Wolfram (1969) recorded in interviews with a Detroit sample of 48 people. Since this feature is markedly absent from white vernacular varieties, except for occasional use among very old "folk speakers" in the South (Bailey and Bassett 1986), its frequent use by young black speakers certainly has the effect of making the black vernacular more distinctive.

One factor which might make us hesitate to accept high frequencies of invariant *be* among teenagers as evidence of change in progress, however, is the fact that, in the 1960s and early 1970s, Labov et al. (1968: 235), Wolfram (1969: 201) and Fasold (1972: 212–14) all found this feature to be commoner in the speech of pre-adolescents and teenagers than in the speech of adults, suggesting that it might represent a stable pattern of age-grading within the community. Both Vaughn-Cooke (1987: 20) and Wolfram (1987: 45–6) draw attention to this possibility, the latter proposing (1987: 46) to:

examine middle-aged V[ernacular] B[lack] E[nglish] speakers in communities where twenty years ago we found habitual *be* to be more frequent among children than adults . . . If current speakers between 30 and 40 show persistent high levels of habitual *be* + *ing*, then Bailey and Maynor are probably correct in proposing habitual *be* + *ing* as a relatively recent change; if not, *be* + *ing* is probably genuinely age-graded.

While the data which Wolfram proposes to gather in Washington DC will undoubtedly be valuable, it should be noted that the "high levels" of invariant *be* use reported for adolescents in eastern cities two decades ago were much lower than those recorded for the East Palo Alto teenagers today. Wolfram (1969: 201) reported an average of 12.8 occurrences of invariant *be* per individual for lower working-class teenagers in Detroit, and 4.8 per individual for upper working-class teenagers.

Bailey and Maynor (1987: 458; 1989: 13–14) argue that intergenerational differences in the use of invariant *be* are not only quantitative, but qualitative – young black speakers in Texas are changing the grammar of *be* by using it primarily as an auxiliary, before Verb + *ing*, while older black speakers use it more often as a copula, before adjectives and locatives – and that they are therefore less likely to represent age-grading. The linguistic and logical inferences that follow from the evidence itself are not that straightforward, as Butters (1989: 6–32) notes in an extended critique, but the intergenerational differences with respect to following syntactic environment are themselves very robust, attested in other cities and data-sets, including our own (Bailey and Maynor 1987: 461–3; Viereck 1988: 295, summarized in Fasold 1989: 28; Rickford 1989). Although the East Palo Alto data are uninformative with respect to adult usage, local teenagers show the marked preference for the use of invariant *be* as an auxiliary, before Verb + *ing*, which Bailey and Maynor (1987) report for young urban Texans: 76 percent of Foxy's invariant *be* tokens and 94 percent of Tinky's occur in this environment (Rickford and McNair-Knox 1987).

Because it accords so well with the theme of this volume, I will now summarize Bailey and Maynor's (1987: 463–96) account of the internal and external factors which seem to them to have facilitated the concentrated rise in the frequency of invariant *be* before Verb + *ing*. On the one hand, this is portrayed (1987: 463–6) as due to internal factors – the unusually wide range of meanings of the English progressive (limited duration, future, extended duration, and habituality), coupled with the apparently unsystematic variation between *be*, zero, and inflected *is* and *are* in adult grammars. In making *be* the almost exclusive marker of extended duration and habituality, the children are seen as effecting a syntactic reanalysis of the form in line with Langacker's (1977: 110) principle of "perceptual optimality," in particular, "transparency," the notion that "the ideal or optimal linguistic code, other things being equal, will be one in which every surface unit will have associated with it a clear, salient and reasonably consistent meaning or function, and every semantic element in a sentence will be associated with a distinct and recognizable surface form." In turn, this internally motivated reanalysis – or at least its spread – is attributed by Bailey and Maynor (1987: 466–9) to an external factor, the increasing segregation of black and white populations which followed the post-World-War I "Great Migration" of Blacks from the rural south to the urban west and north, and the accompanying "White flight" to the suburbs. With less pressure from Standard English and white vernacular varieties, young black-vernacular speakers were freer to reanalyze invariant *be* and use it to minimize the semantic ambiguities of the English progressive.

I discuss Bailey and Maynor's (1987) analysis in more detail elsewhere (Rickford 1989; see also Butters 1989: 6–32), and, since *be* is only one of several features which I want to examine in this paper, I will comment on it only briefly here. Their interpretation of the internal and external factors which triggered the increased use of *be* is quite persuasive, but clearly cannot represent the whole story. With respect to the external factor, for instance, it ignores evidence that even in small communities where Blacks and Whites live together their grammars can remain distinct in fundamental respects because of attitudinal factors and limits on the frequency and quality of their verbal interactions (Rickford 1985). In short, conditions favorable to syntactic reanalysis might have existed within black communities long before the urban migrations of the twentieth century. With respect to the internal factors, a neglected point is the virtually complementary distributions of invariant *be* and zero realizations of inflected *is* and *are* in terms of Following Syntactic environment. Such zero forms are in fact commonest before Verb + *ing* (excluding *gonna* – before which invariant *be* does not occur) and have been for at least a century, on the evidence of ex-slave narrative data in Bailey (1987: 35). The sharp rise in invariant *be* forms before Verb + *ing* could thus reflect a structural filling of this hole or vacuum in the paradigm, as much as a response to the ambiguities of the English progressive. Another factor which Bailey and Maynor neglect is the relationship between invariant *be* Verb + *ing* and present tense Verb (+ *s*) (compare Wolfram 1969: 196–7 and Myhill 1989). As invariant *be* spreads, it displaces present-tense forms as well as inflected and zero forms of *is* and *are*, and until present-tense forms are included in the set of potential environments, an accurate picture of the embedding of this innovation in linguistic structure (Weinreich, Labov, and Herzog 1968: 145) cannot be achieved. Moreover, the older black folk-speakers in Bailey and Maynor's study show a more systematic restriction of invariant *be* to habitual contexts than the authors give them credit for, weakening the authors' claim (1987: 464) that the use of *be* as a marker of habituality and duration is due entirely to the youngest generation.[11] Finally, it should be noted that mesolectal Caribbean-creole grammars show the same preference for explicit preverbal habitual marking which is found with young American black speakers. While these additional factors indicate a need for us to examine other data sets and consider other interpretations before accepting Bailey and Maynor's (1987) analysis of the rise of invariant *be* as an auxiliary in Vernacular Black English, they also reveal the potential richness of this feature for linguists interested in internal and external constraints on syntactic change.

12.3   Zero Copula and Auxiliary *is, are*

The data in table 12.1 on zero realizations of copula and auxiliary *is* and *are* provide relatively strong support for the divergence hypothesis, since three of the four adults omit these forms less than 20 percent of the time, while the teenagers are at the other end of the spectrum, omitting them 82 percent and 90 percent of the time.[12] As noted above, we have no local real-time data from an earlier period, but *is/are*-absence frequencies for black teenagers (14–17 years

Table 12.2   Details of *is* and *are* absence for speakers in table 12.1

	OLD FOLK		MIDDLE-AGED		TEENAGERS	
	John Carbon	*Penelope Johnson*	*Dotsy Boston*	*Paula Gates*	*Tinky Gates*	*Foxy Boston*
0 *is*	11% (54)	5% (39)	0% (45)	8% (48)	67% (129)	79% (72)
0 *are*	25% (69)	38% (16)	44% (32)	54% (67)	96% (127)	99% (82)

old) in Detroit 20 years ago (Wolfram 1969: 179) are lower (30.3 percent for upper working-class and 67.7 percent for lower working-class youths), suggesting that the vernacular of our East Palo Alto youth really may be more non-standard, assuming that the stylistic levels of these data-sets are comparable. By contrast, adult East Palo Alto copula absence is on the whole lower (15 percent –35 percent) than the means reported by Wolfram (1969) for black Detroit adults 20 years ago (27.4 percent and 38.4 percent frequencies for upper working-class and lower working-class speakers 30–55 years old), suggesting that the trend towards increasing vernacularization in this area of the grammar is limited to East Palo Alto teenagers and may therefore be fairly recent.

Furthermore, if we separate the figures for zero *is* and zero *are*, as in table 12.2, Paula Gates's intermediate status in table 12.1 is seen to derive from her *are*-absence data; with respect to *is* absence, she is as conservative as the older folk, and as distinct from the teenagers.[13] The data of table 12.2 also permit comparisons with Labov et al.'s (1968) study of copula absence in New York City, which examined *is*-absence only. The *is*-absence means for the four working-class peer groups in New York City (computed from table 3.14 in Labov et al. 1968: 202) are all lower than those of our East Palo teenagers: 28 percent (57/202) for the 15–18-year-old Oscar Brothers, 36 percent (169/471) for the 9–13-year-old Cobras, 43 percent (200/460) for the 12–16-year-old Jets, and 55 percent (127/232) for the 11–17-year-old Cobras. Labov et al.'s (1968: 292) average *is*-absence figure for New York City adults (about half of them aged 20–39 years, the rest over 40 years old) is lower still – 14 percent (69/506), and in comparison with this the East Palo adults again appear unchanged or closer to the standard.[14]

So far we have isolated two constraints on the absence of *is* and *are*: the internal effect of which form is absent (*are* favoring deletion more than *is*) and the external effect of age (teenagers favoring deletion more than older groups). Table 12.3 provides a more sophisticated perspective on the behavior of this variable in East Palo Alto, for it draws on data from 33 speakers (the six in our core sample plus many more young people), takes into account six potential constraints, and estimates constraint effects in terms of variable-rule probabili-

Table 12.3   Variable rule probabilities for Labov Deletion and Straight Deletion, *is* and *are*, combined, East Palo Alto

Factor group	constraints	is/are Labov Deletion	is/are Straight Deletion
Following	*gonna*	.77	.83
Grammatical	verb-*ing*	.66	.67
	locative	.42	.47
	adjective	.47	.45
	noun phrase	.29	.27
	miscellaneous	.37	.29
Subject	personal pronoun	(.51)	.62
	other pronouns	(.44)	.46
	noun phrase	(.54)	.42
Person/	2nd person, plural	.67	.64
number	3rd singular	.33	.36
Following	___consonant	(.48)	(.48)
phon. envir.	___vowel	(.52)	(.52)
Preceding	consonant___	.59	(.47)
phon. envir.	vowel___	.41	(.53)
Age	old	.22	.23
	middle	.42	.42
	young	.83	.82
Data on each run			
Overall frequency (n's in parentheses):		67% (1,119)	53% (1,424)
Input probability		.62	.35
Formulae:		$\dfrac{D}{C+D}$	$\dfrac{D}{F+C+D}$

ties instead of frequencies. In interpreting these probabilities, it should be borne in mind that factors with values greater than .5 favor deletion, those with values less than .5 disfavor deletion, and those just around .5 have little effect either way. The table presents two alternative computations of *is/are* deletion, but I will concentrate on the Straight Deletion figures in the column to the far right, since this exploits the higher number of tokens (1,424 vs. 1,119) and makes fewer a priori assumptions about the nature of the Vernacular Black English grammar and its relation to Standard English. (See Rickford et al. 1988, included in this volume, for discussion.)

The first observation we might make about table 12.3 is that age is still clearly the single most significant constraint on deletion (the young people are associated with a strongly favoring probability value of .82 while the middle and old groups are progressively more disfavoring), and that the person/number category of the form is also significant (second person plural *are* is more favorable to deletion than third singular *is*). This much, of course, we had already known from tables 12.1 and 12.2, although the supporting data base is now much stronger. But the Straight Deletion probabilities in table 12.3 also provide evidence on other internal constraints which we have not yet considered. The parentheses around the consonant and vowel values in the Preceding and Following Phonological environment indicate that these phonological factor groups did not have a significant effect on *is/are* absence – contrary to what Labov (1969) had found for the Cobras and Jets (for Preceding Phonological environment) – but were in line with a system in which conjugated *be* is underlyingly absent, and inserted by grammatical rule. The other two internal factor groups – subject and Following Grammatical category – are significant, and pretty much along the lines which Labov and other Vernacular Black English researchers (like Baugh 1979) have found: a personal-pronoun subject favors *is/are* absence more than a full noun phrase or any other kind of pronoun; and *gonna* and Verb + *ing* are the Following Syntactic environments most favorable to *is/are* absence, with a following noun phrase least favorable. I will not attempt to explore here why these varied internal constraints work as they do (see Rickford et al. 1988), but it is clear that *is/are* absence is a complex variable, affected by several internal constraints plus the external effect of age.

12.4   Absence of Attributive Possessive -*s*

The table 12.1 data on the absence of attributive possessive -*s* at first seem to provide some support for the divergence hypothesis too, insofar as the adults rarely, if ever, omit this morpheme (Paula Gates is again somewhat an exception) while the teenagers often do (53 percent and 86 percent of the time). However, the quantitative data on this feature are less reliable than those on the other features, because possessive -*s* simply does not occur frequently in everyday speech, and the samples on which the percentages are based are small, ranging from two to 23 tokens.

Earlier studies of this variable in other cities also suffer from limited data,[15] and the evidence they provide of change in real time is, in any case, mixed. The frequencies of possessive -*s* absence which Wolfram (1969: 150) reported for black teenagers in Detroit (36.6 percent and 19.2 percent for upper working- and lower working-class speakers respectively) are lower than those of today's East Palo Alto teenagers, while the frequencies which Labov et al. (1968: 169) reported for New York City peer groups (72 percent and 57 percent in single and group style, respectively) are about the same. In the article in which the divergence issue was first broached, Labov and Harris (1986: 11–12) report even higher possessive -*s* absence frequencies (75–100 percent) for the core group of young Vernacular Black English speakers in Philadelphia who have little contact with Whites. Of the two East Palo Alto teenagers, Foxy is more similar to these core speakers, but it is not clear (especially with the low n's) that Foxy and the Philadelphia core speakers represent a fundamental shift away from the New York city peer group usage of 20 years ago, which led Labov et al. (1968: 170) to conclude even then that "there is no underlying -*s* in the attributive possessive form." Tentatively, on the combined evidence of our apparent-time and real-time data, we might conclude that absence of possessive -*s* is an age-graded feature, but not one which shows significant recent or ongoing change in community norms.

We have not investigated internal constraints on this variable. Its relatively low frequency of occurrence makes such investigation difficult for all researchers, and in any case, earlier studies of this variable report no significant internal effects.[16]

12.5   Absence of Third Singular, Present Tense -*s*

When we turn to the absence of third singular present tense -*s*, the East Palo Alto teenagers are decidedly in line with the Philadelphia "core vernacular" pattern of 75–100 percent third singular -*s* absence reported by Labov and Harris (1986: 8–12), since they both show virtual categorical absence of this form (96–97 percent). Note, however (see table 12.1), that while there is still an appreciable gap between the teenagers and the adults in East Palo Alto, the adults show higher frequencies for this Vernacular Black English feature (44–63 percent) than they do for zero copula or possessive -*s* absence.

The evidence of this variable from studies done in Detroit and New York City two decades ago is somewhat ambiguous. Black working-class teenagers in Detroit in the late 1960s (Wolfram 1969: 150) omitted third singular -*s* 56.4–76.5 percent of the time (upper and lower working-class groups, respectively), while the mean omission rate for the New York City peer groups from the same period (compiled from statistics in Labov et al. 1968: 161) was 68 percent (n = 592/876).[17] While these figures reveal that the tendency to omit this marker more often than not has been manifest for some time, and Labov et al. (1968:

164) had concluded that third singular *-s* was not an underlying part of the grammar of Vernacular Black English, it seems appropriate to characterize at least some of the speakers in these early studies as having the variable third singular *-s* insertion rule which Fasold (1972: 134, 146) found appropriate for Washington DC speakers in the 30–70 percent *-s* absence range. By contrast, Tinky and Foxy's extreme *-s* absence statistics make them more similar to Fasold's Washington DC speakers in the 80–90 percent *-s* absence range, the ones he characterized (Fasold 1972: 146) as having "no concord rule for verbal *-s*." However, at least some of the individuals in the early New York City and Detroit studies must have displayed similar near-categorical frequencies of third singular *-s* absence, so we cannot conclude that Foxy's and Tinky's statistics, dramatic though they seem, represent a fundamental shift in community norms. If further research indicates that most working-class East Palo Alto teenagers display the almost categorical *-s* absence which Foxy and Tinky do, this would provide clearer evidence of divergence.

We have so far found no significant internal conditioning on this variable, except for verb type (compare Labov et al. 1968: 246–8): *have* and *don't* occur without third singular inflections (i.e., *has*, *doesn't*) more frequently (67 percent and 77 percent of the time, respectively) than regular verbs do (54 percent), while zero forms of *say* occur less often (29 percent).[18] Like Poplack and Tagliamonte (1989: 74) we found no significant effect of subject type (personal pronoun versus full NP versus indefinite).[19] We have so far not tabulated our data on potential phonological constraints, which show inconsistent and/or minimal effects in most Vernacular Black English studies. But we have looked specifically for the two novel features which Myhill and Harris (1986) reported for core Vernacular Black English speakers in Philadelphia: the use of *-s* as a marker of narrative past, and the tendency to insert *-s* on the first but not the second member of conjoined verb phrases, as in "she *takes* your clothes out, and *lend* (them) to people." However, neither of these features occurs in our corpus,[20] and their absence cannot be attributed to formal interview style or high-status interviewer effects, as Myhill and Harris (1986) suggest may have been the case with studies prior to theirs. Tinky and Foxy, surrounded by peers and community insiders, relate many excited narratives, but the use of *-s* as a narrative past or historical present is absent from them all, as it is in this extract:

2   This one day, Nita *came* over to that girl house. We *were* standin' – they *were* standin' outside, an' Shanti, she *came* up to that school that day, as this girl just *kep'* pickin – pick – pick – pick – pick. And she had box me three days. Two days she had hit me from – an ah wouldn't hit that girl back. Ah would not hit her back. An Nita *say*, "why you fightin' wid my – you know? Why you messin' wid her?" You know, Anita *was* lookin at her all crazy, "Why you messin' wid her?" An' she *sai'*, "Cause I beat her up." An' ah *looked* at her like this, ah was – ah *was* sick o' that girl then. Ah *say*, "YOU BEAT WHO, WHAT,

WHEN?!! YOU MEAN YOU BEAT ME UP?!!" Ah *looked* at her like dis, ah *start* laughin' – honestly, ah *did*, ah *asked* her, ah *say*, "YOU BEAT ME UP?!!" Ah *ran* through that house like Rambo, a tookin' off earrings an', throwin' things everywhere. Ah *came* out that house, ah – ah *was* Ah WAS BEATIN' her up . . . (Tinky G., East Palo Alto 12, 597–608)

12.6   Absence of Plural -*s* and Past Tense Marking

When we turn to the last two variables in table 12.1, variables not examined in recent discussions of the divergence hypothesis, we find that they provide no evidence that Vernacular Black English has become more divergent or non-standard over time. With respect to the absence of plural -*s* on regular verbs, the East Palo Alto teenagers and old people show the same low relative frequency (10–13 percent -*s* absence), while the intermediate age group is lower still (1–3 percent). Wolfram (1969: 150) had reported comparable frequencies of plural -*s* absence in Detroit: 3.4 percent and 7.4 percent for upper working- and lower working-class black teenagers, and 5.0 percent and 8.6 percent for upper working- and lower working-class black adults. Labov et al.'s (1968: 161) report of 8 percent (n = 132/1707) plural -*s* absence for New York City peer groups two decades ago suggests similarly that no appreciable change has occurred in the interim. We are still tabulating our data on possible internal constraints, but preliminary indications are that a following vowel does inhibit plural -*s* absence, as Labov et al. (1968) also found to be true.[21]

With respect to zero past tense marking (including the presence of -*ed* on regular verbs and stem changing and other inflections on irregular or strong verbs) the picture is similar, except that the tendency, if anything, is towards less nonstandard usage as one descends the age hierarchy. Certainly Mr Carbon, leaving one in five past reference verbs unmarked, is more non-standard with respect to this feature than anyone else in our core sample. As is evident from extract 2 above, the tendency of Tinky and most young vernacular speakers in East Palo Alto is to mark most of their past reference verbs with Standard English past tense forms, especially in the case of irregular or strong verbs. This is pretty much as Labov et al. (1969: 250) reported for black speakers in New York City, and as Fasold (1972: 39) found for black speakers in Washington DC.

The only significant internal constraint on zero past tense marking which we have located to date is verb type. In the combined data for the six core speakers, zero past tense marking is highest (31 percent, n = 156) on weak verbs ending in a consonant not adding a syllable in the past tense, which would yield consonant clusters on suffixation (e.g., /pIkt/ 'picked'), and on the verb *say* (25 percent, n = 222). It is equally low (6 percent) in irregular or strong verbs (n = 622) and on weak verbs like *agree* which end on a vowel (n = 51), and is lowest (2 percent, n = 49) on weak verbs with syllable adding *-ed* like *start* in which the past tense suffix (*start-ed*) is therefore most salient.[22]

12.7 Conclusion: Interpreting the Evidence for Divergence and Convergence

On the basis of the apparent and real-time data we have examined in this paper, particularly for the first two variables in table 12.1, Vernacular Black English in East Palo Alto seems to show some evidence of ongoing change away from the patterns of Standard and Vernacular White English, in line with trends reported for other urban areas. Having said this much, however, several qualifications must be made. In the first place, both our apparent-time and real-time data need to be improved, and we are attempting in our ongoing research to do precisely this – enriching the apparent-time data by increasing the sample size, and trying to locate comparable linguistic data or observations for East Palo Alto ten years or more ago to strengthen our real-time evidence. In the second place, apparent divergence with respect to invariant *be* and the zero copula is matched by stability and/or convergence of other features, particularly with respect to plural and past marking, as shown above, and with respect to the pronunciation of the unstressed syllable in *happy*, *fifty*, and so on as higher, fronter, tenser (more like [i] than [I]) – as shown by Denning (1989), drawing on data from our project in East Palo Alto.

The coexistence of convergent and divergent changes which we find locally is similar to what Anshen (1969) found for Hillsboro, North Carolina,[23] and should of course be no more surprising than the finding that Vernacular Black English is changing. The alternative assumption, that it is standing still, and has been for the past century or longer, would be unwarranted. But the sociolinguistic challenge then becomes, as both Vaughn-Cooke (1987) and Denning (1989) have noted, to explain why some features show evidence of divergence while others remain stable or appear to be converging with Standard English and Vernacular White English.

One external factor that strikes me as very relevant to divergence but one that has been neglected in discussions of it to date, is the differences in attitudes towards black identity and culture, including vernacular language use, between successive black generations. Black teenagers are less assimilationist than their parents and especially their grandparents, and more assertive about their rights to talk and act in their "natural way." By contrast, black adults, affected by the demands of the work-place, seem to be impelled away from distinctively black patterns of language and behavior.[24] Consider, for instance, the following response of Penelope Johnson, a former domestic, to the question of whether one's speech makes a difference:

3   I do think it's – it makes a difference, because in our day an' time, if you don't use your English as near right, people kinda look at you as if, "Oh, I don't want her in – on my job, to speakin' dis way or in my kitchen, aroun' my childrens, you know," so I think it does make a difference how you speak . . .
    (What do you think of your own speech?)
    Oh, it's terrible, sometime.
    (Have you ever tried to change it?)
    Yeah – I'm – I – I have to try, you know, I guess. I – I tries to put the words right, the verbs and things, I try my best to – take my time if I – especially if I'm – speakin' to someone tha's – is – uh – educated, you know. I try to, you know, place my words as near right as I possibly can. Sometimes I slip up.
    (Do you think everyone needs to speak Standard English?)
    I think so. Would be better on us [black people]. (Laughs.) It would be much better on us. (East Palo Alto 6A: 445–78)

Not only do black working-class teenagers from East Palo Alto and surrounding areas not express this kind of insecurity about their own speech,[25] they are also outspoken in their criticism of black peers who act white in speech or any other aspect of social behavior. Consider, for instance, Tinky G.'s scathing comments on a cousin who falls into this category:

4   Then i's these wh – these black girls jus' like – ack lak white girl(s). Ah say, "You wanna be white, go change yo' sk – color. Shut up!" Ah – mah cou' – they ack stupid. Ah got – ah got a cousin, R[. . .], an' she got this black girl, her name is C[. . .], an' she ack so white, po' he'p her. Ah tell her – ah say she love Boy George [a white British rock star]. Ah tell 'er, ah say, "You know what, C[. . .], why'on'choo go live wi' Boy George?" Say, "He not doin anything for you." (East Palo Alto 12: 241–5)

Compare, too, the comments of Reggie, a black teenager from neighboring Redwood City who goes to the same high school as many East Palo Altans, on the taunts that can stick with you for talking white:

5   Over at my school, if they – first time they catch you talkin' white, they'll never let it go. Even if you just quit talkin like that, they'll never let it go! (Reggie, East Palo Alto 50: A530–2)

And consider, finally, the staunch objections voiced by Fabiola, a black teenager from East Palo Alto, to "Oreos" (like the cookie, black on the outside, white on the inside) who try to correct her vernacular usage:

6   It pisses me off when the Oreos – they be tryin to correct your language, and
    I be like, "Get away from me! Did I ask you to – correct me?! No! No! No, I
    didn't! Nuh-uh!" (East Palo Alto 50: A254–8)

For these teenagers, Vernacular Black English is an important means of asserting their black identity, in accord with the "Acts of Identity" model of Le Page
and Tabouret-Keller (1985).[26]

But even if we used the differential orientation of teenagers and old folks to
explain the teenagers' increased use of zero copula, how can we explain the fact
that they are not doing the same with the absence of plural -s or past marking?
At present, neither an external (social identity) explanation nor an internal one
(for instance, pressures to simplify the system by reducing redundant mark-
ings) is capable of discriminating among all the variables of table 12.1 and
accounting for their varied distributions in apparent and real time.

There do seem to be some valid reasons, however, why invariant habitual
be should represent the leading edge of the features apparently undergoing
change. In the first place, it is now very salient as a distinctively black form, one
which in this respect has become the focus of public comment and use by black
entertainers and other public figures,[27] and one which is frequently included by
Whites discussing or imitating black speech (see Butters 1989: 15). One reason
for the rapid dissemination of this form among black youth and for its attracting
the notice of others is that although it functions as a grammatical marker – as
a counter in a set of tense-aspect oppositions marked in the verb phrase – *be* is
an invariant lexical item, which can be consciously adopted and rapidly spread
like slang terms and other lexical items.[28] Futhermore, as a preverbal (semi-)
auxiliary marking tense, aspect, or mood, it occupies a syntactic and semantic
slot in which the distinctiveness of Vernacular Black English has always been
marked, perhaps even more noticeably so over the past two decades. Compare
recent discussions of stressed *BIN* (Rickford 1975), *steady* (Baugh 1984), *be
done* (Baugh 1983: 77–80), *come* (Spears 1982), and *had* (Rickford and
Théberge-Rafal 1989). One can almost bet, as a linguist, that genuine qualitative and quantitative innovations in Vernacular Black English are likely to show
up in the auxiliary (proximate future *finna*, from *fixing to* (Ching 1987), seems
to be increasing in frequency now as a black vernacular marker), and the young
native speakers of Vernacular Black English who are leading in the creation and
adoption of such innovations may well be aware of the dynamic and salient
nature of this grammatical category too.

Ultimately, despite our best efforts to interpret existing apparent- and real-
time evidence, only the future will tell whether the heavy adolescent *be*-users
and copula non-users of East Palo Alto today will adopt their parents' and
grandparents' more conservative linguistic behaviors as they grow older, or
whether they really represent the vanguard of a fundamental change in community norms. We intend to re-record and follow the linguistic development of

Foxy, Tinky, and other individuals in our current sample and combine this with fresh samples of the community to minimize the ambiguities of each kind of real-time evidence (Labov 1986). Regardless of the direction future events take, it is clear that we would be in a much weaker position to interpret them and to untangle internal and external constraints on the grammatical variables discussed in this paper if we did not have the detailed quantitative and attitudinal data for this point in time which we have presented above and which we are continuing to collect.[29]

Notes

This is a considerably revised and expanded version of a paper presented at the annual meeting of the Linguistic Society of America in 1987, and at the International Conference on Historical Linguistics Symposium on Internal and External Factors in Syntactic Change held at Rutgers University, New Jersey, August 15–16, 1989. The research was made possible through research grants provided to myself or the students listed in the next paragraph by the following agencies and individuals: the Program in Urban Studies at Stanford, the Irvine Foundation, and Carolyn Lougee, former Dean of Undergraduate Studies at Stanford.

Many individuals contributed to the research reported in this paper. I am indebted to Faye McNair-Knox (research associate), Jawanza Osayimwese and Keith Denning (research assistants), and participants in a 1987 residential summer research seminar at Stanford who helped to transcribe and tabulate data on several of the variables (Renée Blake, Jeannine Carter, Pamela Ellis, Genine Lentine (graduate supervisor), Diana Loo, Erin Mulligan, Barbara Pearson, Sharon Tu, and Fox Vernon), and the students who were involved in the VARBRUL analysis of the copula data in the summer of 1988 (Arnetha Ball, Renée Blake, Raina Jackson, and Nomi Martin). I am especially grateful to my wife Angela Rickford for feedback and encouragement.

1   These figures are derived from Labov's (1981: 177) observation that the span between comparison points must be "large enough to allow for significant changes but small enough to rule out the possibility of reversals and retrograde movements: . . . from a minimum of a half generation to a maximum of two."

2   In this paper, our focus will be on divergence from Standard English norms rather than local white vernaculars, partly because we have so far been able to locate and interview only a few Whites in East Palo Alto (few non-transient working-class Whites live in the central residential sections of the city), and because the data we have tabulated from those interviews so far (for copula absence and invariant *be* – neither of which the Whites in our sample use) are identical with Standard English norms. For a number of phonological and other variables not examined in this paper, local White Vernacular English does differ from Standard English, however, and it is important to draw the distinction (see Fasold et al. 1987: 68; Butters 1989: 194).

3   For even more recent and comprehensive discussions of the controversy, see Bailey and Maynor (1989) and Butters (1989).

4   Labov and Harris (1986: 5) made this assumption and methodological strategy almost explicit, in noting that, "The extreme character of the core Philadelphia B[lack] E[nglish] V[ernacular] will be evident if the data we present here is compared to that reported for the Jets and the Cobras in New York City in the late 1960s (Labov 1972c)." Labov (in Fasold et al. 1987: 65) was even more explicit: "We have no earlier records in Philadelphia. Our best comparison will be with the work done in New York in 1965–1968." But quantitative comparisons with that earlier work were not provided.

5   As Bailey and Maynor (1986) show, urban and rural black dialects in Texas differ in relation to the expression of habitual aspect, so we at least have to take this demographic difference into account when comparing the data from one black working-class community with another.

6   Since the primary interviewers of black peer group and core vernacular speakers in Labov et al. (1968) and Labov and Harris (1986) were also black (John Lewis in New York City, Wendell Harris in Philadelphia), comparisons between these studies and ours should be particularly pertinent. A neglected issue in current discussions of the divergence issue is the importance of having data sets which are comparable with respect to interviewer characteristics and stylistic level. On this point see Wolfram (1987: 42–4).

7   John Carbon (a pseudonym, like the others) is a retired coal-miner, auto-worker, and construction worker who also earned a living for a while playing in local baseball games. Penelope Johnson is a retired farm-worker, domestic and nurse's assistant. Dotsy Boston is a machinist, and the mother of Foxy Boston (whose father is a construction worker). Paula Gates is a teacher's aide, and the mother of Tinky Gates. Unlike the 1960s studies of Vernacular Black English, we have fairly extensive data on each individual, and more females in our sample than males. Teenage girls in East Palo Alto use the vernacular as vigorously as the male street gangs in New York City in the 1960s did, and in some cases, even more so.

8   For convenience of reference and because such comparisons are basic to the divergence issue, these Vernacular Black English features are described in terms of comparisons with Standard English ("use of invariant *be*," "zero copula"), but it is of course possible to describe them in their own terms, as DeBose and Faraclas (1993) do.

9   Although this variable includes, strictly speaking, both auxiliary (pre-Verb + *ing*) and copula (pre-locative, nominal and adjectival) tokens, we will sometimes refer to it more loosely as "zero copula," following the tradition of the literature on Vernacular Black English.

10 Absolute and relative frequencies for this feature and others in table 12.1 are subject to modification as untabulated data from other tape recordings in our corpus is added. For instance, in a subsequent interview, Paula Gates uses four instances of invariant *be* when talking about "signifying" and other speech events in which she used to engage when she was in school. (Labov et al. 1968: 235 note similarly that New York City adults tend to shift towards *be* use when discussing childhood experiences, and suggests that this may be evidence of age-grading.)

11 What appears to be true from Bailey and Maynor's data (1987: 460, table 6) is that, in the auxiliary environment (before Verb + *ing*), *be* has become almost the exclusive marker of extended and habitual meaning for the children but not for the folk

speakers, who use zero *is/are* for habituals much more frequently than *be* (73 percent vs. 6 percent). However, as I have pointed out elsewhere (Rickford 1989), since auxiliary tokens account for only 12 percent (4/31) of the folk speakers' tokens of *be*, but for 63 percent (62/96) of the children's, this kind of comparison can be misleading. See Butters (1989: 27) for a similar point.

12   In common with virtually all previous studies of the copula, these figures omit tokens which were indeterminate (e.g., contracted *is* followed by a sibilant, as in, "He's sick") or invariant (e.g., clause-final tokens, as in "Yes, he is," never contracted or deleted). See Rickford et al. (1988) for further details.

13   Table 12.2 also reveals that Dotsy follows the majority Mississippi white pattern reported by Wolfram (1974), allowing some *are* absence, but not *is* absence.

14   Labov et al.'s (1968: 202) mean *is* absence figure for white Inwood teenagers is 0 percent (0/218), the same as reported by McElhinny (1993) for Whites in Palo Alto and East Palo Alto. For this grammatical variable, as for absence of third singular and attributive possessive *-s* (see Ash and Myhill 1986: 37, figure 2), divergence from Standard English norms is pretty much the same as divergence from white vernacular usage, at least outside of the South.

15   Labov et al. (1968: 161) report a total of 85 tokens for 44 or more members of the T-birds, Cobras, Jets, Aces, and Oscar Brothers; and Wolfram (1969: 143) reports 38 instances of potential -z possessive for the 24 members of his working-class groups. In both cases, the mean sample size of two or three tokens per individual is considerably lower than in our data. Labov and Harris (1986) provide percentages, but no n's, so we cannot compare their sample size (nor perform chi-square or other significance tests on their data).

16   Wolfram (1969: 143) reported a slight favoring effect of a preceding consonant (especially /n/) over a preceding vowel: 34.6–27.8 percent *-s* absence respectively. Labov et al. (1968: 169) did not have enough data to determine phonological effects.

17   These figures combine statistics for the Thunderbirds, Aces, Cobras, Jets, and Oscar Bros across all styles and phonological contexts.

18   These distributions are based on the data of the middle-aged and old speakers only, since the teenagers are, as noted above, virtually categorical in excluding third-person singular *-s*. Here are the relevant statistics on third-person singular *-s* absence for the adults (n's in parentheses: *have* = 67 percent (21), *do* = 44 percent (9), *don't* = 77 percent (35), *say* = 29 percent (7), regular verbs = 54 percent (222).

19   Relevant statistics – again for adults only – for absence of third person singular *-s*: personal pronoun subjects = 56 percent (174), full NP subjects = 61 percent (92), indefinite subjects = 58 percent (24).

20   Overall, *-s* occurs on semantically past verbs only 1 percent of the time (16 out of 1,100 cases) in our corpus, and never in the speech of the teenagers. Ten of the 16 *-s* tokens occur in the speech of Paula Gates, and they are all tokens of *says*.

21   Combined statistics, for John Carbon and Foxy Boston only: _____## Consonant = 12 percent (85), _____## Vowel = 6 percent (51), _____## Pause = 17 percent (83). Note that Poplack and Tagliamonte (1989: 64–5) also find the same ordering of consonant, vowel, and pause with respect to absence of third singular *-s* in Samaná, and that, as they remind us, Guy (1980: 28) had also found a following pause most favorable for *-t, -d* deletion in contemporary Vernacular Black English.

22   On this point, compare Bickerton (1975: 142ff.), Rickford (1987a: 384–5), and Poplack and Tagliamonte (1989: 64).

23   Anshen's finding – that /r/-lessness diminished with decreasing age while the pronunciation of /θ/ as [t] or [f] increased – is discussed by Vaughn-Cooke (1987: 29), who proposes a two-part hypothesis about Vernacular Black English change: "The majority of features undergoing change in Black English are converging toward standard English; powerful social and linguistic counterforces can reverse the expected direction of a change."

24   Latice, a ninth-grader, perceptively commented (East Palo Alto 50: A067–9) that adults use less Vernacular Black English than children because "when they're in work, they got to try to be like the white people wan' em to be."

25   "I'm not really out to impress anybody," the speaker of Example 5 observed, "I talk the way I want to!" (East Palo Alto 50: A478–9).

26   Note, however, that contrary to the impression sometimes given by proponents of the Acts of Identity model, speakers are still (subconsciously) controlled by applicable internal constraints.

27   Arsenio Hall, the black late-night talk-show host, has even incorporated it into his slogan/theme: "Arsenio Hall – we be havin a ball!" And the late Arthur Ashe deprecated its use by one of his children's teachers in a *Reader's Digest* article. Butters (1989: 15–16) cites other recent examples of public figures using invariant *be*. And it was the single most cited, caricatured, misused, and misunderstood AAVE feature in media coverage of the Oakland Ebonics controversy in 1996 (as discussed in Rickford and Rickford (to appear)).

28   Quite independently, Butters (1989: 20ff.) makes the same point. However, I do not agree with his additional characterization of invariant *be* as a "relatively superficial change" (1989: 24).

29   Note that written attestations of invariant *be* are few and far between. If we had to document current developments in the use of this feature in Vernacular Black English from written records, we would be almost totally at a loss, and this is probably true for most vernacular features undergoing change.

Part III
Educational Implications

13

Attitudes towards AAVE, and Classroom Implications and Strategies

13.1 Attitudes towards AAVE

What people think about AAVE and people who speak AAVE is an important issue for educators, for at least two reasons.[1] First, teachers often have unjustifiably negative attitudes towards students who speak AAVE (Labov 1970b, Di Giulio 1973, Bowie and Bond 1994), and such negative attitudes may lead them to have low expectations of such students, to assign them inappropriately to learning disabled or special education classes, and to otherwise stunt their academic performance (Rosenthal and Jacobson 1968, Smitherman 1981a: 19, Tauber 1997).[2] Second, teachers trying to decide whether and how to take AAVE into account in their classroom pedagogy might benefit from understanding what the attitudes of students, parents, employers, and other teachers are towards this group (see McGroarty 1996).

As it turns out, such attitudes are not uniform (Speicher and McMahon 1992: 400). Even on the existence of AAVE as a distinctive variety, there is disagreement (Shores 1977, Speicher and McMahon 1992: 386–7). Moreover, although educational psychologists such as Bereiter and Engelmann (1966) and Farrell (1983) berate the use of AAVE structures by young children and see them as reflecting or creating cognitive deficits, their conclusions have been persuasively rebutted by linguists (Labov 1970b and Baugh 1988 respectively). Leading African American writers – for example, Maya Angelou, in connection with the Ebonics controversy of December 1996 – have been critical of AAVE (Rickford, in press),[3] but other African American writers – for example, Baldwin 1979, Morrison 1981: 27, and Jordan 1985 – have defended the legitimacy and expressiveness of AAVE just as fiercely. Youth of all races and ages, including pre-school (Rosenthal 1974), elementary and high school (Linn and Pichè 1982, Rickford and Rickford 1995), and college students (Jordan 1985, Jackson and Williamson-Ige 1986) often echo the negative attitudes of their parents, teachers and the media toward AAVE, and their positive attitudes toward SE.[4] At the same time, inner-city African American teenagers sometimes vigorously reject the standard and endorse the vernacular in opposition to mainstream white culture and values (Fordham and Ogbu 1986: 182).

Parents often express concern that if their children were limited to the vernacular, this would negatively affect their chances of going on to college, getting good jobs, and getting ahead in society more generally (Hoover 1978: 85), and the validity of this concern has been demonstrated in empirical research by Shuy (1972), Terrell and Terrell (1983), and Baugh (1996). However, even those parents who preferred the standard for job interviews, for reading and writing, and for schools and formal contexts, accepted the vernacular for listening and speaking, particularly in the home and in informal settings, and some endorsed it positively for solidarity maintenance and culture preservation (Hoover 1978: 78–9, Speicher and McMahon 1992: 398–9).[5]

This ambivalence about AAVE is part of a larger "push-pull" dynamic in African American history (Smitherman 1986: 170), but it is not limited to African Americans. Taylor's (1973) survey of 422 teachers of various races throughout the country revealed that while 40 percent expressed negative opinions about the structure and usefulness of AAVE and other vernacular varieties, 40 percent expressed positive opinions (183). Moreover, their attitudes could not be characterized simply as positive or negative; they varied depending on the aspect of dialect use under discussion, length of teaching experience (those who had been teaching for 3–5 years were most positive), and other factors.[6]

One thing that most teachers, parents, and linguists agree on, regardless of their attitudes towards AAVE, is that children should be taught to read and write fluently as a basis for success in the entire curriculum. Many also feel that they should be assisted in developing bidialectal competence in AAVE and Standard English.[7] Linguists have consistently suggested that these goals would be better achieved if the structural, rhetorical, and expressive characteristics of African American vernacular language were taken into account. In the next section we'll consider some of their observations and suggestions.

13.2   Implications for Teaching Language Arts to Speakers of AAVE

Reading, the subject which parents in Hoover's (1978: 82) study ranked as the most important item in the elementary school curriculum, was the first subject to attract the interest of sociolinguists working on AAVE. Labov (1972c: 33–4) observed that, because of the homonyms produced by regular AAVE rules (e.g. *Ruth = roof; pass = passed*), it might be difficult for teachers to know when they are dealing with a mistake in reading or a difference in pronunciation. For instance, the child who reads "He passed by both of them" as "*he pass' by bof of dem*" may have decoded the past tense meaning and every other semantic component of the original correctly, but simply pronounced the sentence according to the rules of his or her own vernacular. The teaching strategy in this case would be very different from that of a child who had not recognized or understood the significance of the *-ed* suffix. Labov suggested (1972: 34) that teachers in the early grades accept the existence of a different set of homonyms in the speech of African American children to preserve their confidence in the phonic code and facilitate their learning to read.[8]

An alternative strategy, advocated by Baratz (1969), Stewart (1969), and Smitherman (1986), among others, was to introduce AAVE speakers to reading through "dialect readers" which minimize the differences between the printed word and the child's vernacular, and allow the child to concentrate on decoding and comprehension without the additional burden of simultaneously learning a second dialect. Simpkins, Holt, and Simpkins (1977) created the most comprehensive set of dialect materials, a series of *Bridge* readers written in AAVE, a transitional variety, and Standard English, as exemplified in these brief excerpts (Simpkins and Simpkins 1981: 232):

1   *AAVE*: He couldn't find no dictionary, so he split on down to the library . . . He ask the lady there 'bout books to help him learn some big words like redundancy.
   Transition: He didn't have a dictionary so he went down to the public library . . . He asked (the librarian) for a book to help him.
   Standard English: . . . He explained to the librarian that he wanted to increase his vocabulary.

The *Bridge* reading program was field tested with 540 students from seventh through twelfth grade, and the students' progress after several months of instruction was "extremely promising," as measured by scores on the Iowa Test of Basic Skills in Reading (Simpkins and Simpkins 1981: 237).[9] Despite these early successes, the series was not retained, and dialect readers have not been widely adopted, for a variety of political, philosophical, and practical reasons, including negative reactions from educators and community leaders (see Wolfram and Fasold 1969: 142–3, Wolfram 1991: 255–6, Labov 1995, Rickford and Rickford 1995).

Another teaching strategy that was proposed a quarter of a century ago but which is less popular these days is the use of drills that focus attention on differences between AAVE and SE and aim to help children develop competence in switching smoothly between them. Here are some examples of translation drills from Feigenbaum (1970: 92):

2 *Direction*	*Teacher stimulus*	*Student response*
SE→AAVE	Paula likes leather coats	Paula like leather coats
AAVE→SE	He prefer movies	He prefers movies

One virtue of this method is that it recognized and promoted the integrity of both AAVE and SE. Another is that it made use of second language teaching techniques, in accord with Stewart's (1964a) suggestion that SE be taught to AAVE speakers as a "quasi-foreign language." However, the drills were boring, and assumed to a certain extent that the teacher spoke AAVE or had some knowledge of it (Keith Walters, personal communication). Moreover, their value was called into question by theoretical developments in second language acquisition (Wolfram 1991: 225).[10]

One educational implication of AAVE research which was noted early and continues to be emphasized today is that many standard intelligence tests are biased against speakers of AAVE and similar dialects insofar as they include items which involve differences between AAVE and SE but give credit only for the SE response (see Labov 1976, Wolfram 1976, 1986, 1991, Vaughn-Cooke 1983, Smitherman 1986: 237–41, Hoover and Taylor 1987). One example is the ITPA grammatical closure subtest, which includes this item:

3   Here is a dog. Here are two _____. (SE *dogs* is correct; AAVE *dog* is "wrong.")

In response to evidence of bias, some linguists have urged that creators and users of such tests increase their knowledge of the speech of the communities they serve and field test them with dialect speakers (Wolfram 1991: 244–7), while others have called for "a national moratorium on all testing until valid measures are devised" (Smitherman 1986: 239).

With respect to writing, a number of useful suggestions have been made by linguists. Farr and Daniels (1986) have isolated factors associated with effective writing instruction for dialect speakers, including an appreciation of children's native linguistic competence and moderate marking of surface errors (45–6). In a similar vein, Smitherman (1986: 213ff.) urges that, in their responses to students' writing, teachers concentrate on organization, content, and rhetorical power rather than on superficial errors caused by the transfer of grammatical patterns of AAVE. Ball (1992) has drawn attention to special circumlocution, narrative interspersion and recursion styles which occur in the expository discourse of African American students, perhaps reflecting the models of African American sermons and other expressive oral genres. This line of research is similar in some respects to the work of Michaels (1981) and Taylor and Matsuda (1988), who report that African American children often use in oral narratives a "topic associating" style, involving "a series of associated segments . . . linked implicitly" rather than a "topic-centered" style involving "tightly structured discourse on a single topic." The teacher who does not recognize this "topic associating" style, exemplified in 4, may prematurely interrupt or curtail their expressive productions:

> 4 *A topic associating narrative*: I went to the beach Sunday / and to McDonald's / and to the park / and I got this for my birthday / (holds up purse) my mother bought it for me / and I had two dollars for my birthday / and I put it in here / and I went to where my friend / named Gigi / I went over to my grandmother's house with her / and she was on my back . . . (from Michaels and Cazden 1986)

A number of researchers have made other suggestions for adapting language arts instruction to the language and culture of African American youth, advocating, for instance, increased use of call-and-response and tonal semantics in classroom exercises (Smitherman 1986: 220); the use of lyrics from popular songs and rap music to develop poetry appreciation, spelling, vocabulary, and sentence structure (Baugh 1981, Hoover 1991); and a cultural linguistic approach including increased use of the language experience method in which children create and read their own thoughts and experiences (Starks 1983).[11]

Finally, Kochman (1981), Foster (1986) and Morgan (1991) have drawn attention to rhetorical-expressive and/or cultural differences between African Americans and white Americans – for instance, with respect to turn-taking and discussion style. Understanding these differences may improve the teacher's ability to communicate and function effectively in the classroom.

13.3 Classroom Strategies and Exercises Involving Social Dialects

Many of the specific suggestions made in the preceding section in relation to AAVE can be applied to social dialects more generally. The overarching need is that teachers recognize the regularity and integrity of the social dialects which children and adolescents employ in the classroom and in the schoolyard, that they appreciate the powerful attachment to such dialects which students often have – sometimes as a vital part of their social identity – and that they build on such dialects, where possible, in language arts, second language, and foreign language instruction.

One exercise which teachers might do to increase awareness of and sensitivity to social variation is to show and discuss films and videotapes in which distinctive social dialects are exemplified and/or play a significant role. The list might include the following, but the possibilities here are virtually unlimited: *My Fair Lady* (based on George Bernard Shaw's *Pygmalion*), the PBS television series *The Story of English* (with accompanying text by McCrum et al. 1986), the November 19, 1987 discussion of "Black English" on the Oprah Winfrey Show,[12] and *Daughters of the Dust* (see Dash 1992 for screenplay and discussion). Literature which exemplifies similar variation may offer even richer possibilities for reflection and analysis. As examples of the many potential references one might consult on this issue, note Holton's (1984) analysis of the use of AAVE in African American fiction; Brathwaite (1984), Dabydeen and Wilson-Tagoe (1988), and Chamberlain (1993) on Caribbean and Afro-British literature; Lal and Raghavendra (1960) on poetry in Indian English, and James (1986) on Third World literature more generally. Recordings of Third World poets and authors reading their works in their native varieties of English (e.g. Kay, Agard, D'Aguiar, and Berry 1990) constitute another valuable classroom resource.

Finally, teachers should elicit from students examples of age, class, gender, and ethnicity-related differences in language use which they've encountered in their own experience, encourage them to exploit such differences creatively to represent various characters in drama and composition, and engage them in discussion of what these differences reflect about social relations and imply for schooling and careers. The results should be dynamic and richly instructive, for teachers and students alike.

Notes

1   This is a revised and expanded excerpt from Rickford (1996). Many additional references to language attitude studies of AAVE have been added.
2   Contrariwise, teachers who display the most positive attitudes towards AAVE and the greatest knowledge about the history and structure of AAVE as measured by the "African American English test" also show the highest degrees of pupil achievement, in studies by Politzer and Lewis (1979) cited in Hoover, Lewis et al. (1996: 370). Hoover, McNair-Knox et al. (1996) have devised a comprehensive language attitudinal measure for teachers of African American students.
3   For more on Angelou's views, see Rickford (in press).
4   I am grateful to Cathy Harrison of the University of Hawaii for drawing my attention to the work of Linn and Pichè, 1982 and Jackson and Williamson-Ige, 1986.
5   Hoover (1978) interviewed 80 California parents, 64 from East Palo Alto and 16 from Oakland. The "standard" and "vernacular" varieties about which they were asked were African American varieties, spoken by African American interviewers, and sharing AAVE prosodic and phonological patterns while differing primarily in grammar.
6   Renée Blake is currently doing work on language attitudes to AAVE among teachers in New York City, and Anita Henderson is currently studying the language attitudes of employers in Philadelphia.

7   See Sledd (1969) for demurral on this point.

8   For more on the teaching of reading, and on other strategies discussed in this section, see chapter 16, "Using the Vernacular to Teach the Standard," in this volume.

9   Simpkins and Simpkins (1981: 238) reported that the 540 children using the *Bridge* series showed "significantly larger gains" than a control group of 123 students who did not – an average gain of "6.2 months for four months of instruction compared to only an average gain of 1.6 months for students in their regular scheduled classroom reading activities."

10 However, Taylor (1989) has used similar drills quite successfully with college level students, and cites other research (108) in which "the audio-lingual methods, applied to the teaching of Black students, has proved to be a successful tool."

11 See also Heath (1983) and the papers in Brooks (1985).

12 The videotape is available from Harpo Productions, Chicago, Illinois. However, as Keith Walters (personal communication) has suggested, it might be most fruitful to show and discuss this videotape after students have learned about the systematicity of AAVE and other dialects and after they understand some of the factors which influence people's attitudes towards such dialects.

14

Unequal Partnership: Sociolinguistics and the African American Speech Community

This article provides me with the opportunity to talk about a subject that has been of growing concern to me for some years. Its starting point is that American quantitative sociolinguistics has, over the past quarter century, drawn substantially on data from African American Vernacular English (AAVE) and the African American speech community for its descriptive, theoretical, and methodological development, but it has given relatively little back to that community in terms of representation or practical application. While this article focuses on American quantitative sociolinguistics, in relation to AAVE, the criticism can be extended fairly easily to sociolinguistics more generally and to linguistics as a field, in relation to the peoples from whom we have drawn data for our theories and descriptions. So linguists from other sub-fields have no reason for complacency.

Before going on to develop my primary argument, I have a small preamble. In addressing this subject, I am reminded of the reason I originally got into linguistics, as an undergraduate at the University of California, Santa Cruz, at the end of the 1960s. The late Roger Keesing, an insightful linguistic anthropologist (see Keesing 1988), tantalized me into linguistics with his recordings of Solomon Islands Pijin and the radical conception (for me) that creole varieties like my native Guyanese Creole had systematic structure and fascinating, interconnected histories. But what really helped me to abandon English literature and design my own major in sociolinguistics was a paper by Le Page (1968) which dealt with the high failure rate (70–90 percent) of Caribbean high school students on the English language GCE (General Certificate of Education) "O" level exam set by London and Cambridge Universities. Having worked as a high school teacher in Guyana for one year before setting off for college, I was aware of the problem, and I was convinced by Le Page's arguments that it resulted partly from the fact that teachers could not recognize the differences between local creole and Standard English, nor help students to shift smoothly between the two varieties. As a solution to the problem, Le Page recommended that English language specialists should be trained to analyze their native varieties and help teachers improve their methods of teaching English. He outlined the training such specialists should have:

> It is essential that these specialists have a thorough basic training in linguistics, psychological and sociological aspects of linguistic behavior, the psychology of language learning, the processes of creolization, the principles of contrastive analysis, and the structure of the languages involved in their situation (e.g. Creole English, Creole French, English, Spanish, Maya). They must also be trained in the general principles of education, in the preparation of teaching materials, and in the use of audio-visual aids, radio and television. (Le Page 1968: 440)

Armed with Le Page's guidelines and assisted by a liberal and innovative college environment, I combined courses in linguistics, anthropology, and other fields, and graduated with a self-designed major in sociolinguistics in 1971. However, in a quarter century of working as a graduate student and university faculty member since then, I have focussed mainly on descriptive, theoretical, and methodological issues rather than on the applied concerns which originally attracted me to the field.[1] This is partly because of my excitement about the former kinds of research, and partly because of the process of appointment, tenure, and promotion – which rewards theory, and looks askance (if at all) at application. I suspect that, in this respect, my experiences are similar to those of many other sociolinguists; thus, the critique of this article is not just directed at others, but also at myself.

14.1   Contributions of the African American Speech Community to (Socio)Linguistics

The roots of American quantitative sociolinguistics were laid in 1958, in a paper by John Fischer in which the variation between *-in* and *-ing* as present participle suffixes (*walkin/ing*) was analyzed in the speech of 24 New England children. Fischer showed that these were not simply "free variants" – as mainstream linguistics then and now might regard them – but "socio-symbolic variants" systematically constrained by both internal and external factors including verb type, sex, and style. William Labov's studies of Martha's Vineyard (1963) and of New York City (the Lower East Side, 1966) built on these ideas; and with richer data and more significant theorizing about the relation between synchronic variation and change in progress, they essentially established the paradigm of quantitative sociolinguistics. Largely as a result of Labov's work, quantitative sociolinguistics became the dominant sub-field of sociolinguistics.[2]

Until W. Labov 1966, the speech of African Americans had played little if any role in the development of American sociolinguistics. But perhaps as an outgrowth of work by Stewart 1964b and Shuy 1965 which explored the relation among social dialects, non-standard speech, and the teaching of English, W. Labov et al. (1968) produced a two-volume study of the English of (primarily lower- and working-class) African Americans in Harlem, and this was studded with paradigm setting innovations for the field.[3] There were several other contemporaneous studies of AAVE, most of them similarly funded by the Office of Education and/or by private foundations interested in potential educational applications. The list includes studies in Detroit by Shuy et al. (1967) and Wolfram (1969), in Oakland by Mitchell-Kernan (1969), in Los Angeles by Legum et al. (1971), and in Washington, DC, by Fasold (1972). In the 1980s and 1990s, a new generation of urban studies was done in Los Angeles (Baugh 1983), in Philadelphia (Labov and Harris 1986, Dayton 1994), in College Station, Texas (Bailey and Maynor 1987), in East Palo Alto (Rickford et al. 1991), and in Detroit (Edwards 1992). Insofar as these later works were community studies and involved quantitative analyses of selected variables, they can be seen as extensions of the pioneering study by Labov et al. (1968), and they can be considered together in assessing the contributions which the study of AAVE bequeathed to sociolinguistics.

14.1.1   Variable rules

Despite its demonstration that structured variability was a part of language, Labov's 1966 study of the social stratification in NYC English did not attempt to represent such variability directly in linguistic structure; but the study by Labov et al. (1968) of AAVE in Harlem did, via the mechanism of variable rules with variable constraints (ibid., 12). Variable rules – represented notationally by a pair of angled brackets around the output of the rule, matched by at least one such pair in the conditioning environment – went beyond conventional optional rules in specifying that a rule is more or less likely to apply depending on specified factors in the internal or extralinguistic environment. The variable which Labov (1969) used to introduce the concept of variable rules to the field was the contraction and deletion of the copula in AAVE,[4] as in *He Ø nice*, where the deletion was accounted for by the following rule:[5]

$$[+\text{cons}] \rightarrow \langle\varnothing\rangle / \Big\langle \begin{matrix} *\text{strid} \\ +\text{cons} \\ +\text{Pro} \end{matrix} \Big\rangle \# \# \Big[\begin{matrix} \underline{\quad} \\ -\text{nas} \\ +\text{cont} \end{matrix} \Big] \# \# \Big\langle \begin{matrix} +\text{Vb} \\ +\text{Fut} \\ -\text{NP} \end{matrix} \Big\rangle$$

Copula absence in AAVE was to become legendary, insofar as it spawned and continues to spawn more synchronic and diachronic research in sociolinguistics than any other variable. Another AAVE variable – the simplification of word-final consonant clusters, especially *t* and *d* – also led to numerous studies. Copula absence in Harlem was one of three showcase variables used by Cedergren and Sankoff (1974) to introduce VARBRUL, the widely used variable rule computer program. Both variables have played a role in the discussion of central theoretical and methodological issues in quantitative sociolinguistics, including the relation between individual and group grammars (Guy 1980), the relative ordering of variable rules (Labov 1969, Wolfram 1975, Romaine 1982), alternative procedures for computing rule applications and non-applications (Rickford et al. 1991, Blake 1997), the introduction of an exponential model (Guy 1991), and the relevance to variation studies of optimality theory (Guy 1994, Kiparsky 1994).

14.1.2   Analysis of AAVE tense-aspect markers

In addition to copula absence, several grammatical features of AAVE have been the focus of syntactic and semantic analysis by sociolinguists over the past quarter century, beginning with Labov et al. (1968) and with Fasold and Wolfram (1970). The list includes the following tense-aspect markers (adapted from Rickford 1996a):

(a)   Absence of 3 sg. present tense *-s*, as in *He walkØ* for SE *He walks* (Fasold 1972: 121–49).

(b)   Use of invariant *be* to express habitual aspect, as in *He be walkin* for SE *He is usually walking, usually walks* (Fasold 1972: 150–84, Green 1993).

(c)   Use of stressed *BÍN* to express remote phase, as in *She BÍN married* for SE *She's been married for a long time* (and still is), or *He BÍN ate it* for SE *He ate it a long time ago* (Rickford 1975, Baugh 1983: 80–2, Green 1993).

(d)   Use of *done* to mark completive or perfective, as in *He done did it* for SE *He's already done it* (Labov 1972e: 55–6, Baugh 1983: 74–7, Edwards 1991).

(e)   Use of *be done* to mark resultatives or future/conditionals, as in *She be done had her baby* for SE *She will have had her baby* (Baugh 1983: 77–80, Green 1993, Dayton 1994).

(f)   Use of *finna* (derived from *fixin' to* – see Ching 1987) to mark the immediate future, as in *He's finna go* for SE *He's about to go*.

(g)   Use of *steady* as an intensified continuative marker (for actions that occur consistently and/or persistently), as in *Ricky Bell be steady steppin' in them number nines* (Baugh 1983: 86).

(h)   Use of *come* to express the speaker's indignation about an action or event, as in *He come walkin' in here like he owned the damn place* (Spears 1982: 852).

(i)   Use of *had* to mark the simple past or preterite, as in *Then we had went outside* for SE *Then we went outside* (Théberge 1988, Cukor-Avila and Bailey 1995, Rickford and Théberge-Rafal 1996).

Some of these features, such as *come* and *steady*, were only reported in the literature at the beginning of the 1980s; preterite *had*, primarily used by pre-adolescents, was only discovered in the last decade. In addition to the discovery of new tense-aspect forms, there has been considerable recent discussion about the syntax and semantics of previously known AAVE tense-aspect markers like *be* and *done* (Martin 1992, Green 1993 and 1998, Dayton 1994, Green and Rickford, to appear); however, some of this discussion draws on government and binding theory, rather than quantitative sociolinguistics.

14.1.3   Relation to central sociolinguistic concepts

More distinctively sociolinguistic are the ways in which AAVE data have contributed to the analysis of social class, ethnicity, network, and style within the quantitative paradigm. Contrary to what one might think, the number of full-fledged *social class* studies within sociolinguistics – especially those based on random samples – is rather small, and they date primarily from the 1960s. Of these, one of the most significant was Wolfram's (1969) study of AAVE in Detroit – which like its predecessor, Shuy et al. (1967), used a modified version of Hollingshead and Redlich's 1958 education, occupation, and residency scales to yield a stratified random sample.[6] Apart from its methodological innovations, this study was important in establishing that grammatical variables like multiple negation, copula absence, and absence of 3 sg. *-s* tended to show sharp stratification, with major divisions between the middle and working classes; but phonological variables like consonant cluster simplification showed gradient stratification, with smoother transitions between classes (see table 14.1).[7] This pattern has been confirmed in several other studies (Labov et al. 1968, Rickford 1979), so much so that it is stated almost as a general principle in a recent sociolinguistics textbook (J. K. Chambers 1995: 51). Most discussions of the role of *ethnicity* in sociolinguistics refer to research on AAVE and comparisons between black and white Americans; see for instance Wolfram and Clarke 1971, Giles 1979, Fasold 1981, Rickford 1985, as well as the coverage of ethnicity as a sociolinguistic variable in introductory texts like Holmes 1992, Trudgill 1995, and Hudson 1996.

With respect to the analysis of *social networks*, L. Milroy 1980 is rightly given credit for the first substantive use of network theory in sociolinguistics. However, Labov et al. 1968 had effectively used sociometric diagrams a dozen years earlier to reveal the hang-out patterns of the Jets, Cobras, and other African American peer groups that they studied in Harlem; and other studies

Table 14.1 Use of selected AAVE features in Detroit, by social class (adapted from Wolfram 1969)

Feature	LWC	UWC	LMC	UMC
Multiple negation (p. 156)	78%	55%	12%	8%
Absence of copula/auxiliary *is, are* (p. 169)	57%	37%	11%	5%
Absence of 3sg. present tense -*s* (p. 136)	71%	57%	10%	1%
Consonant cluster simplification *not* in past tense (p. 60)	84%	79%	66%	51%

of African American communities (T. Labov 1982, Labov and Harris 1986, Edwards 1992) have drawn on network theory and contributed to our understanding of its utility for the study of sociolinguistic variation.

With respect to the analysis of *stylistic variation*, it was in the study of Harlem by Labov et al. 1968 that Labov turned away from the combined use of interview contexts and channel cues which he had used in 1966 to distinguish *careful* and *casual* styles. The 1968 work, inspired by the work of Gumperz in India and Norway, instead studied stylistic variation in the Harlem study through the contrast between individual interviews and peer group sessions. Subsequently, there were several quantitative studies of stylistic variation according to addressee, but the theoretical conceptualization of style as *audience design* only emerged in the work of Bell 1984. Rickford and McNair-Knox (1994) tested some of Bell's predictions on the basis of repeated recordings of Foxy Boston, an African American teenager from East Palo Alto. Bell's audience design model will undoubtedly continue to provoke discussion and research; but Foxy's AAVE data have, according to Bell (1995: 270), provided one of the most explicit investigations of a sociolinguistic model of stylistic variation to date.

14.1.4 Analysis of narratives and speech events

Another area in which AAVE data have been helpful is the analysis of narratives and speech events. The definition of narrative and the framework for narrative analysis developed by Labov and Waletzky 1967, by Labov et al. 1968, and by Labov (1972: 354–96), using narratives from African American youths and adults, have been widely adopted both within and without sociolinguistics, especially for the study of tense-aspect variation (see Schiffrin 1981, Fleischman 1990, Rickford and Théberge-Rafal 1996). The definition includes reference to temporal ordering or juncture (a change in the order of two narrative clauses "will result in a change of the temporal sequence of their original semantic interpretation" – Labov 1972: 360), and the framework includes recognition of the various structural components of narratives: abstracts, orientation and evaluation clauses, complicating actions, results, and codas.

Moreover, the study of speech events and discourse styles within the ethnography of speaking has perhaps advanced most steadily in relation to the study of speech events and styles within the African American speech community, through studies of sounding, signifying, marking, rapping, hip-hop language, and other speech events (Abrahams 1964, Mitchell-Kernan 1969, Kochman 1972, 1981, Labov 1972: 297–353, H. Foster 1986, Smitherman 1986, 1995, M. Foster 1989, Morgan 1991, 1994b).

14.1.5   Diachronic issues

The main diachronic issues with which sociolinguists have concerned themselves, using AAVE data, are the creole hypothesis, the divergence hypothesis, and grammaticalization. The *creole issue* has to do with whether AAVE was once more different from Standard English and white vernacular dialects than it is now – in particular, whether it was a creole language similar to the Creole English spoken in Jamaica and other parts of the West Indies. In favor of the creolist view are B. Bailey 1965, Stewart 1970a and b, Dillard 1972, 1992: 60–92, Holm 1976, 1984, Rickford 1977, 1995, Baugh 1979, 1980, Rickford and Blake 1990, Singler 1991, and Winford 1992a. More skeptical, however, are McDavid and McDavid 1951, Poplack and Sankoff 1987, Tagliamonte and Poplack 1988, Poplack and Tagliamonte 1991, Mufwene 1992, and Winford 1992b. No single sociohistorical issue dominates annual NWAV and other sociolinguistics conferences as much as the creole issue (cf. Rickford 1995, Winford 1995), and it is likely to do so for years to come.

A more recent and perhaps equally unresolved issue is whether AAVE is currently *diverging* from white vernaculars, becoming more different from them than it was, say, a quarter century ago. This view is favored by Labov and Harris 1986 and by Bailey and Maynor 1987. More skeptical, however, are some of the contributors in Fasold et al. 1987, as well as Butters 1989 and Rickford 1991. One difficulty is that, while the AAVE of the youngest generation shows divergence from white vernaculars with respect to some features, it shows convergence with respect to others. Interested readers should consult Bailey and Maynor 1989, Butters 1989, and G. Bailey 1993 for further discussion.

The most recent diachronic issue to attract the attention of sociolinguists working on AAVE is *grammaticalization*, the process "through which a lexical item in certain uses becomes a grammatical item, or through which a grammatical item becomes more grammatical" (Hopper and Traugott 1993: 2). The only published contributions in this arena to date, using AAVE data, are those by Cukor-Avila and Bailey 1995 and by Rickford and Théberge-Rafal 1996; but given the evidence of ongoing grammatical change in AAVE, this theoretical area is likely to show future growth.

14.1.6   Summary

The African American speech community, with a linguistic repertoire which includes one of the most distinctive varieties of American English (AAVE) – one which richly exemplifies processes of sociolinguistic variation and change – has played a crucial role in the development of sociolinguistic theory and methodology over the past 30 years. It has also, over the same period, fueled the careers of faculty and students alike, through the courses, term papers, conference papers, theses, dissertations, and publications which have used AAVE data and/or focussed on issues in the study of AAVE.

14.2   Contributions of (Socio)Linguistics to the African American Speech Community

What has (socio)linguistics returned to the African American speech community? In some respects, such as attempting to clarify the status of AAVE as a systematic and rule-governed system, a great deal. But overall, I do not believe sociolinguistics has done nearly enough, given that the motivation for AAVE research in the 1960s was the promise which it held out for practical applications in education and other areas. Our contributions to the African American community have been particularly limited over the past decade – a period in which the African American working- and under-class has been, despite its many strengths, worse off than in the 1960s. So we have been returning less, precisely when the community needs us more.

The primary area on which I want to focus is our contributions to the teaching of reading and the language arts at the elementary school level, but I begin by briefly mentioning a few areas in which I think the community has been under-served by us.

14.2.1   Induction of African American linguists into the field

Despite more than a quarter century of concentrated work on AAVE, only a handful of African American faculty of any specialization exist in linguistics. Geoff Pullum claimed a few years ago that not a single US-born African

American faculty member was employed in a Department of Linguistics any-
where in the US; and although I was upset by the claim, I couldn't challenge it.
Arnetha Ball, John Baugh, Carol Blackshire-Belay, Irma Cunningham, Charles
DeBose, Keith Gilyard, Lisa Green, Tometro Hopkins, Faye McNair-Knox,
Marcyliena Morgan, Jerri Scott, Harry Seymour, Geneva Smitherman, Ernie
Smith, Arthur Spears, Ida Stockman, Orlando Taylor, Fay Vaughn-Cooke,
Tracy Weldon, Robert Williams, Selase Williams, and Toya Wyatt are all in
Departments of Anthropology, Black Studies, Communication, Education,
English, German, Pan-African Studies, Psychology, or Speech Pathology –
although Baugh and Spears, at least, were formerly in Departments of Linguis-
tics. On the other side of the coin, Walter Edwards, Salikoko Mufwene, Don
Winford, and I are in Departments of Linguistics; but although some of us
(Edwards, Mufwene, and myself) are now US citizens, we are originally from
the Caribbean or Africa. The only exceptions that I know to Pullum's damning
generalization are John McWhorter – a 1993 Stanford graduate who joined the
Departments of Linguistics and Afro-American Studies at the University
of California at Berkeley in Fall 1995 – and Lisa Green – a 1993 graduate of
the University of Massachusetts at Amherst who joined the Department of
Linguistics at the University of Texas at Austin, also in Fall 1995.[8]

I hasten to add that there is nothing wrong with having African American
linguists in departments other than linguistics, and much that is very right
about it. Given the interdisciplinary interests of many African American linguists and the shortage of jobs in linguistics, the occupational niches provided
by anthropology, Black studies, communication, education, English, speech
pathology, and other departments are most welcome. But African American
linguists could still be better represented on the faculty of linguistics departments than they are, and why they are not is worth consideration.

One reason is, of course, the *pipeline* problem. Data from 51 North American
linguistics departments and programs, surveyed by the Linguistic Society of
America's Committee on Ethnic Diversity in Linguistics (LSA/CEDL) in Fall
1995 (see table 14.2), indicate that only 1.9 percent of all undergraduates and
2 percent of all graduates enrolled in linguistics programs were black, and the
percentage of black faculty recorded by that survey was comparable.[9] A recent
Modern Language Association survey of 49 PhD programs in linguistics similarly revealed that Blacks comprised only 1.5 percent (2 out of 131) of the PhDs
in linguistics granted to students who remained in the US after graduation in
1993–4, while they comprised 3.3 percent (30 out of 916) of corresponding
PhDs in English.[10]

But even with this limited pool, I believe that more can be done to attract
African Americans into linguistics. For one thing, we are sometimes not sufficiently nurturing and encouraging to African American students and others of
color who enroll in our classes. I have heard of students who were initially

Table 14.2 Ethnic distribution of undergraduates, graduates, and faculty in 51 US linguistics departments in fall 1995

Ethnicity	Undergraduate Students	Graduate Students	Faculty (in linguistics departments)
Blacks	11 (1.9%)	23 (2.2%)	6 (1.9%)
Native Americans	6 (1%)	3 (0.3%)	6 (1.9%)
Asians/Pacific Islanders	29 (4.9%)	58 (5.6%)	10 (3.2%)
Whites (non-Hispanic)	467 (79.6%)	791 (75.9%)	278 (88%)
Hispanics	19 (3.2%)	23 (2.2%)	11 (3.5%)
"Minority"	22 (3.7%)	–	–
"International"	26 (4.4%)	138 (13.2%)	1 (0.3%)
Other/Unknown	7 (1.2%)	6 (0.6%)	4 (1.3%)
Total	587 (100%)	1,042 (100%)	316 (100%)

Source: Linguistic Society of America, Committee on Ethnic Diversity in Linguistics survey

attracted to our field, but were discouraged by the insensitivity or impatience of the TAs and professors they encountered in linguistics; African American students and junior faculty alike could benefit from better mentoring. Moreover, some committees on admissions, appointments, and promotions in our field suffer from the institutional racism endemic in American society more generally, and they are simply not proactive enough on behalf of African Americans and other students of color when the opportunities come up.[11] In a period when affirmative action is being dismantled in several states and is threatened at the national level, it will take an even greater effort than linguistics has displayed, in the 20 years since the Equal Opportunity Act of 1964, to increase the representation of African Americans and other students and faculty of color.[12] Nevertheless, it is heartening that the Linguistic Society of America has finally created a Committee on Ethnic Diversity in Linguistics to address the problem. There is evidence that, with commitment and effort, progress can be made.[13]

Overall, sociolinguistics has done better than other fields in attracting African Americans to linguistics; e.g., many of the faculty listed in the first paragraph of this sub-section are primarily or partly in sociolinguistics. But given our debt to the community, and the valuable contributions which the handful of African American sociolinguists has already made to our field,[14] we need to view the under-representation of African Americans in linguistics as an academic limitation for our field as well as a sociopolitical embarrassment. We also need to work with other departments more systematically, and with our university administrations and high schools, to redress the situation.[15]

14.2.2   The representation of the African American speech
community

A second issue is that the representation of the African American speech
community in the writings of sociolinguists, ethnographers, and folklorists has
sometimes been very negative, because of the kinds of examples we have chosen
to include. Geneva Smitherman-Donaldson and Marcyliena Morgan – both
African American women, I should add – have spoken eloquently on this issue,
as the following quotations illustrate:

> Books like Abraham's *Deep Down in the Jungle* (1964), Jackson's *Get Your Ass in
> the Water and Swim like Me* (1974), and Folb's *Running Down Some Lines* (1980)
> – the titles themselves tell you something – conveyed the impression that black
> speech was the lingo of criminals, dope pushers, teenage hoodlums, and various
> and sundry hustlers, who spoke only in "muthafuckas" and "pussy-copping
> raps." Overwhelmingly, the black subjects of the research were predominantly
> male, and the content of their speech data primarily sexual. For example, several
> of the toasts in Jackson's collection were narrated by ex-convicts, and most were
> collected at prisons . . . There is no denying that the "toast world" is a dimension
> of black linguistic tradition; the point, however, is that a slice of black folk
> character was presented as the whole. (Smitherman-Donaldson 1988: 162)

> With few exceptions . . . research on discourse and verbal genres has highlighted
> male-centered activities and male sexual exploits. As a consequence, African
> American women are either erased from the urban landscape because of their
> purported linguistic conservatism or portrayed as willing interlocutors and audi-
> ences for the plethora of street hustler raps and misogynistic boasting reported by
> researchers. Since the speech community, in this case, is viewed as a monistic
> entity, a specific speech event is often presented as a generalized norm rather than
> characteristic of a particular style or genre. Kochman (1981: 75) is emblematic of
> this problem with his statement, "In Black culture it is customary for Black
> men to approach Black women in a manner that openly expresses a sexual
> interest" . . . Kochman contends that this form of "rapping" is a norm, though
> his assumptions are mainly based on male self-reporting of street culture and
> street observations. The fallout that results from this generalization is, once
> again, both the African American community's rejection of research on AAE and
> accusations from linguists of community self-hate. (Morgan 1994a: 137)

The criticisms reflected in these quotations can be extended to the writings
of sociolinguists on a variety of subjects that have nothing to do with speech
events, but still end up with examples involving violence, obscenity, or sex. I do
not believe this is because we are ourselves titillated by these materials, or seek
to titillate our audiences, but rather because we are trying earnestly to demonstrate that we have overcome the "observer's paradox" discussed by Labov

1966, and that we have tapped into the mother lode of the "vernacular." For instance, in Labov and Harris 1986, Harris's skill as an interviewer is presented in these terms:

> he never interviewed anyone until knowledge of the broader, shared background allowed him to go deeper into the emotional and sexual life than sociolinguistic interviews had gone before, and to obtain samples of emotional interchanges that reached a high pitch of intensity. (2)

> Among the many recordings of the core group, none showed a greater level of intensity than a session with Jackie and her close friend "Pam." They met at Harris' house to record their denunciation of the sexual behavior of a man that they both knew. They also dealt with the fighting behavior of a number of other young men in the neighborhood . . . "PAM: They ain't do shit! They ain't do shit! And from that day on we been walking up to they block, and they ain't do shit! Koko big rocks don't mean shit." (4)

When Rickford and McNair-Knox 1994 was in preparation, we had to make a real effort to avoid the stereotypic examples that had gone before. Our paper still includes examples that discuss gang murders and "slamming partners" – but we excised references to "bitches" and other misogynistic posturing which we had originally included in line with sociolinguistic tradition. In the end, our examples were more representative of the *range* of topics and interests of our speakers than they might otherwise have been. According to Morgan 1994a, members of the African American speech community have expressed concern that "the language styles purported to describe the African American community represent the entire social field" (138) and the "multi-situated nature of African American life" (139).

A final comment which can be made in this connection is that concern for the ways African Americans are portrayed in linguistics publications is paralleled by the concern which has been expressed recently about the ways that women are under-represented, or represented in terms of negative stereotypes, in the examples used in linguistics texts (Battistella 1996, Bergvall 1996, Macaulay and Brice 1996, Moonwomon-Baird 1996). Bergvall comments that "the problems of under-representation and misrepresentation . . . , as well as linguists' failure to acknowledge these problems, can be traced to the structuralist separation of the study of form from content or context"; this applies equally to the perpetuation of racism and sexism in linguistic examples.[16]

14.2.3 Prisons, courts, and workplaces

One area in which racial discrimination and injustice are still quite evident in American life is the disproportionate number of African Americans who are arrested, imprisoned, and executed. In 1991, African Americans constituted only 12.3 percent of the population nationwide, but 43.4 percent of the inmates in local jails, and 45.6 percent of the inmates in state prisons.[17] In 1993, African Americans constituted about 12.5 percent of the national population, but 31 percent of all those arrested (*Information Please Almanac* 1996: 853) and 40.8 percent of prisoners under sentence of death (US 1995: 220). Between 1930 and 1993, African Americans constituted 52.7 percent of prisoners executed under civil authority (US 1995: 220).[18] Late in 1995, the Sentencing Project, a national non-profit organization that deals with criminal justice issues, reported that "one in three Black men between the ages of 20 and 29 are within the grasp of the criminal justice system" (as summarized by Jones 1995: 9).

Although the injustices reflected in these statistics extend far beyond linguistics, some undoubtedly include a linguistic component. Sociolinguists have shown, through their involvement in and/or their study of court cases over the past two decades (Lind and O'Barr 1979, O'Barr 1982, J. Milroy 1984, Shuy 1986, Labov 1988, Dumas 1990, Rieber and Stewart 1990), that they can make useful if not always successful contributions to the determination of innocence or guilt and other aspects of the legal process. In the case of African Americans, however, our contributions have so far been limited. Gumperz 1982a provides a discourse- and feature-based defense of a Black Panther community leader who was accused in the 1960s of threatening the life of the president, although the case itself was dismissed before it went to trial. Butters 1997 discusses his testimony on behalf of an African American man in Virginia whose lawyers attempted to appeal his conviction and death sentence on the grounds that the indicting, convicting, and sentencing processes were tainted by racial discrimination.[19] But there is undoubtedly more that we can do. Matsuda 1991 and Lippi-Green 1994 have shown how accent and dialect discrimination in hiring and firing have been tolerated in US courts; the victims in their cases are mainly foreign-born immigrants, but a few are speakers of Hawaiian Pidgin English and of AAVE. Lippi-Green and her students (Arnett et al. 1994, Lippi-Green 1997) have turned more recently to the ways in which Disney animated cartoons teach children how to discriminate against non-standard dialects from an early age.[20] One is led to believe from this and other evidence that language is an element in the disproportionate number of African Americans imprisoned and executed in this country.[21]

The level of *unemployment* among African Americans is also significantly higher than among Whites. In 1993, the unemployment rate among Whites in general was 6.0 percent, and among Whites between the ages of 16 and 24 it was 11.3 percent; for African Americans, the 1993 unemployment rates were 12.9 percent and 31.7 percent, respectively, twice and nearly three times as high as the corresponding white rates.[22] *Under*-employment – including employment in jobs with responsibilities and pay lower than merited by one's training or skill – is somewhat harder to document, but one combined reflection of unemployment and under-employment is annual income. In 1993, the median income for all households, regardless of race, was $31,241; the median for Whites was $32,960, and the median for Blacks was only $19,533 (US 1995: 469). In the same year, the percentage of all US households whose earnings placed them below the poverty level was 15.1 percent; for Whites, the figure was 12.2 percent; for Hispanics, 30.6 percent; and for Blacks, 33.1 percent, or one-third (US 1995: 480). As with discrimination in the judicial system, the roots of these disparities clearly extend beyond language – including "racism, inequality and cultural intolerance," issues which Roberts et al. (1992: 370) felt compelled to include in their cross-cultural communication interventions in the UK. But there are also language elements to the unemployment and under-employment of African Americans (cf. Jupp et al. 1982: 234), and these have not been adequately explored in American sociolinguistics.

As an example of the kinds of sociolinguistic research and intervention which could be done, we might note the work done by the Industrial Language Training (ILT) service established in the UK in 1974 to improve communications in multi-ethnic workplaces, primarily but not exclusively among immigrants for whom English is a second language. In the more than two decades of its existence, the ILT has worked with ethnic minority workers (and would-be workers) as well as with white managers, supervisors, and other staff who interact with ethnic minorities. Not only have they provided training in the mechanics of English, but they have also helped to raise sensitivity on both sides to the deeper levels of interpretation and contextualization at which problems of cross-cultural stereotyping and miscommunication are often manifested. The ILT program has benefited from the scholarship and advice of leading sociolinguists (see Gumperz et al. 1979);[23] and, according to Roberts et al. (1992: 385): "ILT has been a success story in a number of respects. Thousands of people in hundreds of workplaces received training in a complex field. No other public service in the field of ethnic relations has a comparable record."

In the US, little comparable work has been done on behalf of African Americans or other people of color, but what has been done indicates the need to do more. The closest parallel to ILT work is research done by Akinnaso and Ajirotutu (1982) in Oakland in 1976, as part of a project on inter-ethnic communication supervised by John Gumperz. The authors collected data on the performance of 12 African American students in simulated job interviews; and in return, they took over the assessment training portion of the four-week CETA (Comprehensive Employment and Training Act) program in which these students were enrolled. Akinnaso and Ajirotutu examine narratives told by two women in their sample, showing that one of them effectively uses rhetorical strategies and discourse structuring techniques, in order to respond to the underlying intent of the interviewer's question and present herself positively, while the other does not. As they note (143),

> there is common agreement that discourse conventions are very crucial to employability ... Consequently, where several candidates have equivalent qualifications, as is often the case in present-day urban settings, candidates who can linguistically match a standard variety and interact within the discourse conventions of the standard language are normally at an advantage.

This conclusion parallels the results of a very different kind of research done by Terrell and Terrell (1983), who sent six African American applicants out for secretarial positions at 100 sites. Three spoke SE, and three spoke AAVE. The authors report that the SE-speaking applicants were given longer interviews, offered more jobs, and offered jobs with higher pay than the AAVE-speaking applicants. Although most sociolinguists would reject the Standard Language Ideology (Lippi-Green 1994) which lies behind results like these, one cannot reject as easily the reality of its existence. In attempting to increase employment opportunity for AAVE speakers, sociolinguists might follow the model of the ILT program in the UK, working both with employers (to modify their negative attitudes) and with AAVE-speaking job applicants (to increase their bidialectal competence in AAVE and SE, and their sociolinguistic switching abilities).[24] We should also take caution from research by Labov (1995a), showing that the relative frequency of transcription "errors" in SE usage made by an African American word-processor in Chicago (Andrea Ellington) did not correspond to the relative frequency of corresponding features in AAVE.[25] Although plural *-s* absence is low in most AAVE studies, and verbal *-s* absence high, Andrea had more difficulties with SE plural marking (errors 53 percent of the time) than with verbal *-s* (errors only 13 percent of the time). Moreover, it was the absolute rather than relative frequency of her "errors" that affected her boss's evaluation. These findings suggest that we will need to study how AAVE-speaking employees actually perform on the job, rather than predicting such performance on the basis of linguistic regularities uncovered in the existing sociolinguistic literature.

14.2.4   Elementary education

The applied area in which sociolinguistics most self-consciously set out to make a contribution is of course in elementary education, especially in the curriculum-central areas of reading, writing, and the language arts. I think we can claim to have done some useful things here, certainly more than any other field of linguistics. This is particularly true in the aftermath of the December 18, 1996, decision by the Oakland School Board to recognize the "Ebonics"

Table 14.3 California Assessment Program scores (1989–90) for Palo Alto and Ravenswood (including East Palo Alto) School Districts, San Francisco Bay Area, CA

District	*Subject* *Grade*	*Reading* 3	6	8	*Writing* 3	6	*Math* 3	6	8
Palo Alto		337	339	361	329	335	343	348	386
State rank (percentile)		96	99	98	94	99	97	99	99
Ravenswood		237	215	186	246	231	237	230	192
State rank (percentile)		16	3	2	21	3	1	3	1

or AAVE of their African American students in teaching them Standard English. At the general meeting of the Linguistic Society of America in Chicago on January 3, 1997, members unanimously approved supporting the Oakland decision; and linguists of all theoretical persuasions, especially sociolinguists, have since then spoken out repeatedly in the media, attempting to quell the massive public opposition to and misunderstanding of the Oakland proposal.

Despite this most encouraging recent involvement in a vital educational issue, it must still be said that, on balance, we have not done enough, particularly over the past decade – a period in which the educational prospects of lower- and working-class African Americans have, if anything, grown worse. Labov et al. (1968: 1) reported that the African American peer group members they studied in Harlem were perhaps "three, four, or five years behind grade level" in reading. I don't know what the current statistics are for New York, but I doubt that they have improved. In East Palo Alto, my own research base – third-graders in the primarily African American Ravenswood School District – scored at the sixteenth percentile statewide on the reading component of the California Assessment Program in 1989–90; by the sixth grade they had gotten even worse, scoring at only the third percentile (see table 14.3). By contrast, third- and sixth-graders in Palo Alto School District, adjoining but primarily white, scored at the ninety-sixth and ninety-ninth percentiles, respectively (*Peninsula Times Tribune*, November 8, 1990). More recent tests, e.g. the experimental 1993 California Learning Assessment Program (CLAS), continue to document similar disparities (*San Jose Mercury News*, March 9, 1994: 12A). It is perhaps not surprising that, when the elementary school products of East Palo Alto are thrown together with the products of Palo Alto and other peninsula cities in high school, they drop out at an alarmingly high rate, reportedly as high as 70 percent. It may be inevitable that, when education fails them, such students are left with few marketable skills, and get drawn into lives of drugs and crime. East Palo Alto has become a major drug procurement area on the San Francisco peninsula, and the city had a higher per capita rate of homicides in 1992 than any other city in the nation, including Chicago, Detroit, and New York. That rate has since been reduced, but the overall quality of education and life in the city has not improved significantly.

Data from other cities reveal the same grim picture. Michael Casserly, Executive Director of the Council of the Great City Schools (comprising 50 of the nation's largest urban school districts), testified on this topic before a US Senate Appropriations Subcommittee on January 23, 1997. He stated that, in 1994, black students nine years old were 29 points behind their white counterparts; but by age 13, they were 31 points behind, and by age 17 they were 37 points behind (data source: National Assessment of Educational Progress).

What has sociolinguistics said or done about the educational roots of these problems? Through descriptive work funded initially by the Office of Education (see Labov et al. 1968: ii, Wolfram 1969: ix), we have demonstrated the systematicity of AAVE, and have shown how it varies by social class and style. We have rebutted (Labov 1970b, Baugh 1988) the misconceptions about the cognitive limitations of AAVE use suggested by non-linguists like Bereiter and Engelmann 1966 and Farrell 1983. We have also made valuable contributions to changing the perceptions of educators, speech pathologists, and students about AAVE as deficit rather than difference – with the positive effects of these efforts reflected in the position statements on social dialects articulated by the Conference on College Composition and Communication (CCCC) in 1974,[26] and by the American Speech-Language-Hearing Association (1983),[27] in experimental language awareness curricula (Adger et al. 1992, Wolfram 1993), and in handbooks for speech pathologists and teachers (Taylor 1986, Baltimore 1993). However, the wave of negativity elicited by the Oakland Ebonics proposal of December 1996 shows that we need to keep up this educational effort.

We have noted the unfair disadvantages which IQ tests often pose for AAVE speakers (Labov 1976, Wolfram 1976, 1986, 1991: 228–49, Smitherman 1986: 237–41, Hoover et al. 1987, Taylor and Lee 1987). We have considered, particularly in the late 1960s and early 1970s, how dialect readers, drills, and other innovative methods might be used to improve the teaching of *reading* to African American children (Baratz and Shuy 1969, Fasold and Shuy 1970, Labov 1970b, Burling 1973, DeStephano 1973, Simpkins and Simpkins 1981, Starks 1983, Brooks 1985). In the Ann Arbor Black English trial of 1979, we made substantial contributions (Smitherman 1981b, Labov 1982, J. W. Chambers 1983) to Justice Joiner's ruling that the School Board had failed to take appropriate measures to overcome the barriers to equal education posed by the language of the African American children who were faring badly at the Martin Luther King Jr elementary school (more specifically, teachers' negative attitudes toward their AAVE speech). Later on, we drew attention to the "topic associating" style of oral narration used by some African American schoolchildren, and the ways in which they were disfavored by teachers who preferred a "topic centered" style (Michaels 1981, Taylor and Matsuda 1988). We have also recommended, more recently, that African American rhetorical and expressive styles should be more fully accepted and exploited in the classroom (M. Foster 1989, Hoover 1991, Ball 1992, Smitherman 1994b); and that the linguistic needs of students who are native speakers of non-standard English should be considered by policy-makers in allocating federal and local funding for education (Baugh 1998). These are all valuable accomplishments,[28] especially when compared with the little we have accomplished on legal and workplace issues, and with how much less our colleagues in other areas of linguistics have contributed. But because our research involvement and interest in African American education have not been sustained – and because we have generally not stayed in touch with students, their teachers, and their communities – what we have accomplished in the schools falls short of what we might have been able to do, and still can do, in this area.

Take for instance the issue of "dialect readers" as a preliminary aid in teaching reading to speakers of AAVE. The case for them was first made by Stewart 1969, who argued that, for AAVE speakers (as for speakers of West African languages learning to read in English or French), it was pedagogically useful to separate the task of learning to read from that of learning a second language or dialect. In support of his proposal that students first learn to read in their native dialect, and then transfer those skills to reading in a standard variety, Stewart (170) cited experimental research in Swedish by Österberg 1961: "In a Swedish-dialect context, Tore Österberg found that the teaching of basic reading skills in the non-standard dialect of the school children in a particular district (Piteå) increased proficiency, not only in beginning reading in the nonstandard dialect, but also in later reading of the standard language."

Other linguists who contributed to the edited collection in which Stewart's article appeared (Baratz and Shuy 1969) agreed on the general value of dialect readers, and focussed on implementation issues like what orthography to use and how to handle the transition from SE. By the 1970s there were two or three sets of pilot textbooks in AAVE, including the ambitious *Bridge* reading program developed for Houghton Mifflin by Simpkins et al. 1977. The *Bridge* materials included texts and exercises written in three varieties: AAVE, a transitional variety, and Standard English (SE). Here is an example of the opening paragraphs from the AAVE and SE versions of one of their stories, "A friend in need":

No matter what neighborhood you be in – Black, White or whatever – young dudes be havin they wheels. Got to have them. Well, anyway, there happen to be a young brother by name of Russell. He had his wheels. Soul neighborhood, you know. He had this old '57 Ford. You know how brothers be with they wheels. They definitely be keeping them looking clean, clean, clean.

Young guys, Black or White, love their cars. They must have a car, no matter how old it is. James Russell was a young man who loved his car like a baby loves milk. He had an old blue and white '59 Chevrolet. He spent a great deal of time keeping his car clean. He was always washing and waxing it.

The *Bridge* stories were followed by comprehension and other skill exercises, and they were introduced by a recording of a young man speaking to the kids in the vernacular:

What's happenin', brothers and sisters? I want to tell you about this here program called *Bridge*, a cross-cultural reading program. Now I KNOW what you thinkin'. This is just another one of them jive reading programs, and that I won't be needin' no readin' program. But dig it. This here reading program is really kinda different. It was done by a brother and two sisters, soul folk, you know . . .

Simpkins and Simpkins (1981: 237), reporting on their experimental use of the *Bridge* program with 417 seventh- to twelfth-grade students across the US, noted that they showed "significantly larger gains" on the Iowa Test of Basic Skills in Reading Comprehension than the control group of 123 students who were taught with their "regularly scheduled remedial reading instructional activities." In particular (238),

For grades 7–12 , the average gain in grade equivalent scores for the group using *Bridge* was *6.2 months for four months of instruction* compared to only an average of 1.6 months of instruction for students in their regular scheduled classroom reading activities. The group using *Bridge* exceeded the normative level (four months gain for four months of instruction), many of them for the first time in their academic careers. [Emphasis in original.]

However, despite these experimental plusses in its favor, the program did not survive. According to Gary Simpkins (personal communication), the publishers were upset by the fact that they were losing money and by the fact that the program was criticized by columnists and educators. Critics of the *Bridge* approach apparently included African American educators and community leaders, as had also been the case with earlier attempts to incorporate dialect readers in Washington, DC, and to take AAVE into account in addressing the language arts needs of AAVE-speaking children more generally (Stewart 1975).[29] This was also true in 1996, with African American leaders like Maya Angelou and Kweisi Mfume among the harshest critics of the Oakland resolution (although they mistakenly thought that the aim was to teach Ebonics and not Standard English).

Partly because of the demise of the *Bridge*, sociolinguists writing in the 1980s and 1990s (e.g. Baugh 1981: 25, Wolfram 1991: 255–6, Wardhaugh 1992: 340) have almost uniformly rejected the idea of dialect readers (exceptions are Labov 1995b, Rickford and Rickford 1995). But they have done so with little or no regard to the experimental evidence that dialect readers do in fact *help* to teach AAVE-speaking children to read – and without scrutinizing the attitudinal barriers to their use, or asking how they might be overcome.

With respect to the *experimental* evidence (in addition to the positive results reported by Simpkins and Simpkins 1981), Leaverton 1973 reported the use of an everyday (AAVE) and school talk (SE) version of four stories with 37 students in an elementary school in Chicago. He found that students in the experimental group, exposed to both the everyday talk and school talk versions, made more progress in learning to read than those in the control group, exposed only to the school talk version. Hall et al. 1979 also tested 16 African American and 16 white children in Head Start programs in New York City, and found that the African American children did considerably better on a story recall task when the story was presented in AAVE. Robert Williams, who originally created the term Ebonics in 1973 as a replacement for pejorative terms like "broken" and "non-standard" English, also reported in a 1975 article (Williams and Rivers 1975: 104–5) that 900 black children who were tested (Kindergarten, first and second grades) did considerably better on an Ebonics version of the Boehm Test of Basic Concepts than they did on the original Standard English version. Moreover, when four students in my "African American Vernacular English" course (Maroney et al. 1994) tested the response of 20 junior high school students in East Palo Alto to dialect and standard versions of the *Bridge* stories, they found that the students preferred the AAVE stories and did considerably better on stories written in the dialect (see figure 14.1): "Although the students were able to understand concepts from both stories, there was a higher frequency of correct answers for the AAVE versions of the stories: Dreamy Mae – 95.8% correct in AAVE, versus 79.2% in SE; A Friend in Need – 93.8% correct in AAVE, versus 71.9% in SE."

When my wife, Angela, and I attempted to replicate the experiment of Maroney et al. in an East Palo Alto elementary school where we had been volunteering on a regular basis, we found, contrariwise, that comprehension was better with the SE stories than with the AAVE ones.[30] However, there are explanations for the differences between our results, including the possibility that students may have felt more tired and spent less time on the AAVE versions because they always came after the SE versions (Rickford and Rickford 1995: 120). In the face of the largely positive experimental results which dialect readers have yielded to date, we need to continue to experiment with their use in classrooms with substantial AAVE-speaking populations.

With respect to *attitudes*, it is worth noting that attitudes toward AAVE are more positive now among working-class adolescents and young adults than

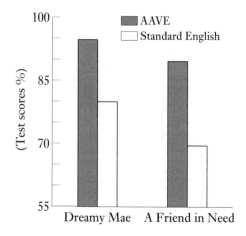

Figure 14.1 Percentage of correct responses on comprehension tests, according to variety used – AAVE vs. SE. (*Source*: Rickford and Rickford 1995: 119, based on Maroney et al. 1994: 21.)

they seem to have been two or three decades ago (Hoover 1978, Fordham and Ogbu 1986); youths and their parents may now be more open to experimenting with dialect readers. Angela E. Rickford (1996: 47, 127), using African American folktales and narratives with students in an East Palo Alto school more recently, has found that teachers and students were very positive about the use of AAVE in dialog. Not all teachers, students, or parents will feel similarly, and some may balk at the extension of AAVE outside of dialog; but to the extent that dialect readers can be shown to increase interest and comprehension and yield positive results, more and more teachers are likely to be willing to experiment with them. Specific suggestions for how sociolinguists might provide leadership in the experimental use of dialect readers are provided by Rickford and Rickford 1995, who note in closing (121–2) that "The idea is not to resurrect the issue of dialect readers as a panacea, but to consider it as one of several possibilities to which sociolinguists should contribute research time and effort as we become involved once more with educational and other applied issues."

14.3 What Can We Do?

My proposal is not that we *stop* drawing on data from the African American speech community: we need the data for our theory and methodology, and our basic research can fruitfully feed back into the needs of the community. But we should start giving back *more*, and training our students to give back more, following the "principle of the debt incurred" which W. Labov (1982: 173) adumbrated: "An investigator who has obtained linguistic data from members of a speech community has an obligation to use the knowledge based on that data for the benefit of the community, when it has need of it." Perhaps as a start we might demand from ourselves and our students one hour of community service or applied work for every hour of tape collected, or every hour spent on theoretical and descriptive issues. There are two different kinds of activities in which we can get involved:

(a) Activities that draw on our expertise and involvement as linguists, including (but not limited to) the ones suggested in this article: training and employing more African American linguists, representing the community positively in our writings, contributing to the solution of legal and employment issues facing the community, getting involved in classrooms with African American students, and doing research on better ways of teaching reading and the language arts at the elementary, secondary, and adult education levels.[31]

(b) Activities that bear little or no direct relation to linguistics, such as tutoring in math, working in soup kitchens, initiating a book drive for a prison or community center, getting involved in building or renovation projects, applying for grants on behalf of community agencies, and helping teenagers to fill out college applications.

Obviously, as a linguist, I believe that the former activities are potentially more important: they draw more uniquely on our expertise, and offer more opportunities for feedback into theory and description. But the latter are relevant, too, and I would rather see us do something than nothing, establishing firmly for ourselves and our students the notion of "service in return." In relation to the former, there are certainly models, both within sociolinguistics and other fields, of what we might do. I would like to close this article by pointing to some of the proactive initiatives which have already been started, and by indicating some ways in which we might do more.

One concept which has been gaining momentum in higher education, but has barely touched linguistics, is the concept of *service learning* – which, when integrated into the academic curriculum, links students' involvement in community service with their academic learning. Like courses in a number of fields at Stanford, my "Introduction to sociolinguistics" and "African American Vernacular English" courses include an optional community service component for an extra unit of credit. Students who take the option engage in community service related to the content of the course, e.g. as language arts tutors in East Palo Alto elementary schools, or as instructors in English as a second language to food service and other immigrant workers on campus.

The students meet in a weekly section with a teaching assistant to share their service experiences and ideas, and to relate what they're doing in the community to what they're learning in the classroom. They are required to submit a paper at the end of the quarter reflecting on their experience, and explicitly exploring ways in which their learning about social dialects, multilingualism, and other topics has contributed to their service within the community, and vice versa.

Although a number of American universities (including Cornell, Indiana, Stanford, and Vanderbilt) have been active in the service learning "movement," the University of Michigan's Office of Community Service Learning (OCSL) is the front-runner in this type of education. The OCSL Press has published two edited collections on the topic, PRAXIS I and II (Howard 1993b, Galura et al. 1993), and they also produce a periodical, the *Michigan Journal of Community Service Learning*. Jeffrey Howard, the OCSL director, has written an article (Howard 1993a) setting out ten "principles of good practice in service learning pedagogy," and linguists interested in establishing service learning in their courses might find it useful to consider them.[32] The principles of Howard's which I have found most helpful are these (Howard 1993b: 5–8):

1   Academic credit is for learning, not service.
2   Do not compromise academic rigor.
5   Provide educationally sound mechanisms to harvest the community learning.
7   Minimize the distinction between the student's community learning role and the classroom learning role.

Within linguistics, the early works of Baratz and Shuy 1969, Fasold and Shuy 1970, and W. Labov 1970b were helpful to teachers, I think; and they would be even today, were it not for their anachronistic language ("Negro Non Standard") and the fact that they do not incorporate research findings of the past quarter century. Fries 1962 was, in my opinion, a remarkable attempt to "bring to the study of the problems of learning to read and of the teaching of reading . . . the knowledge concerning human language which linguistic science has achieved" (vii–viii). One of the things which Fries' book makes clear – as does our involvement in the schools locally – is that we can't just jump in with the expertise of our own discipline: we have to read the literature on the teaching of reading, to learn about phonics, comprehension testing, the psychology of learning, and so on (cf. Rouch and Birr 1984). The panel on "Linguistics in the schools," which Mark Aronoff organized at the 1994 LSA meeting, was a good indication that others feel the need for us to get involved; but I was struck by how much more the participants needed to learn from the discipline of education, and from the schoolteachers and students with whom we have to work.

Another indication of recent interest in the applications of linguistics research is the report of Wolfram and Schilling-Estes 1995b on the deliberations of the linguists who met in September 1995 to identify ways in which linguistics could contribute to the Human Capital Initiative (HCI) launched by the National Science Foundation in 1994. Although brief, this document identifies several research questions which linguists could pursue to contribute to the six foci of the HCI: fostering successful families, building strong neighborhoods, educating for the future, employing a productive workforce, reducing disadvantage in a diverse society, and overcoming poverty and deprivation. The Center for Applied Linguistics (CAL) has of course been involved in some of these areas since its founding in 1959, and some of the applied work relating to AAVE cited in this article (e.g. Baratz and Shuy 1969, Fasold and Shuy 1970) was published under its auspices. More recently it has focused heavily on literacy for adults learning English as a second language, and on the linguistic challenges of US immigrants.

On a different sort of applied tack, the 1995 LSA meeting included papers by Craig 1995 and by Wolfram and Schilling-Estes 1995a, documenting "language preservation" efforts which they are carrying out on behalf of two widely separate communities, at their request – the speakers of the Rama language in Nicaragua and of the Ocracoke dialect in North Carolina, respectively. Wolfram and Schilling-Estes and their colleagues, working with the Ocracoke Historical Preservation Society, have created several products to document and preserve the island's dialect, including an audiotape of speech samples, a video documentary, a dialect lexicon, and a dialect awareness curriculum for schoolchildren. Craig has shared with me copies of the "Illustrated dictionary in Rama" and other materials which she and her students have prepared for use by Miss Nora and Mr Ortiz, local Rama speakers, in Nicaraguan classrooms. She has also shared with me her paper on ethical issues of fieldwork (Craig 1992), which includes a 17-point list of ethical and empowerment issues for fieldworkers. From them I mention only these two: the importance of "producing materials of use to the community" (no. 14) and the importance of "following up, staying in touch" after one's data are collected (no. 15).

Linguists working on Native American languages have also provided a model of how theoretical and descriptive linguistic research can be used to serve community needs, e.g. in the preparation of dictionaries and language learning materials. Hinton 1994 discusses some of the challenges and pleasures of collaboration between linguists and Native American communities, and lists some of the linguists and projects that have been active in California since the 1970s. Among the many sections of her article from which students of AAVE interested in applications might draw inspiration is this one:

> One reason that so many linguists are interested in doing work of the sort that language communities want done is because, despite the professional conflicts,

314 *Educational Implications*

this work is so fulfilling. ALL of us want to do something meaningful with our lives. . . . My experience and feelings [working with the Havasupai and Hualapai communities in Arizona] are probably very close to those of other linguists who have been honored to apply their skills to community needs: the opportunity to be in the language communities, to develop and maintain ties to the people there, and to do something of use gives great personal joy. (253–4)

Nora England, a linguist in the Anthropology Department at the University of Iowa, has worked on Mam, a Mayan language; she has also done important work in training Guatemalan Mayans to be linguists. Akira Yamamoto, of the Anthropology Department at the University of Kansas, is one of the many students of American Indian languages who are involved with community concerns.

A final springboard for sociolinguists contemplating ways to return more to the community is the discussion by Cameron et al. 1992, on "whether and how research could be used to the benefit of both researcher and researched" (1). The authors suggest that researchers should not only be committed to *ethics* ("research on") but also, where possible and appropriate, to *advocacy* ("research on and for") and *empowerment* ("research on, for and with," 22). Cameron's account (1992) of her own involvement with an Afro-Caribbean youth club in London is particularly relevant because it deals with some of the issues addressed in this article,[33] and because it is a good example of empowering research, in which Cameron helped the youths to do what *they* wanted – to make a video dealing with racist language and attitudes toward British Black English. Reflecting on her experience (128), she formulated the following guidelines for her own work, which we may want to adopt more generally:

1 Ask questions that interest the researched group or are generated by them.
2 Be open about your agenda and negotiate at all stages.
3 Make the knowledge and perceptions of the researched group count; do not impose an "expert" framework unthinkingly.
4 On the other hand, share information and analytic tools; the group may reject them but it is wrong to assume from the outset they do not want to know.
5 Present what you learn from research in such a way that the researched group will find it accessible.

Note that these guidelines diverge from both theory and practice within quantitative sociolinguistics; thus guideline 2 advocates more openness about our linguistic interests rather than less (Labov's 1972b response to the "observer's paradox"). But I believe that adopting them would be beneficial for sociolinguistic theory and application alike.[34]

The fundamental rationale for getting involved in application, advocacy, and empowerment is that we owe it to the people whose data fuel our theories and descriptions; but these are good things for us to do even if we don't deal directly with native speakers and communities, and enacting them may help us to respond to the interests of our students and to the needs of our field. Over the years, many of my students, at both the undergraduate and graduate levels, have asked poignantly how they can use linguistics to improve people's lives. I suggest that there are potential uses of this kind, but not ones which we have explored fully enough. With respect to the needs of our field, it is clear that there will simply not be enough jobs in academia for our graduates; university administrations, politicians, and the general public will increasingly ask us to justify their support in terms of the practical good we can offer in return. Increased attention to the kinds of applications I sketch in this article can help us to respond to these needs; and while this will take time, it need not be antithetical to the theoretical and descriptive research in which we are already engaged, but can complement and bolster it. It is also worth noting that the unequal partnership between sociolinguistics and the African American speech community, as documented in this article, represents a far more general problem between linguistics and the communities of speakers whose data fuel our descriptive grammars, theories, and careers. Sociolinguistics is actually less culpable in this respect than other fields, and the need for increased attention to payback and practical application should be recognized and responded to in linguistics as a whole.

Notes

This is a revised version of a paper which I presented in 1994 and 1995 under the title "Sociolinguistic theory and application within the African American speech community," at the Stanford University Linguistics Colloquium, at New York University, and at the conference on African American Vernacular English at Amherst. The lead paper which I presented at the "Service in Return" colloquium at the 1997 annual meeting of the Linguistic Society of America also drew substantially on this article. I am grateful for the comments received from the audiences at those presentations; to Angela Rickford for feedback and encouragement during the writing of this article; and to Bill Bright, Marcyliena Morgan, and Walt Wolfram for their valuable contributions.

1   This is not to say that I have been entirely uninvolved in the applied and service arenas. In Guyana, I participated in workshops dealing with language arts problems, and co-authored a paper dealing with creole interference in English language writing (Rickford and Greaves 1978). My sociolinguistic research on the South Carolina Sea Islands in the 1970s was done through the University of California at Santa Cruz's Cowell extramural and community service program, which required

that community service be primary; in addition to performing a variety of other jobs, I served as classroom aide to Mrs Johnson and Pat Conroy in the two-room schoolhouse made famous by Conroy's 1972 book. In California, I have worked as a classroom volunteer in East Palo Alto, and co-authored a paper on dialect readers in education (Rickford and Rickford 1995), using experimental data collected in the school. In various courses on sociolinguistics or AAVE, I have also included a public service option or requirement; typically students tutor in neighboring schools or teach in adult literacy programs, exploring explicitly the connections between what they learn in the course and the language-related problems they encounter in the community.

2   It is the only sociolinguistics sub-field, for instance, with an annual conference of its own, entitled New Ways of Analyzing Variation (NWAV); and it boasts its own journal, *Language Variation and Change*.

3   Labov et al. 1968 was preceded by an earlier report, Labov in 1965. Labov 1972 is based on Labov et al. 1968, which is more comprehensive and detailed.

4   Baugh 1987 discusses the role which copula analysis played in the development of variable rules and other aspects of sociolinguistic theory.

5   This rule covers only the deletion of the final consonant [z] in *is* after the vowel has been removed by contraction. It states that the copula is most likely to be absent when *is* is preceded by a pronoun or an NP ending in a consonant, and when it is followed by a future verb, as in *He Ø gon try to get up* (12-year-old, Thunderbirds).

6   One could fault Wolfram and his colleagues, as one might Labov and his colleagues, for relying on functionalist or consensus approaches to the analysis of class in the African American community, rather than on the conflict models which are more common in sociology (Kerbo 1983). But this is a very general weakness of the early sociolinguistics studies, as pointed out by Rickford 1986a, Williams 1992, and Milroy and Milroy 1992.

7   Some phonological variables like *th*-stopping also showed sharp stratification, while absence of plural *-s*, a grammatical variable, showed gradient stratification. But in general, the correlation of gradient stratification with phonological variation and of sharp stratification with grammatical variation was maintained:

Voiceless *th* [θ] → *f, t,* or Ø (Wolfram 1969: 84)	71%	59%	17%	12%
Absence of possessive *-s* (1969: 141)	27%	25%	6%	0%
Absence of plural *-s* (1969: 143)	6%	4%	1%	0%

8   The names listed in this paragraph do not represent a complete listing of African American faculty in language related departments in US colleges and universities – there are certainly others (including the contributors to Brooks 1985), and I apologize for their omission – but the general point remains valid that Blacks are under-represented on the faculties of linguistics and related departments.

9   For the sake of simplicity, table 14.2 ignores distinctions between US-born citizens, US naturalized citizens, and permanent US residents in each ethnic sub-category which are available in the LSA /CEDL data. However, I should note that, of the six black faculty in linguistics, three were US-born and three were

permanent residents, while all of the black graduate students and all but one of the
black undergraduate students were US-born. I am grateful to Grant Goodall of
CEDL, and to the staff of the LSA Secretariat (especially Margaret Reynolds,
Executive Director), for making these data available.

10 Percentages of Black PhDs reported by the MLA for Comparative Literature and
Foreign Languages were 1.5 percent (2/131) and 2.5 percent (15/594). Data are
from table 4 of an MLA document (no author or date) entitled, "The MLA's
1993–94 survey of PhD placement: The latest linguistics findings and trends
through time."

11 Another barrier, discussed by Walters (1995: 21) , is the fact that "linguistics as it
constitutes itself – in its practices, in its textbooks, and in its actions – may well be
either irrelevant or insufficient to the concerns of African-American scholars,"
leading them to pursue language related interests in other fields.

12 Ethnic preferences have already been outlawed at all nine campuses of the University of California; and Proposition 209, the mislabeled "California Civil Rights
Initiative" (read: "California Civil Wrongs Initiative"), which was approved by
California voters in 1996, is designed to dismantle affirmative action in California
more generally. According to Morganthau and Carroll (1996: 55), UC regent
and CCRI supporter Ward Connerly "admits that ending racial preferences will
probably lead to a 'precipitous' drop in Black enrollment within the UC system"
(already only 4 percent black).

13 Departments of Linguistics which have managed to admit and graduate better
than average numbers of African American graduate students in recent years
include Stanford, the University of Pennsylvania, and the University of Massachusetts at Amherst. Except in the last case, the African American graduate
students at these universities have all specialized in sociolinguistics and/or pidgin-
creole studies.

14 According to Labov (1982: 165), "The entrance of black linguists into the field was
a critical factor in the further development of the creole hypothesis and the
recognition of the distinctive features of the tense and aspect system [of AAVE]."

15 Some universities are members of consortia which provide departments with lists
of available students of color nationwide; and some provide special funds for
supporting graduate students of color, and/or for helping them to visit departments once they are admitted.

16 See Walters 1995 for a different critique of the representation of AAVE in introductory linguistics texts. One of his main points is that, by treating AAVE as
a special case in a discussion which otherwise refers to "English" (unqualified),
introductory texts fail to challenge students to see themselves as speakers of
dialects which vary by ethnicity, class, region, sex, etc.; and they fail to get white
students "to question their own sense of entitlement or privilege, to remind them
that the standard itself is always and only an idealization" (15).

17 General population data are from US 1995, table no. 18, p. 18. Jail and state prison
data are from Smith and Johns 1995, table 146, pp. 104–5, and table 162, p. 119,
drawing on US Bureau of Justice statistics. A jail is defined as "a confinement
facility administered by a local government agency that holds persons pending
adjudication and persons committed after adjudication, usually for sentences of a
year or less" (Smith and Johns, 105).

18   These figures are worse (48.7–60.8 percent) for the decades between 1930 and 1967, and "better" (40.8 percent and 36.8 percent, respectively) for the 1980s and 1990s. The former period includes a whoppingly disproportionate rate (89 percent = 405/455) of African American executions for rape.

19   Labov 1988 discusses two other legal cases in which he and his colleagues intervened on behalf of African American workers (in 1976) and welfare recipients (in 1982).

20   The "cold-hearted" black crows who jeer the hero in *Dumbo*, for instance, speak a marked variety of AAVE which includes *done, be done, ain't* for "isn't," *don't* for "doesn't," multiple negation, and non-agreement in present tense verbs, as well as phonological features like monophthongization ("Well, hush *mah* feet") and *a* before vowels ("a elephant"). The evil hyenas in *The Lion King* also speak a variety of AAVE, but one marked more by lexical and phonological features than grammatical features.

21   One case with an African American defendant in which the technical expertise of a linguist might have proven useful is the recent "unjust conviction of Chester Schimberg" as reported by Attorney James Sterling Lawrence on "The Injustice Line" Web site (http://home.earthlink.net/~ynot/Schimber.html). Although Schimberg was convicted of rape and sentenced to life imprisonment, the victim said that her attacker, whom she could not see clearly, had a southern accent. Schimberg grew up in the north and apparently does not have a southern accent. According to Lawrence (web site p. 1), "The lawyer never brought out to the jury that she told police the man had a southern accent." Moreover, although the prosecutor claimed that "a person could fake a southern accent, so the failure of the attorney to bring out the fact of Schimberg's accent and heritage was harmless" (Lawrence, web site, p. 2), this claim might have been invalidated by the evidence of recent research showing clear limits on the normal ability of individuals to disguise their voices and/or imitate other accents (Ash 1988, Butters et al. 1993).

22   Data are from US 1995, tables 628 (400) and 635 (404).

23   The *Crosstalk* film referred to by Gumperz et al. 1979 is available from David Thomas Films Inc., 1144 Wilmott Avenue, Chicago, IL 60091 (phone: 312-256-4730).

24   But see Sledd 1969 for objections to promoting this kind of bidialectalism, on the grounds that it gives comfort to the language discriminators and the supporters of white supremacy.

25   For Labov's general comments on Andrea's word-processing errors which are attributable to influence from AAVE, see Duneier 1994.

26   The Executive Committee of the CCCC, a subdivision of the National Council of Teachers of English, passed a resolution in 1972 reversing the centuries-old tradition in which teachers actively attempted to suppress non-standard dialects. The resolution, affirming "the students' right to their own patterns and varieties of language" and suggesting "that teachers must have the experiences and training that will enable them to respect diversity and uphold the right of students to their own language," was approved by the membership of the CCCC in 1974. For a substantial extract of this resolution, see Committee on College Composition and Communication 1978. For a copy of the Linguistic Society of

America's 1997 resolution on Ebonics, see the following website: http://www.leland.standford.edu/~rickford/.

27 See also Cole 1983 and Vaughn–Cooke 1983.

28 For a more comprehensive list of research on AAVE and education, see Harris et al. 1995, and the two-part special issue of *Linguistics and Education* (vol. 7, numbers 1–2), ed. by Tempii Champion and David Bloome, in which it appears. See also, more recently, Adger et al. (in press), and Ramirez et al. (in press).

29 But see the contributions in Brooks 1985 for broad support from African American linguists and educators for recognition of AAVE and systematic attention to it in educational reform.

30 The comprehension edge was slight for "Dreamy Mae" – 70 percent (42/60) correct in AAVE vs. 76 percent (76/100) in SE; but it was substantial for "A friend in need" – 46.3 percent (37/80) correct in AAVE vs. 90 percent (45/50) in SE.

31 These remarks apply similarly to any other populations with whom we happen to work.

32 See also Honnet and Poulsen 1989, which gives several examples for each of its 10 "principles of good practice for combining service and learning" (1).

33 These issues include, for example, negative attitudes toward the youths' British Black English, which Cameron counteracted by telling the youths about the history of pidgins and creoles; the principle of linguistic equality; and the sources of the linguistic prejudice they had encountered.

34 While I am sympathetic to the guidelines of Cameron 1992, I am less persuaded by Rampton's critical comparison (1992) of variationist sociolinguistics and the ethnography of communication, and his conclusion that the latter is intrinsically far more suitable for empowering research.

15

Suite for Ebony and Phonics

15.1   What is Ebonics?

To James Baldwin, writing in 1979, it was "this passion, this skill . . . this incredible music." Toni Morrison, two years later, was impressed by its "five present tenses" and felt that "the worst of all possible things that could happen would be to lose that language." What these novelists were talking about was Ebonics, the informal speech of many African Americans, which rocketed to public attention a year ago this month after the Oakland School Board approved a resolution recognizing it as the primary language of African American students.

The reaction of most people across the country – in the media, at holiday gatherings, and on electronic bulletin boards – was overwhelmingly negative. In the flash flood of e-mail on America Online, Ebonics was described as "lazy English," "bastardized English," "poor grammar," and "fractured slang." Oakland's decision to recognize Ebonics and use it to facilitate mastery of Standard English also elicited superlatives of negativity: "ridiculous, ludicrous, *very, very stupid*," "a terrible mistake."

However, linguists – who study the sounds, words, and grammars of languages and dialects – though less rhapsodic about Ebonics than the novelists, were much more positive than the general public. Last January, at the annual meeting of the Linguistic Society of America, my colleagues and I unanimously approved a resolution describing Ebonics as "systematic and rule-governed like all natural speech varieties." Moreover, we agreed that the Oakland resolution was "linguistically and pedagogically sound."

Why do we linguists see the issue so differently from most other people? A founding principle of our science is that we describe *how* people talk; we don't judge how language should or should not be used. A second principle is that all languages, if they have enough speakers, have dialects – regional or social varieties that develop when people are separated by geographic or social barriers. And a third principle, vital for understanding linguists' reactions to

the Ebonics controversy, is that all languages and dialects are systematic and rule-governed. Every human language and dialect that we have studied to date – and we have studied thousands – obeys distinct rules of grammar and pronunciation.

What this means, first of all, is that Ebonics is not slang. Slang refers just to a small set of new and usually short-lived words in the vocabulary of a dialect or language. Although Ebonics certainly has slang words – such as *chillin* ("relaxing") or *homey* ("close friend"), to pick two that have found wide dissemination by the media – its linguistic identity is described by distinctive patterns of pronunciation and grammar.

But is Ebonics a different language from English or a different dialect of English? Linguists tend to sidestep such questions, noting that the answers can depend on historical and political considerations. For instance, spoken Cantonese and Mandarin are mutually unintelligible, but they are usually regarded as "dialects" of Chinese because their speakers use the same writing system and see themselves as part of a common Chinese tradition. By contrast, although Norwegian and Swedish are so similar that their speakers can generally understand each other, they are usually regarded as different languages because their speakers are citizens of different countries. As for Ebonics, most linguists agree that Ebonics is more of a dialect of English than a separate language, because it shares many words and other features with other informal varieties of American English. And its speakers can easily communicate with speakers of other American English dialects.

Yet Ebonics is one of the most distinctive varieties of American English, differing from Standard English – the educated standard – in several ways. Consider, for instance, its verb tenses and aspects. ("Tense" refers to *when* an event occurs, "aspect" to *how* it occurs, whether habitual or ongoing.) When Toni Morrison referred to the "five present tenses" of Ebonics, she probably had usages like these – each one different from Standard English – in mind:

1 He runnin. ("He is running.")
2 He be runnin. ("He is usually running.")
3 He be steady runnin. ("He is usually running in an intensive, sustained manner.")
4 He bin runnin. ("He has been running.")
5 He BIN runnin. ("He has been running for a long time and still is.")

In Standard English, the distinction between habitual or non-habitual events can be expressed only with adverbs like "usually." Of course, there are also simple present tense forms, such as "he runs," for habitual events, but they do not carry the meaning of an ongoing action, because they lack the "-ing" suffix. Note too that "bin" in example 4 is unstressed, while "BIN" in example 5 is stressed. The former can usually be understood by non-Ebonics speakers as equivalent to "has been" with the "has" deleted, but the stressed BIN form can be badly misunderstood. Years ago, I presented the Ebonics sentence "She BIN married" to 25 Whites and 25 African Americans from various parts of the United States and asked them if they understood the speaker to be still married or not. While 23 of the African Americans said yes, only 8 of the Whites gave the correct answer. (In real life a misunderstanding like this could be disastrous!)

Word pronunciation is another distinctive aspect of dialects, and the regularity of these differences can be very subtle. Most of the "rules" we follow when speaking Standard English are obeyed unconsciously. Take for instance English plurals. Although grammar books tell us that we add "s" to a word to form a regular English plural, as in "cats" and "dogs," that's true only for writing. In speech, what we actually add in the case of "cat" is an *s* sound; in the case of "dog" we add *z*. The difference is that *s* is voiceless, with the vocal cords spread apart, while *z* is voiced, with the vocal cords held closely together and noisily vibrating.

Now, how do you know whether to add *s* or *z* to form a plural when you're speaking? Easy. If the word ends in a voiceless consonant, like "t," add voiceless *s*. If the word ends in a voiced consonant, like "g," add voiced *z*. Since all vowels are voiced, if the word ends in a vowel, like "tree," add *z*. Because we spell both plural endings with "s," we're not aware that English speakers make this systematic difference every day, and I'll bet your English teacher never told you about voiced and voiceless plurals. But you follow the "rules" for using them anyway, and anyone who doesn't – for instance, someone who says "book*z*" – strikes an English speaker as sounding funny.

One reason people might regard Ebonics as "lazy English" is its tendency to omit consonants at the ends of words – especially if they come after another consonant, as in "tes(t)" and "han(d)." But if one were just being lazy or cussed, or both, why not also leave out the final consonant in a word like "pant"? This is not permitted in Ebonics; the "rules" of the dialect do not allow the deletion of the second consonant at the end of a word unless both consonants are either voiceless, as with "st," or voiced, as with "nd." In the case of "pant," the final "t" is voiceless, but the preceding "n" is voiced, so the consonants are both spoken. In short, the manner in which Ebonics differs from Standard English is highly ordered; it is no more lazy English than Italian is lazy Latin. Only by carefully analyzing each dialect can we appreciate the complex rules that native speakers follow effortlessly and unconsciously in their daily lives.

15.2 Who Speaks Ebonics?

If we made a list of all the ways in which the pronunciation and grammar of Ebonics differ from Standard English, we probably couldn't find anyone who always uses all of them. While its features are found most commonly among African Americans (*Ebonics* is itself derived from "ebony" and "phonics," meaning "black sounds"), not all African Americans speak it. The features of Ebonics, especially the distinctive tenses, are more common among working-class than among middle-class speakers, among adolescents than among the middle-aged, and in informal contexts (a conversation on the street) rather than formal ones (a sermon at church) or writing.

The genesis of Ebonics lies in the distinctive cultural background and relative isolation of African Americans, which originated in the slaveholding South. But contemporary social networks, too, influence who uses Ebonics. For example, lawyers and doctors and their families are more likely to have more contact with Standard English speakers – in schools, work, and neighborhoods – than do blue-collar workers and the unemployed. Language can also be used to reinforce a sense of community. Working-class speakers, and adolescents in particular, often embrace Ebonics features as markers of African American identity, while middle-class speakers (in public at least) tend to eschew them.

Some Ebonics features are shared with other vernacular varieties of English, especially Southern white dialects, many of which have been influenced by the heavy concentration of African Americans in the South. And a lot of African American slang has "crossed over" to white and other ethnic groups. Expressions like "givin five" ("slapping palms in agreement or congratulation") and "Whassup?" are so widespread in American culture that many people don't realize they originated in the African American community. Older, non-slang words have also originated in imported African words. *Tote*, for example, comes from the Kikongo word for "carry," *tota*, and *hip* comes from the Wolof word *hipi*, to "be aware." However, some of the distinctive verb forms in Ebonics – he runnin, he be runnin, he BIN runnin – are rarer or non-existent in white vernaculars.

15.3   How Did Ebonics Arise?

The Oakland School Board's proposal alluded to the Niger-Congo roots of Ebonics, but the extent of that contribution is not at all clear. What we do know is that the ancestors of most African Americans came to this country as slaves. They first arrived in Jamestown in 1619, and a steady stream continued to arrive until at least 1808, when the slave trade ended, at least officially. Like the forebears of many other Americans, these waves of African "immigrants" spoke languages other than English. Their languages were from the Niger-Congo language family, especially the West Atlantic, Mande, and Kwa sub-groups spoken from Senegal and Gambia to the Cameroons, and the Bantu sub-group spoken farther south. Arriving in an American milieu in which English was dominant, the slaves learned English. But how quickly and completely they did so and with how much influence from their African languages are matters of dispute among linguists.

15.3.1 The Afrocentric view

The Afrocentric view is that most of the distinctive features of Ebonics represent imports from Africa. As West African slaves acquired English, they restructured it according to the patterns of Niger-Congo languages. In this view, Ebonics simplifies consonant clusters at the ends of words and doesn't use linking verbs like "is" and "are" – as in, for example, "he happy" – because these features are generally absent from Niger-Congo languages. Verbal forms like habitual "be" and BIN, referring to a remote past, it is argued, crop up in Ebonics because these kinds of tenses occur in Niger-Congo languages.

Most Afrocentrists, however, don't cite a particular West African language source. Languages in the Niger-Congo family vary enormously, and some historically significant Niger-Congo languages don't show these forms. For instance, while Yoruba, a major language for many West Africans sold into slavery, does indeed lack a linking verb like "is" for some adjectival constructions, it has another linking verb for other adjectives. And it has *six* other linking verbs for non-adjectival constructions, where English would use "is" or "are." Moreover, features like dropping final consonants can be found in some vernaculars in England that had little or no West African influence. Although many linguists acknowledge continuing African influences in some Ebonics and American English words, (see the *cut-eye* paper in this volume) they want more proof of its influence on Ebonics pronunciation and grammar.

15.3.2 The Eurocentric view

A second view, the Eurocentric – or dialectologist – view, is that African slaves learned English from white settlers, and that they did so relatively quickly and successfully, retaining little trace of their African linguistic heritage. Vernacular, or non-Standard features of Ebonics, including omitting final consonants and habitual "be," are seen as imports from dialects spoken by colonial English, Irish, or Scotch-Irish settlers, many of whom were indentured servants. Or they may be features that emerged in the twentieth century, after African Americans became more isolated in urban ghettos. (Use of habitual "be," for example, is more common in urban than in rural areas.) However, as with Afrocentric arguments, we still don't have enough historical details to settle the question. Crucial Ebonics features, such as the absence of linking "is," appear to be rare or non-existent in these early settler dialects, so they're unlikely to have been the source. Furthermore, although the scenario posited by this view is possible, it seems unlikely. Yes, African American slaves and Whites sometimes worked alongside each other in households and fields. And yes, the number of African slaves was so low, especially in the early colonial period, that distinctive African American dialects may not have formed. But the assumption that slaves rapidly and successfully acquired the dialects of the Whites around them requires a rosier view of their relationship than the historical record and contemporary evidence suggest.

15.3.3   The Creolist view

A third view, the creolist view, is that many African slaves, in acquiring English, developed a pidgin language – a simplified fusion of English and African languages – from which Ebonics evolved. Native to none of its speakers, a pidgin is a mixed language, incorporating elements of its users' native languages but with less complex grammar and fewer words than either parent language. A pidgin language emerges to facilitate communication between speakers who do not share a language; it becomes a creole language when it takes root and becomes the primary tongue among its users. This often occurs among the children of pidgin speakers – the vocabulary of the language expands, and the simple grammar is fleshed out. But the creole still remains simpler in some aspects than the original languages. Most creoles, for instance, don't use suffixes to mark tense ("he walk*ed*"), plurals ("boy*s*"), or possession ("John'*s* house").

Creole languages are particularly common on the islands of the Caribbean and the Pacific, where large plantations brought together huge groups of slaves or indentured laborers. The native languages of these workers were radically different from the native tongues of the small groups of European colonizers and settlers, and under such conditions, with minimal access to European speakers, new, restructured varieties like Haitian Creole French and Jamaican Creole English arose. These languages do show African influence, as the Afrocentric theory would predict, but their speakers may have simplified existing patterns in African languages by eliminating more complex alternatives, like the seven linking verbs of Yoruba I mentioned earlier.

Within the United States African Americans speak one well-established English creole, Gullah. It is spoken on the Sea Islands off the coast of South Carolina and Georgia, where African Americans at one time constituted 80 to 90 percent of the local population in places. When I researched one of the South Carolina Sea Islands some years ago, I recorded the following creole sentences. They sound much like Caribbean Creole English today:

1   E. M. run an gone to Suzie house. ("E. M. went running to Suzie's house.")
2   But I does go to see people when they sick. ("But I usually go to see people when they are sick.")
3   De mill bin to Bluffton dem time. ("The mill was in Bluffton in those days.")

Note the creole traits: the first sentence lacks the past tense and the possessive form; the second sentence lacks the linking verb "are" and includes the habitual "does"; the last sentence uses unstressed "bin" for past tense and "dem time" to refer to a plural without using an *s*.

What about creole origins for Ebonics? Creole speech might have been introduced to the American colonies through the large numbers of slaves imported from the colonies of Jamaica and Barbados, where creoles were common. In these regions the percentage of Africans ran from 65 to 90 percent. And some slaves who came directly from Africa may have brought with them pidgins or creoles that developed around West African trading forts. It's also possible that some creole varieties – apart from well-known cases like Gullah – might have developed on American soil.

This would have been less likely in the northern colonies, where Blacks were a very small percentage of the population. But Blacks were much more concentrated in the South, making up 61 percent of the population in South Carolina and 40 percent overall in the South. Observations by travelers and commentators in the eighteenth and nineteenth centuries record creole-like features in African American speech. Even today, certain features of Ebonics, such as the absence of the linking verbs "is" and "are," are widespread in Gullah and Caribbean English creoles but rare or non-existent in British dialects.

My own view is that the creolist hypothesis incorporates the strengths of the other hypotheses and avoids their weaknesses. But we linguists may never be able to settle that particular issue one way or another. What we can settle on is the unique identity of Ebonics as an English dialect.

15.4   The Oakland School Board Proposal

So what does all this scholarship have to do with the Oakland School Board's proposal? Some readers might be fuming that it's one thing to identify Ebonics as a dialect and quite another to promote its usage. Don't linguists realize that non-standard dialects are stigmatized in the larger society, and that Ebonics speakers who cannot shift to Standard English are less likely to do well in school and on the job front? Well, yes. The resolution we put forward last January in fact stated that "there are benefits in acquiring Standard English." But there is experimental evidence both from the United States and Europe that mastering the standard language might be easier if the differences in the student vernacular and Standard English were made explicit rather than entirely ignored.

To give only one example: at Aurora University, outside Chicago, inner-city African American students were taught by an approach that contrasted Standard English and Ebonics features through explicit instruction and drills. After eleven weeks, this group showed a 59 percent reduction in their use of Ebonics features in their Standard English writing. But a control group taught by conventional methods showed an 8.5 percent increase in such features.

This is the technique the Oakland School Board was promoting in its resolution last December. The approach is not new; it is part of the 16-year-old Standard English Proficiency Program, which is being used in some 300 California schools. Since the media uproar over its original proposal, the Oakland School Board has clarified its intent: the point is not to teach Ebonics as a distinct language but to use it as a tool to increase mastery of Standard English among Ebonics speakers. The support of linguists for this approach may strike nonlinguists as unorthodox, but that is where our principles – and the evidence – lead us.

16
Using the Vernacular to Teach the Standard

16.1 Introduction

I want to begin by congratulating California State University at Long Beach for holding this conference, particularly in a climate in which there is so much ignorance and hostility. I am especially glad to see so many Latino scholars here, indicating that an interest in the language and education of African American students does not imply any lack of interest in the language and education of Latino students, or any other population, for that matter. I begin with these remarks because the director of an educational program in Northern California invited me to speak on Ebonics early in 1997, just after the Ebonics controversy broke, then wrote a little later to withdraw the invitation, since one or two of her Latino Board members felt that attention to Ebonics might detract from attention to (and funding for) bilingual education.

In response to that understandable but misplaced concern, I wrote to tell her what my friend Dr Geneva Smitherman has also emphasized recently: *A rising tide lifts all boats*. We should not be squabbling over crumbs from the table. The needs of various groups of students in our schools are similar in some ways, but different in others. We should be concerned about the success of *all* students and work together to provide each group with the resources it needs to maximize its chances of success in school and life.

In early 1997, I was corresponding often with Don Trujillo, who was at the time a policy representative in Sacramento. He sent me lots of information on California Senate Bill 205, the so-called "Education: Equality in English Instruction Act." Had it been successful, this bill would have wiped out the Standard English Proficiency program (SEP), which is specifically designed to improve the Standard English skills of Ebonics speakers. This would have been a devastating blow not only for schools in the Oakland area, but throughout the state.[1] Trujillo also sent me information on California Assembly Bill 36, which would have gutted bilingual education in California of a lot of its key features, but failed to pass out of committee on April 23, 1997.[2] Trujillo's attitude –

reflecting a concern for the language-related educational challenges of *all* students of color, indeed, for *all* children, regardless of ethnicity – is commendable, and your presence here indicates that you are like him in this respect.

By contrast, California State Assemblywoman Diane Martinez successfully introduced on February 28, 1997 Assembly Bill 1206, which "prohibits school districts from utilizing, as part of a bilingual education program, state funds or resources for the purpose of recognition of, or instruction in, any dialect, idiom, or language derived from English." This bill was clearly aimed at forestalling any attempt to use bilingual education funds for speakers of Ebonics or African American English, and it was eventually approved and signed into law. It represents that defensiveness and terror in the ranks which caused that Northern California director to withdraw my invitation to speak on Ebonics. Hopefully we can dispel that unnecessary defensiveness and fear, and work together for the good of *all* students in California and across the nation.

Let me go on now to explain my title, which is "Using the vernacular to teach the standard." By the *vernacular*, I mean more generally "the everyday [and informal] language spoken by a people as distinguished from the literary language" (*American Heritage Dictionary of the English Language* 1992: 1984) and I mean more specifically the vernacular dialects "which seem to be typified by the use of nonstandard forms" (Wolfram and Schilling-Estes 1998: 13). By the *standard*, and more specifically Standard English, I mean "the variety normally used in writing, especially printing; . . . the variety associated with the education system . . . the variety spoken by those who are often referred to as 'educated people'" (Trudgill, in press: 2–3). As Wolfram and Schilling-Estes (1998: 9.12) point out, what linguists call Standard or mainstream English is often referred to popularly (if ambiguously) as "correct English" or "proper English," and it often tends to be defined negatively: "if a person's speech is free of structures that can be identified as non-standard [e.g. "ain't" for "isn't"], then it is considered standard."[3]

Ninety percent of what was written and said in the media after the Oakland Ebonics resolution of December 1996 represented a misapprehension of the nature of the problem and the nature of the solution which Oakland was proposing. Most writers and commentators made a big fuss of emphasizing how important it was for children to learn Standard English in this society. To this the Oakland School Board might simply have replied, "Yes, we agree. But what's next? *How* are we going to do it?"

16.2   How (Badly) Schools Have Failed to Educate African American Students

Oakland's original aim was to extend the Standard English Proficiency (SEP) program, which had been in place since 1981 throughout the state. That program has as its goal using the vernacular to teach the standard. I want to get that point straight at the beginning. I also want to begin where Oakland began, which is with the facts of *massive educational failure within the African American community*. The fact is that existing methods, throughout the country, are not working. The insinuation of the many vocal critics of Oakland's Ebonics resolution was that Oakland's innovations were misplaced, and that the existing situation in Oakland and in the rest of America was *just fine*, thank you. However, the fact of the matter is that the status quo with respect to the teaching of African American children in American elementary, middle and high schools is far from satisfactory. One of the tragedies of the media coverage of this Ebonics issue is that it never really got to the kinds of problems which started Oakland thinking about Ebonics and other solutions in the first place.

Many of us have heard already of the kinds of failures among African American students which were evident in the Oakland School District in late 1996, for instance, the fact that these students, who comprised 53 percent of the school district population, represented 80 percent of all suspended students, and recorded the lowest grade point average (approximately a C-). For more details, see this web site: http://www.west.net/~joyland/Oakland.htm, and for links to that and other interesting Ebonics web sites, see "Jacqueline's Ebonics Information Page" (http://www.geocities.com/Athens/Forum/2522/). I do however want to point to a number of other examples across the country so you don't think this is just an Oakland or a California problem. You know how people from other parts of the country sometimes think, "Those folks in California are different, and kind of weird, anyhow."

What I want to do, first, is have you look at the test scores from Palo Alto and East Palo Alto ("Ravenswood school district") shown in figure 16.1. The tall bars at the back here represent the children of Palo Alto, California. Palo Alto is right in the middle of Silicon Valley; and includes a lot of professors' kids, many of the children of computer scientists and other highly educated professionals. Palo Alto has some of the best public schools in the country. Looking first at *reading*, the first two tall bars in the back, you'll see that Palo Alto students in the third grade score at the ninety-sixth percentile on the California Assessment Program test; and by the sixth grade, they score at the ninety-ninth percentile. Scoring at the ninety-ninth percentile means, of course, that they are better than 99 percent of students in the state, that is, everybody else! In *writing*, they score at about the ninety-fourth percentile in the third grade, and by the sixth grade, they are at the ninety-ninth percentile and they continue like that. If they were ever to slip to the ninety-second percentile, Palo Alto would have a big national conference to figure out what's going wrong.

Now step across the freeway to the Ravenswood School District in East Palo Alto. As figure 16.1 shows, the primarily African American and Latino students here in the third grade score on the sixteenth percentile on the reading

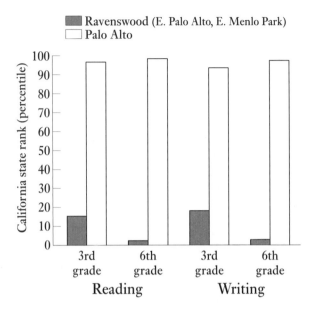

Figure 16.1   CAP test scores for Palo Alto and Ravenswood, 1990 (Source: *Peninsula Time Tribune*, November 8, 1990: A12).

component of the California Assessment Program, but by the sixth grade, they've dropped to the third percentile. (Statistics which I haven't included in this figure show that by the eighth grade, their reading scores have dropped even further, to the second percentile.) If you look at writing, they score on the twenty-first percentile in the third grade, but by the sixth grade they're once again lower, at the third percentile. This represents the regular pattern. Somehow the Palo Alto Schools are able to build on the skills and talents their primarily white children bring to the school and *add value* to them, so that very rapidly students are performing at their maximum potential. Somehow schools in East Palo Alto, with African American and other students of color, fail to do that, *subtracting value* instead: students come in with a certain level of achievement, and do steadily worse with each passing year. This is a forcible demonstration of the point which Claude Steele (1992: 68), made in his important *Atlantic Monthly* article on "Race and the Schooling of Black Americans": "*The longer they* [African American students] *stay in school, the more they fall behind.*"

Lest you think that this is another weird California phenomenon, let us look at some recent data from predominantly African American schools in Philadelphia.[4] In the 1995–6 school year, 41 percent of the students at one Elementary School (Birney) were reading at the Basic Level or above as tested on the SAT-

9, and the school's overall reading score was 56.9. At a high school in the same district, however (Benjamin Franklin), the percentage of students reading at or above the Basic Level was only 7.6 percent, and the overall reading score was 24.4. The 1996–7 statistics show a similar downward spiral, although the extent of the drop between the elementary and high school levels is smaller: 34.4 percent of the students at Birney Elementary School read at or above the Basic Level, and the school's overall reading score was 52.7; at Benjamin Franklin High School, only 14 percent of the students read at the Basic Level or above, and the school's overall reading score was 41.9.[5]

More comprehensively, Michael Casserly, executive director of the Council of Great City Schools, presented data before Senator Specter's US Senate Ebonics panel in January 1997 summarizing the performance of students in 50 large urban public school districts, including between them hundreds and hundreds of schools. Among other things, the data indicated that while white students in these schools show steady improvement in their reading achievement scores as they get older (60.7 percent read above the fiftieth percentile norm at the elementary school in 1992–3, and 65.4 percent did so by high school), African American students showed a steady decline (31.3 percent read above the fiftieth percentile norm at the elementary school level, but only 26.6 percent did so by high school). Moreover, data from the 1994 National Assessment of Educational Progress which he also presented show the same depressing trend in a different way: On a 500-point scale, African American students at the age of nine are an average of 29 points behind the scores of their white counterparts; by the age of 13 they are 31 points behind; and by the age of 17, they are 37 points behind.

I cite these different data sets to make the point quite forcefully that whatever you may think of the Oakland School District and their Ebonics resolutions, the educational malaise of African American students in their District is very general across the United States, particularly in urban areas. Moreover the methods currently being used to teach Reading and the Language Arts to African American students – with which the detractors of the Oakland's Ebonics solution seem to be quite satisfied – are flat out *not* working.

Now clearly, other factors are involved in this kind of failure than language, or even methods of teaching reading. Obviously, there are socioeconomic and class issues (see Rickford, in press), and issues about the kinds of *facilities* which schools in primarily African American and white school districts tend to have. I was present at a meeting which the Rev. Jesse Jackson had with Board members of the Oakland Unified School District on December 30, 1996 (when he announced his revised position on their Ebonics resolution), and I was struck by his statement that the average US prison with large African American populations has better facilities than the average school with large African American populations. There's a frenzy of prison building, expansion, and renovation across the country, as communities discover they're good business.

There's not a similar frenzy of school building and improvement, so we should not be surprised at declining levels of school performance.[6] And unfortunately, those who drop out of schools are more likely to end up in prisons or otherwise fall into the clutches of the criminal "justice" system. As Jones (1995: 9) has noted, drawing on a 1995 report by the Sentencing Project, a national non-profit organization, "one in three Black men between the ages of 20 and 29 are within the grasp of the criminal justice system."

There are also problems in terms of the kinds of teachers which most urban school districts are able to attract, and the training they have, and these problems are related to the fact that urban schools tend to pay lower salaries and have more challenging working conditions. And there are problems in terms of books and supplies. My wife Angela, a reading specialist, was doing a demonstration lesson in the teaching of reading recently at an urban school in the San Francisco Bay area, and she asked the teacher for a story book to read to the class. The teacher said, "Story book?" She didn't have any! The classroom lacked the shelves and tables of gaily-colored and attention-grabbing story books which are customary in suburban schools. Luckily, one of the students in the classroom had in her backpack a book she had happened to bring to school, and that was the book Angela used to demonstrate the teaching of reading.[7] Finally, teachers in schools with primarily African American and other ethnic "minority" populations tend to have lower expectations for their students (Irvine 1990: 54–61) and to ask less challenging questions, and the evidence is overwhelming (see Tauber 1997, A. Rickford 1999) that teacher expectations are closely tied to student achievement. If teachers expect you to do badly, you are more likely to do badly; and if they expect you to do well, you are more likely to do well.

16.3   The Relevance of Ebonics

While factors such as facilities, supplies, teacher pay and training, teacher expectations, parental involvement, and others are indisputably relevant, and I would add my voice to those of others urging that these receive greater attention (see Irvine 1990, Comer 1993, 1997, Cose 1997), I would strongly dispute the claim of Ellis Cose (in *Newsweek*, January 13, 1997: 80) that Ebonics – the language which many African Americans bring to school – is "irrelevant."

On theoretical grounds alone we would assume that the language of African American students plays *some* role in the level of success they achieve in school, since language is so closely connected with cognitive abilities and with performance in other school subjects. As we know, students who do well in English tend to do well in a variety of subjects across the curriculum, and those who don't do well in English, don't do well in most other subjects either.

But there is empirical evidence that language might be related. We know, for instance, that most of the students who fall behind in reading and otherwise fail in inner city schools (see above) are from the working class, rather than the middle class. And we know that the distinctive pronunciation and grammatical features of African American Vernacular English or Ebonics are used most commonly by members of the working and lower class. Consider table 1.3 in chapter 1 of this volume, which summarizes data from Wolfram's (1969) study of Detroit.[8] Except for consonant cluster simplification and absence of plural -*s*, every other Ebonics feature in that table is far more frequent among the working-class groups than among the middle-class groups; for instance, the lower working class uses multiple negation 78 percent of the time, while the upper middle class does so only 8 percent of the time.

Actually, the Detroit figures for working-class Ebonics usage are not even as vernacular as the data we have from East Palo Alto (source of the Ravenswood school district figures in figure 16.1). In the latter community we have recorded working-class teenagers (see Rickford 1992) with copula absence figures of 81 percent and 90 percent, compared with the means of 57 percent and 37 percent in Wolfram's Detroit study, and with third singular present tense -*s* absence of 96 percent and 97 percent, compared with 71 percent and 57 percent in Wolfram's Detroit study. So there's definitely a socioeconomic class boundary which operates with respect to Ebonics usage,[9] and the fact that working- and lower-class African American students tend to do worse in school than their middle-class counterparts may well be related to differences in their language use, or to teacher's attitudes and responses to their language use.[10]

The relevance of negative teacher attitudes to Ebonics was a key element in the 1979 ruling of Justice Joiner that the Ann Arbor, Michigan school district had failed to take adequate measures to overcome the barriers to equal education posed by the language of the African American children at Martin Luther King Jr elementary school (Smitherman 1981a, Labov 1982). But the evidence concerning negative teacher attitudes and responses to the vernacular of African American children had existed even earlier. Williams (1976) reported from a series of experiments that there were regular correlations between teachers' assessment of the relative "standardness" and "ethnicity" of students' speech and their ratings of the children's status, and their confidence or eagerness: students who sounded more non-standard and/or non-white were also rated as being less promising or effective students. What was worse, Williams and his associates also found in a separate experiment that prospective elementary teachers' perceptions of the relative standardness of children's speech were also affected by the children's race; *the same sound track, when accompanying a videotape of an African American or Mexican American child, was rated as less standard than when accompanying a videotape of a white child* (Williams 1976: 105). So students of color got a double whammy negative effect in terms of how teachers perceived and evaluated them in terms of race and language.

We got an even more powerful demonstration of the relevance and role of children's language – and how teachers respond to it in school – in Piestrup's (1973) study of over 200 first-graders in predominantly African American classrooms in Oakland, California. One of the things she found is that there is a very strong inverse correlation between reading score and vernacular dialect score: The lower your dialect score, that is, the *less* of the vernacular you use, the *higher* your reading score, that is, the better you do on standardized tests of reading. This is interesting, but not unexpected, given what we know of the relationship between vernacular English usage and other factors such as socio-economic background which themselves correlate with school success. More interesting, because less well-documented, is the relationship she found between children's reading scores and the different ways in which teachers responded to the vernacular in the classroom. In what Piestrup dubbed the "Black Artful" approach, (1973: 131) teachers "used rhythmic play in instruction and encouraged students to participate by listening to their responses . . . attended to vocabulary differences and seemed to prevent structural conflict by teaching children to listen to standard English sound distinctions. Children taught with this approach participated enthusiastically with the teacher in learning to read." By contrast, teachers using the "Interrupting" approach (ibid.) "asked children to repeat words that were pronounced in dialect many times and interpreted dialect pronunciations as reading errors. Teachers in this group presented standard English sounds for discrimination without ensuring accuracy of response." Some children taught by the Interrupting Approach (131–2) "tediously worked alone at decoding without reading as if they understood; others seemed to guess at almost as many words as they were able to read. Some children withdrew from participation in reading, speaking softly, and as seldom as possible." The latter result was not surprising, because each time they opened their mouths, they were met with rebuke, reprimand, or correction.

Figure 16.2 shows more concretely the difference between these two approaches (and four other approaches which we don't have time to consider) in terms of their correlations with dialect and reading scores. Note that children taught by the Black Artful teachers had higher reading scores overall than children taught by the Interrupting teachers. Moreover, if you look at the slopes for the two groups of teachers (lines 5 and 6), you'll see that the students with the highest dialect scores (i.e., who spoke the most dialect), when taught by the Artful approach, read about as well as the students with the lowest dialect scores (i.e., who spoke the least dialect) when taught by the Interrupting teacher. This is very clear evidence that the way in which teachers respond to and build on the vernacular can have a *powerful* effect on the level of success in reading which African American children attain.

The sad fact, however, is that most teachers do *not* build artfully and skillfully on the vernacular. And most members of the public support them in this. In the hue and cry of the Ebonics controversy in December 1996 and the

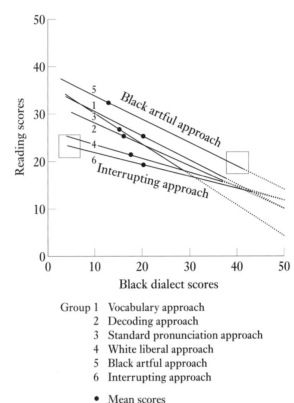

Group 1   Vocabulary approach
      2   Decoding approach
      3   Standard pronunciation approach
      4   White liberal approach
      5   Black artful approach
      6   Interrupting approach

•   Mean scores

Figure 16.2   Correlations between reading scores, dialect scores, and teaching strategies in Oakland first-grade classrooms (Source: Piestrup 1973: 162)
Notes:
(a)   Higher numbers on the "Reading scores" axis indicate higher scores on tests of reading achievement.
(b)   Higher numbers on the "Black dialect scores" axis indicate *more* vernacular dialect or AAVE usage and *less* Standard or mainstream English usage.
(c)   "Solid lines indicate the regression lines for actual scores; broken lines show the extension of these lines" (Piestrup 1973: 162).
(d)   "Children with the highest dialect scores in Group 5 have reading scores approximately equivalent to children with the lowest dialect scores in Group 6. (Indicated by □ at the ends of regression lines for Groups 5 and 6.)" (ibid.)

first few months of 1997 the predominant public response was: "Stamp out Ebonics, or if you can't do that, ignore it, leave it alone, and hope and pray that it will go away. Bury your head in the sand; cover your ears with mufflers. Hear nothing. Don't let that virus anywhere near the classroom." The undeniable fact, however, is that most African American children come to school fluent in the vernacular. It *will* emerge in the classroom, and *how* teachers respond to it can crucially affect how the students learn to read, and how well they master Standard English. Ignoring or condemning the vernacular is not a particularly successful strategy, as shown in Piestrup's study, and as suggested by the massive educational failure associated with this approach nationwide.

If you asked then, "How might the vernacular of African American children be taken into account in efforts to help them do better in schools?" I would say that there are basically three different approaches.

16.3.1   The linguistically informed approach

The first is what I call the "linguistically informed" approach. This encompasses the specific suggestions made by Labov (1995b) based on decades of research on Ebonics or African American Vernacular English (AAVE). One of these is that teachers should "distinguish between mistakes in reading and differences in pronunciation", so AAVE speakers who read "I missed him" as "I miss him" should not automatically be assumed to have misread, in the sense of not being able to decode the letters. On the contrary, they may have decoded the meaning of this Standard English sentence correctly, but they may then have reproduced its meaning according to the pronunciation patterns of their dialect, in which a consonant cluster like [st] – the final sound in "missed" – is often simplified to [s]. Labov (ibid.) also suggests giving more attention to the ends of words, where AAVE pronunciation patterns have a greater modifying effect on Standard English words than they do at the beginnings of words. He also suggests that words be presented in contexts that preserve underlying forms, for instance, words that are followed by a vowel which favors retention of final consonants – *testing* or *test of* – rather than *test* in isolation. He also suggests using the full forms of auxiliary verbs (e.g. *He will be here, He is tall*) and avoiding contractions (e.g. *He'll be here, He's tall*), because of evidence that once you go through a contraction stage, Ebonics is much more likely to proceed to deletion (*He Ø be here, He Ø tall*). These are sound ideas that should not be terribly controversial, but how much of an impact they will make on reading instruction for African American students is not yet clear, since no one has systematically implemented them or assessed their effects.

More recently, Labov and his colleagues at the University of Pennsylvania (Labov et al. 1998) have begun an empirical study of the kinds of decoding errors which African American elementary school students make in attempting to read. Their results are quite striking. Among other things, they report that the children almost never have trouble with single initial consonants (e.g. *b* in *b*at), but they have considerably more with consonant blends and other complex initial consonants, with vowel nuclei, and with the codas or final consonants of words. The details, which will be refined as research in this paradigm

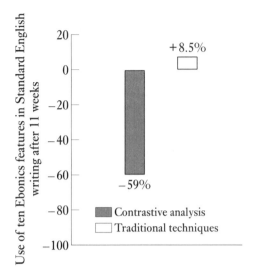

Figure 16.3 Effect of Contrastive Analysis versus traditional techniques on use of Ebonics in English compositions by African American students at Aurora University after 11 weeks of instruction (Taylor 1991: 149)

is extended at the University of Pennsylvania, Stanford, and elsewhere, should prove useful to teachers as well as the designers of phonics textbooks.

16.3.2   Contrastive Analysis

The second approach is to do some form of Contrastive Analysis where you draw students' attention specifically to the differences between the vernacular and the standard language.[11] One of the best examples of this was some work that was done by Hanni Taylor (1989). She's at Aurora University, just outside Chicago, and she was faced with a number of students from inner-city Chicago who used a lot of Ebonics features in their Standard English writing. She divided her students into two groups. With the control group, she used conventional techniques of teaching English and made no reference to the vernacular. But with the other, experimental group, she used Contrastive Analysis, specifically drawing their attention to the points on which Ebonics and Standard English were different. What she found after 11 weeks (see figure 16.3) was that the students who were using traditional techniques showed an 8.5 percent *increase* in their use of Ebonics speech in their writing while the students who had benefited from Contrastive Analysis showed a 59 percent *decrease* in their use of Ebonics features in their writing. This is a very dramatic demonstration of the fact that even if we agree with the pundits across the country that we want students to increase their mastery of Standard English, the Contrastive Analysis approach – essentially what Oakland wanted to do – is more likely to be successful than the conventional approaches that are currently being used. If I can give a very specific example, one of the features that she looked at was third person -*s* absence, as in *He walk* $\boxed{\emptyset}$, instead of He walk$\boxed{s}$. Taylor found that students taught by traditional techniques did show a small reduction (–11 percent) in the use of this feature over the course of 11 weeks, but the students who were taught by Contrastive Analysis showed a massive decrease in the use of this feature (–91.7 percent). The point Taylor made overall is that this process of comparing the two varieties seems to lead to much greater metalinguistic awareness of similarities and differences between the vernacular and the standard and allows students to negotiate the line between the two much more effectively.

There are at least two other instances in which this approach has been successfully used to help Ebonics speakers improve in Standard English and reading. Parker and Crist (1995) both extol the virtues of the Bidialectal Contrastive Analysis approach in teaching minorities to play the corporate language game. In this approach you try to respect the home variety of the students and help them negotiate between that variety and the standard language, teaching them about appropriate contexts for different varieties of speech. The authors say they have used this approach successfully with vernacular speakers in Tennessee and Chicago at the pre-school, elementary, high school, and college levels. There's also a program which I just visited in DeKalb County, Georgia, just northeast of Atlanta; it's the brainchild of Kelli Harris-Wright, and involves use of Contrastive Analysis to help fifth- and sixth-grade students switch between home speech and school speech. According to Cummings (1997), the program "has won a 'Center of Excellence' designation from the National Council of Teachers of English. Last year, students who had taken the course had improved verbal scores at every school." Harris-Wright (in press) also provides specific evidence of annual improvements in Iowa Test of Basic Skills test scores for students in her experimental program, compared with control groups of students in the DeKalb County school district. So we have evidence from these programs that Contrastive Analysis works.

16.3.3   *Introducing reading in the vernacular, then switching to the standard*

The last kind of approach I want to talk about is one in which you actually begin by teaching students in the vernacular – introducing them to reading in the vernacular and then switching to the standard.[12] This follows a principle that was established from research dating back to the 1950s. A classic work is Cheavens' (1957) dissertation on Vernacular Languages in Education.

Cheavens reported on studies around the world which showed that when you began by teaching students in their vernacular or native language before switching to a second language which was not their vernacular, they tended to do better than if you began by teaching them in that second language directly. One of the most dramatic examples was a study done between 1948 and 1954 in 14 schools in Iloilo Province in the Philippines (see Orata 1953). In this study, half of the students were taught completely in English for four grades while other students were first taught for two years in Hiligaynon, their native Philippine language, and then switched to English. What the researchers found is what other researchers have found in many other studies, namely that when the students who began in their own vernacular switched to the second language, they very rapidly caught up with the students who started in English, and even surpassed them. The students who started in the vernacular were outperforming in English the students who started in English, in subjects ranging from reading to social studies, and even arithmetic. This was a massive study done over a fairly long period of time.

The closest parallel to this in terms of the United States and Ebonics or African American English, is the *Bridge* study reported on in Simpkins and Simpkins (1981). This was a study involving 540 seventh- to twelfth-grade students in the United States in 27 different schools in five different parts of the United States. Four hundred and seventeen of the students were taught with an experimental series of *Bridge* readers which began with narratives and exercises written in Ebonics, went through a transitional series written in a variety intermediate between Ebonics and English, and ended up with a final series written entirely in Standard English. A control group of 123 students was taught entirely in Standard English using conventional methods, without the *Bridge* readers. What the researchers found, after four months of instruction and testing, (see figure 16.4) is that the students who were being taught by the conventional methods showed only 1.6 months of reading gain, which would be consistent with the evidence presented earlier that the longer African American students stay in school with existing methods, the further they fall behind. By contrast, the students who were being taught with the *Bridge* readers showed *6.2* months of reading gain after four months of instruction. The experimental evidence was dramatically in support of the approach; the method offered the hope that African American students would finally be able to read above and ahead of the norm rather than below it. But the inclusion of the vernacular in some of the *Bridge* readers elicited knee-jerk negative reactions similar to those which emerged in the Oakland Ebonics debacle of 1996. The publisher of this innovative series of readers, embarrassed by the negative reactions, quickly decided against continuing production of the *Bridge* series, and this very innovative and promising experiment came to an abrupt end despite its dramatically demonstrated pedagogical success.[13]

For many if not most of you, this kind of information about the positive effects of taking the vernacular into account in education is probably brand

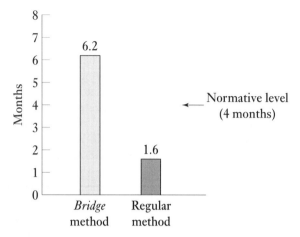

Figure 16.4   Reading gains using Regular vs. *Bridge* (dialect reader) methods, grades 7–12 (Source: Simpkins and Simpkins 1981: 238)

new, even though you may have followed media discussions of the Ebonics issue for months. That's in part because "the print media did little justice to the Ebonics story" (O'Neil 1998: 43), and because of what Noam Chomsky has called more generally the "manufacturing of consent" (see Achbar 1994) – the manipulation of information by the media to present certain sides of issues and exclude others. In keeping with Chomsky's insistence that "the responsibility of intellectuals is to tell the truth and expose lies," several linguists (I know of Geoffrey Pullum, Salikoko Mufwene, and the film-maker Gene Searchinger besides myself) submitted Op-Ed articles on the Ebonics issue to major national newspapers like the *New York Times*, *Washington Post*, and the *Los Angeles Times*. Our submissions were all declined. Some of us managed to get our points of view published in other sources (see Rickford 1996d, 1997c, both reprinted in this volume, and Pullum 1997). But by and large it was an uphill struggle to get anything like a pro-Ebonics or pro-vernacular perspective aired. Sometimes the newspapers would say, "Well, the issue is passé." But the next weekend you would see another editorial or Op-Ed piece ranting and raving about the horror that Ebonics represents or the wrongness of the Oakland resolutions, so it was clearly not the timeliness of the issue that was in question but the take on it which linguists represented. Having seen what the media do with an issue you know well, really makes you wonder about their coverage of other issues. You take on faith that they will follow certain principles of neutrality, and objectivity, and truth, but once you see their betrayal, and misrepresentation, and manufacturing of consent on one issue, it makes you question their reporting on all of the others.

16.4　Some Caribbean and European Parallels

Lest I get entirely wrapped up in lambasting the media and forget my focus on education, let me give you some quick parallels from the Caribbean and Europe to give you a sense that the ways of taking the vernacular into account which I sketched out above have also been proposed and/or successfully implemented elsewhere. I am originally from the Caribbean, and we speak varieties of Creole English there that are very similar to African American English in many respects; in fact I have argued in a number of publications (see Rickford 1977, 1986b, 1997a, the latter two in this volume) that there is a historical relation between these varieties. Way back in the 1950s, Robert Le Page, a well-known British linguist, after going to Jamaica and noticing the appalling failures in the teaching of English and other subjects in the public or state schools, proposed that the first year or two should be taught in creole before Standard English is introduced. One reporter in a local newspaper damned it as an insulting idea (cited in Cassidy 1970: 208) – in fact, if you read some of the press coverage on this issue in Jamaica from the 1950s, it sounds like press coverage of Ebonics from the 1990s in California. But as Le Page (1968) argued, there was a problem with the teaching of English across the "English-speaking" Caribbean: the percentage of students from each country who passed in English on the 1962 GCE "Ordinary" level exam ranged from 10.7 percent to 23.1 percent. Le Page argued that there was systematic interference in the students' English from the creole which was not being recognized by the teachers or the educational system, and an approach that recognized and dealt with this interference would be more effective.

There was similar controversy in Trinidad in 1975, when a new English-language curriculum that took creole usage into effect was introduced (see Carrington and Borely 1977). More recently, teachers working with West Indian students in North American schools similarly feel the need to take their English Creole vernaculars into account; educators in Toronto have been particularly innovative in this respect (see Coelho 1991), as have the developers of the Caribbean Academic Program for Caribbean English Creole speakers at Evanston Township High School, Illinois (see Fischer 1992). For a more comprehensive review of attempts to take pidgin and creole vernaculars into account in the education of their speakers, see Siegel (1998).

In terms of the European scene, I will briefly refer you to two studies, although there are others that are relevant. The first is Österberg's (1961) study of Swedish dialects and education. Österberg conducted an experiment for a few years in which he began teaching one set of students in their vernacular dialect of Swedish and then switching to standard Swedish. A second set of students was taught entirely in standard Swedish for the same period. As you may already have recognized, this was essentially a dialect version of the most famous sets of work that Cheavens had looked at earlier in terms of languages. Again, after 35 weeks, what Österberg found was that the dialect method showed itself superior – both in terms of reading quickly and rapidly assimilating new matter. The same positive results applied to reading and reading comprehension.

Later on a scholar named Tove Bull (see Bull 1990) did a similar study in Norway. She did this between 1980 and 1982 with ten classes of beginning students, with nearly 200 students about seven years old. She used the same kind of design as Österberg did, comparing the progress of speakers of dialect varieties of Norwegian who were experimentally taught in their vernacular and then switched to instruction in standard Norwegian with a control group schooled entirely in standard Norwegian. The results showed that the experimental dialect-instructed students read significantly faster and better than the control group of standard-instructed subjects, and this was particularly true for the children who were doing worse to begin with. Bull attributed this in part to the same kinds of factors that Hanni Taylor talked about – that the explicit attention to the vernacular which the experimental students enjoyed made them better able to analyze their own speech and increased their metalinguistic awareness of language more than the traditional standard-based teaching methods did.

16.5   Summary and Conclusion

I could go on to cite other studies, but my time and space are up. To summarize briefly, the factor which led Oakland to its Ebonics resolution, and which has led many linguists (like myself) to get involved in this issue, is the depressingly poor record of American schools in helping African American students to read and write well, and to succeed in school more generally. While other factors (such as teacher expectations and school facilities) are involved in this failure, the distinctive, systematic vernacular which many African American students speak (AAVE or Ebonics) is certainly relevant, especially teachers' negative and prejudicial attitudes toward it, and their failure to take it into account in helping students master the art of reading and writing in the standard variety. One way of "taking the vernacular into account" is to be more linguistically informed about the kinds of errors AAVE speakers make and the reasons for them, which opens up the possibilities of developing better strategies for helping students avoid or overcome them. A related approach, closer to what Oakland proposed, is to provide Contrastive Analysis between the vernacular and the standard to help AAVE speakers understand and bridge the differences, as has been tried successfully in Chicago, DeKalb County Georgia, and elsewhere. A third approach is to begin with reading materials and instruction in the vernacular and then make the transition to the standard, as has been tried successfully with the *Bridge* program in over two dozen classrooms in the United States and with dialect speakers in Europe. Most people would be surprised to learn of the successes of methods of teaching the standard via the vernacular – the kind of approach the Oakland School Board advocated – but this is partly because of their conditioned prejudices and because of the insidious manufacturing of consent and dissemination of misinformation and ignorance which the media effected on this issue, as on others.

In closing, I would like to turn on its head a comment which the Rev. Jessie Jackson made in his initial remarks on the Ebonics issue, before he learned more about what Oakland was proposing and changed his mind. He was quoted in the *New York Times* of December 23, 1996 as saying that the kind of approach that Oakland was advocating represented "an unconditional surrender, borderlining on disgrace." I would argue that to continue with traditional approaches in the light of their dramatic failure rates, and to ignore innovative methods of taking the vernacular into account, despite their success and promise, represents an unconditional surrender, bordering on disgrace.

Notes

This is a revised version (March 25, 1998 and June 22, 1998) of remarks delivered at the California State University Long Beach Conference on Ebonics on March 29, 1997. I am grateful to the organizers, including Robert Berdan and Gerda de Klerk, for inviting me to take part, and to the editors of the proceedings – see Ramirez et al. (in press) – for permission to reprint this paper.

1   Fortunately, the bill was defeated in committee on April 2, 1997, although there have been subsequent attempts to resuscitate it in a significantly revised form. For further information on this and other California State or Assembly bills cited here, see http://www.sen.ca.gov/www/leginfo/SearchText.html, and consult Richardson (1998) for information on other legislative responses to the Ebonics controversy of 1996–7 at the state and federal levels.

2   More recently, Proposition 227, the Ron Unz "English for the Children" initiative which essentially dismantles bilingual education in California, was approved in California's June 1998 primary election. Interestingly enough, only two ethnic groups voted against it: Latinos and African Americans. The percentage of "yes" votes for the four major ethnic groups in California reveals how divided they are on educational and political issues: Whites: 67 percent, Asians 57 percent, African Americans 48 percent, Latinos 37 percent.

3   The notion of Standard or mainstream English is of course more complex and the subject of greater controversy than can be indicated here, involving considerations of social class and power which go beyond linguistic features. For more discussion, see Wolfram and Schilling-Estes (1998: 8–16), who distinguish between formal or prescriptive Standard English, based more on writing and codified prescriptive

grammars, and informal Standard English, based more on spoken usage, sensitive to regional and social differences, and involving a continuum between standard and nonstandard usage. See also Lippi-Green (1997: 53–62) who assails the notion of standard language or English as an abstraction or myth in light of the considerable variation in usage and judgement which can be found both regionally and socially and even among "educated" speakers; for various reasons, she prefers (building on Heath 1983: 391–2) the term *mainstream* language. See also Bex and Watts (in press), which includes papers focussing more heavily on the notion of Standard English in the UK, although some of them do consider US varieties too. The notion of "vernacular" is less often discussed, but it is subject to ambiguity too (Wolfram and Schilling-Estes, ibid.), and an entire conference on the subject is planned for 1999. Entitled "Vernacularity: The Politics of Language and Style," the conference will be held March 4–7, 1999 at the University of Western Ontario in London, Ontario, Canada. For further information, email Nicholas Watson or Fiona Somerset at nwatson@julian.uwo.ca or fsomerse@julian.uwo.ca or consult: http://www.english.upenn.edu/CFP/

4   These schools were deliberately picked to provide a comparison with data from the *Philadelphia Inquirer* of July 25, 1976 which were cited in Labov (1995).

5   One interesting aspect of the Philadelphia data for 1995–6 and 1996–7 is the fact that the reading data from Cooke Middle School actually show an improvement over those from Birney Elementary School in terms of percentage reading, at or above the Basic Level, for both years (47.5 percent and 40.1 percent respectively) although not in overall reading scores (53.1 percent and 51.2 percent respectively). This is somewhat encouraging since the 1976 data on reading and math combined, which Labov (1995) cited, show a steady and precipitous decline from the elementary level (31 percent of Birney students scored below the sixteenth percentile) through the middle school (50 percent of Cooke students scored below the sixteenth percentile) to the high school (75 percent of Franklin students scored below the sixteenth percentile).

6   As Freccia and Lau (1996) note:

> In 1995, for the first time ever, California spent as much money on its prison system as it did on its universities. Since 1983, the California Department of Corrections has increased its staff by a huge 169%. . . . By contrast, California has decreased its higher education staff by 8.7%. The California Assembly Ways and Means Initial Review of the 1994/95 Budget states, "Corrections spending has grown more than twice as fast as total state spending . . . this explosive growth has come at the expense of spending for other programs, primarily higher education."

Given that African Americans are significantly over-represented in the jail and prison population – "in 1991, African Americans constituted only 12.3% of the population nationwide, but 43.4% of the inmates in local jails, and 45.6% of the inmates in state prisons" (Rickford 1997a: 173) – they are undoubtedly the primary "beneficiaries" of the state's increased spending on prisons. But since spending on prisons comes at the expense of spending on schools, they are also the primary "losers" in this process.

7   By contrast, I recently visited Los Angeles schools participating in the Language Development Program for African American Students, run by Noma LeMoine, and I was impressed by the ready availability of books in each classroom, many of them about African Americans.

8   Unfortunately, we don't have good class-based studies of African American communities beyond the 1960s; it is an area in urgent need of empirical research. I keep encouraging graduate students to do it, but they tend to be daunted by the time, effort, and resources which a randomized study of class in an urban African American speech community would require.

9   The gap in Ebonics use between the working and middle class helps to explain the tremendous denial and condemnation evidenced by African Americans in 1996 and 1997 in relation to Ebonics. By and large, the people whom the media interviewed were not from the African American working- and under-classes; Kweisi Mfume, Maya Angelou, Bill Cosby et al. were very much upper middle-class "representatives of the race," and what they had to say about Ebonics was decidedly influenced by their backgrounds.

10 On this point, see most recently, Wolfram and Schilling-Estes 1998: 297–322, and Wolfram, Adger and Christian, 1998.

11 The handbook of the Standard English Proficiency (SEP) program for speakers of African American language – in use in California since the 1980s, and now used in varying forms in 300 or more schools – contains numerous examples of instructional strategies and drills for contrasting AAVE and Standard English. See also Feigenbaum (1970) and Rickford (1997d). Unfortunately, the SEP program has never been systematically evaluated on a statewide level (Yarborough and Flores 1997), although plans are now afoot to implement such evaluation.

12 Note that this is *not* the approach that the Oakland School Board advocated in 1996.

13 McWhorter (1997) has pointed to a series of studies done in the early 1970s in which "dialect readers were shown to have no effect whatsoever on African American students' reading scores." I think it is important to re-examine and even replicate those studies, but it should be noted that they all differ from the *Bridge* study insofar as they lacked any time depth. The studies cited by McWhorter were one-time studies of the effects of using vernacular or Standard English stimuli on decoding or reading comprehension in the relatively brief (e.g. 30-minute) session or sessions needed to conduct the experiment, rather than studies of the effects of teaching children in the vernacular or in Standard English over an extended period of time, as was the case with the "Bridge" study. This crucial difference may account for the success of the latter study and the failures of the earlier studies. This much is suggested by the authors of one of the most comprehensive earlier studies, Simons and Johnson (1974), who note (355) that "Another limitation of the present study concerns the length of the experiment and the number of reading texts employed. It may be the case that the treatment may have been too brief to show a difference in reading."

References

Abraham, R. C. 1958. *Dictionary of Modern Yoruba.* London: University of London Press.

Abrahams, Roger D. 1964. *Deep Down in the Jungle.* Hatboro, PA: Folklore Associates.

Abrahams, Roger D. 1972. "The training of the man of words in talking broad." In Kochman 1970: 215–40.

Abrahams, Roger D. 1978. *Talking Black.* Rowley, MA: Newbury House.

Achbar, Mark (ed.) 1994. *Manufacturing Consent: Noam Chomsky and the Media: The Companion Book to the Award-Winning Film by Peter Wintonick and Mark Achbar.* Montreal and New York: Black Rose Books.

Adams, G. B. 1977. "The dialects of Ulster." In O'Muirithe 1977: 56–70.

Adger, Carolyn T., Donna Christian, and Orlando Taylor, eds. In press. *Language and Academic Achievement Among African American Students: Making the Connection.* McHenry, IL: Delta Systems and Center for Applied Linguistics.

Adger, Carolyn, Walt Wolfram, and J. Detwyler. 1992. "Enhancing delivery of services to Black special education students from non-Standard English backgrounds." Washington, DC: Office of Special Education Programs. (Cooperative agreement HO23400008-92).

Aitken, A. J. 1984. "Scottish accents and dialects." In Trudgill 1984a: 94–114.

Akinnaso, F. Niyi, and Cheryl Seabrook Ajirotutu. 1982. "Performance and ethnic style in job interviews." In Gumperz 1982b: 119–44.

Akmajian, A., R. A. Demers, and R. M. Harnish. 1984. *Linguistics.* Cambridge: The MIT Press.

Alleyne, Mervyn. 1971. "Acculturation and the cultural matrix of creolization." In Hymes 1971b: 169–86.

Alleyne, Mervyn 1980. *Comparative Afro-American.* Ann Arbor, Mich.: Karoma.

Allsopp, Richard. 1950. "The language we speak." *Kyk-Over-Al*, 3(11): 23–32.

Allsopp, Richard. 1972. "Some suprasegmental features of Caribbean English and their relevance in the classroom." Paper presented at the Conference on Creole Languages and Educational Development, Univ. of the West Indies, St Augustine, Trinidad.

Allsopp, Richard. 1983. *The Creole Treatment of Passivity.* In *Studies in Caribbean Language*, ed. Lawrence D. Carrington, Dennis Craig, and Ramon Todd Dandare, 142–54. St Augustine, Trinidad: Society for Caribbean Linguistics.

Allsopp, Richard (ed.). 1996. *Dictionary of Caribbean English Usage* (with a French and Spanish supplement ed. Jeannette Allsopp). Oxford: Oxford University Press.

The American Heritage Dictionary of the English Language, 3rd edn. 1992. Boston, Massachusetts: Houghton Mifflin.

Asha. 1983. "Position Paper: Social dialects." *Journal of the American Speech-Language-Hearing Association*, 25: 23–4.

Anderson, Barbara A., Brian C. Silver, and Paul R. Abramson. 1988. "The effects of the race of the interviewer on race-related attitudes of black respondents in SRC/CPS national election studies." *Public Opinion Quarterly* 52: 289–324.

Anderson, Monica Frazier. 1994. *Black English Vernacular (From "Ain't" to "Yo Mama")": The Words Politically Correct Americans Should Know*. Highland City, FL.: Rainbow Books.

Andersen, Roger (ed.). 1983. *Pidginization and Creolization as Language Acquisition*. Rowley, MA: Newbury House.

Anshen, Frank. 1969. "Speech variation among Negroes in a small southern community." PhD dissertation, New York University.

Arnett, Carlee, Jennifer Dailey-O'Cain, Rosina Lippi-Green, and Ria Simpson. 1994. "Teaching children how to discriminate." Paper presented at NWAV23, Stanford University.

Ascher, Robert. 1974. "Tin-can archaeology." *Historical Archaeology* 8: 7–16.

Ash, Sharon. 1988. "Speaker identification in sociolinguistics and criminal law." In *Linguistic Change and Contact: Proceedings of NWAV-XVI*, ed. Kathleen Ferrara et al., 25–33. Austin: Department of Linguistics, University of Texas.

Ash, Sharon, and John Myhill. 1986. "Linguistic correlates of inter-ethnic contact." In *Diversity and Diachrony*, ed. David Sankoff, 33–44. Amsterdam and Philadelphia: John Benjamins.

Bailey, Beryl. 1965. "Toward a new perspective in Negro English dialectology." *American Speech* 40: 171–7.

Bailey, Beryl. 1966. *Jamaican Creole Syntax: A Transformational Approach*. Cambridge: Cambridge University Press.

Bailey, Beryl. 1971. "Jamaican Creole: Can dialect boundaries be defined? In Hymes (ed.), 1971b: 341–8.

Bailey, Charles-James N. 1970. "Using data variation to confirm, rather than undermine, the existence of abstract syntactic structures." *Working Papers in Linguistics* 2(8): 77–86. Honolulu: University of Hawaii.

Bailey, Charles-James N. 1982. "Irish English and Caribbean Black English: another joinder." *American Speech* 57: 237–9.

Bailey, C.-J. N., and R. W. Shuy, (eds). 1973. *New Ways of Analyzing Variation in English*. Washington, DC: Georgetown University Press.

Bailey, Guy. 1987. "Are Black and White vernaculars diverging?". In Ralph W. Fasold et al. 1987: 32–40.

Bailey, Guy. 1993. "A perspective on African American English." In *American Dialect Research*, ed. Dennis Preston, 287–318. Amsterdam: John Benjamins.

Bailey, Guy, and Marvin Bassett. 1986. "Invariant Be in the lower south." In *Language Variety in the South*, ed. Michael Montgomery and Guy Bailey, 158–79. University, AL: University of Alabama Press.

Bailey, Guy, and Natalie Maynor. 1983. "The present tense of be in Southern Black folk speech." Unpublished MS.

Bailey, Guy, and Natalie Maynor. 1987. "Decreolization?" *Language in Society* 16: 449–73.

Bailey, Guy, and Natalie Maynor. 1989. "The divergence controversy." *American Speech* 64: 12–39.

Bailey, Guy, and Erik Thomas. 1998. "Some aspects of African American English phonology." In Mufwene, Rickford, Bailey and Baugh (eds) 1998: 85–109.

Baker, Philip. 1982a. "On the origins of the first Mauritians and of the creole language of their descendants: A refutation of Chaudenson's 'Bourbonnais' theory." In *Isle de France Creole*, P. Baker and Chris Corne, 131–259. Ann Arbor: Karoma.

Baker, Philip. 1982b. "The contribution of non-Francophone immigrants to the lexicon of Mauritian Creole." Unpublished PhD dissertation. London: University of London, School of Oriental and African Studies. Ann Arbor, Michigan: University Microfilms International.

Baker, Philip. 1991. "Column: Causes and effects." *Journal of Pidgin and Creole Languages* 6: 267–78.

Baldwin, James. 1979. "If black English isn't a language, then tell me, what is?" *New York Times*, July 29, 1979. (Repr. in Smitherman (ed.), 1981b: 390–2.)

Ball, Arnetha F. 1992. "Cultural preference and the expository writing of African American adolescents." *Written Communication* 9: 501–32.

Baltimore. 1993. *Handbook on Language Differences and Speech and Language Pathology*. Baltimore: Baltimore City Public Schools, Department of Support and Special Pupil Services.

Baltin, Mark. 1973. "A reanalysis of quantifier-negative dialects." Mimeo. University of Pennsylvania.

Banton, M. 1978. "A theory of racial and ethnic relations: rational choice." Working papers on Ethnic Relations, 8. Research Unit on Ethnic Relations, University of Bristol.

Baratz, Joan C. 1969. "Teaching reading in an urban Negro school system." In Baratz and Shuy (eds), 1969: 92–116.

Baratz, Joan C., and Roger W. Shuy (eds). 1969. *Teaching Black Children to Read*. Washington, DC: Center for Applied Linguistics.

Battistella, Edwin. 1996. "The LSA guidelines for nonsexist language." Paper presented at the symposium on "Addressing bias in linguistic example sentences: Are guidelines necessary?" Linguistic Society of America annual meeting, San Diego. January.

Baugh, John. 1979. "Linguistic style-shifting in Black English." PhD dissertation, University of Pennsylvania.

Baugh, John. 1980. "A re-examination of the Black English copula." In W. Labov (ed.), 1980b: 83–106.

Baugh, John. 1981. "Design and implementation of language arts programs for speakers of nonstandard English." In Bruce Cronell (ed.), *Perspectives for a National Neighborhood Literacy Program. The Linguistic Needs of Linguistically Different Children*, 17–43. Los Alamitos, California: South West Regional Laboratory.

Baugh, John. 1983. *Black Street Speech: Its History, Structure and Survival*. Austin: University of Texas Press.

Baugh, John. 1984. "Steady: Progressive aspect in Black Vernacular English". *American Speech* 59: 3–12.

Baugh, John. 1987. "The role of BE copula analyses in the development of a comprehensive linguistic theory." Paper presented at the fifteenth annual conference on New Ways of Analyzing Variation (NWAV-XV), Stanford, Ca.

Baugh, John. 1988. "Language and race: Some implications for linguistic science." In *Linguistics: The Cambridge Survey*, vol. IV. *Language: The Sociocultural Context*, ed. Frederick J. Newmeyer, 64–74. Cambridge and New York: Cambridge University Press.

Baugh, John. 1996. "Perceptions within a variable paradigm: Black and White detection based on speech." In *Focus on the USA*, Varieties of English Around the World, General Studies no. 16. ed. Edgar Schneider. Amsterdam: Benjamins.

Baugh, John. 1998. "Linguistics, education and the law: Educational reform for African-American language minority students." In Mufwene, Rickford, Bailey and Baugh (eds), 282–301.

Bell, Allan. 1977. "The language of radio news in Auckland: A sociolinguistic study of style, audience and subediting variation." PhD dissertation. University of Auckland.

Bell, Allan. 1982. "Radio: The style of language." *Journal of Communication* 32(1): 150–64.

Bell, Allan. 1984. "Language style as audience design." *Language in Society* 13: 145–204.

Bell, Allan. 1991. "Audience accommodation in the mass media." In Giles, Coupland, and Coupland, 69–102.

Bell, Allan. 1992. "Responding to your audience: Taking the initiative." *Language and Communication* 12: 327–40.

Bell, Allan. 1995. "Review of Douglas Biber and Edward Finegan 1994." *Language in Society* 24: 265–70.

Bereiter, Carl, and Siegfried Engelmann. 1966. *Teaching Disadvantaged Children in the Pre-School*. Englewood Cliffs, NJ: Prentice-Hall.

Bergvall, Victoria L. 1996. "'Merely data'? Reflections on/of bias in constructed linguistic examples." Paper presented at the symposium on "Addressing bias in linguistic example sentences: Are guidelines necessary?" Linguistic Society of America, San Diego.

Berlin, Ira. 1980. "Time, space, and the evolution of Afro-American society on British mainland North America." *American Historical Review* 85: 77.

Bex, Tony, and Richard J. Watts (eds). In press. *Standard English: The Continuing Debate*. London: Routledge.

Biber, Douglas. 1988. *Variation Across Speech and Writing*. Cambridge: Cambridge University Press.

Biber, Douglas, and Edward Finegan. 1994. *Perspectives on Register*. Oxford and New York: Oxford University Press.

Bickerton, Derek. 1971. "Inherent variability and variable rules." *Foundations of Language* 7: 457–92.

Bickerton, Derek. 1973a. "The structure of polylectal grammars." In: *Report of the Twenty-Third Annual Round Table Meeting on Linguistics and Language Studies*, ed. Roger W. Shuy 17–42. Washington, DC: Georgetown University Press.

Bickerton, Derek. 1973b. "On the nature of a creole continuum." *Language* 49: 640–69.

Bickerton, Derek. 1974. "Bin in the Atlantic Creoles." *Journal of African Languages*, Special Issue devoted to the English Pidgins and Creoles, ed. I. Hancock.

Bickerton, Derek. 1975. *Dynamics of a Creole System*. Cambridge: Cambridge University Press.

Bickerton, Derek. 1980a. "Decreolization and the creole continuum." In Valdman and Highfield, 109–28.

Bickerton, Derek. 1980b. "What happens when we switch?" *York Papers in Linguistics* 9: 41–56.

Bickerton, Derek. 1981. *Roots of Language*. Ann Arbor: Karoma.

Bickerton, Derek. 1983. "Review of Philip Baker and Chris Corne, 1982, *Isle de France Creole*. (Ann Arbor, Michigan: Karoma). *Carrier Pidgin Newsletter* 11: 8–9.

Bickerton, Derek. 1984a. "The language bioprogram hypothesis." *Behavioral and Brain Sciences* 7: 173–221.

Bickerton, Derek. 1984b. "The role of demographics in the formation of creoles." Paper presented at NWAVE 13, University of Pennsylvania, Philadelphia.

Bickerton, Derek. 1986. "Column: Beyond roots: The five year test." *Journal of Pidgin and Creole Languages* 1: 225–32.

Binnick, Robert I. 1991. *Time and the Verb: A Guide to Tense and Aspect*. New York: Oxford University Press.

Birdwhistell, Ray L. 1970. *Kinesics and Context*. Philadelphia: University of Pennsylvania Press.

Blake, Renée. 1997. "Defining the envelope of linguistic variation: The case of 'don't count' forms in the copula analysis of African American Vernacular English." *Language Variation and Change* 9: 57–80.

Bliss, Alan J. 1972. "Languages in contact: Some problems of Hiberno-English." *Royal Irish Academy Proceedings*, Sec. C(72): 63–82.

Bliss, Alan J. 1977. "The emergence of modern English dialects in Ireland." In O'Muirithe, 7–19.

Bliss, Alan J. 1984. "English in the South of Ireland." In Trudgill 1984a: 135–51.

Blom, Jan-Petter, and John J. Gumperz. 1972. "The social meaning of linguistic structures: Code-switching in Norway." In *Directions in Sociolinguistics*, ed. John J. Gumperz and Dell Hymes, 407–34. New York: Holt, Rinehart and Winston.

Bloomfield, Leonard. 1933. *Language*. New York: Holt.

Blyth, Carl, Jr., Sigrid Recktenwald, and Jenny Wang. 1990. "I'm like, 'Say What?!': A new quotative in American oral narrative." *American Speech* 65: 215–27.

Bolinger, D. 1968. "Judgments of grammaticality." *Lingua* 21: 34–40.

Bourhis, R. Y., and Howard Giles. 1977. "Children's voice and ethnic categorization in Britain." *La Monda Linguo-Problemo* 6: 85–94.

Bowie, R. L., and C. L. Bond. 1994. "Influencing teachers' attitudes toward Black English: Are we making a difference?" *Journal of Teacher Education* 45: 112–18.

Brackenridge, H. H. 1792. *Modern Chivalry*. Philadelphia.

Braidwood, J. 1964. "Ulster and Elizabethan English." In *Ulster Dialects*, ed. G. B. Adams, 5–109. Holywood: Ulster Folk Museum.

Brasch, Walter M. 1981. *Black English and the Mass Media*. New York: Lanham.

Brathwaite, Edward. 1984. *History of the Voice: The Development of Nation Language in Anglophone Caribbean Poetry*. London: New Beacon Books.

Breslaw, Elaine G. 1996. *Tituba, Reluctant Witch of Salem*. New York and London: New York University Press.

Brewer, Jeutonne. 1974. "The verb be in early Black English: A study based on the WPA ex-slave narratives." Chapel Hill: University of North Carolina dissertation.

Bridenbaugh, Carl, and Roberta Bridenbaugh. 1972. *No Peace Beyond the Line: The English in the Caribbean, 1624–1690*. Oxford: Oxford University Press.

Brooks, Charlotte K. (ed.) 1985. *Tapping Potential: English and Language Arts for the Black Learner*. Urbana, Ill.: National Council of Teachers of English.

Brown, Claude. 1968. "The language of soul." *Esquire* (April): 88, 160–1.

Brown, Roger, and Albert Gilman. 1960. "The pronouns of power and solidarity." In *Style in Language*, ed. T. A. Sebeok, 253–76. Cambridge, Mass.: MIT Press.

Bull, Tove. 1990. "Teaching school beginners to read and write in the vernacular." In *Tromsø Linguistics in the Eighties* 11: 69–84.

Bureau of the Census, 1975. *Statistics of the United States: Colonial Times to 1970*, part 2. Washington, DC: United States Department of Commerce.

Burling, Robbins. 1973. *English in Black and White*. New York: Holt.

Burns, Sir Alan. 1954. *History of the British West Indies*. London: Allen & Unwin.

Butters, Ronald R. 1973. "Acceptability judgments for double modals in Southern English." In Bailey and Shuy (1973), 276–86.

Butters, Ronald R. 1984. "When is English 'Black English Vernacular'?" *Journal of English Linguistics* 17: 29–36.

Butters, Ronald R. 1989. *The Death of Black English: Divergence and Controversy in Black and White Vernaculars* (Bamberger Beitrage zur englischen Sprachwissenschaft, 25). Frankfurt: Peter Lang.

Butters, Ronald R. 1997. "'What is about to take place is a murder': Constructing the racist subtext in a small-town Virginia courtroom." To appear in *New Studies of Language and Society*, ed. Joy Peyton and Peg Griffin. Creskill, NJ: Hampton.

Butters, Ronald R., Thomas Espy, and Kent Aschuler. 1993. "The imitation of dialect for illegal purposes: An empirical study." Paper presented at NWAV22, University of Ottawa.

Butters, Ronald R., and Ruth M. Nix. 1985. "The English of Blacks in Wilmington, North Carolina." In Montgomery and Bailey, 255–64.

Bybee, Joan, Revere Perkins, and William Pagliuca. 1994. *The Evolution of Grammar: Tense, Aspect and Modality in the Languages of the World*. Chicago: University of Chicago Press.

Bynon, Theodora. 1977. *Historical Linguistics*. Cambridge: Cambridge University Press.

Cameron, Deborah, Elizabeth Frazer, Penelope Harvey, M. B. H. Rampton, and Kay Richardson. 1992. *Researching Language: Issues of Power and Method*. London and New York: Routledge.

Carden, G. 1970. "A note on conflicting idiolects." *Linguistic Inquiry* 1(3): 281–90.

Carrington, L. D., and C. B. Borely. 1977. *The Language Arts Syllabus, 1975: Comment and Counter Comment*. St Augustine, Trinidad: University of the West Indies.

Carter, Hazel. 1983. "How to be a tone language." In *Studies in Caribbean Language*, ed. Lawrence D. Carrington, Dennis Craig, and Ramon Todd Dandaré, 90–111. St Augustine, Trinidad: Society for Caribbean Linguistics.

Cassidy, Frederic G. 1961. *Jamaica talk: Three Hundred Years of the English Language in Jamaica*. London: Macmillan.

Cassidy, Frederic G. 1966. "Multiple etymologies in Jamaican Creole." *American Speech* 41: 211–15.

Cassidy, Frederic G. 1970. "Teaching Standard English to Speakers of Creole in Jamaica, West Indies." In *Report of the 20th Annual Round Table Meeting on Linguistics and Language Studies: Linguistics and the Teaching of Standard English to Speakers of Other Languages or Dialects*, ed. James E. Alatis, 203–214. Washington, DC: Georgetown University Press.

Cassidy, Frederic G. 1980. "The place of Gullah." *American Speech* 55: 3–16.

Cassidy, Frederic G. 1985 (ed.) *Dictionary of American Regional English*, vol. 1. Cambridge, MA: Harvard University Press.

Cassidy, Frederic G., and Robert B. Le Page. 1980. *Dictionary of Jamaican English*, 2nd edn. Cambridge: Cambridge University Press.

Cedergren, Henrietta, and David Sankoff. 1974. "Variable rules: Performance as a statistical reflection of competence." *Language* 50: 333–55.

Chamberlain, J. Edward. 1993. *Come Back to Me My Language: Poetry and the West Indies*. Urbana and Chicago: University of Illinois Press.

Chambers, J. K. 1995. *Sociolinguistic Theory*. Oxford: Basil Blackwell.

Chambers, John, W., Jr. (ed.) 1983. *Black English: Educational Equity and the Law*. Ann Arbor: Karoma.

Chaudenson, Robert. 1979. *Les Créoles Français*. Paris: L'Harmattan.

Chaudenson, Robert. 1992. *Des Iles, des Hommes, des Langues: Essais sur la Créolisation Linguistique et Culturelle*. Paris: L'Harmattan.

Cheavens, Sam Frank. 1957. "Vernacular languages and education." PhD dissertation, University of Texas, Austin.

Cheshire, Jenny. 1982. *Variation in an English Dialect*. Cambridge: Cambridge University Press.

Cheshire, Jenny. 1987. "Syntactic variation, the linguistic variable and sociolinguistic theory." *Linguistics* 25: 257–82.

Ching, Marvin K. L. 1987. "How fixed is *fixin' to?*," *American Speech* 62: 332–45.

Coelho, Elizabeth. 1991. *Caribbean Students in Canadian Schools*, book 2. Markham, Ontario: Pippin Publishing and the Caribbean Student Resource Book Committee.

Cole, Lorraine. 1983. "Implications of the position on social dialects." *Asha* 25: 25–7.

Coleman, Terry. 1972. *Going to America*. New York: Pantheon.

Collymore, Frank. 1970. *Notes for a Glossary of Words and Phrases of Barbadian Dialect*. Bridgetown: Advocate.

Comer, James P. 1993. *School Power: Implications of an Intervention Project*, 2nd edn. New York: Free Press.

Comer, James P. 1997. *Waiting For a Miracle: Why Schools Can't Solve our Problems, and How we Can*. New York: Dutton.

Committee on College Composition and Communication (CCCC). 1978. "Committee on the CCCC language statement: Students' right to their own language." In *A Pluralistic Nation: The Language Issue in the United States*, ed. Margaret A. Lourie and Nancy Faires Conklin, 314–28. Rowley, MA: Newbury House.

Comrie, Bernard. 1976. *Aspect: An Introduction to the Study of Verbal Aspect and Related Problems*. Cambridge: University Press.

Comrie, Bernard. 1985. *Tense*. Cambridge: Cambridge University Press.

Comrie, Bernard. 1986. "Tense and time reference: From meaning to interpretation in the chronological structure of a text." *Journal of Literary Semantics* 15(1): 12–22.

Conroy, Pat. 1972. *The Water is Wide*. Boston: Houghton Mifflin.

Cooke, Benjamin. 1972. "Non-verbal communication among Afro-Americans – an initial classification." In Kochman (ed.) 1972: 32–64.

Cooper, Robert L. 1982. "A framework for the study of language spread." In *Language Spread*, ed. R. L. Cooper, 5–36. Bloomington: Indiana University Press.

Cose, Ellis. 1997. *Color-Blind: Seeing Beyond Race in a Race-Obsessed World*. New York: Harper Collins.

Coupland, Nikolas. 1980. "Style shifting in a Cardiff work-setting." *Language in Society* 9: 1–12.

Coupland, Nikolas. 1981. "The social differentiation of functional language use: A sociolinguistic investigation of travel agency talk." PhD dissertation, University of Wales Institute of Science and Technology.

Coupland, Nikolas. 1984. "Accommodation at work: Some phonological data and their interpretations." *International Journal of the Sociology of Language* 46: 49–70.

Coupland, Nikolas. 1985. "'Hark, hark, the lark': Social motivations for phonological style-shifting." *Language and Communication* 5: 153–71.

Coupland, Nikolas, and Howard Giles (eds). 1988. "Communicative accommodation: Recent developments." *Language and Communication* 8: 175–327.

Craig, Collete G. 1992. "Fieldwork on endangered languages: A forward look at ethical issues." Paper presented at the XVth International Congress of Linguists, University Laval, Quebec.

Craig, Collete G. 1995. "The Rama language project of Nicaragua: A 10-year perspective." Paper presented at the annual meeting of the Linguistic Society of America, New Orleans, January.

Craig, Dennis B. 1980. "A creole English continuum and the theory of grammar." In *Issues in English Creoles: Papers from the 1975 Hawaii Conference*, ed. Richard R. Day, 111–31. Heidelberg: Groos.

Crozier, Alan. 1984. "The Scotch-Irish influence on American English." *American Speech* 59: 310–31.

Cruickshank, J. Graham. 1905. *Negro Humor: Being Sketches in the Market, on the Road, and at My Back Door*. Demerara: Argosy.

Cruickshank, J. Graham. 1916. *Black Talk, Being Notes on Negro Dialect in British Guiana*. Georgetown, Demerara: Argosy.

Crystal, David. 1980. *A First Dictionary of Linguistics and Phonetics*. Boulder, Colorado: Westview.

Cukor-Avila, Patricia. 1995a. "The Evolution of AAVE in a Rural Texas Community: An ethnolinguistic study." PhD dissertation, University of Michigan.

Cukor-Avila, Patricia, and Guy Bailey. 1995b. "Grammaticalization in AAVE." In *Proceedings of the Twenty-First Annual Meeting of the Berkeley Linguistics Society* (BLS 21), ed. Jocelyn Ahlers, Leela Bilmes, Joshua Guenter, Barbara Kaiser, and Ju Namkung. Berkeley: Department of Linguistics, University of California, 401–13.

Cummings, Doug. 1997. "A different approach to teaching language." *Atlanta Constitution*, Jan 9, 1997: B1.

Cunningham, Irma A. 1970. "A Syntactic analysis of Sea Island Creole ('Gullah')." PhD dissertation, Department of Linguistics, University of Michigan. Available from University Microfilms (#71–4590), Ann Arbor, Michigan.

Curtin, Philip D. 1969. *The Atlantic Slave Trade: A Census*. Madison: University of Wisconsin Press.

Dabydeen, David, and Nava Wilson-Tagoe. 1988. *A Reader's Guide to West Indian and Black British Literature*. London: Hansib.

Dalby, David. 1972. "The African element in American English." In Kochman (1972), 170–86.

Dandy, Evelyn B. 1991. *Black Communications: Breaking Down the Barriers*. Chicago, Ill.: African American Images.

Dash, Julie 1992. *Daughters of the Dust: The Making of an African American Woman's Film*. New York: The New Press.

Dauzat, Albert. 1927. *Les patois*. Paris: Delagrave.

Davis, David Brion. 1986. *Slavery in the Colonial Chesapeake*. Williamsburg, VA: The Colonial Williamsburg Foundation.

Davis, Lawrence M. 1971. "Dialect research: Mythology and reality." In Wolfram and Clarke, 90–8.

Davis, Lawrence M. 1983. *English Dialectology: An Introduction*. University: Univ. of Alabama Press.

Dayton, Elizabeth. 1994. "The *be* element in vernacular African American English *be done*." Paper presented at the Linguistic Society of America, Boston.

Dayton, Elizabeth. 1996. "Grammatical categories of the verb in African American Vernacular English." PhD dissertation, Department of Linguistics, University of Pennsylvania. Available through UMI Dissertation Service, Ann Arbor, Michigan.

DeBose, Charles E., and Nicholas Faraclas. 1988. "An Africanist approach to the linguistic study of Black English: Getting to the African roots of the tense/aspect/modality and copula systems in Afro-American." In *Africanisms in Afro-American Language Varieties*, ed. Salikoko S. Mufwene, 364–87. Athens: University of Georgia Press.

DeCamp, David. 1960. "Four Jamaican Creole texts with introduction, phonemic transcriptions and glosses." In *Jamaican Creole* (Creole Language Studies, 1), ed. Robert B. Le Page and David DeCamp, 128–79. London: Macmillan.

Defoe, Daniel. 1722. *The History and Remarkable Life of the Truly Honorable Col. Jacque, Commonly Called Col. Jack*. London.

De Fréine, Sean. 1977. "The dominance of the English language in the 19th century." In O'Muirithe, 71–87.

Delano, I. O. 1969. *A Dictionary of Yoruba Monosyllabic Verbs*, vol. 2. Ile-Ife, Nigeria: Institute of African Studies, University of Ife.

Denning, Keith. 1989. "A sound change in Vernacular Black English." *Language Variation and Change* 1: 145–67.

Denning, Keith M., Sharon Inkelas, Faye C. McNair-Knox, and John R. Rickford. 1987. *Variation in Language: NWAV-XV at Stanford*. Stanford: Department of Linguistics, Stanford University.

Dennis, J., and J. Scott. 1975. "Creole formation and reorganization: Evidence for diachronic change in synchronic variation." Paper presented at the International Conference on Pidgins and Creoles, Honolulu, Hawaii, 1975.

References   357

DeStephano, Johanna (ed.). 1973. *Language, Society and Education: A Profile of Black English*. Worthington, OH: Charles A. Jones.

Devonish, Hubert St Laurent. 1978. "The selection and codification of a widely understood and publicly useable language variety in Guyana, to be used as a language of national development." DPhil thesis, University of York.

Di Giulio, Robert C. 1973. "Measuring teacher attitudes toward Black English: A pilot project." *The Florida FL Reporter* Spring/Fall: 25–6, 49–50.

Di Paolo, Marianna. 1992. "Hypercorrection in response to the apparent merger of (?) and (a) in Utah English." *Language and Communication* 12: 267–92.

Dickson, R. J. 1966. *Ulster Emigration to Colonial America, 1718–1775*. London: Routledge & Kegan Paul.

Dijkhoff, M. B. 1982. "The process of pluralization in papiamentu." *Amsterdam Creole Studies* IV: 48–61.

Dillard, J. L. 1972. *Black English: Its History and Usage in the United States*. New York: Random House.

Dillard, J. L. 1992. *A History of American English*. New York: Longman.

Dillon, V. M. 1972. "The Anglo-Irish element in the speech of the southern shore of Newfoundland." MA thesis, St John's Memorial University of Newfoundland.

Dorian, Nancy. 1981. *Language Death*. Philadelphia: University of Pennsylvania Press.

Dorrill, George T. 1982. "Black and White speech in the south: evidence from the linguistic atlas of the middle and south Atlantic states." University of South Carolina dissertation.

Dorrill, George T. 1985. "A comparison of stressed vowels of Black and White speakers in the south." In Montgomery and Bailey, 149–58.

Douglas-Cowie, Ellen. 1978. "Linguistic code-switching in a Northern Irish village: Social interaction and social ambition." In *Sociolinguistic Patterns in British English*, ed. Peter Trudgill, 37–51. Baltimore: University Park Press.

Douglass, Frederick. 1855. *My Bondage and my Freedom*. New York.

Douglass, Frederick. 1881. *Life and times of Frederick Douglass, Written by Himself*. Hartford, CT.

Doyle, David. 1981. *Ireland, Irishmen, and Revolutionary America*. Dublin: Mercier Press.

Dressler, Wolfgang U., and Ruth Wodak. 1982. "Sociophonological methods in the study of sociolinguistic variation in Viennese German." *Language in Society* 11: 339–70.

Dubois, Sylvie, and Barbara M. Horvath. 1991. "Examining the effect of interaction on text variation." Paper presented at the twentieth annual conference on New Ways of Analyzing Variation (NWAVE-XX), Georgetown University, Washington DC.

Dumas, Bethany. 1990. "Voice identification in a criminal law context." *American Speech* 65: 341–8.

Duneier, Mitchell. 1994. "Andrea's dream," part 5. *Chicago Tribune*, Dec. 29, sec. 1: 14.

Dunn, Richard S. 1972. *Sugar and Slaves: The Rise of the Planter Class in the English West Indies, 1624–1713*. Chapel Hill: University of North Carolina Press.

Eckert, Penelope. 1988. "Adolescent social structure and the spread of linguistic change." *Language in Society* 17: 183–207.

Eckert, Penelope, and John R. Rickford (eds). In press. *Style and Sociolinguistic Variation*. Cambridge: Cambridge University Press.

Edwards, Jay G. 1974. "African influences on the English of San Andres Island, Colombia." In *Pidgins and Creoles: Current Trends and Prospects*, ed. David DeCamp and Ian F. Hancock, 1–26. Washington, DC: Georgetown University Press.

Edwards, Viv. 1986. *Language in a Black Community*. Clevedon, Avon: Multilingual Matters.

Edwards. Walter F. 1976. "Sociolinguistic models and phonological variation in Guyana." Paper presented at a conference on language and psychology, Stirling University, Scotland.

Edwards, Walter F. 1991. "A comparative description of Guyanese Creole and Black English preverbal aspect marker *Don*." In Walter F. Edwards and Donald Winford 1991: 240–55.

Edwards, Walter F. 1992. "Sociolinguistic behavior in a Detroit inner-city black neighborhood." *Language in Society* 21: 93–115.

Edwards, Walter F., and Donald Winford (eds). 1991. *Verb Phrase Patterns in Black English and Creole*. Detroit: Wayne State University Press.

Eersel, Christian. 1971. "Prestige in choice of language and linguistic form." In Hymes, 1971b: 317–22.

Ellegård, Alvar. 1953. *The Auxiliary Do: The Establishment and Regulation of Its Use in English*. Stockholm: Almquist & Wiksell.

Elliot D., S. Legum, and S. Thompson. 1969. Syntactic variation as linguistic data. In *Papers from the Fifth Regional Meeting, Chicago Linguistic Society*, ed. R. I. Binnick. et al., 52–9. Chicago: University of Chicago.

Elworthy, Frederick. 1879. "The grammar of the dialect of West Somerset." *Transactions of the Philological Society*, 143–253.

Elworthy, Frederick. 1886. *The West Somerset Wordbook*. English Dialect Society publication 50. London: Trubner & Co.

Engblom, Victor. 1938. *On the Origin and Development of the Auxiliary Do*. Lund studies in English, 6. Lund, Sweden: University of Lund.

Ervin-Tripp, Susan M. 1964. "An analysis of the interaction of language, topic and listener." In *The Ethnography of Communication*, ed. John Gumperz and Dell Hymes, 86–102 (*American Anthropologist* 66, 6, pt II).

Escure, Geneviève. 1981. "Decreolization in a creole continuum: Belize." In *Historicity and Variation in Creole Studies*, ed. Arnold Highfield and Albert Valdman, 27–39. Ann Arbor: Karoma.

Escure, Geneviève. 1982. "Contrastive patterns of intragroup and intergroup interaction in the creole continuum of Belize." *Language in Society* 11: 239–64.

Ewers, Traute. 1996. *The Origin of American Black English: Be Forms in the HOODOO Texts*. Berlin and New York: Mouton.

Fallows, Marjorie R. 1979. *Irish Americans: Identity and Assimilation*. Englewood Cliffs, NJ: Prentice-Hall.

Farr, Marcia, and Harvey Daniels. 1986. *Language Diversity and Writing Instruction*. New York: ERIC Clearinghouse on Urban Education and National Council of Teachers of English.

Farrell, T. J. 1983. "IQ and Standard English." *College Composition and Communication* 34: 470–84.

Fasold, Ralph W. 1972. *Tense Marking in Black English: A Linguistic and Social Analysis*. Arlington, VA: Center for Applied Linguistics.

References   359

Fasold, Ralph W. 1978. "Language variation and linguistic competence." In *Linguistic Variation: Models and Methods*, ed. David Sankoff, 85–95. New York: Academic Press.

Fasold, Ralph W. 1981. "The relation between Black and White speech in the South." *American Speech* 56: 163–89.

Fasold, Ralph W. 1990. "Contraction and deletion in Vernacular Black English: Creole history and relationship to Euro-American English." Unpublished MS.

Fasold, Ralph W., William Labov, Fay Boy Vaughn-Cooke, Guy Bailey, Walt Wolfram, Arthur K. Spears and John R. Rickford. 1987. "Are black and white vernaculars diverging? Papers from the NWAVE-XVI panel discussion." *American Speech* 62: 3–80.

Fasold, Ralph W., and Roger W. Shuy (eds). 1970. *Teaching Standard English in the Inner City*. Washington, DC: Center for Applied Linguistics.

Fasold, Ralph W., and Roger W. Shuy. 1975. *Analyzing Variation in Language*. Washington DC: Georgetown University Press.

Fasold, Ralph W., and Walt Wolfram. 1970. "Some linguistic features of Negro dialect." In Fasold and Shuy 1970: 41–86. Repr. in P. Stoller (ed.), *Black American English* (49–83). New York: Delta.

Feagin, Crawford. 1979. *Variation and Change in Alabama English: A Sociolinguistic Study of the White Community*. Washington: Georgetown Univ. Press.

Feigenbaum, Irwin. 1970. "The use of nonstandard English in teaching standard: Contrast and comparison." In Fasold and Shuy, 87–104.

Ferguson, Charles 1971. "Absence of copula and the notion of simplicity: A study of normal speech, baby talk, foreigner talk, and pidgins." In Hymes 1971b: 141–50.

Ferguson, Charles, and Charles E. DeBose. 1977. "Simplified registers, broken language, and pidginization." In *Pidgin and Creole Linguistics*, ed. Albert Valdman, 99–125. Bloomington and London: Indiana University Press.

Ferguson, Charles A., and John J. Gumperz (eds). 1960. *Linguistic Diversity in South Asia: Studies in Regional, Social and Functional Variation*. Bloomington: Indiana University.

Ferrara, Kathleen, Becky Brown, Keith Walters, and John Baugh (eds). 1988. *Linguistic Change and Contact: Proceedings of the Sixteenth Annual Conference on New Ways of Analyzing Variation (NWAV-XVI)*. Austin: Department of Linguistics: The University of Texas at Austin. (Texas Linguistics Forum, vol. 30.)

Fickett, Joan G. 1970. *Aspects of Morphemics, Syntax, and Semology of an Inner-City Dialect*. West Rush, NY: Meadowbrook Publications.

Finegan, Edward, and Douglas Biber. 1989. "Toward an integrated theory of social and situational variation." Unpublished MS, Department of Linguistics, University of Southern California, (revised version published as Finegan and Biber 1994).

Finegan, Edward, and Douglas Biber. 1994. "Register and social dialect variation: An integrated approach." In *Sociolinguistic Perspectives on Register*, ed. Douglas Biber and Edward Finegan, 315–47. New York and Oxford: Oxford University Press.

Fischer, John L. 1958. "Social influences on the choice of a linguistic variant." *Word* 14: 47–56.

Fischer, Katherine. 1992. "Educating speakers of Caribbean English Creole in the United States." In *Pidgins, Creoles, and Nonstandard Dialects in Education*. (Occasional Paper no. 12), ed. J. Siegel 99–123. Canberra: Applied Linguistics Association of Australia.

Fishman, Joshua A. 1977. Language and ethnicity. *Language, Ethnicity and Intergroup Relations*, ed. Howard Giles, 15–57. London: Academic.

Fishman, Joshua A. 1981. Address. Department of Linguistics, Stanford University, April.

Fishman, Joshua A., Robert L. Cooper, and Roxana Ma. 1968. *Bilingualism in the Barrio*. New York: Yeshiva University.

Fishman, Joshua A., Michael A. Gertner, Esther G. Lowry, and William G. Milan. 1985. *The Rise and Fall of the Ethnic Revival: Perspectives on Language and Ethnicity*. Berlin: Mouton.

Fleischman, Suzanne. 1989. "Temporal distance: A basic linguistic metaphor." *Studies in Language* 13: 1–50.

Fleischman, Suzanne. 1990. *Tense and Narrativity: From Medieval Performance to Modern Fiction*. Austin: University of Texas Press.

Folb, Edith. 1980. *Running Down Some Lines*. Cambridge, MA: Harvard University Press.

Foner, Philip S. 1975. *History of Black Americans*, vol. 1: *From Africa to the Emergence of the Cotton Kingdom*. Contributions in American History, 101. Westport, Ct: Greenwood Press.

Foner, Philip S. 1983a. *History of Black Americans*, vol. 2: *From the Emergence of the Cotton Kingdom to the Eve of the Compromise of 1850*. Contributions in American History, 102. Westport, Ct: Greenwood Press.

Foner, Philip S. 1983b. *History of Black Americans*, vol. 3: *From the Compromise of 1850 to the End of the Civil War*. Contributions in American History, 103. Westport, Ct: Greenwood Press.

Fordham, Signithia, and John U. Ogbu. 1986. "Black students' school success: Coping with the 'burden of "acting White".'" *Urban Review* 18: 176–206.

Foster, Herbert L. 1986. *Ribbin', Jivin', and Playin' the Dozens: The Persistent Dilemma in Our Schools*. Cambridge, MA: Ballinger.

Foster, Michele. 1989. "It's cookin' now: A performance analysis of the speech events in an urban community college." *Language in Society* 18: 1–29.

Franklin, John Hope. 1974. *From Slavery to Freedom*, 4th edn. New York: Knopf.

Franklin, John Hope, and Alfred A, Moss, Jr. 1988. *From Slavery to Freedom: A History of Negro Americans*, 6th edn. New York: Alfred A. Knopf.

Freccia, Nico, and Lelaine Lau. 1996. "Sending kids to jail: Progress in California education." *Lift* 1: 02, February. (http://www.lifted.com/1.02/caleducation.html)

Fries, Charles C. 1962. *Linguistics and Reading*. New York: Holt, Rinehart and Winston.

Gal, Susan. 1979. *Language Shift*. New York: Academic Press.

Galenson, David W. 1981. *White Servitude in Colonial America: An Economic Analysis*. Cambridge: University Press.

Galura, Joseph, Rachel Meiland, Randy Ross, Mary Jo Callan, and Rick Smith (eds). 1993. *PRAXIS II: Service-learning Resources for University Students, Staff and Faculty*. Ann Arbor: Office of Community Service Learning Press, University of Michigan.

Gambhir, Surendra Kumar. 1981. "The East Indian speech community in Guyana: a sociolinguistic study with special reference to Koine Formation." University of Pennsylvania dissertation.

Georgia. 1940. *Drums and Shadows*. Georgia Writers' Project. Athens: University of Georgia Press.

Gibson, Kean Amelia. 1982. "Tense and aspect in Guyanese creole: A syntactic, semantic and pragmatic analysis." DPhil thesis, University of York.

Giles, Howard. 1979. "Ethnicity markers in speech." In *Social Markers in Speech*, ed. Klaus R. Scherer and Howard Giles, 251–89. Cambridge: Cambridge University Press.

Giles, Howard (ed.). 1984. "The dynamics of speech accommodation." *International Journal of the Sociology of Language* issue 46. Berlin: Mouton.

Giles, Howard, and R. Y. Bourhis. 1976. "Voice and racial categorization in Britain." *Communication Monographs* 43: 108–14.

Giles, Howard, Justine Coupland, and Nikolas Coupland. 1991. *Contexts of Accommodation: Developments in Applied Sociolinguistics*. Cambridge: Cambridge UP.

Giles, Howard, and P. Powesland. 1975. *Speech Style and Social Evaluation*. New York: Academic Press.

Giles, Howard, and Philip M. Smith. 1979. "Accommodation theory: Optimal levels of convergence," In *Language and Social Psychology*, ed. by Howard Giles and Robert N. St. Clair, 45–65. Oxford: Basil Blackwell.

Givon, T. 1982. "Tense-aspect-modality: The creole proto-type and beyond." In *Tense-Aspect: Between Semantics and Pragmatics*, ed. Paul J. Hopper, 115–63. Amsterdam: John Benjamins.

Gleitman, Lila R. 1967. "An experiment concerning the use and perception of compound nominals by English speakers." Unpublished PhD dissertation, University of Pennsylvania.

Goffman, Erving. 1972. *Relations in Public*. New York: Basic Books.

Gonzales, Ambrose. 1922. *The Black Border*. Columbia, SC: The State company.

Graff, David, William Labov, and Wendell Harris. 1986. "Testing listeners' reactions to markers of ethnic identity: A new method for sociolinguistic research." In David Sankoff (ed.), 45–58.

Green, Lisa A. 1993. "Topics in African American English: The verb system analysis." Dissertation, University of Massachusetts, Amherst.

Green, Lisa A. 1998. "Aspect and predicate phrases in African American Vernacular English." In Mufwene, Rickford, Bailey, and Baugh (eds), 37–68.

Green Lisa A. and John R. Rickford. To appear. *African American Vernacular English and its Contexts*. Cambridge: Cambridge University Press.

Greenberg, Joseph H. 1984. "Some areal characteristics of African languages." In *Current Approaches in African Linguistics*, ed. Ivan Dihoff, 3–21. Dordrecht: Foris.

Greene, Lorenzo Johnston. 1971. *The Negro in Colonial New England*. New York: Atheneum.

Gregg, R. J. 1964. "Scotch-Irish urban speech in Ulster." In *Ulster Dialects*, ed. by G. B. Adams, 163–91. Holywood: Ulster Folk Museum.

Gregory, Michael, and Susanne Carroll. 1978. *Language and Situation*. London: Routledge and Kegan Paul.

Guilfoyle, Eithne. 1983. "Habitual aspect in Hiberno-English." *McGill Working Papers in Linguistics* 1: 22–32.

Gumperz, John J. 1964. Linguistic and social interaction in two communities." In *The Ethnography of Communication*, ed. John J. Gumperz and Dell Hymes, 137–54. (*American Anthropologist* 66: 6, part II.)

Gumperz, John J. 1982a. "Ethnic style in political rhetoric." In his *Discourse Strategies*, 187–203. Cambridge and New York: Cambridge University Press.

Gumperz John J. 1982b. "The sociolinguistics of interpersonal communication." In his *Discourse Strategies*, 9–37. Cambridge and New York: Cambridge University Press.

Gumperz, John J. 1982c. *Language and Social Identity*. Cambridge: Cambridge University Press.

Gumperz, John J. 1982d. "Social network and language shift." In his *Discourse Strategies*, 38–58. Cambridge and New York: Cambridge University Press.

Gumperz, John J., T. C. Gupp, and Celia Roberts. 1979. *Crosstalk: A Study of Cross-Cultural Communication*. Southall, Middlesex: National Centre for Industrial Language Training.

Gumperz, John J., and Robert Wilson. 1971. "Convergence and Creolization: a Case from the Indo-Aryan/Dravidian Border." In Hymes (1971b), 151–68.

Guy, Gregory R. 1975. "Use and applications of the Cedergren/Sankoff variable rule program." In Fasold and Shuy 1975: 59–69.

Guy, Gregory R. 1980. "Variation in the group and the individual: the case of final stop deletion." In W. Labov 1980b: 1–36.

Guy, Gregory R. 1988. "Advanced Varbrul analysis." In *Linguistic Change and Contact: Proceedings of the Sixteenth Annual Conference on New Ways of Analyzing Variation* (NWAV-16), ed. K. Ferrara, B. Brown, K. Walters, and J. Baugh, 124–36. Austin: Department of Linguistics, University of Texas.

Guy, Gregory R. 1991. "Explanation in variable phonology: An exponential model of morphological constraints." *Language Variation and Change* 3: 1–22.

Guy, Gregory R. 1994. "Violable is variable: Principles, Constraints and Linguistic Variation." Paper presented at NWAV-23, Stanford U.

Hall, Robert A., Jr. 1966. *Pidgin and Creole Languages*. Ithaca: Cornell University Press.

Hall, William S., Stephen Reder, and Michael Cole. 1979. "Story recall in young Black and White children: Effects of racial group membership, race of experimenter, and dialect." In *Research Directions of Black Psychologists*, ed. Wade Boykin, Anderson J. Franklin, and J. Frank Yates, 253–65. New York: Russell Sage Foundation.

Halliday, M. A. K. 1978. *Language as a Social Semiotic: The Social Interpretation of Language and Meaning*. London: Edward Arnold.

Hancock, Ian F. 1969. "A provisional comparison of the English-derived Atlantic creoles." *Sierra Leone Language Review* (*African Language Review*) 8: 7–72.

Hancock, Ian F. 1971. "A study of the sources and development of the lexicon of Sierra Leone Krio." University of London Dissertation.

Hancock, Ian F. 1980. "Gullah and Barbadian: Origins and relationship." *American Speech* 55: 17–35.

Hancock, Ian F. 1986. "The domestic hypothesis, diffusion, and componentiality: An account of Atlantic Anglophone creole origins." In *Substrata versus Universals in Creole Genesis*, ed. Pieter Muysken and Norval Smith, 71–102. Amsterdam and Philadelphia: John Benjamins.

Hancock, Ian F. 1987. "A preliminary classification of the Anglophone Atlantic creoles, with syntactic data from 33 representative dialects." In *Pidgin and Creole Languages: Essays in Memory of John E. Reinecke,* ed. Glenn Gilbert, 264–333. Honolulu: University Press of Hawaii.

Handler, Jerome S., and Frederick W. Lange. 1978. *Plantation Slavery in Barbados: An Archaeological and Historical Investigation.* Cambridge, MA: Harvard University Press.

Harlow, Vincent. 1926. *A History of Barbados, 1625–1685.* Oxford: Clarendon Press.

Harris, John. 1982. "The underlying non-identity of English dialects: A look at the Hiberno-English verb phrase." *Belfast Working Papers in Language and Linguistics* 6: 1–36.

Harris, John. 1984. "English in the North of Ireland." In Trudgill 1984a: 115–34.

Harris, John. 1985. "Expanding the superstrate: Habitual aspect markers in Atlantic Englishes." *Sheffield Working Papers in Language and Linguistics* 2: 72–97.

Harris, Ovetta, Vicki Anderson, David Bloome, and Tempii Champion. 1995. "A select bibliography of research on Africanized English and education." *Linguistics and Education* 7: 151–6.

Harris-Wright, K. (In press). "Enhancing bidialectalism in urban African American students." In Adger et al. (eds).

Hatala, Eileen. 1976. "Environmental effects on White students in Black schools." Unpublished Master's Essay, University of Pennsylvania.

Haugen, Einar. 1953. *The Norwegian Language in America: A Study in Bilingual Behavior.* Philadelphia: University of Pennsylvania Press.

Haugen, Einar. 1956. *Bilingualism in the Americas: A Bibliography and Research Guide.* Publications of the American Dialect Society, 26. University, AL: University of Alabama.

Heath, Jeffrey G. 1984. "Language contact and language change." *Annual Review of Anthropology* 13: 367–84.

Heath, Shirley Brice. 1983. *Ways with Words: Language, Life, and Work in Communities and Classrooms.* Cambridge: Cambridge University Press.

Henry, P. L. 1957. *An Anglo-Irish Dialect of North Roscommon.* Zurich: Aschmann & Scheller.

Herskovits, Melville J. 1941. *The Myth of the Negro Past.* New York: Harper & Brothers.

Heyward, Duncan Clinch. 1937. *Seed from Madagascar.* Chapel Hill: University of North Carolina.

Hill, Archibald A. 1975. "The habituative aspect of verbs in Black English, Irish English, and Standard English." *American Speech* 50: 323–4.

Hindle, D. M. 1979. "The social and situational conditioning of phonetic variation." PhD dissertation, University of Pennsylvania, Philadelphia.

Hinton, Leanne. 1994. "Afterword: Linguists and the California languages." In Leanne Hinton, *Flutes of Fire: Essays on California Indian Languages,* 249–54. Berkeley: Heyday Books.

Hobart, Benjamin. 1866. *History of the Town of Abingdon, Plymouth County, Massachussetts.* Boston.

Hollingshead, August B., and F. C. Redlich. 1958. *Social Class and Mental Illness: A Community Study.* New York: John Wiley.

Holloway, Joseph E. (ed.). 1990. *Africanisms in American Culture*. Bloomington: Indiana University Press.

Holloway, Joseph E., and Winifred K. Vass. 1993. *The African Heritage of American English*. Bloomington: Indiana University Press.

Holm, John. 1976. "Copula variability on the Afro-American continuum." *Conference Preprints, First Annual Meeting of the Society for Caribbean Linguistics, Turkeyen, Guyana*, 301–9. Compiled by George Cave, Linguistics Section, Department of English, University of Guyana.

Holm, John. 1980. "African features in White Bahamian English." *English World-Wide* 1: 45–65.

Holm, John (ed.). 1983. *Central American English*. Varieties of English around the World, Text Series 2. Heidelberg: Groos.

Holm, John. 1984. "Variability of the copula in Black English and its creole kin." *American Speech* 59: 291–309.

Holmes, Janet. 1992. *An Introduction to Sociolinguistics*. London: Longman.

Holton, Sylvia Wallace. 1984. *Down Home and Uptown: The Representation of Black Speech in American Fiction*. Rutherford, NJ: Fairleigh Dickinson University Press.

Honnet, Ellen Porter, and Susan J. Poulsen. 1989. *Principles of Good Practice for Combining Service and Learning: A Wingspread Special Report*. Racine, Wisconsin: The Johnson Foundation, Inc.

Hoover, Mary. 1978. "Community attitudes toward Black English." *Language in Society* 7: 65–87.

Hoover, Mary R., 1991. "Using the ethnography of African-American communications in teaching composition to bidialectal students." In *Languages in Schools and Society: Policy and Pedagogy*, ed. Mary E. McGroarty and Christian J. Faltis, 465–85. Berlin: Walter de Gruyter.

Hoover, Mary R., Shirley A. R. Lewis, Robert L. Politzer, James Ford, Faye McNair-Knox, Shirley Hicks, and Darlene Williams. 1996. "Tests of African American English for teachers of bidialectal students." In *Handbook of Tests and Measurements for Black Populations*, ed. Reginald Jones, 367–81. Hampton, VA: Cobbs and Henry.

Hoover, Mary R., Faye McNair-Knox, Shirley A. R. Lewis, and Robert L. Politzer. 1996. "African American English attitude measures for teachers." In *Handbook of Tests and Measurements for Black Populations*, ed. Reginald Jones, 383–93. Hampton, VA: Cobbs and Henry.

Hoover, Mary R., Robert L. Politzer, and Orlando Taylor. 1987. "Bias in reading tests for Black language speakers: A sociolinguistic perspective." *The Negro Educational Review* 39: 91–8.

Hopper, Paul J., and Elizabeth Closs Traugott. 1993. *Grammaticalization*. Cambridge: Cambridge University Press.

Horsmanden, Daniel P. 1810. *The New York Conspiracy, or A History of the Negro Plot, with the Journal of the Proceedings against the Conspirators at New York, in the Years 1741–2*. New York: Southwick and Pelsue.

Howard, Jeffrey (ed.). 1993a. *PRAXIS I: A Faculty Casebook on Community Service Learning*. Ann Arbor: Office of Community Service Learning Press, University of Michigan.

Howard, Jeffrey. 1993b. "Community service learning in the curriculum." In Howard (ed.) 1993a: 3–12.

Hudson, Richard A. 1996. *Sociolinguistics*, 2nd edn. Cambridge: Cambridge University Press.

Hymes, Dell. 1971a. "Introduction to Part 3: General conceptions of process." In Hymes (ed.) 1971b: 65–90.

Hymes, Dell (ed.). 1971b. *Pidginization and Creolization of Languages*. Cambridge: University Press.

Hymes, Dell 1972. "The scope of sociolinguistics." In *Twenty-third Annual Round Table Meeting on Languages and Linguistics*, ed. R. W. Shuy, 313–33. Washington, DC: Georgetown University Press.

Hymes, Dell. 1974. *Foundations in Sociolinguistics: An Ethnographic Approach*. Philadelphia: University of Pennsylvania Press.

Ihalainen, Ossl. 1976. "Periphrastic DO in affirmative sentences in the dialect of East Somerset." *Neuphilologische, Mitteilungen* 77: 608–22.

Information Please Almanac 1996, 49th edn. Boston and New York: Houghton Mifflin.

Inkelas, S., and D. Zec. 1990. "Auxiliary reduction without empty categories." Paper presented at the Syntax Workshop, Department of Linguistics, Stanford University.

Irvine, Jacqueline Jordan. 1990. *Black Students and School Failure: Policies, Practices, and Prescriptions*. New York: Greewood Press.

Irvine, Judith. 1979. "Formality and informality in communicative events." *American Anthropology* 81: 773–90.

Irvine, Judith. 1985. "Status and style in language." *Annual Review of Anthropology* 14: 557–81.

Jackson, Bruce. 1974. *Get Your Ass in the Water and Swim Like Me*. Cambridge, MA: Harvard University Press.

Jackson, Faith, and Dorothy Williamson-Ige. 1986. "White students' judgements of education and social mobility of Black English speakers." Report no. FL 015 599. ERIC Document Reproduction Service no. ED268 783.

Jackson, Juanita, Sabra Slaughter, and J. Herman Blake. 1974. "The Sea Islands as a cultural resource." *The Black Scholar* 5: 32–9.

James, Trevor. 1986. *English Literature from the Third World*. Essex: Longman; Beirut: York Press.

Johnson, Kenneth. 1971. "Black kinesics: some non-verbal communication patterns in Black culture." *Florida Foreign Language Reporter*, 9(1–2): 17–20, 57.

Jones, Charisse. 1995. "Crack and punishment: Is race the issue?" *New York Times*, October 28, 1995, page 1: 9.

Jones, E. D. 1968. "Some tense, mode, and aspect markers in Krio." *African Language Review* 7: 86–9.

Jones, Hugh. 1724. *The Present State of Virginia*. London.

Jones-Jackson, Patricia Ann. 1978. "The Status of Gullah: An Investigation of Convergent Processes." PhD dissertation, University of Michigan.

Jones-Jackson, Patricia Ann. 1983. "The Prayer Tradition in Gullah." *Journal of Religious Thought* 39: 21–33.

Jones-Jackson, Patricia Ann. 1987. *When Roots Die: Endangered Traditions on the Sea Islands*. Athens and London: University of Georgia Press.

Joos, Martin. 1952. "The Medieval Sibilants." *Language* 28: 222–31.

Jordan, June. 1985. "Nobody mean more to me than you and the future life of Willie Jordan." In Jordan, *On Call: Political Essays*. Boston: South End Press.

Jupp, T. C., Celia Roberts, and Jenny Cook-Gumperz. 1982. "Language and disadvantage: The hidden process." In Gumperz 1982b: 232–56.

Kay, J., J. Agard, F. D'Aguiar, and J. Berry. 1990. (Cassette recording of Jackie Kay, John Agard, Fred D'Aguiar, and James Berry reading their own poetry). London: Bluefoot Cassettes and the British Library National Sound Archive.

Kay, Marvin L. M., and Lorin L. Cary. 1995. *Slavery in North Carolina 1748–1775*. Chapel Hill and London: University of North Carolina Press.

Keesing, Roger M. 1988. *Melanesian Pidgin and the Oceanic Substrate*. Stanford: Stanford University Press.

Kerbo, Harold. 1983. *Social Stratification and Inequality*. New York: McGraw-Hill.

Kiparsky, Paul. 1994. "An optimality-theoretic perspective on variable rules." Paper presented at the twenty-third annual conference on New Ways of Analyzing Variation in language (NWAV-23), Stanford University.

Knight, Sarah Kemble. 1865. *The Private Journal of a Journey from Boston to New York in the year 1704*. Albany: F. H. Little.

Kochman, Thomas. 1970. "Toward an ethnography of Black American speech behavior." In *Afro-American Anthropology*, ed. Norman E. Whitten Jr and John F. Szwed, 145–62. New York: Free Press.

Kochman, Thomas (ed.). 1972. *Rappin' and Stylin' Out*. Urbana: University of Illinois Press.

Kochman, Thomas. 1981. *Black and White Styles in Conflict*. Chicago: University of Chicago Press.

Kulikoff, Allan. 1986. *Tobacco and Slaves: The Development of Southern Cultures in the Chesapeake, 1680–1800*. Chapel Hill and London: University of North Carolina Press, for the Institute of Early American History and Culture, Williamsburg, Virginia.

Kurath, Hans. 1949. *A Word Geography of the Eastern United States*. Ann Arbor: University of Michigan Press.

Labov, Teresa. 1982. "Social structure and peer terminology in a black adolescent gang." *Language in Society* 11: 391–411.

Labov, William. 1963. "The social motivation of a sound change." *Word* 19: 273–309.

Labov, William. 1966. *The Social Stratification of English in New York City*. Washington, DC: Center for Applied Linguistics.

Labov, William. 1969. "Contraction, deletion, and inherent variability of the English copula." *Language* 45: 715–62.

Labov, William. 1970a. "The study of language in its social context." *Studium Generale* 23: 30–87.

Labov, William 1970b. "The logic of nonstandard English." In *Language and Poverty: Perspectives on a Theme*, ed. Frederick Williams, 153–89. Chicago: Markham.

Labov, William. 1971. "Linguistic methodology." In *A Survey of Linguistic Science*. ed. W. O. Dingwall, 412–97. College Park: University of Maryland.

Labov, William. 1972a. "Negative attraction and negative concord in English grammar." *Language*, 48: 773–818.

Labov, William. 1972b. "Some principles of linguistic methodology." *Language and Society* 1: 97–120.

Labov, William 1972c. *Language in the Inner City: Studies in the Black English Vernacular*. Philadelphia: University of Pennsylvania Press.

Labov, William. 1972d. "The design of a sociolinguistic research project." Paper presented at the Sociolinguistics Workshop, Central Institute of Indian Languages, Mysore, India. May–June 1972.

Labov, William. 1972e. *Sociolinguistic Patterns*. Philadelphia: University of Pennsylvania Press.

Labov, William. 1973. "Where do grammars stop? In *Report of the Twenty-Third Annual Round Table Meeting on Linguistics and Language Studies*, ed. Roger W. Shuy, 43–88. Washington DC: Georgetown University Press.

Labov, William. 1975. "Empirical foundations of linguistic theory." In *The Scope of American Linguistics*, ed. Robert Austerlitz, 77–133. Lisse: Peter De Ridder Press.

Labov, William. 1976. "Systematically misleading data from test questions." *Urban Review* 9: 146–69.

Labov, William. 1980a. "Is there a creole speech community?" In Valdman and Highfield 1980: 369–88.

Labov, William (ed.). 1980b. *Locating Language in Time and Space*. New York: Academic Press.

Labov, William. 1981. "What can be learned about change in progress from synchronic descriptions?" In Cedergren and Sankoff (eds), 177–99.

Labov, William. 1982. "Objectivity and commitment in linguistic science: The case of the Black English trial in Ann Arbor." *Language in Society* 11: 165–201.

Labov William. 1983. "Recognizing Black English in the classroom." In J. W. Chambers, 29–55.

Labov, William. 1984a. "The continuing divergence of black and white speech in Philadelphia." Paper presented at Stanford University, at a meeting of the Bay Area Sociolinguistics Association.

Labov, William. 1984b. "The transmission of linguistic traits across and within communities." Paper presented at the Symposium on Language Transmission and Change, Center for Advanced Study in the Behavioral Sciences, Stanford.

Labov, William. 1988. "The judicial testing of linguistic theory." In *Linguistics in Context: Connecting Observation and Understanding*, ed. Deborah Tannen, 159–82. Norwood, New Jersey: Ablex.

Labov, William. 1989. "The exact description of a speech community: Short *a* in Philadelphia." In *Language Change and Variation*, ed. Ralph W. Fasold and Deborah Schiffrin, 1–58. Amsterdam/Philadelphia: John Benjamins.

Labov, William. 1995a. Untitled paper presented at the Amherst Conference on African American English, held at the University of Massachusetts.

Labov, William. 1995b. "Can Reading Failure be Reversed: A Linguistic Approach to the Question." In *Literacy among African-American Youth: Issues in Learning, Teaching, and Schooling*, ed. Vivian L. Gadsden and Daniel A. Wagner, 39–68. Creskill, New Jersey: Hampton Press, Inc.

Labov, William, B. Baker, S. Bullock, L. Ross, and M. Brown. 1998. "A graphemic-phonemic analysis of the reading errors of inner city children." Unpublished MS, University of Pennsylvania. (Available at: http://www.ling.upenn.edu/~labov/home.html.)

Labov, William, Paul Cohen, Clarence Robbins, and John Lewis. 1968. *A Study of the*

Non-Standard English of Negro and Puerto-Rican Speakers in New York City. Final Report, Cooperative Research Project 3228, vols I and II. Philadelphia: US Regional Survey.

Labov, William, and Wendell A. Harris. 1986. "De facto segregation of black and white vernaculars." In *Diversity and Diachrony*, ed. David Sankoff, 1–24. Amsterdam: John Benjamins.

Labov, William, and Joshua Waletzky. 1967. "Narrative analysis." In *Essays on the Verbal and Visual Arts*, ed. June Helm, 12–44. Seattle: University of Washington Press.

Ladefoged, Peter. 1967. *Linguistic Phonetics*. Los Angeles: UCLA Press.

Lakoff, Robin. 1971. "Passive Resistance." *Papers from the Seventh Regional Meeting of the Chicago Linguistic Society*, ed. Douglas Adams et al., 149–61. Chicago: Chicago Linguistic Society.

Lal, P., and Raghavendra, Rao K. (eds). 1960. *Modern Indo Anglian Poetry: An Anthology and a Credo*. Calcutta: Writers' Workshop.

Langacker, Ronald W. 1977. "Syntactic reanalysis." In *Mechanisms of Syntactic Change*, ed. Charles Li, 57–139. Austin: University of Texas Press.

Laprade, Richard A. 1981. "Some Cases of Aymara influence on La Paz Spanish." *The Aymara Language in its Social and Cultural Context*, ed. Martha James Hardman, 207–27. Gainesville: University Presses of Florida.

Leacock, John. 1776. *The Fall of British Tyranny*. Philadelphia: Styner and Cist.

Leacock, John, and Andrée Tabouret-Keller. 1985. *Acts of Identity*. Cambridge: Cambridge University Press.

Leaverton, Lloyd. 1973. "Dialectal readers: Rationale, use and value." In *Language Differences: Do they Interfere?*, ed. James L. Laffey and Roger Shuy, 114–26. Newark, Delaware: International Reading Association.

Legum, Stanley, Carol Pfaff, Gene Tinnie, and Michael Nicholas. 1971. "The speech of young black children in Los Angeles." Technical Report no. 33. Los Angeles: Southwestern Regional Laboratory.

Lehmann, Winfred P. and Yakov Malkiel (eds). 1968. *Directions for Historical Linguistic*. Austin: University of Texas Press.

Le Page, Robert B. 1960. "An historical introduction to Jamaican Creole." In *Jamaican Creole*, Creole Language Studies I. ed. Robert B. Le Page and David DeCamp, 1–124. London: Macmillan.

Le Page, Robert B. 1968. "Problems to be faced in the use of English as a medium of education in four West Indian territories." In *Language Problems of Developing Nations*, ed. Joshua A. Fishman, Charles A. Ferguson, and Jyotirindra Das Gupta, 431–43. New York: Wiley.

Le Page, Robert B. 1972. *Sample West Indian Texts*. Department of Language, University of York.

Le Page, Robert B. 1978. "Projection, focussing, diffusion." Society for Caribbean Linguistics, Occasional paper 9. St Augustine, Trinidad: School of Education, University of the West Indies.

Le Page, Robert B., and Andrée Tabouret-Keller. 1985. *Acts of Identity: Creole-based Approaches to Language and Ethnicity*. Cambridge: Cambridge University Press.

Leyburn, James G. 1962. *The Scotch-Irish: A Social History*. Chapel Hill: University of North Carolina Press.

Lind, E. A., and W. M. O'Barr. 1979. "The social significance of speech in the courtroom." *Language and Social Psychology*, ed. H. Giles and R. St. Clair, 66–87. Oxford: Basil Blackwell.

Linn, Michael D., and Gene Pichè. 1982. "Black and white adolescent and preadolescent attitudes toward Black English." *Research in the Teaching of English* 16(1): 53–69.

Lippi-Green, Rosina. 1994. "Accent, standard language ideology, and discriminatory pretext in the courts." *Language in Society* 23: 163–98.

Lippi-Green, Rosina. 1997. *English With an Accent: Language, Ideology, and Discrimination in the United States*. London and New York: Routledge.

Littlefield, Daniel C. 1981. *Rice and Slaves: Ethnicity and the Slave Trade in Colonial South Carolina*. Baton Rouge: Louisiana State University Press.

Lockhart, Audrey. 1976. *Some Aspects of Emigration from Ireland to the North American Colonies between 1660 and 1775*. New York: Arno Press.

Loflin, Marvin. 1967. *On the Structure of the Verb in a Dialect of American Negro English*. Washington, DC: Center for Applied Linguistics.

Loflin, Marvin 1970. "On the structure of the verb in a dialect of American Negro English." *Linguistics* 59: 14–28.

Longacre, Robert E. 1976. *Anatomy of Speech Notions*. Lisse: De Ridder.

Lucas, C., and D. Borders. 1987. "Language diversity and classroom discourse." *American Research Educational Journal* 4: 119–41.

Macaulay, Monica, and Colleen Brice. 1996. "John gives it, Mary gets it: The distribution of gendered NPs in syntactic examples." Paper presented at the symposium on "Addressing bias in linguistic example sentences: Are guidelines necessary?" Linguistic Society of America, San Diego.

Macaulay, Ronald K. S. 1977. *Language, Social Class and Education: A Glasgow Study*. Edinburgh: University of Edinburgh Press.

Major, Clarence, (ed.). 1994. *Juba to Jive: A Dictionary of African-American Slang*. New York and London: Penguin.

Markey, T. L., and Peter Fodale. 1983. "Lexical diathesis, focal shift, and passivization: the creole voice." *English World-Wide* 4: 69–84.

Maroney, Oanh H., Tracey R. Thomas, Gerard Lawrence, and Susan Salcedo. 1994. "Black dialect versus Standard English in education." In *The AAVE Happenin' 1994: Student papers from Linguistics 73: African American Vernacular English*, John R. Rickford, Lisa Green, Jennifer Arnold, and Renée A. Blake (compilers), 3–45. Stanford: Department of Linguistics, Stanford University.

Martin, Stefan E. 1992. "Topics in the syntax of nonstandard English." PhD dissertation, University of Maryland, College Park.

Martin, Stefan E., and Walt Wolfram. 1998. "The sentence in African American Vernacular English." In Mufwene, Rickford, Bailey, and Baugh (eds): 11–36.

Mather, Cotton. 1721. The Angel of Bethesda.

Matsuda, Mari J. 1991. "Voices of America: Accent, anti discrimination law, and a jurisprudence for the last reconstruction." *Yale Law Journal* 100: 1329–407.

McCrum, Robert, William Cran, and Robert MacNeil. 1986. *The Story of English*. London and Boston: Faber and Faber, BBC Publications; New York: Viking. Video-cassettes available from Films Incorporated, Chicago, IL.

McDavid, Raven I. 1972. "Go slow in ethnic attributions: Geographic mobility and dialect prejudices." In *Varieties of Present-Day English*, ed. Richard W. Bailey and Jay L. Robinson, 258–70. New York: Macmillan.

McDavid, Raven I., and Virginia G. McDavid. 1951. "The relationship of the speech of Negroes to the speech of whites." *American Speech* XXVI: 3–16.

McElhinny, Bonnie. 1993. "Copula and auxiliary contraction in the speech of White Americans." *American Speech* 68.4: 371–99.

McGroarty, Mary. 1996. "Language attitudes, motivation, and standards." In *Sociolinguistics and Language Teaching*, ed. Sandra Lee McKay and Nancy H. Hornberger, 3–46. Cambridge: Cambridge University Press.

McManus, Edgar. 1966. *A History of Negro Slavery in New York*. Syracuse: Syracuse University Press.

McTurk, Michael "Quow". 1881. *Essays and Fables in Prose and Verse in the Vernacular of the Creoles of British Guiana*. Georgetown, British Guiana: Argosy.

McWhorter, John. 1995. "Sisters under the skin: A case for the genetic relationship between the Atlantic English-based creoles." *Journal of Pidgin and Creole Languages* 10: 289–333.

McWhorter, John. 1997. "It happened at Cormantin: Locating the origin of the Atlantic English-based creoles." *Journal of Pidgin and Creole Languages* 12: 59–102.

Menard, Russell R. 1975. "The Maryland slave population, 1658 to 1730: A demographic profile of Blacks in four counties." *William and Mary Quarterly*, 3rd series, 32: 29–54.

Michaels, Sarah. 1981. "Sharing time: Children's narrative styles and differential access to literacy." *Language in Society* 10: 423–42.

Michaels, Sarah, and Courtney B. Cazden. 1986. "Teacher–child collaboration as oral preparation for literacy." In *The Acquisition of Literacy: Ethnographic Perspectives* ed. Bambi B. Schieffelin and Perry Gilmore, 132–54. Norwood, NJ: Ablex.

Migge, Bettina M. 1993. "Substrate influence in creole language formation: The case of serial verb constructions in Sranan." MA thesis. Columbus, Ohio: Ohio State University.

Miller, Michael J. 1977. "A brief outline of Black–White speech relationships in the Central Savannah River Area." Paper presented at the Conference on Language Variety in America, University of Chicago.

Milroy, James. 1984. "Sociolinguistic methodology and the identification of speakers' voices in legal proceedings." In *Applied Linguistics* ed. Peter Trudgill, 51–72. London and Orlando: Academic Press.

Milroy, James, and Lesley Milroy. 1992. "Social network and social class: Toward an integrated sociolinguistic model." *Language in Society* 21: 1–26.

Milroy, Lesley. 1980. *Language and Social Networks*. Oxford: Basil Blackwell.

Milroy, Lesley. 1987. *Observing and Analyzing Natural Language*. Oxford: Basil Blackwell.

Mintz, Sidney W., and Richard Price. 1976. "An anthropological approach to the Afro-American past: A Caribbean perspective." Occasional papers in social change, 2. Philadelphia: Institute for the Study of Human Relations.

Mitchell-Kernan, Claudia. 1969. "Language behavior in a black urban community." Working Paper no. 23. Berkeley: Language Behavior Research Laboratory.

Mitchell-Kernan, Claudia. 1971. "Language behavior in a black urban community." Monographs of the Language-Behavior Research Laboratory, no. 2. University of California, Berkeley.

Molloy, Michael. 1946. *The Visiting House*. In *Seven Irish plays: 1946–1964*, ed. Robert Hogan, 29–95. Minneapolis: University of Minnesota Press.

Montgomery, Michael, and Bailey, Guy (eds). 1986. *Language Variety in the South: Perspectives in Black and White*. University: University of Alabama Press.

Montgomery, Michael, and John M. Kirk. To appear. "The origin of the habitual *be* in American Black English: Irish or English or what?" *Belfast Working Papers in Linguistics*.

Montgomery, Michael, and Margaret Mishoe. To appear. "'He bes took up with a Yankee girl and moved up there to New York': The verb *bes* in the Carolinas and its history." *American Speech*.

Moonwomon-Baird, Birch. 1996. "Where are Adam and Steve, Fatima and Eve? Heterosexism in example sentences." Paper presented at the symposium on "Addressing bias in linguistic example sentences: Are guidelines necessary." Linguistic Society of America, San Diego.

Morgan, Marcyliena. 1991. "Indirectness and interpretation in African American women's discourse." *Pragmatics* 1: 421–51.

Morgan, Marcyliena. 1994a. "The African-American speech community: reality and sociolinguists." In *The Social Construction of Identity in Creole Situations*, ed. Marcyliena Morgan, 121–48. Los Angeles: Center for Afro-American Studies, UCLA.

Morgan, Marcyliena. 1994b. "Conversational signifying: Grammar and indirectness among African American women." Paper presented at Interaction and grammar workshop, Los Angeles.

Morganthau, Tom, and Ginny Carroll. 1996. "Affirmative action: The backlash wars." *Newsweek*, April 1: 54–5.

Morrison. Toni. 1981. Interview with Thomas LeClair in *The New Republic*. March 21 1981: 25–9.

Mufwene, Salikoko S. 1981. "Non-individuation and the count/mass distinction." Papers from the Seventeenth Regional Meeting of the Chicago Linguistic Society, ed. Roberta A. Herrick et al., 221–38. Chicago: Chicago Linguistic Society.

Mufwene, Salikoko S. 1982. "Notes on durative constructions in Jamaican and Guyanese creoles." Paper presented at the 4th Biennial Conference of the Society for Caribbean Linguistics, Paramaribo.

Mufwene, Salikoko S. 1986. "Number Delimitation in Gullah." *American Speech* 61: 33–60.

Mufwene, Salikoko S. 1992. "Ideology and facts on African American Vernacular English." *Pragmatics* 2: 141–66.

Mufwene, Salikoko S. 1996. "The founder principle in creole genesis." *Diachronica* XIII: 83–134.

Mufwene, Salikoko S. 1998. "The structure of the noun phrase in African American Vernacular English." In Mufwene, Rickford, Bailey and Baugh (eds), 69–81.

Mufwene, Salikoko S., John R. Rickford, Guy Bailey, and John Baugh (eds). 1998. *African American English: Structure, History and Use*. London and New York: Routledge.

Mühlhäusler, Peter. 1980. "Structural expansion and the process of creolization." In Valdman and Highfield, 19–55.

Mühlhäusler, Peter. 1982. "Etymology and pidgin and creole languages." *Transactions of the Philological Society*, 99–118.

Mullin, Gerald W. 1972. *Flight and Rebellion: Slave Resistance in Eighteenth Century Virginia.* New York: Oxford University Press.

Myhill, John. 1989. "The rise of *be* as an aspect marker in Black English Vernacular." *American Speech* 63: 304–26.

Myhill, John, and Wendell A. Harris. 1986 "The use of verbal *-s* inflection in BEV." In Sankoff (ed.), 25–32.

Newmeyer, Frederick J. 1983. *Grammatical Theory: Its Limits and its Possibilities.* Chicago: University of Chicago Press.

Nichols, Patricia Causey. 1976. "Linguistic change in Gullah: Sex, age, and mobility." Stanford University dissertation.

Nichols, Patricia C. 1983. "Black and white speaking in the rural South: Difference in the pronominal system." *American Speech* 58: 201–15.

Nichols, Patricia C. 1985. "Language and dialect in South Carolina." Unpublished MS.

Nichols, Patricia C. 1991. "Verbal patterns of Black and White speakers of coastal South Carolina." In *Verb Phrase Patterns in Black English and Creole*, ed. W. F. Edwards and Donald Winford, 114–28. Detroit: Wayne State University Press.

Niles, Norma A. 1980. "Provincial English dialects and Barbadian English." University of Michigan dissertation.

O'Barr, William M. 1982. *Linguistic Evidence: Language, Power, and Strategy in the Courtroom.* New York: Academic Press.

O'Donovan, John. 1845. *A Grammar of the Irish Language.* Dublin: Hodges & Smith.

O'Muirthe, Diarmaid (ed.). 1977. *The English Language in Ireland.* Dublin: Mercier Press.

O'Neil, Wayne. 1998. "If Ebonics isn't a language, then tell me, what is? (*pace* James Baldwin, 1979)." In Perry and Delpit, 38–47.

Oomen, Ursula. 1985. "Stages in the decreolization of Black English." University of Trier, unpublished MS.

Orata, Pedro T. "The Iloilo experiment in education through the vernacular." In UNESCO, The Use of Vernacular Languages in Education, 173–8. Paris: Unesco.

Osofsky, Gilbert (ed.). 1969. *Puttin' on Ole Massa: The Slave Narratives of Henry Bibb, William Wells Brown and Solomon Northrup.* New York: Harper & Row.

Österberg, Tore. 1961. *Bilingualism and the First School Language – An Educational Problem Illustrated by Results from a Swedish Language Area.* Umeå, Sweden: Våsternbottens Tryckeri.

Ottley, Carlton R. 1971. *Creole Talk of Trinidad and Tobago.* Port of Spain: Ottley.

Parker, Henry H., and Marilyn I. Crist. 1995. *Teaching Minorities to Play the Corporate Language Game.* Columbia, SC: National Resource Center for the Freshman Year Experience and Students in Transition, University of South Carolina.

Payne, Arvilla. 1976. "The acquisition of the phonological system of a second dialect." University of Pennsylvania dissertation.

Pfaff, C. 1971. "Historical and structural aspects of sociolinguistic variation: The copula in Black English." Southwest Regional Laboratory Technical Report, 37.

Piestrup, Ann McCormick. 1973. "Black Dialect Interference and Accommodation of Reading Instruction in First Grade." University of California, Berkeley: Monographs of the Language Behavior Research Laboratory, no. 4.

Politzer, Robert L., and Shirley A. Lewis. 1979. "Teacher workshops, Black English tests for teachers and selected teaching behaviors and their relation to pupil achievement." Stanford, CA: Stanford University Center for Educational Research (CERAS).

Poplack, Shana, and David Sankoff 1987. "The Philadelphia story in the Spanish Caribbean." *American Speech* 62(4): 291–314.

Poplack, Shana, and Sali Tagliamonte. 1989. "There's no tense like the present: Verbal -*s* inflection in early Black English." *Language Variation and Change* 1: 47–84.

Poplack, Shana, and Sali Tagliamonte. 1991. "African American English in the diaspora: Evidence from old-line Nova Scotians." *Language Variation and Change* 3: 301–39.

Preston, Dennis S. 1986. "Fifty some-odd categories of language variation." *International Journal of the Sociology of Language* 57: 9–47.

Preston, Dennis S. 1991. "Sorting out the variables in sociolinguistic theory." *American Speech* 66: 33–56.

Pritzwald, Kurt Stegmann von. 1938. "Sprachwissenschaftliche Minderheitenforschung; ein Arbeitsplan und eine Statistik." *Wörter und Sachen* n.s. 1: 52–72.

Psathas, George. 1979. "Organizational features of direction maps." In *Everyday Language: Studies in Ethnomethodology.* ed. Psathas, 203–25. New York: Irvington.

Pullum, Geoffrey K. 1997. "Language that dare not speak its name." *Nature* 386: 321–2.

Purcell, A. 1984. "Code shifting Hawaiian style: Children's accommodation along a decreolizing continuum." *International Journal of the Sociology of Language* 46: 71–86.

Quirk, R., and J. Svartvik. 1966. *Investigating Linguistic Acceptability.* The Hague: Mouton and Co.

Ramirez, David, Terrence Wiley, Gerda de Klerk, and Enid Lee, (eds). In press. *Ebonics in the Urban Education Debate.* Long Beach, Cal.: Center for Language Minority Education and Research, California State University, Long Beach.

Rampton, M. B. H. 1992. "Scope for empowerment in sociolinguistics?" In Cameron, et al., 29–64.

Read, Allen Walker. 1933. "British recognition of American speech in the eighteenth century." *Dialect Notes* 6: 313–36.

Read, Allen Walker. 1937. "Bilingualism in the middle colonies." *American Speech* 12: 93–9.

Read, Allen Walker. 1939. "The speech of Negroes in colonial America." *Journal of Negro History* 24: 247–58.

Reichenbach, Hans. 1947. *Elements of Symbolic Logic.* New York: MacMillan.

Reisman, Karl. 1970. "Cultural and linguistic ambiguity in a West Indian village." In *Afro-American Anthropology,* ed. Norman E. Whitten Jr and John F. Szwed. New York: Free Press.

Richardson, Carmen. 1988. "Habitual structures among black and white speakers in East Palo Alto." MA thesis, Stanford University.

Richardson, Elaine. 1998. "The Anti-Ebonics Movement: 'Standard English-Only.'" *Journal of English Linguistics* 26(2): 156–69.

Rickford, Angela E. 1996. "Cognition, comprehension and critical evaluation in a multicultural classroom: A study in literary analysis and appreciation." PhD dissertation, School of Education, Stanford University.

Rickford, Angela E. 1999. *I Can Fly: Teaching Narratives and Reading Comprehension to African American and other Ethnic Minority Students.* Lanham, MD: University Press of America.

Rickford, John R. 1973. "'Riddling' and 'Lying' on a S. Carolina Sea Island." Unpublished TS.

Rickford, John R. 1974. "The insights of the mesolect." In *Pidgins and Creoles: Current Trends and Prospects*, ed. David DeCamp and Ian F. Hancock, 92–117. Washington, DC: Georgetown University Press.

Rickford, John R. 1975. "Carrying the new wave into syntax: The case of Black English BIN." In Fasold and Shuy 1975: 162–83.

Rickford, John R. 1977. "The question of prior creolization in Black English." In *Pidgin-Creole Linguistics*, ed. Albert Valdman, 199–221. Bloomington: University of Indiana Press.

Rickford, John R. 1979. "Variation in a Creole Continuum: Quantitative and Implicational Approaches." PhD dissertation, University of Pennsylvania.

Rickford, John R. 1980. "How does doz disappear?" *Issues in English Creoles: Papers from the 1975 Hawaii Conference*, ed. Richard R. Day, 77–96. Heidelberg: Groos.

Rickford, John R. 1983a. "What happens in decreolization." In Andersen, 298–319.

Rickford, John R. 1983b. "Standard and non-standard language attitudes in a creole continuum." *Society for Caribbean Linguistics Occasional Paper* no. 16. University of the West Indies, St Augustine, Trinidad.

Rickford, John R. 1985. "Ethnicity as a sociolinguistic boundary." *American Speech* 60(2): 99–125.

Rickford, John R. 1986a. "The need for new approaches to social class analysis in sociolinguistics." *Language and Communication* 6: 215–21.

Rickford, John R. 1986b. "Short note [On the significance and use of documentary pidgin-creole texts.]" *Journal of Pidgin and Creole Languages* 1: 159–63.

Rickford, John R. 1986c. "Social contact and linguistic diffusion: Hiberno English and New World Black English." *Language* 62: 245–90.

Rickford, John R. 1986d. "Some principles for the study of Black and White speech in the South." In Montgomery and Bailey 1986: 38–62. University: University of Alabama Press.

Rickford, John R. 1986e. "Riddling and Lying: Participation and Performance." In *The Fergusonian Impact*, vol. 2, ed. J. A. Fishman, 89–106. The Hague: Mouton.

Rickford, John R. 1987a. "Past marking in the Guyanese mesolect: A close look at Bonnette." In Keith Denning et al. (eds) 1987: 379–94.

Rickford, John R. 1987b. "The haves and have nots: Sociolinguistic surveys and the assessment of speaker competence." *Language in Society* 16: 149–78.

Rickford, John R. 1987c. *Dimensions of a Creole Continuum: History, Texts and Linguistic Analysis of Guyanese Creole.* Stanford Cal.: Stanford University Press.

Rickford, John R. 1989. "Continuity and innovation in the development of BEV be 2." Paper presented at the eighteenth annual conference on New Ways of Analyzing Variation (NWAVE-XVIII), Duke University, Durham.

Rickford, John R. 1992. "Grammatical variation and divergence." In *Vernacular Black English. Internal and External Factors in Syntactic Change*, ed. Marinel Gerritsen and Dieter Stein, 175–200. The Hague: Mouton.

Rickford, John R. 1995. "AAVE and the creole hypothesis: Reflections on the state of the issue." Paper presented at NWAV24 (Philadelphia) and at Ohio State University, October.

Rickford, John R. 1996a. "Regional and social variation." In *Sociolinguistics and Language Teaching*, ed. Sandra Lee McKay and Nancy H. Hornberger, 151–94. Cambridge: Cambridge University Press.

Rickford, John R. 1996b. "Preterit had in the narratives of African American adolescents." (With Christine Théberge Rafal.) *American Speech* 71: 227–54.

Rickford, John R. 1996c. "Copula variability in Jamaican Creole and African American Vernacular English: A reanalysis of DeCamp's texts." In *Towards a Social Science of Language: A Festschrift for William Labov*, ed. Gregory R. Guy, John G. Baugh, Deborah Schiffrin, and Crawford Feagin, 357–72. Philadelphia and Amsterdam: John Benjamins.

Rickford, John R. 1996d. "The Oakland Ebonics decision: Commendable attack on the problem." Op-Ed piece in the *San Jose Mercury News*, 26 December.

Rickford, John R. 1997a. "Prior creolization of AAVE? Sociohistorical and textual evidence from the 17th and 18th centuries." *Journal of Sociolinguistics* 1(3): 315–36.

Rickford, John R. 1997b. "Unequal partnership: Sociolinguistics and the African American community." *Language in Society* 26: 161–97.

Rickford, John R. 1997c. "Suite for ebony and phonics." *Discover* 18(12): 82–7.

Rickford, John R. 1997d. "Ebonics and education: Lessons from the Caribbean, Europe and the USA." Paper presented at the national symposium, "What is the Relationship of Ebonics to the Education of Black Americans?" held at Medgar Evers College, City University of New York, Brooklyn, NY, January 25, 1997. To appear in the proceedings of that symposium, ed. Clinton Crawford.

Rickford, John R. 1998. "The creole origins of African American vernacular English: Evidence from copula absence." In Mufwene, Rickford, Bailey, and Baugh (eds), 154–200.

Rickford, John R. In press. "Language diversity and academic achievement in the education of African American students: An overview of the issues." In Adger et al. (eds).

Rickford, John R. To appear. "Variation in the Jamaican Creole copula: New data and analysis." In John R. Rickford and Suzanne Romaine (eds), *Creole Genesis, Attitudes and Discourse: Papers Celebrating Charlene Sato*. Amsterdam: John Benjamins.

Rickford, John R., Arnetha Ball, Renée Blake, Raina Jackson, and Nomi Martin. 1991. "Rappin on the copula coffin: Theoretical and methodological issues in the analysis of copula variation in African American Vernacular English." *Language Variation and Change* 3: 103–32.

Rickford, John R., and Renée A. Blake. 1990. "Copula contraction and absence in Barbadian English, Samana English and Vernacular Black English." In *Proceedings of the Sixteenth Annual Meeting of the Berkeley Linguistics Society*, ed. K. Hall, J.-P. Koenig, M. Meacham, S. Reinman, and L. A. Sutton, 257–68. Berkeley, CA: Berkeley Linguistics Society.

Rickford, John R., and Barbara Greaves. 1978. "Non-standard words and expressions in the writing of Guyanese school children." In John R. Rickford (ed.), *A Festival of Guyanese Words*, 40–56. Georgetown: University of Guyana.

Rickford, John R., and Jerome S. Handler. 1994. "Textual evidence on the nature of early Barbadian speech, 1676–1835." *Journal of Pidgin and Creole Languages* 9: 221–55.

Rickford, John R., and Faye McNair-Knox. 1987. "Conjugated and invariant be in VBE: A West Coast perspective" Paper presented at the sixteenth annual conference on New Ways of Analyzing Variation (NWAVE-XVI), University of Texas, Austin.

Rickford, John R., and F. McNair-Knox. 1994. "Addressee- and topic-influenced style shift: A quantitative sociolinguistic study." In *Perspectives on Register: Situating Register Variation Within Sociolinguistics*, ed. D. Biber and E. Finegan, 235–76. Oxford: Oxford University Press.

Rickford, John R., and Angela E. Rickford. 1976. "Cut-eye and suck-teeth: African words and gestures in New World guise." *Journal of American Folklore* 89: 294–309.

Rickford, John R., and Angela E. Rickford 1995. "Dialect readers revisited." *Linguistics and Education* 7(2): 107–28.

Rickford, John R., and Russell J. Rickford. To appear. *Spoken Soul: The System, Source and Significance of Black Vernacular*. New York: Jonathan Wiley.

Rickford, John R., and Christine Théberge-Rafal 1996. "Preterit *had* in the narratives of African American preadolescents." *American Speech* 71: 227–54.

Rickford, John R., and Elizabeth Closs Traugott. 1985. "Symbol of powerlessness and degeneracy, or symbol of solidarity and truth? Paradoxical attitudes towards pidgins and creoles." In *The English Language Today*, ed. S. Greenbaum, 252–61. Oxford: Pergamon.

Rieber, Robert W., and William A. Stewart, (eds). 1990. "The language scientist as expert in the legal setting." *Annals of the New York Academy of Sciences*, vol. 606. New York.

Roberts, Celia, Evelyn Davies, Tom Jupp. 1992. *Language and Discrimination: A Study of Communication in Multiethnic Workplaces*. London: Longman.

Rodman, Hyman. 1971. Glossary. In *Lower-Class Families in the Culture of Poverty in Negro Trinidad*. New York: Oxford University Press.

Romaine, Suzanne. 1978. "Post-vocalic/r/in Scottish English: Sound change in progress." In *Sociolinguistic Patterns in British English*, ed. Peter Trudgill, 144–57. London: Edward Arnold.

Romaine, Suzanne. 1980. "A critical overview of the methodology of urban British sociolinguistics." *English World Wide* 1: 163–98.

Romaine, Suzanne. 1982. *Socio-Historical Linguistics: Its Status and Methodology*. Cambridge and New York: Cambridge University Press.

Rosenthal, Marilyn S. 1974. "The magic boxes: Pre-school children's attitudes toward Black and Standard English." *The Florida FL Reporter* Spring/Fall: 55–62, 92–3.

Rosenthal, Robert, and Lenore Jacobson. 1968. *Pygmalion in the Classroom: Teacher Expectations and Pupils' Intellectual Achievement*. New York: Holt, Rinehart and Winston.

Rouch, Roger L., and Shirley Birr. 1984. *Teaching Reading: A Practical Guide of Strategies and Activities*. New York: Teachers College Press.

Rousseau, P., and D. Sankoff. 1978. "Advances in variable rule methodology." In *Linguistic Variation: Models and Methods*, ed. D. Sankoff, 57–69. New York: Academic Press.

Russell, Joan. 1982. "Networks and sociolinguistic variation in an African urban setting." In *Sociolinguistic Variation in Speech Communities*, ed. Suzanne Romaine, 125–40. London: Edward Arnold.

Sag, Ivan. 1973. "On the state of progress on progressives and statives." In Bailey and Shuy 1973: 83–95.

Sankoff, David (ed.). 1986. *Diversity and Diachrony*. Amsterdam/Philadelphia: Benjamins.

Sankoff, David. 1988. "Variable rules." In *Sociolinguistics: An International Handbook of the Science of Language and Society*, ed. Ulrich Ammon, Norbert Dittmar, and Klaus J. Mattheier, 984–97. Berlin: Walter de Gruyter.

Sankoff, David., and P. Rousseau. 1989. "Statistical evidence for rule ordering." *Language Variation and Change* 1: 1–18.

Sankoff, Gillian. 1973. "Above and beyond phonology in variable rules." In Bailey and Shuy 1973: 44–61.

Sankoff, Gillian, and Suzanne Laberge. 1974. "On the acquisition of native speakers by a language." In *Pidgins and Creoles: Current Trends and Prospects* ed. David DeCamp and Ian Hancock, 73–84. Washington, DC: Georgetown University Press.

Schiffrin, Deborah. 1981. "Tense variation in narrative." *Language* 57: 45–61.

Schiffrin, Deborah. 1990. "Between text and context: Deixis, anaphora, and the meaning of *then*." *Text* 10: 245–70.

Schiffrin, Deborah. 1992. "Anaphoric *then*: Aspectual, textual, and epistemic meaning." *Linguistics* 30: 753–92.

Schneider, Edgar W. 1983. "The origin of the verbal *-s* in Black English." *American Speech* 58: 99–113.

Schneider, Edgar W. 1989. *American Earlier Black English: Morphological and Syntactic Variables*. Tuscaloosa and London: University of Alabama Press.

Schumann, Howard, and Graham Kalton. 1985. "Survey methods." In *Handbook of Social Psychology*, vol. I: *Theory and Method*, 3rd edn, ed. Gardner Lindzey and Elliot Aronson, 635–97. New York: Random House.

Schumann, John H. 1978a. *The Pidginization Hypothesis: A Model for Second Language Acquisition*. Rowley, MA: Newbury.

Schumann, John H. 1978b. "The relationship of pidginization, creolization and decreolization to second language acquisition." *Language Learning* 28: 367–79.

Schumann, John H., and Ann-Marie Stauble. 1983. "A discussion of second language acquisition and decreolization." In Andersen, 260–74.

Schutze, Carson. 1996. *The Empirical Base of Linguistics: Grammaticality Judgements and Linguistic Methodology*. Chicago: University of Chicago Press.

Scott, Jerrie C. 1973. "The need for semantic considerations in accounting for the variable usage of verb forms in black dialects of English." *University of Michigan Papers in Linguistics* 1: 140–6.

Sells, Peter, John R. Rickford, and Thomas A. Wasow. 1996a. "An optimality theoretic approach to variation in negative inversion in AAVE." In *Sociolinguistic variation: Data, theory and analysis*, Selected papers from NWAV23 at Stanford, ed. Jennifer Arnold, Renée Blake, Brad Davidson, Scott Schwenter, and Julie Solomon, 161–76. Stanford: CSLI.

Sells, Peter, John R. Rickford, and Thomas A. Wasow. 1996b. "Negative inversion in African American Vernacular English." *Natural Language and Linguistic Theory* 14(3): 591–627.

Sheldon, George. 1895–6. *A History of Deerfield, Massachusetts.* Deerfield: private publication.

Sheppard, Jill. 1977. *The "Redlegs" of Barbados.* Millwood, NY: KTO Press.

Shores, David L. 1977. "Black English and Black attitudes". In *Papers in Language Variation*, ed. David L. Shores and Carole P. Hinds, 177–87. University, Alabama: University of Alabama Press.

Shuy, Roger W. (ed.). 1965. *Social Dialects and Language Learning.* Champaign, IL, National Council of Teachers of English.

Shuy, Roger W. 1972. "Social dialect and employability: Some pitfalls of good intentions." In *Studies in Linguistics in Honor of Raven I. McDavid, Jr*, ed. Lawrence M. Davis, 145–56. University, Alabama: University of Alabama Press.

Shuy, Roger W. 1986. "Language and the law." *Annual Review of Applied Linguistics* 7: 50–63.

Shuy, Roger W., Walter A. Wolfram, and William K. Riley. 1967. "Linguistic correlates of social stratification in Detroit speech." Final Report, Cooperative Research Project 6-1347, US Office of Education.

Siegel, Jeffrey. 1998. "Applied creolistics in the 21st century." Paper presented at the Symposium on Pidgin and Creole Linguistics in the 21st Century, held at the combined annual meetings of the Society for Pidgin-Creole Linguistics and the Linguistic Society of America, New York, January 1998. To appear in the symposium proceedings, ed. Glenn Gilbert.

Simons, Herbert D., and Kenneth R. Johnson. 1974. "Black English syntax and reading interference." *Research in the Teaching of English* 8: 339–58.

Simpkins, Gary A., G. Holt, and Charlesetta Simpkins. 1977. *Bridge: A Cross-Cultural Reading Program*, 1st edn. Boston: Houghton-Mifflin.

Simpkins, Gary A., and Charlesetta Simpkins. 1981. "Cross cultural approach to curriculum development." In Smitherman (ed.) 1981a: 221–40.

Singler, John Victor. 1984. "Tense, modality and aspect of Liberian English." Los Angeles: University of California dissertation.

Singler, John Victor. 1991. "Copula variation in Liberian settler English and American Black English." In *Verb Phrase Patterns in Black English and Creole*, ed. Walter F. Edwards and Donald Winford, 129–64. Detroit: Wayne State University Press.

Singler, John Victor. 1995. "The demographics of creole genesis in the Caribbean: A comparison of Martinique and Haiti." In *The Early Stages of Creolization*, ed. Jacques Arends 203–32. Amsterdam: John Benjamins.

Sledd, James. 1969. "Bidialectalism: The linguistics of White supremacy." *English Journal* 58: 1307–15.

Sledd, James. 1973. "A note on buckra philology." *American Speech* 48: 144–6.

Smith, Abbot Emerson. 1947. *Colonists in Bondage: White Servitude and Convict Labor in America, 1607–1776.* Chapel Hill: University of North Carolina Press.

Smith, Ernie. 1975. "Ebonics: A case history." In *Ebonics: The True Language of Black Folks*, ed. Robert L. Williams, 77–85. St Louis, Miss.: Robert L. Williams and Associates.

Smith, Ernie. 1997. Ebonics: *The Historical Development of African-American Language. A monograph: The Africanist-Ethnolinguist Theory.* San Francisco, CA: Aspire Books.

Smith, Jessie Carney, and Robert L. Johns. 1995. *Statistical Record of Black America.* New York: Gale Research, Inc.

Smith, Julia Floyd. 1985. *Slavery and Rice Culture in Low Country Georgia, 1750–1860.* Knoxville: University of Tennessee Press.

Smitherman, Geneva. 1981a. "Introduction: Black English and the education of black children and youth." In Smitherman 1981b: 11–31.

Smitherman, Geneva (ed.). 1981b. *Black English and the Education of Black Children and Youth: Proceedings of the National Invitational Symposium on the King Decision.* Detroit: Wayne State University, Center for Black Studies.

Smitherman, Geneva. 1986. *Talkin and Testifyin: The Language of Black America.* Detroit: Wayne State University Press. (Orig. pub. 1977 by Houghton Mifflin, Boston. The 1986 edition includes an additional "Afterword.")

Smitherman, Geneva. 1994a. *Black Talk: Words and Phrases from the Hood to the Amen Corner.* Boston and New York: Houghton Mifflin.

Smitherman, Geneva. 1994b. "The blacker the berry, the sweeter the juice: African American student writers and the national assessment of educational progress." In *The Need for Story: Cultural Diversity in Classroom and Community*, ed. Anne Haas Dyson and Celia Genishi, 80–101. Urbana, IL: National Council of Teachers of English.

Smitherman, Geneva. 1995. "If I'm lyin, I'm flyin: An introduction to the art of the snap." In *Double Snaps*, James Percelay, Stephan Dweck, and Monteria Ivey, 14–33. New York: Quill/William Morrow.

Smitherman-Donaldson, Geneva. 1988. "Discriminatory discourse on Afro-American speech." In Smitherman-Donaldson and van Dijk, 144–75.

Smitherman-Donaldson, Geneva, Teun A. van Dijk. 1988. *Discourse and Discrimination.* Detroit: Wayne State University Press.

Smyth, J. F. D. 1784. *A Tour of the United States of America.* London.

Sommer, Elizabeth. 1986. "Variation in Southern Urban English." In *Language Variety in the South*, ed. Michael B. Montgomery and Guy Bailey, 180–201. University: University of Alabama Press.

Sommer, Elizabeth, and Robert Trammell. 1980. "On the Distinctiveness of Southern Black and White Speech." Paper presented at the 22nd Meeting of the Southeastern Conference on Linguistics. Memphis State University.

Spears, Arthur K. 1982. "The Black English semi-auxiliary *come*." *Language* 58: 850–72.

Speicher, Barbara L., and Seane M. McMahon. 1994. "Some African-American perspectives on Black English vernacular." *Language in Society* 21: 383–407.

Starks, Judith A. 1983. "The black English controversy and its implications for addressing the educational needs of black children: The cultural linguistic approach." In *Black English: Educational Equity and the Law*, ed. John Chambers, Jr, 97–132. Ann Arbor: Karoma.

Stavsky, Lois, I. E. Mozeson, and Dani Reyes Mozeson. 1995. *A 2 Z: The Book of Rap and Hip-Hop Slang.* New York: Boulevard Books.

Steele, Claude. 1992. "Race and the Schooling of Black Americans." *Atlantic Monthly*, 4 (April): 68–78.

Stewart, William A. 1962. "Creole language in the Caribbean." In *Study of the Role of Second Languages in Asia, Africa and Latin America*, ed. Frank A. Rice, 34–53. Washington, DC: Center for Applied Linguistics.

Stewart, William A. 1964a. "Foreign language teaching methods in quasi-foreign language situations." In Stewart (ed.) 1964b, 1–15.

Stewart, William A. (ed.) 1964b. *Non-Standard Speech and the Teaching of English.* Washington. DC: Center for Applied Linguistics.

Stewart, William A. 1965. "Urban Negro speech: Sociolinguistic factors affecting English teaching." In *Social Dialects and Language Learning*, ed. Roger W. Shuy, 10–18. Champaign, Illinois: The National Council of Teachers of English.

Stewart, William A. 1967. "Sociolinguistic factors in the history of American Negro dialects." *Florida Foreign Language Reporter* 5: 11–29.

Stewart, William A. 1968. "Continuity and change in American Negro dialects." *Florida Foreign Language Reporter* 6: 3–14.

Stewart, William A. 1969. "On the use of negro dialect in the teaching of reading." In *Teaching Black Children to Read*, ed. Joan C. Baratz and Roger W. Shuy, 156–219. Washington, DC: Center for Applied Linguistics.

Stewart, William A. 1970a. "Historical and structural bases for the recognition of Negro dialect." In *20th Annual Round Table*, ed. James E. Alatis, Monograph Series on Language and Linguistics, no. 22, 239–47. Washington, DC: Georgetown University Press.

Stewart, William A. 1970b. "Toward a history of American Negro dialect." In *Language and Poverty*, ed. F. Williams, 351–79. Chicago: Markham.

Stewart, William A. 1974. "Acculturative processes and the language of the American Negro." In *Language in its Social Setting*, ed. William W. Gage, 1–46. Washington, DC: The Anthropological Society of Washington.

Stewart, William A. 1975. "Teaching Blacks to read against their will." In *Linguistic Perspectives on Black English*, ed. Philip A. Luelsdorff, 107–131. Regensburg: Hans Carl.

Sullivan James P. 1973. "The genesis of Hiberno-English: A socio-historical account." New York, Yeshiva University dissertation.

Tagliamonte, Sali, and Shana Poplack. 1988. "How Black English Past got to the present." *Language in Society* 17: 513–33.

Taniguchi, Jiro. 1956. *A Grammatical Analysis of Artistic Representation of Irish English.* Tokyo: Shinozaki Shorin.

Tanna, Laura. 1984. *Jamaican Folk Tales and Oral Histories.* Kingston: Institute of Jamaica.

Tarone, Elaine. 1985. "Variability in interlanguage use: A study of style shifting in morphology and synytax." *Language Learning* 35: 373–403.

Tauber, Robert T. 1997. *Self-Fulfilling Prophecy: A Practical Guide to its Use in Education.* Westport, Ct: Praeger.

Taylor, Hanni U. 1989. *Standard English, Black English, and Bidialectalism.* New York: Peter Lang.

Taylor, Orlando L. (ed.). 1986. *Nature of Communication Disorders in Culturally and Linguistically Diverse Populations.* San Diego, CA: College Hill Press.

Taylor, Orlando L. 1973. "Teachers' attitudes toward black and nonstandard English as measured by the language attitude scale." In Roger W. Shuy and Ralph W. Fasold (eds), *Language Attitudes: Current Trends and Prospects*, 174–201. Washington, DC: Georgetown University Press.

Taylor, Orlando L., and Dorian L. Lee. 1987. "Standardized tests and African Americans: Communication and language issues." *Negro Educational Review* 38: 67–80.

Taylor, Orlando L., and Maryon M. Matsuda. 1988. "Storytelling and classroom discrimination." In Smitherman-Donaldson and van Dijk, 206–20.

Terrell, Francis, Sandra L. Terrell, and Sanford Golin. 1977. "Language productivity of Black and White children in Black versus White situations." *Language and Speech* 20: 377–83.

Terrell, Sandra L, and Francis Terrell. 1983. "Effects of speaking Black English upon employment opportunities." *Asha* 26: 27–9.

Thakerar, J. N., H. Giles, and J. Cheshire. 1982. "Psychological and linguistic parameters of speech accommodation theory." In *Advances in the Social Psychology of Language*, ed. C. Fraser and K. R. Scherer, 205–55. Cambridge: Cambridge University Press.

Théberge, Christine. 1988. "Some sixth grade rappers, writers and readers." Senior Honors Essay, Department of Linguistics, Stanford University.

Thelander, M. 1982. "A qualitative approach to the quantitative data of speech variation." In *Sociolinguistic Variation in Speech Communities*, ed. Suzanne Romaine, 205–55. London: Edward Arnold.

Thomason, Sarah Gray. 1981. "Are there linguistic prerequisites for contact-induced language change?" Paper presented at the Language Contact Symposium, University of Wisconsin, Madison.

Todd, Loreto. 1974. *Pidgins and Creoles*. London: Routledge & Kegan Paul.

Traugott, Elizabeth Closs. 1972. *A History of English Syntax. A Transformational Approach to the History of English Sentence Structure*. New York: Holt Rinehart & Winston.

Traugott, Elizabeth Closs. 1976. "Pidgins, creoles, and the origins of Vernacular Black English." In *Black English: A Seminar*, ed. Deborah Sears Harrison and Tom Trabasso, 57–93. Hillsdale, NJ: Erlbaum.

Traugott, Elizabeth Closs. 1989. "On the rise of epistemic meanings in English: An example of subjectification in semantic change." *Language* 65: 31–55.

Traugott, Elizabeth Closs. 1994. "Subjectification in grammaticalization." To appear in *Subjectivity and Subjectification*, ed. Susan Wright and Dieter Stein, 31–54. Cambridge: Cambridge University Press.

Traugott, Elizabeth Closs, and Bernd Heine (eds). 1991. *Approaches to Grammaticalization*, vols. I and II. Amsterdam: John Benjamins.

Traugott, Elizabeth Closs, and Suzanne Romaine. 1985. "Some questions for the definition of 'style' in socio-historical linguistics." *Folia Linguistica Historica* VI/1: 7–39.

Trudgill, Peter. 1974. *The Social Differentiation of English in Norwich*. Cambridge: Cambridge University Press.

Trudgill, Peter. 1981. "Linguistic accommodation: Sociolinguistic observations on a sociopsychological theory." *Papers from the Parasession on Language and Behavior*, 219–317. Illinois: Chicago Linguistics Society.

Trudgill, Peter. 1983a. *On Dialect: Social and Geographical Perspectives*. New York: New York University Press.

Trudgill, Peter. 1983b. *Sociolinguistics: An Introduction to Language and Society*, rev. edn. Harmondsworth, England: Penguin.

Trudgill, Peter (ed.). 1984a. *Language in the British Isles*. Cambridge: Cambridge University Press.

Trudgill, Peter. 1984b. "Dialect contact and the transmission of linguistic forms." Paper presented at the Symposium on Language Transmission and Change, Center for Advanced Study in the Behavioral Sciences, Stanford.

Trudgill, Peter. 1986. *Dialects in Contact*. Oxford: Basil Blackwell.

Trudgill, Peter. In press. "Standard English: What it isn't." In *Standard English: The Widening Debate*, ed. Tony Bex and Ian Watts. London: Routledge.

Trudgill, Peter. 1995. *Sociolinguistics*, 3rd edn. London: Penguin.

Turner, Lorenzo Dow. 1949. *Africanisms in the Gullah Dialect*. Chicago: University of Chicago Press.

US. 1995. *Statistical Abstract of the United States*, 115th edn. Washington, DC: Bureau of the Census.

Valdman, Albert, and Arnold Highfield (eds). 1980. *Theoretical Orientations in Creole Studies*. New York: Academic Press.

Van den Broeck, Jeff. 1977. "Class differences in syntactic complexity in the Flemish town of Maaseik." *Language in Society* 6: 149–81.

Vaughn-Cooke, Fay Boyd. 1983. "Improving language assessment in minority children." *Asha* 25: 29–34.

Vaughn-Cooke, Fay Boyd. 1987. "Are Black and White vernaculars diverging?" In Fasold et al., 12–32.

Viereck, Wolfgang. 1988. "Invariant *be* in an unnoticed source of American Early Black English." *American Speech* 63: 291–303.

Wakin, Edward. 1976. *Enter the Irish-American*. New York: Crowell.

Walser, Richard. 1955. "Negro dialect in eighteenth century American drama." *American Speech* 30: 269–76.

Walters, Keith. 1989a. "Social change and linguistic variation in Korba, a small Tunisian town." PhD dissertation, Austin: University of Texas.

Walters, Keith. 1989b. "The interviewer as variable in quantitative sociolinguistic studies." Paper presented at the annual meeting of the Linguistic Society of America, Washington, DC.

Walters, Keith. 1995. "Contesting representations of African American language." Keynote address, SALSA III conference, the University of Texas, Austin.

Warantz, Elissa. 1983. "The Bay Islands English of Honduras." In *Central American English*. ed. John Holm, 71–94. Heidelberg: Julius Groos Verlag.

Wardhaugh, Ronald. 1992. *An Introduction to Sociolinguistics*, 2nd edn. Oxford: Basil Blackwell.

Weiner, Judith, and William Labov. 1982. "Constraints on the agentless passive." *Journal of Linguistics*. 19: 29–58.

Weinreich, Uriel. 1953. *Languages in Contact: Findings and Problems*. Repr. 1968. The Hague: Mouton.

Weinreich, Uriel, William Labov, and Marvin L. Herzog. 1968. "Empirical foundations for a theory of language change." In Lehmann and Malkiel (eds), 95–189.

Wells, J. C. 1982a. *Accents of English*, vol. II: *The British Isles*. Cambridge: Cambridge University Press.

Wells, J. C. 1982b. *Accents of English*, vol. III: *Beyond the British Isles*. Cambridge: Cambridge University Press.

Wells, J. C. 1983. "The Irish element in Montserrat Creole." In *Studies in Caribbean Language*, ed. Lawrence D. Carrington, 124–9. St Augustine, Trinidad: Society for Caribbean Linguistics.

Welmers, William E. 1973. *African Language Structures*. Berkeley and Los Angeles: University of California Press.

Weltens, B. 1983. "Non-standard periphrastic DO in dialects of South West Britain." *Language and Lore* 3(8): 56–64.

Westermann, Diedrich, and Ida Ward. 1957. *Practical Phonetics for Students of African Languages*. London and New York. Published for the International African Institute by Oxford University Press.

Whinnom, Keith. 1971. "Linguistic hybridization and the 'special case' of pidgins and creoles." In *Pidginization and Creolization of Languages*, ed. Dell Hymes 91–115. Cambridge: Cambridge University Press.

Whitney, William Dwight. 1881. "On mixture in language." *Transactions of the American Philological Association* 12: 1–26.

Williams, Frederick. 1970. *Language and Poverty*. Chicago: Markham.

Williams, Frederick. 1976. *Explorations in the Linguistic Attitudes of Teachers*. Rowley, MA: Newbury House.

Williams, Glyn. 1992. *Sociolinguistics: A Sociological Critique*. London: Routledge.

Williams, Jeffery P. 1985. "Preliminaries to the study of the dialects of White West Indian English." *Nieuwe West-Indische Gids* 59: 27–44.

Williams, Robert L. (ed.). 1975. *Ebonics: The True Language of Black Folks*. St Louis, Miss: Robert L. Williams and Associates.

Williams, Robert L., and Wendell L. Rivers. 1975. "The effects of language on the test performance of Black children." In R. Williams (ed.), 96–109.

Wilson, John. 1987. "The sociolinguistic paradox: Data as a methodological product." *Language and Communication* 7: 161–77.

Winford, Donald. 1979. "Phonological variation and change in Trinidadian English: The evolution of the vowel system." Society for Caribbean Linguistics, Occasional paper 12. St Augustine, Trinidad: School of Education, University of the West Indies.

Winford, Donald. 1988. "Verbs, adjectives and categorical shift in CEC." Paper presented at the seventh biennial meeting of the Society for Caribbean Linguistics, College of the Bahamas, Nassau.

Winford, Donald. 1992a. "Another look at the copula in Black English and Caribbean Creoles." *American Speech* 67: 21–60.

Winford, Donald. 1992b. "Back to the past: The BEV/creole connection revisited." *Language Variation and Change* 4: 311–57.

Winford, Donald. 1993. "Variability in the use of perfect *have* in Trinidadian English: A problem of categorial and semantic mismatch." *Language Variation and Change* 5: 141–87.

Winford, Donald. 1995. "Decreolization, divergence, and dialect distance in African American Vernacular English." Paper presented at the Amherst conference on African American English, University of Massachusetts.

Winford, Donald. 1997. "On the origins of African American Vernacular English – A creolist perspective. Part I: The sociohistorical background." *Diachronica* XIV (2): 305–44.

Winford, Donald. 1998. "On the origins of African American Vernacular English – A creolist perspective. Part II: Linguistic features." *Diachronica* XV (1): 99–154.

Wolfram, Walt. 1969. *A Sociolinguistic Description of Detroit Negro Speech*. Washington, DC: Center for Applied Linguistics.

Wolfram, Walt. 1971. "Black–White speech differences revisited." In *Black–White Speech Relationships*, ed. Walt Wolfram and Nona H. Clarke. Washington, DC: Center for Applied Linguistics, 139–65.

Wolfram, Walt. 1974. "The relationship of white southern speech to Vernacular Black English." *Language* 50: 498–527.

Wolfram, Walt. 1975. "Variable constraints and rule relations." In Fasold and Shuy 1975: 70–88.

Wolfram, Walt. 1976a. "Levels of sociolinguistic bias in testing." In *Black English: A Seminar*, ed. Deborah S. Harrison and Tom Trabasso, 263–87. Hillsdale, NJ: Erlbaum.

Wolfram, Walt. 1986. "Black–White dimensions in sociolinguistic test bias." In *Language Variety in the South*, ed. Michael B. Montgomery and Guy Bailey, 373–85. University: University of Alabama Press.

Wolfram, Walt. 1987. "Are Black and White vernaculars diverging?" In Ralph W. Fasold et al., 40–8.

Wolfram, Walt. 1991. *Dialects and American English*. Englewood Cliffs, NJ; Prentice Hall.

Wolfram, Walt. 1993. "A proactive role for speech-language pathologists in sociolinguistic education." *Language, Speech and Hearing Service in Schools*. 24: 181–5.

Wolfram, Walt. 1994. "The phonology of a sociocultural variety: The case of African American Vernacular English." In *Child Phonology: Characteristics, Assessment, and Intervention with Special Populations*, ed. John E. Bernthal and Nicholas W. Bankson, 227–44. New York: Thieme Medical Publishers, Inc.

Wolfram, Walt, and Carolyn Adger. 1993. *Handbook on Language Differences and Speech and Language Pathology: Baltimore City Public Schools*. Baltimore, Maryland: Division of Instruction, Department of Support and Special Pupil Services, Baltimore City Public Schools.

Wolfram, Walt, Carolyn T. Adger, and Donna Christian. 1998. *Dialects in Schools and Communities*. Mahwah, NJ: Erlbaum.

Wolfram, Walt, and Donna Christian 1989. *Dialects and Education: Issues and Answers*. Englewood Cliffs, NJ: Prentice Hall.

Wolfram, Walt, and Nona Clarke (eds). 1971. *Black–White Speech Relationships*. Washington: Center for Applied Linguistics.

Wolfram, Walt , and Ralph W. Fasold. 1969. "Toward reading materials for speakers of Black English: Three linguistically appropriate passages." In *Teaching Black Children to Read*, ed. Joan C. Baratz and Roger W. Shuy, 138–55. Washington, DC: Center for Applied Linguistics.

Wolfram, Walt, Kirk Hazen, and Jennifer Ruff Tamburro. 1997. "Isolation within isolation: A solitary century of African American Vernacular English." *Journal of Sociolinguistics* 1: 7–38.

Wolfram, Walt, and Natalie Schilling-Estes. 1995a. "Dialect preservation and community collaboration: A proactive program." Paper presented at the Linguistic Society of America, New Orleans.

Wolfram, Walt, and Natalie Schilling-Estes. 1995b. "Linguistics and the human capital initiative." Report to the National Science Foundation. Department of Linguistics: North Carolina State University.

Wolfram, Walt, and Natalie Schilling-Estes. 1998. *American English*. Malden, Massachusetts, and Oxford, UK: Basil Blackwell.

Wolfson, Nessa. 1976b. "Speech events and natural speech: Some implications for sociolinguistic methodology." *Language in Society*. 5: 189–209.

Wolfson, Nessa. 1979. "The conversational historical present alternation." *Language* 55: 168–82.

Wood, Peter H. 1975. *Black Majority: Negroes in Colonial South Carolina from 1670 through the Stono Rebellion*. New York: Knopf.

Wood, Peter H. 1989. "The changing population of the colonial South: An overview by race and region, 1685–1790." *In Powhatan's Mantle: Indians in the Colonial Southeast*, ed. Peter H. Wood, Gregory A. Waselkov, and M. Thomas Hatley, 35–103. Lincoln and London: University of Nebraska Press.

Wright, Joseph. (ed.). 1898. *English Dialect Dictionary*, vol. 1. London: Froude.

Wright, Joseph. 1905. *The English Dialect Grammar*. Oxford: Henry Froude.

Yarborough, Sophie, and Laura Flores. 1997. "Using Ebonics to Teach Standard English." Press telegram, Long Beach, CA.

Yeager-Dror, Malcah. 1991. "Linguistic evidence for social psychological attitudes: Hyperaccommodation of (r) by singers from a Mizrahi background." *Language and Communication* 11: 1–23.

Yetman, Norman K. 1967. "The background of the slave narrative collection." *American Quarterly* 19: 534–53.

Youssef, Valerie. 1991. "Variation as a feature of language acquisition in the Trinidad context." *Language Variation and Change* 3: 75–101.

Zentella, Ana Celia. 1989. Personal communication to the author at NWAVE 18. October.

Index

Page references in italics refer to figures, maps, and tables